ISBN 978-1-331-84598-0
PIBN 10241372

1 MONTH OF
FREE
READING

at

www.ForgottenBooks.com

By purchasing this book you are eligible for one month membership to ForgottenBooks.com, giving you unlimited access to our entire collection of over 700,000 titles via our web site and mobile apps.

To claim your free month visit: www.forgottenbooks.com/free241372

Similar Books Are Available from
www.forgottenbooks.com

BY THE SAME AUTHOR.

1.—Cathedralia; a Constitutional History of Cathedrals of the Western Church, and of the Various Dignities, Offices, and Ministries of their Members. 5s. Masters.

2.—The English Ordinal, its History, Validity, Catholicity. 7s. 6d. With an Introduction on the three Orders of Ministers. Rivingtons.

3.—Church and Conventual Arrangement. (Illustrated.) 15s. Atchley.

4.—William of Wykeham and His Colleges. (Illustrated.) £1. 1s. Nutt.

5.—Memorials of Westminster. (Illustrated.) 7s. 6d. Rivingtons.

6.—Plume's Life of Bishop Hacket, with large additions and copious notes. 3s. 6d. Masters.

7.—Cathedrals of the United Kingdom. 5s. Stanford. 2nd edition.

8.—Minsters of the United Kingdom. 2s. 6d. Stanford.

9.—History of the Benedictine Abbey of St. Martin, Battle, Sussex. (Illustrated.) 5s. Ticehurst.

10.—History of the Austin Canons' Priory, Christchurch, Hants. (With a plan.) 1s. Tucker. 2nd edition.

11.—Memorials of Stamford, Past and Present. (Illustrated.) 3s. 6d. Johnson.

12.—The Double Choir Historically and Practically Considered. Rivingtons.

13.—The Interior of a Gothic Minster. 1s. Masters.

14.—The Precinct of a Gothic Minster. 1s. Masters.

15.—The Cathedral Cities of England and Wales. Parts published separately :—*Bath and *Wells (Peach); *Canterbury (Drury); *Bristol (Chilcott); *Carlisle (Thurnam); *Chichester (Wilmshurst and Mason); *Chester, *Manchester, *St. Asaph, and *Bangor (Phillipson and Golder); Durham (Walker); Ely (Hills); *Exeter (Pollard); *Rochester (Bracket, Tunbridge Wells); *Lichfield (Bemrose, Derby); *Lincoln (Akrill); *Norwich (Stacy); *Oxford (Mowbray); *Peterborough (Clarke); *Salisbury (Browne); *Winchester (Doswell); *Worcester (Wright, Birmingham); York and *Ripon (Hollins, Harrogate); *Llandaff and *St. David's (Mason, Tenby

* Published; the rest are at Press.

SACRED ARCHÆOLOGY.

SACRED ARCHÆOLOGY;

A POPULAR DICTIONARY

OF

ECCLESIASTICAL ART AND INSTITUTIONS,

From Primitive to Modern Times.

BY

MACKENZIE E. C. WALCOTT, B.D.,

OF EXETER COLLEGE, OXFORD;

PRÆCENTOR AND PREBENDARY OF CHICHESTER; MINISTER OF BERKELEY CHAPEL,
LONDON; M.A., F.R.S.L., F.S.A., F.R S N.A.; MEMBER OF THE ROYAL ARCH.
INST. OF GT. BRIT. AND IREL.; MEMB. CORR. SOC. FRANÇ.
D'ARCHÉOL., SOC. DES ANTIQ. DE NORMANDIE,
ETC.

"Mutabuntur, Tu autem idem Ipse es."
"Catholicum, quod semper et ubique et ab omnibus
creditum est."—VINC. LIRIN.
"In necessariis unitas, in dubiis libertas, in omnibu
caritas."—S. AUGUST.
"Plus semper Veneranda primorum sæculorum anti-
quitas quàm novella cujusquam institutio."

LONDON:

L. REEVE AND CO., 5, HENRIETTA STREET,
COVENT GARDEN.

1868.

PRINTED BY J. E. TAYLOR AND CO.,
LITTLE QUEEN STREET, LINCOLN'S INN FIELDS.

TO ALL MEMBERS

OF

THE ONE HOLY CATHOLIC CHURCH

DISPERSED THROUGHOUT THE WORLD,

WHO DESIRE THE DAY

WHEN THERE SHALL BE ONE FOLD UNDER THE ONE SHEPHERD,

This Volume

IS INSCRIBED.

107, *Victoria Street S.W.*

PREFACE.

——◆——

THE history of a book can hardly be without interest to the
reader. The present volume is an endeavour to render a
subject (which in all its departments has been investigated
by me during many years) intelligible and interesting to others
who have not the leisure for similar research, or who want
the opportunities furnished by a large and accessible library.
Even under the most favourable circumstances the advanced
student is liable to be at fault to find the volume which
contains the precise information of which he is in search on an
emergency; and the earlier and greater part of a literary life
is spent in discovering the titles and the nature of the contents
of books. My pages, I trust, therefore, may be welcome even
to him, and, if interleaved, prove a convenient index for
annotation.

Wherever I experienced a difficulty in my own ordinary
reading, I at once sought for its solution and noted it down.
Every rare fact or curious illustration-which I discovered was
added to my store, whilst conversation, inquiries, and the
current literature of the day suggested what were the requirements of a large class of inquirers. As far as was practicable,
technicalities have been avoided, and explanations given which
are easy and popular. Those who are experienced in literary
labour will know that this volume is no mere compilation of

fragmentary and disjointed extracts, but has been slowly, and
with critical effort, constructed out of a mass of conflicting
evidence, and has been elaborated as much amid historic
monuments and the archæological wealth of museums as under
the shadow of bookshelves. It is not a doctrinal or polemical
essay, its purport and scope being purely archæological. My
object has been to combine under one comprehensive and
systematic scheme, in the full and true meaning of the word
archæology, and for the purpose of mutual illustration, the
varied information derived from the silent architecture and
material remains of ecclesiastical antiquity, with the written
records of the manners and customs of those who were their
authors, and to exhibit the religious and social condition of
our forefathers as if they lived again. To discuss one without
the other of these essential elements of information is to produce an incomplete and unsatisfactory view of a subject which
must, when an author writes in the interest of no party,
embrace both. The history of dogma is thus studied by the
aid of direct and incorruptible evidence, whilst the changes and
diversity of ritual and discipline, the forms of popular superstition, and lingering tradition, lend their visible or oral
testimony to the facts of the past for all who would understand
the spirit of the Church, the shadow itself being but a
deepened light.

The subjects treated will be found to range themselves
under the two great classes indicated above.

I. THE ARTS.—1. Architecture, religious buildings, the crypt,
the catacomb, chapels, basilicas, baptisteries, churches and
their various divisions, minsters, altars, tombs. 2. Sculpture,
statues, wood-carving, bas-reliefs, diptychs, sacred vessels,
effigies, gems. 3. Painting, mural fresco, and diaper, stained
glass, mosaics, iconography, symbolism, emblems, colour. 4.
Engraving, inscriptions, brasses, slabs. 5. Furniture and
plate, vestments, veils, hangings, apparel of the altar, ecclesiastical ornaments of ministers, and divine service.

II. PRACTICES, RITUAL, TRADITION, CUSTOMS.—1. The orders

of the sacred ministry, and the office of minor clerks. 2. Ecclesiastical dignities, offices, and ministries in the service of the Church. 3. Religious communities, rules, and conventual arrangement of buildings. 4. Distinctions of the faithful, catechumens, and penitents. 5. Divine service, sacraments, rites and ceremonies in all their details, their administration and accessories. 6. Discipline and ordinances. 7. Sundays, festivals, and fasts. 8. Usages and institutions.

My great difficulty has been to compress my accumulated notes within the compass of a single volume, to arrange them under a methodical classification, to select carefully appropriate headings for all points of primary and general interest, as well as to avoid repetition. For the sake of conciseness, although with extreme reluctance, as a matter of necessity, references have been omitted, except to Holy Scripture. Foot-notes would have seriously enhanced the cost of the book, and increased its size beyond the conventional limits of a single volume. Most readers, however, it may be fairly assumed, would choose to have concise summaries and definitions which, after careful sifting and comparison of evidence, have recommended themselves for final adoption, in preference to the modern fashion of constructing catenæ of names, which are found on examination to be altogether conflicting. It is a display of erudition and of error, as easy as the mere citation of authorities only to refute them is ungenerous, and also disrespectful to the reader. I have, however, given a list of general authorities, and a subsidiary index of synonyms and words of kindred or approximate import, which occur under the principal headings.

Another point which I have, above all, endeavoured to secure, is the absence of all controversy. Facts are here stated without the irritating adjuncts of those needless disputes which have been so frequently raised upon them, that the most sacred and solemn subjects have been desecrated by the unchastened language of human passion. Whatever may be my failures or shortcomings in other respects, I trust that I have nowhere offended against Christian truth, Catholic doctrine, or the spirit of charity; and even in those matters of practice or observance which, as a sincere and conscientious English Churchman I could not recognize, and with which I had no sympathy, I hope I have not marred a dispassionate and candid statement by involuntary misrepresentation, or a single line which, hereafter, I could wish unsaid.

Every publication of the archæological societies of this and foreign countries which fell in my way; the classified indices of Migné's Patrology; the volumes of the Parker Society, and the Anglo-Catholic Library; 'Notes and Queries'; the works of Cardwell, Strype, and Burnet, Maskell, Rock, Palmer, Dr. Neale, and Archdeacon Freeman; local histories and topographical illustrations; all available MSS. in the British Museum, the Public Record Office, and the University Libraries of Oxfor and Cambridge, and the statutes of cathedrals—have been consulted. The general list, which the student can consult on particular points, is as follows, besides the well-known works of Bingham, Riddle, Augusti, Siegel, Herzog, Britton, Gally-Knight, Hope, and Willis; Couchaud, Texier, De Vogué, and Gailhabaud; Assemanni, Baronius, Thomassin, Du Pin, Mabillon, Muratori, Morin, Renaudot, Catalani, Grævius, D'Achery, Martene, and the series of historians issued under the direction of the Master of the Rolls :—

Albertis, ' De Sacris Utensilibus,' 1783.
Amé, ' Carellages Émaillés,' 1859.
André, ' Droit Canonique.'
Assemanni, ' De Ecclesiis,' 1766.
Beleth, ' Rationale Divinorum Officiorum,' 1562.
Beyerlinck, ' Magnum Theatrum Vitæ Humanæ,' 1678.
Binterim, J., ' Die Vorzüglichsten Denkwürdigkeitien der Christ. Katholischen Kirche.'
Blavignac, ' Histoire de l'Architecture.'
Bock, F., ' Geschichte der Liturgischen Gewander des Mittelalters, 1856.
Boissonet, ' Dict. des Cérémonies et des Rites Sacrés,' 1847.
Bona, ' De Divina Psalmodia,' etc.
Borromeo, ' Instructions,' trans. by Wigley.

Bourassé, ' Dict. d'Archéologie Sacrée, 1851.
Brand, ' Popular Antiquities,' ed. Ellis, 1853.
Brandon, ' Analysis of Gothic Architecture,' 1847.
Cassalio, ' De Veteribus Christianorum Ritibus,' 1645.
Cavalieri, ' Opera Liturgica,' 1764.
Colling, ' Gothic Ornament.'
Daniel, H. A., ' Codex Liturgicus,' 1847 ; ' Thesaurus Hymnologicus,'
   1841.
Dansey, ' Horæ Decanicæ Rurales,' 1844.
David, E., ' Histoire de la Peinture au Moyen Age.'
De Caumont, ' Architecture Religieuse,' 1854 ; ' Architecture Civile,'
   1853.
De Douhet, ' Dictionnaire des Mystères,' 1854.
De Vert Claude, ' Explication de la Messe,' 1726.
Didron, ' Annales Archéologiques.'
Dollman, ' Ancient Pulpits.'
D'Ortigue, ' Dictionnaire de Plein Chant,' 1853.
Du Cange, ' Glossarium Mediæ et Infimæ Latinitatis.'
Durand, ' Rationale Divinorum Officiorum,' 1484; and Neale and
   Webb's Introduction.
Ellacombe, various publications on Bells.
England, Bishop, ' Ceremonies of Holy Week,' 1847, ' Construc-
   tion, etc., of a Church, Vestments of the Clergy, and the Mass,'
   1845.
Expilly, ' Dictionnaire Géographique,' 1762-8.
Ferguson, ' History of Architecture.'
Ferrari, O., ' De Re Vestiaria,' 1654. B., ' De Ritu Ecclesiæ Veteris
   Concionum,' 1713.
Ferraris, L., ' De Disciplina Ecclesiastica.'
Ferrarius, A., ' Bibliographia Antiquaria.'
Fosbrooke, ' British Monachism,' 1843 ; ' Encyclopædia of Anti-
   quities.'
Frances, ' De Ecclesiis Cathedralibus,' 1665.
Freeman, E. A., ' History of Architecture ;' ' Origin of Window
   Tracery.'
Gavanti and Merati, ' Thesaurus Sacrorum Rituum,' 1749.
Genebrand, ' Traicté de la Liturgie,' 1602.
Gerberti, ' Vetus Liturgia,' 1776 ; ' De Cantu et Musica Sacra,' 1775.
Goar, ' Euchologium,' 1647.
Guenebault, ' Dictionnaire Iconographique,' 1850.
Habert, Is., ' Archieraticon,' 1643.
Haines, ' Monumental Brasses.'
Hallier, ' De Sacris Ordinationibus,' 1739.
Hampson, ' Kalendarium Medii Ævi,' 1841.
Hefele, C. J., ' Beiträge zur Kirchengeschichte,' 1864.
Helyot, ' Dictionnaire des Ordres Religieux,' 1847.

'Hierurgia Anglicana.'

Hittorp, 'De Diversis Catholicæ Ecclesiæ Officiis,' 1624.

Hopkins, 'History of the Organ.'

Hurtaut, 'De Coronis et Tonsuris.'

Isabelle, 'Édifices Circulaires.'

Jebb, 'Choral Service ;' 'Ritual Law.'

Kennett, 'Parochial Antiquities,' 1695.

King, 'Rites and Ceremonies of the Greek Church,' 1772. (T. H).,
   'Medieval Architecture,' 1859.

Kugler, 'Handbuch der Kunstgeschichte,' Band II., 1861.

Labarte, 'Arts in the Middle Ages,' 1855.

Lenoir, 'Architecture Monastique,' 1862.

Lingard, 'History and Antiquities of the Anglo-Saxon Church,' 1844.

Lipsius, 'De Cruce,' 1540.

Littledale, Dr., 'Offices of the Holy Eastern Church,' 1863.

Lorenzano, 'Liturgia Mozarabica,' 1850.

Lübke, W., 'Geschichte der Architektur,' 1865.

Lyndsay, Lord, 'Christian Art.'

Lyndwood, 'Provinciale,' 1679.

Macri, 'Hiero-Lexicon,' 1677.

Maillane, 'Du Droit Canonique,' 1776.

Maringola, 'Antiquitatum Christianarum Institutiones,' 1857.

Martigny, 'Dictionnaire des Antiquités Chrétiennes,' 1865.

Martin and Cahier, 'Mélanges Archéologiques.'

Martini Poloni Chronicon, 1574.

Mérimée, 'L'Ouest de la France.'

Molanus, 'De Historia Imaginum,' 1771.

'Monasticon Anglicanum.'

Moreri, 'Le Grand Dictionnaire Historique,' 1740.

Muller, 'Manuel d'Archéologie.'

Paley, F. A., 'Manual of Gothic Mouldings ;' 'Illustrations of
   Baptismal Fonts ;' 'Manual of Gothic Architecture.'

Parker, J. H., 'Glossary of Architecture.'

Pascal, 'Liturgie Catholique,' 1844.

Petit, 'Remarks on Church Architecture,' 1850.

Petrie, 'Ecclesiastical Architecture of Ireland.'

Polydore Vergil, 'De Rerum Inventionibus.'

Portal, 'Des Couleurs Symboliques,' 1837.

Pugin, 'Glossary of Ornament,' 1844.

Rheinwald, R. F., 'Die Kirchliche Archæologie,' 1830.

Rocca, 'Opera Liturgica,' 1712.

Roth, 'De Disciplina Arcani,' 1841.

Rubenius, 'De Re Vestiaria,' 1665.

Scarfantoni, 'Animadv. ad Lucubr. Canonic. R. F. Cecoperi,' 1751.

Schayes, 'Histoire de l'Architecture Belgique,' 1849.

Sharpe, 'Decorated Windows,' 1849.

Shaw, 'Ancient Tile Pavements,' 1858 ; 'Dresses and Decorations of the Middle Ages,' 1840.

Sicard (1150-1215), 'Mitrale,' 1844.

Simpson, 'Ancient Fonts,' 1828.

Sivry, 'Des Pélerinages,' 1850.

Stephani, 'Thesaurus,' ed. Dindorf., 1848.

Street, 'Gothic Architecture in Spain,' 1865.

Texier, 'Dictionnaire d'Orfévrerie;' 'Les Émaillons et les Argentiers de Limoges.'

Thiers, 'Sur les Autels;' 'Sur les Jubés.'

Vice-Comes, J., 'Observationes Ecclesiasticæ,' 1615.

Viollet-le-Duc, 'Dict. Raisonnée de l'Architecture Française,' 1854 ; 'Du Mobilier Français,' 1855.

Wakeman, 'Architectura Hibernica,' 1848.

Webb, B., 'Continental Ecclesiology,' 1848.

Whewell, 'Architectural Notes.'

Winston, 'On Glass Painting.'

Wilkins, 'Concilia Magnæ Britanniæ,' etc.

Wollhouse's 'Moller.'

Zaccaria, 'Bibliotheca Ritualis,' 1776.

I trust that readers of chroniclers and medieval MSS. will find their researches rendered more easy, and that many travellers at home and abroad will be enabled to visit old minsters and investigate the precious remains of antiquity with some better result than that of a mere confusion of images, which vanish wellnigh as soon as they are created, or of an ignorant belief in a medley of arrangements in themselves perfectly distinct, and the propagation of infinite mistakes and misapprehension. I shall be still more glad if I have contributed my share towards the spread of that knowledge which can alone (by showing the true value of what has been bequeathed to our keeping) protect the contents of muniment chests, and stay the hands of irrational and ruthless destruction. A fury which is more dangerous than the ravages of armies, mobs, or fanatics, has recently, under the specious plea of restoration, chiselled over the fronts of walls and defaced mouldings, swept away ancient remains of woodwork and internal ornament, and made of glorious fabrics a havoc, now, alas! irreparable, and a subject of lasting national shame.

I have so often been indebted to critics, hostile and friendly,

that I am quite prepared to receive their suggestions, advice,
and corrections with a grateful spirit. I will only remind
them, in the words of Lord Bacon, that a work of this nature
"is a thing of exceeding great weight, not to be compassed
without vast labour, and that which stands in need of many
men's endeavours; our strength, if we should stand alone, is
hardly sufficient for so great a province, for the materials are
of so large an extent that they must be gained and brought
in from every place."

SACRED ARCHÆOLOGY.

Abacus (from *abax*, Gr., a tablet). The uppermost part or crown of a capital.

Abbey. A community of men or women under the rule of an abbot or abbess. In the middle ages the Abbeys were the guardians of literature, science, and civilization; protesting against force by learning, against corrupt morals by purity, against the abuses of wealth by poverty, against the licence of power by submission. Agriculture, music, and the arts were all indebted to these houses of religion. Monasticism commenced in the East during the third century. In Egypt there were communities of thirty or forty monks living in one house, and a corresponding number of such dwellings formed a monastery under the rule of an abbot; the subordinate houses were governed by a provost or prior, and over each ten monks a dean presided. From the fifth to the seventh century in the West each monastery had its abbot, who owed obedience only to the diocesan; and its dependent houses or cells were governed by removable priors. In the tenth century the reform of Clugni took place; one abbot presided over the whole order,—all subordinate heads of houses being called priors. The Cistercians in the eleventh and twelfth centuries appointed an abbot in each monastery, all of whom were required yearly to attend the General Chapter; but the parent Abbey of Citeaux preserved a large amount of authority over her "four daughters," La Ferte, Pontigny, Clairvaux, and Morimond.

The Mitred Abbeys were—

Abingdon, St. Mary.	Hyde, SS. Peter and Paul.
Alban's, St.	Malmesbury, St. Aldhelm.
Bardney, St. Oswald.	Peterborough, St. Peter.
Battel, St. Martin.	Ramsey, St. Mary and Bennet.
Bury, St. Edmund's.	Reading, St. James.
Canterbury, St. Austin's.	Selby, St. German.
Colchester, St. John.	Shrewsbury, SS. Peter and Paul.
Crowland, St. Guthlac.	Tavistock, St. Mary.
Evesham, St. Mary.	Thorney, St. Mary.
Glastonbury, St. Mary.	Westminster, St. Peter.
Gloucester, St. Peter.	Winchcomb, St. Mary.
Hulme, St. Benet.	York, St. Mary.

St. Alban's long claimed precedence, but at length Westminster succeeded in securing the first place.

At Rome there are nine Mitred Abbots General, Benedictines of Monte Casino, Basilians, Canons Regular of St. John Lateran, the orders of the Camaldoli and Vallombrosa, Cistercians, Olivetans, Sylvestrinians, and Jeromites; they sit on the left of non-assistant bishops.

Abbot. The Superior of a Monastery of Benedictines, Cistercians, and some Clugniac and Præmonstratensian houses. In the eighth century some presidents of secular colleges, with the confusion of names all signifying simply jurisdiction, were called abbots; and about the same time in France there were many intruders, lay-abbots, who usurped the revenues; but Hugh Capet restored the election to the monks. In England the Crown frequently interfered, either by presenting its nominee or withholding its consent to the elect of the convent. In France, parish priests were called abbés; the religious took the name of father. At Westminster the abbot was buried with an Indulgence and cross of candles laid upon his breast. In some cathedrals abbots held stalls; as the abbots of Sion and Sherborne at Salisbury, the abbot of Grestein at Chichester, those of De Lyra and Cormeille at Hereford, of Athelney and Muchelney at Wells; there are other instances at Coire, Gerona, Palencia, Toledo, Valence, and Auxerre; and the priors of Nostell and Hexham were prebendaries of York.

The abbot was the chief officer and president of the house: where monastic churches were also cathedrals he was called a prior, the bishop being treated as the abbot, and at Ely occupying his stall in choir. If a mitred abbot, as at Gloucester, he wore the same vestments and ornaments as a bishop, although originally it appears that the mitre was made of less costly materials, and the crook of the staff turned inwards, to mark that his jurisdiction was internal over his house. At Abingdon he had his (1) abbey proctor, who was his bursar, and alternately with the seneschal his court-holder and man of business; (2) keeper of courts, who was granarer and larderer, and receiver of guests; (3) chaplain, who was one of the hebdomadarii, or weekly celebrants, and his constant companion. At Durham the chaplain was his chamberlain and comptroller. At Gloucester the abbot might have five esquires : one to be seneschal; the second, marshal, to regulate the expenses as comptroller of the household, and regulate the fare in hall and number of guests; the third, cook; the fourth, chamberlain; the fifth, usher of the table; one only to have a horse; also a subchamberlain, pantryman, butler, a cook as drysalter, farrier, and messenger; four palfreys for himself and his chaplains, four grooms of the robes, a page, and a long chariot; eight dogs of the chase, four harriers, a groom, and page; but the hounds were to be driven out of the hall at meal-time by the ushers. At Peterborough, in the twelfth century, they swore in twelve seniors as electors, who assembled in the abbot's chamber, while the prior and convent sang and prayed in the chapter-house for their direction. Sometimes abbots resigned; and one at St. Alban's then occupied a chamber under the hall, and at Meaux another built a chamber on the east side of the infirmary.

There were two abbots at Toledo and Osma, one at Pampeluna, Valence, and Auxerre, and four at Palencia, capitular members. Pope John XX., at the beginning of the eleventh century, allowed abbots to-wear pontificals; in the twelfth century, notwithstanding the opposition of the bishops, those abbots received the grant of mitre, ring, and sandals : their use is only by Papal indulgence, and the mitre must be plain white, except in the case of exempt abbots, who may have orphreys; but they have a conventional right to use the pastoral staff, as an ensign of authority and spiritual charge; but it was distinguished by a veil-banner, *sudarium*, or *orarium*, in token of subjection to the bishop, except when the bearer was an exempt abbot. Abbots also claimed to give the benediction, and confer the clerical tonsure and minor orders within their churches : the Cistercian abbots in Italy were permitted by Pope Innocent VIII., and those in Spain by Gregory XIII., to consecrate altars and plate in their own minsters with chrism obtained from the bishop. Pius IV. extended the right to the abbots of Monte Casino.

Abbots, Lay. In the time of Charles the Bald, many persons were allowed to hold abbeys on terms of military service, who were called field abbots, or abbot counts, and these appointed clerical deans in their place (see DEAN and PRO-VOST). The Duke of Cleveland is now Abbot of Battle, and Earl of Kilmorey of Newry ; and by an arrangement at the Reformation, each alternate Bishop of Osnaburg is a Protestant prince. James Stuart, son of King James V. of Scotland, was Prior of St. Andrew's.

Ablution. Wine and water used by the priest after Communion to cleanse the chalice and his fingers. At one time he was required to drink it ; the water-drain was always erected near the altar to receive the ablution.

Ablutions. (1.) *Capitilavium*, head-washing ; a Spanish rite, adopted in France. It took place on Palm Sunday, the Sunday of Indulgence, out of respect to the sacred chrism with which the catechumens were anointed on the solemn day of baptism. Possibly the custom ceased after the Council of Mayence, in 833, required baptism to be celebrated after the Roman manner. (2.) *Pedilavium*, ablution of the feet, which see. (3.) Ablution of the hands. In the Tabernacle there was a laver, and a brazen sea in the Temple, symbolical of holy baptism, cleansing by the blood of Christ, and the blessings conveyed by the stream of evangelical doctrine. Washing of the hands before the Eucharist was received was common to the whole Church from the earliest times ; as St. Cyril of Jerusalem says, it is symbolical of the purifying of the heart that should accompany the worshipper. The priests, after receiving the offerings in kind, also washed their hands before the consecration, so as to minister with clean hands, and purified from all touch of earthly things ; and the laity, who always received the sacred element of bread in their hands, washed them beforehand,—a discipline which died out between the sixth and ninth century, as appears by a canon of Tours.

Abracadabra. An amulet used by the Basilidian heretics to cure fevers ; connected with—

Abraxas. Little images of metal, with inscriptions and symbols, used by Gnostic and Basilidian heretics. The letters in Greek make up the number 365, the days of the year, as St. Augustine has pointed out. This figure appears on the ring of a Norman Bishop of Chichester.

Accent. *Grave accent* is the fall of a perfect fifth in the *Cantus Collectarum;* the *accentus medius,* the fall of a note ; the *accentus moderatus,* or *interrogativus,* the rise of a note ; the *acute accent* the rise to the second note above it.

Acclamations. Set forms of address used by the early Christians at funerals ; on the monuments of the dead [*in pace, vivas in Deo,* etc.] ; or on inscriptions to the living, as brotherly greetings, or to put them in remembrance of holy things.

Acolyth. A servant; follower : an order of subordinate ministers mentioned by St. Cyprian ; and in the Greek Church in the reign of Justinian. By the Fourth Council of Carthage their duty was to furnish wine for the Lord's Supper and light the candles, and at a later period to clear the way in processions. In the Eastern Church the subdeacons apparently discharged the office of the acolyth. The name was given to this minor order because the duty of such clerks was to accompany bishops and priests. Pope Cornelius is the first writer who mentions the order, and he enumerates forty-two at Rome ; there they carried the eulogies, and also the Eucharist to those absent from church. They went up to the altar, each with his bag in his hand, some on the right and others on the left, with the subdeacons, who held the mouth of the bags open whilst the archdeacon put into them the consecrated bread for the people. The acolyths then presented the bags to the bishop on the right and priests on the left, and the latter broke the bread on two patens presented by the subdeacons. This ceremonial ceased in the time of Gelasius ; then they were ordered to hold the paten and calamus, assisted at the scrutiny of catechumens, and recited the Creed with them. There were three orders of

acolyths at Rome : the Palatines, who assisted the Pope in
the palace and Lateran basilica; Stationary, who served in
the stations in churches; and the Regionaries who assisted
the deacons each in his region.

Acrostics. (1.) The initials of several words, forming a sacred
word, as in the case of *Ichthus* (fish), representing the Divine
Sonship and attributes of the Saviour.   (2.) *Akroteleutia*, end
verses; the final symphony alluded to by the Apostolical
Constitutions, Philo and Socrates.   Eusebius of Cæsarea
and St. Chrysostom mention that a single voice began the
Psalm, and the rest sang only a portion.   Cassian says in
the monasteries a single voice sang the Psalms.   In the
Book of Common Prayer, the verse and answer in the Preces
and suffrages in several cases make up one petition, the
answer being the end or part of the foregoing verse.   St.
Augustine also notes the dipsalma (the Hebrew Selah), the
point in the middle of a verse where the reader preceded and
the people began to respond.   At length the people became
so vociferous, that it was found necessary by the canons of
Laodicea and Carthage to provide an order of Singers.

Acts of Martyrs. The lives and acts of the early martyrs
were written at an early date on thin leaden tablets; as
Gregory of Tours mentions.   Dionysius of Alexandria and
Eusebius Pamphilus were the earliest martyrologists: they
were imitated by Anastasius the Librarian, in the ninth century; Metaphrastes at Constantinople in the tenth century;
Surius in the sixteenth; Ruinart in the seventeenth; and
the colossal compilations commenced by Bolland, and still
continued by laborious successors.   The authentic acts are
divided into several classes : (1) proconsular or presidential,
founded on official documents; (2) original or autobiogra-
phical; (3) contemporaneous; (4) memorial and abbreviated; (5) traditions recorded in sermons, hymns, and pane-
gyrics.

Administration.   The distribution of the Sacred Elements
in the Holy Communion; during this time the organ continues
to play at Durham Minster.

Adult Age, by the canon law, is fourteen years.   Infancy
terminates at the seventh year; childhood [*pueritia*], in the
fourteenth; youth, in the twenty-fifth or twenty-eighth year;
manhood [*juventus*], in the fifty-fifth year; *ætas senilis s.*

gravitas, middle-age, in the seventieth. Old age has no definition by years; extreme old age [*senium*] ends in death.

Advent. The season called after the coming of Christ in flesh, and instituted for the preparation of Christian minds for a holy life and pious meditation on the Nativity of the Lord. It commences always between Nov. 26th and Dec. 4th, and includes a period of four weeks. It has been said to be mentioned by Maximus of Turin in the fifth century, but is certainly spoken of in the Council of Lerida, A.D. 524. Formerly the Sundays were reckoned inversely to our present computation, that next Christmas being called Advent Sunday. This is one of the four Ember seasons. At Marseilles, after matins and before lauds begin, the choir kneels down, and the anthem is solemnly chanted until Christmas Eve, " Send forth the Lamb, the ruler of the earth." In France, in early days from the sixth century, Advent was most rigorously fasted.

Advertisements of Queen Elizabeth, The, were put forth in 1564–5 to stop irregularities in divine service.

Ædituî. Officers at Milan, who take charge of the fabric

Affusion. Aspersion, or sprinkling, although previously praotised, did not become general until the thirteenth century in the Western Church, which permits it, although the ancient practice of immersion, or dipping, has never been formally abolished, in favour of pouring water on the person to be baptized. Affusion was probably an indulgence to Clinics, or persons baptized at the point of death, and then extended to infants in delicate health. The Eastern Church retains dipping, and insists on rebaptism by immersion in all cases where it has not been observed.

Agapæ. Love feasts; a meal taken, in primitive times, as supplemental to the Holy Communion on Sunday evenings, when the candles were lighted; after prayer, religious conversation and instruction; and- followed by collections of alms for widows, orphans, and the poor. It probably was instituted in memory of that which was technically called the Common Supper of the Lord and the Twelve, in distinction to the Pasch, or Legal Supper, and the Eucharistic Supper, and as a mark of brotherly affection and equality in the Gospel. It is mentioned by St. Jude (v. 12) and St. Paul (1 Cor. xi. 16, 34). The third Council of Carthage permitted a supper after Holy Communion on Maundy Thursday. Such feasts were kept also on martyrs'-days, at weddings and burials, and dedications of churches in the daytime. The Council of Gangra, in the fourth century, mentions them as occasions of almsgiving to the poor; but abuses crept in, the original design was lost sight of, and St. Augustine at Hippo, and St. Ambrose at Milan, suppressed the custom altogether. St. Chrysostom and St. Gregory of Neo-Cæsarea, the Councils of Laodicea, III.; Carthage in the fourth century; Orleans, 535; and that in Trullo, 692, forbade the keeping of agapæ in churches. Pope Gregory the Great allowed the Kentish Converts of Augustin to observe the dedication of a church as a holiday with festivities; but the repast was served under tents made of leaves, and not inside the church.

The agape was long used before the Communion in Africa, and the custom has been traced to apostolic times (Acts ii. 46; xx. 11). The Jews kept an agape after funerals, called the bread of grief and cup of consolation (Ezek. xxiv. 17; Jerem. xv. 5–7; Deut. xxvi. 14; Prov. xxxi. 6).

Agatha's, St., Letters. A superstitious charm against· fire; the heathen took her veil from her tomb to extinguish a conflagration. When Frederic II. was about to-lay Catania in flames, the legend says that at the reading of the Gospel he saw these words written in letters of gold on the book :— "Harm not Agatha's birthplace, for she avengeth injury."

Agenda. The ritual of a church, with the books embodying it, in contrast to the Credenda, or Articles of Faith.

Agnus Dei. A little round cake of perfumed wax, stamped with the figure of the Holy Lamb bearing the standard of the Cross. When these cakes were hallowed by the Pope, a post came in haste, saying, " My Lord, my Lord, these are the young lambs that have announced Alleluia; now are they come to the font." They are distributed on the Octave of Easter to be burned as perfumes, symbolically of good thoughts, or in memory of the deliverance of men from the power of the grave at Easter by the Lamb of God. Matthew Paris says that the French shepherds used the agnus-dei during the time of the Crusades.

The custom took its origin in the distribution of the ends of the paschal of the past year, which the people burned in their own houses as a safeguard against evil spirits. At Rome the archdeacon, instead of this plan, blessed wax moulded with oil and stamped with a lamb on Easter Eve, and these little medals were given out on Low Sunday to the baptized. In the form of medals it dates from the sixth century, but in its earlier form from the fourth century. St. Gregory the Great sent an agnus-dei to the Empress Theodolinda.

Agnus Dei. An anthem in the Canon of the Mass, sung between the fraction of the Host and the Pax. It occurs in the Sacramentary of Gelasius, and was sung by the clergy only until Pope Sergius I., c. 700, ordered the people also to join in it. When Pope Innocent III. mentions that it was repeated thrice, owing to the prevalence of a schism, it appears that the words, "Grant us thy peace," had been introduced; but the ancient custom of saying three times only, "Have mercy upon us," is retained at St. John's Lateran, except when the Pope celebrates.

Aire. A linen napkin, embroidered with coloured silk, used as a chalice veil at Canterbury in 1635, and by Bishop Andrewes.

Aisle (*ala*, a wing). A word used by Strabo in describing an Egyptian temple; the Greeks called the colonnades of their sacred building *diptera* or *periptera*, with the same notion of a wing. It is the collateral division or member of a church, flanking the nave, choir, or transept. In many foreign cathedrals the aisle is doubled, as at Cologne, Ulm, Pisa, Milan, Gorlitz, Strengnas, Seville, Toledo, Bazas, Amiens, and Toulouse, and trebled at Antwerp. The earliest instance of the double aisle is in basilicas and at St. Paul's Without, Rome. At Chichester, Manchester, Edinburgh, Melrose, Elgin, Amiens, Evreux, Rouen, Paris, Bourges, Troyes, Beauvais, and in other places, the additional aisle was divided into chapels. The nave aisles were occupied by lay persons to view processions; and at Norwich the rings remain in the pillars through which the ropes were drawn on such occasions. At Canterbury the only access to the east end for lay people was by the south aisle, that on the north being blocked up by altars: the additional aisle was a great relief, both in capabilities of accommodation, and in furnishing room for chapels. In Cistercian churches the eastern aisle

of the transept was divided into chapels, two or three in each
wing. In the Basilica, the aisle on the right-hand was allotted to men, as the women occupied that on the left side, according to the old arrangement of suitors for justice, when
the building retained its original character as a court of law.
Aisles, when enclosed with screens, were sometimes called
CHANCELS, as forming memorial or guild chapels; the aisle
behind the high-altar was THE PROCESSIONAL PATH, serving
for the passage of the procession; the aisles at the back of
the stalls were the RETRO-CHOIR.

There are aisleless transepts at Carlisle, St. Mary's
Overye; St. Bartholomew, Smithfield; Christchurch, Hants;
St. Alban's; Sherborne; Binham, Bromham, and Le Puy;
but there are both east and west aisles at Winchester, Westminster, Ely, Byland, Wells, York, Milan, St. Denis (as
once in Old St. Paul's); and at Winchester, Caen, Upsala,
Pontigny, and formerly at Canterbury, an additional aisle on
the north and south. The Cistercian transept had invariably an eastern aisle divided into chapels.

Bolton, Brinkburne, Weybourn, Hulne, Bayham, Easby,
Carcassone, Angers, Wechselburg, Pforte, Geneva, and
Meissen have aisleless choirs. Solignac has an aisleless
nave; Lanercost and Hexham had only a south aisle, and
Brinkburne only a north aisle. At St. Denis there is an internal western aisle. At Leominster the parish church
formed an enormous south nave aisle; the Dominican and
Franciscan friars had only one aisle, usually on the south,
which was allotted to the congregation at sermon times.
Their choirs were ordinarily aisleless. At Gloucester and
Ghent the friars' nave had two narrow aisles, barely sufficient to form passages. The arcade of the triforium opens
directly into the aisles at Rouen, Waltham, and Rochester.

Ajuleios. Tiles of a blue colour, used in Spain; there are specimens in the Gaunt Chapel, Bristol.

Akephali. Bishops independent of superior jurisdiction.

Albe (white). A close, white linen garment, which was ordered to be worn by deacons by the Fourth Council of Carthage, 398, and Ælfric's canons in 957. It is the " white
habit " [candida vestis] mentioned by St. Jerome as worn
by all the clergy at the time of the Holy Communion; the
Father also mentions the tunica mundior (the fairer tunic) or

camisia, whence the modern word 'chemise,' or bed-gown, worn "*in camis.*" It reached down to the heels, and in the twelfth century at St. Alban's was ornamented *acu pluma-ria* : the sleeves were tight; and on the cuffs and edges of the skirt were pieces of rich work, called apparels. It was bound with a girdle or zone, which was originally a rich, broad belt, but gradually dwindled into a narrow cord. The albe was said to typify the white robes which had been washed in the blood of the Lamb, and the garment of right-eousness and salvation; whilst the girdle symbolized discre-tion, and the constraining love of God and our neighbour. Cranmer explained it as symbolical of the robe which our Lord wore in the presence of Herod, and of the innocency of life and purity of conscience which beseem the celebrant; and the girdle as suggestive of the close attention of mind which he should exhibit at that time. An ancient albe is preserved at Shrewsbury.

Album. The official register of a church.

Alchemy. Metal; a counterfeit of gold, as latten was of brass.

Alexander. A stuff of Alexandria; work Alexandrine is mosaic.

Alien Priories. Cells belonging to foreign religious houses in England; they were dissolved by stat. 2 Henry V. One of the most perfect is that of Wilmington, Sussex.

Alleluia. The singing of this Hebrew word, meaning Praise the Lord, like Amen and Sabaoth, has been derived from the use of the Church of Jerusalem. It is attributed to Pope Damasus. Pope Gregory allowed it to be sung out of Easter-tide. The *alleluiæ inclusio* was the close of the time for singing alleluia, from Christmas to Epiphany. The famous Alleluia Victory was won by St. Germanus and the Britons chanting Alleluia, 492, at Easter time over the Saxons and Picts. The Saturday before-Septuagesima was called Alle-luia, because it was sung for the last time then until Easter-tide.

The name Alleluia is also given to certain Psalms, the XLV. and those following, of which the word forms the close. St. Gregory ordered the alleluia to be sung not only at Easter, but throughout the year. It was allowed at fune-rals. Alexander II. prohibited the alleluia in the liturgy in the interval between Septuagesima and Easter Eve; and the Fourth Council of Toledo forbade it on all fast-days. It was used in the Mass to represent the Hebrew title of the Cross, as Kyrie Eleison was a reminiscence of the Greek. Victor of Utica called it the alleluiatic melody; on the Circumcision, which was fasted as a protest against heathen revelry, the alleluia was not sung. The people sang it together in divine service, monks assembled to its sound, and the labourer in the field and the seaman on shipboard chanted it in the early days of the Church.

All-Hallows, *i. e.* All Saints. There are thirteen churches with this dedication, eight of which are in London. In the time of Elizabeth, bells were tolled during the whole night, commencing after evensong, and continued on the morrow on All-Souls' Day.

All-Souls' Day. The morrow of All Saints, Nov. 2. In Shropshire and Cheshire children go round the parish, singing a peculiar song and collecting alms,—probably a relic of the old custom of asking for money to pay for Masses for the dead.

Almery, *or* **Aumbry.** The medieval hutch; a cupboard; occasionally used for keeping broken meat; hence a confusion was made in calling the almonry, the place of almsgiving, the almery, where the dole of fragments from the conventual tables was daily made. The word is derived from *armarium,* and usually designates the wall-closet or locker for keeping the church books or altar-plate, the chrism used in baptism and confirmation, and the holy oil for the sick. In many cases the Eucharist reserved for the last Communion was stored in an aumbry near the altar, as is still the case in Italy. In the cloister the books used in reading-time were kept in an aumbry placed either within the church, close to the door, or else in a locker adjoining it at the north-east angle. At St. Alban's it was in the former position, and enriched with colour. The Greeks had an aumbry for holding the vestments of the religious,—a sort of hanging wardrobe over the altar; from the fifth century presses for the same purpose were erected in the sacristies of the Western Church. There are sometimes two, but more generally one aumbry on the Epistle side in French churches. At Chester there are two on the Gospel side. The Carthusians had two aumbries, one on the right for the vessels, and another for books. Aumbries to contain processional crosses, the bier, taper-stands, and burial furniture, occur in walls near the cloister and cemetery. Three of wood, formerly behind the reredos, are preserved at Carlisle, two of these of the fifteenth century, and one of earlier date, and carved. Several of the fifteenth century are remaining at Selby. Two remain behind the high-altar at Hythe and Sompting. At Salisbury there are several good stone specimens, one retaining its original doors. At Durham there are double aumbries on either side of the altar platform, which held the ewer, books, cruets, chalices, patens, and altar linen. All the keys were locked up by the sacristan at night in a master aumbry until early in the morning. Usually the aumbry is provided with a slab. At Selby there are some good specimens of wainscot aumbries.

Up to the thirteenth century the piscina had a small upper shelf for the chalice; and even in later examples a little cre-dence for holding the cruets and vessels is found. Some-times a small ledge for the calamus appears; and until the thirteenth century the marks of holes for the hinges of doors are visible; after that date, however, the aumbry became common. The vestibule of the Franciscan Convent, London, attached to the chapter-house, was provided with book aumbries and water from the common conduit; and at Wen-lock there are three large arched recesses for aumbries at the north-east angle of the cloisters.

Almond-tree. The symbol of St. Mary, in allusion to Aaron's rod, which blossomed in a night; but M. Montalembert conceives the plant to be dedicated to the Holy Trinity.

Almoner. He distributed the alms, doles, and fragments, and wine-leavings from the various halls, to the poor; provided the expense of the processions in Lent and on Rogations; found mats for the chapter-house and cloisters, dormitory stairs and choir; the necessaries for the Maundy, and a staff of boxwood, which he gave to each monk at processions in Rogations, before which his men cleared the way. At Nor-wich he found wine on certain feasts, and for the clerks of St. Nicholas and boy bishop; under the great almoner was the sub-almoner. He had charge of the bridges at Durham at an early date. At Gloucester the sub-almoner distri-buted the fragments from the refectory and halls of the abbot, infirmary, and lay brothers. The almoner still remains at Metz. The office was founded at Segorbe in 1358. At Lincoln the almoner was called the hospitaller. A minor canon, after the Reformation, discharged the duties at Gloucester, Rochester, Chester, Durham, and Ely.

Almonry (from *Eleemosine*, alms). The place where the daily dole was given to the poor, and therefore invariably adjoining a principal entrance to the monastery. At Canterbury and St. Paul's and Durham, the choristers lodged in it ; and were called, as in St. Mary's College, Winton, the children of the Almonry. At Rome, Pope Vitalian had the choirboys of the Papal chapel lodged and boarded in the Parvise, as, centuries after, the choristers of St. Mary's, Warwick, had their sleeping-room adjoining the church. The almoner, one of the minor canons of St. Paul, had charge of the eight singing-boys.

Almsbox, *or* **Poor Men's Box.** A box in which alms for the poor are placed at the entrance of churches ; there is a good medieval example at Selby, and one of iron, of the fifteenth century, at St. George's, Windsor.

Almsmen. At Gloucester there were thirteen St. Peter's-men, or fraternity of the Holy Cross, founded 1516, by Abbot Malvern, who wore a black gown, hood, and scapulary, with the arms of the monastery on their right shoulder, and a cross of red and blue on their breast.

At Durham there were four aged women of the Infirmary living without the south gate, maintained from the prior's table ; the master of the infirmary said Mass for them on holidays and Fridays in the infirmary chapel.

Almuce, *or* **Amess.** A habit of grey fur, worn in winter by monks and canons. It was at once a cap and tippet ; the outside was of cloth, and the inside was lined with fur, costly, and of a silver-grey colour, as worn by dignitaries, or of dark-brown hue, known as Calabre, from Calabria, whence it was imported, by inferior ministers. The canons' cloth was black, that of the Doctor of Divinity scarlet, and covered the shoulders. The vicars wore the black amess in England and at Vienne ; but violet at Monte Regale, Cefalu, Mazzana, and Messina ; and black with violet edges and ends at Otranto and Palermo. At Langadoc the canons' amess was purple, in honour of martyrs, with a hood [*pœnula*] of lambs' fur.

At Setabis it was of ermine; at Syracuse, black or violet, according to the season; at Neti, of black silk; at Vienne, in summer, of green material; and at Otranto, violet, with crimson edges. At Astley the canons' hoods were lined with linen or fine taffeta from Michaelmas to Easter. In 1242, the Benedictines of Canterbury obtained the Pope's licence to cover their heads during divine service, owing to the cold; the same privilege was allowed at Durham, Peterborough, and Crowland. The Clugniacs and French and Italian canons wore the amess either over the head as a hood, or carried it on the left arm. It sometimes had a stole-like form, as in the portraits of Archbishop Warham, Abbot Bewforest, of Dorchester, and a famous wall-painting at Chichester. Strype calls it a tippet, and, in 1571, it was prohibited by the Council of London, although Parker wore it as "a collar of sables" at his consecration. In a medieval miniature of a præcentor of Salisbury, preserved in the Book of Life of St. Alban's, and on the brass of J. Courthope, 1559, the shape is that of a cape with pendants formed of the tails of animals. But the habit in either shape is not earlier than the thirteenth century, the cape being added two centuries later; its material, the skins of dead animals, typified deadness of spirit to the world. It is the French *aumasse* and Italian *almutzio*. In Italy, during summer time, it is a convenient compromise for the large and heavy cappa. At Cambridge the proctors wear the hoods "squared" like a tippet on formal occasions.

Altar (Latin *altare*, from *altus*, elevated; *ara*, from Gr. *airo*, to raise) (St. Matt. v. 23; xxiii. 18; Heb. xiii. 10). Bishop Ridley renders it Thusiasterion, the place of sacrifices. It consists of the mensa [*lapis integer*], or upper slab, which should be of one piece, to denote the unity of Christ's person; and of a substructure composed of legs, shafts, slabs; or a solid construction, in front of which was an ornamental sculpture, called the tabula, or a hanging of rich material, known as the pall, and recently as the ante-pendium [*devant l'autel*], parafront, or frontal. The true altar was reputed to be the Holy Stone, being the seal of the place of relics, and large enough to contain upon it the chalice and paten; this was let into the slab. The superaltar was a superb covering of the upper slab, used on great occasions.

Minucius Felix, Origen, and Arnobius, say that the Christians had no altar, but their meaning was to distinguish it from the Jewish and Pagan *bomos*, whereon sacrifices of blood were offered, as the Christian altar is spoken of by our Lord and St. Paul. The first altars were, no doubt, tables shaped in memory of the Last Supper; but the tombs of martyrs and confessors in the Roman catacombs were afterwards, during times of persecution, used and covered with sacred sculptures or the image of the Good Shepherd. When the Church had peace, the form of these primitive altars was preserved, and the altar itself built over the grave or confession of a saint, in allusion to St. John's vision of the souls beneath the altar in heaven, or, in lieu, the relics of a saint's body were placed within it. The erection of the first permanent altar is attributed to Pope Sixtus II., and the use of stone in their construction, after the Oriental custom, to Pope Sylvester, *c.* 315. Altars of wood are mentioned by Optatus, St. Athanasius, and St. Augustine; an example exists in St. Praxedes, at Rome; that of St. John's Lateran is of great antiquity,—wooden, hollow, and tomb-shaped, resembling that of the Holy Cross, at Poictiers, as described by St. Gregory of Tours. William of Malmesbury states that St. Wolstan of Worcester first introduced stone in England as the material for altars in place of wood. St. Cyril speaks of British altars in his time without mentioning their make. Erasmus saw one of wood about the period of the Reformation in Canterbury Cathedral. The material of wood symbolized the cross of Calvary.

About the beginning of the fourth century several Councils required the employment of stone, which was preferred from its symbolical reference to Christ, the Rock (Ps. cxviii. 22; Dan. ii. 35), or, expanding the idea of the martyrs' memorials to the holy sepulchre of Him who was made perfect through suffering. St. Gregory of Nyssa, *c.* 370, mentions stone altars in the East, and, in the West, the Council of Epaone, which was enforced in England in 740, and by Lanfranc in 1071, confirmed the practice by ordering that only altars of stone should be consecrated with chrism. The earliest consecration was made by order of Pope Felix I., *c.* 276, in imitation of the anointing of Jacob's pillar. In Belgium stone altars began to be erected in the sixth century.

The earliest form of the altar was a table,—a slab supported on a single shaft, called the reed, like one still existing in the crypt of St. Cecilia's at Rome, or resting on several columns, such as Symeon, Bishop of Ptolemais, describes, which varied in number, from four, six and seven, to eight. To these fugitives clung; and Pope Vigilius, when pursued by the soldiers of Justinian, fled to St. Peter's, and put his arms for sanctuary round the shafts of St. Euphemia's altar, in the sixth century, and the people compelled the prætor and soldiers to retire from the church. The earliest form represented in the catacombs is that of a table on legs, such as remain at Valogne, *c.* 693, St. John's Ravenna, SS. Nazarus and Celsus in the same city, and St. Vincent aux Trois Fontaines. In Belgium, from the sixth to the twelfth century, the altars were composed of a slab resting on five or seven supports; in France they were of the same form, and occasionally raised on mere brackets, but in the thirteenth century they became oblong. In the Greek Church the single altar was small and table-shaped,—a slab supported on five shafts, one in the centre and four at the angles, probably, as in the parallel instance of fonts, symbolizing Christ and the Evangelists.

The old Byzantine altars of Vienne and Spires are of unusual form, being composed of a single block of stone. From the thirteenth to the fifteenth century the tomb-like altar appears; there are ancient examples at St. Vitalis, Ravenna, St. Francis Perouse, Avenas, St. Germer, and the Museum Cluny, but formerly at Basle. In England we possess similar instances of late medieval date, usually of solid construction and with panelled fronts at Arundel, Porlock, Dunster, Abbey Dore, Christchurch (Hants), and Magdalen Hospital, Ripon. In a side altar, at Jorevalle, the recess for relics remains in the frontal. The tomb-like form in many places was preserved with the primitive cavity for relics; the French sub-altars, carried on legs like tables, are believed by some authorities to have served as credence-tables. At Veruela the high-altar, of the twelfth century, is solid with an arcaded front, whilst the sub-altars stand on five shafts.

In the Greek Church there is only one altar. At Milan, according to the Ambrosian rite, the single altar stands detached from the wall; the other altars are modern, having been erected by Cardinal Borromeo. There was at first only a single altar in a church, typifying the unity betwixt Christ and His Church; and the fact is recorded by St. Ignatius, St. Irenæus, St. Cyprian, Tertullian, and Eusebius of Cæsarea; the tradition is still preserved in England with the necessary modification of having an additional altar for early or additional services as at Salisbury, Hereford, St. Paul's, Wells, Chester, Lichfield, Norwich, Carlisle, Christchurch (Hants), Romsey, and, till recently, at Chichester. In Sweden there are usually two unused altars at the ends of the aisles. At length altars were multiplied; Constantine the Great erected three altars in the church of the Holy Sepulchre at Jerusalem, and four in St. Mary's, in the valley of Jehosaphat; in 326, Bishop Aventius consecrated three altars at Avignon. Pope Leo the Great, in the sixth century, mentions thirteen altars erected by Palladins, Bishop of Saintes, in memory of the Apostles. St. Gregory of Tours speaks of two altars in St. Peter's, Bordeaux, and celebrated on three altars in the church of Brennes. St. Benet d'Anian, in the time of Constantine, erected seven altars in his minster of St. Guilhem du Desert. In the eleventh and twelfth centuries, when the aisles were continued eastward, and apses were converted into chevets, with a processional path and radiating chapels, altars necessarily were multiplied. In the fourth century, there were seven in the Lateran; in the fifth century, St. Ambrose mentions the soldiers, when leaving the basilica of Milan, embracing the altars to announce peace accorded to the Church by Valentinian, and St. Hilary dedicated three altars in the baptistery of the Lateran. St. Gregory mentions two in St. Peter's, Bordeaux, and thirty in another church. The Greeks retain a single altar in a church, but build a number of external oratories for the celebration of Mass.

The primitive altar stood in the centre of the church as at Tyre, described by Eusebius, on Mount Olivet, and still later at Seligenstadt. The celebrant was thus distinctly seen by the whole congregation, whom he faced, and the site corresponds to that of the rood altar in a medieval church. It had a passage all round it in allusion to the words of the Psalm (xxvi. 6), "I will compass Thine altar." St. Chrysostom mentions curtains which draped it about, just as the bankars on either side, and the dorsal at the back fenced in the medieval altar. A curious relic of the ancient custom of the celebrant to front the people is preserved in the remarkable altar of Bologna, which has two faces; and at Canterbury, in Parker's time, when there was no communion, the priest stood on the east side of the altar, facing the people; and Jewel mentions that it was also the custom at Milan, Naples, Lyons, Mayence, Rome, and St. Laurence, at Florence. It is still observed at St. John Lateran, St. Peter's in the Vatican, St. Mary Major, St. Mary in Trastevere, and St. Peter's at Cirate. By the Ambrosian rite, the priest, in memory of ancient usage, does not turn to give the benediction or say "Dominus vobiscum," as he is supposed to have the people in front of him. The high-altar ought always to front the east in cathedrals and collegiate churches; minor altars and chapels might front any point of the compass. The ancient altars had four columns at the corners, which supported a domelike canopy, called the ciborium or Baldacchino, to which were affixed large curtains of silk, which fell at the moment of consecration, and remained drooping during the Communion. Sometimes the materials used in an altar were precious marbles and porphyry resting on columns of the same rich stone; if the altar was of simple masonry, it was covered with magnificent draperies of silk, with sumptuous embroidery, and encrusted with gold and precious gems. Pope Sylvester, at the beginning of the fourth century, erected an altar of silver and gold, with rich jewelled work; to it Leo III. and Leo. IV. gave altar-cloths of tissue of gold, with scenes from our Lord's life. There is a magnificent altar, the Palliotto, in St. Ambrose's, Milan, which was executed by Wolvinius, in 835, and erected by Bishop Angilbert, with plates of precious metals and enamelling. The altar of Basle, c. 1019, now in the Hôtel Cluny, is of gold; one at Monreale is of silver; that of St. Germer, near Beauvais, of the twelfth century, is of bronze; that of Ratisbon is of silver; and other examples of metal occur at Aix-la-Chapelle, Pistoia, of the fourteenth century, and Florence. A portable altar, cased with silver, of the tenth century is preserved at Oviedo, and another of the twelfth century at Munich. Whilst the altars of cathedrals and minsters were overlaid with mosaics and enrichments of great value, in the country churches the altar was of plain stone, and covered with a cloth of pure linen or lace. In the crypts of Spires and St. Savin there are five altars of this simple character; but sculptured frontals of the same date have been preserved, which adorned the richer altars. At Brussels, Amiens, Rouen, Abbeville, and other Belgian and French churches, there are modern wooden altars.

Where the front of the altar is plain, it was intended to be concealed with hangings. In Spain, Italy, and France, owing to modern innovations, ancient altars are rare, but in Germany they are common; and of all varieties, the Baldacchino, or ciborium, remains at Prague, at Castle Transnichts, of the thirteenth century, in Bavaria; early fourteenth-century altars, with rich ciboria, may be seen at Ratisbon; at Erfurth there are fronts of canopied images, or mere interlacing arches; and in the Alte Dom Chapel of the Cloisters, Ratisbon, one of the ninth century has crosses within circles; another there, of the eleventh century, rests on four columns; another, in the cathedral of Brunswick, is Romanesque, and composed of a marble slab resting on four bronze shafts; the superb high-altar of Cologne is of the earlier part of the fourteenth century; the materials are black and white marble, and the frontal consists of canopied images. Triptych altars of wood of the fourteenth and fifteenth centuries are preserved in the same cathedral, and superb examples of the reredos at Lorsch and Erfurth. The fifteenth-century type was a wooden altar and reredos, with a large triptych, carving in deep relief and pictures as at Oberwesel.

There were several altars in a large church :—

I. The High Altar, distinguished as the great, chief, or principal, which stood at the east end of the sanctuary. It was called also the chapter or cardinal altar, because used for the high, cardinal, chapter, or conventual Mass, which was sung after prime in summer and after tierce in winter. Anciently, always isolated, and aloof from the wall, in distinction to minor altars.

II. The Altar of the Rood, the Cross, the Crucified, or Jesus, which was placed in the rood-loft, facing the nave, and formed the high-altar of the parish or laity.

III. The Middle, or Matin Altar, which stood at Worcester

and St. Alban's under a rood beam, at the east end of the choir, before the entrance of the Presbytery. It was used for the early or matin Mass of a convent; it stood, however, sometimes behind the high-altar, and, where there was an apse, between it and the throne of the bishop. In Cistercian churches, and at Pisa, Bourges, Chartres, and Rheims, it was used for the reservation of the veiled cross on Good Friday, which was borne in procession by two of the clergy singing the anthem, "Popule Meus," "O my people." At Canterbury, in 950, as in the old cathedral of St. Peter's, Rome, there were three altars in a row, one behind the other, —the high, matin, and rood altars..

IV. At the lower end of the choir was an altar at Toulon, Orange, Noyon, Sées, St. Germain des Prés, Padua, Turin, Verona, Bologna, Sienna, and several Roman churches, used for the conventual Mass or as a rood altar.

V. The altar of St. Mary, usually in a chapel eastward of the presbytery; besides other minor altars of saints, arranged in chapels at the ends of aisles, or against the nave-pillars. These were attached to chantries, and maintained by the endowment of founders or at the expense of guilds and brotherhoods.

At the Reformation, many altars were destroyed in England and tables of wood erected, but the demolition and change were regarded with popular disfavour, and some bishops, like Day of Chichester, refused to take any part in the desecration. In some places, where the choir or chancel was too confined to hold the communicants, the altar was removed, at the time of Communion, into the nave, thus occupying the site of the old rood-altar, and afterwards restored to its proper position at the east end of the chancel, standing altarwise. In the first Prayer-book of Edward VI., it was also called God's board, and the Lord's table. In the 'Consecration Service,' the 'Statutes of Hereford,' and other authorized documents, it retains its ancient name of altar. At Durham and Worcester in the reign of Charles I., at Bolton in Craven in 1703, at Stratford on Avon in the present century, stone altars were erected. That of St. George's, Deal, was brought from Northbourne Priory; there are other examples at Westminster Abbey and New College Chapel, Oxford.

The slab of the altar at its dedication was ensigned with five crosses, one in the centre and four at the corners, in memory of the five wounds of Christ, and also with the name of the saint in whose honour it was raised, according to an English council held in 816. It was divided into three parts in front, *medium altare*, before the altar, and the right-hand, or Epistle side, and the left-hand, or Gospel side, according to the English use; but in Roman churches, since 1458, the position is reversed, being assumed from the crucifix on the altar, and not as before, from the celebrant's arms, facing the reredos. Altars were washed with wine and water on Maundy-Thursday, in allusion to the blood and water which flowed from the Saviour's riven side. The Emperor was set upon the altar of Mayence on his consecration, and the Pope on the altar of St. Peter's after his election by the cardinal bishops. In England, in 896, slaves were manumitted at the altar, and oaths of purgation made before it, and donations of lands by the gift of a sword, or a horn or cup laid upon it. Altars were required by English councils to be anointed in 740, and hallowed in 960.

The Greeks, in the ninth century, charged the Western Church with presenting a lamb at the altar on Easter Day, with a symbolical reason; and Sir Thomas More speaks of the hallowing of the fire, the fount, the Paschal Lamb. At Westminster Abbey, in the thirteenth century, a salmon was yearly presented at the high-altar in commemoration of the monks having succeeded in establishing their right of the conservatorship of the Thames from Yenlade, below Greenwich, to Staines Bridge; and at the same date until the reign of Elizabeth, before the altar of St. Paul's every year a doe in winter time and a buck in summer, garlanded with roses and flowers, was offered by the bequest of a knightly St. Baude, in lieu of 22 acres of land granted to him by the chapter. At York, a lamb was offered by the tenants on Lammas Day, and a stag was annually presented at Durham on St. Cuthbert's Day by the Nevilles. At Léon, one quarter of a bull, which had been killed in the last bull-fight, was annually offered at the high-altar on August 27.

There is an altar-cloth at Emneth which was given in 1570, and exhibits a resemblance to medieval embroidery. Some at York are of stamped leather.

Until the ninth century the altar was unornamented, but in the tenth century the cross was put on it; but before the fourteenth century no candles or crosses were permitted to be permanently set on altars, but were invariably brought in by two acolyths when Mass was to be said. Until the thirteenth century the bishops sat at the end of the apse, but in the fourteenth century altars were multiplied and the throne was displaced. The next step was to bring in at the time of Mass portable retables or diptychs; and then, in the fifteenth century, the contre-retable appeared, a wainscoted decoration above an altar, designed to receive the altar-piece or retable, either a picture or bas-relief of the saint to whom the altar was dedicated, and at the end of that period Germany was pre-eminent in the delicacy of the carvings of such works of art.

Altarage. Altar-dues, the offertory-alms for a priest's maintenance.

Altaristæ, *or* **Officiatores.** Deputy chaplains appointed for saying Masses.

Altar-piece. A picture over an altar. At Gloucester there is a painting of the early part of the fifteenth century, representing the Crucial Judgment, which is supposed to have formed the altar-piece.

Alure. A passage, alley, walk, in a church or cloister; a parapet; a gutter.

Ambon. (Greek, *anabainein*, to mount, because ascended by stairs; or *ambo*, because there were usually two ambons.) An elevated desk or pulpit, used for reading the Holy Scriptures, the Epistle and Gospel, and placed in the centre of the nave, either in the middle or on one side. When there were three ambons, the Epistle was read from the southern, and the Gospel from the northern lectern. Where there was only a single ambon, the Epistle was read from its lower step by the subdeacon turning towards the altar, and the Gospel by the deacon on a step higher, in the direction of the nave; and a large chandelier or candlestick, attached to the ambon, supported the Gospel light. It usually had two flights of stairs, one on the left, towards the east, for ascending it, and the other on the right, facing westwards, for descending; but in some churches, to mark due honour to the Gospel, the subdeacon and deacon used different staircases.

At the ambon were recited the diptychs, the acts of martyrs, letters of peace or communion; sermons were delivered; and the newly-converted made profession of faith. Towards the nave were iron prickets for tapers where there was no great chandelier or Gospel candlestick. Beneath it was the privileged place for the choir, from the time of St. Gregory, when the singers had their special duties, as the deacon was always a Gospeller, and none but priests could celebrate.

The Council of Laodicea applies the word 'ambon' to the place of the singers; the choir, not the lectern; just as St. Gregory Nazianzen contrasts the great *bema* of the readers with the sacred bema, or sanctuary. This name of bema is also occasionally transferred to the ambon, which was known by other names, as, pulpit, lectern, *purgos* (tower), *suggestus*, *gradus* (the step), *auditorium*, or *ostensorium*. St. Cyprian, St. Gregory of Tours, and Prudentius called it the tribunal of the church, as bishops like St. Chrysostom preached from it; and Walafrid Strabo, in allusion to the crowd of hearers grouped around it, gives the derivation of the word, *ambire*, to surround. The great royal, or beautiful gate, the entrance to the ritual choir, rose over the ambon. The most ancient ambon existing, that in the Holy Ghost Church, Ravenna, is of the sixth century; the most modern, dated 1249, is preserved in St. Pancras, at Rome. At St. Sophia's, Constantinople, the ambon was jewelled and hung with lights. The ambon for the Epistle at St. Mary's Cosmedin, St. Clement's, and St. Laurence Without, at Rome, is square, and on the north side; the Gospel ambon, on the south side, is octagonal, and reached by two flights of stairs. Toledo possesses ambons of bronze, and those of Seville are still used for chanting the Gospel and Epistle. The ambons of Toscanella, St. Mary in Ara Cœli, and St. Nereus, Rome, and St. John, Pistoia, of the thirteenth century, have a large eagle in front. The ambon was the original from which the pulpit, the lectern eagle, and rood-loft were derived. A pulpit on the north side of the chancel of Compton Martin, Somerset, may have been used as the Gospel ambon.

Ambrosian Liturgy. A Mass used at Milan, and also by the Cistercians.

Ambulatory. An aisle; the processional path.

Amen. The Puritans, according to Stapleton, had a trick used by their preachers to make their audience cry Amen, which was a poor imitation of the applause and clapping of hands used in ancient times, and condemned by St. Chrysostom and St. Jerome; although Burnet, at a later date, sat down in the pulpit of St. Margaret's, Westminster, to enjoy the humming approbation of the congregation manifested at one of his political discourses. It was a primitive practice to answer Amen at prayers (1 Cor. xiv. 16), and St. Jerome says, "In church, at the tombs of the martyrs, the Amen, like the heavenly thunder, booms again." St. Chrysostom says it took the place of the Greek acclamation of the orator by his audience, and was uttered in a kind of chant. St. Justin mentions that after the Holy Communion the people cried out together Amen; and St. Augustine, St. Cyril of Jerusalem, St. Ambrose, Tertullian, and Eusebius mention that the communicant, on receiving the Eucharist, used the word to express that he had received the Body and Blood of Christ. "With the same mouth," says Tertullian, "you say Amen in honour of the King of Saints and to glorify a gladiator." St. Athanasius speaks of the use of Amens in the church of Alexandria, and St. Gregory Nazianzen bids his mother speak only in church by replying with an Amen to what the priest had said.

The word means True, or, according to Eusebius, So be it, or, as Aquila explains it, Faithfully. St. Hilary defines it to be the response to pious words.

Amice. An oblong or square piece of fine linen; a covering of the head and neck introduced in the seventh and eighth centuries to preserve the voice, as Amalarius suggests, and also as a decent ornament. At a later date it was regarded as the counterpart of the Jewish ephod or humerale, and was made sufficiently ample to cover the shoulders and chest. At Rome, about the year 900, it was used as a covering for the head, and wound round the neck at the time of Holy Communion. In the tenth century it received an ornamental border, called the Apparel. The amice is not enumerated among church vestments until the ninth century, and it was not until the thirteenth century that the clergy covered their heads during the sacred office; it is probable that the bishops also did not wear their mitres at such times previous

to this date. The other names of this appendage were
epomis, and, about the beginning of the ninth century, superhumerale and anabologion. It was supposed by some
writers to symbolize the helmet of salvation; but Cranmer
considers it to represent the veil with which the Jews
covered the face of the Saviour at His mocking, when they
buffeted Him, and also faith, the head of all virtues.

Ampulla. (Latin, *vas amplum*, or *olla ampla*.) The cruet
for chrism oil, and holy oil, and sick men's oil. The most
famous was that preserved at Rheims, until broken by a
miscreant after the death of Louis XVI.;—a portion of the
oil was saved and used at the coronation of Charles X.;—it
was made of glass, and used at the coronations of the kings
of France from the time of Clovis, who had been baptized
with it. An idle legend declared that it had been brought
from heaven by a white dove to St. Remi. The real fact
was, that the holy oil used at the baptism of Clovis was enclosed in the figure of a dove suspended over the baptistery.
2. A leathern pouch given in England to pilgrims to the various greater shrines.

Amula. The ancient name for a cruet for the wine used at the
Eucharist. When personal offerings in kind ceased, the ampulla, or burette, replaced the round amula, which was often
jewelled and of precious metal.

Amulet. A preservative; from the Arabic *hama-il*, a small
Koran hung as a necklace, as a safeguard; from *hamala*, to
carry. It was applied to the Holy Eucharist by Christians.
The Christian amulet, from being carried in the breast, was
often called encolpium, or philacteria; sometimes they were
in the form of a medal of bronze, marked with a cross, and
of a hand, with the salutation *Zekes*, 'Mayest thou live;' a
portion of the Gospels hung round the neck; a relic; or a
formulary within a box of precious wood, like one preserved
at Monza.

Analogion. A reading-desk.

Anaphora. In the primitive Liturgies, the Oblation, analogous to the Canon of the Mass; and in the English Liturgy
to the portion following the words, " Lift up your hearts."
It commenced with the triumphal hymn.

Anchor. One of the earliest symbols used by Christians on
their rings, as by good George Herbert in later days, as the

pledge of hope of safety against shipwreck, in allusion to
Heb. vi. 18. The mystic fish is often associated with it, and
its shape below the ring is cruciform, which, no doubt, contributed to its popularity. Other authors regard it as a
symbol of constancy or conscience; or the wholesome effects
of poverty and tribulation on the soul.

Anchoret. A hermit, says Giraldus, is a wanderer; an anchoret is a recluse. In the Middle Ages, there was a.regu-
lation, called the Ancresse Rule, for inclusi, men or women
recluses who lived immured in a peculiar chamber in or near
a church for life, as at Norwich, Westminster, Leicester, and
Peterborough; in the churches of the Holy Innocents and
St. Médard, at Paris, in the fourteenth and fifteenth centuries. They were admitted by the bishop, and retained their
civil rights; in certain cases the door might be reopened.
At Mas d'Azil, the chamber in which an idiot was confined
is still shown. At Westminster, the cell was in an aisle; at
Peterborough, near the Lady Chapel; at Durham it was approached from the north choir aisle by a staircase. At Norwich, a gallery still existing in the north choir aisle communicated with the sanctuary men's chamber, which, before the
fifteenth century, was the reliquary chapel of St. Osyth, and
occupied by a recluse. At St. Peter's, in St. Alban's, there
was a recluse in the twelfth century, and at Mantes in the
time of William I. At Durham, the anchorage was a porch
with a rood standing between two pillars at the east end of
the north choir aisle. It contained an altar for Mass, and
was reached by stairs from the shrine. It had been, in ancient time, the dwelling of an anchoret. There was an anchorage at Leicester, and the Dominican Friary, in Norwich.
Frequently, the anchoret was a priest who was not permitted
to open any church door, but preached or conversed with
lay persons through a low grated window on the south side
of the chancel, which was also used to communicate lepers.
Sometimes the anchoret had a separate dwelling, with an
oratory attached to it. At Markyate, a recluse, Christina,
lived in a cell barred with a heavy wooden bolt, provided
with a stone seat, and secluded from view by an inner screen.
Near it six hermits lived. Women who had renounced the
world were permitted to have a chamber within the church,
having only a grated aperture, which opened into the build-

ing. One such inmate at a time only was permitted. Sometimes the recluse was an involuntary occupant of a cell, accepting it as a commutation for death due to a criminal offence.
These cells must not be confounded with the chambers of the
sacrist, chantry priests, or church watchers over chapels or
in parvises. Occasionally, the cells were wooden structures
in a cemetery, and provided with a garden.

Ancien et Nouveau Diacre. Two of the junior canons at
Cologne, Lubeck and Osnaburg; probably so called as of
two foundations for deacon canons.

Angelic Hymn. The "Gloria in Excelsis," so called because
sung by the angels in Bethlehem on the night of the Nativity.

Angelic, *or* **Heavenly Hierarchies.** St. Augustine professes
that he did not know the distinction between the orders
mentioned in the Apostolical Epistle to the Colossians. But
at a later date, nine companies have been enumerated,
divided into three hierarchies —

1. Seraphim (perfect love), cherubim (perfect wisdom),
thrones (perfect rest, and in contemplation as dwelling
nearest to God).

2. Dominions, Virtues, Powers; holding the general
government of the Universe, the gift of miracles in God's
service, and the office of resisting and casting out devils.

3. Principalities, Archangels, Angels: intrusted with the
rule of nations, of provinces and cities, and individual man
as a guardian.

The nine choirs are represented in the glass of New College Chapel, Oxford, and at Chartres in the thirteenth century, Vincennes fourteenth century, and Cahors fifteenth
century, in sculpture; on the roof of St. John's, Stamford,
and on the beautiful Pillar of the Angels, at Strasburg. At
Lincoln, the "Angel Choir" contains figures of angels in
the tympana of the triforium. They are often represented
in priestly vestments, but more correctly with unsandalled
feet, wings of gold, and robes of pure white; sometimes
their wings, in the latter part of the fifteenth century, are
painted in various colours, as in the stained glass of Tattershall, Warwick, Wells (Norfolk), and Southwold; or in earlier examples with peacock's-tail feathers, to represent the
eyes within and without, as on the chapter-house walls of

Westminster. St. Michael appears at first in an albe, but in the fifteenth century, with far less propriety, in armour.

The conventional delineation is as follows :—

1. *Angels:* ministers and messengers of grace ; with albes flowing to the feet, with golden girdles [as they are represented in the Apocalypse], and green stoles ; they carry a ring of gold in their right hand and the seal of God, $\times$, in their left hand ; or they are in armour with girdles of gold, battle-axes, and lances ; or they bear a book and ring ; are represented as in the bloom of youth, with white robes of purity and golden ornaments of holiness and glory.

2. *Archangels:* angels sent as messengers on God's greatest matters, as St. Gabriel at the Annunciation, and to Zacharias, and St. Michael, the Archangel of the Doom, mentioned by Daniel and St. Jude, ambassadors extraordinary. They carry a cross-banner, the emblem of victory, and a javelin or axe.

3. *Seraphim,* whose chief is Uriel, chant for ever the praises and love of God. Their spiritual swiftness is represented by their wings, and their ardent love by a burning heart, and are compared to pure fire. They have six wings : two about their head, two about their feet, and two outspread, as if to fly, and they carry in each hand a scroll inscribed, " Holy, Holy, Holy " (Isaiah vi. 2).

4. *Cherubim:* angels, so called, says St. Jerome, from their exceeding knowledge, or their swiftness (Ps. xviii.). They are under their chief, Jophiel ; sometimes they appear with four wings, to veil their feet and faces, and looking towards each other ; or are represented by winged heads ; or of red colour, or standing upon burning wheels (Ezek. i. 19, 20).

5. *Thrones:* who stand always at the throne of God, as in Ezekiel's vision. They appear as wheels of fire, with wings studded over with eyes ; or they carry a palm and crown, emblematical of justice and equity, and are kneeling. Their chief is Zaphkiel. At Chartres, they have green wings and sceptres, and are enclosed within a crimson elliptic aureole.

6. *Dominations:* whose chief is Zadkiel, carry a sceptre, sword, and cross. By their ministry, God exercises His power in the world.

7. *Virtues:* under Haniel, carry a crown of thorns in one

hand and a chalice of consolation in the left hand. At New College, they have a battle-axe and spear, with a pennon marked with the cross.

8. *Powers :* the host, from whom God is called the Lord of Sabaoth; guardian angels under Raphael, who carry a levin bolt and flaming sword. At New College, they wear a jupon, sword-belt, an ermine tippet and furred cap, and carry a spiked bâton.

9. *Principalities :* the guardians of princes, under Kamiel, hold sceptres, and wear a belt with a cross over their breast.

Angels usually are vested in a white pall or tunic, and a blue stole; they are represented in human form as ministering to man (Heb. i. 14); winged, from their readiness to aid man (Ps. xci. 11); with a censer, as offering the prayers of men (Tobit iii. 24, 25, xii. 12; Rev. viii. 3, 4); as youths, because immortal; beautiful, because holy (Exod. xxv. 18; 1 Chron. vi. 23, 27, 28); armed, in allusion to 2 Macc. xi. 8; girdled (Rev. xv. 6); white-robed, from their sinlessness; with jewels, as symbolical of their virtues (Exod. xxviii. 17); barefooted, as God's ministers (Joshua v. 13, 16; Exod. iii. 5; St. Matt. x. 9, 10); and among clouds, as dwelling in heaven.

St. Clement of Alexandria taught a transmigration of human souls into angels, and, by successive stages, into archangels. Like Justin Martyr, he believed that angels fell from their first estate for love of earthly women. An angel often crowned a spire, tower, or flèche; for this reason, the central tower of Canterbury was called the Angel Steeple; and still a great angel with a cross stands over the Apse of Rheims.

After Arianism appeared, two angels were usually represented on either side of our Blessed Lord, as witnesses to the Divinity and Consubstantiality of the Word. Angels were always represented round the choir, and especially in the sanctuary and about the altar (eminently by the Carthusians), in allusion to their presence in divine worship (1 Cor. xi. 10). Sometimes angels carry a measuring rod (Rev. xxi. 15; Ezek. xl. 3); a sword, as the ministers of God's wrath; the instruments of the Passion, as executing His mercy; or scales, as performing His judgments. The trumpet relates to the Last Judgment, and other instruments of music recall the divine melody of their heavenly home.

Angelus. "Hail, Mary!" the salutation of St. Gabriel to the Blessed Virgin, is commemorated by a prayer said at the sound of a bell called the Angelus, which is rung at dawn, noon, and evening. The latter was ordered by Pope John XXII., 1316–34, the first by the Council of Bourges in 1369, and enforced by Archbishop Arundel in 1399, who required a Paternoster and five Aves to be said. It was often called the Gabriel Bell. The midday bell was instituted by Louis XI. in 1472. The modern form was introduced into France in the sixteenth century. In the thirteenth century, at St. Alban's, three peals were rung for the Lady Mass; and the Angelus has been attributed to Pope Urban II., when he enjoined prayers to be made for the Crusaders; or Calixtus III. in 1455, when the Christian army was engaged in repelling the Turks. The Curfew, which is as ancient as the time of King Alfred, was probably adopted for the evening Angelus. St. Augustine and St. Jerome say that our Lord went to His Passion at night, rose in the morning, and ascended at noonday, and the three hours are indicated in Ps. lv. 17.

Animals and living creatures are often represented in sacred buildings within mouldings and on tombs, merely as ornaments from early days; such as dolphins, doves, griffins, monsters, birds, and the like. In the medieval period, effigies rest their feet on a lion or dog, the types of constancy and strength; but in the catacomb and church, the lion, the horse, the lamb, the hart, the stag, the dove, peacocks, fish, are emblems. The lion represented vigilance; the lamb, innocence; the hart, flight from sin; the hare or the horse alluded to the Christian course (1 Cor. ix. 24; 2 Tim. iv. 7); the dolphin typified speed and diligence, and, from heathen fables of Ælian and Pliny, loving affection; whilst birds, amongst foliage and flowers, portrayed the deliverance of the souls of the blessed from their earthly habitations (Ps. cxxiv. 6). In the ceremony of canonization, the Pope is offered, among other presents, caged birds, as emblematical of the virtues of saints. Doves and serpents refer to St. Matt. x. 16.

Anker-hold. A cell of a recluse in a church. At Kilkenny Cathedral, there was one at the north-east angle of the choir, "through which, by a stone window placed on the right horn of the altar, that is, the Gospel side, the anchoret could see the mysteries ;" an account which fully describes the true intention of those openings hitherto pedantically known as hagioscopes and lychnoscopes, words of recent coinage, and erroneously explained. This cell was four feet below the choir-floor, but the recluse was enabled to see the altar by means of an open niche, to which he went up by stairs; it contained a fireplace and rude lockers or aumbries. In Bavaria, each cell had three windows, one to see the Sacrament, a second for the admission of food, and a third for light, being closed with horn or glass. Some of the women recluses had also a servant in the adjoining chamber, and three windows in their own cell; one, of the parlour, for conversation, curtained with a black veil, which was embroidered with a white cross; another, the home-window, for light and ventilation; and the third for communion. Several anker-holds still exist: at Fore, in Ireland, in the church; at Wilbraham, in the tower; at Stanton, Somerset, adjoining the church; and in the south arm of the transept at Norwich : each had its altar, crucifix, and images. In Pembrokeshire, at Othery, Somerset, and several cruciform Cornish churches, especially at Mawgan, the chamber or passage is pierced through the wall at the junction of the transept and chancel, or where the end of the roed-screen would terminate. These all have their external low-side windows; and at Elsfield it is provided with a stone book-desk and seat.

Annates. First fruits paid to the Pope when an ecclesiastic was promoted. They were made a settled duty by Pope Boniface IX. in the reign of Henry IV., but claimed many years before by the Pope. Henry VIII. seized them. Queen Mary refused to receive them, but Queen Elizabeth accepted their restoration. Queen Anne nobly gave them up for the better maintenance of the poorer clergy, as a fund called Queen Anne's Bounty.

Annuals. Annals, yearminds, or obits; anniversary Masses for the dead.

Annuellars. Chaplain priests who celebrated the Commemoration Masses for the departed, on their annuals. Their usual pay was three marks yearly. At Exeter there were twenty-four, who acted as subdeacons in choir; at Wells, fourteen : both corporations lived in a collegiate manner. The name was preserved at Llandaff so late as 1575.

Annunciation. Lady Day. The feast is mentioned by St. Athanasius, St. Augustine, St. Chrysostom, Gelasius, and Gregory [and by the Council of Toledo, on December 18, in 654] ; it was confirmed by Boniface IX. in the fourteenth century.

Ante-church. In some churches, as Vezelay, Clugny, Dijon, Sherborne, Glastonbury, and Lewes, there was a large ante-church, which corresponded with the ancient Prior Porticus, or Pro-Naos. The ante-chapel is a transeptal approach to a college chapel, as at Merton, New, Magdalen, All Souls', and Wadham, at Oxford.

Ante et Retro. To bow before and behind in choir to the abbot or dean, and to the altar, in entering or leaving the choir. At Windsor and Durham and Oxford, a trace of the custom lingers : in the Royal Chapel, the canons bow to the Sovereign's closet, and in the cathedrals to the altar. At Canterbury, the statutes prescribe bowing to the altar and to the dean.

Ante-pane, *or* **Ante-pendium.** The front-cloth ; frontal. (1.) A curtain hung in front of the ciborium. (2.) An altar-cloth covering the western face of an altar. Bishop Hacket calls it a suffront.

Anthem. A corruption of the word Antiphon, an alternate chant ; it is also used to designate a passage selected from the Holy Scripture or the Psalter (according to the rule prescribed by the second Council of Braga), and sung to music, either by a single voice or in chorus ; and it is employed to mark the sentence prefixed to a Psalm or canticle, giving the key-note to its meaning, pointing out in which of its mystical senses it is at the time to be recited, as well as the tone according to which what follows is to be sung antiphonally. The word 'anthetime' occurs in the sense of a text for Bishop Story's sermon, and another by Dr. Chadsey, at St. Paul's ; and in Edward VI.'s First Book for the sentences, " Remember not," and " O Saviour of the world," in the Visitation of the Sick, and " Turn Thou us " in the Commination Service. It is still retained in the notice of the Easter Hymn sung instead of the 'Venite,' and in the rubric after the Third Collect at matins and evensong. Anthems were sung in the steeple of St. Paul's after the Reformation, and a metrical hymn, composed about the

D

same time, and another so lately as 1585, bear the same name.

On Easter Day the anthem is used in place of the ninety-fifth Psalm, which was the usual invitatory of matins as early as the fourth century, and also called an anthem,—the name given at that date also to the verse which precedes the intonation of a Psalm. In its modern sense, of a piece of sacred music for the use of the Church, it first occurs in the time of Elizabeth. In Queen Mary's reign they sang anthems about the steeple of St. Paul's; and to this day, in memory of the battle of Neville's Cross, three anthems are sung on the central tower of Durham on May Day, one side being omitted owing to the fall of a chorister some years since. The anthem was at first repeated before a Psalm, but in later times also after it.

Anthony, St., of Egypt, Order of. Founded by Gaston Frank in 1095, to attend on those struck with leprosy or erysipelas, called the sacred fire; hence one of the symbols of the Saints; another is the hog, which suffers from cutaneous disease. The rule is Augustine; the dress a cassock, patience, a black hood and plaited cloak, with a Tau cross in blue cloth on the breast. The first monastery was at La Motte, near Vienna.

Antilegomena. (Greek; controverted.) Certain books of the New Testament, which were doubted before admitted into the canon of Scripture, as, for instance, the Apocalypse.

Antiminsion. A portion of the covering placed on an altar at its dedication, and used in the Greek Church for the same purpose as a super-altar in the West; that is, as a portable altar for Communion where there was no consecrated building.

Anti-pasch. The Sunday after Easter Day.

Antiphonal. Alternate singing (from *anti*, opposite, and *phone*, a voice). Socrates attributes its introduction to St. Ignatius in the Eastern Church; but Theodoret says it was the invention of two priests of Antioch, Diodorus and Flavian, during the Arian heresy in 350. St. Ambrose brought the custom into vogue in the Western Church at Milan. The original idea, no doubt, was borrowed from Isaiah's vision, where the angels are represented as crying one to another. The Psalms, Responses, Suffrages, Gloria Patri, Kyrie,

Creed, Sanctus, Agnus Dei, and Canticles, are sung in this manner.

Antiphonar. A Church-book containing the music for the hours, anthems, hymns, Psalms, noted in plain chant. It is divided, like the Gradual, which contained the chant for the Mass, into the "Proper of Time" and the "Common of Saints." Every French diocese had its own antiphonar; at Milan the rival Roman and Ambrosian uses, and at Toledo the Roman and Mozarabic antiphonars, formed the subject of a long controversy. As the anthems principally compose its contents, they have given name to the book. Pope Gregory the Great compiled the first antiphonar, which he called a Centon, having selected an antiphon from the Psalms as an introit, and others for the Responsory, Offertory, and Communion.

Antipopes. The rival occupants of the Papal Chair from Urban VI., 1389, to Alexander V., 1409, respectively resident at Avignon and Rome, and supported by the Italians or French.

Apocalypse. (Greek.) The Revelation of St. John the Divine.

Apocrypha. (Greek; hidden, obscure, spurious; called also ecclesiastical or deutero-canonical.) The Books not belonging to the canon of Scripture, being not regarded as authentic. They were, however, generally read in church for religious instruction, as St. Athanasius, St. Jerome, and Ruffinus mention, and are used in the Church of England. They include III. and IV. Esdras, Tobit, Judith, the rest of Esther, Wisdom, Baruch, the Song of the Three Children, Susanna, Bel and the Dragon, Prayer of Manasses, the I. and II. Maccabees. St. Jerome first uses the term Apocrypha, as Ruffinus explains, because they were not ordinarily read in church. At a later date the Shepherd of Hermes and the Epistles of Clement were included in the term. The Third Council of Carthage in 401 ordered that only the Canonical Books should be read as Scripture in church.

Apokrisiarii. (1.) Legates of the Patriarch of Constantinople. (2.) Commissaries of foreign churches in the Imperial city.

Apologia. The Confession and Absolution in the Gallican Liturgy.

Apostles' Creed. "Symbolum commune sive Apostolorum;"

is so called commonly, and by St. Ambrose, because it contains the substance of their teaching, and from the Latin initial word, *credo*, I believe. It is given in substance by Tertullian, referred to by St. Irenæus, Origen, Gregory of Cæsarea, and Lucian the Martyr, was summarized by St. Ignatius, and in the old offices of Holy Baptism; and is called the Canon of Right and Standard of Faith by St. Basil, the Key of Peter by St. Ambrose, and the Rule of Faith by St. Augustine. The words "life everlasting" were added in the time of St. Cyprian; "the resurrection of the body," in the time of St. Augustine; "He descended into hell," in the Creed of Aquileia; and "the communion of saints," in the sixth century. It was adopted by Charlemagne, and in the eleventh century in Spain. Cranmer alludes to "the painters showing the twelve articles," which an old tradition (distinctly alluded to by St. Ambrose and Leo the Great, and preserved by St. Augustine, Ruffinus, Isidore of Seville, and Honorius) attributed to the several Apostles, as they were often delineated holding scrolls containing each a distinct sentence. And certain of the Prophets —for instance, Joel iii. 12, Amos ix. 6, Hosea xiii. 14, Is. vii. 14, Jer. iii. 19—correspondingly held a parallel and anticipative text from their writings, foreshadowing it. The order of the Articles, with the authors assigned at their last meeting in a grotto on Mount Olivet, are as follows :—St. Peter, " I believe;" St. John, "Maker;" St. James, "and in Jesus Christ;" St. Andrew, "who was conceived;" St. Philip, "suffered;" St. Thomas, "He descended;" St. Bartholomew, "He ascended;" St. Matthew, "from thence;" St. James, "I believe;" St. Simon, "the communion;" St. Jude, "the resurrection;" St. Matthias, "life everlasting." The Greek Creed adds the words, "and in one Lord." It was called a Symbol, as a common test of the Apostles' doctrine and fellowship. The ancient creeds of the Churches of Jerusalem, Cæsarea, Alexandria, Antioch, Rome, and Aquileia, and that preserved in the Apostolical Constitutions, resemble it in every main particular. It was adopted at Antioch.

Apostoli. Documents granted by judges in appeals to the Court of Rome.

Apostolical Canons. A work first alluded to by name in the

Council of Constantinople in 394, and probably compiled in the third century; they have been reckoned at ninety-five or seventy-six, according to different arrangement and divisions. They represent, no doubt, Apostolic tradition, rules of discipline established before the Council of Nice, and decisions of synods or bishops made in the second and third centuries. Pope Gelasius, in 494, passed a censure on them, —mainly in regard to their claim to the title of Apostolical,— with the exception of the first fifty, which Dionysius Exiguus, a Roman abbot, published in the beginning of the sixth century from the original Greek. These were accepted at Rome and in the West; and in England also, it is believed, about the year 670. The Greek Church has also received these, with an addition of thirty-five made by John, Patriarch of Constantinople. The Council in Trullo adopted them as Apostolical, and the second Council of Nice regarded them with the same respect as the edicts of general councils. With the exception of John Damascene and Photius, the Oriental writers generally referred them to an Apostolic origin.

Apostolical Constitutions. A work in eight books, first mentioned by Epiphanius at the close of the fourth century, and probably composed during the third century, but embodying remnants of earlier records preserved in the Greek Church, which include a most interesting description of Church ceremonial.

Apostolical Succession. The spiritual pedigree by which bishops, priests, and deacons of the Catholic Church trace their authority to minister back to the Apostles, according to the Saviour's promise, that He would be with them always, even unto the end of the world. The King of Hungary derives his title from St. Stephen's crown, which is called Apostolical.

Apparitor. The medieval Sompnour or Summonitor; an officer of an ecclesiastical or bishop's court, who summoned persons to appear.

Appurtenances. (*Pertinentiæ.*) Appendages or complement of the vestment, viz. the albe, stole, amice, maniple, and girdle.

Apse. (From the Greek word, meaning an arch or vault.) The semicircular termination of the end of a church, choir, tran-

sept, or chapel. The Council of Tours prohibited the entrance of women into an apse. The form is borrowed from
the tribune of the Roman basilica, which was occupied by
the judges and their assessors. When the basilica was converted into a church, the bishop took the place of the presiding judge, the prætor or quæstor, at the head of the apse,
which became the sanctuary, whilst the priests and deacons
occupied the semicircular seats on either hand, which had
formerly been tenanted by the assistant judges, and now
form the luna, or moon, of the Italian churches. By an au-
dacious symbolism, derived from the apocalyptic vision of
the Elders seated round the Throne, twelve stone chairs for
suffragans were set on either side of the bishop's chair in
St. Ambrose's, Milan; and in the majority of Italian churches
the stalls of the clergy are arranged in a semicircle behind
and eastward of the altar.

From its semidomical vault the apse was called the *concha*,
or shell, and when approached by steps, the *bema*. The
stalls were called *synthronoi* by the Greeks, and *consessus* by
Latins, and the whole space was called the presbytery,
sanctuary, or tribunal. The early symbolism imagined our
Blessed Lord stretched upon the cross in the ground-plan
of the church, His body in the nave, His expanded arms in
the transept, and His head laid upon the altar; and from this
circumstance the apse was called the *capitium*, or chevet, the
head; and the east wall its front. The round and arched
apse represented the vault of heaven. St. Jerome calls it
the apse; Procopius Paul the silentiary, and St. Paulinus
speak of it as the concha, from its shell-like form. St. Augustine gives it the name of exedra. It seems that the un-
roofed churches built in the time of persecution were of this
form, as St. Theodotus of Ancyra is said to have prayed
near the concha of the Church of the Patriarchs, where the
altar was; the heathen having barred the doors.

Curtains—so lately as the time of Durand—or veils separated the apse from the rest of the building. In early
times the altar, like that of libations in the basilica, stood in
the chord of the apse, and the bishop's throne was placed
against the east wall, as at Canterbury, Norwich, Vienne,
Lyons, Autun, Rheims, and Monreale. The apse is generally the most ancient portion of a church, as the choir was

always the portion first built, and only reconstructed with the greatest reluctance, being devoted to the most sacred offices of religion. During the Early English period, when the eastern ends were rebuilt, the altar was removed to the square east wall, and the stalls of the clergy arranged on both sides of the choir. Where the apse was preserved, a circle of chapels was erected round it, introducing a new symbolism of the crown about the Saviour's head. This was after the eleventh century, when the aisles were con- tinned round the apse, and apsidal or radiating chapels were built outside them, each usually maintained by some guild or brotherhood, which, on certain holydays or in great cere- monials, posted themselves there under their banners or attended a special service. Sometimes a principal chapel,— such as the Baptistery of Drontheim, the Becket's Crown of Canterbury, and the Three Kings of Cologne,—approach- ing a circular form, were placed eastward of the apse ; whilst in other places, in lieu of a coronal of chapels, a transeptal form,—as at Lilienfeld, and like the Nine Altars of Durham, the New Work of Peterborough, or the eastern range of Bridlington, Hexham, and Fountains, — was adopted.

From an early date the great central apse had been flanked often by two lateral apses, one forming the Sacristy, and the other containing the Credence Table. In the Nor- man Period the apse was round at Peterborough, Norwich, Waltham, Crowland, Haarlem, Lund, Strengnäs ; but in the Pointed Style it became polygonal, as at Westminster, Tewkesbury, and Pershore, and in the Lady Chapels of Lichfield and Wells. Apses were rare in Scotland, but were found at Stirling, Leuchars, and Dalmeny. In the thirteenth century the square end became common in England, and a single window, as at Ely, Lincoln, York, and Carlisle, formed its great eastern feature ; this form also exceptionally occurs at Poictiers, Soignies, Bari, Laon, Dol, Angers, Sienna, Prato, and Vercelli, and was adopted in the earlier churches of Belgium. This was also the Cistercian arrangement, with the exception of Beaulieu (Hants), Altenberg, and Veruela.

The Continental chevet is of various forms ; of three, six, seven, or even, as at St. Anthony's, Padua, of eleven sides ;

it opens into three, five, or seven chapels ; in England there were five at Tewkesbury and Pershore, seven at Westminster, three at Norwich, Leominster, Waltham, and Gloucester, and at Battle three polygonal chapels, under that of the Virgin, in the crypt.

Each arm of the transept had usually in Norman times an apsidal eastern chapel, or sometimes two. One remains at Christchurch, Hants, but most have been rebuilt. The same arrangement occurred at Rheims, Marburg, and Florence. Tournay had both north and south apses.

Some churches along the banks of the Meuse, Rhine, and Moselle, possess both an eastern and western apse, as Mayence, Treves, Bamburg, Worms, Spires, Laach, Nuremberg, Oppenheim, Augsburg, Nevers, Besançon, some churches at Cologne and Verdun ; that on the west was originally a baptistery. At Florence and Pisa the external baptistery fronts the west door. The bronze font of Münster, of the fourteenth century, still occupies the western apse of that Cathedral ; the same was the case at Worms originally, and at St. Gall in the ninth century. At a later date the eastern apse was reserved for the chapter services, and the western held the parish high-altar. At the west end of the old cathedral of Canterbury, the bishop's throne was in the western apse, fronting the Lady Altar. In councils he sat next to the Bishop of Ruffina, until the Pope called up St. Anselm as the Pope of the other orb, or apse, to a seat next himself at the Council of Bari. In the ancient cathedral of Cologne there were two choirs, one on the east dedicated to St. Peter, and that on the west, containing the altar of St. Mary ; at Liége and Besançon there were also two choirs. In churches dedicated to St. Peter and St. Paul, the eastern apse was consecrated to the latter, and the western to the former saint, in allusion to the Pontifical throne of Rome and the eastern labours of the Apostle of the Gentiles. In cases where the original arrangement of churches has been turned from east to west,—as at Nevers, St. Bénoit (Paris), St. Lorenzo (Rome), and many German churches,— the ancient apse will be found at the west, and the more recent apse at the east end. When the high-altar was placed against the east wall, or in the chord of the apse, the matin altar for the lesser or conventual Mass stood at the east end of the choir.

Aquæ Bajulus. The bearer of holy-water. The priest's clerk or assistant, who lived on the alms of the people, certain fees on Sundays and festivals, and certain sheaves of corn in harvest : the medieval parish-clerk.

Arabesques. Fanciful ornamentation used by the Spanish Arabs, who were forbidden to delineate animal life.

Arca. A name used by St. Gregory of Tours for an altar composed of three marble tablets, one resting horizontally on the other two which stand upright on the floor ; there is one at St. Vitalis, Ravenna, of the sixth century.

Arch. The central voussoir in the component stones is the key-stone; the underpart of the arch is the soffit, or intrados ; the outer side is the back, or extrados.

Archbishop. A title given in the fourth and fifth centuries to the bishops of the chief cities; it occurs, perhaps for the first time, in the writings of St. Athanasius, and is applied to the Bishop of Alexandria. The title was officially given by the Councils of Ephesus, 430, and Chalcedon. In the East it was simply borne as an honorary distinction by certain prelates, but in the West all Metropolitans bore the title ;—Canterbury, York, Armagh, Dublin, Cashel, Tuam ; St. Andrew's, Glasgow ; Rheims, Rouen, Dol, Tours, Sens, Bordeaux, Bourges, Auch, Narbonne, Lyons, Besançon, Vienne, Tarantaise, Arles, Aix, and Embrun ; Gran, Hamburg, Cologne, Magdeburg, Mayence, Saltzburg, Treves, Gnesen, Dioclea, Rome, Salerno, Grado, Ravenna, Milan ; Toledo, Oviedo, and Seville and Mechlin.

Archdeacon. This dignitary was probably at first simply the senior deacon, chosen by the deacons with the bishop's sanction, (as the archpriest was the senior priest,) and served as his almoner and assistant at the altar, as *primicerius diaconorum* to the bishop, but afterwards was put forward, as Origen says, as the bishop's man of business, and at one time was known as the bishop's eye, being his delegate. This occurred about the fourth century, when the bishops became jealous of the power of priests, and especially of their chief, the archpriest. So late as the beginning of the twelfth century in England the archdeacon was in deacon's orders. Optatus mentions an archdeacon, the office having been founded in the third century. By the canon law he discharged the duties which afterwards devolved on the chancellor, in having charge of the readers and regulating the lections, and also, as the treasurer did in later times, kept the plate and provided incense and the sacred elements; he also announced the coming fasts and festivals. Between the sixth and ninth centuries his precedence over the inferior archpriest, or rural dean, was established, and after the year 1000 he was regarded as an ordinary, but within two centuries the bishops and the Council of Saumur and Tours were compelled to restrict his jurisdiction, which was confined to the presentation of candidates for ordination, visitation, proving wills, institution to benefices, suspension, and excommunication. At Rome, Liége, Constantinople, and in many French dioceses his name was suppressed, owing to the arrogance of the archdeacons. In England his office dates at Canterbury from 798, and at Llandaff from 914; in the eleventh century six, in the twelfth century thirteen, and in the thirteenth century three archdeaconries were founded. There were frequently, as at Salisbury, St. Paul's, and Lincoln, several archdeacons in a cathedral; at Toledo there are six. In the cathedrals of the Old Foundation the archdeacon had his own stall, but was regarded as a " person." In some places, however, he succeeded to the superior archpriest's rank, as Llandaff, Conserans, St. Bertrand, St. Fleur, Placenza, Rieti, Forli, Barcelona, Malta, Bergamo, Otranto, and Aix, he was President of Chapter. At Lavantz there was a provost archdeacon, and at Saltzburg, where he wore pontificals; and at Astorga the deaconry and archdeaconry were held by one person; in England the dean exercised archidiaconal jurisdiction in the close city and commune of prebends, another relic of the original system. In the East the office ceased in the eighth century. St. Jerome denounced their immoderate pretensions, and mentions that at Alexandria they were elected by the deacons. In the time of Gratian they were invariably priests. They now visit their archdeaconries, and present candidates for Holy Orders.

Arches, The. A court of the archbishop, so called from having been held in the Church of St. Mary-le-Bow, or De Arcubus. The dean has jurisdiction within thirteen parishes in London, and fifty-seven others lying in various dioceses, which are peculiars of the primate, that is, subject to his jurisdiction.

Archimandrite. A Greek abbot, who presided over one of the Lord's Mandrai, or sheepfolds.

Archpriest. The protopapas of the Greek Church. There were two kinds of archpriests ; one, urban, the superior of a community ; the other rural, the superintendent of a district ; the first merged in the capitular dean, the second in the rural dean. An officer of this name mentioned by the Council of Chalcedon, St. Jerome, Socrates, Sozomen, and St. Gregory Nazianzen, who acted as the bishop's vicar-general, and usually succeeded to the See when vacant. Again, Pope Innocent III., it is said, subjected the arch-priests to the archdeacon, but Isidore incorrectly refers the subordination to the seventh century ; but these were clearly rural deans, as Isidore speaks of them as " archpriests, by many called deans." They were also called urban deans, presiding in greater churches as the bishop's delegates over the city clergy, and at Padua and Turin retain their presi-dency. By the fourth Council of Carthage the archpriest had charge of the orphans, widows, and pilgrims, and in the second Council of Aix is called the bishop's minister. From the seventh to the ninth century the archpriest acted thus as dean of the city clergy, and the bishop's deputy in matters of jurisdiction and hearing confessions of priests, until his powers were transferred to the archdeacon. At Louvaine, Brussels, Vilvorde, Tene, and Mechlin, he stood in the same capacity as the chorepiscopus of Utrecht, the dean of deans of Liége, or the city prior of Seville, being dean of the city. And no doubt the real distinction of the names, at first common, but in later days attached to different persons, con-sisted in this,—the dean presided over the internal chapter, ministers, and servants ; the archpriest ministered in the close or city, and the provost attended to the secular affairs. In Southern Europe the parochus corresponds to the Western archpriest, the parish priest of the close, the French arch-priest, and the subdean of our old foundations. The true archpriest, as a dignitary in some cathedrals and collegiate churches, held the same power as a dean at Cremona, Ratis-bon, Osma, Siguenca, Aberdeen, Bergamo, Ager, Motuca, and in addition exercised episcopal jurisdiction during a vacancy ; he also, within the precinct, administered sacra-ments and celebrated marriages. On the death of the de-

prived Bishop of Lincoln, Dr. Watson, in 1584, and before the
consecration of a bishop of Chalcedon in 1623, the Pope appointed three archpriests for the Roman communion in England.   At Ghent, Teruel, Jaca, Toledo, Osca, Forli, Milan,
Monreale, and in France, he was a dignitary ranking after
the archdeacon, and performing the duties of a parish priest
in the close.   There were three at Saragossa and six at
Angers.   At Lyons he celebrated in the archbishop's presence, and then occupied the dean's stall.   At Ratisbon he
was called provost-archpriest, as at Ely in 673, and had the
right of a mitre and staff, but a dean had the supervision of
divine service.   In the Italian collegiate churches and in the
cathedral of Cremona, he was the chief dignitary, the
primicier usually ranking next to him ; at Forli his office
was founded in 1519 ; at Aire there are two archpriests.
By the canon law he clearly stood in the place of a dean, as
his duties were defined to consist in constant attendance in
choir, the supervision of all the priests, and the right of
celebration in the absence of the bishop ; and Lyndwood
distinctly says of the (urban) archpriest, " he is one with a
dean."   The term " monk of Gloucester " seems to have
been the dean of this kind.   He is called in the Councils of
Autun and Orleans a provost, and probably at that time
only exercised external jurisdiction in the cathedral city.
Like the penitentiary, he was a canon having cure of souls.
He also bore the name of Dean of Christianity, as his chapter was a court of ecclesiastical jurisdiction, and maintained
discipline within the precinct.   The superior archpriest
generally merged in the capitular dean and provost, but occasionally the title was preserved abroad, and in England
also.   There was an archpriest of Dunbar, as the dean's
junior, until the Reformation ; and in the thirteenth century
the collegiate archpresbyters of Ulcombe, Kent, and in the
fourteenth century those of Haccombe, Penkwell, Beerferris,
and Whitchurch, in the county of Devon, were founded, but
they were subordinate to the jurisdiction of the ordinary and
archdeacon.   A late Rector of Haccombe absurdly tacked on
lawn-sleeves to his M.A. gown, and claimed precedence after
the bishop.   The inferior archpriests were rural deans in
1188 in England, or rural archpriests, and are identified with
them in the 'Margarita Decretorum,' and the Reformation

of Laws Ecclesiastical of the time of Henry VIII., and by the Council of Tours in 1163, when they are mentioned as stipendiary delegates, or vicars of bishops and archdeacons in causes ecclesiastical. The office in this sense did not exist in Italy. At Bourges the archpriest, or city rector, ranked before canons only during the life of the bishop who appointed him. The canonists say the Parochus (the town incumbent), Plebanus (the country incumbent), and rural archpriests, differ only in name. In the Greek Church the archpriest is the chief minister in a parish.

Arcosolium. A recess in a catacomb (from *solium*, a sepulchral urn, and *arcus*, an arch), divided by little ˉwalls into family burying-places in those allotted to the faithful, are ranged lengthwise in the subterranean galleries ; but the tombs of martyrs were made in the chapels where religious service was held.

Armenians. Founded by Eustachius in Armenia in 320. They adopted the Dominican rule in Italy, and came to England in 1258 ; their scapular was black.

Arms-Royal. These unauthorized additions in a church were made before 1555, when we find the taunt made to Cranmer, " Down with Christ's arms (the rood), and up with a lion and dog " (the Tudor greyhound). Wolsey first changed the arms of York into their present form, the keys of St. Peter with the crown, instead of gules, a pall, and crozier or.

Ascension Day. ˑA festival established in the latter.half of the third century, and mentioned in the Apostolical Constitutions as the Analepsis. St. Chrysostom speaks of it under the name of Sozomene, implying that the work of man's redemption was thereby completed. It probably had been simply included in the long pentecost of festivals between Easter and Whit-Sunday, or else was thought to have been sufficiently consecrated for observance by our Lord's own great act. St. Austin includes it with the anniversaries of the Passion, the Resurrection, and Descent of the Spirit, as those days which were of apostolical institution, or by a plenary council of the Church. At St. Magnus, London, the clergy on this day are presented with ribbons, cakes, and staylaces. The common name for the day was Holy Thursday. In some medieval churches, as Durham and Gloucester, the Ascension was represented by the elevation of a figure of Christ by ropes, or a vice, through a hole in the vault, whilst the priests stood together, like the Apostles, and looked up. By a beautiful symbolism, in fine contrast to this coarse parody, the Church of the Ascension at Jerusalem was left without a roof. In the south of France it is called Alms-Thursday, owing to the doles which were bestowed, in allusion to the gift of the Spirit on this day.

Ascetics. (Fr. *askesis*, exercise of virtue.) (1.) Devotees who gave themselves to prayer; so called from the time of St. Anthony, imitating St. John Baptist and the prophets. (2.) Confessors distinguished by extraordinary acts of charity, as St. Martin is called. Probably in the ascetic we may see the prototype of the monk.

Ashlar. Squared stone.

Ash-Wednesday. (*Dies Cinerum.*) The first day of Lent, or Head of the Fast. Amalarius says that the singers used the words, " We have changed our garb for haircloth and ashes, let us fast and pray before the Lord." The ceremony of the priest scattering ashes over the congregation, with the words, " Dust thou art, and to dust shalt thou return," from which the day took its name, is attributed to Pope Gregory the Great, towards the end of the sixth century, and was established by Celestine III. in 1191. The morrow was called Embering Thursday.

Aspergil. The sprinkler. A brush used in scattering holy-water contained in the holy-water vat. It was made of hyssop, in allusion to the prayer in the Miserere.

Ass-worship was attributed to the Jews by the Gentiles, according to Josephus and Tacitus, and afterwards to the Christians, owing to the mention of the animal in the history of Balaam, the victory of Samson, the stable of Bethlehem, the flight into Egypt, and the entry on Palm Sunday into Jerusalem. At Beauvais, on January 14, the Feast of the Ass was observed yearly : an ass bearing the image of the Madonna was led in procession to St. Stephen's Church, where an absurd prose was sung, with the refrain, " Hez, Sire Asne," during the Mass. At Chalons-sur-Marne the bishop of fools rode mounted on an ass. At Autun the principal canons held the four corners of the golden housings of the ass, and at Cambray a picture of the ass was placed behind the high-altar from Palm Sunday to Maundy Thursday. Naogorgus says, that on Palm Sunday a wooden ass with a rider was drawn upon wheels through the streets to the church door, where the priest blessed the palms as talismans against storm and lightning, and then lay down before it, and was beaten with a rod by another priest. Two "lubborers" then alluded to the entry of our Lord into Jerusalem, and the ass smothered with branches was drawn into the church. In some places the ass was hired out, and led through a town, whilst boys collected bread, eggs, and money, half of which was given to the hirer.

Aster, *or* **Asterisk.** An instrument used by the Greeks in the Liturgy; a star of precious metal, surmounted by a cross, which is placed on the paten to cover the Host, and support a veil from contact with the Eucharist; it recalls the mystic star of the magi, which is commemorated as the priest censes the aster.

Athanasian Creed. A hymn, or canticle; called also the Psalm "Quicunque vult," being pointed and divided into verses. From the tenth century, at least, it has been sung antiphonally; and Abbo, in 997, mentions (as quoted by Waterland), that he had heard it in alternate choirs in France and England. It is not mentioned earlier than the seventh century, and then by writers of the Latin Church, and the Council of Autun in 677. It was probably the composition of some divine in that Church about the fifth or sixth century, and has been attributed to Vincent of Lerins, Eusebius of Vercelli, Pope Anastasius, Hilary of Arles, Venantius Fortunatus, Vigilius Tapsensis (an African bishop), or Victricius of Rouen. In all probability it is of Gallican origin. The Abbot of Fleury, in 970, alludes to it, and Hincmar of Rheims, in 850, required all priests to learn it by heart.

Atrium. Rendered by Eusebius, *aithrion,* open to the sky; like area, it denoted the precinct in front of a basilica; and was also called *Aule,* the large outer open court of the Basilica, in front of the narthex, surrounded by screened colonnades, and containing a fountain, or phiala, often canopied and enclosed in the centre. Penitents of the first class were placed in the cloister of this court. The fountain in which the faithful made their ablutions before entering church, was blessed on the Vigil and Feast of Epiphany, but, at length, the bénitier at the entrance of churches took its place.

Attrition signifies, says Aquinas, in spiritual cases, a displeasure on account of sins done, but not perfect. Contrition is when it is perfect, a first and full sorrow.

Audience. A court formerly held by the archbishops of either province ; that of Canterbury was removed from the palace to the Consistory Place of St. Paul's. All cases, whether contentious or voluntary, which were reserved for the archbishop's hearing, were tried here, and the evidence was prepared by officers called Auditors. When the court was no longer held in the palace, the jurisdiction was exercised by the master and official of the Audience. He is now represented by the Vicar-General, official of the Arches and audience, whose court was held in the hall of Doctors' Commons.

Audientes. Hearers ; the second class of penitents, who were allowed to stand in the narthex at the reading of the Scriptures and sermons, but were forbidden attendance at Common Prayer or Holy Communion.

Auditor. The inspector of the house accounts in a monastery.

Auditory. (1.) A parlour. (2.) The alley of the cloister in which the Clugniacs and Cistercians kept the school of novices.

Aumbry (*see* **Almery**). Where there was no sacristy the vestments were kept either in a large coffer, or a niche chamber in the wall ; an example of the former remains at Notre Dame de Valére. There is a remarkable relic aumbry of the fifteenth century, and made of oak, at Chichester, containing a slit in the cross-bar for the reception of alms.

Aureole. An extended nimbus. The representation of a transparent cloud, or a field of radiance and splendour, enveloping the whole body with a mantle of light. The nimbus (cloud), which is of earlier date, is an aureole, or luminous disk, which only encloses the head. (Ps. civ. 2.) In later Italian art it is an equilateral triangle, or of lozenge shape. The aureole, which is never found in the catacombs, is usually an oval or elliptic in shape, and often filled with stars or figures of angels. Where persons are seated the aureole is circular, or a quatrefoil. Its origin has been traced to the *imagines clypeatæ* (images within bucklers) of the Romans, in which a bust stands out from a shield-shaped round or orb. This was imitated by the Christian architects in early times, who placed a bust of the Saviour in a round blind window in the west front of a church. The vulgar name invented by Albert Dürer, and now exploded, for this form, when resembling the intersections of two circles, was *vesica piscis.* The aureole also assumes the form of a quatrefoil, sometimes is rounded, and occasionally foliated. In Greek paintings of the Transfiguration rays extend beyond the aureole. The *Glory* is the combination of the nimbus and aureole, and is applied to the rays of gilded wood seen over the altars of Amiens and St. Roch at Paris, or to the appearance of fire, in which the Divinity was shrouded. (Ezek. viii. 2, 3; ix. 3; Exod. xxiv. 17.) As the nimbus and aureole are supposed to be a luminous irradiation of the head and body, and take colouring, like the stars, of light under different aspects, ranging from blue or red to white,—this is often symbolically applied; thus Judas has a black nimbus, virgins have it of red, married persons of green, penitents of pale yellow, worthies of the Old Testament of silver, and saints under the Gospel of gold.

The nimbus is a sign of saintliness, as applied to angels and saints, or of power in the case of emperors and kings. When of triangular form, it is used only in depicting the Holy Trinity. From the fifteenth century it denoted God the Father; and, by the Greeks, is augmented with three rays, inscribed with the letters sacred, *O˘ON.* It is of rare occurrence in France, but common in Italy. Sometimes a triangle is enclosed within a circle, to represent the Eternal Trinity in Unity. When of square form it denotes a living person, and is peculiar to Italian art. Virgins are distinguished by a round nimbus.

When the nimbus encircles the Saviour's head, it is round, and receives the mark of a cross upon it, and also when He is represented as the Lamb of God, or the Lion of Judah. The interstices sometimes are powdered with crosses, and, by the Greeks, are filled with the letters O ōn, "Which is" (Rev. i. 4, 8), or by the Latins with LVX, the light. The round nimbus of saints and angels is without the cross, but is often engraved with their names. The heads of the symbols of the Evangelists frequently have a nimbus. The Greeks exceptionally give a nimbus to the heads of worthies of the

Old Testament. The medieval artists put a circular nimbus as the symbol of heavenly bliss about departed saints, and one of square form (the symbol of earthly honour) around living dignitaries in Italy. The nimbus does not occur earlier than the fifth or sixth century; before the twelfth century it was supposed to be transparent; in the thirteenth and fourteenth centuries it became opaque, and after the fourteenth still denser. The disk is often pearled, jewelled, or represented as blossoming. It typifies the imperishable crown of glory promised to the redeemed (1 St. Peter v. 4; St. James i. 12; Rev. ii. 10; Ps. vi. 13; Wisd. v. 17), and its brightness and rays allude to St. Matt. v. 14, as they are the light of the world. After the fifteenth century the disk-form disappeared, and for two centuries it became a circlet or ring hovering over the saint's head; in the seventeenth century it fell into total disuse.

Auricular Confession. Pope Innocent III., in the fourth Council of Lateran, 1215, ordered that the faithful of either sex should confess their sins alone, and once a year at least, under pain of losing Christian burial. Leo the Great, in the fifth century, owing to some scandals in public confession, also authorized the parish priest to receive confessions; but the Council of Chalons in 813, and later authorities left confession immediately to God or to a priest optional.

Austin Canons. Regular canons, who assumed their title after the Council of Lateran in 1139, when Pope Innocent imposed upon them the rule drawn up by St. Augustine of Hippo in his cix. epistle. Lyndwood says some wore a linen rochet and black open cope; some white linen or woollen, and a close black cope and cross on it; and some wore all white and a cross; some wore boots like monks, and some shoes like seculars. They were introduced into England in 1105, through the influence of Athelwolph, confessor to Henry I. at Nostell. They held 161 priories in England, including the cathedral of Carlisle, and the churches of Bristol, Hexham, Christchurch (Hants); Oxford, Waltham, Dunstable, St. German, Lanercost, Cirencester, Cartmel, Dorchester, Oxon, Walsingham, Newstead, Worksop, Bolton, Dunmow, Bridlington, St. John's (Colchester); Guisborough, Kirkham, Thornton, and St. Bartholomew's and St. Mary's Overye, London. Their naves were also parish

churches, and served by vicars. They held several cathedrals,—Carlisle, St. Andrew's, Milan, Palermo, Patti, Cefalu,
Chiemsee, Tortosa, Pampeluna, Saragossa, and Saltzburg.

Austin Friars, *or* **Eremites.** Volaterranus and Alvarez place
the Augustinians after the Dominican and Franciscan orders;
but Adrian of Ghent and Polydore Vergil give them the first
rank. Their earliest appearance as hermits has been referred to a very early date, but according to the most trust-
worthy authors, they were founded by William, Duke of
Aquitaine and Earl of Poitou about the year 1150, and
were known as Williamites. Alexander IV. gathered their
scattered communities into a single order, under a prior-
general, and removed them into cities and towns. In 1254
they settled in England at London, where the nave of their
church remains; and at Woodhouse, in Wales, in 1255, they
left the wild for towns. They wore a black robe and girdle,
and observed the so-called rule of St. Augustine, which was
adopted by all the other mendicant orders. They were
famous in disputation, and the "keeping of Austins" formed
a material part of the act of taking a M.A. degree at Oxford.

Avercorn. Reserved rent, as corn, paid to monasteries.

Avoury (*Avowes*). The picture of a patron saint depicted on a
square gilt vane of metal, which was attached flag-wise to a
staff, and carried in funeral processions.

Badge, Sepulchral. An emblem of the sex or occupation of an
interred person; as, for instance, the comb, mirror, or scis-
sors for a woman, as at Iona; shears or a sword for a man.

Bailey. The court between the keep and outer defences of a
castle. Churches were sometimes built within these en-
closures, as at London and Oxford, and retain the name of
"In the Bailey," although all traces of the surrounding
buildings have disappeared.

Balcony. A name introduced by the Venetians and Genoese.
It was originally a palcus or advanced tower over a gatehouse, intended to carry the machicolations. In the fifteenth century it was built as an ornament in front of private
houses. At St. Bartholomew's, Smithfield, there is a glazed
balcony; in the south nave aisle of Westminster is one of
timber, and both communicated with the superior's lodge;
at Durham, the old anchorage or porch in the north choir

aisle was used by the prior to hear High Mass; it was reached
by steps; and on the south side of the choir of St. Alban's
a similar raised platform was discovered, which was probably used for the same purpose. At Westminster, processions could be conveniently viewed from the projecting oriel.

Baldachino (from *Baldacca*, cloth of Babylon or Bagdad). A
small dome which overshadows a high-altar, and is usually
carried on four columns. It was formerly called the ciborium; it supported the altar-curtains, and was crowned with
a cross, which subsequently was placed upon the altar itself.
When there was no canopy of this kind, a covering of precious stuff or plain linen, such as was ordered by the Council
of Cologne in 1280, adorned the altar. The baldachino was
ornamented with tapers on festivals, and composed of marble, wood, stone, bronze, or precious metals. It was sometimes
erected over tombs. St. Chrysostom says the silver shrines of
Diana resembled small ciboria. Another name for the baldachino was Munera. In 567 the Second Council of Tours ordered that the Eucharist should be reserved not in a little receptacle, like images, but under the cross which crowned the
ciborium. Wren designed a baldachino for the altar of St.
Paul's. In St. Mark's Cathedral at Venice is a beautiful specimen, and another at Lugo; that of Toledo is of blue velvet.
The Baldachino at Gerona, 1320–48, is of wood, covered
with plates of metal, and stands upon four shafts, supporting
a flat quadripartite vault covered with small figures. At
Brilley and Michael Church there are canopies of wood over
the altar. The word in Italian and German is used as a
synonym of the French crown and English canopy—an ornamental projection, which covers the tops of stalls, doorways, niches, and windows. The canopy carried over the
sovereign in processions was called a *ceele*, from *cœlum*.
Baldachino also designates the canopy which Italian bishops
have a right to erect over their chairs in church.

The ciborium was originally the receptacle of the host,
dove or tower-shaped, and suspended over the altar; but as
luxury increased, under the name of tabernacle it extended
itself into an architectural erection above the altar, like a
canopy supported by four columns, forming four arches, over
which were hung rich curtains, reaching to the ground, and
only drawn aside at certain periods of the Mass. In the

centre hung the vessel containing the host. Latterly curtains were abolished, and the form became changed into that now called the Baldachino. Justinian's ciborium at St. Sophia was of silver gilt, with a canopy of silver, topped by an orb of massive gold.

Baldric. Baudrey; a bell-rope; the leathern strap for suspending the clapper from the staple in the crown of a bell.

Baleys. A ruby of an inferior kind.

Ball-Flower. An ornament of the " Decorated Period," like a flower closed up into a ball, with three petals rounded closely upon it.

Baluster. A small, round pillar, found in the windows of pre-Norman towers.

Bands (in the Oxford University Statutes, rendered *collare*). An introduction of the Tudor period, either a relic of the amice, or an adaptation of the broad, flowing bands then worn by all classes. In France and Italy the clergy wear bands of a black material, edged with white. Lawyers in England use very long bands. The small Genevan bands are a tradition from the seventeenth century and the Puritans, for Dr. Hammond has in his portrait the broad cavalier band. In 1566 the out-door dress of the English clergy consisted of the square cap, tippet, long gown, and bands; and in church, of the surplice and cope. In the Statutes of Hereford, 1630, they are defined as linen fragments, which some bind about their necks.

Banker. A covering for a bench; hangings of cloth; the side-curtains of an altar.

Banners in church and processions were adopted from Constantine's use of the labarum—the cross-banner,—which was carried in the van of his army. They were used to commemorate the Easter victory of our Lord. The sacred banner of the Maccabees had the initial letters of the Hebrew words, forming the text Exodus xv. 11. The Emperor Heraclius, in 621, took a picture of the cross to battle in his war with Persia, and carried the cross on his shoulders up Calvary, as an act of thanksgiving, which was the origin of the Festival of the Exaltation of the Holy Cross. The earliest instances of banners in England are those of two guthfana, war-vanes or standards, which were given by Bishop Leofric to Exeter Cathedral. But St. Augustine

before had entered the gates of Canterbury with a banner
of the Cross carried before his procession, singing a litany.
The banner of St. Cuthbert was of white velvet, with a red
cross of the same material, and contained in the centre St.
Cuthbert's corporax cloth. It was fringed with red silk and
gold, and had three silver bells attached to it. It was of
great weight, and five men assisted the bearer when it was
carried in procession. Pope Gregory III. sent a banner
which he had blessed to the King of France. Leo III. gave
one to Charlemagne; and Alexander II. sent another to
William of Normandy, for his invasion of England. Philip
II. of France also received a Papal banner. King Henry V.
carried a Cross banner in his expedition against the Lollards; and in the rising of the North in 1570 the rebels
carried a banner embroidered with the five wounds, a chalice, and a cross, with the legend *In hoc signo vinces* ("thou
shalt conquer by this sign"). The banners of St. John of
Beverley, St. Peter of York, and St. Wilfrid of Ripon were
carried on a sacred car, crowned with a cross, by Archbishop Thurstan in 1138, at the Battle of the Standard, or
Northallerton, an imitation of the caroccio invented by
Eribert, Archbishop of Milan in 1035; and beneath the banner of St. John, carried by a priest, Edward I. fought
against the Scots. Henry II. carried the banner of St.
Edmund of Bury to the Battle of Fornham, October 16,
1673. Round the shrine of St. Cuthbert at Durham, the
banners of the King of Scotland, Lord Neville, and other
noblemen were placed as ornaments and acts of homage.
The Earl of Surrey borrowed St. Cuthbert's banner (which
was carried at Flodden), and, as Skelton says, that of St.
William of York in his Scottish campaign. Ferdinand and
Isabella chased the Moors out of Granada, led by the Cross-
banner. Our own Henrys and Edwards fought beneath the
banners of St. Edmund the Confessor and St. George. In
later days, captured flags were suspended round the dome of
St. Paul's, and the banners of the Bath and St. George at
Westminster and Windsor. Henry VII. offered the banner
of St. George at St. Paul's after his victory at Bosworth.
The *oriflamme* or banner of St. Denis was always carried before the kings of France in battle, as by Philip le Bel and
Louis le Gros; and regimental colours invariably receive

benediction by a priest before their presentation. Pope Pius V., in 1568, " baptized " the Duke of Alva's babel, or standard, by the name of Margaret. After the Reformation in England, Cartwright mentions " bells and banners in Rogations, the priest in his surplice saying gospels and making crosses." In parish processions banners are still carried in front of choirs at Peterborough, Southwell, and other places. At Salisbury, before the Reformation, three large banners were carried on Ascension Day—two in the midst, of the Cross, and one in advance, representing the Lion of Judah; whilst in the rear was his trophy, the image of a dragon. At Canterbury they included the arms of noble benefactors. In some places, till recently, a lingering relic of banners might be seen in the garlands suspended upon the poles which were carried at the perambulation of parishes. Casalins says the procession resembles a celestial host rejoicing in the triumph of Christ, and displaying the sign of the Cross and banners to the discomfiture of the powers of the air. And Cranmer said, " We follow His banner as Christ's soldiers, servants, and men of war, for the remembrance of Him, declaring our proneness and readiness in all things to follow and serve Him;"—a thought which beautifully harmonizes with the admonition at Holy Baptism, that we should serve under Christ's banner, and fight manfully against His enemies, continuing His faithful soldiers and servants unto our lives' end. (Psalm xx. 5.) Banners were used at weddings and funerals; the lesser guilds borrowed those of the parish church.

Banns. Proclamation; public notice of marriage intended to be solemnized. The first canons of councils which ordered this publication are those of Lateran in 1139, and the Fourth Lateran in 1215. Three publications were required by the Canons of Westminster in 1200; and on three Sundays or festivals distinct from each other, by Reynolds's Constitutions in 1322; that is, as Lyndwood says, on three several, even if successive days, in Easter or Whitsun week, or at other times with a break of a day : the intention being that only a single publication should occur on one day. In 1328, Archbishop Meopham directed special attention in the matter ; meaning, as Lyndwood says, at least publication in the parish churches of the parents and kindred, as well as those of the contracting parties.

Baptism. The Fathers distinguish three kinds of Holy Baptism: (1) of water (St. Matt. xxviii. 19; St. Mark xvi. 16); (2) of the Spirit (Acts i. 5; St. John iii. 3–5), in case of the desire of baptism where it cannot be had; or of penitence, pains and tears; (3) of blood (St. Mark x. 38; St. Luke xii. 50), where a martyr or confessor was prevented by death or persecution from baptism by water (St. Luke xii. 24; St. Matt. v. 10). "The blood of the martyrs is the seed of the Church" is a sentiment of Tertullian in his Apology against the Gentiles, and adopted by St. Augustine in his 109th Sermon.

The types of baptism are the Deluge (1 St. Peter iii. 21), the Red Sea (1 Cor. x. 2), the water flowing from the rock struck by Moses' rod (St. John iv. 14), water of Jordan sanctified by the Saviour's baptism. Jordan is sometimes represented as a human figure with a water-pot; the hart desiring the waterbrooks, and a child mounted on a fish, are also used in ancient monuments.

Baptism was called Indulgence by the Council of Carthage; remission or ablution of sins by St. Augustine and St. Gregory Nyssen; regeneration by St. Cyril of Jerusalem; unction by St. Gregory Nazianzen; illumination or the seal of Christ by Clement of Alexandria; the royal character, Christ's gift, initiation, and consecration; and, in the language of the Discipline of the Secret, on many ancient tombs the day of acceptance, that is, admission into the Church: and in some cases, where baptism had been deferred, we find "he laid down his albs at the grave;" or "he passed away," or "fell asleep in his alb."

In Apostolic times neither place nor time were prescribed for the administration of baptism; but Tertullian mentions Easter and Pentecost as the proper seasons, the first being selected in memory of the death and rising again of the Lord, with Whom we are buried in baptism, and by being lifted up out of the water are reborn to the new life; and Whitsuntide, as the festival of the Holy Ghost, of Whom the baptized are reborn. These times were enforced by the Councils of Mayence 813, Gerona 517, Autun 578, Tribur 895, Macon 583, Cealcythe 785, Excerpts of Egbright 740, Winchester 1071, and Otho the Legate in 1237. Othobon in 1268 mentions the eves of Easter and Whitsunday.

Epiphany was a baptismal season in Africa and in Asia, but the Western Church repudiated the custom. At Christmas, and on the festivals of apostles and martyrs, children were baptized. Pope Felix IV. allowed private baptism only in case of extreme necessity.

In medieval times the font was hallowed with special solemnity on Easter and Whitsun Eves, but the practice was forbidden in 1547. The usual hour for baptism was 3 P.M., the hour when our Lord gave up the ghost and the angel appeared to Cornelius; but at a later period, an hour some time previous to dinner or noonday was prescribed, in order to guard against intemperance.

If born within eight days of either Easter or Pentecost; children, by Archbishop Peckham's injunctions, were to be reserved for baptism at those times. In the Synod of Africa, held under St. Cyprian, the second or third day after birth was appointed, or at least one within eight days. By Ina's laws, 693, baptism was to be administered within thirty nights; by Edgar's canons, 960, within thirty-seven nights; and within nine nights by the Northumbrian canons, 950. The Church of England appoints no later day than the first or second Sunday next after birth, or other holyday falling between. The time for the administration is after the Second Lesson at Matins or Evensong. There is only one baptism for the remission of sins: to re-baptize is to commit sacrilege.

Baptism for the Dead. St. Paul, to reprove those who denied the Resurrection, may have used the authority of heretics like the Cataphrygians, who baptized the dead bodies, not as approving the act, but quoting it as it served his argument. The Marcionites baptized living proxies for the dead; the Third Council of Carthage condemned those who actually christened the dead: some heretics baptized children yet unborn; and in the primitive Church Christians were baptized over the graves of the departed, in token that the dead should rise again; possibly to this custom the Apostle alludes.

Baptisteries. The early Christians were baptized in water by the roadside (Acts viii. 36–38); or in a river (Acts xvi. 13–15); or a prison (Acts xvi. 33); in a spring, or at sea, or in private houses (Acts ix. 18; x. 47, 48); or in any place.

Bede mentions Paulinus baptizing in the Swale; at Rome
there was an early baptistery in the house of Cyriacus, in
the Pontificate of Marcellus.   Constantine erected baptisteries in the suburbs, and on the Cælian hill.   Gregory of
Tours says that baptisteries were introduced into France
under Clodovic.   St. Cyril of Jerusalem mentions baptisteries
with an outer part for the preliminaries, and an inner part
for the administration.   The Novels of Justinian prohibited
the administration of baptism in private houses, and the only
exceptions permitted by the Canon Law are in cases of extreme necessity, or children of the Royal family and princes.
Baptism was to be administered in church under pain of
deposal in the priest, and of excommunication in lay persons ; for many persons deferred their baptism until the hour
of death, that they might depart more undefiled out of the
world.   Councils were sometimes held in the large Italian
baptisteries.

In the fifth and sixth centuries baptisteries became common, and were known as the Place of Illumination, the Baptismal Church, the Hall of Baptism : the terms Columbethra
and Font also occur.   They were at first detached buildings.
The baptistery of Frejus is separated from the cathedral by
a porch; that of Aix was formerly isolated; St. Frort of
Poictiers is reputed to have been an ancient baptistery ; and
those of Constantine, at St. John Lateran, a modern restoration, and St. Constance, near the Church of St. Agnes Without
at Rome, are detached.   One baptistery only was originally
allowed in each city or town, as until recent times at Parma,
Bologna, Pisa (1160, measuring 129 feet in diameter and
179 feet high) ; and till 1791 at Puy, Barbastro, Saragossa,
and Siguença.   There is only one baptistery, in accordance
with ancient rule, at Florence, Pisa, and Bologna.   And at
Milan, by the Ambrosian rite, the parish priests went to the
Basilica on the eves of Easter and Pentecost, and carried in
procession to their churches the water which had received
benediction.   The Councils of Auxerre and Meaux, in the
sixth century, first allowed the use of a baptistery in parish
churches.   There are fine examples at Aix, Frejus, Florence
(90 feet in diameter), and Strasbourg, the latter dating from
453.   At Lampaul, Brittany, the baptistery is domed, stands
on eight columns, and has innumerable decorations of the

seventeenth century. In England, at St. Peter's Mancroft
(Norwich), Luton, Trunch, Aylsham, and Mellifont, there is
an octagonal building or screen, being an enlarged canopy,
or rather a reduced baptistery, within the church, to seclude
the font. At Luton it is of stone, and the Decorated period;
at Trunch it is a rich covering of oak, with an hexagonal
closure carried on pillars outside the font; at St. Peter's
Mancroft it is of wood, built in the fifteenth century.
There is a similar enclosure at Cividal de Friuli, of the
eighth or ninth century. The Becket's Crown of Canterbury, and the eastern octagon of Drontheim, may have been
used as gigantic baptisteries.

They were always dedicated to St. John Baptist, as still
at Ravenna, Verona, Milan, and St. Restituta, at Naples;
and the altar contained his relics. They were almost invariably, as symbolical of the Regeneration, octagonal, as at
the Lateran, St. Tecla's (Milan), Aix, Florence, St. Zeno,
Verona, and Frejus; but polygonal buildings occur at
Canosa and Bologna; hexagonal at Sienna, Parma, and
Aquileia; and circular at Pisa and Pistoia. One described
by St. Paulinus resembled a tower. At Bari, one of the
fourth century is circular without, and within of twelve
sides, once adorned with figures of the Apostles. The Lom-
bardic architects continued to build baptisteries in front of
the churches until the thirteenth century; but, with this exception, in other places they ceased to be erected after the
eleventh century, when parish churches were permitted to
have a font; and in Germany they merged into the western
apse. At Tours the baptistery was used as a chapter-house,
as in the old cathedral of Canterbury, when archbishops
were buried in it. As infants were communicated immediately after baptism, altars were erected in the baptistery;
and they remain at Pisa, Florence, and Ravenna, in the
latter case with a cross, dated 658. At Padua and Pistoia
the baptistery had a chancel, and one at Bonn has a nave
and porch. At Cambrai, in the fourteenth century, a large
piscina was added for the sponsors to wash their hands, and
to receive the rinsings of the vessel used for pouring the
consecrated water. The ancient baptistery of Vercelli contains two seats, one for the priest, and another for the
sponsor. In countries northward of the sunny South and

Italy, the baptisteries were, at an early period, removed within the church.

Barge Board. An ornamental board, used in the front of gables, which became common in the fourteenth century; in the fifteenth century they were cut in rich and beautiful patterns.

Bartonar. A monastic officer; the overseer of bartons, granges, and farms; a granarer.

Base. The lower part of a pillar, or wall.

Basilians. Students in religious colleges founded by St. Basil.

Basilica. The king's house. The word, adopted from the Roman courts of justice, is said to have been at an early date, not before the time of Constantine, applied to such buildings when consecrated; to churches which contained the bodies or at least the relics of martyrs or saints; and to larger churches, like the Lateran and Vatican. In the Council of Gangra they are expressly named as the Martyrs' Basilicas, and another title was Martyrs' Memorials. In 398 the Council of Carthage prohibited the erection of churches except on such sites. In the fourth and fifth centuries Basilica invariably implied a memorial church. In France small mortuary chapels are still called basilicas, and in the sixth and seventh centuries the word designated a minster in France, but in 1237 an unconsecrated building in England; whilst all inferior houses of God were called simply churches. In the Council of Cealcythe the basilica is a synonym for parish church, that is, in 816. Basilica and oratory were often used as the designation of churches other than cathedrals. The only example north of the Alps remains at Tréves. Alby is a perfect basilica. Two pillars of that of Reculver are preserved at Canterbury; and portions of others are said to exist at Bosham, Lympne, and Stow. There were two kinds of basilicas, the smaller and larger. The smaller basilicas, like that of SS. Sixtus and Cecilia at Rome, were exact copies of the little chapels of the Catacombs; a rectangular, aisleless nave, terminating in a central and two transeptal apses, containing altars; and the same plan is observable in St. Petronilla, SS. Nereus and Achilles, and SS. Mark, Marcellinus, and Tranquillinus.

In front of the larger basilica, both in the East and the West, was a forecourt (*atrium, aithrion,* or *aula*), surrounded

by colonnades (*tetrastulon, quadriporticus*), and containing a
covered fountain (*phiala* or *cantharus*) in the centre ; this
court served as a cemetery, and station of penitents, catechumens, and neophytes, whilst the faithful washed their
hands at the spring.   We see here the origin of the cloister,
the galilee, and holy-water stoup.   In front of the church
was the vestibulum, or pronaos, a narrow portico or porch,
which was supported on columns and fenced in with an iron
screen, on which were rings for the support of rich veils
on great festivals.   The vault, usually covered with sacred
pictures, was called the impluvium.   Here was the station of
the strati, or acroomenoi ; and a water stoup, the malluvium,
phiale, or cherñibozeston, was placed for washing the hands.
The central porch, when there were others on the north and
south, was called the narthex, or ferula, from its reed-like
shape and greater length than the others.   This opened into
the naos, or *atrium laicorum,* or nave, with its aisles, the
andron on the right, which was larger than the other at St.
Sabina, at Rome, St. Sixtus (Pisa), and Narni Cathedral,
for men, and the matronikon on the left for women, as in the
old heathen court, the six entrances being restricted to the
different sexes, as the great west door was to the clergy.
The upper galleries and end of the matronikon were occupied by widows and young religious women ; the western
portion of the nave was allotted to catechumens and penitents,
and the eastern to the faithful ; the monks sitting in the eastern
part of the andron.   A marble balustrade, called the septum,
podium, or peribolos, breast high, formed the entrance of the
ritual choir (the choir of singers), which was raised on a traverse, or platform, and known as the *suggestum lectorum,* or
tribune, extending into the nave līkē the choir in a Norman
minster, and shut off by the chancel rail (*cancelli*), which
had a central door.   The solea was the western part, outside
the door of the bema ; at Rome it was called the Senatorium,
being reserved to persons of rank.   The word tribune is still
preserved in Italy and Germany.   At Constantinople the
Emperor sat within the enclosure, but at Milan St. Ambrose
compelled Theodosius to sit outside among the laity.   On
either side of the chancel-door was a pulpit or ambon ; one
on the south for reading the gospel, and a pulpit, the ambon
proper ; the other, the analogion, a lectern for the Epistolar,

the reader of the Prophecies, and chief singer. The solea of
the clergy, eastward of it, was occupied by the minor clerks,
subdeacons, and singers. In the Carlovingian period these
desks were united. Martene also mentions an arrangement
of two ambons on the right of the entrance; one facing the
altar, for the Epistle, and the other fronting the people, for
reading the prophets, whilst the Gospel ambon, still more
elevated, occupied the left side. The Paschal candlestick
adjoined the ambon. The use of the ambons ceased about
1309, when the Popes removed to Avignon. We observe
here the germ of the medieval roed-screen and loft. The
Secretarium of the Western Church was usually on one side
of the solea. The eastern end of the church formed the
holiest of all, the sanctuary, bema, presbytery, or suggestum,
reached by a flight of steps. It was fenced by a rail with a
central door; but in larger churches with three entrances,
one facing each of the great alleys of the nave. In the chord
of the apse, concha, or semicircular end, stood the altar;
behind it was the bishop's throne, with the stalls of the
clergy on either side. The altar stood above a crypt, memorial, or confession, the grave of a martyr or saint; and
above it, until the thirteenth century, was a cupola, called
the ciborium, or baldachino, which has been preserved at
Rome, Venice, Brie, and in some other churches. In Eastern
churches, on the right side was the secretarium, sacrarium,
diaconicum, paratorium, or oblationarium, the credence table,
chamber and aumbry for plate; and on the left, gazophylakion, skenophylakion, or vestry, library, and muniment
room, where the offerings of the faithful were kept. Some
of the principal Roman churches still retain the distinguishing title of Basilica, and John de Athon, the Canonist, applies
the term to great churches.

Basins. Before the high-altar, and above the steps to it,
were usually three basins of silver, hung by silver chains,
with prickets for serges or great wax candles, and latten
basins within them to receive the droppings; these tapers
burnt continually, night and day, in token that the house
was always watching unto God. Basins were used for carrying the cruets and the ewers for the ablution of the priest's
fingers; they were usually in pairs, one being used for
pouring, the other for receiving the water; thus we find one

engraved with the mortal life and a second with the Divine life of Christ. The material was sometimes enamelled copper or silver gilt, and the embellishment was frequently of a heraldic rather than religious character. At Durham one basin and two cruets were used at a time. There is a beautiful basin of the time of Edward II., wrought with figures of a knight helmed by a lady at a castle gate, in St. Mary's, Bermondsey, which once belonged to the abbey there. Two enamelled basins of the thirteenth century at Conques are called Gemellions; one is used a's a ewer, and the other as a jug. There was also a large basin for alms, usually double gilt, used upon principal festivals, and a smaller one of less value for ordinary days. Alms-basins of Flemish manufacture and latten are preserved at St. Margaret's, Westminster.

Bath-house. A large building for bathing at certain times, was a usual adjunct to a Benedictine monastery; at Canterbury it occupied the site of the deanery.

Baths were used by the faithful before Communion, by catechumens before Baptism, with the use of the strigel and perfumes, and by the clergy on the eves of festivals. The latter had by the grant of Theodosius the right of sanctuary; and Constantine having built one at Constantinople, near the Apostles' Church, St. Hilary Damasus, and Adrian I. followed his example at Rome. Paintings and mosaics adorned them, and bishops in their visitation enjoined their use. One at Puzzuoli still bears the name of the Bishop's Spring.

Baton (anciently *Bourdon*). The staff carried as the badge of office by a præcentor, chanters, chancellors, and choir-masters. Honorius of Autun mentions the præcentor's silver staff and tablets. The wand was only carried at High Mass and Second Vespers. At Dijon, Puy-en-Velay, and St. Chaffre, the præcentor used it to beat time and as an instrument to correct those who misbehaved; at Lyons batons were carried by the choir-master and oldest vicar to keep off the crowd in processions. At Angouléme on great days the canon who sings the office still carries a silver baton. The staff of the rector of choir and the præcentor is frequently mentioned in English inventories. It had no crook, but usually a Tau-shaped cross-beam at the end for images. There is a good silver staff in the Treasury of Cologne.

Battels. Payments at Oxford for college expenses (called sizings at Cambridge) ; from an old word signifying a coin.

Batter. To slope inwards.

Battlement. A crenellated parapet ; in Ireland they are often multiplied in graduation so as to form corbie steps. At Carlisle Cathedral they carry upright crosses,—a very remarkable feature.

Bawdkyn. Cloth of gold ; from *Bagdad, Babylon,* or *Baldacca ;* brocade.

Beacon Turrets occur at Llandrillo yn Rhos, at St. Burian's, Hadley, and St. Michael's Mount, under the modern name of St. Michael's Chair ; they carried a light in a pot suspended on an iron frame, to guide travellers or ships. The cage for the cresset remains at Hadley Tower. Octagonal lanterns are found at Boston, in the west tower of Ely, at All Saints', York, and other places which served the same purpose. St. Hilary Tower was yearly whitewashed by the port of St. Ives, to render it conspicuous at sea. At Bow Church, Cheapside, and Winchester, there were beacons.

Beam-Light. The lamp which burned before the Holy Sacrament ; so called, because set on the rood-beam above the altar, in distinction to a light set upon a perch or swinging stand, or those placed in bowls suspended from the vault.

Bearing-Cloth. A christening robe or mantle, in which children were carried to the font. One of the sixteenth century, made of blue satin, and embroidered with silver lace and fringes and gold vignettes, is preserved at Bitterley Court, Salop.

Beauseant Avant. The war-cry of the Templars, in allusion to their colours—black for their foes, and white for friends, side by side ; for which the old French word was *bauçant* (piebald). The Hospitallers' flag was red with a white cross.

Bede. A prayer. Bede-roll was a catalogue or list of the departed, who were prayed for every Sunday from the pulpit. Beadman or precular is a prayer-man, one who says prayer for a patron or founder, hence an almsman. In all the Cathedrals of the New Foundation, there are several bedemen on the Foundation, who wear the Tudor rose on their breast, and serve as bellringers and assistant-vergers. Beads of jet were regarded as having virtue to help ; beads of mystill were mixed beads ; they were sometimes of wood and sometimes of stone, and, in England, often called a pair of paternosters, or, by the common folk, *preculæ*, or Ave-beads. A belt of paternosters is ordered to be said at the death of a bishop in the English Council of Cealcythe, of the ninth century. Abbot Paul, who inhabited the desert of Seeta, according to Sozomen, recited the same prayer three hundred times a day, and counted them by means of an equal number of little stones, like the cubes used in mosaic work, which he kept in a fold of his robe, and cast away one by one. In a painting of the eleventh century, representing the burial of St. Ephraem, the monks carry chaplets in their hands, or suspended at their girdles. Alan, Archbishop of Mechlin, in the sixteenth century, says that such crowns lasted in England from the time of Bede until the seventh century, and were hung upon church walls for public use. The famous Lady Godiva, of Coventry, according to William of Malmesbury, bequeathed a threaded chain of jewels, used by her at prayer-time, as a necklace to St. Mary's image. A similar chaplet is mentioned in the Life of St. Gertrude in the seventh century. Most probably Peter the Hermit, *c.* 1090, introduced the fashion with the Hours of our Lady among the Crusaders, having seen the beads of the Mahometans. The Indians use beads, and the Jews have a chaplet called Meah Beracot. The ascription of the chaplet to Venerable Bede is no doubt due to the similarity of name; but St. Dominic, in 1230, may be regarded as the author of the permanent use of the beads. The Rosary is a modern name. The Lady Psalter consisted of fifteen Paternosters, and a hundred and fifty Aves, the latter representing the Psalms of David, in place of which they were recited. The name of Bede was translated to the knobs on the prayer-belts, and when pilgrims from the East introduced chaplets of seeds or stone, to round beads strung upon a string, which were used in place of a girdle, studded with bosses or notched on the part which trailed upon the ground. "Hail Mary" was formerly unknown till 1229 or 1237, and then was used simply in the Angelic Salutation. (St. Luke i. 28–42.) Urban IV., in 1261–4, added the rest of the words to "Jesus Christ;" but the prayer or invocation is barely three hundred years old.

Bedel. A bidder, crier, or summoner.

Belfry. A corruption of the Low Latin word *belfredus*, which Ducange derives from bell-fried (peace) ! the French *beffroi* is said to be only another form of *effroi*. Penitents were placed here in England. Latimer speaks of "Poor Magdalene under the board and in the belfry." The possession of a bell-tower by the laws of Athelstan, 926, conferred on the owner the thane's right of a seat in the town-gate, corresponding to a place on the grand jury. At Aberdeen and Glasgow, in early times, the bells were hung on trees ; and usually in England the belfries were detached when there was a heavy peal of bells. See *Detached Towers*.

Belgian Architecture. There are three styles. 1. Primary and transitional, tenth to thirteenth century ; the porches are lateral, the towers mostly at the west end, and the choirs small and apsidal. 2. Secondary, pointed, or rayonnant, fourteenth to latter part of fifteenth century ; distinguished by the chevet, size of the windows, and elaboration in towers. 3. Third, pointed, or flamboyant, latter part of fifteenth to latter part of sixteenth century.

Bell (from *pelvis*, a bowl). The earliest mention of bells occurs in the descriptions of the dress of the Jewish High Priest in Exodus and Ecclesiasticus. They were not unfamiliar to the ancient nations, as they are alluded to by Martial, Pliny, Suetonius, Porphyry, Zonaras, and Lucian, in association with the public baths ; the chariot of Camillus at his triumph, the rites of a Syrian goddess, Indian philosophers assembling for prayer, pyramidal towers, clocks, and the covering of Jupiter's temple by the Emperor Augustus. The invention of bells has therefore been erroneously attributed to Paulinus, Bishop of Nola, by Durandus, Honorius of Autun, and Walafrid Strabo. The word 'nola' applied to a bell does not date earlier than the fourth century, and that of 'campana' not until the eighth century. Possibly Paulinus may have introduced the distinctive use of church bells at Nola, and the famous brass of Campania lent colour to the tradition. Pope Sabinian at Rome in 604 ordered the hours to be sounded on the bells ; and they are mentioned in the Ordo Romanus about this date, as being used to announce Tierce, Mass, and processions. St. Owen, in the Life of St. Eloy, *c.* 650, speaks of the bell (campana) ; and Bede mentions, about half a century later, Hilda, a nun of Hackness, whilst lying in her dormitory, hearing the well-known sound of the bell for prayers; and a monk of St. Gall has recorded the casting of a bell for Charlemagne. The Greeks employed a symbol—a wooden clapper—as they still do; but in 865 Patriciacus Ursus, Doge of Venice, sent a present of a peal of bells to the Emperor Michael at Constantinople. In 874 a Venetian bell was forwarded to the Emperor Basil. In 550, Odoceus, Bishop of Llandaff, is said to have removed the cathedral bells during a time of excommunication. In 740, Pope Zachary allowed the Benedietines of Monte Casino to use bells for the hours and Mass; but John XXII., owing to the complaint of the secular clergy, allowed the regular communities to possess only one bell. The Council of Lateran imposed a fine of one hundred ducats upon any church which rang its bells before the Cathedral on Easter Eve; and at Bath, on Sundays, no parish church was allowed to ring before the Abbey had chimed for High Mass; whilst at Winchester the abbey of St. Mary was removed to another site, owing to its bells and organs clashing with one another. Bells were rung for the canonical hours; Masses; the burial of the dead, according to old custom; to still storms, such bells bearing the legend of *Maria gratiœ plena* or *Verbum caro factum est;* at the Angelus three times a day, under the invocation of St. Gabriel during processions; and by the ordinance of Pope Gregory IX. at the elevation of the Eucharist. The TOCSIN, or alarm-bell, was common to all countries; but the PASSING-BELL, even in medieval times, was peculiar to England.

The uses of the church bells are summed up in the following lines :—

" Laudo Deum verum, plebem voco, congrego clerum,
Defunctos ploro, pestem (nimbum) fugo, festa decoro (*or* que honoro)."

Their use was founded on the employment of the silver trumpets, under the Law according to Numbers x.; and Josephus, describing these instruments, says, "They ended in a bell-like form." Cassiodorus called an organ a tower of pipes, and Honorius of Autun and Walafrid Strabo give to bells the name of the clangers or trumpets of the Church. By the Council of Limoges they were called the clamours of metal; and by the Ritual of Beauvais the messengers of God's people.

Evigilans stultum (waking the unwise) was the monastic nickname of the matin-bell, used also at Angers. At Chartres, six large bells, the Commanders, gave the signal for the after-peal to ring before service. At Bayeux, they were called *moneaux* (the warners), and the death-bell is named the *mortuaise*. At Strasburg, one which summoned the assembly of the Council, bore the name of magistral. Hexham possessed a foray-bell and a fire-bell. The fire-bell of Sherborne Abbey is dated 1652; one of the most ancient church bells in use is that of Barcelona, dated 1293. Another at Fontenailles was made in 1202; and one at Bayeux has ears. In England the most common dedications of bells were the following, arranged according to their relative numerical proportions :—St. Mary, St. John, Jesus, St. Catherine, Trinity, St. Margaret, and St. Peter. Great Tom of Lincoln (1610) was dedicated to the Holy Ghost, and that of Westminster to St. Edward the Confessor. The Bell of Lambourne was rung nightly as a guide to travellers over the interminable downs of Berkshire; and one at York, as a signal to persons traversing the Galtres Forest. The Sanctus-bell was rung during the singing of the Ter Sanctus, and the sacring-bell at the elevation of the Eucharist. Campana was a large bell; nola, a smaller specimen. The squill (or onion-shaped) or *tintinnabulum*, was rung in the Refectory, the cymbal in the cloister, the nola in choir, the nolula in the clock, the campana in the belfry, and the sign in the tower. The Irish and Celtic bishops carried hand-bells, a campana, bajula, or clocca; those of St. Kentigern and St. Medan had hereditary custodians. The capped bell of St. Cullan, *c.* 908, in a shrine of the twelfth century; the bronze bell of St. Cuana, *d.* 650; another of St. Ruadhan, *d.* 584; and St. Cummin's bell, *d.* 662, are in the British Museum. In the time of Charlemagne, in Northumberland, in 950, and even in the last century in Carthusian houses, priests rang the bells. An abbot, as a rector and vicar do now, at his induction rang the church bell as a sign of his new power. The pilgrims to St. Thomas's Shrine entered the city piping, singing, and jangling their Canterbury bells. The bell of Lincoln, Great Tom (*grand ton*) (1835) weighs five tons eight cwt.; Tom of Oxford (1680), seven tons; and Peter of York (1845), ten tons fifteen cwt. Peter of

Exeter has, perhaps, the finest tone of all. In 1099, Godfrey
de Bouillon set up bells at Jerusalem; and the Crusaders introduced peals into the East; but in 1452 the Emperor Mahomet prohibited their use to the Greek Christians after the capture of Constantinople, so that again the use of the sign or
primitive bell,—a rude but not unmelodious clapper,—is again
practised. The sign is mentioned by St. Ephrem, c. 370, as
the call to Holy Communion; and by St. Gregory of Tours, c.
570, and the Canons of Cealcythe, 816, as the call to prayers.
Charlemagne adopted the word when he mentioned the
ringing to Mass; and in the Chronicle of Battle Abbey, in
the twelfth century, the familiar term again appears. In
830, Amalarius mentions that these clappers were, in his
day, called Little Rome. On the three last days of Holy
Week, at least from the time of Albinus and Beleth, the
bells are silent and wooden tablets employed in order to
mark the solemnity of the season, and in memory of the
tribulation of the early Christians, who met only by concert,
or by the oral summons of a public notice in their assemblies on the previous evening. Even after the conversion of
Constantine, they were apprised of the hours of prayer by
a *præco*, or runner, as St. Jerome says, or else by the sound
of a wooden instrument, according to Fortunatus and Metaphrastes; whilst in the monasteries, as St. Jerome mentions, they were called with the cry of Alleluia. At Chartres there was a belfry over the crossing, which contained
a wooden instrument called the *grue*, used in Holy Week,
when the bells were silent. Probably the first step to fixed
bells was made by the use of portable or hand-bells, which
are mentioned by Giraldus, speaking of the time of Germanus, c. 430, and specimens of these are still preserved. The
hand-bell is still rung at Oxford, in front of funeral processions of members of the University. At Congleton, on the
eve of the parish wake, St. Peter ad Vincula, a man in whose
family from time immemorial the belts have been preserved,
walks through the streets, shaking three belts covered with
bells, and this is called " Ringing the Chains " (of St. Peter).
A hand-bell is invariably used at funerals in Italy, Sicily, and
Malta, and commonly so in France and Spain, as a signal to
clear the way, and elicit a prayer for the departed. Criminals
were sworn on St. Evin's bell by the justices of Munster.

Tin trumpets, preserved at Willoughton and Thorney, are said to have been used to call the congregation together. At Canterbury, by Lanfranc's Constitutions, the convent was summoned to attend the dying by the blow of a mallet on the cloister door.

Bell, Book, and Candle, By. The form of the greater excommunication.

Bench-table (*banc*). A line of stone seats occurring in churches, cloisters, and porches. Medieval benches are found in England and France, but nowhere in Spain or Italy, where kneeling only was permitted, as in England even in the time of Archbishop Arundel, when all persons sat on the floor in sermon time. When permanent pews, or benches for the purpose of hearing sermons, were built in the fifteenth century, the bench-table disappeared. In the latter part of the seventeenth century the French began to use fixed seats.

Benedicite. The hymn of the three children, Ananias, Azarias, and Misael, sung in the furnace on the plains of Dura, which, in the first Prayer-book of Edward VI. is ordered to be sung daily in Lent. Its use seems very appropriate to the First Morning Lessons on Septuagesima and the nineteenth Sunday after Trinity. The Council of Toledo, 633, ordered it to be sung on all Sundays and festivals in the pulpit at Mass.

Benedictines. Black Monks, founded by St. Benedict at Monte Casino in 530, from whom monachism, hitherto without aim and use, took life. There were six principal congregations or branches of the order: the Clugniacs, Grandmontines, Vallombrosa, and Camaldoli of the eleventh century ; Carthusians and Cistercians, Savigny, or Grey Brothers, and Tiron ; besides the minor and modern communities of Monte Casino (1408) St. Maur (1621) and others. The order gave to the Church 40 popes and 2000 cardinals, 7000 archbishops, 5000 bishops, 15,000 abbots, and most of its learned members in all ages. They held all the cathedrals of the new foundation in England except Carlisle, and also those of Monte Casino and Monreale. The magnificent churches of Tewkesbury, Battle, Pershore, Glastonbury, Tynemouth, Selby, Sherborne, Milton, St. Mary's (York), Crowland, Ramsay, also belonged to them. A parish church for their labourers will always be found adjoining their close ; which included workshops of every trade, and a mill, in order to render them independent of the outer world.

Their dress consisted of boots and woollen hosen, breeches, a stamine, or linsey-woolsey shirt, a black tunic, or under-robe with long sleeves, a leathern girdle, a black cowl, a frock like a mantle, and, for manual work, a scapular, consisting of a hood, and two pieces of cloth hanging down one behind the other in front of the wearer. Richard I. said that he would bequeath his luxury to Black Monks, his avarice to the Grey, and his pride to the Templars.

Benediction. The Latin or Western form of benediction is purely symbolical, and made by extending the thumb, first and second fore fingers, with the third and fourth closed upon the palm, as symbolical of the Holy Trinity; but in the Greek Church the first finger extended represents I; the third finger is bent towards the palm and crossed by the thumb like an X (Ch), at the same time the second finger is curved inwards to form C (s), and the fourth finger is similarly bent into a C; this arrangement gives the Greek monogram for the four letters which begin and end the name of Jesus Christ (JesuS CHristoS). It is also supposed to represent the conjunction of A and Ω, Alpha and Omega, the title of the Saviour; or the aspiration of the soul to the Holy Trinity, and faith in His eternal benefits, represented by the circle made by the thumb and ring-finger. The rite of Constantinople prescribes benediction by the patriarch holding in his right hand a three-branched candlestick, as emblematical of the Triune God, and in his left one with two lights, symbolical of the two natures of our Lord.

Benediction of Bells. Bells improperly are said by Ivo of Chartres and Alcuin, c. 770, and oven by Durand and Martene, to be baptized; and Charlemagne in his Capitulars, 789, forbade the baptism of clocks or bells. The canonical term for the ceremony of consecration is Benediction. Pope John IV., in the seventh century, gave his name to the great bell of St. John Lateran; and John XIII., in 968, first gave positive instructions for the benediction of a bell, the gift of the Emperor Otho, in the same church, and oil and chrism were used in its unction. Bells were named after some saint or some distinguished person, and instances of this nomenclature occur in the Hautclere, Douce, Clement, Austin,

Mary, Gabriel, and John,—the Bonnie Christchurch bells;
Mary and Jacqueline of Notre Dame, Paris, the George
d'Amboise of Rouen, the Rolin de l'Huys and Benet, the
Bauda of Vienne, and the Great Roland of Ghent, which was
the gift of Charles V. Recently the Bishops of Oxford and
Salisbury have dedicated bells, as in the parallel instance of
former prelates consecrating altar plate, and the font, and
other church furniture, including the names of Andrewes,
Lake, Wren, and Hacket. Dr. Tresham having had the
Mass-bell of Christchurch, Oxford, repaired, when Pro-Vice-
Chancellor, called it Mary. Baptism was simply a French
term which took its origin in sprinkling a new bell with
holy-water: and by some of the older canonists, churches
were said to be baptized when the rite of dedication only
was intended. The superstition against which Charlemagne
in 789 protested was an immersion of the bells in water
known as baptism; a matter very different from a consecration of the dull metal as an instrument of God's praise.

Benediction of Grapes. At Clugny there were numerous benedictions: of the new beans, the freshly pressed juice of the
grape, and on August 6th of the ripe grapes which were
blessed on the altar during Mass, and afterwards distributed
in the Refectory.

Benediction of Ships. The benediction of inanimate things is
founded on 1 Tim. iv. 4, 5. A relic of this ceremony remains
in the practice of breaking a bottle of wine over the bows of
a ship at its launch.

Benediction of Swords. On the Sunday in Lent called Lætare
and on Christmas Eve the Pope blessed a sword, which he
afterwards sent to some favoured king. Pius II. gave one
to the Duke of Burgundy, and another to Louis XI., King of
France, each with a suitable inscription.

Benedictus. The song of Zacharias at the birth of St. John
Baptist, which is not to be used as a Canticle when it oc-
curs in the chapter for the day, or as the Gospel on St. John
Baptist's Day (Feb. 18; June 17, 24; and Oct. 15).

Benefice. The perpetual right of enjoying the fruits of ecclesiastical goods, accruing to a clerk from a special office.
About the ninth century, and towards its close, the clergy
no longer were paid from a common fund, but by a fixed
portion of land or income, as a title or usufruct. They were

divided into secular, held by secular clergy; or regular, when occupied by monks. Doubles were benefices of popes, bishops, and abbots; intermediate doubles, those of capitular dignitaries; and minor doubles parochial cures; whilst chapelries were designated as simple.

The right of ADVOWSONS arose from the permission given by bishops in early times to those who founded and endowed churches to nominate the incumbents. The word is derived from *advocatio*, the reception of a client by a patron, who was bound to be advocate or protector of the rights of the Church, and the clerk presented. An advowson appendent is one annexed to a manor; that which has been separated from it is said to be in gross. NOMINATION is the offering a clerk to the patron. PRESENTATION the offering a clerk to the bishop. The donative invests the clerk by the patron's simple deed, without presentation, institution, or induction; and this was the usual practice where the clerk was already in orders, until the middle of the twelfth century, when the bishops established a right to institution as spiritual investiture in all cases, although formerly they had only claimed it when the nominee was a layman.

BENEFICES are (1) presentative, in which the patron presents the nominee for institution to the bishop, and the bishop commends him to the archdeacon for induction; (2) collative, those in the gift of ordinaries, who forward him to the archdeacon to induct him; (3) donative, exempt from the jurisdiction of the ordinary, where the patron puts his nominee into possession by an instrument under his hand and seal, without institution.

Benefit of Clergy. Previous to the Act 28th Henry VIII. c. 1, a clerk convicted of felony could not be condemned or sentenced by a temporal judge, but was committed to the bishop's prison on a bread-and-water diet, with the privilege of compurgation; but if he failed to establish his innocence (or, as it was said, purge himself), he was given over to the secular arm.

Berefellars. Seven persons in Beverley Minster, who acted as rectors of choir; their amesses were probably lined with bear-skin, or fells, whence their name.

Beryl. (1) A precious stone, or deep-red cornelian; (2) fine glass-like crystal.

Bethlehem (Order of). Reformed Dominicans, distinguished by a blazing star on the breast, who founded a house at Cambridge in 1257.

Bid Ale. A feast where an honest man, being decayed in his estate, was set up again by the contributions of his friends at a common meal.

Bidding Prayer (*bede*, to pray). A form of prayer inviting supplications in church for all estates of men, which may be traced back to the people's prayer mentioned in the Council of Lyons in 517. Similar prayers were made in Africa and Germany, and are alluded to by Ivo of Chartres in 1092. St. Chrysostom used the form, "Blessed be God." St. Ambrose had his own form, preserved by Ferrarius. Optatus says sermons began and terminated with the name of God. The Apostolical Constitutions enjoin the Pauline benediction. Old forms of the Bidding Prayer occur at the time of the Reformation, and these, or one at present used in cathedrals and the Universities, were employed by Parker, Sandys, Gardiner, Latimer, Jewel, and Andrewes; but Fletcher, Ravis, and Hacket used forms of their own.

Birretta (from *pyrrhus*, or *purros*, red). A cap so called from the colour of the fur, its original material. The cappa was also called a birrhus, and worn with a fur hood to cover the head. Copes in 1281 were ordered by Archbishop Peckham not to be worn birretted behind and before, that is, without folds (another meaning of birrhus), and not slit down the back or the centre in front. The earlier birrhus, a cloak, as Sozomen explains it, loose and of woollen material, was usually red in colour, and common to all the clergy. St. Cyprian wore a beros together with his tunic, and the habit is alluded to under the same name by the Council of Gangra. St. Austin speaks of a precious birrus, probably made of rich silk. At the coronation of William and Mary some of the clergy wore square caps, resembling flat-topped birrettas. The birretta, a scull-cap, is mentioned in 1298 as the instrument of investiture of a rector by the Archbishop of Canterbury. Birrus was also a tippet worn on the tunic, and sometimes buttoned over the chest, or else flowing over the shoulders: it was used by the clergy, of a ruddy black or brown, or more usually fire-red colour, as its name, *purros*, as an adjective implies; but as a substantive, indicating a dress, it was spelt *beros*. It had sometimes a hood attached to it, and is represented by the modern mozzetta.

Bishop. (Gr. *episcopos*, an overseer or superintendent.) The first of the sacred order of ministers; to whom consecration by three bishops is indispensable. Bishops are divided into four classes: (1) suffragans, titulars, and *in partibus infidelium;* (2) archbishops and metropolitans; (3) primates; (4) patriarchs. The bishop holds a stall at Lichfield, Lincoln, Salisbury, Limerick, Cashel, St. Patrick's, and Deventer, as formerly at Ross, in Scotland. At Durham he was a Count Palatine and Earl of Sadberg, until 3 & 4 Will. III. c. 19. In several cathedrals, and in all of the new foundations, the bishop was abbot; and to this day the bishop occupies what otherwise would be the dean's stall at Carlisle and Ely, and at Durham on certain occasions. At Carlisle and Monreale, houses of Canons Regular, the superior was the bishop; and at Monte Casino and La Cava the Benedictine abbot was also the bishop. The Bishop of Norwich sits in the House of Lords as Abbot of Hulme, the barony having been severed from the see in 1535. The sees of Carlisle and Rochester are held in frank alms. In cathedrals of the old foundations he summons the Great Chapter, interprets the statutes, celebrates at the Holy Communion, and gives the benediction. He has the right of visitation, and confers the dignities and prebends, and in most cases the residentiaryships. In many cathedrals of the new foundation he can celebrate when he pleases. The several sees were founded or in existence in the following order: CANTERBURY, 596; YORK, 314; LONDON, 604; WINCHESTER, 634. [Llandisfare, 635–854; Hexham, 678–821. United in Chester-le-Street 854, and merged in] DURHAM 990. [Sherborne taken out of Winchester, 705, including the sees of Wiltshire, 920–1058; Bath, 1088; Wells, 909, united 1136; Cornwall and Devon, 904, united in Exeter 1041; Bristol, 1542; the see at Sonning and Ramsbury from 920, and at Old Sarum 1058, removed to] SALISBURY in 1075; HEREFORD, 680; [Mercia, see at Leicester 655, at] LICHFIELD (or Chester) *c.* 750, and COVENTRY 1102: the latter cathedral was destroyed at the Reformation; [Devon, see at Tawton or Crediton, 905; Cornwall, see at Bodmin, St. German's, 850, or St. Petrock, united in] EXETER, 1056; [Dorchester owen

636, Lindisse or Stow 678, Leicester 658, united at Dorchester 886, removed to] Lincoln, 1076; [Ely, taken out of Lincoln, 1109; [Selsea, 681, removed to] Chichester in 1085; Carlisle, 1133; Worcester, 680; Rochester, 604; [East Anglia 630, Dunwich 673, North Elmham 673–870, East Anglia 955, Thetford 1078, translated to] Norwich 1094; Wells 909; Bath, c. 1088, united 1135 [called Bath and Glastonbury 1206–1218]; Peterborough, formed out of Lincoln; Gloucester, out of Worcester; Chester 1541; Bristol, out of Salisbury, 1542; [Osney, out of Lincoln 1542, removed to] Oxford, 1546; Sodor and Man, 360; St. Asaph, 560; Llandaff, c. 500; Bangor, 516; St. David's, 436.

In 1075 Lanfranc, in conformity with the Canons of Sardica 347, and the decree of Pope Leo, gave order for the removal of the sees out of villages into large towns: from Sherborne to Salisbury, Selsea to Chichester, Lichfield to Chester, and on the King's return Lincoln and Norwich were made sees.

By the Act of 3 & 4 Will. IV. c. 37, two archbishops, Tuam and Cashel, and eight out of eighteen bishoprics were suppressed. Scotland had two archbishoprics; Glasgow and St. Andrew's, eleven ancient bishoprics, and one, that of Edinburgh, founded in 1633.

The archbishops of France are those of Besancon, Bordeaux, Lyons and Vienne, Paris, Rheims, Aix, Arles and Embrun, Alby, Auch, Avignon, Bourges, Cambray, Rennes, Rouen, Sens and Auxerre, Toulouse and Narbonne, Chambéry, Tours, with seventy-three suffragans. Of Spain: Toledo, Seville, Burgos, Santiago, Granada, Saragossa, Tarragona, Valencia, Valladolid, with forty-six suffragans. Austria has one patriarch, four primates, and eleven archbishops: Agram, Colocza, Erlau, Fogaras, Gran, Gueritz and Gradisca, Limburg, Olmutz, Prague, Saltzburg, Udine, Venice, Vienna, Zara, with fifty-eight bishops. In Belgium the episcopate includes the prelates of Mechlin (archbishop), Bruges, Ghent, Liége, Namur, and Tournai. In Greece there are seven archbishops and nine bishops. In Portugal there are three archbishops, those of Lisbon, Braga, and Evora, with thirteen suffragans. In Russia are twenty-nine archbishops, twenty-eight bishops, and eleven suffragans; two Roman archbishops and ten bishops. In the kingdom of Italy the archbishops take their titles from Bologna, Cagliari, Ferrara, Genoa, Milan, Modena, Orislano, Ravenna, Sassari, Turin, Vercelli. In Holland, Utrecht, Haarlem, Bois-le-duc, Breda, and Ruremonde, are episcopal sees. There were twenty-four archbishoprics in the kingdom of the Two Sicilies. The Pope had eighty-nine suffragans. In Sicily the archbishoprics are those of Palermo, Messina, and Montereale, with eight suffragans.

English bishops sign with their Christian names, and the Latinized title of their see, as—Cantuar (Canterbury), Ebor (York), Carliol (Carlisle), Exon (Exeter), Dunelm (Durham), Cicestr (Chichester), Winton (Winchester), Oxon (Oxford); which is a relic of the time when Latin was the language of correspondence, and also a necessary distinction from temporal lords deriving their title from a cathedral city. Ely alone in England has never given title to a nobleman.

Bishoping. The vulgar name for Confirmation.

Bishopric (*bishop* and *ric*, region). When a See is vacant in England a writ issues out of the Exchequer to seize the temporalities into the hands of the Crown, leaving the spiritualities to the archbishop, or dean and chapter, according to the custom of the place. Then the Crown issues the *Congé d'eslire*, or licence to choose a bishop, to the dean and chapter, with a royal missive containing the name of the elect, who must be chosen under pain of *præmunire;* and they, within a certain number of days, choose a bishop, and certify their election to the Crown, sealed with the chapter seal. The Crown then issues a commission under the great seal to the primate or certain bishops to examine and confirm the election, which is done at Bow Church, London, with the assistance of the chief ecclesiastical judges of the realm. After the confirmation, consecration follows within certain days; then the archbishop certifies the consecration under his seal; the sovereign receives the new bishop's homage and fealty, and commands him to be put in possession of his See. He is then enthroned in his cathedral, and then enjoys his spiritualities; and, lastly, a writ issues out of the Exchequer to the sheriff to restore to him his temporalities. 1 Eliz. c. 1, § 7.

Black Rubric. The declaration on kneeling at the end of the office for the Holy Communion.

Bloodletting. Owing to the coarse and heating fare of the monks, quarterly bloodlettings or minutions were in use, during which the brethren were excused choir services, and received indulgences and relaxations of diet. An abbot of Peterborough was held in grateful memory because he allowed the terms to be kept punctually.

Body of the Church. The nave, of which the transept forms the arms, and the choir the head.

Bonhommes. Friars, introduced into England by Richard, Earl of Cornwall, in the time of Henry III. They settled at Berkhampstead, in the latter half of the thirteenth century, and at Ashridge and Edgington.

Book of Common Prayer. The English ritual, founded on the Salisbury use of St. Osmond, 1085, the Salisbury Breviary, 1530, and Missal, 1533, reformed; and adopted 1541 throughout the southern province. The English Litany was first used in 1544; the Communion Service, March, 1548; the first Prayer-book of Edward VI., June, 1549; the Ordinal, $15\frac{49}{50}$; the second Prayer-book of Edward VI., 1552; restored Latin Prayer-book of Queen Elizabeth, 1560, with some alterations, 1559. The Book of Common Prayer was revised 1661–2: the present use, with the exception of the Form for the Queen's Accession, a later addition of the time of Queen Anne.

Book of Cries. The book used for entries of banns, proclamations, and the like.

Books. (1.) When books were rare they were often placed in a public position in churches for use by students and the devout, and it is said the former occasionally slipt off the margins to write their love-letters on the parchment. So early as the twelfth century at St. Alban's a Bible with the best commentaries was placed in a painted aumbry in the nave; at Hereford, in 1369, Bishop Charlton bequeathed a copy of the Holy Scriptures with Books of Devotion to the Cathedral; in the sixteenth century Erasmus saw books chained to the pillars of Canterbury for the use of the laity, and at Lincoln a similar custom is on record. Books with their chains attached are preserved still at Hereford, Wimborne, Stratford-on-Avon, Malvern, St. Mary Redcliffe, Little Stanmore, Frampton, Cotterall, Hanmer, and Bridlington. Upon the altars of great churches was placed a splendidly illuminated volume called the 'Book of Life,' which, like the ancient diptychs, contained the names of benefactors who were commemorated in certain Masses. Those of Durham and St. Alban's are now preserved in the British Museum. Probably these suggested the introduction of the Bidding Prayer. (2.) The stalls at Chichester were called books. In many of the monastic MSS. some curious illustrations of the period occur in little pen-and-ink sketches made at the foot of the pages by readers. It is observable that the common types, Primer, Pica, Brevier, and Canon, preserve the names of the ancient church books.

Boots were introduced by the Benedictines, and worn by masters of arts at their inception, until the doctors of faculties appropriated them to their own use, and masters were reduced to pantables or sandals. The boot was buttoned up the side of the leg like a gaiter; hence, probably, the modern use of the latter by the bishops, who have always a doctor's degree. The Doctor of Divinity stood booted and spurred at his act, as if shod with the preparation of the Gospel, and ready always to preach God's word.

Bowcer. A bursar.

Bowing at the Name of Jesus. In harmony with the apostolic injunction, Queen Elizabeth and Archbishop Parker ordered all persons to take off their hats in church, and bow their knees at the pronouncing of the name of Jesus, and, by the canons of 1603, no man is allowed to cover his head, except in case of infirmity, when he may use a nightcap or coif; and when in Divine Service the Lord Jesus is named, due and lowly reverence is to be done by all present, as had been accustomed. This is now usually made simply by bowing the head. The monks of Peterborough, St. Augustines, Canterbury, Crowland, and other minsters, were allowed, by Papal indulgence, about the year 1243, a covering for their heads in time of cold weather, and in 1343 black caps (*pileoli*) were worn in Exeter Cathedral. The Bishop of Worcester, as commissioner of Cardinal Pole in 1558, enjoined in the Cathedral of Hereford that at the naming of Jesus in singing or saying every man should give token of reverence with vailing (removing) their bonnets and bending their knees; and likewise when the verse, " Blessed be the name of the Lord " is sung, and the Psalm

"Praise the Lord, ye servants;" also in the Creed, at the saying of the verse, "Incarnate of the Holy Ghost," and these words, "and was made man." See *Ante et Retro*.

Bowling-green. An ordinary adjunct of a Benedictine Abbey. At Westminster it lay south of the infirmary garden, and at Durham in the same direction, near the common house.

Bowls. The Glastonbury Bowl, standing on four lions and carved with figures of Apostles, is preserved at Wardour Castle. At Waltham Abbey when they put the conventual loaves into the oven, as many as drank in the bakehouse had pardon, Latimer says. At Bury St. Edmund's, Becon relates there was a pardon bowl, of which whoever drank received five hundred days' pardon. The pardon bowl given by Archbishop Scrope is preserved at York Minster. There were two mazers at Durham, Bede's Bowl and Judas's Cup. There was also a famous St. Leonard's Bowl. The bowl of St. Giles's, London, was also brought out and presented to a criminal on his way to execution at the Elms of Tyburn. In Aubrey's time, in Herefordshire, a large loaf and a mazer bowl were brought out at funerals and given to a "sin eater," who thereby took upon himself all the sins of the dead.

Bowtell. A small pillar, or shaft.

Boy Bishop. The most deserving chorister or scholar was appointed on St. Nicholas' Day, during the chanting of the Magnificat, the bishop of boys until the day of the Holy Innocents, and wore the ornaments of a bishop. The custom prevailed in the great schools of Winchester and Eton, and was perpetuated by Dean Colet in his foundation of St. Paul's, no doubt as a stimulus to Christian ambition in the boy, just as the mitre and staff are painted as the rewards of learning on the school walls of Winchester, or in honour of the holy child Jesus. The ceremony was observed at Tours, Antwerp, Beauvais, Vienne, Toul, Senlis, Noyon, and Amiens, at the Nunnery of Godstow, and in the Couvent aux Dames at Caen, as in our own cathedrals, in many collegiate and several parish churches tiny pontificals being provided for them. At Rouen, the choristers in albs and copes and tunics, holding tapers, on the eve of the Feast of Holy Innocents, assembled in the sacristy, and there went in procession, headed by the boy-bishop, mitred and pontifi-cally vested, to the altar of the Holy Innocents, where the child gave his benediction to the people. On the festival Mass was sung by a canon, the boy-bishop singing the Prose and Offertory. At vespers, at the singing of the words, "He hath put down the mighty from their seat," he resigned his staff and office (the people giving money), having first said Mass and preached in church. They were called St. Nicholas' clerks. At Salisbury, in the procession of the boy-bishop, the dean and residentiaries went first, followed by the chaplains, the bishops, and petty preben- daries; the choristers sat in the upper stalls, the residen- tiaries furnished the incense and book, and the petties were taper-bearers. The boy-bishop gave the benediction. At Zug the boy-bishop was preceded by a chaplain carrying a cross, and followed by a fool in motley, whilst his fellows, dressed like canons, brought up the rear. After going to church he levied a tax on all the booths in the fair. In England, in Henry VIII.'s time, the boys counterfeited bishops, priests, and women, singing and dancing from house to house, blessing and gathering. In many parts of France the boy-bishop was master of the festival under an unpleas- ing aspect, the day being called the Feast of Fools, and kept on Easter Monday; May 1; or at Paris on January 1, and on Holy Innocents' Day at Cognac. The chief actor was dressed in bishop's robes reversed, with spectacles of orange-peel; his companions, grotesquely dressed, placed themselves in the stalls, parodied divine service, and burned old shoes as incense; and the mummery concluded with dances, buffoonery, songs, and a shameless procession through the streets, with the sham bishop mounted on a car. Al- though these indecent levities were forbidden by the Councils of Cognac, 1260, Nantes, 1431, and Basle, 1431, by the Legate in 1198, and the Chapter of Troyes in 1445, they did not die out until the sixteenth century. In England the custom was suppressed in 1542.

Branch. (1.) A light consisting of three tapers, as an emblem of the Holy Trinity, carried in funeral processions and set upon the coffin when it rested. (2.) A large cumbrous corona, consisting of branches of brass for lights, used in the seventeenth and eighteenth centuries, in England; few specimens now remain; one still hangs in the sanctuary of Chichester.

Brasses. Monumental plates, representing the canopied effigy of the departed, made of brass, or the mixed metal called latten or Cologne plate, inlaid on large slabs of stone; introduced owing to the inconvenience offered by raised stones and effigies on the floors of churches. The earliest form was the enamelled work of Limoges, about the middle of the twelfth century; the earliest instance occurring in this country, however, in Rochester Cathedral, in the tomb of Walter de Merton, 1277. The earliest recorded brass dates from 1208; the indent of one c. 1246 remains at Salisbury. The first brasses came from Flanders, and were introduced in the thirteenth century. In England they consisted of several plates, or pieces, having a background of stone; round the edge runs an inscription with merchant's mark, coats-of-arms, and evangelistic symbols at the corners, the unoccupied portions being filled with an ornamental diaper. About four thousand are preserved, more than exist in any other country; and these examples are most common on the east coast, from Kent to Norfolk and adjoining counties, Surrey, Sussex, Middlesex, and Berks; but are rare in the north and west, being chiefly confined to the cathedral and conventual churches, as in Herefordshire. In Ireland, Wales, and Scotland they were also far from common.

North Germany and Belgium possess some good examples, but in other parts of Europe they were either confined to the upper classes, or have been destroyed.

Brattishing. A cresting.

Breviary. A name for the Office Book, not earlier than the fifth century. In fact, Micrologus is, perhaps, the first writer who uses it, in 1080; but the actual thing signified, the breve orarium, or shortened prayer, is far older; as St. Benedict abridged the canonical prayers, and directed the Psalter hitherto said daily to be spread over an entire week.

Bridget, the XV. Oes of St. Fifteen prayers (*orationes*, of which *oes* is the abbreviation), composed by St. Bridget (whose revelations were fervently credited in medieval times), and used before the crucifix daily in St. Paul's church at Rome. They were formerly very popular.

Brief. (1.) A mortuary bill or roll sent by a messenger to affiliated or associated religious houses to announce the death of a brother, and beg the prayers of the inmates on his behalf. (2.) Letters patent issued by the Sovereign, declarations and recommendations authorizing the collection of alms for a specific work of charity, and read after the Nicene Creed. They were abolished by 9 Geo. IV. c. 28 in 1828.

Broche. (1.) A spit. A spire rising straight from the sides of the tower, as was common in early English; but the term is not earlier than 1521, and then applied to that of Louth. (2.) The morse of a cope. (3.) A leaden ornament, with the head of Becket, worn by pilgrims to Canterbury.

Bruges. Satin. Rich material of tissue from Flanders, often spelt Bridges, the English medieval form of the town of Bruges, used for vestments.

Budge. Fur of kids, employed in trimming robes.

Bulla (*boule*, bullet). A seal made of two circular pieces of lead, and attached to Papal documents, which at length took the same name. A beautiful bull, attributed to Benvenuto Cellini, is preserved in the Public Record Office. Ecclesiastical seals were usually oval, until the fourteenth and fifteenth centuries, when they became circular; and up to the thirteenth century the seal was suspended by silk threads or a slip of parchment, but was then attached to the document.

Bull's Eye. The circular window in the west front of an early Italian church, which became the rose of the Gothic period.

Burials. The Christians paid great reverence to the body, which had been the temple of the Holy Ghost, and was to be raised from sleep into a glorious incorruption by an immortal change. They therefore assembled for vigil and exequies before the funeral; and, according to the tradition of the Church, sang hymns and canticles, the service being held at night. Prudentius mentions the use of the Psalm cxvi., and St. Augustine relates that Psalm ci. was chanted with responses at the death of his mother, Monica. St. Jerome says, that in his time Alleluia was sung on such occasions by the whole congregation, shaking the gilded roofs of the temple. The anthems sung on such occasions are actually preserved to us, such as Psalm cxvi. 7–15, Prov.

x. 17, and Wisdom iii. 1 in the Apostolical Constitutions, and Psalms xxiii. 4 and lix. 16, by St. Chrysostom. The exequies were kept on the third, seventh, ninth, thirtieth or fortieth day after death, as appears from the Apostolical Constitutions and the writings of St. Augustine; and St. Ambrose attributes the custom to the mourning for Jacob by the survivors for forty days, the lamentation at Atad during seven days by Joseph (Gen. l. 3–10), and the weeping for Moses in the plains of Moab thirty days (Exod. xxxiv. 8.)

In former times, when a person was dying, he was laid on ashes, and ashes were strewn upon his chest in the form of a cross, with these words, "Thou art dust, O man." The body was always washed until the tenth century, as a sign that the soul was now cleansed from all stain and pollution, and that its companion should at the last day be given purity and eternal glory. It was the practice in apostolic times (Acts ix. 37). St. Chrysostom thought that our Lord's body was washed for His burial after the manner of the Jews (St. John xix. 40). St. Gregory, Bede, and Gregory of Tours refer to the practice in their days; and at Canterbury, in St. John's Chapel, there was a special stone slab set apart for the ceremony. The eyes were closed tenderly, perfumes were burned, and unction was also made in imitation of the anointing of the Saviour's body (St. Mark xiv. 8; xvi. 1). The bodies were steeped in aromatic preparations during two or three days, in which myrrh, balsam, and honey were the principal ingredients, as a preservative against corruption. The graves were closed with marble slabs; and the dead laid upon two winding-sheets, which contained a layer of lime, to prevent the escape of any offensive smell into the catacomb. The body was swathed in rollers of pure linen, in allusion to the white garments of the just, and a napkin wrapped about the face; and shrouds also were employed, often tied above the head and below the feet, like a child in swaddling bands; and there are examples of this singular practice at Frampton, Dorset, and in Dr. Donne's effigy in St. Paul's crypt. The persons employed in these last offices were called the *Fossarii*, or diggers. The Council of Auvergne forbids the covering of the dead with palls or the fair cloth for covering the elements (*ministeria opertoria*) in the case of priests ; and the Council of Autun also prohibited the employment of veils and palls, or the giving of the Eucharist, or kiss of peace. The bishop or priest anointed the dead with oil before the burial procession set out, and said certain prayers, which were followed by chants of thanksgiving to God; and lastly by funeral sermons, as St. Melitius pronounced for Gregory of Nyssa ; Eusebius on Constantine, St. Gregory Nazianzen for St. Basil and St. Cæsarius, St. Ambrose for Valentinian, and others partially preserved by Theodoret and Nicephorus. The usual practice was to wrap the martyrs in precious stuffs ; but bishops, abbots, and priests were interred in their sacred habits, as Nadab and Abihu had been buried under the law (Levit. x. 5). St. Augustine was buried in his mitre, and with his staff. St. Cuthbert was laid to rest in his habit, his shoes on his feet, and the chalice and oblata, a fragment of the Eucharist, on his breast; and when the body of St. Birinus was exhumed, it was found with the doubled stole, the red mitre of silk, and a metal cross upon his heart, with the chalice below it. Martyrs were usually buried in the dalmatic or colobium, and their severed limbs were carefully rejoined. Great captains who died in battle were buried standing upright; so were the Claphams at Bolton Abbey, and Ben Jonson at Westminster. The imposition of a fragment of the Eucharist on the heart of the dead was forbidden by Councils. At the head of a dead priest a seal of wax, stamped with a cross, was placed : at Westminster and Hereford the abbots and bishops were buried with a cross of candles, two tapers laid saltier-wise on the breast ; a chalice of earthenware or pewter was laid with a paten in the grave ; forms of formal absolution on metal plates were also sometimes interred with the dead ecclesiastic. The clapper was used to give notice of the setting out of the funeral procession; but in the eighth or ninth century bells were employed for the same purpose. As early as the fourth century palm and olive branches, as symbols of victory, were carried; and at a later date rosemary was added, and sometimes incense was burned. A cross occasionally during the sixth, and commonly in the ninth century, preceded the bier. Laurel, or ivy leaves, were often placed in the coffin, and lighted torches carried, in allusion to the virgins' lamps burning at the marriage of the

Lamb. At Durham, at the interment of a monk, his blue
bed was held above the grave, and became the barber's
perquisite. There was also a pretty custom of placing
crowns of flowers on the heads of virgins, which is alluded
to by St. Jerome, St. Augustine, and St. Gregory Nyssen.
A lingering trace of it was observable in England till very
recently in many places, and the stand on which a crown of
this kind was suspended is still pointed out at St. Alban's.
During the ages of persecution the dead were carried on
two-wheeled country carts to the grave, in order to escape
notice. The position in the grave was on the back facing
the east, after the manner of our Lord's burial, as Bede describes it. "Entering from the east into that round house
cut in the rock, they saw an angel sitting on the south side
of the place where the body of Jesus had lain; that is, on
the right side, for to the body lying with its head to the
west the south was on the right." The head placed to the
west, and the feet turned to the east, betokened the posture
of prayer in life, and the readiness of the departed to hasten
from the set of time to the day-spring, from the world to
eternity. Priests, however, were buried with their faces to
the west, as if waiting to follow the Lord when He rises in
the east, and so to lead their flocks as their joy and crown
of rejoicing when the Chief Shepherd shall appear. The
custom was introduced in 1614 by Pope Pius V. Owing to
the position of the faithful in their graves, as if expecting
their Lord's return, the east wind is called in Wales, " the
wind of the dead men's feet." The departed were placed
on their backs because death to the Christian is but a little
sleep, with their face to Heaven, whereon their hope relies,
and to the east in sure hope of the resurrection to eternal
life.

In France, Durandus mentions that evergreens, ivy, and
laurel were spread under the heads of the faithful, in token
that though in the body they die, yet in the spirit they are
living unto God. Vases of holy-water and crosses; cruses
with the oil of martyrdom; the instruments of passion; the
chain rings and haircloth of the ascetic were often interred
in the tomb. Sometimes the acts of a martyr, engraved on
leaden tablets, were placed inside; and his name or his
symbol, the palm (Ps. xcii. 12), which was said to flourish

under weights and pressure (Rev. vii. 9), or the emblem of victory, was carved outside the monument. Confessors were indicated by the symbol of X, the monogram of Christ. Every grave was to be kept for its own single tenant by the Councils of Autun and Macon. Interments were made by the primitive Christians always, when practicable, in daylight.

St. Chrysostom and St. Augustine have beautifully observed that funeral ceremonies are for the comfort of the living, not for aids to the dead. They betoken the pious belief that God's providence watches over the sleepers, and that such good offices please Him because done in faith in the Resurrection. Constantine the Great established a Guild of Bearers, who were freed from all civil duties and dues, in order to attend upon the burial of the dead. These undertakers were called collegiates and deans, from forming a society, and Kopiatæ, from a word signifying rest, and also lecticarii, as carriers of the bier. In the seventeenth century, in England, sermons were commonly delivered at the funerals of bishops and persons of distinction. The Holy Communion was generally administered; and St. Ambrose, Prudentius, and St. Jerome mention the graceful practice of loving hands scattering flowers over the tomb,—the violet, rose, lily, and purple blossoms,—and laurel or ivy leaves placed in the coffin. To this day, in some parts of Wales, women strew ivy leaves in the way of a funeral procession.

Lights, in token of victory and union with Christ at the marriage of the Lamb, were carried before and behind the bier at funerals which were celebrated in the day-time, as St. Chrysostom, Theodoret, St. Jerome, the Gregories of Nazianzum and Nyssa, Eusebius, and the Novels of Justinian record; and the custom prevailed in France in the time of St. German of Auxerre. The Council of Elvira forbade the placing of lights in cemeteries simply because of some local abuses which had followed on the practice of praying around graves at night. The Emperor Julian compelled Christians to bury at night. St. Gregory of Tours mentions that interments were made within four days after death.

Interments were not permitted in the church, as Optatus mentions, and the Councils of Braga 563, Tribur 895, and Vaison under Leo I., and that of Winchester in 1071, distinctly prescribe. The Emperors were buried in the porches, or forecourts, as Arcadius and Theodosius and Constantine the Great, who, as St. Chrysostom says, lay before St. Peter's at Constantinople, like the doorkeeper and chamberlain of the Fisherman of Galilee. Sidonius Apollinaris says Christians were buried outside the city suburbs. At length, about the seventh century, the bodies of nobles, priests, clerks, and men of eminence were interred within churches, as appears by the Councils of Meldi and Mayence, and the sole prohibition was that there should be no burial near an altar; and if the bones could not be removed from an altar, then by Theodulf's Capitula, 994, the altar itself should be taken down. In 960 burials in churches were permitted in England as an old custom. In the fourth century the atrium was not used generally for burial, but within two hundred years the practice became general. At Canterbury bishops were buried in the north porch, and kings and queens at St. Martin's porch, in the early minster, about the seventh century. At Durham the bishop's chariot bore his body through the nave to the choir door in the fourteenth century, but noblemen were carried on men's shoulders from the entrance of the nave. At Glastonbury, for a very long period, there were two pyramids, each of several stories, inscribed with the names of benefactors in the cemetery; but there were no other monuments, interments being made simply under the turf, as the case was at St. Alban's in the thirteenth century. From 1096 to 1311 bishops were buried in the chapter-house of Durham; but the first prior buried within the minster was Fosser, in 1374; the first bishop Anthony Bec; and the first laymen the Lords Neville, in consequence of their defeat of the King of Scotland. In Spain interment within a church was not permitted until the thirteenth century. At Winchester, Stigand was the first bishop buried in the nave. At Dunstable, Ourscamp (there called the Hall of the Dead), and Gloucester, noblemen were buried in the chapter-house. At Hereford the bishop, and at Westminster the abbot, was buried with two candles laid crosswise on his breast; at Chichester a bishop was found to be buried with a leaden Indulgence. Burial in a friar's coat was not uncommon, as if a passport to a happy future; pardons, cloths, and relics were also laid in graves.

One of the most singular and painful superstitions connected with this subject was that condemned by the Council of Arles (and the canons of Ælfric in 957) as devilish, unchristian, and inhuman,—singing of songs, dancing, jesting, making merry, laughing, and being drunken. A vestige of a somewhat similar practice is discernible in the funeral baked meats and burial dinner, not yet extinct in England. The Second Council of Tours found it necessary to suppress the monstrous ignorance which delighted in offering meat and wine in February and on the day Cathedra St. Petri on the tombs of the dead. St. Augustine condemned it as heathenish; but even in the seventeenth century it survived in France and Spain; and Casalins says, in the Spanish Chapel of St. Ildefonso at Rome an inscribed stone recorded that on a certain day—that of All Souls—an offering of a carpet and two tapers was to be laid on the tomb, and at its feet bread and wine of the value of four carlins, according to the custom of Spain, were to be placed. In England we find vigils, or memories of the dead, prohibited by the Archbishop of Canterbury, except when kept by priests and the immediate relatives of the departed; and again by Archbishop Thoresby of York, in 1367, owing to the vile abuses which turned the house of mourning into a scene of merriment and excess. The monstrous impiety of placing the consecrated elements within the lips of the dead was forbidden by the Councils of Trullo, III. Carthage, and Autun; and the superstition of giving the kiss of charity was also abolished. But the celebration of the Holy Communion at funerals is as old as the time of St. Augustine, and is mentioned by the Council of Carthage and Eusebius. In the time of Alexander III., on the first day of Lent, the Pope at his first station was presented with a roll of paper dipped in oil by an acolyte; the chamberlain afterwards took it, and it was carefully preserved until the Pope died, and then was placed under his head as a pillow, and buried with him. No doubt, like the oil and thread of the heathens, it conveyed a symbolism of life and death.

After the burials of princes, noblemen, and soldiers, their coat, armour, flag, sword, headpiece, and recognizance were set up in churches. Pardon letters were buried with the dead; doles of provisions and money were made in their name; black gowns and mourning cloaks were distributed to all who attended their obsequies; and the body was watched previously to the funeral with lights burning at the head and feet, and then carried to the grave with torch and taper, bells and banners. The month's mind, a Mass said on the thirtieth day, was common in England; and the day's mind, or memorial, on the Continent; the anniversary or annual was also kept; and the names of benefactors inscribed in the Book of Life—a memorial laid upon the altar, and read out during Mass. St. Augustine strongly condemns the use of black mourning, in which he agrees with St. Jerome, St. Cyprian, and St. Chrysostom.

The Cistercians, at the approach of death, were laid in their blanket on the ground, which was strewn with ashes in the form of a cross, and covered with a mat. In the Benedictine houses the Passion was read out to the dying; and when his body was carried into the chapter-house the whole convent received it with dirge and requiem: while it was in the infirmary chapel previous to this removal, two monks nearest in kin or kindness knelt at the feet of the bier, and the almonry-children, standing in their stalls, sang psalms. One peal was rung upon the bells when the interment was completed. -

Bye-Altars, *or* **Tables,** as called by Bishop Ridley, probably designate minor or secondary altars, in distinction to the high-altar; but in the primitive Church were two tables, one for holding the vestments on the right side, and the other on the left for the vessels; and so the term may indicate a credence.

Byzantine Architecture prevailed through Christian Asia and Africa, and extended to Sicily. It was the modification of Roman architecture by an Eastern element. There were four periods of the art. I. 330-537: rock churches, and round or octagonal churches. II. 537-1003: marked by the multiplication of domes and polygonal apses. III. 1003-1453: when the narthex became less prominent, and choirs were made more important; frescoes were replaced by mosaics; the women's galleries, hitherto erected over the aisles and narthex disappeared; and the cruciform shape lost its significance by the absorption of the aisles. IV. 1453 to the present time. The arrangement was originally an external square, containing a circular building within; but there are several modifications : (1) the round church; (2) the basilica, with apsidal ends to the transept; and (3) the cross of four equal arms, with a dome over the crossing and each arm. The style penetrated to Provence, through commercial relations between Marseilles, Greece, and Constantinople, and thence to the north and centre of France; and also to the banks of the Rhine, under the patronage of Charlemagne. The dome took the place of the Western vault, as most suited to a circular building; and to Procopius poetically seemed to be suspended by a golden chain from heaven, and the whole style combined the basilica with the round church of the Holy Sepulchre of Jerusalem. Like the Basilica, the Eastern Church had its colonnaded atrium, or forecourt (peribolos), the narthex (propyla, pronaos), or advanced portico; galleries for women over the aisles of the nave or trapeza; the chorus cantorum known as the solea; the presbytery was in it; the holy bema, a raised stage, so called from its steps, or hierateion, or hagion; and the sacristies (pastophoria) here called the paratrapezon, or prothesis, on the north, and the skeuophylakium, or diaconicum minus on the south. Over the bema of the readers, which resembled the basilican ambon, rose the royal door. There was only a single altar, but in some cases parecclesiæ, or side churches for daily services, with altars, were added; the chancel screen was called, from its pictures, the iconostasis, with its central door curtained, and two lateral doors : the kiklis occupied the place of the podium; over the altar rose the dome, or trullus. There were four doors, the holy, which were veiled, between the bema and solea, called the holy; the royal, between the solea_and nave; the angelic, between the nave and narthex; and the beautiful, great, or silver, between the narthex and anterior porch (prothyrum). The influence of the style is seen in the cupolas of Russia; those of France, introduced by Venetian colonists and commerce, the ornamentation of capitals, the polygonal apses, and round churches of Western Christendom. A stream of Italian art came to the south and south-west of France, and thence moved northwards in course of gradual development, and also spread down the Rhine, diverging right and left, influencing the border provinces of France; the two developments meeting in the Ile de France; as they had previously been combined at Torcello : the Byzantine modification of the Basilica in Italy received a new form in Rhineland and again in France ; and the turret-like treatment of steeples, the huge triforium, and low central lantern, became common features.

Calabre. A dark or ruddy fur from Calabria, used for the almuces of minor canons and priests vicars in English cathedrals.

Calamus. (1.) The reed; the single upright shaft which supported the table of an altar, called also columella. In the fifth century there were, according to local rite, two or four pillars, and a fifth in the centre, which supported the place of reliques, was sometimes added, as in that of St. Martha at Tarascon, St. Agricola's at Avignon, and one at Marseilles, formerly at St. Victor's Abbey. The space between these columns served as a sanctuary for fugitives. (2.) Called also Fistula, Siphon, and Canna, a narrow tube or pipe of precious metal, which was for some time used after the tenth century, or, as some say, a still earlier date, in the Western Church by the communicants for suction when partaking of the chalice. Bishop Leofric, in 1046, gave a silfrene pipe to Exeter Cathedral ; William Rufus gave others to Worcester. The custom was long retained at St. Denys, and Cluny, at the coronation of the kings of France ; and the Pope still, at a grand pontifical Mass, uses a golden pipe at communion when he celebrates in public together with his deacon and subdeacon. The Benedictines. and Carthusians communicated the laity with a reed in Italy, in memory of the bitter draught of vinegar, gall, and myrrh offered in a reed to the dying Saviour on the cross, and also to avoid any risk of spilling the consecrated wine, and to indulge the insurmountable repugnance of some persons to drinking of one cup.

Calefactory. Pisalis, or pyrale, called the Common House at Durham ; a chamber provided with a fireplace or stove, used as a withdrawing-room by monks, and generally adjoining the refectory. It very often is a portion of the substructure of the dormitory. Here the brethren met before the dinner-time, and in winter time for warmth. Canons regular greased their boots in it, and were let blood. Where there was no Galilee, processions were marshalled here. The præcentor of Benedictines dried his parchment, prepared the waxen tablets and liquefied ink, and the censers were filled by the sacristan's servants in this room. At Winchester a chamber in the south wing of the transept, used for the latter purpose, still retains the name. At the Grey Friars, London, it was furnished with aumbries and water from the conduit; at Kirkham it had a bench-table, and at Thornton a series of stalls.

Calendar. (1.) Sculptures of agricultural labours within medallions, found in Norman churches and those of the thirteenth century as ornaments over doors and porches. (2.) A martyrology, a roll of saints inscribed on the days of their festivals, called by the Greeks Menologium.

Calliculæ (*kallos*, beauty) *or* **Trochades,** small roundles of purple stuff or precious metal worn by the Christians on the lower part of their dress, or upon their shoulders, as distinctive ornaments.

Caloyers. Greek monks of the order of St. Basil.

Calvary. A wayside crucifix.

Camail. (1.) A tippet of black worn by French clergy, but edged, lined, or furred to mark canons. (2.) An aumusse, or cape of fur, adopted by the English dignitaries, with edging of the animal's tail, or pendants, and by canons in a modified form in the fifteenth century.

Camaldoli. A reformed order of Benedictines founded by Romuald of Ravenna, *c.* 1009. They wore a cassock, scapular, and hood of white wool, and a large-sleeved gown. They lived in mountainous and solitary places.

Cameo (*camahutum, camahuija*). A stone, usually onyx, carved in relief. They were greatly prized in the Middle Ages, and often set in the church plate and as ornaments of vestments, fetching enormous prices, and considered to be the chief and most precious articles in royal treasuries.

Campanile. A detached bell-tower, of round or square form, common in Italy. Those of Cremona, Pisa, Bologna, Florence, and Venice are noble examples. At Bologna, Pisa, Padua, Ravenna, and St. Agnes, Mantua, they lean out of the perpendicular. In England they were not uncommon, usually occurring on the north side of the close, as still at Chichester and Evesham, and formerly at Salis-

bury, Lichfield, Worcester, St. Alban's, Ely, Westminster;
but at Canterbury on the south; and at Bury St. Edmund's
one still is standing on the west.   These belfries were
expressly constructed for the bells in order to save the
church-towers from injury through the vibrations of enormous masses of resonant metal.

Candle-beam. A beam for holding the candles over an altar.
On it also were placed the crucifix, images, and reliquaries.

Candles. There is a marble candelabrum, taken from the catacomb of St. Agnes, in the baptistery of St. Constante at
Rome. Prudentius mentions candlesticks of gold for tapers,
used at the nightly assemblies; and in the Middle Ages
lights were, on festivals, lit about the graves of bishops and
the shrines of saints. St. Gregory of Tours speaks of a
similar practice in France in his own day. Candles were
placed on prickets between the pillars of the ciborium,
carried at the administration of baptism, in translations of
relics, in processions, specially at the time of holy communion, during funerals, and during festivals, on rood
beams and in crowns. Bede alludes to the illumination of
churches on feast days. Perpetuus, Bishop of Tours in
475, gave lands to maintain a light round St. Martin's
tomb. St. Jerome alludes to the Eastern practice of
burning lights at the reading of the gospel; and at the
close of the fourth century Constantine gave a pendent
chandelier, to hang above the altar, for his church in the
Lateran. The acolyth's duty, by the Council of Carthage,
was to kindle the lights, the archdeacon at his ordination
making him touch a candlestick containing a taper. The
Greeks have two tapers on a side altar, which at certain times
are brought in by the lectors or acolyths before the celebrant
and deacon, and large candles before the iconostasis. In
the earliest times, until the eighth century, the book of the
gospels and the sacred vessels for holy communion only
were placed upon the altar. The next arrangement was,
after the Greek manner, to place at the corners of the
altar four lights at the beginning of the holy office, and
these were removed by the acolyths at the conclusion of
the service. In fact, it has been asserted by competent
authorities that candles have not been regarded as per-

manent or indispensable accessories of an altar for more than four centuries. In the catacombs lamps or tapers were used, and set on stands called *canthara* and *cerostata*, or suspended by chains. Paulinus, Bishop of Nola, speaks of the bright altars encircled by many lights (*lychni*), burning day and night, and of painted candles. But candles were not set upon the altar until the tenth century, having been previously arranged around it or on the ground, and even long after that date the lights were suspended in silver basins in front of the altar, arranged in crowns upon the candle-beam or over the altar, in standing candelabra, and on the altar step, or round the altar, according to the dignity of the festival. Tapers were also kept burning before shrines and the altar of holy cross in the rood-loft and round the Easter sepulchre. To maintain these lights the treasurer in the cathedral found wax, as the sacristan did in the monastery; in some cases a special rent being paid out of a dependent church in their patronage and allotted for the purpose; whilst in parish churches a cow or ox was bequeathed to the wardens, who sold the milk, or leased out the labour of these animals to furnish the necessary funds. In 963 and 994 we find in England the parishioners required to bring their lights with them at evensong and matins, besides, as in 878 and 1017, paying their light scot, a tax for the supply of church lights,—a half-penny-worth of wax for every plough land on Easter eve, Allhallowmas, and the Purification. In the laws of Wales altar candles were required to be of wax, "because bees derive their origin from paradise." All the remnants of wax which was unconsumed were carefully preserved and sold to the chandlers who supplied the tapers. Immediately before the Reformation there were three pairs of candlesticks provided for the high-altar of Salisbury, but there is no evidence that they were used at one time; and at Durham at the same time the high-altar had, we know, only two tapers; and still earlier, at Bury St. Edmund's, two candles burned between the high altar and shrine, placed on a retable (*tabulatus*). At Gerona on doubles four lights, and on semidoubles two lights are used on the high-altar. The modern Roman rule is to have two candles at private Masses, six on Sundays and festivals, on ferials four, and on great festivals eight or more, but any extreme attention to numbers is regarded as superstitious. There were only two at Durham up to the time of the Reformation —two double gilt for festivals, and two of parcel gilt for ordinary days, on the high-altar. The first instance of several candles being placed upon the altar occurs in the case of the chapel of Henry VIII. on the Field of the Cloth of Gold, which had five pairs of gold candlesticks. At William III.'s coronation there were twelve lighted candles on the altar. Durandus mentions only two as in use in his time. King Edgar's canons, in 960, enjoined burning lights at the time of Mass; and in the canons of Ælfric, 957, it is said the acolyth holds the candle or taper when the gospel is read or the housel hallowed at the altar,—not as if he were to drive away the obscure darkness, but to signify bliss by that light, to the honour of Christ, who is our light. At Salisbury in medieval times there were five lights attached to the wall of the pulpit or rood-loft when the lections were read. Candles—either five or seven, according to Gregory of Tours—were carried before the gospeller proceeding to the ambon in France. It is probable that the direction in King Edward's injunction of 1546 providing "two lights upon the high-altar before the sacrament, for the signification that Christ is the very true Light of the world," was worded from the old English canon already quoted, whilst the expression *before the sacrament* seems to allude to the hanging lights of a later date, suspended in front of the altar. The candlesticks were always low, and the tall candles now in use are of modern introduction. Two candles were burning at the coronations of James I. and Queen Anne, on the altar. Candlesticks standing upon a tripod base are still preserved; that of St. Bernevald (tenth to eleventh centuries) at Hildesheim, Hanover, of electrum; another, formerly at Gloucester and Mans, of bronze gilt, of the twelfth century, now at Kensington; two of iron at Noyon; one, a tree with seven branches, such as Dante saw in the vision of Purgatory, still exists at Milan; it is of bronze gilt and the thirteenth century, and is called, from its sculptures, "the tree of the Virgin;" the branches in other instances were supposed to represent the seven virtues, and reproduce the Jewish candelabrum of the Mosaic tabernacle; the four rivers at the base typified the liberal arts, music, rhetoric, logic, and geometry. It stood at the entrance of the sanctuary, flanked by the great and little paschal. The altar candlesticks of Bristol Cathedral are of Spanish workmanship of the seventeenth century. At York there were two large tapers for the altar, seven large branches, and on certain vigils a branch of seven candles set before the four grand dignitaries of the Church a century since. At Bury St. Edmund's there was a procession made, with tapers, through the wheat-sown fields, in order to preserve the corn from weeds and blight.

A SEVEN-BRANCHED CANDLESTICK stood also before the high-altar, in allusion to the seven lamps of the Apocalypse, as at Long Melford. In the Gallican Church it was probably a relic of Eastern ritual. It was in use at Rouen, Milan, Clairvaux, and Rheims. One remains at Lichfield, and another, called the ratelier (*rastrum*, or harrow), at Lyons; and a third at Tours, still used on high festivals; and a fourth at Lund. In some churches there was a magnificent series of branches grouped together, called the Tree. A superb seven-branched candlestick was presented to Canterbury by Prior Conrad in the twelfth century, and another to the shrine of St. Birinus at Winchester by King Canute in 1035. At Bourges and Pistoia there were two placed on either side of the entrance to the sanctuary. At Stockholm there is one at the present time, and at Ribe a specimen with only five branches. Martene mentions seven candles burning before the altar at Eastertide. At the close of the eleventh century Abbot Paul gave three precious candlesticks to be lighted in front of the high-altar of St. Alban's, and a silver basin for a light to be hung above it. At solemn Masses the seven acolyths each carried a taper, which they placed on the ground either behind the altar or in the middle of the choir, or on the first step of the altar; and when the gospel was sung two, or sometimes all seven accompanied the deacon to the ambon and ranged themselves round him. At St. Clement's, Rome, the places for the candles were marked on the pavement. In the south of France, before the first communion, the seven-branched candlestick is placed in a recess in the aisle, and the young men and women holding tapers light them from it, symboli-

H

cally of obtaining the graces of the Holy Spirit. A candle-stick is composed of a foot, a stem, a knob for handling it, a bowl, and a pricket on which to set the taper.

THE TENEBRÆ CANDLES. The triangular candlestick—called the herse in English cathedral statutes—used at the service of the Tenebræ, varied in its number of tapers, which were nine at Nevers, twelve at Mans, thirteen at Rheims and Paris, twenty-four at Cambray and St. Quentin, twenty-five at Evreux, twenty-six at Amiens, and forty-four at Coutances. Calfhill says that in England it was called the Judas Cross. The Lady Candle was the single taper left burning when all the rest, representing the Apostles, had been extinguished one by one. Sir Thomas More says that it symbolized St. Mary standing beneath the cross of Calvary. At Seville, entre-los-Coros is a tenebrario of bronze, twenty-five feet in height, which was made in 1562.

THE PASCHAL CANDLE was a type of the pillar of fire which led the Israelites through the wilderness. St. Gregory mentions the Exultet, the form of benediction of the paschal attributed to St. Augustine or St. Ambrose. The deacon either in the ambo or choir near the presbytery steps blessed the paschal, which was enjoined throughout the Latin Church, instead of in basilicas only, by Pope Zosimus in 417; and the calendar of feasts was required to be attached to the paschal by the Council of Nicæa. At Paris and St. Denis the candlestick stood on the top of the sanctuary step; that of Gloucester, the gift of Abbot Peter c. 1115, and made of bronze, is now in the South Kensington Museum. At Durham it was nearly as broad as the choir, and the long square taper almost reached to the vault. Below it were seven flower-shaped branches for tapers. The light burned behind the three pendent altar-lights from Maundy Thursday until the Thursday after Ascension Day. At other times it was kept under the stairs leading to St. Cuthbert's shrine. It was lighted through the vault, at Coutances from the clerestory, and in St. John's Lateran by a deacon, who was wheeled up in a portable pulpit for the purpose. By the Salisbury use it burned throughout the octave of Easter at Matins, Mass, and Vespers, and from its light every taper on the eve was rekindled. In the basilica the paschal candle was set upon the top of a pillar, on the left-hand side of the ambon. A shaft of this kind, though not of undoubted antiquity, remains in the church of St. Agnes at Rome. There is a candlestick on the north side of the altar at St. Anthony's, Padua, and another of the twelfth century, of colossal size, at St. Paul's Without. At Durham the stand was of latten, glistening like gold, and enriched with figures of the evangelists, flying dragons, curious antique work of archers, bucklermen, spearmen, knights, and beasts. The weight of these high, ponderous tapers was very considerable, being at Chartres of 72℔., at Rheims 30℔., at Rouen 40℔., and at Westminster, and Canterbury in 1457, of 300℔. There is an orifice in the vault of Norwich choir, through which the sacrament light was let down and the paschal taper kindled. The paschal stand remains at St. Clement's, Rome, and another in the atrium of the cathedral of Capua, where three other lights, in honour of the Holy Trinity, are kindled on a staff or paschal post below it. The paschal contains five grains of incense, representing the five sacred wounds, according to the Fourth Council of Toledo. Whilst the canticle Exultet is being sung, a deacon, vested in white, pronounces it blessed, in memory of women announcing the tidings of resurrection to the Apostles. The candle is then lighted with the new fire. Bede mentions that the date of the year was inscribed on the candle; afterwards a long label, the original of an almanack, inscribed with a calendar of feasts, was attached to it. St. Stephania, Naples, was burned down by fire caught from the paschal candle on Easter night, during which it was the local custom, in the eighth century, to leave it unextinguished. The paschal candlestick still stands near the altar of Southwell, and the socket for the post remains in the pavement of the Presbytery of St. David's on the north side. The four superb candlesticks which adorned King Henry VII.'s Chapel, Westminster, and are marked with the Tudor rose, are now in the Cathedral of Ghent.

In the transept of St. Alban's there was a tall candle set before the image of St. Mary, called the Mariola, which on great festivals was gracefully wreathed with flowers.

PROCESSIONAL TAPERS. Seven or nine candles were carried in procession in France, according to the dignity of the festival.

FUNERAL TAPERS. P. Gregory in 684, and Wheatley in the last century, speaking of this practice in their times, express the pious hope that the departed, having walked here as children of light, are now gone to walk before God in the light of the living.

As a lighted taper was placed in the hand of the newly-baptized, baptism was called Illumination. On Christmas Eve so many lights were kindled that it was called the Vigil of Lights, and the faithful sent presents of lights one to another. An early instance of a perpetual light was that of the firehouse of St. Bridget, at Kildare, which burned unquenched from the fifth century to 1220. It may have been connected with a beacon, and the offerings made for its maintenance in part supported the poor. From the number of burning tapers which were used in churches on Easter Eve, St. Gregory Nazianzen calls it the "holy night of illuminations;" whilst Easter Day was alled the Bright Sunday, in allusion to the tapers and white robes carried by the neophytes. Tapers were also used at consecration of churches.

Candlemas Day, February 2, so called from the blessing of the candles on that day, the anthem being " A Light to lighten the Gentiles." Even at the close of the last century, Ripon Minster, on the Sunday before Candlemas, is described as being ablaze, in the afternoon service, from the multitude of lights; and a similar custom apparently was observed at Durham in the seventeenth century.

HERSE LIGHTS were placed round the bier of the dead in church, upon a barrow-like structure of iron. These resemble the lights set before the tombs of martyrs in the catacombs.

CANDLESTICKS, in Germany, were often placed upon shrines, and some, of pyramidal shape and of the fifteenth century, still remain. In Chichester Cathedral lights, on particular days, were set round four tombs in the Presbytery. Candlesticks of bronze remain at Nuremberg, Mayence, Aix-la-Chapelle, and Leau ; at Bruges there are four of copper-gilt in the Jerusalem church, and in the Louvre there are three, with enamel-work of the twelfth century.

Cannibalism, *or* **Infanticide,** it appears from the writings of Justin Martyr, Minucius Felix, Tertullian, and Origen, was at first attributed to the Christians, in depravation of the doctrine of the spiritual communion of the Body and Blood of Christ.

Canon (from *canon*, or *canna*, a straight reed used for ruling lines). (1.) A rule (Gal. vi. 6) ordained by the Fathers; a Constitution of the Church. (2.) The Creed, as the criterion for distinguishing a Christian; the rule of faith of Tertullian, St. Irenæus, and St. Jerome. (3.) A clerk who observes the Apostles' rule, or fellowship—*koinonia* (Acts ii. 42); one borne on the list, or canon of a cathedral or collegiate church, as the term is used by the Councils of Nice and Antioch, and bound to observe its statutes or canons, and the rule of a good and honest life. Hence, in later times, when the names of benefactors were inserted in the rolls or canons of numberless communities, the Popes confined the term Canonization to those whom they admitted to the title of Saint. The word is one of rank and precedence, and should be prefixed in addressing a prebendary. Canons are primarii among all others of the clergy of the city and diocese. The name is attributed to Pope Pelagius or Gregory, and was certainly common in the reign of Charlemagne; in the sixth century it designated all clergy on the Church register, affording a perfect example of liturgical obedience, and receiving a canonical portion—a regular annual pension —out of its revenues. This list is called Album by Sidonius Apollinarius; Matricula by the Council of Nicæa; and by St. Augustin the Table of Clerks. There were several kinds of canons :—

I. CANONS SECULAR. Those of cathedral and collegiate foundations, who mixed more or less with the world, and ministered the offices of religion to the laity. The title first appears in 1059, when it was used by Pope Nicholas in the Council of Rome; but the existence of such canons in England, who had separate houses, may be traced back three centuries earlier. Such are the canons of cathedrals of the old foundation, and collegiate churches. Their oldest title was in Germany, senior, retained in the ancien of some Rhenish cathedrals; or brother, then canon and lord; and lastly capitular, as being members of the chapter. As Christianity spread, the number of the clergy augmented, and the bishop chose from them some of the most learned to live in common with him in the episcopium, or bishop's house, as his assistants and advisers. In time similar colleges were founded in other places, where the clergy lived in a building called the canonica, minster, or cloister, and performed religious worship, receiving food and clothes from the bishop: they were termed canons, and the bishop's vicarius was called prior, provost, or dean. From this ancient arrangement of common habitation and revenues, the custom survives in some parts of the collation to canonries by the joint consent of the bishop and chapter. A single trace remains in England at Chichester, where the dean and chapter have six stalls in their patronage. Prebends at length were instituted, by a division of the common fund; and although the canons lived apart in their separate houses, yet, from their aggregation in one close, their daily presence in choir and union in chapter, they were supposed still to dwell together. After the Reformation the vicars were required to occupy their college and halls, and the last trace of the common life was only recently lost. In the eighth century the Councils of Aix and Verne, and in the ninth century those of Tours (813), Meaux (845), and Pont-sur-Yonne (876), required clerks to live the canonical life in a cloister near the cathedral, with a common refectory and dormitory, observing the teaching of the Scriptures and the Fathers under the bishop, as if he were their abbot. In Germany the canons were called Dom-Herren, and in Italy dom(ini), the masters of the cathedral; as at Lincoln, the dignitaries were known as masters of the fabric; at Liége they were called trefonciers (terræ fundarii), lords of the soil; at Pisa, ordinarii, by special privilege of Nicholas II., owing to their jurisdiction as ordinaries over the inferior ministers; at Constantinople, decumans; at Cologne and Lyons, Counts; and at Besançon, Compostella, and Seville, cardinals; at Evreux, barons. Sometimes, from their right of electing the bishop and their president, they were known as electors; and as being graduates, and in recognition of their rank, domini, or lords. Every canon is a prebendary—a canon as borne on the church list, and a prebendary as holding a prebend or revenue. In cathedrals of the new foundation, residentiaries, by the new Act, are no longer called prebendaries, but simply canons. In the old foundations all are canons and prebendaries, residentiary, stagiarii, stationarii, nati; or non-residentiary; the latter at Lichfield were called exteriors, or extraneous. In the foreign cathedrals were three classes: (1) capitulars, perpetuals, simple or ordinary; numeral, or major canons in actual possession of stalls; (2) the German domicellares or domicelli, the chanoines bas-formiers of Angers, Sens, and Rouen; bye-canons, minor canons, or lordlings in distinction to the majors domini, or dom herren; expectants of vacancies; honorary, or supernumeraries, elected by the bishop and chapter, who augmented the efficiency of the choir and received small payments, but ranked after the vicars or beneficiaries; and (3) canons elect, not yet installed. Every canon in England and France gave a cope to the fabric; in Italy, the Peninsula, and Germany they paid a stipulated sum. Canons had the right of wearing mitres at Lisbon, Pisa, Besançon, Puy, Rodez, Brionde, Solsona, Messina, Salerno, Naples, Lyons, and Lucca; these were plain white, like those of abbots, as a sign of exemption from the jurisdiction of the ordinary, and probably a corrupt use of the end of the almuce. Some canonries are attached to archdeaconries or livings, like St. Margaret and St. John, Westminster, 1840; and some to university offices, as those of Christchurch to the professors of Divinity, 1605; and Hebrew, 1630; of Worcester to the Margaret Professor, 1627, now exchanged for a stall at Christchurch, 1860; of Rochester to the Provost of Oriel; of Gloucester to the Master of Pembroke College, Oxford; and of Norwich to the Master of St. Catherine's Hall, Cambridge, by Queen Anne. The Principal of Jesus College, Oxford, had formerly a stall at St. David's. By a recent Act the Professors of Greek and Hebrew at Cambridge have stalls at Ely, and the occupants of the chairs of Pastoral Theology and Ecclesiastical History at Christchurch. James I. confiscated a stall at Salisbury to endow a Readership at Oxford. The Professors of Greek and Divinity hold stalls at Durham.

At Lisieux the bishop was earl of the city, and the canons exercised the criminal and civil jurisdiction; on the Vigil of the Feast of St. Ursinus, two, habited in surplices, crossed with bandoliers of flowers, and holding nosegays, rode to every gate, preceded by mace-bearers, chaplains, and halberdiers in helmet and cuirass, and demanded the city keys;

they then posted their own guard, and received all the fees
and tolls, giving to each of their brethren a dole of wine
and bread.

II. REGULAR CANONS. Clergy at first not bound by vows,
but by canons derived from the Fathers and monastic rule,
yet at a later date confined to a cloister, and professing the
three vows of obedience, poverty, and chastity : in fact, the
monks of Canterbury in the eleventh century were called
canons, and their president was known as dean. The institution of these canons has been attributed to St. Jerome or
St. Augustine : no doubt they were at first merely colleges
of priests and divinity students, having a common dormitory
and refectory, clothed from a common stock, and keeping
fixed hours of devotion, such as those established at Repitz,
and by Eusebius of Vercelli. In the first four centuries
clerks lived in the midst of the faithful, each in his family,
until St. Augustine established a monastery, and compelled
his clerks to reside in it. Such persons observing the common life according to the canons, were called clerks canonical. The custom spread from Africa to France in the time
of the Second Council of Tours ; Spain at the period of the
Fourth Council of Toledo ; and England at the coming of
St. Augustine, the bishops and their clergy living together. St. Gregory established the discipline of canons at
Rome. The common life for bishops and priests lasted until
the ninth century. The so-called "Three Rules of St.
Austin" were observed by the great order of Austin canons,
and their branches. In the sixth century, St. Gregory
of Tours mentions canons of Tours and Tournay : in the
latter half of the eighth century, St. Rigobert at Rheims
and Chrodegang at Metz introduced a modification of the
Benedictine rule, in a congregation of clergy living under a
stricter collegiate discipline and in common, like monks ;
and so popular was this institution of Chrodegang, that it
was taken as the model for the foundation of collegiate
churches erected out of those hitherto simply parochial ; and
within two centuries, before 997, the canons of Spires, Arras,
Worms, Tours, and Mayence carried the change further,
and became secular canons ; whilst in Lorraine, and at Bayeux after 1000, the common dormitory and refectory were
observed ; which in 1068 Pope Alexander, in a synod of Rome,

reinforced, but Rheims and Paderborn in the thirteenth, Liége in the twelfth, and Cologne and Utrecht abandoned about the close of the eleventh century; when at Wells and Exeter, regular Canons replaced Benedictines, and, under a provost, occupied a common dormitory and refectory as in Lorraine, contrary to the English mode of secular Canons, as William of Malmesbury states; they soon gave place to secular Canons; but for a time, in 1219, at Exeter, Bishop Simon made the chapter have a common table and steward; and in 1300 Besançon was the last French cathedral which abandoned the common life, having until that date daily read the rule of the Council of Aix-la-Chapelle in chapter, after the martyrology. Probably the grand distinction between canons regular and secular was drawn about the middle of the eleventh century, when an abbot, Arnulphus, in 1066, is said to have permanently founded the Canons Regular, who assumed the latter name—in point of fact, a tautology—in order to express that they held the rule of common life and income inviolably, whilst the secular canons had their private households and special revenues, called prebends. In Germany, until this period, all canons were on an equal footing, the bishop alone having a separate table; but with the increase of wealth they took the title of Dom Herren, lived apart, and established vicars; the bishops then interfered, and bound all those who continued to live in common by a vow of poverty, under the name of regular canons: all those who did not retain the common life were called seculars. At Canterbury, Durham, Rochester, and Norwich the Benedictines ejected the regular canons at the end of the eleventh century; but at Exeter and Wells the case was reversed. The colleges of secular canons in cathedrals are not earlier than the Norman invasion. Alcuin says, that in monasteries the priests were called canons, and the rest monks; and at the same time colleges of clerks assumed the style of canons.

III. HONORARY CANONS. Canons exempted from observing the hours. Sovereign princes and nobles were occasionally regarded as honorary canons of cathedrals; as the Emperor at Strasbourg, Liége, Bamberg, Ratisbon, Cologne, Spiers, Utrecht, Aix-la-Chapelle, St. Peter's and St. John Lateran, Rome; the King of France, at Poictiers, Chalons, Sens, Anjou, Tours; being Warden of St. Quentin and Abbot of St. Hilary; the King of Spain at Burgos, Toledo, and Leon; and the Queen of England first Cursal of St. David's. The prerogative was due to the unction of the sovereign at coronation. The Dukes of Bourges and Burgundy had stalls at Lyons; the Count d'Astorga at Toledo; the Duke of Brabant at Utrecht; the Count de Chasteluz at Autun; and the Counts of Anjou at Tours. The Princes of Mecklenburg held four prebends at Strasbourg. The twenty extravagantes at Toledo assisted only on certain anniversaries. In cathedrals of the new foundation twenty-four honorary canons, so called by a blunder, may be appointed by the bishop, pursuant to a recent Act of Parliament; they may be called upon to take duty in church, but have no vote in chapter. In foreign cathedrals they are called supernumerary, fictitious, or improper canons, not being regarded as of the body.

There are three classes in foreign churches. (1.) Expectants, *canonici in herbâ*, with right of succession to the next vacancy. (2.) Honorary, *canonici in aere*, merely titulars, without succession, but having a stall if the chapter concede it. (3.) Supernumeraries, bye-canons, added by a new foundation. The honorary canon is not bound to residence, can retain a living requiring continuous residence, and is not to be called canon, but always honorary canon.

Canon Law. A collection of the decisions of Councils, the decrees of Popes, and Papal bulls and letters. In 520, Dionysius Exiguus, a monk of Rome, compiled a Codex Canonum, comprising Papal decrees from 398 to 1154, and Charlemagne's Capitulars, which lasted until the twelfth century, when Ivo, bishop of Chartres, in 1114, began—and Gratian, a Benedictine, in 1150 completed—his famous " *Decree*," in three books; and containing the canons and decisions made from the time of Constantine the Great, in the fourth century, to that of Pope Alexander III.

The next portion of canon law are the *Decretals*, rescripts of Alexander III., Innocent III., Honorius III., and Gregory IX., on all subjects coming within the cognizance of the Ecclesiastical Courts, first published in five books by Raimond de Renafort, chaplain to Gregory IX., in 1234. In

1298, Pope Boniface VIII. added a sixth book of decisions, called the *Sext*. Clement V., in 1308, published the *Clementines;* and in 1317 Pope John XXII. added the *Extravagants*. These five portions constitute the body of canon law. In the Ecclesiastical Courts, or Courts Christian, and in the University Courts, canon law is still used, and in force where it is not contradictory to the common or statute law of England. It is based on the 'Provinciale' of Bishop Lyndwood, of St. David's, who embodied in it all the Provincial Constitutions applicable to England and adopted by the Archbishops of Canterbury, sitting in provincial synods, from 1206 until 1443, and afterwards received by the Province of York in convocation in 1463. To these must be added the Legatine Constitutions of Cardinals Otho and Othobon, legates of the Pope, put forth in the thirteenth century. In the twenty-seventh year of his reign, Henry VIII. forbade the University of Cambridge to confer degrees in canon law; hitherto it had been common for English jurists to graduate as doctors in both laws, canon and civil.

Canonical Age. For a bishop, 30 years; for a priest, 24; for a deacon, 23, unless he have a faculty from the archbishop in the English Church. The canon law prescribes 30 years for a priest, 25 years being regarded as a permissible year. In 417, the diaconate could be taken at 25 years, and the priesthood at 30 years; but Siricius, *c.* 390, made the ages 30 and 35 years; in the Roman Church they are 23 and 25 years, but in the Greek Church 25 and 30. The Council of Ravenna (1314), defined 20 years of age as the lowest for the reception of the diaconate; but 21 years are accepted by the American and Scotch Churches, the age permitted before the Reformation to monks of Westminster, and in the Ordinal of 1552 : it is now the age required for the Roman subdiaconate. The Councils of Adge (506), III. Carthage (397), and II. Toledo (531), give the age for the diaconate at 25; that of Melfi (1089) at 24, and for priesthood at 30, the age required in the old English laws and the Councils of Neo-Cæsarea (314), IV. Toledo (633), IV. Arles (524), and in Trullo (691), as that in which our Lord began His ministry. The age for a bishop was, by the Apostolical Constitutions and Pope Boniface, in the eighth century, 50; in the Novels 30 or 35; and by Popes Siricius and Zosimus (417), 45.

Canonicals. The dress prescribed by the Canons to be worn by the clergy, and in actual use in Fielding's time. In 1766 the Connoisseur alludes to the appearance in the streets of the doctor's scarf, pudding-sleeve gown, starched bands, and feather topgrizzle. George Herbert, when ordained priest, laid aside his sword which he had worn as a deacon, and adopted a canonical coat.

Canonization. The declaration of a name as that of a saint, and its insertion in the catalogue of saints. The name of "saint," used in the Apostolical Epistles as a synonym for Christian, was, in lapse of time, restricted to those recognized as eminent for holiness or martyrdom; and in the several dioceses the bishop, at least as early as the time of St. Cyprian, appointed their names to be commemorated during divine service on the day of their decease or suffering, called their "birthday" (into immortality). The recognition of their sanctity was called their "vindication," a term used by Optatus. In the time of St. Augustine reference was made to the Primate of the province, who, with the College of Bishops as his assessors, decreed the admission of the names of such as were to be reputed martyrs. At length, when certain bishops were found to be easy in the matter of inserting names in the Catalogue of Saints within their dioceses, decisions of this nature were restricted to the See of Rome. In the primitive Church all bishops might, with consent of their metropolitan, propose to the veneration of the faithful the martyrs who had suffered within their dioceses, having first approved the Acts, which were drawn up in form and submitted to episcopal sanction, after which their names were inscribed on the diptychs to be read. Such was the simple process of canonization, from the time of St. Augustine till the tenth century. The last recorded instance of this mode occurs in the case of St. Gualtier of Pontoise, raised to the honours of a saint by the Archbishop of Rouen in 1153. The first formal act of canonization, or insertion in the Canon or list of saints, was made in the case of St. Swibert, at Verda, in Germany, by Pope Leo III., on September 4, 804, at the request of the Emperor Charlemagne; and after fast and prayer, during the celebration of Mass, the cardinals and bishops then present assenting. Others say that the canonization of St. Ulrich, Archbishop

of Augsburg, in 993, by Pope John XV., was the earliest regular act. The doctors and Fathers of the Greek and Latin
Church, as Athanasius, Basil, Nazianzen, and St. Chrysostom,
—or Jerome, Ambrose, and Augustine,—are reputed saints
by tacit assent. In modern canonization, the following requirements are made :—that the life should have been blame-
less throughout, eminent for good works, and adorned by
miracles. The Pope is thrice adjured to canonize, and twice
refers the petition back to the prelates assembled : on the
third application he yields. The prerogative of canonization
was first confirmed to the Pope in 1170, by Alexander II. ; but
at an earlier date the Papal sanction was required, whilst
the bishop still initiated. In still older times, down to the
tenth century, the saint was exalted by the suffrage of the
people conjointly with the bishop. It now consists of a formal process of inquiry into the acts of the person named,
followed by a decree of beatification. In case miracles are
proved, canonization follows. The Japanese martyrs were
canonized in 1862.

Canon of Scripture. The formal list of books regarded as
composing Holy Scripture, written by inspiration of God as
the Rule of Faith. The Old Testament was divided by Ezra
into Moses, the Prophets, and Hagiographa, or Holy Writings. Our Lord notices this arrangement, only using the
word Psalms apart for the whole of the last section. (St.
Luke xxiv. 44.) The first division included the Pentateuch ;
in the second were comprised the Historical Books and
Prophets, except the Chronicles, Esther, Daniel, and Ezra,
which were included with Ruth, Psalms, Job, Ecclesiastes,
Canticles, and Lamentations in the third division, making
in all twenty-four books. To these was added the New Testament. The Canonical Scriptures of the Old Testament
are enumerated by Eusebius, Epiphanius, Gregory Nazianzen, and the Council of Laodicea, held in the third century.
Eusebius gives us the first formal list of the books of the
New Testament. The word "canonical" is first applied to
the Scriptures in the third Council of Carthage.

Canon of the Altar. A kind of triptych, containing in the
centre the Consecration, on the left the Gloria, Credo, and
Offertory, and on the right the Commemorations and Communion Prayers.

Canon of the Mass. This portion of the service, commencing after the hymn Ter-Sanctus, ' Holy, Holy, Holy,' and forming a body of prayers before and after the consecration of the Eucharist, was drawn up according to different authorities by one Scholasticus Voconius, Bishop of Castellana; Musæus, Priest of Marseilles; Alexander I., Leo, Gelasius, Gregory I., Gregory III., or Innocent III.; the latter, however, distinctly refers it to the Redeemer and His Apostles. It has, however, been traced back to the time of Pope Celestine, and, yet earlier, to a period apostolical, in its essential features—the prayer for the Church militant, the words of institution, and use of the Lord's Prayer. It was said secretly by the priest,—Cranmer says, "not because it is unlawful to be heard, read, or known of the people, but that it is expedient to keep silence and secrecy at the time of such a high mystery, and that both the priest and people may have the more devout meditations, and better attend about the same." It was called by the Synod of York, 1195, the Secret of the Mass, from this circumstance, which does not date further back than the sixth century in the Latin Church; although the term Secret shows that the practice was not always uniform to say it in a loud voice, as Justinian enjoined at that date in the churches of the East. Gregory the Great calls it the Canon. It is the Rule by which the Eucharist is consecrated, and by some authors is called the Mystic or Canonical Prayer, as by Pope Vigilius, Innocent I., Amalarius, St. Gregory the Great, and St. Augustine; the Church Rule, by St. Ambrose; the Agenda or Action, by Walafrid Strabo; the Secret, by St. Basil; the Order of Prayers, by Isidore; the Lawful, by Optatus. The archdeacons were required to see that the purity of the canon was preserved intact. In the first three centuries martyrs only were commemorated in it, and afterwards the names of confessors were introduced.

Canonry. A special prerogative and an ecclesiastical benefice; the spiritual right of reception as a brother, a stall in choir, a voice in chapter, and receiving a prebend or canonical portion annexed to it out of the Church revenues, in consideration of ecclesiastical duties performed in it. Every canonry has of necessity a prebend, and every prebend of necessity a canonry belonging to it.

Canons of Eusebius. Ten tables, composed by Eusebius for the comparative study of the Gospels, indicating by numbers the parallel passages of the Evangelists and those peculiar to each.

Canopy. (1.) A tent-like covering for the pendent pyx at Durham, on which was a pelican of silver. (2.) A sounding-board of a pulpit, expressively called in French *abat-voix*, from its use to hinder the preacher's voice from being lost among the vaulting. Good specimens occur at Winchester and Worcester of the sixteenth century; but most of those remaining are of the Jacobean period, one of the earliest occurring at Sopley, Hants, 1604. There are much finer specimens at Ulm, Mayence, Strasbourg, and Vienna. In the centre of the under part is often a dove, in allusion to St. Mark i. 10; and on the summit an angel called the Messenger of the Word, or an incongruous ornament, often nearly resembling a heathen Fame or Glory. At Beaulieu and St. George Faye la Vineuse, the refectory pulpits being partly corbelled out and partly set within the wall, the vault overhead forms the sounding-board. The open-air pulpit of Magdalen College, Oxford, is of similar construction.

Cantatorium. A name for the Antiphonar.

Cantharus, Nymphæum, *or* **Phiala.** (1.) A fountain, usually of porphyry or marble, placed in the atrium or a laver in the impluvium, where the faithful washed their face and hands before entering the basilica; sometimes called the Leontarion, from standing on lion-supporters; occasionally the water flowed from a central figure; and in fine examples it was enclosed in a group of pillars and arches. St. Chrysostom and Tertullian allude to the previous washing by worshippers. (2.) An oil-lamp or torch held by the subdeacon; or at High Mass, by a deacon, whilst he waved the censer with his other hand by the Ambrosian rite.

Canticles. The Te Deum, Benedicite, Benedictus, Magnificat, and Nunc Dimittis. The Songs of Moses, Miriam, Deborah, Hannah, and Isaiah are Canticles; hymns inspired at the moment on a special occasion. After the fifth century Canticles were added to psalmody. The Benedictus is mentioned by Amalarius in 820, and by St. Benedict, nearly three centuries before, as the Canticle from the Gospel. Te Deum was sung at Matins every Sunday before the Gospel-lectern, by the rules of St. Benedict and St. Cæsarius of Arles, *c.* 507. The Magnificat occurs in the office of Lauds in the latter rule, and in the office of the Eastern Church; in the time of Amalarius it was used at Vespers. By the Apostolical Constitutions the Song of Symeon, or Nunc Dimittis, was also sung at that hour, that is, probably, in the fifth century.

Cap. A square-topped cap is worn in the universities, like that of the theologists before the Reformation, except that it has stiffening, and a tassel in lieu of a tuft. In Flanders the priest wore his cap at baptisms. A round, low cap, sometimes having a broad brim, which was doubled down on reaching the choir, was worn often by canons from the end of the thirteenth century: at Antwerp the colour was purple; at Pisa and Cologne it was scarlet. The red cap was also used by doctors of divinity at Oxford; it was square and steepled, but just before the Reformation was worn square. In foreign universities tassels served by way of distinction. The D.C.L. and D.M. still retain the use of the round cap, which in 1605 was worn by all undergraduates. When the cap was worn in choir the upper part of the amess was thrown back like a hood, when it looked like a low mitre and muffled the shoulders, having a fringe made of the tails of the animals of whose fur it was made. Then the amess was stitched in front, with a hole for the wearer's head, and about the beginning of the fifteenth century became a tippet, or short cape. In the early part of the next century it was worn like a shawl, longer behind than before, and with two strips like a stole narrowing to a point, but appearing as a ruff over the shoulders. The use of the cap lined with fur was permitted by the Pope Honorius III. at Canterbury, at Peterborough, and Croyland, from Michaelmas to Easter, in consequence of the cold. Canons were allowed to use it in church, except during the Canon of the Mass, the verse, " And was incarnate," and the Benediction. The assistant-deacon and subdeacon were forbidden to use the cap. At Stoke College caps and not hoods were worn. The golden cap which Pope Sylvester sent to St. Stephen in 1000 is used at the coronation of the kings of Hungary.

Capitilavium. Head washing. A name for Palm Sunday in France and Spain, because the heads of the Competentes, who were to receive the baptismal unction, were then washed. In 813 the practice was abolished by the Council of Mayence. At Milan the feet of the candidates were washed.

Capitula. Little chapters ; sentences from Holy Scripture. The Council of Agde mentions little chapters taken from the Psalms.

Capuchins. Franciscan friars; so called from the form of their round capuchon, or hood, unlike the pointed form used by the Carthusians. A reformed order of the Observants, founded by Matthew Basci, of Monte Falconi, in 1525. They have a vicar-general and guardians, and were principally found in France and Italy.

Carde, *or* **Care Cloth.** A fine linen cloth held over a bride and bridegroom at their marriage until they had received the benediction. It was usually made of rich silk, possibly of the material known as Carde of Inde, whence its name. It fell into disuse in the sixteenth century.

Cardinal. The word, when applied to an altar, means the high or principal altar, and from their attendance upon it two minor canons at St. Paul's are still called the senior and junior cardinals. Their duties were to take charge of the choir, to present defaulters to the dean on Fridays, to act as rectors of the choir, to administer sacraments, enjoin penances, hear confessions, bury the dead, and receive oblations.

Cardinals were the incumbents of the principal parishes, suffragan bishops of the Patriarchate of Rome; to these were added the deacons of the chapels of hospitals, and the priests of ordinary churches. The incumbents of Angers, at a later date, when assisting their bishop at solemn Mass called themselves cardinals. In the eleventh century the Roman cardinals established their superiority to bishops. Their number varied, until in 1586 Sixtus V. fixed it at seventy, comprising six bishops, fifty priests, and four deacons. The priest-cardinals received the privilege of a mitre before 1130, and the deacons also previous to the year 1192. These are said to have been of silver.

As applied to clergy, the title appears to have implied that they were permanent and stationary, and not employed only for a time; and we find that clerks expatriated or exiled from their own countries were received into churches at Ravenna or Rome, and were said to be incardinated or transplanted. The idea of the Church hinging on the prince cardinals of Rome is not earlier than the Council of Basle. The origin of the latter dignitaries may be traced back to the seven Curators or Regionaries, heads of quarters of the city, who were appointed shortly after the time of Nero, like the seven deacons, for the supervision of secular matters. In course of time prebends or revenues were founded by gift or legacy, from which these officials took their titles, several using the same designation. The next step was a nomenclature adopted from the names of saints and martyrs. In 1125 Pope Honorius appointed seven cardinal bishops to assist him when acting as the celebrant in the basilica of St. John Lateran ; they bore the names of Hostiensis (his office was to consecrate the Pope and carry the pall), Portuensis, St. Rufinæ, Sabinensis, Prænestinus, Tusculanus, and Albanensis. To these Pope Nicholas III. added three priests and four deacons. . With the allegorical disposition of the middle ages, which was repeated among the Grandmontines at Winchester College and St. Paul's School, Paul IV. enlarged the entire number of the College to seventy members, in allusion to the seventy elders who assisted Moses, and the seventy Disciples of our Lord. Their duties were to exercise spiritual jurisdiction over their own churches, to act as the Pope's privy council and household, to serve as envoys or legates à latere, to administer affairs in the vacancy of the Popedom, to conclude synods and councils, and to elect the Pontiff. From holding this important position they were called Cardinals. Popes Clement V. and John XXII. elevated them in rank above all bishops, and a series of honours were showered upon them. A red cap was allowed them by Pope Innocent IV. at the Council of Lyons in 1245, which was borne on their armorial coat in testimony of their readiness to shed their blood for the Church. Until this date only legates à latere had been thus distinguished, and Regulars who were Cardinals retained the head-dress of their orders, until Pope Gregory XIV. in 1592 granted the privilege to them. In 1299 Pope Boniface gave the cardinals a purple dress, in imitation of the Roman consuls ; but in 1213, Cardinal Pelagius, as Legate à latere, wore it when ambassador at Constantinople. Paul II., 1464-71, gave them the episcopal dress, a white silk mitre with damask work, the red coif, the right of using a white horse and purple housings, and a red hood or cope. At the same time they received the scarlet bonnet formerly reserved to the Pontiff, and resembling the causia, a purple, broad-brimmed hat, usually worn as a sunshade by the Macedonians and sailors. It has been suggested that red was adopted as the colour of supreme dignity and royal purple by these heads of the spiritual militia of the Church. Pope Stephen IV. gave into their hands the election of the Popes. In 1586 Pope Sixtus declared men of any nation, and not Italians only, capable of being raised to the dignity of cardinals, who, on January 10th, 1630, received the title of Eminence, in lieu of that of Most Illustrious or Most Reverend. They formerly rode on mules with rich trappings ; but in the middle of the sixteenth century adopted the use of carriages, until the Duchess of Mantua and other ladies of fashion followed their example, when they again, but only for a very short period, resumed the practice of riding on horseback. The Pope appoints a cardinal in a consistory, the chief ceremony being the delivery of the scarlet hat, with the words *Esto Cardinalis,* "Be a Cardinal ;" he is then presumed to be a brother of the chief Pontiff. At first the hat had three scarlet knots, fringes, or tassels on each side ; these were increased to five, while archbishops had four of purple colour, and bishops three of green material ; but during the last two centuries bishops have worn four green ones ; and prelates, abbots, and prothonotaries three of purple or black. Their dress consists of a red soutane, or cassock, with a cincture with tassels of gold, red caps and stockings, a rochet and a large cloak, with an ermine cappa in winter. The large hat is depicted over Sherborne's arms at Chichester, although he was a simple bishop.

The cardinals form the Pope's Privy Council and Senate of the Roman Church. Six of their number are cardinal bishops, ordinaries of the suburban churches, the Bishop of Ostia being dean, and the Bishop of Porto subdean. There are fifty priests and fourteen deacons ; the two seniors of the latter class assist on the right and left of the Papal throne ; the priests and deacons take their titles from the principal parish churches and ancient stations of Rome, of which they are titular rectors. Every cardinal has his chaplain, who wears a purple soutane and cincture, a surplice, and stole-like scarf, with which he supports his master's mitre when not actually worn. When the Pope officiates, or in a procession, the cardinals wear white damask mitres, red shoes, and, if bishops, a cope, if priests, a chasuble; if deacons, a dalmatic. In times of penance the colour of their robes is violet, and on a few particular days rose instead of red. Their dress of state when not engaged in sacred functions consists of a large purple mantle called the croccia; on less important occasions, of a mantelet, or short cloak, through which they put their arms, and worn over the rochet, and over this is a mozzetta, or tippet, showing only the chain of a pectoral cross. Paul III. and Pius V. abrogated the title of cardinal in the other cathedrals, but Compostella by special indulgence retains the privilege. The curate of St. John de Vignes was also called the Priest Cardinal.

The institution of cardinals was imitated in several foreign cathedrals,—at Ravenna, Syracuse, Milan, Orvieto, Salerno, Naples, Orense, Oviedo, and Seville. In the latter church there were four canons so called, and at Milan twenty-four cardinal canons, twelve of them being priests, nine deacons, and three subdeacons, who officiated weekly in their course. Pope Leo IX., in 1054, appointed seven cardinal priests canons, at Besançon, Rheims, Cologne, and Aix-la-Chapelle, who officiated pontifically at the high-altar, as at Magdeburg, Mayence, Treves, and Compostella. At Besançon they wore mitre, dalmatic, gloves, and sandals; and the assistant deacons and subdeacons were called cardinals.

Carmelites, *or* **White Friars.** An order of friars who took their origin in a congregation of hermits on Mount Carmel, who were associated by Albert, Patriarch of Jerusalem, in 1122. During the Holy War they came over to Europe, and were taken under the protection of the Popes. Honorius IV. gave them the white cloak, which had hitherto been worn only by the Præmonstratensians, and called them Brethren of St. Mary. Innocent IV. bound them under conventual rule, and John XXIII. exempted them from the jurisdiction of bishops. Eugenius VI. allowed them to eat flesh. They were brought by Earl Richard de Grey from Carmel into England, c. 1250, and established themselves at Alnwick; when they first came into towns. In 1258 Alexander IV.

allowed them to imprison all renegades from the order. They usually had an image of St. John Baptist in their cloisters, with the hope of gaining greater estimation as under the protection of him who came in the spirit of Elias of Carmel. Their chief was called the Provincial. They wear a cassock, scapular, patience and hood of brown colour and a white cloak. When the Saracens recovered the Holy Land white as a royal colour was prohibited, and they adopted grey; but when they came to England they resumed the white over grey. Their house at Coventry remains in almost complete preservation.

The DISCALCEATES, or Unshod, were founded by St. Theresa at Avila, and her rule was confirmed by Pope Pius IV. in 1562. They were nicknamed Kitchen Friars; they went barefooted, and wore a very coarse habit. A portion of the Carmelite Friary remains at Aylesford, near Maidstone.

Carnary. A "skull house," or charnel. A vault stacked with bones and skulls of skeletons; as at Grantham, Hereford, Rothwell, Ripon, and Christchurch (Hants), and the Franciscan church at Evora. A charnel chapel was built near the west end of the Cathedrals of Worcester and Winchester, over a crypt devoted to this pious purpose of preserving human remains disinterred in the formation of new graves.

Carnival. [Farewell to flesh.] The week before the first day of Lent.

Carol (*quadril*, from its square shape, *quarrée*, through the Norman word *carole*). (1.) A *grille*, cage, closure, or chancel; railings round the tombs of martyrs or persons of sanctity or importance; a screen of wood or metal, designed to preserve them from indiscreet devotion by pilgrims, and from injury by ignorant or mischievous visitors. They are mentioned frequently in the Inventory of St. Paul's. The Confession in the basilica was always fenced with a balustrade of this kind.

(2.) An enclosed study or reading-place in a cloister, used by the scribes or ordinary monks and regular canons. Carols of stone remain in the cloisters of Beaulieu, Melrose, and Gloucester, the south and west walks at Chester, the south and east walks at Worcester, and were in the south alley of Canterbury. At Durham there are three carols in each window; at Worcester apertures for communication remain between the recesses. In foreign monasteries they are usually placed in the little cloisters.

(3.) A spiritual song or hymn in English, sung in honour of the Nativity. The French word *Noël*, which resembled it, is said to be a corruption of Emmanuel. The famous carol, the Boar's Head, is still sung on Christmas Day in Queen's College Hall, and the dish is carried in procession to the sound of silver trumpets.

Carthusians. A very strict order of monks for study and prayer, founded, in 1086, under the Benedictine rule, by St. Bruno of Cologne, at the Chartreuse, in the diocese of Grenoble. They came to England in 1180; and established themselves at Witham, in Somersetshire. They had also houses at the Charterhouse (London), Shene, and Mount Grace. No woman was permitted to enter their gates. They lived almost as solitaries, keeping the hours in their three-roomed cells and copying books ; maintaining a perpetual silence ; meeting in hall only on great festivals, and rarely speaking, and then only from necessity rather than choice. They did not have a daily Mass. Their habit was a hair-cloth shirt, a white tunic, a black cloak, and a cowl out of doors. Their houses were restricted to a prior, and twelve monks, and eighteen lay brothers.

Cassock. The ancient caracalla of the Roman. A close linen coat, with sleeves which came down to the calf of the leg, and was worn by soldiers, and afterwards adopted by the clergy. In its earlier ecclesiastical form it was fur-lined, and called the pelisse. The Greeks button it on the shoulder, the Roman clergy down the front. The habit of the Doctor of Divinity at Oxford is scarlet ; and the same colour was given for doctors to the University of Paris by Pope Benedict XII.; as portrayed in old manuscripts, on the Continent minor clerks and choristers still wear red or purple cassocks, but priests now wear black. Roman bishops have purple, cardinals scarlet, and the Pope a white cassock.

Catacombs. Rome stands on an alluvial soil, and also one that is volcanic. Of the latter are three kinds, pure puzzolana, from which sand was dug ; stone tufa, forming the quarries for building materials ; and granular tufa, useless for either of these purposes, in which the Christians exclusively excavated their catacombs, as burial-places for their

departed, hence called cemeteries, and also as churches,—
the Christian catacombs having nothing in common with
their heathen prototypes. The latter contained large spaces,
and wide passages for the transit of loads, carts, and
horses; whilst the former consist of narrow galleries,
straight pathways, and tiers of tombs. The heathen emperor had his mausoleum, which the patrician imitated; the
wealthier provided the columbaria; the ashes of the middle-
class man filled a small urn; and the hideous puticellus received the poor. The Christian alone was buried in his own
separate chamber, like his Master (St. Matt. xxvii. 60), beneath
the soil which he purchased or the bountiful bestowed.
The word 'catacomb' does not occur earlier than the time of
Pope Gregory I., that is, in the sixth century, but the use of
such burial-places dates from the first age of Christianity.
The Christians called their additions "new crypts to the
catacombs." Some caves near St. Sebastian are supposed
to have been the first occupied by Christian worshippers,
and the phrase *ad catacumpas* of the seventh century, and
juxta catacumbas of the thirteenth century is limited to the
space between that church and the tomb of Cæcilia Metella.
Catacumbæ was the title of an oratory built in the middle of
the fourth century, over the burial-place of SS. Peter and
Paul. The word is derived from *kata*, down, and *kumbe*,
the hold of a ship, or *kumbos*, an excavation. *Katatumbæ* is
another reading. Catacombs also exist at Chiusi and Milan,
and numerous other places. Steep stairs lead down to them,
some from amongst vineyards outside, as at St. Calixtus and
SS. Nereus and Achilles; or from the church built over the
crypt in later days, as at St. Lawrence and St. Sebastian.
The catacombs present an intricate labyrinth of corridors;
in the walls are graves; the *loculus*, so called from the Vulgate rendering of Gen. l. 25; St. Luke vii. 14, the solitary
tomb of an individual; and the *cubicula*, groups of family
vaults, with a martyr's tomb and altar in one at one end,
forming the early churches of Christ. Actual chapels comprised a chamber for either sex, for men on the east and
women on the west, with separate approaches; a choir and
sanctuary; and chancel seats; and smaller stations for religious meetings and the commemoration of the departed.
Shafts furnished light and a wholesome atmosphere, or

afforded a passage for the bier. Paintings on stucco adorned the vaults; lamps of clay, set on brackets and in niches which yet bear the stain of smoke, lighted the Christian through the maze of paths; and wells supplied water for holy baptism. Here St. Alexander, St. Calixtus, St. Caius, Liberius, and St. Boniface sought sanctuary in times of persecution, and St. Stephen and St. Sixtus died the death of martyrdom. The catacombs, long the object of pious pilgrimages, ceased to be stations and places of devotion after the incursions of Lombards, Goths, and Saracens in the neighbourhood of Rome had induced the Popes to remove the martyrs' bodies to the churches of the city; and from the eighth century, when these translations of relics became common, few persons visited the crypts, and then only those of the Vatican and St. Sebastian. The absence of Popes in the fourteenth century at Avignon, and the extravagant devotion to classical and pagan lore in the following age, diverted persons from interest in the catacombs. The influence, however, of these sacred places has never been lost; it appears in the Gothic crypt, and still more plainly in the basilica, with its separate aisles for the sexes, and the arrangements of the sanctuary, where the ciborium or baldachino was copied from the arch which was hewn out over the martyr's tomb, before which the worshippers met; and the tomb itself suggested a form for the altar raised over the confession. There were many of these cemeteries outside the city of Rome, as intramural interments were forbidden by the Twelve Laws. They were known also as *Areæ*, the tomb, catacomb, and crypt in the sand. The names of upwards of sixty are preserved. At length, by the edicts of the Emperors, about the year 260, the Christians were forbidden to hold meetings or bury within them; but they were again allowed these privileges, as appears from the writings of St. Jerome and Prudentius, who picturesquely describe the catacombs, then disused; and the custom only ceased when the bodies of the saints and martyrs were translated into splendid tombs in the upper churches built aboveground. The latest catacombs were excavated by Pope Julius in the fourth century. Mass is said in the Kallixtan catacomb yearly on November 22nd.

Catechumen. [Rom. ii. 18; Gal. vi. 6.] A novice or tyro. A candidate (so called from wearing a white robe at baptism), to whom the mysteries of the faith were taught preparatory to holy baptism. This course in the early Church lasted from forty days to three months, or as many years. They had finally to profess their belief from an elevated place three times, in memory of St. Peter's confession, and, as if made with heart, in word and deed, facing the East. Until their reception, they left the church after the Gospel had been read. There were three classes, (1) hearers; (2) praying kneelers, or prostrate, who attended prayers and received the benediction; (3) competents, seekers of the grace of Christ, who were taught the mystery of the Trinity, the doctrine of the Church, and remission of sins. They received the appellation on Palm Sunday. The hearer placed in the hands of the clergy a written desire for baptism, and then received the sign of the cross on his forehead, with imposition of hands, and permission to enter the church to hear the Holy Scripture and homilies by the bishop. They were not taught the Creed or Lord's Prayer. The next class, who came to pray as well as hear, left church before the oblation, when the Mass of catechumens ended; and then the penitents followed, in order that the discipline of penitence and ceremonial of reconciliation might not be divulged to the canons. But in order to maintain reserve in communicating divine doctrine, the catechumens were not allowed invariably to attend sermons, until the fifth century in France, and in the sixth century in Spain. When the competents had been accepted, and given in their names forty days before baptism, they were called elect, and required to observe a strict penitential discipline. In the Western Church, on the fourth Sunday in Lent, but on the second among the Greeks, the names of the elect were inscribed on the church register, and the name of an apostle or saint was given to them. A special confession was made by them; and they passed a scrutiny for seven days preceding their baptism, which consisted in exorcism, repetition of the Creed,—a custom dating back to the third century. A catechist, or *doctor audientium*, sometimes acted as the bishop's deputy, as Origen, though a layman, did during eighteen years. In the catacombs there are still lofty chambers, one for each sex, where the catechumens received instruction.

Cathedral-Church. The See, or seat, of a bishop, who takes his title from it; so called from his *cathedra*, throne or chair; and it was also called *parochia*, the principal or mother church, and in some places still the High Church. In it coronations, ordinations, councils were held, manumissions of serfs made, and academical honours conferred. The word is confined to the Western Church, and is not older than the tenth century. The *cathedraticum*, or payment to the bishop for the honour of his See, called in Italy *La chierica*, was paid in the time of Honorius III. by all the diocesan clergy; and in later days St. Richard's pence at Chichester, St. Chad's pennies at Lichfield, Pentecostals and smoke-farthings elsewhere, were the tribute of the diocese to the cathedral church, and a compensation for an omission to visit it at Whitsuntide. A cathedral is composed of a corporation of canons presided over by a bishop. In some rare cases, as Pistoia and Prato, Lichfield and Coventry, and Bath and Wells, a bishop had two cathedrals; and occasionally a collegiate church was united to a cathedral, as at Dublin. The system was established in large towns for mutual aid, and as a central station for missionary operations. They were of two kinds: cathedrals served by a composite body of monks and clerks under rule, and immediately governed by the abbot-bishop as his family and household; and collegiate churches, with chapters of clerks under an archpriest, but having the bishop as the head of the capitular body. Gradually the itinerant clergy, who were sent out on Sundays and festivals to the surrounding district, settled down as permanent parish priests, whilst those who remained about the bishop became his standing chapter. There were cathedrals of regular canons in many places, of Præmonstratensians at Littomissel, Havelburg, and Brandenburg, and of Austin canons, as already noticed, in nine cities. The cathedral of Alcala is called magistral, because all the canons have the degree of D.D. Ramsbury, exceptionally, although a see, had no chapter. At Canterbury and Worcester, two minsters, occupied by the clerks and monks respectively, adjoined each other, till the bishop definitely assumed one as his cathedral. At Winchester, and in London, at Westminster, the monks built a separate minster; at Worcester and Winchester they absorbed the canons; at Exeter they gave way to them; at Canterbury, Durham, Rochester, and Norwich, they only gradually gained the ascendant when the Norman policy removed sees from villages into towns, as in the instance of the translation from Thetford to Norwich, and Selsey into Chichester, as, about forty years earlier, had been the case of Exeter removed from Bodmin, and Salisbury from Wilton; and half a century yet earlier, in the foundation of Durham. With the exception of Monreale and Monte Casino, and some early foundations in Germany, colonized from this country, in England only there were monastic cathedrals. These were Canterbury, Winchester, Durham, Bath, Carlisle, Ely, Norwich, Rochester, Worcester; and being refounded at the Reformation as secular cathedrals, along with the newly-created sees of Chester, Bristol, Peterborough, Oxford, Gloucester, and Westminster, are known as cathedrals of the new foundation. Those of the old foundation, which always had secular canons, are York, St. Paul's, Wells, Chichester, Exeter, Hereford, Lichfield, Lincoln, Salisbury, and the four Welsh cathedrals. The bishops of Meath, Ossory, Sodor and Man, Argyll and the Isles, Caithness, Moray, Orkneys, and Galloway, did not take their titles from their sees. Some German cathedrals, as Bamberg, Camin, Breslau, Laybach, Meissen, Olmutz, like those of Trent and Trieste, are exempt, that is, free from visitation by the archbishop of the province, and immediately subject to the See of Rome.

CATHEDRALS OF THE NEW FOUNDATION. Those which were, before the Reformation, held by Benedictines, or by Austin canons, as Oxford, Bristol, and Carlisle, or as Ripon and Manchester, had been collegiate churches. The chapter consists only of residentiaries, who, till the recent Act, were called prebendaries; the corps of the prebend being the dividend or yearly income of each stall. The minor canons were originally equal in number to the major canons; and out of their number the precentor and sacrist are annually chosen.

CATHEDRALS OF THE OLD FOUNDATION. Those which have always been held by secular canons, and underwent no change at the Reformation. These consist of four internal dignitaries,—dean, precentor, chancellor, and treasurer; archdeacons, in some cases of a subdean, and subchanter of canons, and prebendaries and canons, residentiary or non-resident, internal or extraneous. Each was represented by his vicar. Strasbourg, in France, alone retains its full complement of members and ancient organization; but in Spain, Italy, Germany, and Austria, all are preserved intact. The cathedrals of Elgin, Ross, Aberdeen, and Caithness were modelled on Lincoln, which followed Rouen; those of Dunkeld, Glasgow, and St. Patrick's (Dublin), on Salisbury, which followed Amiens; as St. Paul's imitated Paris in its constitution, and is now the model for Carlisle and Peterborough.

Catholic. Universal. A term used by the Apostolical Fathers, and adopted by the Eastern and Western Churches; and from the third century all who retained the Apostolic faith, and were members of the true Church, called themselves Catholic. The Creed of the Council of Nicæa, A.D. 325, gives the Church the name of Catholic.

Cautelæ Missæ. Certain regulations concerning the office of Holy Communion, like those at the end of it in the Book of Common Prayer, only more minute, and entering into extreme detail.

Celestines. A Benedictine Order, founded by Peter Molon, Pope Celestine V., at Majella, in the thirteenth century; or by Peter Damian, c. 1078. They wore at first a blue habit, whence their name, perhaps; but afterwards a white cassock, black patience, scapular, hood, and cowl. They were numerous in France, where they were remarkable for their particular neatness of dress, and called the "pleasant Celestines." They came to England in 1414. The Order was suppressed in 1778.

Cell. (Obediences, or Abbatiales.) Dependent religious houses founded on Abbey estates, under the jurisdiction of the Abbot of the Mother Church. About the middle of the eleventh century, owing to the creation of a new dignitary, the prior, in the Abbey of Clugni, these establishments received the designation of priories. (2.) The small dwelling of a hermit or a Carthusian; that of the latter contained a bedroom, dayroom, and study. (3.) A cubicle, or partitioned sleeping-room in a dormitory.

Cellarage. The store-chambers of the cellarer or house steward were formed under the refectory at Kirkham, Sawley, Lewes; under the guest-hall at Chester; but more usually below the dormitory. It commonly was divided longitudinally into two alleys by a range of pillars, and laterally by wooden screens into separate rooms. At Fountains one enormous range on the western side of the cloister was filled with wool, with which the Cistercians supplied the conventual market. At Chester, a similar vaulted space was stocked with fish, which the Abbey boats brought up the Dee. At Durham, it was divided into various apartments, and devoted to many uses. The substructure of the refectory contained the food, and that of the dormitory the materials for furniture and clothing. At Canterbury, in the western range of vaults were the beer and wine cellars; and at the north end, as at the Charterhouse, the turn remains in the wall—an oblique opening through which the cup of wine asked for by a weary monk was passed to him. At Battle Abbey two magnificent specimens remain; one under the guest-house, and the other on the west side of the cloisters, as at Beaulieu, where a wall divides it from the cloisters.

Cellarer. (1.) The same as the Economist. The office exists at Aichstadt, Augsburg, Hildesheim, Wurtzburg, Bamburg, Halberstadt, and Basle. At Amiens he furnished wine for Masses, but had been caterer of the common table. (2.) One of the great monastic Obedientiaries, who acted as commissary-general, manciple, purveyor, proctor, and bursar. He presided over the goods, hospital, granaries, cellars, kitchens, and stables. He bought furniture, cheese, beverages, hay, fuel; appointed the pittances, and ordered the daily provisions. He found wine and minstrels on the great festivals. He weighed the bread, and gave out beer for ink to the precentor, and was excused frequent attendance in the minster, owing to his onerous duties. At Canterbury he was "father of the monastery," and kept a court-mote in his hall.

Cemetery. A resting-place; a churchyard; because our Saviour has declared death to be only a sleep. Tertullian calls it an area, when used for religious meetings. The enormous Campo Santo, built between 1218 and 1283, by John of Pisa, is the most remarkable in Europe, forming a great cloistered quadrangle. The burial-place of unbaptized infants was called the Cemetery of the Innocents. In foreign cemeteries, and commonly in the north of France, a light—the dead man's lantern—burned in a phare, or tower, to mark the resting-place of the dead; one of the thirteenth century remains at Fontevrault; and it is not improbable that in many cases a low side-window contained a lantern, or lych-light, in England for the same purpose. There are sometimes two churches within one churchyard, as at Altrincham, Evesham, Willingale, Cockerington, Hackford, Reepham, and Gillingham; as formerly also at Fulbourne, Trimley, and Staunton. The monastic cemetery was usually on the south side; and the laymen's yard, on the north of the Presbytery in England, but in France eastward of it; and a light burning at night gave light both to the crypt and this garth. At Durham, after dinner, the monks, bareheaded, went in procession daily to pray around the graves of their departed brethren. At Canterbury, the southern close was divided into the outer cemetery for lay persons, and the inner for ecclesiastics and religious. The cemetery-gate, called at Gloucester and Worcester, until their destruction, the Lych gate, remains at Ely and St. Augustine's, Canterbury.

Censer (*Acerra, thymiatorium, fumigatorium, succensum,* or thurible). A vessel for burning incense, which is supplied by a spoon from one shaped like a ship or boat. Censers of gold or silver were given by Constantine to St. John Lateran; and by Pope Sixtus III. to churches. An ancient silver censer is at Louvaine, and one of German work at St. Anthony's, Padua. The censer originally was, probably, in the form of an urn, which the priest took by the base when incensing the altar; then the cover, full of holes, was added for the escape of the perfumed smoke; and lastly, in the twelfth century, the idea of balance-chains suggested itself. The ship after the twelfth century received a foot and jointed cover. The censer was always round, and divided into two halves; the lowermost, containing the charcoal-fire and perfume; the upper, pierced with holes for the escape of the scented air; three or four chains were fixed to the lower portion, and a single chain to the cover. Censers were sometimes made like a keep and towers, or like a church with many apses, like those of the twelfth century at

Treves; sometimes the New Jerusalem, or the Three Children in the Furnace of Dura, crowned the cover, as in the copper censer of the twelfth century at Lille.

Ceremony. The derivation of this word has been much debated; it has been traced from *caritas*; from Cære, the town where the Roman relics were preserved during an invasion of the Gauls; from *cerus*, sacred, or from *carendo*, because those who observe it stand aloof from what it proscribes. It is defined as usage by Cranmer, and implies the observance of a rite: its administration and accessories, forms and actions relating to the minister, place, time, and mode of worship, which are appointed as pertaining to decent discipline and godly order. Ceremonies, according to the Injunctions of King Edward, "be no workers nor works of salvation, but only outward signs and tokens, to put us in remembrance of things of higher perfection."

Certain. A lesser endowment for a mortuary Mass; where the person was prayed for with a number of others, and not individually; the names being written all together on a board or plate above the altar.

Chain Gate. A not uncommon name for a gate protected by a chain originally, as at Winchester, Wells, St. Paul's, and Westminster.

Chair. In a chapel of the Catacombs at St. Catherine's, Chiusi, the altar, a marble table on a column of travertine, stands at the end of the apse, and the bishop's chair is placed on the Gospel side. In the catacombs, the bishop's chair cut in the tufa constantly appears in the apse. At St. Agnes there are two, one possibly having been used at enthronization, and by a bishop assisting at Mass; or perhaps the chair of some sainted Pope. Even at the close of the sixth century, consecrations of bishops were held in the catacombs at Chiusi. A bishop's chair has on either side a priest's chair in the catacomb. In the crypts there were also movable chairs, like one on which St. Stephen was martyred, and taken out of the catacomb of St. Sebastian by Innocent XII. as a gift to the Grand Duke Como III. These are said to have been taken often from the Roman Warm Baths. When they received steps at a later period, they were called Gradatæ, and, if curtained, Velatæ. Sometimes the back was ornamented with a dove—the emblem of the Holy Spirit; and the arms were decorated with lions, unicorns, or griffins, typical of strength and vigilance, or dogs of fidelity, as on the throne of St. Hippolytus, in the Lateran. In France they sometimes buried bishops sitting in their chairs; and the latter were at length removed, as a throne, to the upper church. A marble chair of the twelfth century, formerly used by the Primates, is preserved at Lyons. Another, called St. Gerard's Fauteuil, of the thirteenth century, and of stone, is at Tours. There were others at Rheims, Autun, Arras, and Metz. Several of the Roman and Italian churches retain the pontifical chair in the apse, as St. Ambrose (Milan), St. Gregory on Mount Cælius, St. Stephen the Round, St. Mary Cosmedin, St. Clement, St. Agnes, and St. Mary in Trastavere. Martene says that the French bishops usually sat on a faldstool set upon the steps or on one side of the altar; but that at Lyons and Vienne they, with their clergy, sat in stone chairs, as in the basilica; and he mentions that the stone chair in which bishops were enthroned then remained at Autun. The Pope's marble chair of the fourteenth century is preserved at Avignon. At Canterbury the primatial throne is of the twelfth century, and made of marble; formerly it was placed behind the high-altar, and occupied by the archbishop until after the consecration of the elements. At Dijon and St. Vigor the thrones were also of stone; that of marble, in Palermo, stands at the west end of the cathedral. Ivory was also employed. There is a silver chair with pierced tracery, c. 1395, at Barcelona; and the Coronation chair at Westminster, containing the Stone of Scone, is of oak, of the time of Edward I., and was used by the celebrant at St. Edward's altar. St. Peter's chair of wood, in the apse of St. Peter's in the Vatican, resembles a curule chair. *See* THRONE.

Chair Organ. The same as a choir organ. One placed behind the organist's seat, as in Winchester College chapel, and facing the choir.

Chalice. (*Calix*, a cup; 1 Cor. x. 16, *poterion*.) The cup used at Holy Communion to contain the consecrated wine, and called the Lord's cup by St. Athanasius, and the mystic cup by St. Ambrose. There were four kinds,—(1) Communical, that used by the celebrant; (2) the ministerial, large and small, for communicating the faithful; (3) offertory, in which the deacons received the wine offered by communicants. Possibly the chalices found in tombs of the catacombs were those into which the deacon poured the wine, and were religiously preserved for burial with their late owners; (4) the baptismal, used for communion in the case of the newly baptized, and for administering to them milk and honey. It was formerly made of wood, as St. Boniface said, when permitting its use: "Once golden priests used wooden chalices; now, on the contrary, wooden priests use golden chalices." At St. Denys there was a medieval chalice of sardonyx. Pope Zephyrinus, c. 202, ordered the material to be glass; and St. Jerome speaks of a bishop of Toulouse who bore the Lord's body in a wicker canister and His blood in glass. Tertullian also alludes to the latter material. Wooden chalices were in use until the ninth century. The Council of Rheims, in 226, forbade glass, and in 883 the use of wood, tin, glass, and copper. Pope Leo, in 847, prohibited wood or glass; the Council of Tribur, in 897, proscribed wood; the Council of Cealcythe, in 785, forbade wood; but Ælfric's canons, in 957, allowed wood, probably owing to the devastations of the Danes; but, three years later, King Edgar's canons allowed only molten metal. Honorius, Cæsarius of Arles and St. Benedict used, or at least mention, glass chalices, which certainly were not disused in the eighth century. Glass was considered improper, owing to its fragility; horn, from blood entering into its composition, by the Council of Cealcythe; wood, from its porousness and absorbent nature; and brass and bronze, because liable to rust. In 1222 the Archbishop of Canterbury forbade tin or pewter; but tin was used in France so lately as 1793, and by the canons of 1604 the wine was to be brought in "a clean and sweet standing pot or stoop of pewter, if not of purer metal." St. Columban used bronze or tin, in memory of the nails of the cross. The most precions metals and materials were, however, at an early date used. Onyx, ivory, sardonyx, and agate are mentioned by early French writers; marble is spoken of by Gregory the priest; gold and silver are mentioned by St. Augustine; in 227 Pope Urban required the latter; in the time of Pope Gregory II. chalices were jewelled, and Tertullian mentions that they had carvings of the Good Shepherd; from the

K

sixth to the thirteenth century their handles were sculptured
with animals or foliage, and blue, red, and green enamel
was used in their ornamentation. At Clairvaux,'St. Malachy's
chalice was surrounded with little bells; one at Rheims, of
gold, was inscribed with an anathema, imprecated upon any
person who should steal it. Sometimes the maker's name
was engraved upon it. One, formerly belonging to St.
Alban's Abbey, is now at Trinity College, Oxford; and another ancient specimen remains at Corpus Christi College in
the same University; and a third, of the twelfth century, at
Chichester. Three of early date are at York. Chalices of
earthenware or pewter were buried in the grave with priests.
There is a chalice, that of St. Remigius, of the twelfth century,
at Paris; St. Wolfgang's cup, c. 994, and the chalice of
Weintgarten are preserved at Ratisbon; another is at Mayence. St. Jerome's, in St. Anastasia's at Rome, has a copper
foot and earthenware bowl. There is a Jacobean chalice of
wood at Goodrich Court, and a German chalice, of the
fifteenth century, is in a case in the British Museum.. Until
the twelfth century the communion was given in both kinds,
but subsequent to that date the chalice was administered
only to the celebrant and his acolyths; the vessel, therefore,
which had previously been of large dimensions, for the use
of all the faithful, and was provided with two handles, shrank
into a cup-like form about that period in the Western
Church. The Greeks retain communion in both kinds, and
consequently the two-handled chalice. Several of this
shape are still preserved in the treasury of St. Mark's,
Venice. In the eleventh and twelfth centuries the stalk was
short, the foot large, the knop in the centre thick, the bowl
wide; after that the cup became small, the stalk long, and
the knop tall and flat, and in some cases enriched with
tabernacled figures of saints. In the fifteenth century it
underwent a further modification, the knop became diamond-
shaped in profile, the cup more long and shallow, and the
foot indented, like the petals of a flower. There are several
chalices still preserved, one of ivory and silver, of the fourteenth century, at Milan; that of Rheims, of gold, with
enamels and gems, of the twelfth century, now in the
Imperial Library at Rome; that of Troyes, c. 1220; and
one of Cologne, of the thirteenth century, with the Apostles

under niches below the rim,—sometimes sacred subjects from the life of our Lord adorn the base; another at St. Gereon's, of the fifteenth century, has only an arabesque pattern; but a beautiful specimen at Hildesheim, of the thirteenth century, represents, in compartments, the offering of a lamb by Abel, and Melchisedech's oblation of wine, the brazen serpent, and the bunch of grapes from Eshcol. The pomel, or knop, and foot were usually covered with nielli, gems, and elaborate chasings. The foot was indented in order to keep it steady when laid down to drain upon the paten, according to ancient usage, before the affusions were drunk by the priest, or at the commencement of Mass. At York the curves are wanting, but one foot has a crucifix. The *ansatæ* in the sixth century, being of great weight, were often suspended by chains above the altar.

In 418 Pope Zosimus restrained the use of the chalice to the cells of the faithful and of clerks. Pope Martin V. gave it to the Roman people, and the Council of Basle permitted it to the Bohemians. The Emperor of Constantinople, at his coronation, partook of the chalice; and Clement VI. allowed the King of Gaul to partake at pleasure, although other princes were permitted the privilege only at their coronation and at the hour of death. The Pope, at solemn celebration, communicates the cardinal deacon with the chalice. The monks of St. Bernard dipped the bread in the wine. Pope Victor III. and the Emperor Henry of Luxembourg are said to have been poisoned by the chalice.

According to Alexander of Hales, and Leo of Chartres, the chalice should stand on the right side of the paten, but by the Salisbury use it is placed behind it.

The denial of the cup to the laity by the Roman Church was introduced at the close of the twelfth century, and confirmed in 1414 by the Council of Constance.

Chamberlain. In a monastery he was overseer of the dormitory, and purchased clothes, bed furniture, and other necessaries. He received all considerable sums of money or account. He acted as treasurer, having the charge of nearly every considerable payment. At Durham his chequer was near the abbey gates, under which was the tailors' shop for making linsey-woolsey or stamyne shirts, and tunics for the monks and novices, and whole and half socks of white woollen cloth. His chamber was in the dormitory at Abingdon. He provided copes, albes, cowls, coverlets, hoods, shoes, and boots, towels, combs, knives, beds, straw palliasses, stools, bed-perches, hot water, tools for the tailors and cordwainers, five lights burning in the dormitory from twilight to dawn, and baths three times a year. At Canterbury he provided mats, blankets, razors, all the monks' clothing, horseshoes for the farriers, and glass for the dormitory. The old clothing was distributed by him to the poor. Under him were the laundry folk, peltmen or skin dressers, tailors, shoemakers, etc. In a cathedral he was often called the provost, and like the massarius in Italy, chamarier of Lyons, Strasbourg, and Saragossa, was the receiver of rents and paymaster of the stipends and money for pittances, and general accountant of income and keeper of the common chest. He was annually elected, and took precedence of canons whilst in office. At St. Paul's he found the necessaries for divine services and posted the summonses of prebendaries to chapter on their stalls, and at York acted as punctator of the absences of the vicars. In the latter instance he might be a vicar.

Chamfer. A slight splay in an angle of buttresses and capitals.

Champlève enamels have the ground hollowed out to receive the colours.

Chancel, as a division of a church, is a diminutive of the full phrase *infra cancellos,* within the chancels. The word was also applied, in England in the thirteenth century, to chantries, or side chapels next the choir. But usually the chancel in a parish church corresponds to the choir of a cathedral and minster, and is directed to remain as in times past, that is, with its appropriate furniture and seats or stalls for the clergy and singers. The old English name is Theo- or Theofod-steal, holy or altar-place.

Chancellor of the Choir. The dignitary in a cathedral next in rank to a precentor, who presided over the readers of the lections in church, and the schools of the city and cathedral. The office was instituted in England in the twelfth century, but in France apparently not until the thirteenth century. The dignitary bore the name in foreign chapters of Scholasticus Scholarca cabiscol, that is, *caput scholæ,* head of the school, magistral and theologal. Like the Greek charte-phylax, he was the librarian and secretary of the chapter, and sealed the capitular correspondences. He also acted as the theological lecturer and reader in canon law. The chancellor's name is derived from that of the law officer who stood at the bar *ad cancellos* to receive the pleas of suitors, and was keeper of the court seal. The chancellor of a university has the sole executive authority within the precinct.

Chancellor of the Diocese. The judge of the bishop's consistorial court, official and vicar-general of the diocesan. The office does not occur earlier than the reign of Henry II., and was instituted to supply a substitute for the bishop when absent in parliament or attendance at court, and must be held by a graduate with the degree of M.A. or B.C.L.

Chancels. Cancelli,—screens, often of great beauty and richness, set round an altar, or the choir, or tombs of saints. The original chancels were those which divided the choir from the nave, forming a line of demarcation between the clergy and laity. Leo III., in the time of Charlemagne, erected a chancel of pure silver, and Stephen IV. placed another of the same material round an altar. The Second Council of Tours enjoined the people not to stand near the altar among the clerks at Vigils or Mass, because that part of the church which is divided off by chancels is restricted to the use of the singing clerks. St. Gregory of Tours mentions a chancel in the chord of the apse in St. Pancras' Church near Rome, and at St. Sophia's, Constantinople; the chancel fenced the entrance to the sanctuary.

The chancel-screens round the choir were called, in Spain, rejas, and elsewhere pectorals, being a wall breast-high at which the faithful communicated and received the palms and ashes when they were distributed. It was identical with the peribolos which was introduced when the Hours were first sung in choir during the fourth century. The solid and taller screen does not date earlier than the twelfth century. Sometimes the chancels had a balustrade and columns, called Regulars, placed at intervals; on these curtains were suspended, so as to resemble the Greek *iconostasis;* St. Gregory of Tours notices that they were embroidered and painted with sacred images in France. At certain times in the service these veil-like draperies were drawn back and again closed, unlike the modern custom of leaving the whole vista of the interior and the altar in full view; this utter change from the more ancient idea of seclusion of the sacred mysteries emanated from the Jesuits, and contemporaneously with the introduction of the ceremony of Benediction, and has resulted in a wholesale destruction of the rood-screens. The latter, which is the true representative of the primitive chancels, marked the separation between the clergy and laity, and also symbolized the entrance to the Church triumphant. For this reason it was painted, as at Hexham, with figures of saints, or with the sentences of the Creed, or with the destruction of the dragon, or the Last Judgment. Two of these screens, of open work of the time of Wren, exist at St. Peter's, Cornhill, and All Hallows the Great, Thames Street, London; whilst beautiful specimens of lateral choir-screens remain at Alby, at Paris of the fourteenth century, at Chartres and Amiens of the fifteenth century, and of the thirteenth century at Canterbury. The chancels mostly, however, have shrunk into the mere altar-rail round or in front of the altar, dividing, not as before, the nave from the choir, but the choir from the sanctuary.

Changeable Taffeta. A material like shot-silk used for vestments.

Chant, Ecclesiastical. Singing is mentioned in the Apostolical times, Acts xvi. 25; 1 Cor. xiv. 26, just as our Lord and His Disciples sang a "hymn," that is certain Psalms; but what the music was is unknown. The church song was probably founded on Greek music; and antiphonal singing, alluded to by Pliny, took its origin at Antioch, and was adopted by St. Basil at Neo-Cæsarea, in Egypt, Palestine, and Arabia. St. Ambrose introduced it into the West at Milan, employing the use of the East in Psalms and hymns, which were responsively sung in the night hours during the Arian persecution by the Empress Justina to relieve the weariness of watching. Previously, in many times and in many churches, single voices chanted whilst the congregation merely joined in at the end, and meditated in silence. The people now joined zealously in the chanting, until at length their extreme vociferation necessitated the institution of a distinct order of singers or choristers by the Councils of Laodicea and Carthage, and at length, despite popular opposition, in the West. Milan became the school of music for Western Europe, and the name of the old melody for the Te Deum, the Ambrosian Chant, preserves the name of its originator, although St. Gregory's name, as that of the later reformer, is now more commonly associated with it. In the East, St. Chrysostom, with melody and sweet harmony at night,—the choral processions accompanied by tapers which were carried in cruciform stands,—endeavoured to outvie the attractive hymnody of the Arians. St. Athanasius, at Alexandria, caused the reader to intone the Psalms with so slight an inflection of the voice that it was more like singing than reading, and St. Augustine contrasts it with the agreeable modulation used at Milan. St. Jerome complained of theatrical modulations in singing. P. Gelasius, in 494, condemned the abuse, and in the sixth century Pope Gregory introduced the plain chant, a grave and natural tone which repressed the caprice of the singers, and reduced them to uniformity. In 705 Charlemagne enforced its observance throughout the Western Church. The Gregorian school at Rome was imitated by those of Lyons in France, and of Africa, mentioned by St. Gregory of Tours: St. Patrick in Ireland, Benedict and Theodore at Metz and Soissons, Augustine and Theodore at Canterbury, Precentor John of Rome at Wearmouth, James the Deacon at York, Eddi in Northumbria, c. 668, Putta at Rochester, and Mabran at Hexham, were the founders of the ecclesiastical chant in this country. The Councils of Cloveshoe and Trent, St. Bernard and John of Salisbury, in the reign of Henry II., reprobated a florid style in church, for as early as the eleventh century Thurstin of Caen, Abbot of Glastonbury, endeavoured to introduce a more pleasing melody than the Gregorian tones. Trumpets, cornets, pipes, and fiddles in 1512 are mentioned in English churches by Erasmus; virginals, viols, harps, lutes, fiddles, recorders, flutes, drones, trumpets, waits, and shawms by Bale; bagpipes, lutes, harps, and fiddles by Whitgift. In 1635, lyres and harps were used at Hereford, and two sackbuts and two cornets at Canterbury; and at the Chapel Royal, Lincoln, Westminster, Durham, and Exeter, orchestral music accompanied the chant after the Restoration. Country churches only recently lost such accessories. The early Anglican single chant was founded upon the latter, and the double chant occurs first in Dean Aldrich's MSS. Several of the Roman school rose to the Pontificate, as Gregory II., Stephen III., and Paul I., on the Continent, and in England many of the precentors were raised to the episcopate or an abbacy, and were usually recommended for their office by their learning as well as for their musical skill, like Eadmer and John of Thanet at Canterbury, Symeon of Durham, Somerset of Malmesbury, and Walsingham of St. Alban's. Monks in their monasteries followed the example of the clergy in their churches, and Lérins became the school of southern France. Some conventual rules, such as those of St. Hilarius, St. Macarius, and Serapion, allowed only the abbots to chant. Women joined in the chant, as appears from St. Gregory of Nazianzum, and Isidore of Damietta. The Capitulars permitted them to sing the rite antiphonally with men at funerals, St. Augustine and the Council of Chalons and Aix-la-Chapelle, in the nineteenth century, desired nuns to sing their office.

Chanter. 1. The Precentor. 2. A ruler of the choir. 3. The Succentor.

Chapel. By Casalins the name is derived from huts covered with goat-skins, *capellarum*, like that in which St. Apollinaris celebrated ; the Jewish tabernacle was in the same manner roofed with badger-skins. It has also been supposed to come from *capella*, a reliquary chest or cabinet, or *cupella* as it is termed in ancient inscriptions in the catacombs, for a funereal vase, a grave or place of burial during the fifth century ; capella, in the sense of *cup* or *cop*, a roof or top, covering or canopy of an altar which contained relics. The chape or cope of St. Martin was the ordinary covering of his tomb in the Cathedral of Tours, and the Counts of Anjou carried it to battle before the King of France. The tent which contained it was called the capella, or chapel, hence the name of chaplains for the priests who served with the army, and also celebrated in the oratories of the palace, in which during time of peace, these shrines were deposited. Socrates mentions centuries before that Constantine carried out to his wars a tent or tabernacle shaped like a church. In Spain the choir is still called the capilla mayor.

There are several kinds of chapels. (1.) Isolated or detached buildings for religious worship annexed or affiliated to mother churches, without the right of having a font or cemetery; called in the statutes of Canute, "a field church," and in modern times chapels of ease. (2.) Those attached to a palace, castle, mansion, or college, less generally known as oratories; the earliest recorded in a college of a university is at Paris in 1254. (3.) Chantries, or internal buildings within a church. (4.) An aisle furnished with its own altar, chalice, paten, cruets, basin, pyx, and sacring-bell. (5.) A set of vessels and vestments used in the service of the church, as when we read that a bishop bequeathed his chapel to a cathedral. (6.) A well chapel, like that of the Perpendicular period at Hempstead, Gloucestershire, or the still more famous St. Winifred's at Holywell, where the bath, which was a place of great resort, is star-shaped, and was formerly enclosed with stone screens; round it is a vaulted ambulatory, and in front there is an entrance porch; in the upper storey there is a chapel. The chapels of the first class are not permitted to contain a font, and usually have no cemetery. The Saintes Chapelles of Paris, Vincennes, Dijon, Riom, Champigny, and Bourbon, so called as containing presumed relics of the Cross, were peculiar to France. That of Dijon is called the Palatine, from the palace of the Dukes of Burgundy in which it stood.

In the eleventh century, when the practice of building crypts or subterranean churches fell into desuetude, the chapel became an integral portion of the upper structure; usually there were three at the east end, one in the centre dedicated to St. Mary, set between two adjuncts. In the twelfth century, chapels were multiplied round the sanctuary; throughout the Norman style they were apsidal, but gradually became polygonal. In the thirteenth century, the Eastern chapels were added in still greater numbers round the choir; at Tours there were as many as fifteen. In this and the succeeding century chapels were erected between the buttresses of the nave-aisles. These are common abroad; and occur at King's College (Cambridge), and at Windsor, at Lincoln in the presbytery, and formerly there was one in the nave at Canterbury.

In England we have a group of chapels round the presbytery at Westminster, Tewkesbury, Pershore, radiating from the main building, but it was an uncommon arrangement, like the external range of chapels in the naves of

Chichester and Manchester ; and the lateral or transeptal
line (as at Gurk), of those at Fountains, Peterborough, the
Nine Altars of Durham, formerly at Bridlington, and that
recently destroyed at Hexham, and the second or choir
transept, as at Salisbury, Lincoln, and Canterbury. Chapels
were usually founded as sepulchral chantries and supported
by families of distinction, by the bequest of ecclesiastics,
and very frequently by confraternities and guilds. They
resemble in many particulars the cubicles or side rooms of
churches, which Paulinus of Nola says were allotted for
prayer, devout reading, and commemoration of the departed ;
but they were no doubt rendered indispensable by the multiplication of altars which blocked up the nave and aisles, and
by the enclosure of the choir with screens, and in foreign
churches to strengthen the enormous stride of the buttresses
which was necessary to support the vast height of the walls,
weakened by being pierced with a large clerestory. In
order to provide still more room, aisles were added on either
side of the transept, and in some cases there were both upper
and lower chapels, as at Christchurch (Hants), and St. John's
(Chester), like that built over the Clugniac antechurches.

In conventual establishments there was a chapel of the
infirmary and a chapel of the guest-house. Occasionally
we find chapels in towers, as at Canterbury and Drontheim ;
in western towers the dedication was usually to St. Michael,
as the conductor of souls to Paradise. In Christchurch
(Hants) (7), and at Bury St. Edmund's (9), and Abingdon
(11), there were several chapels built in the cemetery and
close, and this may have been a not uncommon arrangement, until such parasitical buildings were absorbed into the
central minster after its reconstruction with larger dimensions
on a grander scale. In the Eastern Church at Moscow, Blan-
skenoi, and on Mount Athos, and in several parts of Ireland,
there were similar groups, usually seven in number, probably
to preserve the principle of having only one altar in a church.

Chaplain. (1.) A priest who officiates in a collegiate or private chapel at a particular altar. (2.) A clerical vicar or
beneficiatus in a foreign cathedral. (3.) The domestic chaplain of a peer. An archbishop may have eight, a duke or
bishop six, a viscount four, the Lord Chancellor, a baron, and
K.G., three, a marquis or earl five, a dowager, the dean of

the chapel, the Master of the Rolls, Lord Almoner, the Lord Treasurer, and Secretary to the Queen, each two ; the Lord Chief Justice of the Queen's Bench and the Warden of the Cinque Ports each one. (4.) Chaplains in ordinary to the Queen, priests who serve in rotation as preachers in the Chapel Royal, the Dean of St. Paul's, if a royal chaplain, or if no royal chaplain is present, presides at the opening of each new convocation. The word chaplain designated an assistant priest, and generally an officiating priest. Their annual wage was six marks in the fourteenth century. They were called vice-curates in absence of the parish priest ; the assistant curate was properly called a conduct. They were removable by the rector. Chaplains at Pisa are divided into two classes. (I.) Thirty-two participants in the daily distribution, wearing a violet robe, and called Chaplains of the Quinterno, from the name of the register-book. They form a college called the Chaplains' University, which is presided over by four superintendents, and has its own chancery seal and buildings. (II.) Twenty simple chaplains, without any share in the quotidian, wearing a cowl on the left shoulder ; they do not attend the Hours, and are incapable of promotion into the staff of the cathedral ; but simply serve chantries.

CHAPLAINS, MILITARY, *Aumôniers d'Armée.* St. Boniface, in his first council in Germany, ordered that every commander should keep a priest to shrive his soldiers at the eve of a battle. In the time of Charlemagne and before the Battle of Hastings, it was the custom to confess and communicate the troops before an engagement.

Chapter. (1.) A paragraph ; a lesson from the Bible ; a statute under one rubric. (2.) An assembly of persons for conference on common business. (3.) As properly applied to a cathedral, a sacred congregation of persons set apart for the worship of God in principal churches, and forming the council of the president of the foundation, from whom, as their head (*caput*), the chapter (*capitulum*) derives its name. As monks and canons regular had their chapters, so when secular canons had their common table divided into separate prebends, they were formed into chapters, "little heads," as the bishop was the principal head. The monks and regulars derived their chapter from the daily reading of the little chapter, a portion of their rule, in their assembly, about the

seventh century, when the word occurs in the capitulars of
Charlemagne and the Councils of Aix and Mayence, instead
of the older term 'congregation,' employed by St. Benedict
and Bishop Julian of Marseilles in 480.   Properly speaking,
a chapter was in a cathedral church; a convent was a church
of regulars, and a college an inferior church, with its members living in common.   A chapter cannot be composed of
less than three persons.   Uusually it assembled on every
Saturday, and was then often called a parliament; now it
meets ordinarily once in every quarter.   A curious complaint
was made in the fifteenth century at Lincoln that the dean
brought armed followers into chapter.   At Rouen it was
convened annually; at Mayence four times a year.   In the
new foundations, fortnightly chapters are enjoined.   The
bishop is the principal head; the dean the numeral head.
Its members are canons, having a stall in choir and a vote
in chapter, with prebends, a foundation and estate, and the
right of a common seal, being assembled under their head,
and convened by the sound of a bell.   Absent canons are
represented by proxies.   It can enact statutes, which must
be ratified by the visitor, and has all the rights of a parish;
and before it and the dean all members of the body are to
be tried.   It forms the bishop's council, and must furnish
assistants to him at ordinations, and on the vacancy of a see
exercises episcopal jurisdiction.   There are various kinds of
chapters :—

I. A close chapter, where the number of members is limited.

II. The lesser or ordinary chapter, composed of residentiaries only, at least two-thirds of the number, and meeting
under the dean.

III. The great or extraordinary chapter, consisting of all
the canons, resident or non-resident, convened by the bishop.
It was also called the Pentecostal chapter, because it met at
Whitsuntide, and continued to do so at Salisbury until 1811.
At Hereford it is convoked twice a year; and at Chichester,
and in other cathedrals, it is still convened on special occasions.   Sometimes there were two regular chapters in one
church, as at St. Ambrose's, Milan, and St. Augustine's,
Pavia, each having its own superior; or two churches constituted the bishop's collective chapter, as at Bath and
Wells, Lichfield and Coventry, Hamburg and Bremen.

Chapter, Monastic. This was held in winter after Tierce, but after Prime in summer. At the sound of a bell, rung by the prior, the monks entered two-and-two, and bowed to a cross in the centre of the room, to the superior's chair, and to one another. The ordinary business transacted comprised reading the martyrology, announcement of coming festivals, reading the rule, or, on Sundays and holy-days, a homily of the Fathers, commemoration of the departed and living bene-factors, nomination of celebrants and the officiating priest for the week ensuing, public confession of faults, infliction of penance and discipline, and once a year recital of charters. The novice was admitted in chapter; the superior was elected, and the great officers of the house were confirmed in it; the inventory of the library was also carefully inspected in chapter every Lent. In the secular chapter, held after Prime, all business connected with the church, the services, and lands was transacted, and all disputes determined. Every canon had his voice in chapter, and his stall in choir. In 1279 there were two general archidiaconal chapters, and four quarterly ruridecanal chapters held yearly in England.

Chapter-house. The conventual or capitular parliament-house, rare in France and Germany, was used daily by the regulars, and on every Saturday by the secular canons. In it also the bishop convened the community at his visitation or dio-cesan synod. It derived its name from the little chapters or rubrics of the statutes being read over in it in the monastery, it is said. At Valencia and Hereford the pulpit for the theological lecture stood in it until recently. In the ninth century, the north alley served for the purpose of the chap-ter-house, as at St. Gall; but in the tenth century, a sepa-rate building was erected at Fontenelle, and Edward the Confessor built one of a circular form at Westminster. The chapter-house in a convent was almost invariably an oblong, sometimes terminating in an apse, and round or polygonal in a secular establishment. The latter form may have been suggested by the column with radiating arches which is found at the east end of an apsidal crypt, or by the Italian baptistery, in which councils were sometimes held. The rectangular form was more convenient for the judicial character of the buildings, as the polygonal was for synodical meetings convened by the diocesan. There are two apparent, but not real exceptions, at Exeter, where the chapter-house is oblong, and the Benedictines were replaced by canons; and at Worcester, where it is polygonal without and circular within, and canons were superseded by Benedictines. At Bari, the baptistery, round on the exterior, is twelve-sided within, each compartment formerly having a figure of an Apostle. At Wells, Lincoln, Lichfield, Southwell, York, and Elgin, this council chamber stands on the north side of the church, connected with it by a passage for marshalling processions; but at Salisbury it occupies its normal position in convents, the centre of the east side of the cloister. At Chichester and St. David's it is in an upper storey, adjoining the transept. In the secular canons' chapter-houses a large crucifix stood in the centre, near a pulpit for sermons and reading; and stalls were ranged round the sides of the walls; the dignitaries occupying the east end, and the canons sitting in order of installation, reckoning from the east to the west. In the Benedictine houses the walls were generally arcaded to form stalls, and a large coffer, called the trunk, was placed at the entrance, as the place of offenders. The abbot's or prior's chair fronted it, and every monk who approached it performed the *venia*, an inclination of reverence. The apse of the chapter-house possibly contained an altar, as the building was regarded to be only less sacred than the church, and a light burned constantly in it, and before the door. At Tongres the altar remains; and at Exeter the chapel of the Holy Ghost adjoins it in the usual position of the slype. At Belvoir and St. Paul's, it stood in the centre of the cloisters. At Bristol, Exeter, Beaulieu, Haughmond, and Chester, a large vestibule, with a central door and windows opening eastward, is built in front of the chapter-house, in order to afford additional accommodation to the general assemblies of the orders. The Cistercians had sermons in the chapter-house; and, like the other regular orders, admitted novices, administered punishment, and transacted general business in this room, which abroad was known as the chapter-hall. It was a peculiarity with the Cistercians to subdivide their chapter-houses into alleys by ranges of pillars; and between it and the transept they invariably placed a large aumbry or cloister library; and the Clugniacs at Wenlock followed the example; but in the

Benedictine houses the slype, or way to the cemetery, always intervenes in this position. Burials were permitted in the chapter-house to bishops, priors, and eminent laymen, before interments within the church itself were suffered to be made. At Durham and Norwich penitential cells adjoined the chapter-house, the offenders being at once taken to them, after sentence had been delivered.

Chapter, or Conventual Mass. The High Mass or Mass of the day, usually sung before 10 A.M.; in France the hour is 8 or 9 A.M.

Chartulary. A book of charters and endowments. It was kept in the cartaria.

Chasse. (*Capsa.*) (1.) A coffer for holding the relics of a saint. It formerly had the shape of a long bottle, with a little roof-like covering. It was made of copper, gilt, and sometimes enamelled. From the thirteenth century it took the shape of a little church. (2.) An embroidered case or covering for the book of the Gospels; sometimes called the camisia.

Chasuble. [*Casula,* a little house.] So called, says Isidore of Seville, from its covering the whole person. A garment at first common to clerks and laymen, but in the former case made of richer stuff. In the Fourth Council of Toledo it was reckoned a sacred habit. Its old English name was Massa hakele, the mass mantle. Its proper shape is a complete oval, with a single aperture, through which the head is passed. The word occurs first in the year 474, in the will of St. Perpetuus, of Tours. The Greek chasuble was of equal width all round, from the top to the bottom. The Western form was that of pointed ends behind and before; and the early mosaics of the sixth century show it thus sloping and hollowed, but reaching to the feet; but there are other examples which portray it shorter, as it is worn at present, the ends being frequently rounded. The other names of this vestment were *penula* or *phelone* (2 Tim. iv. 13), a thick upper cloak, and *planeta,* as Ducange amusingly explains, owing to the many changes through which it had wandered from its original shape; of course the true derivation is from its flowing folds. A remarkable vestment of this kind at St. Apollinaris, Ravenna, bears the name of the Chasuble of the Diptychs, as it is covered with an auriclave, orphrey, or superhumeral, a band of golden stuff, like an ancient archiepiscopal pall, sewn behind and before, and divided round the neck, covered with the names and heads of thirty-five bishops of Verona, in succession, from the foundation of the See to the middle of the eighth century. By the Second Council of Nice such representations were permitted on ecclesiastical habits and sacred plate. The name of auriclave, like orphrey, meaning the "gold-bordered," was given to the chasuble from its peculiar embroidery on the onophorion or laticlave, a band originally of a different colour from the robe, and called the auriclave when made of cloth of gold. One of this kind, of the fifth century, is preserved in the cathedral of Ravenna. St. Stephen's chasuble, made by Grisella, Queen of Hungary, in 1031, is preserved at Buda, and worn by the Sovereign at his coronation ; its colour is green. That of St. Boniface is at Mayence, and another at St. Rambert-sur-Loire. There are two at Madeley, of the fourteenth century, which were probably brought from Much Wenlock. One at Talacre is said to have come from Basingworth. There is one at Salisbury in green and gold, of the sixteenth century. The pall of an archbishop was often called the superhumerale, or rationale, in allusion to Levit. viii. 7, 8; so the orphreys of the chasuble were sometimes called the rationale, as being in front, and the superhumeral as falling over the shoulders. The chasuble called *palliata* had the pall sewn upon it. Until the twelfth or thirteenth century the pectoral or front did not differ in form from the dorsal or back. The superhumeral dwindled into a narrow collar, and the cross on the back of the chasuble is the last relic of the auriclave. On the medieval chasuble this did not appear ; but from the orphrey, called the pectoral or pillar, which covered the breast, two bands, called humerals, sprang over the shoulders, forked like the upper part of a Y, and ended in a single band of gold lace, known as the dorsal. From an early date chasubles were ornamented with sacred designs, flowers, and symbolical animals and birds, a usage permitted by the Second Council of Nicæa. The processional chasuble had a hood, which was worn in France until the latter half of the ninth century. In England the ends of the chasuble took the shape of the reversed arch of the pointed style of architecture. From being used specially at the time of celebration it was emphatically called the vestment. Cranmer says, " The over-vesture or chesible signifieth the purple mantle that Pilate's soldiers put upon Christ after that they had scourged Him ; as touching the minister, it signifies charity a virtue excellent above all other."

Chef. A reliquary head. There is a fine one of St. Candidus of the ninth or tenth century, of wood plated with silver, and preserved in a church of Geneva. One of St. Eustace, from Basle, of the thirteenth century, is in the British Museum. At Chichester there was a Chapel of St. Richard's Head.

Chequer. The office of a monastic obedientiary.

Cherubic Hymn. In the Greek Church, a hymn sung by the choir before the great entrance, " Let us, who mystically represent the cherubim, and sing the holy hymn of the quickening Trinity, lay by at this time all worldly cares, that we may receive the King of Glory, invisibly attended [literally, borne on the spears like an emperor] by the angelic orders. Alleluia." The Greeks, in their liturgy, distinguish between the many-eyed cherubim and the six-winged seraphim.

Chests (Cope or Vestment) are of triangular shape, and remain at Gloucester, York, Salisbury, and Westminster. In the thirteenth century the synod of Exeter required a chest for books and vestments in every parish. Such parish chests of Early English date remain at Clymping, Stoke d'Abernon, Saltwood, and Graveney : of Decorated date at Brancepeth, Huttoft, and Haconby ; and of the Perpendicular period at St. Michael's, Coventry, and St. Mary's, Cambridge, and Oxford Cathedral. A " Flanders chest " remains at Guestling. Some very rude coffers, bound with iron, are preserved in some churches, and others are enriched with colour ; these are probably of late date. The material was often cypress or fir. Others are curiously painted, like one in the vestry of Lambeth Palace. Several Early English chests are preserved in the triforium of Westminster Abbey ; one is at Salisbury ; and another was removed from the Pyx Chapel to the Record Office.

Chevet. [*Capitium.*] The place representing where our Lord's head appeared upon the cross on the ground plan of a church, in which the altar represented His head, and the radiating

chapels the glory about it. Like the apsé, it took its origin
from the junction of the circular mortuary chapel with the
choir, by the removal of the intermediate walls in a basilica.
The tomb-house has been preserved at Canterbury, Sens,
Drontheim, Batalha, Burgos, and Murcia. The chevet
appears at Westminster, Pershore, and Tewkesbury. In
France its screen of tall pillars is very striking.

Chevron. An ornament of zigzag form used in Norman architecture.

Childermas. The old English name for Holy Innocents' Day.

Chimere. [*Zimarra, cymar.*] A mantle with sleeves, made
with a slit at the armpit, like the gown of a B.A. of Cambridge, which could be put on at pleasure. Archbishop
Scroop, when led to death, wore his blue chimere with sleeves
of the same colour ; and Archbishop Warham, in Holbein's
portrait, is represented in a dress of this kind over his
rochet. It was the everyday dress of a bishop, and, as
Becon says, its "black colour signifieth mortification to the
world and all worldly things, as the rochet purity and innocency of life." It was made of velvet, grogram, or satin,
and was open down the middle, for convenience in riding.
It is now made of black satin, and has the lawn sleeves of
the rochet sewn on to it; but really represents the scarlet
habit or sleeveless cope of a D.D., which was worn by
bishops in the reigns of Henry VIII. and Edward VI., as
now in Convocation and at the opening of Parliament.
Hooper objected to the colour ; and late in the reign of Queen
Elizabeth the present hue was adopted. It has been said
that the Parliament robe of bishops represents the old Cambridge D.D.'s gown, which, having been worn by Parker
when primate, was adopted by his suffragans at the time.

Choir. From a passage in an Epistle of Isidore Pelusiota,
it appears that in early times men and women singers
sang together. "The Apostles of the Lord, desiring to restrain unseemly talking in church, showing themselves to us
as masters of modesty and soberness, wisely permitted women
to sing in church." This custom was afterwards repealed,
and men placed on the south side and women on the north.
Durand says, that in secular churches the laity joined with
the choir, until the canons erected high screens as a shelter
from cold.

The word "choir" is first used by writers of the Western Church, and Isidore of Seville and Honorius of Autun derive it from the *corona* or circle of clergy or singers who surrounded the altar, as in the Temple of Jerusalem: the term occurs in the 18th canon of the Fourth Council of Toledo. Other writers have suggested *chorea* or *corona*, following Isidore's explanation; or *concordia*, from the concord of the singers, or the Greek *chara*, joy. But *chors* or *cors* (*à coercendo*) is Latin for an enclosed place, and may be allied with *Cor* in *Corwen* and *Banchor*, the *Kirrock* of Westmoreland, the Welsh *carreg*, Gaelic *carragh*, and Breton *chreach;* a circular form is said to be implied in the latter words, as in the Greek *choros*, Latin *corona*, etc.

The choir proper did not exist until the conversion of the Emperor Constantine, when the clergy were able to develope the services of the Church. In the Norman period it was very small, usually under the lantern, but was enlarged in the twelfth century, and still more in the thirteenth century, when it received a great expansion, from a length of two or three bays into a size equal to half or the whole of the western arm of the church. In the Norman period, the roof is often lower than that of the nave, and usually the choir itself is raised above the level of the western arm.

In the south-western districts of France and throughout Spain, as in the Lateran, St. Clement, St. Laurence Without, and St. Mary the Great at Rome, the choir occupies the centre of the nave with an enclosed passage to the sanctuary, the congregation being arranged between it and the sanctuary; this is probably an arrangement of modern times, as at Westminster in our own time. In parts of Italy the choir still retains its ancient position behind or eastward of the altar. In the Duomo of Fiesole, and at Lucca, there are two choirs, one behind and the other in front of the high-altar. In the north of Germany choirs are usually elevated upon crypts (as that of Milan stands raised over the confession), and shut in with solid stone screens: the same arrangements may be seen at Canterbury, Auch, Augsburg, Alby, Chartres, Bourges, St. Denis, Amiens, and Notre Dame, Paris; whilst Christchurch (Hants), Rochester, and Trebitsch Abbey are actually walled off from their aisles. At Winchester and St. Alban's, stone parcloses serve the same purpose. The Jesuits only never had a distinct choir, and the Franciscans and Dominicans severed their choirs wholly by the erection of a tall thin tower before their entrance. At one period, in France, Durandus mentions that it was the practice to hang a curtain in front of the choir, like the Lenten veil. In Continental cathedrals there is frequently both a summer and winter choir. Ceccoperius affirms that the bishop, in consideration of cold in winter, may allow the sacristy to be used for divine service; and if it or the tribune has a window or door in the direction of the high-altar, through which the people can hear and attend, the canons may use it without his licence, except upon festivals. The place is then called the choir, if four canons are present. At St. Peter's at Rome, the architectural choir is not used, and is known simply as the tribune; but, as in parts of Tuscany, the choir is placed in front of the altar. At St. Denis, a side chapel, as in other places a sacristy or chapter-house, serves as the winter choir. The present Rubric allows Morning and Evening Prayer to be used " in the accustomed place of the church, chapel, or chancel." At Canterbury, at one time, the early morning service was said in the chapter-house; at Oxford, Durham, and Lichfield (and formerly at Westminster), in the Lady Chapel; at St. Paul's, Salisbury, Lincoln, Gloucester, and Christ Church, Dublin, a side chapel was occupied for the same purpose; and the custom in several of these churches has not yet become obsolete. The Hours are sung at St. Peter's, Rome, in the Clementine Chapel. The south side of the choir is the right side, the left is that on the north, these positions being determined from the entrance on the west. The east walls of many churches, otherwise destroyed, often were allowed to stand, out of respect to their sanctity, even during the destruction at the Reformation,—as at Guisborough.

Choir Transept. The choir transept is the Ala Superior of Gervase, as Leland calls " the second transept of Salisbury, a light and division between the choir and presbytery." It usually marks the termination of the sanctuary, as the main transept marks the entrance of the choir. This additional structure would not only accommodate altars, but also sick and infirm monks and canons, who were permitted to attend in the retro-choir. M. Vitet gives twenty-four examples of this transept on the Continent, and attributes its origin to an Oriental source. M. Didron likewise refers it to the influence of Byzantium. M. Martin found it ordinarily in churches built before the Ogival period.

Choral Habit. In England the canons wore a surplice, a black close, and sleeveless cope, and the grey almuce or hood : regulars used the rochet, and monks their proper habit, but on the Continent the colours are more brilliant. At Pisa, in winter, they wear a large red cope, and in summer a red mozzetta over a rochet; at Salerno, crimson tunicles and rochets, and the hebdomadary wears violet ; at Urgel the cope was red, but at Tortosa and Gerona black ; at Valencia the cope worn over a rochet is superbly furred, and has a violet hood lined with ermine in winter, and with crimson silk in summer ; at Besançon the camail, or hood, is of blue silk, lined with red taffeta ; at Strasbourg the cope of red velvet is lined with ermine, and has gold guards ; at Catania the mozzetta of black cloth is worn over the rochet ; at Syracuse the mozzetta is violet, as at Malta, where it is used with a rochet and cope ; at Vienne the cope was black, at Rouen it was violet. At Burgos the canons wear in winter a cope, mozzetta, and a surplice with sleeves elevated on the shoulders. By the Council of Tortosa, 1429, the use of furs was restricted to dignitaries and cathedral canons ; but in some special cases in England priests vicars, who represented dignitaries or priest-canons, as at Exeter, and the subdean of minor canons at St. Paul's, wore a grey almuce, lined with black cloth ; at Burgos the vicars' surplices reached to the ground, and were rolled over the hands. At St. Paul's the vicars wore a plain almuce of black cloth, and lined or doubled cap. As early as 1386, the Council of Saltzburg required a distinction to be made in the choral dress of canons and vicars. Canons formerly wore violet only in their robes, until the Council of Trent changed the colour to black. At Ratisbon the choir-tippet, or mozzetta, is of red silk ; in France the camail is black, edged with the same colour, in the diocese of Bayeux ; in the south, as at Montauban, where it is crimson ermined, it is often rich in hue. At Verona blue cassocks are worn ; in Normandy they are scarlet for the choristers ; at Milan the scarlet cape and mantle are worn by canons ; the vicars carry furred capes on their arm, and the lay singers have hooded black mantles, faced with green.

Chorepiscopus. (1.) In the primitive Church the periodeutai, superintendents on circuits, as the Council of Laodicea calls them, or rural bishops without territorial titles, existed at an early date, certainly in the fourth century in the East, and were common in Africa. They cannot be traced before the fifth century in the Western Church; they acted as vicars or coadjutors of the city or diocesan bishops, who at length grew jealous of their authority, and the office was suppressed in the tenth century in the East. By the writings of St. Basil, it appears that they administered Confirmation, consecrated churches, gave the veil, superintended the clergy of the churches over which they presided, recommended candidates for ordination, in the presence of the bishop ordained deacons and priests, and, in his absence, clerks in minor orders, by the Councils of Antioch and Ancyra. They sat in councils along with bishops, and subscribed synodal acts at Neo-Cæsarea, Nicæa, and Chalcedon. In the West, from the seventh century, their rights were limited, as by the Council of Seville; in the eighth century Pope Leo II. forbade them to ordain priests, consecrate churches and chrism, or receive nuns; and at length, in the ninth century, their only authority extended over minor clerks,—the Council of Ratisbon, in 800, being the first to restrict them; until, in the tenth century, their powers were transferred to archpriests, plebans, or vicars-general, and the dignity and office of chorepiscopus had ceased to exist at the end of that period. They appear, however, to have exercised their functions in France in the twelfth, and in Ireland in the thirteenth century; indeed, in the latter country groups of bishops in one district or city were very common, and a trace of the custom survives in the titles of the Bishop of Meath, an aggregate of dioceses, and the Bishop of Ossory, whose See is St. Canice's, Kilkenny. (2.) The precentor of Cologne, as overseer of the choir, was called chorepiscopus. At Utrecht there are four chorepiscopi, or arch-subdeacons, acting as chief rural deans.

Choristers. Called in France children of the albs, or simply children of the choir. Those of Pope Vitalian, 659–669, were lodged and boarded in the parvise, as at Canterbury, Durham, and St. Paul's, they were known as the boys of the almonry. It is recorded of Gregory the Great, St. German, and Nizier, Archbishop of Lyons, that they used to attend the choir-boys' music school; and children were required to be church singers by the Councils of Aix-la-Chapelle and IV. Toledo. Pope Urban IV. was once a chorister of Troyes. We find them sometimes called clerks of the first or third form, according to the manner in which the rows of seats were numbered. They were usually under the charge of the succentor; but at Salisbury, where they were endowed, were intrusted to a canon, called the warden of the twelve boys. They carried the cross, censers, and tapers, and were promoted to be thuriblers, to hold minor orders, and, if worthy, advanced to the office of vicars. Their numbers varied between four and sixteen in various churches; all received the first tonsure, and were maintained at the tables of one of the canons, whom they regarded as their master, and attended. Probably the ordinary arrangement was, that a portion of the number acted as singers, and the rest as assistants at the altar. In the seventeenth century, at Hereford, they were required to be taught to play on the lyre and harp in choir. In process of time they ceased to subsist on the canons' alms; and at Lincoln they appear first to have been boarded in a house, under a master; and the excellent precedent was followed at Lichfield at the close of the fifteenth century. Their dress was a surplice.

Chrism *and* **Holy Oil.** By the Council of Melde, the priest on Maundy Thursday had three cruets brought to him, in which were the consecrated oil of the catechumens, chrism, and oil of the sick. There were two kinds of holy oil. (1.) Chrism, or myron, called principal, a compound of oil and balsam, with which candidates for baptism were anointed upon the head and confirmed on the forehead; and clerks to be ordained received unction with it. (2.) Simple: the pure oil of olives; also consecrated by a bishop for the anointing of the sick and energumens, and of catechumens on the breast, shoulders, and forehead. Chrism at first was made only of oil by both Latins and Greeks. In the sixth century, balm brought from Judæa was mixed with it; and this kind was in use in the West until the sixteenth century,

when the Spaniards, by permission of Paul III. and Pius
IV., adopted balm from India. The Greeks use, instead of
balm, forty different kinds of aromatic spices. Unction was
regarded as the spiritual preparation of Christians to wrestle
against the devil, and in memory of the anointing of Christ
to His burial. A bishop is anointed on the head and hands.
The baptized was anointed previously with oil on the breast
and between the shoulders, and after baptism with chrism
on the head and brow. In allusion to 1 St. John ii. 17;
2 Cor. i. 21; 1 Peter iii. 9, kings at their consecration,
altars and churches at dedication are anointed. The baptismal unction is mentioned by Pope Sylvester in 324.
Priests anointed the breast, and bishops the forehead of
candidates. Chrism is called myrrh by the ancient writers;
it was symbolical of the sweet savour of Christ, and of the
anointing of His members by the Holy Spirit to be His
peculiar people—a royal priesthood. (Exod. xxx. 25-30;
Numb. iii. 3; 1 Sam. xxiv. 6; St. Luke iv. 18; Acts iv. 27,
x. 38; 2 Cor. i. 21; 1 Peter ii. 9.) Consecration of chrism
was reserved to bishops only who distributed it to the parish
priests. In the fifth century this ceremonial was fixed to
Maundy Thursday, and during the second of the three
Masses celebrated on that day, which, in consequence, was
called the Mass of Chrism. However, in France, the Council of Meaux, in 845, permitted consecration on any day, as
in primitive times; and the Greeks, although regarding
Maundy Thursday as the principal occasion, still follow the
same practice, but reserve it to the patriarchs, who perform
the office with great pomp. The vase for keeping chrism,
from its shape, was called the chrism-paten. In the tenth
century it was fetched by the priest before Easter, or by a
deacon or subdeacon in the thirteenth century. All that
remained over from the last year was carefully consumed by
fire. By the Council of Orange, 441, chrism was used once
for all in baptism. The chrism and holy oil were kept
under lock and key, to provide against any abuse to purposes of sorcery and witchcraft, in the thirteenth century.
In 1549 children were still anointed with chrism on the
forehead in England. In lieu of this ceremony, we now
invoke the grace of the Holy Ghost. Bale says that the
chrism was kept in alabaster boxes.

Chrismarium. The place where confirmation was administered at Rome and Naples; called also consignatorium—the place of sealing. Sacristies were frequently used for this purpose.

Chrismatory. A vase for holding chrism; that used by William of Wykeham is preserved in New College, Oxford.

Christian Name. (St. James ii. 7; 1 St. Peter iv. 14–16.) As the name of Jesus is incommunicable as that of the Saviour, His disciples were called Christians, because they receive of His fulness, and have the unction of the Holy Spirit communicated to them. A name was given to children at baptism to remind them of their solemn profession, and that worthy name by which they are called. A similar custom prevailed at circumcision—the analogous Jewish rite. Clement I. required candidates for baptism to go to their priest, and give in their names, and then be taught the mysteries. Heathen names were prohibited, and those of apostles or saints usually adopted as memorials and examples of godly living. This spiritual name was entered in the Baptismal Register. In case of an immodest or uncomely name being given in baptism, the bishop at Confirmation might alter it, by Peckham's 'Constitutions.' In 1549 the bishop mentioned the Christian name of the candidate at Confirmation.

Christmas. The birthday of our Lord; which Pope Julius I. confirmed to be kept on December 25; and St. Chrysostom, in the fourth century, speaks of the feast as of great antiquity; Clement of Alexandria, in the beginning of the third century, speaks of it, but refers it to April 19 or 20, or May 20; and sermons of St. Basil and St. Gregory Nazianzen, preached on this day, are still extant. St. Epiphanius reckons it on January 6, but St. Augustine on December 25. From the West the observation of the day passed to the Eastern Church in the fourth century; as Chrysostom says, the feast was unknown at Antioch ten years before the time he was preaching, that is, probably as kept on December 25, the day hitherto observed having been January 6. The Latins, and Africa, and the Greek Church, generally, however, held the Nativity on December 25, as appears from St. Jerome, St. Augustine, St. Chrysostom, St. Basil, and St. Gregory Nazianzen. The Orientals in Egypt,

Cyprus, Antioch, and Palestine, appear to have observed, for a time only January 6, as the feast of the Nativity and Epiphany, or Theophania, a name equally applicable to both, as St. Gregory Nazianzen observes. However, about the beginning of the fifth century the Nativity was commemorated, in the East, on December 25, and the Epiphany on the later day. In the sixth century, beyond doubt, East and West agreed in their observance. The Basque call it the New Day, because all things are become new—old things are passed away. Christmas Eve is called in Celtic the Night of Mary; in Germany, the Holy Night; in Portugal, the Pasch of the Nativity; and in old English, Yule Merriment. In the Isle of Man the peasants bring tapers to church, and sing carols; and in Germany they beat with mallets on the house door, to symbolize the anxiety of the spirits in prison to learn the glad tidings of the Nativity. There were three Masses on this day,—one at midnight on the eve [except in the Gallican, Mozarabic, and Armenian rites], commemorating the actual birth of our Lord; the second at dawn or cock-crow, its revelation to man in the shepherds; and the third at noon, the eternal sonship of the Holy Child Jesus. Two Masses were said in France in the time of St. Gregory of Tours; but three Masses were not introduced into Spain until the fourteenth century, nor at Milan until the fifteenth century. In the Medieval Church there was a representation of the shepherds, as at Lichfield, with a star gleaming in the vault; and so lately as 1821 the Flemish preserved the same custom, and the peasants entering with sheep offered eggs and milk, whilst Midnight Mass was being said at the high-altar. From the time of St. Augustine, Midnight Mass was said on the eve; and the Councils of Orleans and Toledo required all persons to attend their cathedral church, under pain of excommunication for three years by the Council of Agde. The Christmas-box was a box made of earthenware in the seventeenth century, in which apprentices placed the rewards of their industry given them at that season.

Chronogram. Words in an inscription, so placed that the numeral letters give the date of a certain event thus recorded. The earliest instance occurs in stained glass, c. 1062, at St. Peter's, Aix. There is another, of the time of

Charles I., on the cieling of the lantern of Winchester. The only letters which can be used are M, C, L, X, V, I.

Chrysom. A white linen vesture, tightly fitting and girdled, which reached to the feet, was given to the newly-baptized as a warning to put on the new robe of regeneration and holiness, that they might hereafter, in the resurrection, walk in white (Rev. vi. 11). The form of words was as follows :— "Take this white unspotted robe that ye may bear it without spot before the judgment seat of our Lord Jesus Christ, and have life eternal." This albe having been worn seven days, in recollection of the sevenfold gifts of the Spirit, was put off in the church or baptistery, and, having been washed, preserved there. After the disuse of this albe children to be baptized were brought in a chrysom, casula, or sabanus, which was delivered to the sponsors as a token of the innocency given by God's grace in baptism and of that to which the baptized should give themselves. At the churching of the infant's mother the chrysom was presented to the priest to be used for making surplices, or coverings for the chalice, or for some similar purpose.

Church. In Greek *kyriake*, used by Eusebius, the Councils of Ancyra, Laodicea, and Neo-Cæsarea, like the Latin *dominicum*, the Lord's house ; in Germany a cathedral is called, by a union of these terms, the Dom Kirche ; in Italy simply Duomo, as Mayence was known as the Dom ; and in Lancashire there is a Church-kirk. In Scotland and in the Danish settlements in England the form "kirk" was adopted. We have also the Latin word *ecclesia* preserved in Eccleston, Eccleshall, Eccles, and Beccles. The earliest church property so called dates from the reign of Alexander Severus, 222–235. Optatus of Milevi mentions forty churches at Rome. From the time of Gallienus (260) to the edict of Diocletian for their destruction in 303, the Christians had their use ; and the Acts of St. Theodotus of Ancyra, martyred by that Emperor, allude to an apsidal church. The original Christian churches were oblong, looking eastward, with the chambers of the clergy on either side, and two western doors as separate entrances for men and women. Afterwards churches were built in various forms,—in the shape of a cross, square, or round ; the former were vaulted, and the latter had wooden cielings. All were apsidal, and their orientation is called by Paulinus "the more usual form;" but Stephen, Bishop of Tournay, speaks of it as a peculiarity of St. Benet's, Paris, in a letter to Pope Lucius III., and in some Italian churches at his day, the celebrant at the altar faces the west. About the year 1000—the fancied millennium of some ancient writers—architecture came nearly to a stand-still. Churches were not repaired, much less rebuilt; for, as William of Tyre said, the evening of days seemed to have fallen upon the world and the coming of the Son of Man to draw near; whilst charters of foundation, rare as they were, bore the ominous heading, "forasmuch as the world's end approacheth." But about the beginning of the eleventh century confidence was restored, and an era of church building so universal set in that Ralph Glaber says that it seemed "the world was putting off its dingy vesture and donning a pure white robe."

Churches, in their threefold longitudinal division of nave, choir, and sanctuary, correspond to the arrangement of the Temple, with its court of the Gentiles, the worldly sanctuary, and holy of holies. They have also a triple elevation, containing the base-arcade, triforium, and clerestory, and also three parts laterally formed by the main body of the structure and its aisles.

Churches are distinguished into various grades, the patriarchal, primatial, and metropolitan, according to the rank of their presidents : cathedral, as containing a bishop's cathedra or See; collegiate, which are composed of a chapter and dean; conventual, if belonging to a religious community; abbeys, those under an abbot, or priories, if governed by a prior; minsters, when attached to a monastery or of imposing size; parochial, if furnished with a font.

Church-Ales. Festivals at which the benefactions of the people at their sports and pastimes being collected, were devoted to recast the bells, repair towers, beautify churches, and raise stocks and funds for the poor.

Church Books were divided into several classes. There were six reading books: the 'Bibliotheca,' a collection of the books of the Bible by St. Jerome; the 'Homilar,' the homilies used on Sundays and certain festivals; the 'Passionar,' containing the acts of martyrs; the 'Legendary,' an account of confessors; the 'Lectionary,' the Epistles of St. Paul;

and the 'Sermologus,' sermons of the Popes and Fathers read on certain days. The song and ritual books are mentioned under their titles. It was the custom till of recent years for women-servants to carry their church books in a clean white handkerchief,—a relic of the old custom in the Western Church for women to receive the Eucharist in a linen cloth. To this day the altar-rail at Wimborne Minster is covered at the time of Holy Communion with a white cloth.

Church Reeves (from *greefa*, a steward). Church wardens, officers chosen to maintain order during divine service and as trustees of the church goods and furniture. In Spain they are called operarii, and in France marguilliers (*meriglerii*), from the marel, or token of lead which was given by them to the priests who attended service as a qualification for receiving payment. .They appear as Melinglerii at Cefalu, Catania, and Monte Regale.

Churchyards. The dead were not buried, in the earlier times, in the outer court of the church, but examples of the praotice occur in the fourth century, and after the sixth century it became general. The churchyard, under the name of atrium, is first mentioned with the garden near the church in 740 in the 'Excerptions' of Ecgbright. Cuthbert, Archbishop of Canterbury, is said to have introduced the use of churchyards as burial-places into England. So lately as 1791 the burial-yard of the cathedral only was used at Hereford. Fairs and markets were prohibited in churchyards by Act of Parliament in 1285, and another Act of Henry VI. proscribed the former in them on Sundays; but at the period of the Reformation they were often profaned by the revellings of summer lords in May, and by mummers in winter time, and noisy revels and banquets were held under tents in them on the former occasion. The indecent practice was at length suppressed, and in 1623 the privilege of sanctuary was taken from churchyards. The first recorded instance of a formal consecration of a churchyard is mentioned by Gregory of Tours in the sixth century.

Ciborium. (1.) A pavilion or dome-shaped canopy or cupola, mentioned by St. Chrysostom, resting upon two, four, or six pillars, with arched faces, erected over the altar of a basilica. It resembled a little church, and so some medieval churches were called *ciboria*. Its curtains were called the four veils or *circitorium* (enclosure). These were raised at the elevation only. The priest on entering within them used the appropriate prayer of the veil. A curtain, called the *antependium*, or frontal, hung before the tomb-like part of the altar or sepulchre containing the relics of saints. It was usually surmounted with a cross, and under it was suspended a dove or cup of gold or silver containing the reserved Eucharist. Occasionally, the larger included a smaller ciborium, which was called the peristerium, from covering the dove in which the sacrament was reserved; as we often find mention both of the peristerium and dove together. Sometimes, from its floral ornament, the ciborium was called lilia or malum. The curtains being in memory of the veil of the Temple, probably disappeared when palls and corporals were introduced. Bishop Jewel calls it the "meat tent;" and it took its name from the sacred food (*cibus sacer*) reserved in it; or more probably, from kiborion, the outer cup-like covering of the Egyptian bean, which its dome resembled. The Greeks still use it in this sense, having a silver bottle in the tabernacle for the element destined for the communion of the sick. (2.) A pyx; a silver vase, like a chalice, for the reserved host,—a modern use. At Battle in 1140 a dove-shaped ciborium is mentioned. The cross which had covered the ciborium, at length, was placed on the altar.

The ciboria or domes were used until the thirteenth century, and Gothic examples remain at St. Paul's Without, St. Clement, St. Agnes, St. John Lateran, St. Mary Cosmedin, St. Cecilia Trastavere, Rome, Gercy Abbey, Brie, and Lugo. They were imitations of the sepulchral recess of the catacomb. The first silver ciborium was erected at Rome, with four pillars, by Pope Symmachus, and another in 824 by Pope Eugenius II. All the tapers round the ciborium on great festivals, like those of the Gothic rood-beam, were lighted. The Greeks have ciboria, with the calendar of feasts, in their naves. In 1549 it was called "some other comely thing prepared for the purpose" of holding the Eucharistic bread.

Cieling. (*Ciel, cœlum.*) The under part of a roof. There are painted ·cielings at Peterborough and St. Alban's. The Norman cieling was usually flat. There are wooden cielings at Winchester and York with bosses, an Early Decorated one of plaster at Rochester, and a very rich wooden cieling at Cirencester. Ely has a superb modern specimen.

Cimeliarch. The muniment keeper in a foreign cathedral.

Circumcision. The octave of Christmas. Its present name does not date earlier than the sixth or seventh century, and commemorates the shedding of our Lord's infant blood in conformity with the Mosaic law. The festival was established in the time of Leo the Great, but its occurrence of January 1 is not mentioned before the Council of Tours, held in 567. It is marked in the ancient calendars, and in the martyrology of St. Jerome, Bede, and Usuardus. The 'Sacramentary' of St. Gregory defines it "in the Lord's octave." The day was fixed in order to efface the relics of pagan superstition; and so in ancient missals two Masses are appointed, one being called the Mass to divert from idols. A fast was also observed at Milan and elsewhere, until the ninth century. In 578 the Council of Auxerre prohibited Christians from disguising themselves as stags or calves on the kalends of January, and a penitential of Angers enjoined three years' penance for a similar offence. The Second Council of Tours, in 567, required all priests and monks to have public prayer in church on this day; and the Council in Trullo forbade the observation of the kalends.

Cistercians. Grey or white monks; a reformed order of the Benedictines, founded by Robert of Molesme and Stephen Harding, an Englishman, at Citeaux, in Burgundy, in 1098. They came to England and settled at Waverley in 1128. From their eminent refounder, Bernard of Clairvaux, in 1113, they were often called Bernardines. They were distinguished by their silence, austerity, labour in the field, their grey or white habit, and dislike to ornament in their buildings. They erected their abbeys in lonely places, usually well-wooded and watered valleys, far away from human habitation, and were principally noted by their success as graziers, shepherds, and farmers. The short choir, the transeptal aisle, divided into certain chapels, the low central tower, the grisaille glass in the windows, the solitary bell, the absence of tessellated pavements, pictures, mural colour, and many lights in their churches; the regular and almost invariable arrangement of the conventual buildings, with the dormitory at the eastern side of the cloister, communicating with the transept by a flight of stairs ; the refectory set at right angles to the cloister; the chapter-house divided into aisles, except at Margam in Wales, are unfailing notes of the houses of the order.   There were in later days modifications of this extreme rigour in the towers of Fountains and Furness, and noble choirs of the former church, Rievaulx, and Sallay; in the exceptional apse of Beaulieu, and the chevet of Croxden, with its crown of radiating chapels and the use of stained glass and armorial tiles.   But in general the character of extreme simplicity, verging on baldness, was preserved.   Only one abbey church, that of Scarborough, remains in use; the rest are in ruins or destroyed.   At Buildwas, Jorevalle, Melrose, Byland Rievaulx, Ford, Merevale, Boyle, Tintern, Lilleshall, Kirkstall, and Netley, it is still possible to trace the ground plan, or reconstruct the arrangement of the ancient buildings.   The absence of an eastern Lady Chapel in England is always observable.   No such adjunct was ever built, because the entire church was dedicated to St. Mary.   The square east end may be said to have been universal in this country, for there were but two instances to the contrary ; but, with the exception of Citeaux, which was square-ended, the finest minsters on the Continent presented an apse or chevet.   The triforium story was rare in England.

Clamacteria.   Little bells attached to crowns of light.

Claustrals, or persons of the house.   In a Benedictine monastery, the abbot, prior major, subprior, third and fourth priors, who held chapter and collation, celebrated Mass, and presided in hall, the precentor, master of the novices, and succentor.

Claviger.   A canon who keeps the keys of the chapter seal and chests.   There are usually two or three such officers at a time.

Clavus.   A broad band of embroidery arabesque or rich stuff of purple coloured, worn on vestments.   The deacon wore it narrow ; the priest had a broad stripe.   The laticlave of the colobium was a wide band, reached from the neck to the feet.   In the chasuble it was pall-shaped, and called the pectoral, dorsal, and onophorion, auriclave, and orphrey.   It also occurs reaching no lower than the chest, where it is covered with roundles of metal and edged with little balls.

Clear-story, or over-story. The upper range of windows in a church, in contradistinction to the triforium, or blind-story.

Clergy. [From *kleros*, a lot or heritage.] God's inheritance. The bishops, priests, and deacons of the Church, who are called clerks in holy orders. As they were at one time the only educated persons in the country, all scholars were known as clerks.

Clerk-ales. A feast in which, when the clerk's wages were small, the richer parishioners sent in provisions for a banquet, and gave him more liberally than his quarterly payment would amount to in many years.

Clerk of the Closet. The confessor to the Sovereign, whose office it is to attend at the right-hand during divine service, to resolve all doubts respecting spiritual matters, and to wait in the private oratory or clóset, where the chaplains in turn said prayers.

Clerks of the Vestry or Vestibule. Men in charge of the sacristy, with the furniture for High Mass, and the copes. At Durham they slept at night over the west end of the vestry, and, with two others, acted as bell-ringers. The latter slept in a chamber opposite the sacristan's chequer in the north alley. There were three clerks of the vestibule at York.

Clochier. A detached campanile. At St. Paul's it contained the mote bell, which summoned the citizens to folkmotes, or musters of arms, on their parade ground.

Clock. A mechanical clock at Clugny, made by Peter de Chalus, is mentioned in the middle of the fourteenth century. A contemporaneous clock, with automata to strike the hours, formerly at Glastonbury, is now preserved at Wells. In the fourteenth century, Abbot Wallingford gave an astronomical clock to St. Alban's; and in 1324 T. de Louth, treasurer, presented to Lincoln a clock "as was common in cathedrals and the greater conventual churches." At Padua, Bologna, and Paris, church clocks are mentioned of the same date. At Dijon, Wells, and Strasbourg, there are curious processions of little moving figures made at the hours, which are struck also by automata. The invention of clocks with a wheel and escapement is attributed variously to Pacificus, a deacon of Verona, in the ninth century, and to Gerbert of

M

Rheims, subsequently Pope Sylvester II., who died in 1003.
A clock to mark the hours in choir for commencing divine
service remains at Toledo, with automata; at Rheims, in the
north wing of the transept; at Westminster, in the south
wing, near the vestry; and at Beauvais, in the north choir
aisle. There is also a mechanical clock of 1508 at Lyons.
The choir bell, or nota, of Durand was formerly hung at the
entrance of the choir for the same purpose, of giving due
warning; and then the great campana in the belfry and the
signa of the tower sounded the summons to the faithful. The
choir bell inside the church is also mentioned by Reginald
of Durham.

Cloissonné. The older method of enamelling, where the hollows in the ground were made by thin strips of metal sol-
dered on to it.

Cloister. (*Claustrum*, an enclosure; Germ. Kreuzgang.) A
court surrounded by covered ways, called alleys; the central
space, or garth, was planted with trees and flowers; and at
Oseney, Chester, Durham, and other places had a conduit
and fountain in the centre. It was known as the laurel
court at Peterborough; the palm court, as connected with
the ceremonial of Palm Sunday, at Wells; and the Sprice
at Chester, a corruption of Paradise, as it was called at
Chichester and Winchester, having been either filled with
earth from the Holy Land, or, more probably, because it
was the Lord's garden, sown with the seeds of the resurrection "harvest." The enclosed portion of the forecourt of
the basilica was also called the paradise, and from the surrounding porticoes the cloister took its origin. Each alley of
the quadrangle in a monastery was placed under the government of the obedientiary, or officer whose chequer or place of
business adjoined it; it was considered to form part of the
church. The usual arrangement was this: the refectory
invariably on the side opposite or parallel to the minster;
the dormitory on the east, or otherwise on the west; sometimes the latter site was occupied by the guest house, or the
bedchamber of the converts, or lay brothers; a large central
space for air, light, and recreation was thus secured in the
utmost privacy, whilst passages communicated with all the
principal buildings. The alleys were allotted to various
uses: that lying next the hall being forbidden to the bre-

thren at most times. The western alley was occupied by the novices, and the northern alley by the monks in times of study; the eastern side was used at the maundy, and the usual Sabbatical feet-washing. The abbot, or superior, sat next the east door of the cloister, near the entrance of the church.

In some monasteries, as Fountains, Beaulieu, Jorevalle, Netley, Stoneley, Wroxhall, Kirkstall, and originally at St. Alban's, there were only, it would seem, alleys of timber-work, which have long since perished. Other cloisters, such as Durham and Peterborough, were enriched with a superb series of stained glass; and the fan-traceried vaulting at Gloucester is a marvel of the most elaborate stone-work.

At night four lanterns were lighted at the four angles of the cloister, and in front of the chapter-house door. A procession was daily made through its entire circuit. In the eighth century abbots were frequently buried in the centre of the garth.

Many secular cathedrals, as three in Wales, Lichfield, and York, and most collegiate churches, as Southwell, Ripon, and Manchester, were unprovided with cloisters. In many foreign minsters, as Maulbronn, Pay, Münster, Caen, Pontigny, Puy-en-Velay, Braga, Batalha, Siguença, Leon, Toledo, Gerona, Huesca, Mayence, and Toulouse; the cloisters were on the north side, to secure shade in a hot climate, or rather, perhaps, for water-supply and drainage, as at Sherborne, Canterbury, Gloucester, Chester, Magdalen College (Oxford), Cartmel, St. Mary Overye, St. David's, Tintern, Malmesbury, Milton Abbas, Moyne, Muckross, Adare, Kilmallock, and the Dominican churches of Paris, Agen, and Toulouse. In some other churches they occupied an abnormal position on the north of the choir at Tarragona and Lincoln, and southward of it at Burgos, Rochester, and Chichester; and at Lerida, Olite, New College (Oxford), and Brantome on the west of the church. At Hereford there was a chantry of Our Lady Arbour, over the vestibule of the chapter-house; and chapels, in the centre of the sward at Winchester College, Hildesheim, and Old St. Paul's, in which Masses of Requiem were sung for the repose of the souls of persons buried in the garth. The cloisters of Verona, Pisa, and Subiaco, of Zurich, Batalha, Beauport,

Fontenelle, and Caen are among the finest foreign examples. At Bamberg there are two cloisters, one on the north and the second to the south; at Tarragona and Ratisbon, are two on the north-east of the church; at Hildesheim the cloister is eastward of it. Sometimes the ordinary fourth alley of the quadrangle is wanting, as at Wells, Toul, Canigo, and Hereford. At Evesham there were, and at Norwich there still exist, rooms over the cloisters. The infirmary in England had often its separate cloister, as at Gloucester, Westminster, and Canterbury; and in foreign monasteries the subordinate cloister was allotted for the use of the copyists and communication with the lodgings of the conventual officers. At St. Paul's there was a two-storied cloister, enclosing the chapter-house. There is another instance at St. Juan in Toledo. The Carthusians built round their cloister cells of solitaries, containing three rooms, in one of which *missæ siccæ* might be celebrated; the Certosas at Florence and Pavia still preserve the arrangement, which, at the foundation of monasteries, was a necessity, as we find the monks at Battle living at first in little houses, and at Stoneley the Cistercians occupying " dwelling-places of tents," whilst at Fountains the earliest brotherhood lodged under the yew-trees that grew upon the slopes. Marburg presents the remarkable type of two choirs, two rood-screens, two towers at each end, and two cloisters,—one on the north and another on the south.

The Eastern monasteries have usually a large central space, round which is a colonnade communicating with the houses of the inmates. In Ireland, Spain, Italy, and France, the windows were unglazed, resembling open arcades.

Close. The enclosure of a cathedral, surrounded by a wall, and bordered by the houses of the dignitaries, canons, and minor members of the foundation. In the fourteenth century, Wells, Lichfield, Lincoln, and Exeter were enclosed with walls; and in the following century St. David's (Hereford), and St. Paul's, owing to the acts of violence perpetrated within the precinct by robbers, and the danger accruing to the canons on their way to church. In the twelfth century the canons in English cathedrals had their separate houses, and the dignitaries possessed oratories attached to them. The close included also a chapter-house, library, school, vicars' college, and, in some instances, a cloister, as at Hereford, Chichester, Wells, Salisbury, St. Paul's, St. David's, Exeter, and Lincoln. Large gate-houses at various points gave access to the precinct. At Bury St. Edmund's the precinct, in the tenth century, was marked by four crosses, at the four cardinal points of the abbey-jurisdiction. Some of the ancient houses remain at Chichester, Exeter, Wells, and Bayeux. Markets, fairs, and every kind of traffic were forbidden in the close, which usually extended to a distance of 180 feet on each side of the church. The well-kept close is peculiar to England.

Clugniacs. A reformed order of Benedictines, founded by Berno, abbot of Gigny, in 912, at Clugny, in Burgundy. In 1077 they came to England, in the time of Henry II., and established their first house at Lewes, under the patronage of the Earl Warrenne. The parent house was Clugny, and they had also noble minsters at Charité-sur-Loire, Vezelay, Taunus, Bromholm, Meaux, Pontefract, Castle Acre, Wenlock, Bermondsey, and Thetford. The chief peculiarity of their churches in France was a large ante-church for penitents. The transept was usually without aisles; but St. Bernard, in 1127, inveighed against their luxury, the enormous height, excessive breadth, empty space, and sumptuous ornament of their churches. The dress of the order was a black frock, a pelisse, a hood of lamb's wool, red hose, a white woollen tunic, and black scapular: and in choir, copes of linen: in cloister and refectory, a white pall; and in times of labour a white scapular. Their first churches, like those of Cistercians, were dedicated to St. Mary; their rule was a composition of those of St. Benedict and St. Augustine. They prohibited the use of organs, and all superfluous carving and pictures, but allowed painted crosses of wood. In England their churches were very irregular in plan. At length they became the most luxurious order in their mode of living: and Peter of Clugny upbraids them with their extravagance in no measured terms. Some of their monasteries were double, composed of men and women. The early peculiarities of their rule were, the dipping of the Eucharist in the chalice; the use of furs for the sick or delicate; admission of novices before a year's probation; the reception of a fugitive monk after three cases of offence; absence of manual labour, and the custom for abbots to dine always with the brethren. The Clugniacs wore a pelisse, a frock, and a cowl of scarlet cloth, to show their readiness to shed their blood for the sake of Christ; they slept in their shirts. They had three or four courses at dinner, two being regarded as a caritas, and shared among two monks; electuaries, spiced and perfumed, and delicate cooking were used; the abbot entertained his guests, and any monks whom he invited, in the hall. Women might enter the monastery; and convents of nuns were placed under the rule of the abbots; the bishop appointed and deposed them, and acted as visitor in difficult cases. No manual labour was practised, and conversation was freely allowed. The churches were beautifully and richly adorned; incense was much used, and the ceremonial was elaborate. The guests' feet were not washed, but in lieu three poor men were admitted to the lavanda. After vigils they returned to sleep in their dormitory. Their houses were built in populous places.

Clustered Column. A combination of several shafts to form one pillar.

Coadjutor. An assistant to a bishop, or to a dignitary, or a canon, called " fictitious ;" in the latter cases having the right of succession, and taking precedence of canons in the representatives of dignitaries.

Cock is set on church-towers in Germany, France, and England, as a symbol of the resurrection at the dawn of the great day, as Christ's rising took place at cock-crow; of Christian courage; of pastoral vigilance, and a warning of St. Peter's fall. It occurred on the top of the Norman tower of Winchester.

Coffin (*cophinus*). Joseph was carried from Egypt to Canaan in a coffin, and the early Christians adopted the custom of the heathens in using coffins. Stone coffins were ordered for the interment of monks by Abbot Warin, of St. Alban's, 1183-95; they had hitherto been buried under the green turf. In the tenth and two following centuries a low coped coffin of stone, with a hollow for the body, and a circular cavity for the head, was in use; one palm deep in St. Anselm's time. The boat shape is the most ancient, the ridge being next in point of age. St. Richard of Chichester, in the thirteenth century, was buried in a wooden coffin. Those of the Templars, in the Temple Church (London), are of lead, decorated with ornaments of elaborate design in low relief. An old legend represents St. Cuthbert, in his stone coffin, floating down the Tweed.

Collar. The neck-cloth worn by the clergy does not date earlier than the beginning of the eighteenth century. The ruff of the time of Elizabeth fell into desuetude before the falling collars of the time of James and Charles I.

Collation. (1.) The free assignment of a vacant canonry or benefice. (2.) Reading of devout books from the pulpit by the reader of the week, followed by an exposition from the superior in chapter. (3.) A sermon after a funeral. (4.) A lecture on the Catechism in 1622. (5.) The monastic supper. During the first four centuries there was but one meal taken a day, and that was supper (*cœna*). When the midday meal was adopted, a slender repast of bread, wine, and dry fruit, not worthy of the name of supper, was taken after Vespers, during the reading the Scripture or Fathers, called the collation—and so the name was given to the meal, and adopted by laymen and priests. The jentaculum, or breakfast, was made on a basin of soup.

Collect. (1.) A church appointed as the starting-point and place of assembly of a procession going to a station, as, for instance, the collect was at St. Sabina, on the Aventine, when the station was fixed at the basilica of St. Paul. (2.) A prayer so called, because collected into one form out of many petitions, or from the people being joined in as one, or because offered for the whole collective Church, or a particular church. Most collects end "through Jesus Christ," because the Father bestows His gifts through the mediation of Christ only. The five parts of a collect are the invocation, the reason on which the petition is founded, the petition itself, the benefit hoped for, ascription of praise, or mention of the Lord Jesus, or both. The collects in the Mass were composed by Pope Gelasius. At St. Alban's, in the twelfth century, they were limited to seven. The collects were included in the Collectar, and the collects at the end of the Communion Service, Matins, and Evensong, etc., fulfil the definition of Micrologus, as the concluding prayer in an office, in which the priest gathers up and collects all the prayers of the people, to offer them to God. Out of the eighty-three used in the English Church, fifty-nine are traceable to the sixth century.

College. (Many collected into one.) (1.) In the province of Canterbury the bishops form a college, in which the Bishop of London is dean, the Bishop of Winchester subdean and chancellor, the Bishop of Salisbury precentor; since the time of St. Osmund, in place of the Bishop of Winchester, the Bishop of Lincoln is vice-chancellor, the Bishop of Worcester chaplain, and the Bishop of Rochester cross-bearer to the primate. In the absence of the latter, the Bishop of London presides in the provincial synod. (2.) A church inferior to a cathedral, which is served by persons living in common. At Oxford, Gloucester College was composed of halls which were filled with Benedictine students of Gloncester, Abingdon, St. Alban's, Tewkesbury, and Tavistock.

Collegiate Churches took their origin in the impossibility of receiving all the applicants for canonries in cathedral, so that it was necessary to turn parish churches into capitular foundations. They were also attached to great schools, as Winchester and Eton, and to hospitals. They are inferior churches, with members living in common, and not possessing a bishop's chair. They were always built in towns or cities of importance, and their president was a graduate. At Southwell and Beverley, the Archbishop of York was head of the chapter; at Bosham, the Bishop of Exeter; at Penkridge, the Archbishop of Dublin. St. Patrick's (Dublin) is united to the cathedral of Christchurch; and there are similar combinations at Mantua, Cremona, Sisteron, Montauban, Calahorra, and Calcada; but Bath and Wells, Lichfield and Coventry, were examples of Benedictines united to secular canons, to form a combined chapter. The Pope distinguished some of these churches by the title of *insignis*, or eminent, when united to another foundation, or by special favour; but the title was conveyed in common report also, or by position in a town of great importance. In Italy, and by canon law, the chapter had the patronage of the canonries.

Collet. The English name for an acolyth.

Colobium. [Gr. *kolobos*, curt.] A white tabard, or sleeveless tunic, which was at length superseded by the use of the dalmatic. It was also called the *lebitonarium*, as proper to deacons; was ornamented with the *clavus*, or purple band, or with *calliculæ*, or the *paragaudas*, little disks, and a fringe of balls.

Colours, Ecclesiastical. Festivals were distinguished by white, as emblematical of the purity of the life of saints, and by red, as symbolical of the heroism of the death of martyrs. VIO-LET, mentioned by Durandus, in addition to white, red, black, and green, was used on common days and in Advent, Lent, and on vigils, as the penitential colour nearest to black; and GREEN, the hue of hope and spring, from the octave of Epiphany to Septuagesima, and from the octave of Pentecost to Advent, in anticipation of the joys to which the doors have been opened by the resurrection and ascension of our Saviour, and by the descent of the Holy Ghost. At burials, Masses of the dead, and on Good Friday, BLACK is worn; and by the Salisbury use, Crocus or SAFFRON, gold colour, on feasts of the confessors, emblematical of the preciousness of their faith; but at Laon on Good Friday, in allusion to the envy of the Jews. RED, by the Salisbury use, was used on Ash Wednesday, Sundays in Lent, and the three latter days of Holy Week, as the symbol of sin (Isaiah i. 18); as the sign of majesty and might on Sundays (Isaiah lxiii. 1); and of blood in the commemoration of the passion, death, and burial of our crucified Lord; and so on Good Friday at Bourges, Sens, Mans, and by the Ambrosian rite. The latter uses it also on Corpus Christi, as the great mystery of Christ's love, and, like the Church of Lyons, on the Circumcision, in memory of the first shedding of His blood, and the first act of His love; whereas the Roman use employs white on the former day, in allusion to the mystery of faith; red on Pentecost personifies the divine love of the Holy Spirit; and in funeral services of the Greeks, and the ancient rites of France, and by the Pope on Good Friday, as showing that love is the cause of their sorrow. Red is the ordinary colour of the Salisbury and Ambrosian rites, as green is of the Roman. Red was used in Lent, being the vigil of the Passion, from Septuagesima to Easter eve, at Bourges, Nevers, Sens, and Mans. Black chasubles with red orphreys were used from Passion Sunday to Easter at Paris, and at funerals in parts of Germany and Flanders. Red and white were the Dominical colours in England. BLUE (*indicum, blodium*) was worn on the Continent, like violet, on All Saints' Day, in Advent, and on Septuagesima, and on feasts of St. Mary, as in England, in Spain, and Naples. It was probably used at Salisbury on ferials in Advent. Our Lord and St. Mary wear red and blue. In some foreign churches the dignity of feasts was attempted to be shown by a graduated scale of colours. A curious analogy has been traced between the three common chord notes, the third, fifth, and eighth, with the three primary colours of the solar ray; and of the seven notes of the major diatonic scale with the colours of the solar spectrum, so that various instruments have been ingeniously represented as colours,—the oboe as yellow, the flute white, the trumpet scarlet, etc. St. Jerome mentions that one dress was worn in sacred ministrations, and another in ordinary life; and in 260 Pope Stephen III. enjoined the ecclesiastical vestments to be used only in church. Possibly about the sixth century the fashion of vestments became fixed. Salvian, Paulinus of Nola, and Pope Celestine, in 428, allude to the adoption of a distinct dress by priests. In France it was the practice in the fifth century; and the monks, by the adoption of a habit, promoted the movement. At Constantinople, in the fourth century, the Catholics wore black, and the Novatians white out of doors. St. Chrysostom celebrated in white, which he mentions as the church-dress. In the early times of the Church white was used, certainly in the fourth century, as appears from the writings of St. Jerome, Gregory of Tours, Isidore of Seville, and Fortunatus. Anastatius speaks of it in the lives of Popes Leo III. and IV., Gregory IV., and Sergius II.; and in the mosaics at St. Paul's Without, at Rome, white robes, sometimes adorned with bands of violet or gold, were worn by the early Popes. From the ninth century red, blue, and green were gradually permitted in vestments, but prescript colours were not generally adopted until the eleventh or twelfth century, white being retained for the amice, albe, surplice, and the cope and chasuble on feasts of the Nativity, Epiphany, All Saints, and St. John the Baptist. They are first mentioned by the author of the 'Treatise on Divine Offices' about the eleventh century, and afterwards, in the thirteenth century, by Durand, Bishop of Mende, and Innocent III. The Greeks, about the same period, adopted these colours, reserving red, however, for fast-days and memorials of saints. The Greek Church requires white at Christmas, Epiphany, and Easter; blue or violet in Passion Week, in Advent, Lent, and at burials; and white and green at Pentecost. Red is regarded as the symbol of ardent love; green of the life of grace; violet of penitence; and white of truth. No doubt the common colour for altar-cloths,—which is red, and the ordinary colour of the Salisbury rite,—was observed in England, owing to the Sarum use being prescribed for the whole southern province in 1541. The national use differed greatly from the Roman, as in the use of red instead of violet on Sundays in Lent, and from Septuagesima to Easter, on Ash Wednesday, Maundy Thursday, Good Friday, and the Great Saturday or Easter eve, on Sunday in Trinity, and in processions; whilst gold colour was used instead of white on confessors' days.

COLOURS, EMBLEMATICAL. Colours have been called the hieroglyphics of heavenly secrets, and the idea has been carried out in the mosaics of churches, the paintings of the catacombs, and in the ornaments of divine worship. White, the union of all luminous rays, is the colour of divine truth (Rev. xxii.; Dan. vii. 9), as seen in the description of the Ancient of Days and the Great Throne of Judgment; of angels, who are represented appearing in white; of the Saviour as God (St. Mark ix. 2; St. Luke xxiii. 11; Rev. i. 13); and, therefore, worn on the festivals of Christmas, Easter, and other holy days consecrated to Him; of purity, life, light, joy, peace, and innocence. Saints are often represented in white (Rev. vi. 11), and in a mosaic in St. Paul's (Rome), they are thus portrayed casting down their crowns before the throne; the converts from paganism have their heads bare, and those of the Jewish dispensation wear veils (2 Cor. iii. 14; Is. iii. 23). Catechumens wore white robes during the octave after their baptism. The Pope wears white; and on great days the bishop's chair was draped in white to represent divine truth. The dead were wrapped in white, in memory of our Lord's winding-sheet.

Red, as that of fire, is the colour of burning love, as on the wings of seraphim; of the fiery tongues, at Pentecost; of power, dignity, and martyrdom, as worn on Good Friday; or the sacred fire of Christ's doctrine (St. Luke xii. 49). Mar-

tyrs were buried in a scarlet colobium or dalmatic, the symbol of charity and blood-shedding.   Cardinals wore red as a
type of love and the Passion of our Lord, which they should
have always in remembrance.

Green, the token of life in the vegetable kingdom, is the
colour of immortality, as in the robes of angels ; of the life
of grace (Ezek. xx. 47; Rev. ix. 4; St. Luke xxiii. 31),
just as evergreens and laurel were laid in the graves beneath the bodies of the departed, in token that they shall
rise again ; of hope, as when a cypress is carved on a tomb ;
of the creation of life and the regeneration in the world to
come, when used in vestments on Sundays from Epiphany
to Septuagesima, and from the third Sunday after Pentecost
to Advent; and of life in Jesus in the veil used in the Ambrosian rite to cover the altar after communion, and the
cloth which covers the holy stone upon it.   It also represents
bounty, youth, prosperity, faith, and, when palish in hue,
baptism.

Violet, worn on Embers and vigils, being a mixture of
black for sorrow and red for love, betokens penitence, grief
for sins, inspired by the love of Christ.   Our Lord wears
violet sometimes as a type of the Man of Sorrows.   St. Mary,
in her grief, St. John as the preacher of repentance, and
angels sent on errands of warning are robed in violet.   Nuns
wore violet; so did Benedictine abbots until recent times,
and penitents in primitive times.   Violet was the colour of
the parchment used for church books in the time of St.
Jerome and at a later date.   Violet typified truth, deep love,
and humility.

Blue, the colour of heaven, used on feasts of St. Mary,
was the emblem of piety, sincerity, godliness, contemplation,
expectation, love of heavenly things.

Jacinth represents Christian prudence ; purple royalty
and justice.

Yellow, worn on confessors' days, betokens brightness and
faith.

Black is the symbol of death, humiliation, mourning, and
penance.

Pale yellow, as in the dress of Judas, signifies deceit.

Comb. The comb of ivory or metal with which the first tonsure was made and the hair was arranged in the sacristy, is

sometimes found in the graves of medieval priests. That of St. Cuthbert is of ivory, preserved at Durham; and St. Loup's, of the twelfth century, at Sens. The latter is jewelled and has symbolical animals.

Commandery (*commenda*, a benefice), *or* **Preceptory** (*præceptio*, a first share). A cell of the Templars and Hospitallers, for collecting demesne-rents; and a home for veteran members of those orders; the president paid himself first his own pension, and then accounted for the residue. These houses remain at Swingfield, Clibburn, and Worcester.

Commemoration takes place when two double festivals concur, and the office for the greater is used, whilst the collect only of the lesser is said; or when a double coincides with a greater Sunday; or a double of the second class falls on a greater week-day, and the same rule is observed. In Lent, Advent, on ember-days, and greater ferials a special collect is used.

Commemoration of Benefactors. In colleges a form of prayer, prescribed in Queen Elizabeth's reign, is used during term, in pious memory of founders and benefactors. The proper Psalms are cxlv., cxlvi., cxlvii.; the lesson, Eccles. xliv. The suffrages are :—

" The just shall be had in everlasting remembrance ;
He shall not be afraid of evil tidings.
The souls of the righteous are in the hand of God ;
Neither doth any torment touch them."

Then follows a collect. At Oxford the commemoration by the university is called encænia.

Commendatory. One having the grant of a benefice in trust for life, and enjoying the revenues.

Commissary. The judge of a bishop's court in a peculiar, and holding jurisdiction in those parts of a diocese for which he holds a licence.

Commixtion of the body and blood of Christ together, as Cranmer explained, signifies the joining together of His body and blood at the resurrection, which before were severed at the time of His passion. It consisted in the immersion of a fragment of the Host in the chalice.

Common House, *or* **Parlour.** The calefactory. A common room, with a fire in winter, for the monks.

Communar. (1.) The bursar in a cathedral, who distributed the commons or general capitulary fund, and paid stipends. (2.) An officer, called the master of the common house, who provided a fire in the calefactory and certain luxuries on festivals.

Communion, Holy. In early times, after the Benediction by the bishop, which followed the Lord's Prayer, the deacon called the people to Communion, saying "Attend;" and then the celebrant said, "Holy [things] for holy [persons];" to which the answer was, "One holy, one Lord Jesus Christ, to the glory of God the Father, blessed for ever, amen;" followed by the Gloria in Excelsis. The Eucharistic bread was broken before the ministration, and in the Greek Church immediately after the consecration. The Latins divided each bread into three, the Greeks into four parts. The latter used two fractions; one before consecration, into three parts, at the words "He brake it;" and the second, properly so called, when each part was subdivided, before the Lord's Prayer and after the reading of the diptychs. The Mozarabic rite prescribes nine parts to be made, in allusion to the nine mysteries of the life of Christ, the conception, nativity, circumcision, transfiguration, passion, death, resurrection, glory, and kingdom. The fraction was succeeded by the mixture mentioned by the Councils of IV. Toledo and Orange in 441. After the call "Holy for the holy," the congregation communicated, the bishop, priests, clergy, ascetics, women, deaconesses, virgins, widows, children, and then the rest present. The distribution was made by deacons, but in later times the priest ministered the bread, and the deacon the chalice. Deacons sometimes administered the bread, with the restriction that he was not to do so to priests or to the people without the order of a priest. In Spain priests and deacons communicated at the altar, minor clerks within the choir, and the people at the chancels. The Greeks also allowed only the former within the sanctuary. Persons in the East received either prostrate, kneeling, or standing, bowing the head at the ministration. In the West priests alone received in the latter posture. The words of ministration were at first "The body of Christ, and the blood of Christ;" to which the faithful replied, "Amen." In the time of Gregory the Great they were expanded thus, "The body of our Lord Jesus Christ preserve thy soul;" and in the age of Charlemagne, "The body of our Lord Jesus Christ preserve thee to everlasting life." Men received in the hollow of the right hand, bare, crossed over the left, throne-like, as St. Cyril of Jerusalem says; and women in a linen cloth, called the dominical, from which they raised the element to their lips. The chalice was administered by the deacon, who held it by its two handles, and at length the calamus was used by the people.

Communions. Ps. xxiii., xxxiv., xlii., cxviii., or cxlv., sung during the administration in the Greek Church; and mentioned by St. Jerome, St. Cyril of Jerusalem, the Apostolical Constitutions, and early liturgies.

Communion of the Sick. Although the church is the proper place for a celebration, yet in cases of necessity the Holy Communion was administered, in ancient times, in crypts, at the tombs of martyrs, in a prison, on the celebrant's breast, in the deacon's hands, in a tent, a hut, a house, in the fields, at sea, by a bedside—anywhere, except in the burial-places of the heathen. *See* VIATICUM.

Compass, *or* **Span-roof.** One reaching from side wall to side wall, unlike a lean-to roof.

Competentes, *i.e.* seekers of the grace of Christ; an advanced class of candidates for Baptism, who had received adequate instruction. They received this name on Palm Sunday, when the Creed was delivered to them; on the second Sunday following the Lord's Prayer was explained in their hearing.

Comprising Arch. The large exterior arch of a window which encloses the subordinate lights and tracery.

Concha. An ancient name of the apse, from its shell-like or volute form.

Conclave. The meeting of the cardinals for the election of a Pope.

Concomitance. The Roman doctrine that, under the form of bread the blood of Christ is also received, although the chalice is not ministered.

Concordance. The first Biblical concordance was commenced in 1236, by Cardinal Hugh de St. Cher.

Concordat. A treaty of agreement in ecclesiastical matters between the Pope and some sovereign or church.

Conduct. (*Conductitius, stipendiary.*) A chaplain without endowment.

Confederated Monasteries. Those in union for prayer for the dead members, mutual hospitality, and admission to chapter. Westminster was confederated with Bury, Worcester, Malmesbury, St. Alban's, Winchester, York, Colchester, Wenlock, Reading, Bermondsey, Tavistock, Tewkesbury, Rochester, Ramsey, Hulme, Canterbury, Shrewsbury, Cirencester, Malvern, Hurley, and Fécamp.

Confession. (1.) General; made by a congregation. (2.) Auricular; private to the priest's ear. (3.) Martyrdom, or memorial to a saint; a tomb beneath an altar containing a window, called the jugulum, or cataract, through which the pilgrim let down a cloth (called the pall, brandeum, sudary, or sanctuary) to touch the body of the sleeper. It was surrounded by a screen of perforated marble, or a rail of bronze, and was often closed in with pillars, covered with metal plates, and illuminated by lights and candelabra. The theory was, that every church was erected over a catacomb: and where it was impossible to have a real confession, relics were enclosed within an altar, which was erected on an elevated platform, and called the confession. The true confession was the germ of the crypt; in old St. Peter's it formed a subterranean Chapel of St. Peter. At the beginning of the thirteenth century the steps to it were removed, and the entrance closed. The altar built over the actual grave was the lower confession; the upper confession was the larger altar of marble, erected above it, in the church itself, as at St. Prisca, St. Sylvester, St. Martin, and St. Laurence at Rome.

Public confession of sins prevailed in the fourth century, and lasted longer in the West than in the East. Private confession is supposed to have been first appointed during the Decian persecution, 249-51; but public confession in the East was first given up at Constantinople, owing to a scandal in 390. Theodulph, Bishop of Orleans (835), ordered confession to be made once a year; and the rule was made absolute by the Council of Lateran (1215). It was usual to confess on the first Sunday in Lent. Tertullian, Origen, and St. Cyril are supposed to allude to private confession.

Confessional. A stone chair in the catacombs. A small recess at the foot of the dormitory stairs of St. Alban's, and a stone chair with two armed warders in the south arm area of the transept at Gloucester, and two wooden structures at Bishop's Canning and Tavistock, are said to have served as confessionals. The usual place was a seat in the chancel, in the face of day, and open to all passers-by; the modern closed boxes are of recent introduction. In 1378 women were confessed without the chancel veil, and in an open place, that she might be seen though not heard by the people. Men confessed at Easter, Pentecost, and Christmas. Bedyll, writing to Cromwell, recommended the walling up of "the places where the friars heard outward confessions of all comers at certain times of the year." Probably these apertures were in friary churches in the form of low side windows. One of the fourteenth or fifteenth century remains at Nuremberg. It consists of five canopied compartments; the central was occupied by the priest, and the two lateral portions by penitents, who entered by the outermost doors. An open metal screen fills the apertures only halfway up. In England confession was ordinarily made openly in the chancel, the priest sitting in the stall on the north-east side, and the penitent kneeling before him. Roger Van der Weyden, who died 1464, represents a confessional chair on the north side of the nave, next the stairs to the chancel, and outside the rood-screen. In Flemish churches the IV. Coronati, still used by the Austin canonesses, and St. Helen's, Bishopsgate, orifices in the wall served as confessionals.

Confessor. (1.) The name of a singer in the Councils of Carthage and Toledo in 400, when anthems were forbidden to be sung by nuns and widows with singers, except in the presence of a bishop. Confession of God's name (Psalm cvi. 1) is synonymous with its praise. (2.) Martyrs without bloodshedding, who by a good life have witnessed to Christ. Their names were first inserted in the diptychs in the fourth century.

Confessor of the Household. The subdean or one of the priests in ordinary of the chapel royal, who read daily prayers to the household, visited the sick, and prepared persons for Holy Communion. The dean of the royal chapel Stirling, who was always Bishop of Glasgow or Dunblane, was the Scottish kings' confessor, and the Bishop of Chichester was confessor to the Queen of England. At St.

N

Paul's the cardinals acted as confessors. The confessor of
the Papal family is a Servite. *See* PENITENTIARY.

Confirmation. (1.) A term first employed by St. Ambrose, and
adopted by Popes Leo and Gregory. This holy rite was also
called the seal, the perfection, conclusion, or complement [of
holy baptism], and the sacrament of chrism, or, from the act
of signing on the brow, the reception of the cross. Chrism
was, in the fourth century, called the confirmation of confession of faith. In baptism we are made Christians; the
proper effect of Confirmation is the gift of the Holy Ghost.
In the former we are new-born to life, in the latter strength-
ened for the conflict. The laying on of the Saviour's
hands upon the heads of little children, and the example of
the practice, of the Apostles, in the Acts, furnish the Scriptural warrant for this sacramental ceremony, which is mentioned in the third century. St. Cyprian and the Council
of Meaux call it a sacrament in the wide sense of the term.
A bishop only can administer it. It seems from Tertullian
that confirmation immediately followed on holy baptism.
Tyndale and others, at the time of the Reformation say that
children were confirmed, at eleven or twelve years of age,
by bishops in their visitation, coming once in seven years,
and then, perhaps, only within seven miles of the appointed
place; and Cosin mentions that it had been commonly administered in the streets, in the highways, in the common
fields, without any sacred solemnity. The change of the
baptismal name or an addition to it at confirmation was an
innovation of a later period. In medieval times adults went
to confession before confirmation; and the rite was never to
be repeated, on pain of severe penalty to the parents, and of
irregularity and incapacity to receive holy orders in the
recipient, by English councils in the fourteenth century.
(2.) The ceremony or process of confirming a bishop at Bow
Church, London, including the citation of all who have any
objection to advance against the Crown's nominee.

Congregation. The ancient name for a chapter, used by St.
Benedict. It designates some religious orders, and in the
University of Oxford the assembly of all regent graduates
mainly for the purpose of granting degrees.

Consecration. (1.) The ordination of a bishop. (2.) The
dedication of the sacred elements in the Holy Communion;

that the faithful, receiving these, God's creatures of bread and wine, may be made partakers of the body and blood of Christ, given, taken, and received verily and indeed, after a heavenly and spiritual manner. The consecration is effected by virtue of the words of the Saviour (1 Cor. xi. 23, 26). Gregory the Great thought that the Apostles consecrated with the Lord's Prayer. Amalarius simply says that it was used at the same time. (3.) The dedication of a church to God's service. St. Ambrose alludes to consecration of churches as an immemorial and universal custom. Eusebius says it was a sight full of beauty and consolation to see the solemn dedication of churches and oratories rising on every side, as if by enchantment, and attended by all the bishops of a province. The Councils of Jerusalem and Antioch were held on the occasion of consecration of churches built by Constantine. Eusebius, in 315, preached at the dedication of the basilica of Tyre. The ancient ceremonial consisted of prayer, thanksgiving, and praise of the founders, as in the discourses delivered by St. Ambrose and Gaudentius. The Holy Eucharist was then celebrated. The later ceremonial and a form of prayer date from the ninth century ; but the unction with holy oil, the crosses on the walls, and the tapers burning before them are probably older; and the Pontifical Mass, on the authority of Paulinus, is traceable to the fourth century. The diocesan always consecrated, or at least performed the preliminary rite of saying certain prayers and erecting a cross on the site, according to the First Council of Braga and that of Chalcedon. In the vacancy of a See the nearest bishop officiated. Churches were always dedicated to God only, as the name Dominicum implies, when St. Jerome mentions the consecration of the Golden Dominicum at Antioch, and Eusebius speaks of Constantine's kyriakai. St. Augustine adduced the consecration of churches in His honour as a proof of the Godhead of the Holy Spirit. Churches built on the site of a martyrdom or the tomb of a martyr were called memorials, and occasionally the founder's name was preserved, as in three at Carthage, and some more at Rome and Antioch. A church at Jerusalem was called the Cross, because built on the site of the Passion ; or Anastasis, because the doctrine of the Holy Trinity was definitely established in it through means of St.

N 2

Gregory Nazianzen. Another church, at Carthage, having been recovered from the Arians, was called the Restituta. Sunday became the usual day for consecration only in later times. The annual feast of dedication was observed in the time of Sozomen. Gregory the Great enjoined its observation in England. So sacred were churches after dedication that the faithful washed their hands and faces before they entered. The monks of Egypt laid aside their sandals on the threshold; princes put off their armour and crowns, and dismissed their guard at the door; loving worshippers bowed down in the porches and kissed the very gates. St. Gregory Nazianzen mentions that the devout never turned their back towards the holy table, and St. Ambrose alludes to the deep and reverential silence observed.

St. Cyril of Jerusalem says that the Apostles consecrated the upper chamber of Pentecost; and early writers record the dedication of houses by the Apostles and their successors. Evaristus divided the Roman churches among his priests, and in the time of Cornelius there were forty-six churches. Some of the earlier dedications, dating back to the fourth century, were those of St. Saviour, St. John Baptist, and St. Peter in the reign of Constantine; St. John Baptist at Constantinople, built by Theodore, and St. Peter at Alexandria. St. Ambrose mentions a church of the Apostles, and St. Jerome speaks of the basilicas of the martyrs. St. Augustine calls the temples of God the memorials of martyrs, because dedicated to God only, although they bear the names of saints. In the ninth century consecrations in England are distinctly mentioned. By the canon law the site was first marked out by a cross, in token that the ground was devoted to God. Hence it was called a title, owing to the Vulgate rendering of Genesis xxviii. 18, where the Authorized Version gives the word as "pillar." Round the newly-built church twelve lamps were lighted, symbolically of the twelve Apostles, or the light of the gospel; and, according to Egbert's canons, on the exterior also. The bishop knocked with his staff thrice on the door, saying, "Lift up your heads, O ye gates;" and, the door being opened, he went in with the clergy and people, saying, "Peace be to this house." He then drew an alphabet on the pavement, from east to west, in the shape of a cross saltier, to signify the rudiments of religion and the teaching of the cross. He then consecrated the altar by making the sign of the cross with holy-water on the four horns, as if the four corners of the earth were purified by the laver of regeneration and the suffering of faith. He then sprinkled it seven times, to signify the gifts of the Spirit; and then the walls of the church whilst the 68th Psalm was sung. He afterwards made the sign of the cross with chrism on the centre and four horns of the altar, and twelve crosses on the walls of the church, in memory of the twelve Apostles, the teachers of the Gentiles. Mass was then celebrated, and the deed of endowment exhibited.

The dedication or wake-day was kept during an octave on each anniversary. Our Lord kept the feast of dedication (St. John x. 22); and Eusebius alludes to the practice in his own time. Sometimes, as at Thorney, the choir and nave had different dedications. Christchurch and the Holy Trinity formed an interchangeable title for a church. This anniversary was called Encænia, a term formerly given to the dedication of a heathen temple. In Ireland it is called the Patron [saint's day].

Consignatorium Ablutorum. Confirmation of the baptized.

Consistentes. Bystanders, called by the Greeks synistamenoi. The third class of penitents, who were allowed to be present, but neither to make an oblation nor to communicate.

Consistory. The diocesan court of a bishop, in which are tried causes of *voluntary* jurisdiction, that is, affecting visitations, licences, institutions, and sequestrations; and *contentious* or judicial, touching probate of wills and hearing of cases to be decided, the former by his vicar-general, the latter by an official, but now by the chancellor of the diocese. Criminal clerks were committed to the bishop's prison by this court.

Consuetudinary. (1.) Ritual or book of constitutions for ceremonials and official duties. (2.) A custumal or rental of estates.

Convent. A house and church of monks, regular canons, or religious women.

Conversi. Lay brothers of a monastery, who had forsaken the world.

Conversion of St. Paul. Venerable Bede alludes to this festival.

In the twelfth century it appears to have been observed, after an interval of desuetude; and in 1200 Pope Innocent, and in 1250 a Council ordered it to be kept. Pope Clement VIII., in the latter end of the sixteenth century, distinguished it as a double major. Formerly he was commemorated on June 30th, as his "birthday," and associated with St. Peter on the day before and on February 22nd.

Convocation. (1.) A representative council of the clergy in each province, convoked originally, in the time of Edward I., for the purpose of self-taxation, at the same time as the lay Parliament, which gradually assumed synodical action. It is assembled by writ of the Crown, but prorogued and dissolved by the archbishop's mandate. The Lower House consists of deans, archdeacons, a proxy or proctor from every chapter, and two from every diocese in Canterbury; and from each archdeaconry in York province, elected by beneficed clergy. It assembles under a prolocutor or president. The Upper House is composed of bishops only, under each primate. Convocation met at St. Paul's until the time of Cardinal Wolsey, who assembled it in the exempt precinct of Westminster, to free it from the jurisdiction of Canterbury and the jealousy of York. Convocation lost the privilege of self-taxation when the clergy were allowed to vote for knights of the shire in 1664. (2.) The Convocation in the University of Oxford consists of all persons admitted to regency, who have their names on their college books, and have paid all their fees. This assembly gives assent to statutes passed in congregation, confirms leases of lands, makes petitions to Parliament, elects burgesses, and confers honorary degrees, or those given by degree or by diploma.

Cope. (*Cappa;* from *cop,* a covering, or *caput,* the head, over which it was thrown, or *capere,* from taking in the whole body.) There were several kinds of this cloak-like vestment. A ceremonial cope, called the *Pluviale,* one worn out-of-doors, whence its name,—a protection from rain in processions; the close cope and the choral cope. It appears to have been modelled by Pope Stephen, in 286, on the Roman *lacerna,* a large square-hooded cloak, fastened with a brooch upon the breast, and worn by soldiers and by civilians in the last age of the Republic, and it resembled the Greek *mandyas* or *chlamys,* a habit of smaller dimensions than the *pallium*. The *lacerna* was usually sad-coloured, purple or red. The latter were called *byrrhi*. The open part of the cope represented that eternal life was offered to the minister of holy conversation; and the entire habit was an imitation of the purple robe of mockery, or *sakkos*, which our Lord was compelled to wear. It was also often called the *byrrus*. The cope was originally a great cloak worn in processions principally, which in time was gradually enriched with embroidery and gems, so that in the thirteenth century it had become one of the most magnificent vestments in use, and was known as 'precious.' It frequently had superb orphreys and a hood splendidly worked with figures of saints and other patterns. In pre-Norman times they had, in England, tassels and movable hoods of thin beaten gold and silver, such as William's stole at Ely. Some examples had fringes of bells, like one at Canterbury, which had a little chime of 140 in 1108, and others sent by William I. to Clugny, or presented by Lanfranc, Ernulph, and Conrad to their minster. One is still preserved at Aix-la-Chapelle, having silver bells round the hem, said to have been given by Pope Leo III. at the coronation of Charlemagne. There are three copes of the fourteenth century at Durham, one given by Queen Philippa, 1346, another of crimson silk, with the beheadal of Goliath, presented by Charles I.; two at Langharne; one of green velvet of the fourteenth century at Ely; two at Carlisle of the fifteenth and sixteenth century; one of crimson velvet, with crowns and stars of Bethlehem, at Chipping Campden; some of the date of James II., at Westminster; several of the fourteenth century at Spires; one of the fifteenth century, found at Waterford Cathedral, at Oscott; some of Caroline date at Riseholme, worn by the Bishops of Lincoln at coronations; and others at Wardour Castle, Weston Underwood, and Stonyhurst; some traditionally being said to have been brought from Westminster. The silken copes were distributed in choir by the precentor to the various members upon great festivals; at other times they were carefully folded and put away in triangular cope-chests. Every canon, at his installation, presented one of these precious or processional copes to the fabric; and every abbot or bishop gave a cope of profession, on his appointment, to Canterbury Cathedral.

THE CANONICAL OR CHORAL COPE was a large, full, flowing cloak of black woollen stuff, worn by canons and vicars in cathedrals. It is mentioned at Chichester, in the twelfth century, as without corsets and open. It opened downwards from the breast, and was sewed up as far as the throat, round which was a hood. In the fifteenth century, the almuce was sewn on to the cope like a hood, except when it was carried across the shoulders, or thrown over the left arm.

THE CLOSE OR SLEEVELESS COPE, an ample hood lined with fur, did not open in front, whence its name. The hood was of ermine, like that of the proctors at Oxford. It is seen depicted on the famous wall-painting of Chichester Cathedral,—Bishop Sherborne being habited in it. In the thirteenth century all clerks were required to wear close copes in synods, and in the presence of prelates and parochial clergy in their parish; they were to be laid aside on journeys. Black canons, Benedictines, and nuns were to use black, and not coloured copes, and faced only with black or white fur of lambs, cats, or foxes. They were forbidden caps by H. Walter's canons in 1200. In 1195 priests were forbidden to wear sleeved copes. In 1222 monks and canons were proscribed burnet or irregular cloth, or girdles of silk or gold embroidery in their habit, and the nuns were to use no veil of silk. At the close of the twelfth century, dignitaries were allowed the use of sleeved copes; but in 1222, it was found necessary to forbid the gay colours of red and green adopted for copes. The monk retained the sombre hue of black. At Cambridge the D.D. still wears, on formal occasions, a cope of scarlet cloth with ermine bands in front. By the Laudian statutes of Oxford, Doctors of Divinity on formal occasions are required to wear either the close or open cope; and Bachelors of Arts, when reading in the Bodleian Library, were enjoined to be attired in "their habit or cope, cowl, and cap."

The *Cappa Magna*, worn in processions and during certain functions in Italy at this day, corresponds to the English close cope. It is a large violet-coloured habit, with a train and an ermine cape when worn by bishops, but only furred when canons use it.

In England, at the Reformation, the precious copes were,

unhappily, too often desecrated to garnish beds as coverlets. Bishop Cosin wore a cope of white satin. Portions of copes are still, in several English churches, used as altar or pulpit cloths.

Coping. The capping or slanting cover of a wall, acting like a large drip-stone.

Corbel (Fr. *corbeau*) *or* **Source.** A bracket. A projecting piece of stone to carry a parapet, an image, or beam.

Corbie Steps. Graduated battlements up the side of a gable, as at Caen, and on the towers in Ireland and Scotland and Flanders.

Corner Stone. The first stone of a church, laid on the northeast side, as determined by the orientation of the sun on the day of the feast, or patron saint. At Beaulieu only one stone was found on the site on the ground, and it was in this position; that of Avranches, the solitary relic of a cathedral, is still pointed out.

Cornice. A corruption of the Latin term *coronis;* that which crowns and completes a structure.

Coronation. The investiture of a sovereign. The Archbishop of Canterbury crowns the king, and the Archbishop of York the queen.

Coronet. This ornament first appears in the effigy of John of Eltham, who died 1332. The addition of a marquis's coronet to an archiepiscopal mitre does not date back before the time of Sheldon. Edmundson speaks of it as a novelty. It has since then been drawn as a ducal coronet. The Bishops of Durham, who took their title by the grace of God or by divine providence [in distinction to other bishops, who are styled by divine permission], whilst still palatine, until 1833, used the coronet by right, or in lieu of it a plume of feathers.

Corporal. A word used in the ' Sacramentaries,' by Pope Gregory, Isidore of Seville, and in the capitulars of the Frank kings in 800, meaning a fine linen, or canvas cloth of pure white, according to the Council of Rheims, on which the sacred elements are consecrated, and hence called the corporal in allusion to the body of Christ, of which bread is the sacrament. Isidore of Pelusium called it the eileton, the wrapping-cloth; and Isidore of Damascus speaks of it as the winding-sheet. The centre, on which the chalice and paten stood, were quite plain, the ends alone being of silk, or worked with gold or silver. It was ordered to be used by Pope Sixtus in 125, and Sylvester, c. 314, directed it to be of linen and not of stuff, as before. It was also known as the pall-veil, or sindon, and represented the fine linen in which Joseph of Arimathea wrapped the Lord's body in the garden tomb. The altar, by canon law, had two palls, and one corporal of plain linen cloth. The removal of the cloth from the consecrated elements typified the manifestation of the mysteries of the Old Testament by the death of Jesus. The earliest corporals covered the entire altar, and hung down at each side; two deacons were required to spread it.

Corporal Acts of Mercy. (1) Feeding the hungry; (2) giving drink to the thirsty; (3) clothing the naked; (4) harbouring the stranger; (5) visiting the sick; (6) ministering to prisoners; (7) burying the dead. (St. Matt. xxv. 35; Tob. i. 17.)

Corporax Cups. Vessels of precious metal, suspended by a chain under a canopy, and used for the reservation of the Eucharist for the sick. It sometimes took the form of a tiara of crowns, in allusion to Rev. xix. 12, and was covered often by a thin veil of silk or muslin, called the " kerchief of cobweb lawn." At Durham it was of very fine lawn, embroidered with gold and red silk, and finished with four knobs and tassels. That used by St. Cuthbert formed the banner carried to victory at the Red Hills.

Corpus Christi. (*Fête Dieu.*) The feast of the Body of Christ, kept on the Thursday after Trinity Sunday (or the octave of Pentecost), was instituted in 1264, by Pope Urban IV., for a procession bearing the Eucharist, with an office and prose composed by Aquinas; the office is also attributed to Robert, Bishop of Liége, in 1249. Colleges at Oxford and Cambridge bear this dedication. It afterwards became the chief occasion on which the mysteries were acted by the clergy, and the miracle plays by guilds. The mother churches began the procession on this day, and subordinate churches on or within the octave. It was an immemorial custom in Spain for the priests to carry the tabernacle upon these occasions raised upon their shoulders. In England, on Corpus Christi Day, they carried the silver pyx under a canopy of silk and cloth of gold, borne by four men, preceded by a pageant— Ursula and her maidens, St. George with spear and dragon, the Devil's house, St. Christopher bearing the Infant, St.

Sebastian pierced with arrows, St. Katharine with sword and wheel, St. Barbara with the chalice and cakes, followed by banners, crosses, candlesticks, reliquaries, cups, and images, which the priests lifted on high, whilst before them went many sacring bells and musicians, St. John pointing to the Lamb, upon which two clad as angels cast sweet-smelling flowers. The highway was strewn with boughs, every wall and window was decorated with branches. In villages the husbandmen went among the cornfields with crosses and banners; and the priest, carrying the blessed bread in a bag round his neck, read the Gospel at certain stations, as an amulet against wind, rain, and foul blasts.

Corrody. (1.) A payment, in kind or pension, in money made by a monastery to the nominee of a benefactor, who had the right of appointing often an indefinite number of such persons. (2.) An allowance by a monastery to servants or outliers.

Corse. A platted or woven silk ribbon, used as an ornament of vestments.

Corsned (from *kur*, trial, and *snœd*, a slice). An ordeal, mentioned in 1015, which was made by eating barley-bread and cheese, over which prayers and ceremonies had been used by the priest, to discover whether the eater were guilty or not. In Christian times the Host was used.

Cotta. An Italian tunicle of linen reaching to the knees. Ducange says it was a closed circular surplice.

Coucher. (1.) A register or accompt book. (2.) A church book couched, or lying, on the chancel desk.

Council. A solemn assembly of the representatives of independent Churches, convened for deliberation and the enactment of canons, or ecclesiastical laws. The first ever held was at Jerusalem (Acts xv.). Eusebius mentions synods in the East in the second century, and Firmilian, in the middle of the third century, speaks of them as annual in Africa. These were provincial, held under the presidency of the metropolitan. After the conversion of Constantine, the Byzantine emperors exercised authority in convening councils in the East; and in the West, at a later date, the Pope assumed similar powers.

The four general or œcumenical councils recognized by all Churches are those of Nicæa, 325, held against the Arian heresy; Constantinople, 381, against Apollinarius; Ephesus,

431, against Nestorius; and Chalcedon, 451, against Euty-
ches and Nestorius. The four following words, in their
order, give a summary of these decisions with regard to
Christ:—*alethōs*, perfect God; *teleiōs*, perfect man; *adiai-
retōs*, one altogether; *asynchetōs*, not by confusion of substance. The Greek Church adds to these II. Constantinople,
553; III. Constantinople or in Trullo, 680, so called from
the domed chamber in which it was held; and II. Nicæa,
787. To these the Church of Rome adds IV. Constantinople,
869; the Four Laterans, 1122, 1139, 1179, 1215; two
at Lyons, 1245, 1274; Vienna, 1311; Florence, 1439;
V. Lateran, 1512; Trent, 1545. Some add Pisa, 1409;
Constance, 1414; and Basle, 1431.

The acts of councils were read out from the ambon during
the time of Holy Communion, and during their tenure the
gospels were laid open on a throne covered with rich stuffs,
to remind all present to judge right judgment, as at Ephesus, 1st Lateran; 3rd in the Vatican; Ferrara; Florence,
and Basle. It is so represented in Italian bronzes and
mosaics of the fifth century.

Counterpoynt. (1.) Counterpane. A coverlet composed of
counter-points or panes of different colours, contrasting with
each other. (2.) Music written in several distinct parts, so
called from the notes being placed over against or above
the other in the score.

Cowl. (From *cucullus*, an abbreviation of *cucus* or *kokkos*, a
helmet.) A hood sown on the cope, oblong in shape and
ending in a point, worn by monks. From its use to cover
the head it was also called capitium. Canons wore it
slightly different in shape from that of the monks, and from
them it passed into the universities.

Cramp Rings are attributed by Hospinian to the claim of
Westminster Abbey to the possession of the ring given by
St. John, in the guise of a pilgrim, to Edward the Confessor.
On Good Fridays the kings of England used to bless finger-
rings for the cramp, which were worn by sufferers in full
belief of recovery.

Cream Box. A chrismatory.

Credence. (It. *credenza*, a sideboard, or buffet.) The bystand-
ing table, called also the prothesis, oblationarium, and ministerium; a bracket or recess by the Cistercians. It either

takes the form of a little table covered with a linen cloth,—
at Brabourne it is on the south side and formed of black
marble, with a cross in a circle carved on it,—or is made
like an aumbry in the wall. On it were placed the oblations
of the faithful; and in the Greek Church, at Tours and
Rheims, the offering is still made in procession. It also
carried the basin, cruets, and sacred elements. In some
churches a second table held the Mass vestments of the
bishop. The wall credence is often connected with a drain,
is rare in the twelfth [one occurs at Lausanne], but is usual
in the following century. Sometimes it occurs on the north
and south sides of an altar; often it is divided by a thin
slab of stone. In the fourteenth century it is sometimes
doubled, as at Chester and Caen, one recess holding the
plate and books, the other containing the tapers and cruets.
There are beautiful specimens in the Sainte-Chapelle, Paris,
and there is one on the south side in St. Antonio's, Padua.
Where there are two credences, that on the epistle side has
a drain and shelf, to hold the basin and cruets; and that on
the gospel side, which has no drain, held the books, candles,
and ornaments of the altar, being, in fact, an open aumbry;
but when it had doors attached, the Sacrament was reserved
in it. When the Pope celebrates on Easter Day, there are
three credences,—two on the epistle side, one containing
the deacon's plate, the second supporting two candles and
necessaries required by the sacristan. The third, or Pope's
credence, is on the gospel side, where, at the end of the
Creed, the sacristan washes the sacred vessels; the sacristan
drinks of the wine and the water, and finally at the offertory
tastes the particles from which the hosts are prepared, at
the command of the cardinal deacon, as a precaution against
poison. The French call the folding part of a stall a credence. The table credence is sometimes a little table of
stone, as at St. Cross and Fyfield, carried on a shaft; or a
moveable sideboard of Jacobean date, of wood, on legs, as
at Battle, Manchester, Queenborough, Cobham, Chipping
Warden, St. Michael's, Oxford, and one of the time of
Charles II. at Islip. A slab of stone under an arcade, of
the latter part of the thirteenth century, remains at Sées.
In the Greek Church there are two recesses in the east wall,
the aumbry being on the north and the credence on the

south.   In England the credence is sometimes, as in Lincolnshire, on the south, but ordinarily on the north of the
altar, as at Lyons and Mans.   Side-altars were used as
credences for the preparation of the chalice at Soissons,
Amiens, Chalons-sur-Saône, and St. Germain des Prés; a
ministerium was used at Bayeux.   At Lyons it was of stone,
and at Beauvais of wood.   The name has been derived from
the ceremony of pregustation of the elements in the Pontifical Mass, but Bishop Hickes derives it from an old English
word, meaning the place of preparation.   The first use of
credence in the Roman ritual occurs in the time of Leo X.,
in 1516, and apparently was introduced when the custom of
personal offering fell into desuetude.   A fit place simply is
enjoined in an ' Ordo' of the fourteenth century.   The Cistercians used a recess or wooden shelf.   The Cistercian " ministry" held only the corporal veils and chalice, as, like the
Jacobins and Carthusians, they placed the elements on the
altar itself.

Creed.   (From *credo*, Latin, I believe.)   The Belief, the form
containing the articles of the Christian faith.

Creeping to the Cross.   Alcuin mentions that on Good-Friday
a cross was prepared before the altar, and kissed in succession by the clergy and people.   Sometimes it was laid on a
cushion in a side-chapel.   By Ælfric's Canons (957), the
faithful were required to pay their adoration, and greet
God's rood with a kiss   " We humble ourselves to Christ
herein," Cranmer says, " offering unto Him, and kissing the
Cross, in memory of our redemption by Christ on the Cross."
The practice was forbidden in 1549, but was observed at
Dunbar in 1568 by the congregation, barelegged and barefooted.   During the ceremonial the hymns " Pange, lingua "
and " Vexilla regis prodeunt" were sung, followed by the
" Improperia," or reproaches, an expansion of Malachi iii. 3, 4.

Crenellation.   The fortifying of a monastery or close, permitted by the king only, or in Durham by the bishop palatine.
The earliest instance of the former is in Edward III.'s reign,
and of the precinct in the time of Edward I. at Wells and
Lichfield.

Cresset.   A stationary lamp.

Cresting.   The ornamental brattishing, or finish, which sur-
mounts a screen or roof, taking the form of a battlement;

open work of metal or stone, and of flowers. That of Exeter Cathedral is of lead.

Crewell. Lightly-twisted worsted.

Crockets. (From the French *croche*, a bishop's crook.) The curved projections on the sides of pinnacles, supposed to represent the slipperwort. The earlier form is a leaf curved down, the later of leaves returned, or pointing upwards.

Crop. The top or finial of a pyx.

Cross. The royal standard of Christians, as Fortunatus of Poictiers calls it, reminding us by its four arms of the height and depth, the length and breadth of the love of Christ. St. Ambrose, Tertullian, and Maximus of Turin mention a custom of the primitive Christians to pray with their arms extended in the form of a cross. St. Ambrose speaks of the cross as the mast of the ship under the shadow of which the Christian need fear no wreck. St. Jerome, Origen, and Thomas Aquinas, following Lucian and Tertullian, say that its earliest form was the Hebrew Tau.

The use of the sign of the cross is very ancient, and expressly signifies the Passion of Christ as a strength against unholy thought and sinful deeds. Tertullian says that the Christians before they would undertake any work, at going out and coming in, at sitting down and rising up, at board, bath, or bed, at the bringing in of lights,—in all occupations, in fact, made the sign of the cross upon their forehead. St. Chrysostom recommended its use before and after meals, and St. Jerome extended it to every act, and especially in going out. Prudentius, in his hymns, alludes to the custom; and Ruffinus mentions that every house in Alexandria had its doorpost, entrance, windows, walls, and pillars painted with the sacred sign. The Second Council of Ephesus required every private house to possess a cross. St. Jerome says that it formed the military standard, and adorned the imperial purple and the crown of the diadem; and St. Augustine exclaims, "Kings wear the cross on their brow, of more price than all the jewels of their diadem."

With the cross the priest signed the Sacrament at consecration. Soldiers signed themselves with the cross when the trumpet sounded for battle. Ships carried the cross; the martyr's tomb bore it; it glittered over the altar; Valentinian III. and Eudoxia set it on their crowns. In the fifth century it was carried in processions. In the sixth century consuls carried the cross on their sceptres. The sign of the Son of Man will be seen in heaven at the last day, and with it angels seal the elect (Rev. xiv. 1). The ancients made the sign with the hand extended, but with the thumb only. The Greeks make it with three fingers joined, in honour of the Holy Trinity,—towards the mouth from the forehead downwards, in honour of the incarnation ; and from right to left, in honour of the session at the right hand of God. The Western Church makes the sign with the hand from right to left,—with the right hand from brow to breast, and from one shoulder to the other. The latter is probably of monastic origin, and not earlier than the eighth century.

The cross, according to an old legend, was made of the palm of victory, the cedar of incorruption, the olive for royal and priestly unction. The fourth material is variously given as the aspen, cypress, box, or pine. In medieval times it was usually green, as the symbol of everlasting divinity. Crosses, by the Council of Constantinople, 706, were forbidden to be laid down on a pavement.

Justinian required that no church should be built without having a cross affixed to it, but the Emperors Valens and Theodosius, in 427, required that every sign of our Saviour Christ, whether engraved or depicted or painted, should be effaced. By the canon law no one could build a church except the bishop first came and set up a cross upon the site ; and in the eleventh and twelfth centuries the whole cemetery was marked out ·by boundary crosses. Crosses were set at the head of graves as early as the time of St. Patrick, and before the middle of the eleventh century there was always a central cross erected in churchyards, to remind people of the reverence due to the sacred spot. In Italy the altar-cross is represented both in the eleventh century and by Giotto and Fra Angelico. In the interval, it is often omitted on works of art. Pope Leo IV. ordered that the only ornaments which should be set on the altar were the capsa or reliquary, the gospels, and pyx with the viaticum. In France the stations, where processions carrying the relics halted, were marked by a cross or calvary, such as abound with magnificent sculptures in Brittany, or as wayside crosses in many parts of the Continent. In Italy they frequently mark the scene of a murder. There are beautiful calvaries at Traon Houarn, Plougastel (1602), Llanrivam (1548), Plouçomen, and at Lampaul and Grinnillian (1581–88), in Brittany, consisting of a stone basement, surmounted by an extraordinary number of figures representing the life and passion of our Most Blessed Lord. At Lewes and Chichester the calvaries stood on large green mounds. It is possible that the blue cross at the west end of the nave of Durham (a line of demarcation to women), may have marked the last station of processions. Grindal forbade persons to "rest at any cross in carrying any corse to burying, or to leave any little crosses of wood there." The Eleanor crosses of Geddington, Waltham, and Northampton commemorate the resting-places of the bier of Queen Eleanor on her way to burial in Westminster Abbey, and were erected by King Edward I. There is a beautiful churchyard cross, with a canopied crucifix, at Bitterley in Shropshire, and another at Somerby. Remarkable crosses, with runic knotwork or grotesques and monsters remain at Hawkswell, Penrith, Bedale, Walton in Yorkshire, Kirk Braddon, and Kirk Andreas. Those on the shores of Lough Neagh are covered with sculptures of Scriptural subjects; one at Kirkmichael (Isle of Man) represents a stag-hunt. There are several cemetery crosses at Iona, and one with sculptures at Gainton.

The use of the cross on the brow in holy baptism, as the sign or seal of faith, is mentioned in the time of St. Cyprian. It was made twice in the Eastern Church, but in that of the West only once, with a triple afflation according to the old rituals. It was made on the breast in love, on the forehead as a profession, on the arm for work, says St. Ambrose; and in baptism in England, by the first Prayer Book of Edward VI., on the breast and forehead. The sign was made with the right hand, according to Justin Martyr; or with the whole hand, to signify the five wounds of Christ, as Durando suggests; or with three fingers, if we follow Innocent III., as invoking the Holy Trinity; or with two, to signify the two natures of Christ; from above to below, and from right to left, to denote Christ's descent from heaven to earth, and his passing from the Jew to the Gentile and from

o

death to life, as Gavanti and Merati inform us. The heretical Jacobites, who refused to use water, invented a baptism
of fire by printing a cross with a hot iron on the cheek or
forehead of the baptized; and the Flagellants used "a
voluntary baptism of blood," produced by violent scourging.

Cross for Preaching. Crosses, at which sermons were delivered,
existed on the north side of Norwich and Worcester Cathedrals and St. Paul's, and on the south at Hereford. A beautiful example remains in the Dominican friary at Hereford.
St. Oswald used to preach at the cemetery cross of Worcester.

Crossing. [*Crocia; croix.*] The intersection of the arms of
a church.

Cross, Market. A vaulted open structure, crowned with a
cross, usually built in the centre of the cross streets, for the
shelter of persons attending market. Examples remain at
Elgin, Chichester, Malmesbury, Congresbury, Salisbury,
Glastonbury, Shepton Mallet, and Cheddar. The cross of
Winchester is pyramidal, with statues. The staple cross
still remains near Christchurch (Hants). At the market
cross of Chichester, by Bishop Sherborne's endowment,
people were regaled with wine on St. George's Day, and
dismissed with the words, "All is over. Pray for Lord
Robert's soul."

Cross, Memorial. A beautiful structure of stone was erected
near Durham, in memory of the victory of the Red Hills,
and called Neville's Cross, whilst a humbler crucifix of wood
marks the spot on which the monks had stood, praying for
the rout of the Scots.

Cross of Absolution. A metal cross, inscribed with a Papal
absolution, buried in graves. Specimens have been found
at Meaux, Mayence, Périgueux, and Bury St. Edmund's.
One of a bishop, *c.* 1088, is preserved at Chichester.

Cross of Boundary, Wayside, and Sanctuary. Crosses engraved on boundary stones are mentioned by Louis le
Debonnaire in 807; and standing crosses for the same purposes are frequently alluded to in old English cartularies.
Near Hereford, there is a good example, of the fourteenth
century. At Bury and Beverley, the whole precinct was
distinguished at the cardinal points of the compass by tall
crosses. In Cornwall and the Isle of Man crosses are very

common; in the former county they sometimes have a rounded head. One at Towednack has a curious double-incised cross, like a patriarchal cross, which may mark the boundary of a religious house. St. Burian's has a church-yard cross of the thirteenth or fourteenth century; and at a little distance a sanctuary cross, with a crucifix. At Battel, as late as the seventeenth century, the boundaries were marked by watch crosses. There is a wayside cross, of the fourteenth century, in Burleigh Park.

Cross of Consecration. Twelve crosses were made by the bishop with chrism at the dedication of a church, which were afterwards cut in stone (usually within a circle or quatrefoil), or distinguished by colour. Of the latter kind, one occurs in the Palace Chapel of Chichester; and, simply cut, in two choir chapels of the cathedral; and, of more ornamental character, there are examples at Salisbury, Ottery, Uffington, Moorlinch, Tours, and St. Giles d'Ile. At Exeter, two of the twelve exterior crosses remain. They do not occur earlier than the eleventh century.

Cross of Prelates, *or* **Crozier,** which reminded bishops of their duty, as the pastoral staff was for the direction of the laity. The archiepiscopal cross of Canterbury was distinguished from the processional cross (which had but one) by two crucifixes, behind and before. The double-crossed patriarchal cross, so called, formed by the addition of the scroll, was used in Greece, but in the West is merely a conventional and arbitrary invention of painters (it resembles, however, the cross of Lorraine); and the triple-barred cross of the Pope is equally modern and unauthorized. The cross was carried by a subdeacon in front of Pope Leo IV., when he rode on horseback, according to the custom of his predecessors. The Archbishop of Ravenna was allowed to have his cross borne before him throughout his province, and within three miles of Rome. Augustin entered Canterbury with a cross borne before him; Thomas à Becket was preceded by his silver cross; and St. Anselm refused to allow the Archbishop of Dublin such a privilege in England; whilst Archbishop Peckham, in 1279, excommunicated all persons selling victuals to the Archbishop of York, if the latter persisted in having his crozier carried in state within the province of Canterbury. After the ninth century,

o 2

legates apostolic were permitted to enjoy this distinction; and in the twelfth century, it was extended to metropolitans who had received the pall; but in the thirteenth century, it became common to all archbishops. Celestine III. and the Council of Lateran, in 1213, granted the use of the banner of the cross to be carried before the Patriarchs of Alexandria, Antioch, and Jerusalem, except in the city of Rome. The cross-bearing is a prerogative, not an act of jurisdiction, but simply a sign of honour and reverence due to a dignity. The Bishop of Lucca wears the pall, and, like the Bishop of Pavia, has his cross carried before him by grant of Alexander II., 1070; his canons walk mitred in processions, like cardinals. The kings of Hungary also carry the cross, in memory of King Stephen, to whom it was granted, in 1000, by Pope Sylvester II. The Archbishop of Nazareth had the right of using the cross everywhere; and the Archbishop of Toledo throughout Spain. In 1452 Booth, of York, by a compact made in 1353, gave an image of himself to Canterbury, having carried his cross within the province. The Bishop of Funchal, on certain days, has a crozier carried before him, instead of the staff, in memory of the See having once been metropolitan. The Pope never carries a crozier, unless he should be in the diocese of Tréves, where St. Peter is said to have given his staff to its first bishop, Eucherius. The reason is, that the bend at the top of a crozier betokens restricted jurisdiction, whilst the Pontiff claims unlimited sovereignty. It is certain, however, that originally he received a *ferula*, or staff, at his inauguration. The Bishop of Capetown was the first colonial metropolitan who carried a crozier. There is a fine crozier of the fifteenth century at Toledo, the guion which Cardinal Mendoza, in 1492, planted on the Alhambra; and another, with enamel work, at Cologne. Ragenfroi's cross, of the twelfth century, with Goliath in the head, is at Goodrich Court; a third, with enamel and figures, is in the British Museum.

Cross on Spires. The usual crest of a spire is a cross set upon a circle or mound to represent its empire over the world. The cross of Amiens dates from 1526. Over the cross is usually a cock. At Edinburgh and Newcastle the tower is covered with an actual crown of stone.

Cross, or Rood Cloth. (1.) A veil or hanging drawn in front of the rood-loft. (2.) A cloth to cover the images of the rood in time of Lent, that could be raised, lowered, or drawn aside by a rope.

Cross, Pectoral. (*Crux collaris, enkolpion, periama.*) A cross worn by a bishop on his breast, in imitation of the high-priest's heart-plate, or the gold plate upon his brow, according to Innocent III. The Greeks call it the enkolpion. It is not reckoned among the episcopal ornaments by that Pope, Aquinas, or Durand, although it was worn in their time, and at an earlier date by St. Gregory of Tours, Rottard, Bishop of Soissons, at a council in 863, Pope Leo III. in 811, and St. Alphege of Canterbury in 1012. In the fourteenth century prayers were enjoined to be said when it was put on; and probably at that date it became an ordinary mark of a bishop, worn on his breast, as the stole, which symbolizes Christ's cross, is laid on the shoulders of a priest. St. Cuthbert's crosses are still preserved at Durham.

Cross, Red or Blue. The mark set on houses infected in times of plague.

Cross Week. The days of the rogation were so called in 1571; the name formerly designated the week in which the Invention of the Holy Cross, May 3, was kept.

Cross, Weeping. One at which penance was performed.

Crown. The symbol of victory and recompense (Rev. ii. 10; 2 Tim. iv. 8) was the emblem of martyrdom: first the cross was crowned, and then crowns of laurel, flowers, palm, or precious metal were suspended or carved over the tombs of martyrs and confessors. Sometimes the Divine hand offers the crown; sometimes two crowns are represented for a virgin martyr; or doves carry crowns of olive, emblems of peace bought by the martyr's triumph; or the palm and cross are associated, to represent the merit, the labour, and prize. Hence came the hanging crown of light; and the " oblations," the representation of the Blessed offering their crowns to the Redeemer. The Christian emperors gave their soldiers crowns of laurel, adorned with the monogram of Christ. Clovis II., in 508, Canute at Winchester, and Henry II. offered their crowns at the altar, and never wore them again. Two of the most ancient royal crowns now extant are those of Charlemagne of the ninth century, at Vienna, and St. Stephen of Hungary, consisting of two parts; one sent by Sylvester II. to that king in 1000, and the other, of Byzantine workmanship, the gift of the Emperor Michael Ducas, and about eighty years later in date. The famous iron crown of Lombardy, long preserved in the Treasury of Monza, the gift of Theodolinda, c. 616, is of the sixth century, and remarkable for its enamels and the thin rim of iron, said to have been made out of a nail of the true cross, which is attached to it on the inside, and is the origin of its name. A number of gold votive crowns, of the seventh century, found at Guerrazar, are now in the Museum of Clugny. The Archbishop of York always crowns the Queen Consort.

Crown of Saints. The origin of the aureole, which was at a later period placed about the head, instead of being carried by a dove, or laid on a pillar; sometimes two are represented—one for chastity, the other for martyrdom.

Crown of Thorns. In the catacombs the triumphal sentiment rather than that of suffering is often seen; as, for instance, the Roman soldiers are seen crowning the Saviour's head with flowers, as though the thorns had blossomed. The Saviour's head is said to have been bound with the buckthorn, rhamnus nerpruna, the Arabic alhausegi, and the spina sancta of the Italians. St. Louis IX. was believed to have brought it to Paris, where it was preserved in the Sainte-Chapelle.

Crowns of Candles and Tapers, or, as they were often called in France and Greece, *phares*, in distinction to *canthari*, or oil lamps, were at an early date suspended in the choir; they weré circles covered with tapers or lamps, hung by chains or ropes from the vault. At Tours a standing lamp, with three tapers, is a lingering relic of the custom in France, where glass lustres are now common, but the hanging crown has been revived in England. At Aix-la-Chapelle there is an octagonal crown of the latter part of the twelfth century, which was the gift of the Emperor Frederick Barbarossa; it is made of bronze, gilt, and enamelled, and supports small circular and square towers, which serve as lanterns, sixteen in number; between them are courses of tapers tripled, making in all forty-eight lights. It appears to descend from the dome, as from the vault of heaven, over the tomb of Charlemagne. Another crown of great beauty, the gift of Bishop Odo, brother of William of Normandy, adorned the choir of Bayeux, until its destruction in 1562. The earliest on record is that given by Pope Leo, which was made of silver, and had twelve towers and thirty-six lamps. Another, of cruciform shape, was hung before the presbytery of St. Peter's at Rome, and lighted with 1370 candles, by Pope Adrian. Constantine gave a pharus of gold to burn before St. Peter's tomb; and Leo III. added a lustre of porphyry, hung by chains of gold, to burn before the confession of the Apostles. Sixtus III. gave a silver pharus to St. Mary Major; Hilary presented ten to St. John Lateran; and Walafrid Strabo mentions one hanging by a cord before the altar at St. Gall. At Durham, in the twelfth century, we read that in honour of St. Cuthbert lights were arranged like a crown round the altar, on the candelabrum, and lighted on greater festivals. This is the earliest instance in England. Crowns had little bells, called clamacteria, pendent from them. The corona, the luminous crown or circlet of lights, whether a single hoop or a tier of many, is the most beautiful of all modes of lighting,—hanging and flashing like a cloud of fire before the sanctuary in some grand cathedrals, such as those suspended in the midst of the choir of St. Remi at Rheims, Clugny, Toul, and Bayeux, and representing the heavenly Jerusalem with its gates and towers, and angelic warders. The crown of Hildesheim, of the thirteenth century, is of large dimensions, and is enriched with statues; thirty-six oil lamps burn upon the double gateway towers; seventy-two wax tapers, arranged in threes, blaze on the intermediate battlements; when these hundred and eight lights, like diamonds of living fire, are seen from a distance, they fuse into a disk-like glory, or a sun to which the inscription alludes, being as beautiful as the marigold windows of brilliant glass, which are, in point of fact, crowns in the form of a nimbus, set vertically, and of another kind. In the Greek churches now there is often a wooden cross, hung with ostrich eggs, suspended from the dome, which, almost in mockery of ancient splendour, is furnished with lights upon festivals. Formerly hanging phari burned before the altar; a lustre of seven branches in the

centre of the church, and twelve lights on the sides of the
chancel-screens. The lights arranged along the rood-beam
were only another form of the crown, in a right line instead
of a curve. Three or seven lights typified the divine graces,
and twelve the Glorious Company of the Apostles. . At the
Temple Church (Bristol), there is a beautiful crown, with
twelve branches; on the top is the Blessed Mother and the
Holy Child, and under them are St. Michael and the dragon.
A luminous cross of copper, with intersecting arms, and oil
lamps hanging by chains, of the thirteenth century, is suspended under the dome of St. Mark's (Venice), and is lighted
on great festivals. A Perpendicular crown, formerly at Valle
Crucis Abbey, and now at Llanarmon, has a figure of the
Blessed Virgin, canopied, and four tiers of branches for lights.

Crucifix. No existing monument at Rome, it has been said,
before the fifth century, exhibits a cross either of the Latin or
Greek form; one of Tau shape occurs in 370. The bare cross
never appears before the middle of that century; and those
found in the catacombs were the work of pilgrims, more
pious than intelligent, in comparatively recent times. A
portrait of the Saviour in the middle of a church, is mentioned in Lactantius. It was necessary to be very guarded
in the use of the cross, and its earliest form is that of four
gammas united in the centre like a rude saltier; but possibly, about the fourth century in Africa and distant countries, the cross may have been used more freely. It appeared as the ansata of Egypt on the coinage of Valentinian I., who died in 375: and on that of Constantine,
struck at Aquileia and Tréves; and as a cross on some
Italian monuments of the fourth century. In the time of St.
Paulinus of Nola it was painted amidst crowns, and is represented as jewelled on mosaics at St. Vitalis (Ravenna);
and in the Papacy of John I., who died 400, was carried in
procession. The next step was to exhibit the allegorical
Lamb, with the attributes of the Saviour, the monogram,
and the bare cross, which, in the sixth century, received a
development; first the Lamb carries the cross-banner, then
as it had been slain, is lying at the foot of the cross; next,
bleeding from the riven side and pierced feet; at last,
painted in the centre of the cross, only to give place to the
figure of the Redeemer. In the famous Vatican cross the

Saviour appears in half-length, holding a cross; on the cruets of Monza, the gift of Gregory the Great, the Saviour's head, with a cruciform nimbus, and a cross, flowering, are hesitatingly represented; in another He appears with extended arms, the cross only being wanted. Then the cross, jewelled or flowering, was portrayed below the Saviour's bust or above a lamb. On the pectoral cross of Monza of the same date, the actual crucifix appears in enamel; at first it was simply etched in outline, then it was painted on wooden crosses; at length, in the ninth century, in the pontificate of Leo III., it became a bas-relief. St. Gregory of Tours mentions a painted crucifix which had a loin-cloth at Narbonne, c. 593; and Fortunatus speaks of one in relief —the first on record—in 560. In the East the Council of Constantinople, in 680 and 692, prescribed historic representation in lieu of emblems, and then, probably, the Greeks first used the crucifix even in delineation, and its use was confirmed by Adrian I. The earliest crucifix in the catacombs is said to be of the end of the eighth, though others refer it to the seventh century. There is a painting of one in a Syrian gospel, c. 586, preserved at Florence. In 706 Pope John VII., a Greek by birth, consecrated the first crucifix in mosaic in St. Peter's at Rome, although an earlier portraiture of the kind has been alleged to have been traced to the time of John V., c. 686. However, it was not generally admitted into the sanctuary until the pontificate of Leo III. It occurs on the marble pulpits of Pisa and Sienna, wrought by Nicolo Pisano in 1260-7. Benedict Biscoss brought back from Rome to England a picture of the crucifixion; but St. Augustin, when he entered Canterbury singing litanies, was preceded by a silver cross and a picture of Christ. The crucifix was set on the altar at King Charles I.'s coronation. There is a Norman crucifix still remaining on the west wall of the transept of Romsey, near the south cloister door. There is a crucifix upon church crosses at Sowerby, St. Burian's, and Bitterley. A very remarkable specimen of a raguly cross exists in a hermit's cave at Carcliff Tor, with a lamp-niche near it; another instance of the raguly cross and crucifix, with a dove on the top, occurs on a monument at Bredon. The altar crucifix, paten, and a portion of the processional cross, with a lantern

carried before the viaticum and in funerals, are preserved at
Malen, Isle of Man. At first the Saviour was represented
in a colobium, with sleeves, and reaching to the feet, as in
those of Lucca, Louvain, Ratisbon, Rheims, St. Denis, Senlis, and Langres. In the ninth century the gradual baring
of the figure commenced; it was portrayed always as living
until the eleventh century, but as dead, or with agony depicted in the face, afterwards. The earliest extant example
of this occurs in a fresco of St. Urbino, above the valley of
Egeria, c. 1104. No crucifix in bronze dates before the
tenth century; and possibly the rule of the Council of Byzantium, in 692, enjoining historic rather than symbolic
treatment of sacred subjects in art, may have led to their
adoption; but it was not until 1754 that Benedict XIV.
made them an indispensable accessory of the altar. Few
Italian crucifixes are more ancient than the fourteenth century, except that painted on cloth, stretched on a wooden
cross, c. 1020, in the Vallombrosans' Church at Florence;
another in the Dominican Church at Naples; and the wooden
crucifix of Nicodemus at Lucca, which is clothed like
that of Sienna, and said to have been carried before the
army at the battle of Montaperti, in 1260. A crucifix in
relief, c. 888, on an ivory triptych, given by Agiltruda to
the monastery of Rambona, is now in the Vatican Museum.
The Saviour is supported on a tablet called the suppedanea
(footstool), and His hands and feet are affixed to the cross
with four nails, the number indicated or expressly mentioned by St. Cyprian, Gregory of Tours in the sixth century,
and Innocent III.; and it is borne out by the ancient specimens at Monza and Pisa; but in and after the thirteenth
century, three only are depicted. Cimabue and Marga-
ritone at Florence first represented the Saviour's feet laid
one on the other; an ancient medal portrays His legs
crossed. The famous Vultum de Lucca, by which Rufus
swore, is a crucifix of the eighth century, clothed in a dark
priest's robe; it may be of Byzantine workmanship.

Cruet. (*Urceolus, amula, burette.*) A vase for holding the water
and wine used at Holy Communion. John de Garlande,
writing c. 1080, says there should be two cruets—one for
wine, the other for water. The ancient cruets were very
rarely of crystal or glass, and generally of enamelled copper,

and, in consequence, about the fourteenth century, were distinguished by the letters V and A to mark their contents. Several ancient examples are preserved,—one of the thirteenth century at Paris; one, in the form of an angel, of the fourteenth century, at Aix-la-Chapelle; and another of the fourteenth or fifteenth century in the same cathedral, silver gilt. Sometimes the handle was made in the form of a dragon. After the time of the Renaissance the cruets were made of transparent material; there was one at Grandmont Abbey, however, of crystal, mounted in silver, of the thirteenth century, with an eagle engraved upon it. A cruet for oil, in bronze, used at the coronations of the emperors, and shaped like an antique bust, is preserved in the Treasury of Aix-la-Chapelle. Four of silver, of the ninth century, are preserved in the Vatican; they are of classical form.

Crypt. The earliest crypts which we possess are those of Hexham and Ripon. They contain entrances; one used exclusively by the priest serving at the altar, the others for the ascent and descent of the worshippers, and opening into a chapel containing relics and recesses for an altar. In the wall are niches, with funnel-headed openings for lamps. At Winchester, a low, arched doorway, below the screen of the feretory, led down to the relic chamber, which was in consequence called the Holy Hole. In later times, aumbries and secret hiding-places for plate and treasures were generally provided. In the eleventh, twelfth, and thirteenth centuries, crypts became developed into magnificent subterranean churches, like those of Canterbury, Gloucester, Rochester, Worcester, Winchester; St. Peter's, Oxford; Bayeux, Chartres, Saintes, Auxerre, Bourges, Holy Trinity, Caen; St. Denis, Ghent; Fiesole, Padua, Florence, Pavia, Palermo, and Modena. The earlier examples are of moderate dimensions, resembling cells, as in the pre-Norman examples at Lastingham, at St. Mellon, at Rouen, of the fourth century; St. Maur, and Faye la Vineuse. After the fourteenth century the crypt was replaced by lateral chapels built above ground. In fact all crypts—called in some places the crowds,—the shrouds or undercroft, were built to put Christians in remembrance of the old state of the Primitive Church before Constantine. The crypts of the

Duomo and St. Ambrogio, Milan, Parma, and Monte Cassino, are still used as a winter choir; and the parish church of St. Faith, in the shrouds of St. Paul's, was occupied until the Great Fire. Several of our largest cathedrals, built on unfavourable sites for excavation, as Durham and Chichester, have no crypt. The crypts of Winchester, Rochester, Gloucester, Worcester, and Canterbury were all made before 1085; and after that date the construction of crypts was laid aside, except where they were a continuation of existing buildings, as at Canterbury and Rochester. There is, however, an exceptional Early English example under the Lady Chapel of Hereford, and one of Decorated date at Waltham. A curious Decorated contrivance for erecting a crypt in an earlier church, which was never designed to have one, may be seen at Wimborne Minster, where the crypt under the presbytery lies open to the aisles. At Bosham and Dorchester (Oxon) there is a small crypt in the south alley of the nave, under a raised platform, for an altar or chapel, which is only another specimen, on a much smaller scale, of the same principle which, at Lubeck, Hildesheim, Naumberg and Halberstadt and Rochester and Canterbury, left the crypt floor on a level almost with the nave, and raised the choir level to a great height, enclosing it with stone screens. At Christchurch and Gloucester there was a crypt under each arm of the cross, except the western one. At Auxerre and Bourges the crypt, like the subterranean church of Assisi, was useful as a constructional arrangement to maintain the level of the choir. Occasionally the crypt assumes rather the character of a lower church, as in the Sainte-Chapelle, Eton, and St. Stephen's, Westminster. There is no example of a crypt in the Peninsula or Ireland, and Scotland possesses only one at Glasgow. At Westminster, Glasgow, and Wells, there is a crypt under the chapter-house, which contained an altar. The crypt was frequently brilliantly lighted on great festivals, and its chapels were constantly thronged with pilgrims and visitors, so that at present we can hardly portray to ourselves, in their cheerless desolation, that once they were much frequented places of prayer.

Culdees. (*Colidei*, as Giraldus Cambrensis Latinizes the word when speaking of those of Bardsey and Tipperary; or rather *gille-de,*God's children ; or *kyll-dce,* the house of cells.) Worshippers of God ; communities of secular priests and canons in Scotland, mentioned first in the ninth century. They held the cathedrals of St. Andrew's, Dumblane, and Brechin until the thirteenth century, and until Henry I.'s time survived at York ; and at Armagh till the reign of Elizabeth, where they were vicars choral, their chief or prior being the precentor. Fordun, in the fourteenth century, invented the legend of the Culdees being monks and priests without bishops. In the Columban monasteries the resident bishop exercised all episcopal functions, but was subject to the abbot, being under monastic rule. But this subordination lasted only whilst the whole Scottish Church was monastic; whereas in the Roman Church everywhere the episcopate was supreme, but the monasteries were always seeking exemption from the rule of the diocesans.

Cup. The English name fôr the repository or vessel containing the Host in the pyx, used by Matthew Paris and in the inventories of St. Paul's and other churches.

Cupella (from *cupa,* a cinerary urn). The smaller loculi, used for the burial of children in the catacombs.

Cupola. A small dome. From the same root as *cup,* meaning hollow, and *cap* or *cop,* high.

Curate. A clerk having cure of souls. Until the fourth and fifth centuries in the East there were country curates, and St. Cyprian mentions town clergy. In the large cities, from the fourth to the fifth century in the East and at Rome, the churches had their own priests, who instructed the people, the communion being given only in the cathedral. In the beginning of the fourth century Pope Marcellus established twenty-five titles for preparatory instruction before baptism and reconciliation of penitents. In the Greek Church cardinal priests discharged the same duty. In the beginning of the fifth century the bishop sent the Eucharist for distribution to the parish priests : then by degrees the latter received power to reconcile penitents in case of necessity and heretics in danger of death, in the absence of the bishop ; to visit the sick, to administer extreme unction. and to choose singers. In the seventh century they augmented or diminished the number of assistant clerks according to the condition of the church revenues, as in the sixth century

they had received authority to celebrate in their churches
and oratories, chapels of ease required by the increase in the
numbers of the faithful.   The bishops gradually regarding
them as fellow-workers, subordinated their assistants to
them in all touching divine worship and burial.   It was not
until the close of the sixteenth century in England that the
word was restricted to assistant clergy, deputies, or substitutes.   In France the latter are still called vicars.   In England in the Middle Ages the distinction was drawn between
temporary and perpetual curates.

Cusp. *Cuspis,* a spear point; or *genesse,* the projecting part of
the foliation or curve in Gothic tracery.

Custos. (Warden.) The treasurer or chief sacristan in a
foreign cathedral.   There were also various custodes : the
custodes ordinis, the great monastic officers, the third and
fourth priors, who acted as the rounds; the custos feretri,
the shrine keeper; the custos operis or fabrice, the canon
in charge of repairs of the building in secular cathedrals;
the four custors at Exeter, attendants in the sacristy, bell-
ringers, and marshalmen in processions; and the custos
puerorum at Salisbury, a canon who had the supervision of
the choristers.

Daily Celebration of the Holy Communion is mentioned in
Acts ii. 42–46; and by Tertullian, St. Cyprian, St. Irenæus,
St. Ambrose, St. Gregory, and Stephen of Autun, and is pro-
vided for in the Church of England.

Dais. (1.) Tabernacle work, canopies.   (2.) The raised platform for the principal table in a hall, hence called the high
table.   (3.) The canopy over a president's chair.   The stall-
like seat of the Archbishop of Canterbury remains at Mayfield, and forms the centre of the table.

Dalmatic. A tunicle, originally reaching to the feet, with
large sleeves as long as the elbow, introduced authoritatively,
according to Alcuin, by Pope Stephen in place of the
colobium (*kolobos*), which was sleeveless but had a cowl, being
a tight scanty tunic worn, by effeminate civilians and senators,
and resembling the Greek sakkos.   The dalmatic has the
form of a cross; and is white in colour, in memory of the
Incarnation.   It was sometimes decorated with calliculæ.
It has two red bands behind and before, as symbols of Chris-

tian love, and two purple stripes to represent the blood of Christ. The sleeves originally had double stripes at the wrist. Each side has large fringes, symbolizing the active and contemplative life. It derived its name from Dalmatia, where it was first made in the second century, and was a royal vest worn by Commodus and some other emperors. It resembles the Greek stoicharion. It was formerly restricted to the use of deacons at Rome, but about the tenth century it was adopted as the proper habit of deacons on Sundays. Ferrarius says the white tunic or camisia was girdled, and was replaced by this dalmatic; and Amalarius informs us that it was originally a military dress; but it was worn by bishops in the time of St. Cyprian, and the body of St. Cuthbert, buried in 687, was found clad in a purple dalmatic. It was at first the vestment of the Pope when he officiated pontifically, as in the time of St. Gregory the Great. At an early period its use was permitted to bishops as a distinction and reward of service, and at their request to deacons. Vienne in the time of Zacharias, and in the pontificate of St. Gregory, and Orleans in that of Symmachus, received the privilege as the pledge of communion with Rome. Until the time of Adrian I. deacons of the Gallican Church used only the albe and stole, and up to the fifth century it was reserved to bishops and priests elsewhere than at Rome, where it was the mark of deacons. In the following century it was granted generally to deacons. Strabo, in the ninth century, mentions that priests, in imitation of bishops, wore dalmatics under their chasubles; and until the close of the last century the celebrant at Orleans preserved the custom. Kings, being consecrated with chrism and permitted to bear their part in religious services, were allowed the use of the dalmatic. It is still worn by the sovereign of England at a coronation as a supertunic over the tunic surcoat or colobium. In this country there appears to have been no perceptible difference between the dalmatic and tunicle, although the latter, which was appropriated to subdeacons, is said to have been shorter and less full-sleeved than the former. Probably as the gospeller and epistoler were ranged on either side of the celebrant, for the sake of uniformity it was considered desirable to permit no marked dissimilarity in costume. The hanging plaits now worn represent the ancient full-sleeves. Several tunicles and dalmatics of the fourteenth century are preserved at Spires, and some, formerly at Waterford, are now at St. Mary's, Oscott. The dalmatic of the time of Leo III., or at least of the ninth century, and of Greek manufacture, at St. Peter's, Rome, is vulgarly called the cope of Pope Leo, whereas it was worn by the emperors when created, at their coronation, canons of that basilica. It is of blue silk, embroidered in silver, gold, and silk thread of various colours, with figures, groups, and sacred subjects. The emperors at their coronation, being created canons of St. Peter's, put on dalmatic cope, sandals, and mitre; and, after receiving the crown, officiated as subdeacon at the Mass which followed. All the ancient specimens had orphreys, apparels on the breast and shoulders, and ornamental fringes.

Damascene. *Ferruminatio*, the ornamentation of iron or steel with designs made with the use of acids, and afterwards filled up with gold or silver. The name of this art is derived from Damascus, which was famous for workers in this art.

Dance. As early as the ninth century Pope Eugenius II. prohibited dancing and singing base songs in church; and St. Augustine mentions that dancers invaded the resting-place of St. Cyprian at night and sang songs, but that, on the institution of vigils, the vile practice ceased. In 858 Gautier, Bishop of Orleans, condemned the rustic songs and women dancers in the presbytery on festival days. In 1209 the Council of Avignon prohibited, on the vigils of saints'-days, theatrical dances and secular songs in churches. After the capture of Constantinople, in the fourth crusade, the Latins danced in St. Sophia. Sir T. More speaks of women dancing and singing ribald songs in English cathedrals. At Seville still, on the Immaculate Conception, the last three days of the carnival, and the feast of Corpus Christi, the ten choristers or Seises, dressed in the costume of pages of the time of Philip III. and plumed hats, dance for half an hour, to the clinking of the castanets, a grave measured minuet within the iron screens in front of the high-altar, in blue and white for the Blessed Virgin, and red and white for Corpus Christi. At the conclusion the organ peals out, the bells ring, and the veil is drawn before the Host. At Christmas, in Yorkshire, so lately as Aubrey's time, there

was dancing in churches with songs of Yule, Yule. The
custom may probably be traced to King David, as recorded
in 2 Sam. vi. 14, which is more than can be said for the monks
of Peterborough, who were delated to the Bishop of Lincoln
for dancing in their dormitory at late hours of the evening,
in the fifteenth century. In 1212 processions danced round
the churches of Paris, and women danced in the cemeteries.
A council at Bayeux, in 1300, and another at Bourges, in
1286, condemned dances which took place in churches and
churchyards. There was a curious custom in France for
priests to dance with women after celebrating their first
Mass. On the Feast of Fools dancings were made by the
vicars in the porches of French cathedrals. In the fifteenth
century the faculty of theology branded as bad priests
those who danced in the choir masked and disguised in
women's dresses during the divine office, whilst the clerks
indulged in coarser levities. About the same time, in private,
they laid aside their scutaries before putting on pourpoint
and dyplers. Cardinals joined in the dance : those of Narbonne and St. Sauveur, in 1501, at Milan before Louis XII.;
and the Cardinal of Mantua, in 1562, in fêtes given to Philip
II. at Trent. In 1687 the Jesuits mingled characters sacred
and profane, and entertained the Archbishop of Aix with a
ballet. In 1702 the nuns of Artois and Cambrai used to put
on men's clothes and dance in their cloister. In England, after
the Reformation, in Queen Elizabeth's time, the lords of mis-
rule, between All-hallows Eve and the Purification, and the
summer lords and ladies in May, used to flock on Sundays
and holidays to churches and cemeteries with pipes and drums,
dances, mummings, and masks, bells, and hobby-horses in
the midst of divine service, and then feasted all night in
arbours and bowers. In the seventeenth century the apprentices and servants of York used to keep a sort of saturnalia
in the old minster on Shrove Tuesday.

Dance of Death. A series of pictures in which Death, portrayed as a skeleton, is the principal figure, and represents
all the animation of a living person, sometimes amusingly
ludicrous, and at others mischievous, but always busily employed. It is interesting, as it exhibits the costumes of all
ranks and conditions of life at the period. Hans Holbein
painted a dance of death in the royal galleries at White-

hall. There was also a fine example in the cloisters of the chantry chapel of St. Anne, called the Pardon Church House, on the north side of St. Paul's in London, which dated from the reign of Henry V.; and others were painted in the cloisters of the Holy Innocents at Paris; at Basle and Lubeck in the fifteenth century, at Minden in the fourteenth century; and at Dresden, Leipsic, and Annaberg. In the fourteenth century it is alluded to in the "Vision concerning Piers Ploughman," and has been said to have been acted as a spiritual masque by clerks. Prior speaks of "imperial death leading up Holbein's dance." Possibly it was at once a memorial of a fatal plague as well as a moral lesson.

It was known also under the title of the DANCE MACHABRE, either from an imaginary poet of Germany called Macabar, who was said to have written the appropriate distichs placed under each set of figures, or more probably from the hermit saint of Egypt, Macarius, who is still portrayed on iconostases of Greek monasteries, as he was frequently introduced. The English name was Dance of Pouli's (St. Paul's).

Deacon. (*Diaconos*, a server or minister.) The lowest of the three sacred orders : his office is to assist the priest in divine service, and especially to help in the distribution of the Holy Communion; to read the Holy Scriptures and homilies in the church, to catechize youth, to baptize infants in the priest's absence, to search out the poor and sick, and preach if admitted thereto by the bishop. The priest only is named in the latter part of the Litany, and the office of matrimony and burial. The canonical age for the diaconate is twenty-three years, unless he have a faculty, and then he must continne a whole year, to the intent he may be perfect and well expert in things appertaining to the ecclesiastical administration, except for reasonable causes it shall otherwise seem good to the bishop. The first deacons (Acts vi. 1–7) were appointed as almoners or overseers of the poor, and preachers (Acts viii. 27); but in the Philippians i. 1, and 1 Tim. iii. 8–13, they appear as an ecclesiastical order. By the Fourth Council of Carthage they were regarded as assistants to the priest, and their ordination was reserved to the bishop alone on this ground. In the third century, c. 251, there were only seven deacons at Rome, and at Saragossa in the time of Diocletian,—the complement appointed in large cities by the

Council of Neo-Cæsarea. In the time of Justinian they were numerous at Constantinople; and Sozomen says their numbers varied in other cities. Besides those duties which they discharge in the Church of England, they also absolved penitents, acted as the bishops' representatives in councils, reported to him of the lives of the clergy and laity, collected alms, and had charge of the martyrs' tombs. They were called often Levites, and their dress was alb and stole, then the colobium, and latterly the dalmatic.

Deaconess. (Rom. xvi. 1.) A woman who prepared candidates for baptism, watched the women's door and the conduct of women in church, and visited the sick and poor, like a modern Sister of Charity. Their chairs, cut in tufa, remain in the crossway of the catacombs. The usual age of appointment varied from forty to fifty years of age; occasionally, in earlier times, it was fixed at twenty years, and usually a widow was appointed; imposition of hands and benediction were employed at their ordination. In the fifth and sixth centuries the office was abolished in France, and died out in the Western Church between the eighth and eleventh centuries, but was retained in the Greek Church for a hundred years later. In 173 Pope Soter prohibited them touching the sacred plate or incensing the altar.

Dead Man's Chamber. The room in which a dead monk was laid previous to removal into the infirmary chapel, from whence he was carried into the chapter-house, where the last service was said.

Dean. I. By the Benedictine rule deans in monasteries were subordinate officers presiding over groups of ten monks, and they are mentioned by St. Augustine and Cassian; the canons subsequently adopted the arrangement, which resulted in the single dean with cure of souls. Whence we observe, in order to avoid confusion, that in every Benedictine house the prior was the provost, and under him were the several deans: in the German cathedrals the provost, as president, was charged with the administration of the property, whilst the dean was head of the chapter which he convened, and had the control of the choir and services, being the spiritual chief, as the other was the head in matters temporal. In the Continental churches, where there were provosts, the deans, as their inferiors, like those in the

colleges of our universities, exercised supervision over the
internal discipline. Lyndwood gives the terms dean, archdeacon, archpriest, provost, as applicable to one office. The
canonists say the various terms of prior, dean, and provost
all mean one thing—a president charged with jurisdiction;
and in 1126 the provincial canons of Canterbury apply the
designations priory or deanery to the same office.

The word "dean" was a military title, denoting the officer
in command of ten men; at Constantinople the canons were
called decumans, and the chief cardinal and the highest
auditor rotæ are called deans. In conformity with the de-
cimal system of tithes and tithings, dioceses were divided
into divisions, or districts of ten churches or parishes, presided over by deans urban and rural; and the titles passed
into chapters. The transition from dean to provost, or of
provost to dean was smoothed by the fact that the monastic
deans, superintendents of ten monks, præpositi denis, "pro-
vests of tens," furnished food and clothing to them. In
813 the Council of Mayence substituted deans for provosts;
in 817, by the Council of Aix-la-Chapelle, the provost was
made subordinate to the dean. Chapters having gradually
emancipated themselves from the absolute presidency of the
bishop, changed the name of his immediate vicegerent, till
then known as the provost; and at Lichfield, until 1222, the
deanery was in the bishop's nomination; or when princes
and nobles assumed the revenues and title of lay provosts,
abbots, and priors, the word dean was adopted to denote
the spiritual head; and the provosts became financial officers. At Liége there was a "dean of deans." The change
was gradual; at Rouen in the tenth century, at Upsala and
Urgel it occurred in the thirteenth century, and at Solsona
in 1409. In England the deanery was founded in three
cathedrals in the eleventh century, in five during the twelfth
century, and at Brechin, Dunblane, and Exeter in the thirteenth century. The Dean of Salisbury held Heytesbury,
and the deanery of Windsor and Wolverhampton were held
together.

The dean in England was often the first residentiary, as
at St. Paul's, Salisbury, Lincoln, and Wells; and at Wells,
Chichester, and Lichfield held a prebend. His seat is on
the right-hand side on entering the choir; every member on

coming in or going out bowed to him in his stall. He celebrated in the bishop's absence on the great festivals, and
preached on certain occasions; had the cure of souls, and
supervision of morals; presided in chapter; installed dignitaries and canons; exercised archidiaconal jurisdiction with
the chapter in the prebendal churches, and personally within
the precinct and in the city. He gave leave of absence to
residentiaries for certain times. Until the Reformation he
was elected by the collective chapter, and the right lasted
at Exeter even in the present century. If he visited a prebend he received entertainment for a limited period; and at
York blessed the ashes on Ash Wednesday, the palms on
Palm Sunday, and the candles at Candlemas, and entertained
forty poor folk daily. A dean is now bound to reside eight
months in the cathedral; and the recent Act (3 & 4 Vict.
c. 113, s. 3) placed all the deaneries of the old foundation,
except the Welsh, which are in the bishop's patronage, in
the gift of the Crown. Deaneries of the new foundation were
donatives of the Crown. By the Canons of 1603 a dean was
to reside ninety consecutive days in a year. In the new
foundations the dean has the exclusive control of divine
service "cum decoro," i. e. with befitting propriety and majesty.

There can be no dean without a chapter; at St. Burian's
the deanery was preserved when the chapter was extinguished; at Southwell and Beverley, the Archbishop of
York was virtually, though not nominally, the dean, and,
like the Bishop of Durham, at Bishop's Auckland and
Chester-le-Street, occupied his ordinary stall on the south
side of the choir.

II. RURAL DEANS. Subordinate, temporary officials, under
an archdeacon, appointed by the bishop, removable by him
and the archdeacon, and holding office only during the lifetime of him who nominated them. They are inspectors of
morals and churches, and referees in disputed matters, within
certain assigned districts. In former times they acted as
penitentiaries to receive the confessions of priests, and held
a seal of office in 1237: a meeting of the clergy under their
presidency is called a rural dean's or ruri-decanal chapter.
In 1571 they were required to instruct the people in sermons.

The rural deans held a similar office to that of the chorepiscopus, the rural or inferior archpriest of the seventh and eighth centuries; but he is not mentioned until the eleventh century in England, and then in the laws of King Edward the Confessor as the bishop's dean with his chapter, in 1064. The Council of Tours in 1163 mentions, that in some dioceses there were paid deans, or archpriests, vicegerents of bishops or archdeacons, in matters delegated to them, and judges in ecclesiastical causes. In Italy the office is unknown. Citations were committed to their care in the thirteenth century, and in 1281 they were sworn annually in the bishop's synod not to be guilty of abuses in such matters. In 1222 they were forbidden to demand aid or subsidies from the clergy; and in 1200 were desired to visit with only two horses. By Canons made in 1195, if any person was suspected of crime he was to be admonished privately by the dean-rural, then in presence of two or three persons, or lastly in the chapter, where he might be punished. Sometimes they were beneficed within their deanery, but not in all cases. These deans collected the taxes imposed upon the clergy.

III. DEANS OF CHRISTIANITY. (1.) Delegates of the bishop in priest's orders, afterwards or otherwise known as officials, judges ecclesiastical, delegated by the bishop or archdeacon to hear causes in their courts. From this exercise of ecclesiastical or spiritual jurisdiction, their courts were called Christian Courts, because the bishops were called in the ancient edicts Christian, and their jurisdiction and courts, being founded on the law of God and the Church, bore the same name. (2.) Rural deans. (3.) Capitular deans in the cathedral cities or prebendal churches and estates.

IV. DEANS OF PECULIARS. There are only two deans of spiritual promotion—the Rector and Dean of Bocking a Peculiar of Canterbury, and the Dean and Vicar of Battle— nominated by the abbot of the monastery as the parish priest, with archidiaconal power within the leuga or precinct. There were similar deans, members of their houses, in the convents of Carlisle, Evesham, Canterbury, Waltham, and Worcester. The town monk of Gloucester had similar duties; and in a Clugniac monastery the dean was the prior's suffragan and villæ provisor. In Cenignola, in Italy, the archpriest of the collegiate church claimed similar privileges within his territory. There are several deans in covenant or condition, some of lay promotion, presiding as commissary or principal official, having jurisdiction but no cure of souls, within peculiars of the Archbishop of Canterbury—those of Croydon, Malling, Pagham, and Tarring, and the Arches.

V. DEAN OF THE PROVINCE OF CANTERBURY. The Bishop of London, who was so called because he executed the archbishop's mandate summoning the bishops to Convocation; he is also honorary dean of the chapel, so styled on account of the dignity of the sovereign, whose oratory it is.

Decade. The tenth bead in a rosary. One formed of brass, having a disk carved with the sacred monogram, a cross, and the three nails, was found at Huntingdon.

Decorated Architecture is divided into two periods: (1.) Early, with geometrical tracery (1300-1325). (2.) Late, with flowing tracery (1325-75). The characteristics of the style consist in tracery, which, in the reign of Edward II., was reticulated like network; under Edward III., flowing; and, in the time of Richard II., gradually changing into Perpendicular. At Gloucester, the work resembles the later style, but the mouldings are still Decorated. The tracery appears in the orbs, or ornamented spaces upon walls. The circles become pointed and flowing ovals; crockets and finials receive a more undulating outline; buttresses support angles obliquely; pinnacles are square or polygonal, with crockets and finials; the vaulting has the main ribs tied together by transverse, diagonal, and cross ribs; diaper-patterns cut in stone are profusely used; the triforium is a mere gallery; bosses are multiplied, and the ribs entangled on the vaulting. The windows are of large dimensions; their tracery formed of geometrical figures; and, later in the style, flowing in wavy lines; while mullions divide the window below into many compartments. The doors resemble Early English doors, but are not so deeply recessed; the arches in large examples are pointed, in smaller of ogee form; niched statues are introduced in the jambs; and windows and doors have often triangular or ogee canopies. The feather mouldings are seldom found wanting. Iron scroll-work is still employed on doors. Mouldings have usually large shallow hollows, ovolos, and ogees, the curve of contra-flexure; fillets and splays are often used; round mouldings have generally a sharp edge, or are convex in the middle and concave at the ends; enrichments are fanciful, leafage, heraldic, or masks; arches are drop, equilateral, or ogee. Stone-work is foliated, *i. e.* cut into small hollows like spear-heads; buttresses are niched, and have triangular pediments or pinnacles; pillars, in plan like a lozenge, have clustered shafts; walls are diapered, and hollows enriched with ball-flowers—a three-petal flower, enclosing a grenade or ball (the pomegranate of Castile, or the Temple of Jerusalem, or, possibly, copied from the bells on the hem of the priest's robe), or a flattened blossom of four petals; arches form equilateral triangles; and the Lady Chapel is a prominent building. The scroll moulding is freely used. Tombs began to have canopied effigies introduced in the sides; slabs to be inlaid with brass, and sepulchral inscriptions added to them; and later, the sides were enriched with quatrefoiled panels.

Decretals. Decisions of the Pope in ecclesiastical matters of law. They were in force until the fourteenth century, when the Papal influence began to decline.

Defender of the Faith. A title given, October, 1521, by Leo X. to Henry VIII. The King of France is called the Eldest Son of the Church and Most Christian; and the King of Spain the Most Catholic.

Degrading. To deprive a clerk of holy orders. In 1529 there is a curious ceremony on record, when a bishop scraped the finger nails of both hands of one Castellane with a piece of glass, saying that by it was taken from him all the power which had been conferred by the anointing of his hands at Ordination. From a priest, the paten, chalice, and chasuble; from a deacon, the New Testament and stole; from the subdeacon, alb and maniple; from the acolyth, the taper and cruets; from the exorcist, the office of his order; from the reader, the lectionary; and from the ostiarius, the church keys and surplice were taken; and in all cases the tonsure was shaven off.

Degree. The steps of an altar, which ought always to exceed two; three is the most common number.

Deodand. A gift to God. A personal chattel forfeited to the king, and applied to pious uses, having been the immediate cause of a man's death.

Deosculatory. The pax bread.

Deposition. (1.) Death. (2.) Burial of a saint or ecclesiastic, in the sense of consignment,—the temporary trust of a treasure to the tomb, in sure hope of another life.

Desk. A low desk for the Litany, erroneously called a 'faldstool ;' is often placed in the central alley of the church, before the chancel door, or in the choir of a cathedral or collegiate church. It is, no doubt, a modification of the ancient lectern, at which the cantors stood. A small prayer desk and seat are in a side chapel of King's College, Cambridge. At St. Ruan Major there are two carved desk-ends, for gospeller and epistoler, within the reod-screen, one of them supported by an angel kneeling. The bishop's desk, of the early part of the sixteenth century, remains at Palencia.

Despotica. Great holydays in the Greek Church,—Christmas, Easter, Ascension, Pentecost, Good Friday, Annunciation, Presentation, Palm Sunday, Transfiguration, Raising of Lazarus, and the Lord's Baptism, answering to our Trinity Sunday.

Detached Bell-towers occur at Spalding, Fleet, Berkeley, Torrington, Pembridge, Bosbury, Richard's Castle, Ledbury, and Yarpole ; Beccles, Walton, Woburn, Mylor, Brynnlys, Hennlan, Llangyfelach, Gunwalloe, East Dereham, Marston-Morteyne, Lapworth, Elstow, Magdalen and New Colleges (Oxford), Dunblane, Kilkenny, Evreux, Groningen, Namur, and the Jesuits' Church (Antwerp). At Talland a covered way connects it with the church.

Deviation. An inclination of the direction of the ground plan of a church to the right or left, symbolical of our Lord's drooping upon the cross. In some instances, the cause may be, at first sight, attributed to the inequality of the site, in very rare and peculiar instances, as at Eastby and Auxerre ; but even this doubt disappears in view of the fact that De Caumont found that in one hundred French churches of the thirteenth and fourteenth centuries there was invariably a northward inclination ; whilst in most English churches, the deflection lies southerly, as at Geneva and Nevers.

Diaconicum Majus. (1.) The Greek sacristy for keeping the books, vestments, and plate. It was also called the aspastorion or salutorium, because bishops received guests and visitors in it. (2.) *Diaconicum Minus.* A vestry with a little sub-altar, placed on the right of the high-altar, to hold candles, fire, incense, vestments, and the eulogies or blessed bread. Here the celebrant and assistants robed. It was called also *skeuophylakion* and *bematis diakonikon*.

Diadem. An ornamental band round the head.

Diaper. From Ypres or *diaspro*. (1.) Cloth with a pattern woven into it. (2.) An ornament of flowers for walls, which came into use in the eleventh century. Good specimens occur at Bayeux, Canterbury, Gloucester, Rochester, and Westminster. In the fifteenth century it passed from the sculptor into the hands of the painter. At St. Alban's we discover traces of successive stages of mural enrichment;— representation of joints of masonry in the thirteenth century; rich diapering of the fourteenth, in imitation of stained glass; and in the fifteenth, Scriptural or legendary illustrations. At Worcester and Bristol the chapter-houses have courses of green and white stone, after the Italian fashion of using particoloured marbles. The chapter-house of Westminster has rich colouring; and at Gloucester, the great arcade of the nave was elaborately painted. At Rochester the shafts and arches were painted red, green, and yellow; the whole face of the stone-work was filled with the same tint, not distinguishing the moulding, both in the nave and transept. At Carlisle the choir pillars were painted white, and diapered with red roses nearly a foot in diameter, with a gold monogram, "IHC," or "J.M." of the fifteenth century. In Conrad's "glorious choir" of Canterbury, the vault was painted like a sky. At Peterborough the Norman cieling,—that of Abbot Wheathamstead, at St. Alban's,— and those at Chichester, and Bolton, of the Early Tudor period, are good specimens of their style.

Dignity. A term, not earlier than the eleventh century, implying pre-eminence in rank, administration with jurisdiction for life, superior place in choir and chapter. Besides archbishops and bishops, deans, by pontifical right, and the precentor and archdeacon, by common law, are dignitaries; so also, by custom, are the chancellor and treasurer of a cathedral. Canons are quasi-dignitaries. Dignities were founded for the preservation of church discipline. In foreign churches, they are called prelacies. In Spain, dignitaries had a special stall, but no voice in chapter. Dignities are conferred by collation. Between the thirteenth and fifteenth centuries, the dignitaries in Germany prefixed the noble " Von " to their names.

Dimity. Stuff from Damietta. A kind of fustian.

Diocesan Synod. An assembly of the bishop and his priests to put in force the canons of general councils, national and provincial synods, and to agree upon rules of discipline for themselves.

Diocese. (Greek *dioikesis*.) (1.) A district subject to the jurisdiction of a chief Roman governor. In the Byzantine empire a union of several provinces or churches under a supreme viceroy, præfectus prætorio, who resided in the chief city. There were four of these divisions. An ecclesiastical district, in the third and fourth centuries, corresponding with the civil district, under the rule of the metropolitan archbishop, and comprising sees or *parochiæ*, parishes of bishops. (2.) The district of an individual bishop, including the parishes presided over by priests. In the Roman empire every city, with its proasteia or suburb, had its senate and president. In imitation of this plan the Church had its presbytery and chief, called apostle, angel, or bishop, with jurisdiction over the paroikia, corresponding with the civil circuit (Titus i. 5). A term used during the first three centuries, as by St. Jerome, St. Epiphanius, and the Councils of Antioch. Parish priests were established in the towns which had civil magistrates. The whole empire was divided, at first, into provinces, under a prætor or proconsul living in the metropolis, and then into dioceses, comprehending many provinces, under an exarch, vicar, or imperial prefect. To these corresponded the metropolitan or primate in the ecclesiastical metropolis and province, and the exarch or patriarch in the chief city of a diocese. At length the paroikia became the parish of a priest, the diocese the district of a bishop, and a province remained primatial.

Diptychs. (Greek, *dis*, twice, and *ptussein*, to fold.) (1.) Two writing tablets joined together. On one were inscribed the names of the living, and on the other those of the dead ; or when the leaves became numerous, enclosed within two covers of ivory ; thus forming the church roll or catalogue of benefactors and worthies, with the names of the magistracy, the clergy, saints, martyrs, confessors, and the faithful

dead, to mark the strict tie and communion that binds in one
the Church triumphant and militant. It was read out by the
deacon during the Holy Communion from the fourth century,
until the names became too numerous for recital, and only a
general commemoration mentioned by St. Augustin was made.
The use of the diptych, if not of apostolical date, is to be traced
to the second century. St. Cyprian alludes to it in the third.
The practice was continued until the twelfth century in the
Western Church, and until the fifteenth century in the
Greek. It is clear, however, that a book of life stood on the
altar at Durham and St. Alban's until the Reformation; and
even in the seventeenth century, at Chichester, SS. Wilfred
and Richard were commemorated, and a list of benefactors
set up in a public place in the cathedral. The diptychs of
Fulda, Amiens, Trèves, Arles, and Rambona are preserved.
(2.) A picture which folds together, with ivory sculptured
covers, such as those preserved in the Vatican, at Vercelli,
St. Maximus, Trèves, Besançon, and the Barberini Library.
Sometimes the tablets, according to their number, were
called triptychs, pentaptychs, or polyptychs; or, from their
use and contents, holy or mystic tablets, ecclesiastical cata-
logues, anniversaries, the matriculation roll of the church,
and the book of life or the living. There are several classes
of diptychs :—(1) diptychs of the baptized, a baptismal
register of the citizens of heaven, corresponding to the
Roman fasti, or roll of new citizens; (2) diptychs of the
living, containing the names of the sovereign, clergy, and
benefactors, each in its own column, the titles of œcumenical
councils from the time of Justin I., and names of saints.
The last entries became the origin of calendars and also of
hagiologies or legends; (3) diptychs of the dead, containing
the names of bishops and other worthies. After the recitation of the names by the deacon, the celebrant said the
" Prayer after the Names," or " On the Diptychs," " O Lord
and Master, our God, grant these souls rest in Thy holy tabernacles;" and in the case of bishops the people replied, " Glory
be to Thee, O God." The diptychs were usually read at the
time of commemoration of the dead in the Canon of the Mass,
but in some churches of Gaul and Spain after the Offertory,
where the " Collect after the Names " followed the oblation
by the people. In some places the deacon read out of the

diptych from the ambon, or at the foot of the altar; in others the subdeacon recited it softly to the celebrant, or behind the altar. In private Masses the celebrant himself read them. Sometimes names were erased, and heretics in this way retorted on Catholics. So Theodoret attributes the reconciliation of the Churches to the restoration of St. Chrysostom's name upon the diptychs of Constantinople thirty-five years after his death.

Dirge. (*Dirige.*) The use of the Psalm from which the words *dirige gressus meos,* "direct my steps," (Psalm cxvi. 9) are taken has been ascribed to St. Isidore or Gregory. It was daily said in choir during Lent after the Hours, except on the three last days of Holy Week; and frequently at other times, with the exception of Eastertide. It is now said, by obligation, in the Roman communion, yearly, on November 2. It occurs in the Office of the Dead, and was often called the Placebo, from the antiphon (Ps. v. 8, Vulgate version), or the vigil of the dead. The word dirge, a funereal song, is derived from it. The price paid for singing a dirge was a groat, or fourpence.

Discant. Measured music, pure and simple. (1.) Two chants, a double chant, the Greek diaphonia. (2.) The accompaniment to a chant or melody,—harmony. Part singing with the principal or leading voice, the tenor, called often the motet, triplum, and quadruplum, according to the number of additional voices.

Discharging *or* **relieving Arch.** A blind arch built into the wall in order to relieve the masonry or opening below from the superincumbent weight.

Disk. The Greek paten, which is larger than that of the Western Church. At the time of the communion it contains the wafer for the priest, with the seal (sphragis) and the letters IC XC NI KA, the abbreviation of Christ the Conqueror, within four compartments, of the shape of a Greek cross. Round the hollow of the disk are the small altar-breads for the communion of the clergy and laity.

Diversity of Ceremonies. In the Holy Communion different countries had diverse rites, as the ancient liturgies were drawn up independently, and bishops added to them what appeared to be edifying. At length the use of the metropolitan church was ordered to be followed throughout the province; and the Fourth Council of Toledo prescribed one order in the Mass, Vespers, and other offices to be observed in Spain and Gaul. About the year 800 Gaul and Germany adopted the singing of the Nicene Creed from Rome, and in 1073 Spain adopted the Roman use in great part. In England the uses of York, Lincoln, Hereford, Bangor, and Salisbury did not exhaust the diversity of rites; and in France the various customs are hardly extinct. For instance, at Lyons as at Milan and by Maronites the amice is worn outside the alb in Holy Week. The Ambrosian rite at Milan, the Mozarabic rite of Toledo, the Benedictine and the Cistercian uses stand apart from the forms observed by other Churches.

Divine Liturgy, The, representing the Saviour saying Mass and served by angels is represented on the walls of the apse and the drum of the dome in Greek churches, and was imitated at Lyons and Rheims. In the latter cathedral the ideal passed into a ceremonial, for at grand Masses, before the Offertory, the choristers, dressed like angels, came out one by one with measured steps from the sacristy and laid upon the high-altar or a side credence the vessels for divine service.

Division of Sexes. In 1549 the communicants were "to tarry still in the choir, or in some convenient place nigh the choir, the men on the one side and the women on the other side," and "all other" were to "depart out of the choir except the minister and clerks." And in the existing Rubric the communicants are invited to "draw near." In 1633 Archbishop Abbot also desired the communicants after communion "to return to their seats and places in the church." In the Jewish Temple the men occupied a different place from women, and the Christian Church adopted the arrangement. At Rome the gospel was read on the south side of the altar towards the men, whereas St. Augustine says it was usually read on the north, in allusion to Jer. iii. 12 ; and the Clugniac deacon turned to the east. In the basilica the right-hand aisle was allotted to men, and that on the left to women. Tribunes on this side were occupied by widows, and the opposite galleries by young religious women. The separation was no doubt originally an Eastern arrangement, but was observed at Florence, St. Ambrose

(Milan), St. Mark's (Venice), Modena, St. Michael (Padua), Andernach, Boppart, and Bonn. At St. Bride's (Kildare) there were two doors, two chancel arches, and a partition running along the centre of the nave, from east to west. It still lingers in the diocese of Bayeux and many parts of England. A gallery for women was erected under the roof of the nave aisles at St. Lawrence, St. Agnes, and the Four Coronati at Rome. In Brittany men occupy the nave, and women are seated in the aisles.

Doctors, The Four, of the Church. These are Saints Ambrose, Augustine, Jerome, and Gregory. The Angelic Doctor is St. Thomas Aquinas ; the Divine Doctor, J. Ruisbroek ; the Doctor of Grace, St. Austin; the Invincible Doctor, W. Occham ; the Mellifluous Doctor, St. Ambrose ; the Profound Doctor, Thomas Bradwardine, Archbishop of Canterbury ; the Seraphic Doctor, Bonaventura ; the Subtle Doctor, Duns Scotus. The Scholastic Doctors were Aquinas, Scotus, Gabriel, Bill (1480), and Roger Bacon (1270). Doctors of Divinity had a ring given to them as an ornament of honour and authority, and appeared in boots as a sign of being always ready to preach the gospel. They wore scarlet as the colour of dignity, and were permitted to wear a gold ring, except when acting as celebrants.

Dog Whipper. An official in many post-Reformation churches and cathedrals, as Durham and at Ripon ; in Queen Elizabeth's time, at St. Paul's, he paid a special visit on Saturdays. In the cathedral of Lima there is a perrone. In Germany he is called Hundfogde, or Spögubbe, and in France Roy de l'Eglise. At Amsterdam there is, in the New Church, the dog-whipper's chapel ; and in Portuguese churches a common adjunct is the kapella dos execuçães.

Dole. (1.) A boundary, as in the word dolemeads at Bath. (2.) A distribution, or deal of alms at funerals or on anniversaries of the dead. Bread is still given every Sunday on the founder's tomb at Tidswell, and loaves are distributed at Chichester and in many churches still in pursuance of a bequest. These were often called the livery, *i.e.* delivered dole. According to some monastic rules the commons of a dead abbot were laid before his chair daily, and given to the poor after hall, for forty days. Casalins says that in his time the same practice was prescribed in France at the demise of sovereigns and princes of the blood.

Dom. A title of respect given to the Benedictines and canons, being the short for dominus, the medieval ser (sieur), and sir of the Reformation, applied to non-graduate priests. The B.A. of Cambridge is now designated dominus, but the M.A., as at Oxford, is dominus magister, and the D.D. dominus doctor.

Dome. A cupola, probably so called as being the distinguishing ornament of the cathedral; the Italian *duomo*, the German *dom*, and Latin *domus Dei*, God's house, the dominicum of St. Cyprian, Ruffinus, and St. Jerome. The dome is the necessary constructional development as the fittest covering for a round building; at first it had a flattened form; as the builders grew bolder it was elevated, and received additional height by means of a story or drum set under it. This beautiful ornament was used in pre-Norman times in England; it is seen at Valencia, Zamora, Salamanca, Clermont, Le Puy, Cahors, Angoulême, of the early part of the twelfth century; in Poitou, Périgord, and Auvergne; at Aix-la-Chapelle, Cologne, Antwerp, and along the banks of the Rhine; at Florence (1420), Artor, Venice, Ravenna, Parma, Piacenza, Verona, Milan, Como, Pavia, and Antwerp; in the Santa Sophia of Constantinople, the bulbous domes of Russia, and the flattened cupolas of the Saracen. It became the lantern in English Gothic art, but is closely approached in the superb octagon of Ely. Whether elongated, spherical, or polygonal, it is one of the noblest crowns of the exterior of a church, and perhaps the most effective in adding dignity to its interior. Span of domes—Pantheon, 144; Florence, 142; St. Peter's, 139; St. Paul's, 115; St. Sophia, 100.

Dominant. The note which most frequently recurs in a Gregorian chant or psalm.

Dominical Altar. The high-altar.

Dominical, or Sunday Letter. Seven letters of the alphabet, from A to G, marking Sundays in the calendar. If Sunday falls on January 1, then A is the Sunday letter; but if on a Saturday, then B; in retrograde order, as in the case of leap-year, when from March the next letter backward is taken.

Dominicans. The Black Friars or Preachers, an order founded by St. Dominic of Calagorra, Canon of Osma, in 1205, and confirmed by Pope Honorius III. in 1216. The rule, a modification of that of St. Austin, was strict abstinence from flesh: fasts of seven months' duration, from Holy Cross Day to Easter, and on all Fridays; maintenance wholly by the alms of the faithful; the use of woollen clothes only; and at first a mere white tunic and scapular, without a cowl. In time this rigour was abated, and they wore a white serge tunic, a black cappa or cloak, and a hood for the head; and their simple, unadorned chapels became magnificent churches, rich in every ornament of architecture, colour, and carving. From their devotion to the Blessed Virgin, they called themselves at first, until the Pope forbade it, Brothers of the Virgin Mary; and they always had a Madonna and crucifix in their cells. There was a general chapter held annually. The superior was called master of the order, and the greater officers, priors and superiors. A Dominican, since the time of Pope Honorius III. (1216–27), is always master of the sacred palace, the interpreter of the Holy Scripture, and censor of books. The order was instituted for preaching at home and for missions to the heathen; the crusade against the Albigenses and the horrible Inquisition in Spain were carried on by the Black Friars: the order has produced 1458 cardinals. It used to take mere children and enrol them before the conventional age of probation. They held that the Virgin was conceived in original sin, consecrated Saturdays to her honour, and were, in scholastic theology, stout Thomists: as the leader of that party, Thomas Aquinas, was of their order. Their preaching-cross remains at Hereford, their refectory at Canterbury, the nave of the church and other buildings may be seen at Norwich, and part of their convent at Lynn, Beverley, and Gloucester. There were three divisions of the order—the preaching friars, who occupied a convent; cloistered nuns; and the militia of Jesus Christ, who engaged in actual war on heretics; they afterwards admitted brethren and sisters of the Penitence of St. Dominick, who were approved in 1360 by Innocent VI. Bishop Pecock says they evaded their rule, which forbade them to touch money, by counting with a stick. The early Dominican churches were plain, without images, carvings, or pictures, and provided

Q

with only one bell. The use of the organ was not common. Women were not allowed to sit in the choir-aisles, and large high screens parted off the friars from the congregation, for whose use, at the elevation of the Host, windows were opened in these partitions. The lay brothers sat apart. Occasionally their churches, as at Venice and Pistoia, were cruciform, but usually terminated in a square end; the naves of Perugia and Spoleto are aisleless, but sometimes they had narrow recesses, as at Ghent, or lateral chantries for altars; or, as at Pisa, Sligo, Brecon, Kilmallock, Gloucester, and Roscommon, a single aisle for the accommodation of the congregation at sermons; lateral chapels were added at a later date. Apsidal choirs occur at Monza, Milan, Toulouse, Antwerp, Oberwesel; and at Paris, Agen, and Toulouse the church was double, consisting simply of two aisles of equal length. At Louvaine and Norwich the nave has aisles of the usual size. The choirs had no aisles. The chapter-house at Toulouse was apsidal, and had three aisles. They were also called Jacobins, from their first house in Paris, in the Rue St. Jacques. In England they established themselves at Oxford, in 1221. The preacher for the Papal family was a Dominican, until Benedict XIV. appointed a Capuchin. This order prays more than any other for the dead, the friars chanting the " De Profundis" every time they pass through the cloister.

Dominus Vobiscum. The Lord be with you. The Council of Braga, 563, said that this form of blessing, with the response, was retained in the East from the times of the Apostles. It occurs in Scripture, Judges vi. 12; St. Luke i. 28. In early times the salutation was confined to the faithful only. In the fourth and fifth centuries the strictness of this observance was relaxed. When the Mass of the catechumens was joined to the Mass of the faithful the bishops alone used the form, " Peace be with you," as the representative of Christ; whilst a priest said, " The Lord be with you." But in 561 the Council of Braga, and Pope Innocent III. at a later date, directed the bishop to say *Dominus vobiscum*, in order to show that he was a priest as well as prelate. The response is derived from 1 Cor. vi. 19; xvi. 18; Gal. vi. 18; Rev. xxii. 17, in allusion to the indwelling Spirit.

Doors. The principal door of a Gothic church fronted the centre of the nave, but did not receive any ornamental decoration of sculpture, in France, until the twelfth century, as at Clugny, Vezelay, and Moissac. About that period, in France, and in the Early English style, the door was usually divided into two sub-arches, symbolically of Christ, in His two natures, as the door; and constructionally, one as an entrance for persons coming in, and the other as a means of egress, set under a lintel at the base of the outer comprising arch. The tympanum, a triangular space between the lintel and crown of the arch, and the voussoirs, the stones composing the arch, were often filled with images and tabernacle-work; whilst the older doorways were religiously preserved, as at Auxerre, Sens, and St. Denis. Bishop Ralph of Chichester, in his quarrel with the king, barred the cathedral door with thorns against the laity. The lateral doors usually present a mere archway, without a central pillar, but closed with folding-doors. Sometimes they are highly enriched with sculpture. In cathedrals the north door was used for the passage of funerals, and by the laity. In parish churches where there were two, one on the west wall of the transept, as at Hythe and Sompting, the second was used by women. The western doors were only opened for the reception of a bishop, the primate, or a sovereign prince. But there is no such entrance at Romsey, which was the minster of a nunnery, or in churches with western apses. At Canterbury the south door was used as a spiritual law court in early times; but, as in other cathedrals, where the cloister was on the north, became the ordinary entrance for lay persons. At the church door marriages and the churching of women were commenced, but from 1549 to 1552 the latter ceremony was removed to the choir door, where a light was always kept burning in minsters; and before it the offending novices of Bury did penance, lying down to be trodden over by the convent; and in cathedrals peccant vicars kept involuntary vigil.

Doors often bore names of saints, as at Paris and Amiens, or of adjoining buildings, as at Rome. At Paris; Romsey, and other English churches there were red doors in the transept. The superb bronze doors of the baptistery of Florence, by Ghiberti and Andrew Ugolini, cannot be matched even by those of Aix-la-Chapelle, Mayence, Augsburg, Hildesheim, or Novgorod. In the first church of St. Denis, in 1140, three portals of gilt bronze adorned its western front; but in France, throughout the thirteenth and fourteenth centuries, the taste of the people achieved what Italian artists could not produce,—statuary such as that which flows over the portals of St. Denis, Angoulême, Poictiers, Paris, Vezelay, Autun, Chartres, Sens, Auxerre, Laon, Rheims, and Amiens; whilst at the same time the richest patterns in wrought-iron work adorned the doors of the treasury of Sens, of the thirteenth century, and the great entrances of Paris, of the same date. Besides these were massive knockers in the twelfth and thirteenth centuries. The latter were rings, set in a square or round plate of metal, which, during the fourteenth and following centuries, became either square or oblong, and the knocker was moved by the tail of a lion or dragon, as at Bayonne, of the thirteenth century. The Brazen-noses of Oxford and Stamford are well known. At Chartres, Arles, and Provence, lions form the colossal warders of the doors.

The Norman doorways are usually enriched with ornament, with various patterns, grotesques, and signs of the zodiac. The arch is round or segmental; and occasionally a pediment projects over it. The tympanum has generally some Scriptural sculpture, or the zodiac, as at St. Mary's Walmgate, at York. The doors have as their only ornament hinges and scrollwork of iron. The Early English doorways are almost universally pointed. The panels are filled with distinct shafts, and the opening divided by a single or clustered shaft into two arches. The scrollwork of the doors is more delicate, elegant, and elaborate than in the former style. The Decorated doorways are less deeply recessed, and the shafts are slighter; a weaker moulding over the arch is common, and the terminations of scrollwork usually are in the form of foliage. In the Perpendicular period the square lintel of the outer moulding, the spandrils filled with carving, small shafts, large spaces in the joints, and panelled doors are characteristic of the style.

Dormitory. The sleeping chamber, placed under the charge of the chamberlain in a monastery or house of regular canons or friars, invariably built either on the west or east side of the cloister, and with few exceptions, as at Merevale and Byland, in the latter position. In the Cistercian houses the dormitory always adjoined the transept, and extended over the chapter-house and calefactory. In the Austin canons' church of Hexham a noble flight of stairs communicates with the south wing of the transept; and at Westminster a bridge afforded communication with the triforium and staircase, running across the end of the sacristy. At St. Alban's a confessional recess has been detected at the foot of the staircase, where the monks were shriven on descending for matin Mass. In this instance, and at Durham, it was on the west side of the cloister. Occasionally it stood east and west, at right angles to the cloister, as at Worcester, Winchester, and Chester. The dormitory was divided into cells by partitions [called intermedia, which were introduced by the Clugniacs] from one another, and from the central alley, by doors, hung with curtains, or made three-parts of trellis-work. This external screen only was preserved by the Dominicans, and did not exceed a cubit in height. Each cell had its own window and book-desk, used for study during the meridian or noonday repose. It was furnished with an oaken bedstead, a bolster, rug, palliasse, blankets, and a coverlet of fur or sheepskin; with a round mat at the side, a bench at the foot, and a perch overhead, on which the monk's day clothes were hung. A light burned at each end of the chamber, which was strewn with rushes, hay, or mats. In the centre was a cross, at which any occupant who disturbed the brotherhood was required to do penance. A patrol and watchman saw that order was kept, and the prior visited every cell before retiring to rest. After matins, for which they were awoke by a deputed officer, they returned to the dormitory for a short time, and after dinner were allowed another interval for repose or study, which was passed in their cells. At a later date, in the diocese of Winchester, the Austin canons kept pet birds; and the nuns of Romsey and some members of religious houses in Lincolnshire took children into their dormitories. The monks of Peterborough were once delated to the bishop of the diocese in the fifteenth century for dancing in their dormitory at night.

Dornyx. Coarse damask, made at Doornix, or Tournay.

Dorsal, *or* **Dossal.** (From *dorsum* Latin, and *dos* French, the back; Germ. Postergule.) (1.) The hinder part of a stall. (2.) The hanging behind the choir stalls, or an altar, and rendered tapecium. At St. Alban's, at the close of the eleventh century, it was wrought with the martyrdom of the saint; and two others, in the twelfth century, represented the prodigal son and the traveller who fell among thieves. Some heraldic tapestries were in use behind the stalls of Exeter. Possibly dorsals were the origin of the linen pattern on panelling.

Double Chant. An innovation on the ecclesiastical or single chant, arising out of a mistake made by a deputy-organist at Gloucester Cathedral in the last century. The earliest instances, probably, were those of Turner and Isam, in Dean Aldrich's collection.

Double Churches. (1.) Those of Monte Subiaco, like that of Assisi, were due to the peculiarities of the site; but, in fact, every minster provided with a crypt formed a double church; so did the chapels built in the fourteenth century on the model of the Sainte-Chapelle at Paris; St. Stephen's, Westminster; St. Etheldreda's, Holborn; the prior's chapel, Ely; and that of Chichester House, London, which had an external approach to the upper chapel. Of the same kind were the chapels in the Holy Sepulchre of Jerusalem; those of Lynn, Egra, Landsburg; Ottmar's Kapella, Nuremberg; Swartz-Rheindorf, which belonged to a nunnery; St. Gothard's, attached to the transept of the cathedral of Mayence; the Lady Chapel and St. Michael's loft at Christchurch (Hants); one formerly existing at St. John's, Chester, and another in the cloister of Hereford: that of St. Cormac's, Cashel; and at St. Benignus, Dijon, the baptistery had a Chapel of St. Mary over it, and in a third stage the Trinity Chapel. The conventual chapels of Russia are usually double. The lower chapel served for public worship or a sacristy, whilst the upper storey contained relics, or, where there is an opening in the centre, to allow two congregations to attend one service. In some cases the lower chapel may have served as the founder's burial-place. (2.) There was a modification in this plan, in having an upper and lower chancel, the uppermost being used by the principal persons of the congregation, as at Compton (Surrey); Browne's Hospital (Stamford); and in noblemen's houses. In the Holy Ghost Church,

Wisby, of the twelfth century, the nave is double, and the upper storey was used by the nuns of an attached hospital. The Bridgetines and nuns of Fontévrault attended service in the upper "doxale," and the men of the order in the lower building, where two convents had a common church. Walsingham tells us the women were above, under the roof, and the men on the ground floor. (3.) The two-aisled church of Pakefield served for two distinct parishes; and the Bridgetines of Hovedoun (Norway), had a similar church; and in England the Gilbertines assembled in the nuns' church, being separated from the sisters by a veil. The Dominican churches of Paris, Agen, and Toulouse were of two aisles.

Double Monasteries. Separate convents, composed both of men and women, in the Fontévrault, Gilbertine, and Bridgetine orders, who met only in church, the monks in the nave and the nuns in choir; and in yet earlier times at Tynemouth, Whitby, Repton, Wenlock, Wimborne, Ely, Barking, and Coldingham, in East Anglia; at Jouarre, Farmoutier, Remiremont, Chelles, Les Andelys, in Ireland and Belgium; in these early Celtic monasteries the monks acted as chaplains, and were under the abbess, who was seigneur of the lands.

Doubles. These chief feasts included, according to the Salisbury use, *Christmas, *Ascension, *Easter Day, *Whit-Sunday, and the *two days following the latter festivals; *First Sunday after Easter, Trinity Sunday, *Epiphany, *Annunciation, *Purification, Circumcision, *St. John Baptist, *St. Peter, St. Andrew, St. Michael and All Angels, and *All Saints. Those marked with a star were greater doubles, the rest, with other saints' days and ordinary Sundays, were semi-doubles. On the doubles the antiphons to the Benedictus and Magnificat were doubled, that is, sung entire before and after the canticle, hence the name of these days; at other times the initial words only were sung. On these feasts the choir was governed by four rulers or cantors, who alternated with the choir in singing the verses of the Psalm Venite, or invitatory, hence called the quadruple Invitatory. The doubles had first and second Vespers. The semi-doubles resembled them in this particular, but the antiphons were not doubled. All that are preserved in our calendar are ordinary Sundays, certain holydays, and those falling within the octaves of great feasts. In cathedrals of the new foundation the dean is to officiate on great doubles and principal feasts, the subdean on semi-doubles, and the canons on other days.

Dove. A dove, for eleven centuries accepted as the symbol of the Holy Ghost, was suspended in baptisteries, and over the altar. The earliest example occurs in 359, on a tomb, hovering over a lamb, and shedding the divine blessing. The colour, white, denotes purity; and the crimson feet and beak denote love; and its nature is gentleness. In the Baptism of Jordan it showers a bright stream of rays from its beak. The nimbus is yellow, with red rays, or else the rays are black; sometimes the nimbus is red, and the rays gold. Occasionally the seven gifts of the Spirit are represented by as many doves, or lamps (Isaiah xi. 1, 2; Rev. v. 6, 11, 12). The dove also typifies modesty, humility, gentleness, charity, contemplation, prudence, harmlessness (St. Matt. x. 16); apostles, martyrs, mourners (Nahum ii. 7); deliverance of the soul (Ps. cxxiv. 7); the devout soul (Song of Sol. ii. 10); and, with an olive-branch in its beak, is equivalent to the prayer of "Requiem in pace." Amphilochius, in the 'Life of St. Basil,' speaks of a golden dove above the altar; and in 537 the clergy of Antioch accused the heretic Severus, in the Council of Constantinople, of having rifled the font and altar of the gold and silver doves which were suspended over them. The dove, then used for reservation of the Eucharist for the sick, no doubt typified Christ himself, the messenger of peace,—as Tertullian calls a church the dove's house. The symbol was also often represented on the summit of a cross, as St. Paulinus says, to typify the opening of heaven to the simple; and hung about the tombs of confessors and martyrs, and sometimes by loving hands over those of friends and relations. In the Greek Church the dove above the altar is not used for purposes of reservation of the Eucharist. Matthew Paris, in 1140, speaks of the dove with the reserved Host falling down during the time of High Mass, and in the presence of King Stephen, in Lincoln Minster; and Casalius, in the seventeenth century, says that the Sacrament was reserved in a pendent dove at Paris, and in many French churches. The dove of the baptistery contained the chrism and holy oil. In Italy Cranmer says the Sacrament never was seen hanging over the altar; and Mabillon also mentions that there the dove stood on it. It appears that the dove, in such cases, was enclosed in a tower, usually of silver, as in those given by Constantine, St. Hilary, and Pope Innocent to Roman churches. Martene saw one suspended in a monastery at Tours; and in the churches of St. Clement, St. Agnes, and St. Laurence at Rome, the hook is said to remain still on the ciboria. The Eucharist, wrapped in a napkin, was laid within the dove, which was placed within a tower, often crowned with a cover, and then both were placed in the under-canopy (peristerion), below the great ciborium.

Doxology. (1.) The Greater; the Gloria in Excelsis. (2.) The closing paragraph of the Lord's Prayer, which occurs in St. Matthew's but not in St. Luke's Gospel, and is used as an antiphon in the Greek Church after the Embolismus, which follows the Lord's Prayer. In the English Church, where the service is of praise, it is used, but is omitted where the tone is penitential or one of prayer. (3.) The Less; the Glory be to the Father, at once a creed and a hymn. In some places, as at Manchester Cathedral, the choir turns to the east during its repetition; and elsewhere the custom is to incline the head during the first verse, in imitation of the angels, who veil their faces when singing to the glory of the Holy Trinity (Isa. vi. 9). The words, "as it was in the beginning," etc., were added in the Western Church, except by the Spaniards, in the seventh century, who added "honour" after "glory," as appears by the Canons of Toledo. It is said that the addition was made by the Council of Nicæa as a protest against Arianism; it was certainly ordered by the Council of Vaison in 529. The doxology itself is attributed to Flavian of Antioch, and was employed by St. Clement, St. Justin, St. Basil, St. Irenæus, St. Dionysius, St. Gregory Thaumaturgus, and Firmilian. In the West it was recited after every psalm, but at the end óf the last only in the East. The use of this hymn occurs in the rule of St. Benedict in the sixth century.

Drain. (*Piscina* [the Roman bath], *lavacrum, sacrarium, cuve.*) A basin, on the gospel side of the altar, introduced for the convenience of ablutions and washing the sacred vessels.

Formerly it was in the pavement at the base of the altar, used as a laver for the washing of the priest's hands and for pouring away the water used in washing the altar-plate. At Paris external gurgoyles carried off the ablutions. John of Avranches ordered the use of a special vessel for the purpose. In Clugniac churches it was lined with tiles. At Rouen, Lyons, Chartres, and in Carthusian churches the acolyth brought a hand-basin for the priest to wash his fingers. Probably until the twelfth century, when one occurs at Lausanne, the piscina was a moveable metal basin, set on a detached pillar. About that time it was united and became a constructional portion of the building. It had for its type the horn of the Hebrew altar, which resembled the crest of a dwarf pillar, with a cup-shaped mouth and a grooved throat to receive and convey the superfluities of the sacrifice into a cistern beneath. One of the most ancient remains at Morwenstow. Pope Leo IV. ordered a "place" to be prepared in the sacristy, or near the altar, with two orifices and a clean hanging towel, or cloth, for the priest to wash his hands after communion, and for the ablutions of the chalice. This was in the ninth century. About the same period Hincmar, Archbishop of Rheims, recommended its use; and Walric, a monk of Clugny, mentions two piscinæ, near each other and close by the high-altar, made of brick, and used, one for cleansing the chalice by the deacon, the other for washing the celebrant's hands with wine. Ivo of Chartres mentions the ablution of the priest's fingers after communion. No example of a drain of this description remains of earlier date than the eleventh century, nor in England before the middle of the twelfth century. Norman drains remain at Leicester, Romsey, Kirkstall, Gloucester; and one of transitional date is in King's College, Cambridge. After the thirteenth century the niches containing the drain were left open, as closed aumbries had come into general use. Before the priest consumed the ablutions of the hands and the wine and water of ablution of the chalice, which might be supposed to retain some particles of the elements, and the water in which the corporals were washed, they were poured down the drain; and where the drain was double, as at Troyes, in the fourteenth century, the remains in the cruets, the ablutions of the priest before the office, and the water used in washing the ordinary church-linen and the hands of the servers, were emptied into the other orifice. In this instance the drain is on the right-hand side of the altar. The Clugniacs had two drains, lined with tiles, which were also used by the deacon and subdeacon. At Rothwell the drain has three cavities; possibly one for the ablution of the priest's fingers and of the chalice, the second for the use of the assistants and ministers, and the third for ablutions of other substances. By the statutes of Constance every altar was provided with a drain, having a cover and three towels,—one for the first ablution, the second used after the Gospel, and the third after the Communion. In the Greek Church the drain was in the sacristy or at the base of the altar. In the West there was a drain inside chapels for the water poured over the celebrant's hands, and another for the rinsings of the chalice. In the thirteenth century a double drain was provided for these purposes; but in the fourteenth century the assistants ceased to wash at the altar, the perfusions with wine and water of the celebrant's fingers were disused, and the priests were persuaded to drink the water of the ewer, and then one drain only was provided. Drains for pouring away other substances and the ablutions of corporals, etc., are frequently found at a distance from any altar. In 1287 Martene says that the cloth used for wiping the chalice or any portion of dress, or a towel which was stained with the consecrated wine was burned, the ashes being thrown down the drain. In Italy the drain is almost unknown. In England it is often connected with an upper credence shelf, and enclosed in a niche in side chapels; but at the high-altar is almost invariably on the east side of the sedilia. At Cambrai, in the fourteenth century, the baptistery contained an open drain, used by the sponsors who held the child to wash their hands and to receive the rinsings of the shell or vessel used at baptism.

Dromikos. The term applied, from the shape of the circus for races, to describe the apsidal oblong of the early St. Sophia at Constantinople.

Dyzemas. (1.) *Dismes, decimæ,* tithe-day. (2.) The name of the penitent thief in the apocryphal gospel. His fellow is called Gesmas or Gestas, and the soldier Longinus, from his spear [*lonche*].

Eagle. St. Gregory considered this bird to typify the contemplative life; other fathers regarded it as an emblem of resurrection (Ps. ciii. 5). It is the symbol of St. John the Evangelist, as it soars up to heaven and the sun; and he dwells in his Gospel and the Revelations specially on the divine discourses and the celestial glory of the Sun of righteousness. It also represented the regeneration of the neophyte; the resurrection of the Saviour (says St. Ambrose); and renewing of the soul on earth, as glory hereafter will renew body and soul; the power of grace when it is pourtrayed drinking at a chalice, or in combat with a serpent, the type of evil.

The eagle desk, or lectern, was used at first in the choir only to carry the gospels, but at a later date the gradual, antiphonar, and choir chant-books were laid upon it. In England brazen eagles remain, of the fifteenth to the seventeenth century; there are specimens at Winchester, Lynn, Wells (1660), York (1686), Canterbury (1663), Lincoln (1667), and Salisbury (1719). At Toledo there are two eagles of gilt bronze (1570), and one of brass (1646), represented vanquishing the dragon; the whole being supported on six crouching lions, and the pedestal, dated 1425, adorned with tabernacled statuary. There are brass eagles, of the fifteenth century, at St. Symphorian-à-Nuits, and Merton College, Oxford. They are used for reading the lessons. At Bourges, and at Exeter till recently, the eagle stood in front of the altar. At Aix-la-Chapelle there is an ancient specimen; and another at Southwell, formerly in Newstead Abbey. One was given to Peterborough in 1472, and another in 1519 to Canterbury. At Durham there was a pelican of brass, on the north side of the altar, for reading the epistles and gospels, and a brass eagle for the legendary stood in the choir. The earliest eagle does not date earlier than 1300, but it was often carved previously on the front of the pulpit. An eagle dated 1683, and formerly in the cathedral, remains in the church of St. Mary-le-Port, Bristol. A late Decorated pelican is preserved at Norwich; and an eagle, dated 1496, in St. Gregory's in that city.

Early English Architecture lasted from the reign of Richard I. to that of Henry III. (1200–1275). The pointed arch contains the germ of the vertical principle, and buttresses were enlarged to resist the lateral pressure on the exterior from the roof downwards, which was caused by its introduction; hence arose the pyramidal form which distinguishes the style; the ribs cross the vault at right angles, or run diagonally along the groins. The use of materials of small size produced the round arch; the pointed style took its origin in mechanical necessity and requirements, and the Decorated rose out of the constructive features. The development of the shallow buttress, as an artificial abutment, and the introduction of the pointed arch, from its greater capability of resisting and supporting the pressure of a heavier superincumbent load, reduced the outward thrust of the round arch when bearing a weight. The windows are long, narrow, and lancet-shaped, and often combined in triplets, or arranged in pairs side by side; circles are often interposed in the space between these lights and the comprising arch; the mouldings are more boldly cut; and foliage, or a " dog-tooth" ornament, forming a square edge, notched like a St. Andrew's cross, is used in their hollows. They are called by the French violets, and were employed in the first half of the thirteenth century. They have also been supposed to represent the cyclamen, or gazelle's horn, just as the ball-flower is said to have had the red anemone, the lily of Scripture, for its type; both ornaments having been introduced from the East. The arches are lancets (acute-angled), drop (obtuse-angled), foliated; or form equilateral triangles; the roofs have a high pitch; the ceiling is ribbed and groined, and usually stone-vaulted. Spires and the triforium are prominent features; flying buttresses are used; buttresses are divided into stages, with sharply sloping set-offs, and are usually pedimented; the angles are often chamfered. Capitals resemble inverted bells, and are wreathed with foliage. Crockets and knobs are set on the edges of pinnacles, usually circular, octagonal, or square, and sometimes shafted. Pillars are circular, octagonal, or shafted. The doors are deeply recessed, with small shafts in the jambs, are often flat, sometimes round-headed, the featherings are often trefoiled or cinquefoiled; when double they are divided by a single shaft, their chief ornaments consisting of iron scroll-work. Mouldings have outlines of rectangular recesses, or are alternate rounds and deeply-cut hollows:

sometimes splays and small fillets are used. The vault has ribs along the apex, and additional ribs between the cross springers and diagonals. Piers frequently divide windows. Stone coffins of this and the preceding style are coped, ornamented with crosses, or bearing effigies of the dead, sometimes placed in low recesses, and occasionally simply canopied. The growth of this style may be traced in the gradual development of the raising of the aisle roof to the height of the nave-roof, light being admitted through a gallery; then the outer roof of the aisle was cut through, mere ribs being left as flying buttresses, and then the central vault was cut up with intersections, in order to obtain space for the windows to the very height of the ridge, and this last expedient necessitated the adoption of pointed windows. The first instance of plate tracery occurs at Lincoln. The period of transition to the Decorated style lasts from 1275 to 1300; the reign of Edward I. mainly embraces it, but there are some buildings of a Decorated character of the time of Henry III.

East (the). The Jews turned to the West in prayer, in the direction of the Holy of Holies (1 Kings viii. 48; 2 Chron. xxix. 6; Dan. vi. 10; Ezek. viii. 16, 17); the Christians, at least from the second century, turned to the East, as to the true Light of the World, our Blessed Lord, who came in the East. In several churches at Rome, in the Castle Chapel (Caen), at Seville and Haarlem, and St. Benet (Paris), the entrance is on the east and the altar to the west,—the latter the invariable practice of the Jesuits. In such cases the priest, standing on the west side of the altar, which was interposed between himself and the people, faced east, as in churches of true orientation; whilst in the latter the celebrant stood between the altar and the people, with his back to the latter; but it is an irregular arrangement, although a curious relic of the early parallelism between the Law and the Gospel.

Easter Day, so called from Urstand, the Resurrection, of which it is the commemoration; the name is as early as the time of the venerable Bede. The Greek term *lampra*, or bright day, is also connected with the idea of the uprising of the great light of the Sun of Righteousness. The original title was Pascha, a form of the Hebrew name of the Passover: as

Good Friday was called the pasch of the Lord's Passion, so Easter Day was styled the pasch of the Lord's resurrection. In the time of Leo the Great, pasch was used as the designation of Easter in the Latin Church; and the coloured eggs, still given on this feast in the north of England, are spoken of as pasch eggs. Melitus, in the second century, wrote on the paschal festival. Tertullian says it was the highest occasion for holy baptism, and St. Cyprian mentions the Easter solemnities; the Council of Ancyra calls it the most holy feast, or the great day, and St. Gregory Nazianzen denominates it the feast of feasts, the great Lord's Day, the queen of festivals.

There was, at an early date, a great controversy about the proper day for observing the festival, and Polycarp and Anicetus, Bishop of Rome, in 158 held a friendly consultation on the matter. The quartodecimian, or Jewish method, which was advocated by Polycarp as following the teaching of St. John, aimed at its observance on the actual anniversary of the great act of our Lord, on the third day after the fourteenth day of the month Nisan; whilst the Western Church, imitating the example of SS. Peter and Paul, held it on the next Lord's Day. In England the former use was maintained until the arrival of St. Austin, and in the north as late as 714. Although Anicetus and St. Polycarp had reconciled their differences by mutual toleration, Pope Victor and Polycrates, Bishop of Ephesus, at the close of the second century, respectively assembled councils, which ended in each maintaining his own opinions; but the Pope anathematized the churches of Asia for their adherence to their ancient custom. The Council of Arles, in 314, decided the celebration of Easter should be held on one fixed day; and the Council of Nicæa, in 325, ruled that it should be a Lord's Day, and directed the Church of Alexandria to send timely notice of that day, in order to secure its universal observance. On the Feast of Epiphany the deacon, by the Ambrosian rite of Milan, announced the exact day of the month.

It is the only festival for which we have express Scriptural authority, for St. Paul says " Christ our Passover was sacrificed for us, therefore let us keep the feast;" and the ancient Church discerned a prophecy of it in the words of the Psalmist, " This is the day which the Lord hath made, let us be glad and rejoice in it." Constantine, in his rescript about Easter, mentions that it was then observed in Britain. In the Greek Church the usual greeting is, "Christ is'risen;" to which the answer is immediately made, "Alleluia;" and in our own service the special anthem contains the words, "Christ is risen again." The primitive Church observed the day by solemn Communion, the administration of baptism, liberation of prisoners, suspension of all secular spectacles, the manumission of slaves, hospitality, almsgiving, and a general holiday. Bishops sent the Eucharist to each other under the form of Eulogies, till the Council of Laodicea forbade it, in the middle of the fourth century.

It was long a vulgar error that the sun danced for joy on this morning, and even grave Bishop Hacket, like the lively Suckling, alludes to the superstition. In Wales, Salop, Cheshire, Lancashire, and the counties of Warwick and Stafford, there is an old practice of lifting persons aloft in chairs on this day, evidently as a rude memorial of the rising on this morning, or the lifting of the Cross out of the Easter sepulchre in churches. At Rouen, York, Lichfield, and Durham that ceremonial was observed with peculiar solemnity. At University College, Oxford, the Fellows, on leaving hall, chop with a hatchet at a huge block of wood, which is set up by the master cook, possibly in allusion to "the accursed tree."

Easter Eggs. The egg was the symbol of creation in Egypt, and of hope and the resurrection among early Christians; and the custom of giving coloured pasch-eggs on Easter morning is found in the East, in the Tyrol, in Russia, in Greece, in many parts of England, where it may be traced back to the time of Edward I., and was observed at Gray's Inn in the reign of Elizabeth. In France the pasch egg is eaten before any other nourishment is taken on Easter day. Tansy pudding, according to Selden, is a memorial of the bitter herbs eaten by the Jews; and peculiar cakes in some places formed the staple fare on this day. Paul II. issued a form of benediction of eggs for England, Scotland, and Ireland. Henry VIII. received a paschal egg in a case of silver filigree from the Pope. The Jews regarded the egg as a symbol of death. De Moleon says that at Angers, on Easter Day, two chaplains standing behind the altar, addressed two cubiculars or corbeliers, vested in dalmatic, amice, and mitellas, as they advanced towards them, "Whom seek ye?" and to the reply, "Jesus of Nazareth, the crucified," answered, "He is risen; He is not here." Then those who personated the Marys took from the altar two ostrich eggs wrapped in silk, and descended chanting, "Alleluia, the Lord is risen."

Easter Eve. The Sabbath high-day of the Jewish ritual, when all presented themselves before the Lord and the sheaf of the first-fruits was offered. In the Christian Church it was called the Great Sabbath in the second century. The Portuguese designate it the Sabbath of Alleluia. The vigil of Easter is mentioned by Tertullian, the Apostolical Constitutions, Eusebius, Lactantius, St. Gregory Nazianzen, St. Jerome, and St. Chrysostom. The churches were lighted up so that it seemed like day, in honour of the illumination of the grave by the resurrection, and of the Light of life and the world arising from the dead. The services were continued past midnight to welcome the dawn. Ordinations were held, baptism (towards the end of the fourth century) was administered; and in the Medieval Church the font, the paschal candle, the incense, and new fire received benediction. The Holy Communion was celebrated after Vespers, in anticipation of Easter; Gloria in Excelsis formed the Introit, and the bells rang joyously for the dawn of Easter. At Milan the deacon thrice announced in the Mass, "Christ, our Lord, is risen," and the choir thundered back the words, "Deo gratias," thanks be to God. Easter Eve is the only Jewish Sabbath retained by the Church. A strict fast was maintained on the vigil, in reference to St. Matt. ix. 15; and according to Lactantius, St. Jerome, and others there was a tradition that Christ should return to judgment on this night. In consequence of abuses following the nocturnal assembly, it was forbidden by the Council of Autun in 578. The paschal taper can be traced back to the sixth century. Two candles, symbolical of Apostles and Prophets, were also lighted from a fire of branches (St. John xv. 5). By an Irish Council, held in 456, and the Sarum use, the Holy Communion was administered on this eve, probably after midnight.

HALLOWING THE NEW FIRE was performed in the east

R

alley of the cloister in cathedral and conventual churches, and in parish churches in the porch. At Salisbury the septiform litany, led by the precentor in person, was chanted by seven choristers; and at Canterbury the convent, in albs, singing the Miserere, assembled on the morning of Easter Eve to watch the kindling of the flame by the deacon, either by the burning-glass or flint and steel, but at Clugny with a precious beryl, or sometimes a triple candle. The sacristan lighted a taper on the top of a lance-like staff, the master of the boys kindled his lantern, and the procession, often led by the primate with incense and cross, returned to the choir chanting the hymn Inventor rutili, whilst the servant of the cellarer rekindled, with the fire remaining in the cloister, all the hearths which had previously been extinguished. At Rome, also, formerly the fires in the city were relighted from the holy fire. No doubt there is intimate relation between this custom and the blessing of the candles still preserved at Rome, and the lighting of the tapers from the sacred fire in the Holy Sepulchre at Jerusalem on Easter Day. In England, at the time of the Reformation, the parishioners on the eve carried away a brand from the holy fire to rekindle their cold hearths, and marched nine times in procession round the font. On Easter morning they brought in meat and other provisions at Matins, to be blessed by the priest.

HALLOWING THE FONT. By the Councils of Gerona in 517, of Ireland 456, and several English synods of the eleventh and thirteenth centuries, baptism was only administered on the eves of Easter and Pentecost, except in cases of necessity. St. Ambrose alludes to the washing of the feet of the newly-baptized, in imitation of our Lord's great condescension in the paschal chamber. In later times the font, like the waters at Epiphany by the Greeks, was solemnly hallowed, the water being expressly consecrated in remembrance of the Easter baptism. In the fourth century, in the East, the Greek Church observed the custom of baptizing catechumens and consecrating the water in the font on this eve. At Salisbury, on every day in Easter week, a procession was made with four rulers of the choir to incense the font.

Easter Offerings. Easter is one of the three seasons at which all parishioners are bound to communicate by the Council of

Adge, 506; Canute's laws, 1017; canons of Eanham, 1009; Gloucester, 1378; Gran; Paris, 1429; Cologne, 1310; Lateran, 1215; Pope Calixtus, and the English Church. A priest was permitted to say two Masses on this account by the Council of Oxford, 1222. The people then made their oblations, in kind, to furnish the Eucharistic elements, or compounded by a payment of money, which became the origin of Easter offerings. In the time of Edward VI. these payments, which constituted an important revenue of the Church, were ordered to be paid at Easter, if they had not been rendered on one of the four statutable offering days. By the rubric, parishioners are still required to pay at this time "all ecclesiastical duties customably due." Possibly the offerings also included personal tithes. 2d. or 4d. for adults, and ½d. for children and servants formed the customary offering.

Easter Sepulchre. At Tours the canons, on Good Friday, recited the Hours, not in their stalls, but standing round a tomb of marble. This is the earliest notice of the ceremonial of laying the crucifix, and the Eucharist, which was reserved in a ciborium on Maundy Thursday, and placed in an Easter sepulchre. At Poictiers the Host was wrapped in a folded corporal between two patens, with a gold cross above it; and then, being placed in clean linen, was enclosed with holy water and incense, within a repository, which was locked, guarded by five watchers, and surrounded by numerous lights. Cranmer says this was done "in remembrance of Christ's sepulture, which was prophesied by Esaias to be glorious, and to signify there was buried the pure and undefiled body of Christ, without spot of sin, which was never separated from the Godhead, and therefore, as David expressed it in the fifteenth Psalm, it could not see corruption, nor death could detain or hold Him, but He should rise again, to our great hope and comfort; and therefore the Church adorns it with lights to express the great joy they have of that glorious triumph over death, the devil, and hell." The sepulchre was (1) a chapel, as at Winchester; (2) a wall recess, usually in the north side of the chancel, as at Bottesford and Stanton St. John; (3) a temporary structure sumptuously enriched, as at St. Mary, Redcliffe; (4) a tomb, under which a founder, by special privilege, was buried; (5) a vaulted enclosure, as at Norwich, which, like a sepulchre at Northwold, has an aperture for watching the light, without requiring the person so employed to enter the choir. At Seville a magnificent structure of wood, in three storeys, raised over the tomb of F. Columbus and brilliantly lighted, serves as the sepulchre. Neogorgus says that the people standing at the barriers used to cast violets and all kinds of sweet flowers on the sepulchre, and made their offerings whilst the choir chanted a dirge. In some places the steps of the sepulchre were covered with black cloth. Soldiers in armour kept guard, and a bright flash of fire burst from the tomb as the priest removed the crucifix. There was a constant succession of watchers and worshippers in most churches. At Lichfield three persons kept unbroken vigil and sang psalms until Matins were said on Easter morning. At Wells a light burned in the sepulchre. Beautiful tombs, of Decorated or Perpendicular date, remain at Heckington, Navenby, Patrington, Northwold, Holcombe, Burnell, Southpool, Woodleigh, and of the thirteenth century at Lincoln and Hawton, where the Roman sentinels are carved on the lower panels, and in the latter instance within a groined recess the risen Saviour appears to the three Marys. At Durham a framework, with rich hangings of red velvet and gold embroidery, was erected on Good Friday, and from it on Easter Day, between three and four A.M., two of the most aged monks took a figure of the risen Saviour holding a cross, and laying it on a crimson cushion, brought it to the high-altar, singing Christus Resurgens; then it was carried to the south choir-door where "four ancient gentlemen held over it a rich canopy of purple velvet, faced with red silk and gold fringes, and so round the whole church, the whole choir attending with goodly torches and great store of other lights, all singing and praising God, till they came again to the high-altar." Archbishop Parker defended such choral processions and singing that hymn as an "open protestation of faith and willingness to follow Christ in all holy conversation." Cardinal de Joyeuse, Archbishop of Rouen, abolished the ceremonial, as in France it had been profaned by attempts at positive personation.

Easter-tide. During Easter week there was an ancient custom that no one should touch the ground with the bare foot;

all stood during prayer-time, and, in the age of Tertullian and that of St. Chrysostom, expanded their arms and stretched their hands towards heaven, as if they were not content because they could not soar up to it. St. Ambrose describes the whole season until Whitsun Day as one long Lord's Day. Balsamon mentions that artisans did not work on Monday or Tuesday in Easter week, and St. Augustine and St. Gregory Nyssen speak of their observance. The Church of England appoints a special Preface for the whole octave, and epistles and gospels for the Monday and Tuesday. The Councils of Constantinople, Macon (585), and Ingelheim (948), and the Constitutions of Ecgbright, enjoined that the whole week should be kept with equal solemnity,—it was called the neophytes' octave,—and during every day the competents who had been baptized on Easter Eve came in their white robes, and with lights in their hands (which gave the name of Bright Day to Easter), until the Sunday in Albes, the eve of which was called the close of Easter, and the custom lasted from the time of Tertullian till after the date of Gratian. St. Chrysostom, St. Augustine, and the code of Theodosius show that the whole octave was kept; and the Sacramentary of St. Gregory and the Salisbury use contain a service for each day, but the Council of Mayence (813) and the Canons of Ælfric (957) restrict the celebration to four, and the Council of Constance (1094) confines it to three days; the latter period is alluded to by St. Gregory Thaumaturgus in the third century.

Economist. A steward; called by Possidius provost of the church-house. A priest, mentioned by Isidore Pelusiotes, appointed by the Council of Chalcedon in 451, and elected by the clergy in the East; to discharge the same duties as devolved on a medieval treasurer, provost of canons, and almoners in an English cathedral. In the Western Church he is mentioned in the fourth century, and was a deacon at Milan in the time of St. Ambrose. His office was contemporaneous with the restriction of an archdeacon to spiritual duties. In the vacancy of the See by the Councils of Chalcedon and Trent he acted as receiver-general and administrator of the episcopal revenues. At Kilkenny, St. David's, and Exeter, as now at Windsor, he received the capitular rents, and at Westminster provided the common table, and paid the servants' wages. At Hereford two economists, or bailiffs, rendered half-yearly accounts of the great commons.

Effigies and Grave-stones. Some very early sepulchral monuments, or standing stones, probably associated with idolatrous respect, as it appears, in England, in 1018, were christianized by the addition of a cross; St. Sampson is known to have done this. In Wales, and Brittany, as at Rungleo, there are frequent examples. The Jewish monuments took the form of pillars (1 Sam. x. 2; Gen. xxxv. 20; 2 Sam. xviii. 18), and the same form of unhewn stone, inscribed with the name of St. James, is mentioned by Eusebius, near the Temple of Jerusalem. The ancient monuments of Glastonbury were pyramidal. St. Jerome and Prudentius mentioned inscribed grave-stones; and SS. Basil and Chrysostom inveigh against the extravagance lavished on such memorials. In the catacombs pious inscriptions, sacred emblems, and marks of the sex or profession of the dead were carved on the titles, or marble slabs which closed the grave; and for the rich, sarcophagi, called bisomi, trisomi, or quadrisomi, according to the numbers interred, were ornamented with figures in relief, and incidents recorded in Scripture. Pelagius II. and Councils in Spain, Germany, and France resisted burials within churches; in the eighth century they were permitted in Italy; but the well-known legend connected with the translation of St. Swithin, in 862, shows the repugnance of the English to the practice; and several bishops, as late as the eighteenth century, declared that churches were for the living, and the cemetery for the dead. The earliest church tombs in this country are of the eleventh and twelfth centuries, ridged in form, and covered with a cross, or in the latter period a recumbent figure; the width of the slab diminishing from the head to the feet. Canopies were sparingly used, and supported by shafts. At length tombs were recessed in the wall. Incised stones, monumental slabs of marble and stone, and even alabaster, with figures engraved on them, came into use in the middle of the thirteenth century, and were cheaper than brasses; one of the earliest examples exists in Wells Cathedral. This use lasted till the time of Charles I., but in Germany and France was more common than in England. There are instances of inlaying the portions representing flesh with material of a lighter colour, and brass is also employed. In the thirteenth century plain pediments were erected over the tombs, but at its close finials and crockets were employed, armorial badges, traceried panels, and tabernacled figures were added, and then at length the high tomb and effigy were detached from the wall, and in many cases placed beneath splendid canopies, pyramidal structures of great size, as at Gloucester, Westminster, and Canterbury, or of stellated form, as at Tewkesbury and Gloucester. At length chantry chapels were erected between the piers of the great arcades, as at Winchester, York, Ely, Tewkesbury, Salisbury, and St. Alban's. In the middle of the thirteenth century flat stones, with brasses, were used; only one is known to remain in France; but there are five incised slabs at Rheims and St. Ouen, and at Chartres of the fourteenth century. At the close of the fifteenth, and in the sixteenth century, the monuments became debased, as in Sir T. Pope's tomb, Trinity College Chapel, Oxford, and the flat tester, supported on pillars, over the Montague tomb at Bath. During this period alabaster was freely used for effigies. At Murcia, Burgos, and Batalha magnificent tomb-houses were built at the east end, as in the earlier instances of Bury St. Edmund's, Canterbury, and Drontheim. Iron slabs occur, of the fourteenth century, at Burwash, Crowhurst (1591), and Himbleton (1690).

The chivalret, or effigy, is often of metal, as at Augsburg, of the eleventh century; those of two bishops of the thirteenth century at Amiens; and at Westminster, the De Valences, Henry III., Queen Eleanor, Richard II., Queen Anne, Henry VII., Queen Elizabeth, and Margaret, Countess of Richmond; the Black Prince at Canterbury (1376), Earl Richard at Warwick (1435), the Earl of Portland at Winchester; those of W. de Merton and Sheppey at Rochester, Bishop Oldham at Exeter, and Wykeham at Winchester are of alabaster, and retain their colour. There are also effigies of oak at Brancepeth, St. Giles (Durham), Gloucester, Little Horkesley, Danbury, Ashwell, Woodford, (Northhants), Burnham, Gayton, Fersfield, and that of Isabella of Angoulême at Fontévrault. There are some fine effigies at Marburg, Verucla, Burgos, Avila, Miraflores, and Toledo, some appearing in the Spanish examples, as if sliding on their backs. Weepers or mourners, friends of the departed, were also set in niches on the sides of tombs, as on St. Richard's at Chichester.

Effigies often are represented as holding a pot of unguent, or a heart (Sam. iii. 41; Ps. li. 10), inscribed Jesu Mercy (Job xix. 25, 26, or Ps. cxxxi. 5), possibly embodying the old invitatory Sursum Corda, "Lift up your hearts." Occasionally angels bear up the head of the effigies, as on the tomb of Aymer de Valence at Westminster, in allusion to the angels sitting on our Lord's sepulchre (St. John xx. 12; St. Mark xvi. 5); or their carrying up the soul to heaven (St. Luke xvi. 22); sometimes, as on a tomb at Lisieux, the naked soul is held in a sheet by Abraham. Three chantry priests, or bedemen, support the head of figures at Bedale Staindrop and the effigy of Wykeham. St. Oswald and St. Wolstan are at each side of King John's head at Worcester. There are also minor accessories: dogs at Gonalston, a dog, hare, and bird on King Richard's tomb at Rouen, a little lion on the Lyons' tomb (c. 1385), the head of a horse and a diminutive henchman at a knight's feet at Minster; four henchmen at Arbroath arrange the folds of drapery on the figure. Sometimes these accessories are of great size: the bronze monument of Maximilian I. has twenty-eight colossal statues; four kneeling knights carry on a litter the armour of Sir F. de Vere; knights watch the Duke of Bavaria at Munich; Sixtus IV. sleeps on a bed, guarded by all the virtues, at Rome.

Occasionally the effigy is of miniature dimensions, and has been mistaken for memorials of children, as in the so-called boy-bishop's tomb at Salisbury, at Horsted Keynès, Haccombe, Tenbury, Ayot St. Laurence, Bottesford, Mapouder, Cobberley, Little Easton, Anstey, and Long Wittenham. At Lichfield and Worcester there are half effigies, the central portion of the figures being imbedded in the wall. At Llanfihangel two pilgrims hold their arms crossed, and their breast is ensigned with a cross. The cross-legged effigies of knights represent those who had taken the vow of a Crusader, or pilgrim; those whose hands are drawing their swords were actually engaged in the holy war. From the attitude of the former the death's-head and cross-bones took their origin, or from the lifted arms of those represented as praying in their sleep. The crossed legs are said also to indicate a judicial capacity.

Effigies were constantly carried on the hearse at funerals; and even in his lifetime Edward I. gave to Chichester cathedral a mensura, or waxwork figure, of himself. Until the time of Henry V. the actual body was usually carried exposed; but from the reign of Edward III. the waxwork effigies were brought to Westminster Abbey and preserved; some, indeed, still remain. These formed the model for the effigy made in more durable material; it must be remembered that the illusion of the coloured wax was heightened by the fact that funerals of great personages were conducted by torch-light until the close of the last century.

Sometimes the tomb is in two stages : the lowermost contains the cadaver, skeleton (le gisant or jacens), as in Bishop Gardiner's at Winchester; on the uppermost was laid the effigy, robed and in prayer (Le Priant or orans); in this case attendant angels show that his prayer has been heard. Captain Stanley, at Lichfield, is represented naked, and with a scroll of confession, as on this condition his burial was permitted, as he had died either unreconciled or under the displeasure of the Crown.

Electrum. (1.) A composition of gold and silver mixed, used in medieval metal-work. (2.) Enamel. (3.) Copper gilt.

Elevation of the Host. The lifting up of the paten and consecrated element of bread was instituted by Pope Honorius III. (c. 1210), and he directed that it should be adored when elevated, or being carried to the sick, the people reverently bowing. Casalius quotes as his authority (Ps. lxxii. 16). Anastasius Sinaita alludes to this ceremony; and it appears as early as, perhaps, the fourth century in the Greek Church; it has been traced in England in the eleventh, in France in the twelfth, and in Germany and Italy before the thirteenth century. Thomas Aquinas and Bonaventure mention the elevation of the paten only; the elevation of the chalice was of later date. The ringing of little bells at this time was introduced by William of Paris, and generally enjoined by Gregory XI.

Emancipation. A curious ceremony in Germany by which a domicellar was promoted to be a capitular canon. He knelt down in the sacristy before the precentor and scholastic, holding two rods crossed over his breast, and being asked,

"What seekest thou?" replied, "I desire to be emancipated, for Christ's sake." He was then thrice struck with the rods, in the name of the Holy Trinity, and so emancipated from the yoke of chanter and chancellor, and once by each canon; the precentor and scholastic afterwards led him up for installation to the dean.

Ember. *Ymbren* (so called in the laws of Alfred and Canute), "circuits" from being, says Leo in 442, fasts occurring at stated periods in the revolution of a year, but their origin is lost in the night of ages; *Quatuor tempora*, the four times: and the German *quatember*, called in Welsh the procession weeks, and in Germany the holy fasts. The word appears in the canons of Eanham in 1009. Micrologus says that these weeks were given to the English by Gregory the Great, A.D. 600. Gelasius, 492, and Cuthbert in 747, mention only three weeks, but Ecgbright, at the same date, speaks of four, that of Lent including the fourth. The Councils of Mayence, 813, and Salegunstadt in 1022, and Durandus, mention for their occurrence the months of March, June, September, and December; but the Council of Clermont, 1095, more precisely, names the first week in Lent, Whitsun-week, the week before the autumnal equinox, and the fourth week in Advent. Gelasius first speaks of them as stated seasons for ordinations. It is probable that they were imitated from the four Jewish fasts, and instituted to beg God's blessings on the fruits of harvest,—in spring for sowing, in summer when growing, in autumn at the harvesting, and in winter when they are garnered into the barns. The Ember-days are the Wednesday, Friday, and Saturday after the first Sunday in Lent, after Whitsunday, after September 14, Holy Cross, and after December 13, St. Lucy. The days kept varied in different countries, and the present arrangement was not fixed until the eleventh century, certainly after the Council of Clermont.

Emblem. A symbol is the representation of some dogma of religious belief, a revelation from God derived direct from Holy Scripture; whereas an emblem is an arbitrary representation of an idea of human invention, and created by the imagination. A symbol may be used as an emblem, but an emblem cannot be employed as a symbol. For instance, a sword is the symbol of martyrdom, but the peculiar emblem of St. Paul. An anchor may be either a symbol or an emblem.

The earliest symbols were derived from Scripture: the Good Shepherd, disused between the seventh and ninth centuries; the door of the fold; the Lamb of God; a light; the dove; the keys of St. Peter; the chased hart desiring the water-brooks; the anchor of the soul; and later, the lamb standing on the mountain of God's house, or, after the sixth century, bearing on its shoulders the cross-banner. The early Christians saw the cross prefigured in the out-stretched arms of Moses on the hill and in his rod, which they delineated crowned with a **T** or cross; the pole of the brazen serpent, with its transverse beam; the two sticks of the widow of Sarepta; and the sign mentioned by Ezekiel. In the catacombs the reserve of reverential tenderness, or the fear of betraying to scorn the object of faith in the sacrifice of Calvary, induced the early Christians to symbo-lize rather than paint it; thus they drew the types of it found in the Old Testament, or, less commonly, incidents in the Saviour's life,—the Fall, Noah's ark, Moses receiving the law, striking the rock, Abraham's sacrifice, Elias's translation, the three children in the furnace: the adoration of the magi, the miracle of the loaves, and that of Cana, the healing the cripple, the raising of Lazarus, St. Peter's denial, and the smiting with the reed. Then a lion, as an emblem of soli-tude, was given to St. Jerome, as having been a recluse in Syrian deserts. Then hieroglyphs were employed. St. Anthony appears with fire, the emblem of Divine love; a swine at his feet, typical of sensual desire trodden down, and a bell, expressive of vigilance, and with the Tau, a form of the cross. St. Christopher, by his height, represents loftiness of heart; by his sacred infant-burden, Christ in the soul; by his staff, holding to the cross; and by wading through a stormy river, passage to the better country through martyrdom. His wolf's head, converted by the old English into that of a dog, refers to his birthplace in Lycia. St. George, armed as the Christian warrior (Eph. vi. 12–17), and on horseback, as borne up by Divine grace, transfixes with his lance the devil (Rev. xii. 9), whilst the Church, or perhaps the Virgin soul, watches the victory. Constantine, pourtrayed in the Palatine, a knight with a cross on his hel-met, warring with the dragon of idolatry. St. Lucy carries the eyes typical of constancy and Divine illumination, whilst the

legend of St. Ursula and the eleven thousand virgins, which
is mentioned in the tenth century, is a perverted record of a
historical fact which occurred on October 21, 237, or in 451,
being indicated by a careless copyist as XIM. instead of MM.
(martyrs), or a corruption into a single name, Undecimilla,
the latter M being taken for a numeral.

In monasteries the acts of their founders, but in cathedrals
a metaphysical system of symbolism, obtained the preference.
A frequent warning against sacrilege is offered by the terrible angel on his horse treading on Heliodorus, from the
thirteenth century.   Under the feet of saints impersonations
of holiness are carved, and horrible beasts as the embodiment
of evil.   The bishop thrusts his staff into the mouth of a
writhing lion, and the Virgin treads on the old serpent, as
our Saviour goes upon the lion and dragon.   Very often the
evangelical subjects are ranged with the corresponding
events of the Old Testament, as in the glass of King's College, Cambridge, round the chapter-house of Salisbury, and
formerly over the stalls of Winchester, till destroyed in the
civil wars.   Of an inferior class are the bestiaries, or fables
sculptured on the folding seats of stalls, as a visible teaching
of morality under an allegorical form.   Beleth, St. Isidore,
and Durand, Bishop of Mende, followed some code of
canons which applied a complicated symbolism to the whole
structure of a church in its minutest details, but Durand's
Italian leanings render him comparatively silent with regard
to carved imagery.   The Decretal of Gratian contains some
allusions to symbolism.   From the twelfth to the fourteenth
century external corbels and gurgoyles take the most grotesque forms, often masks, like that of the "devil looking
over Lincoln," and with their mocking expressions reproducing "the grin of Arius," who, at the Council of Nicæa,
was convulsed with demoniacal mirth.

The emblems on ancient and medieval tombs included
badges of sex or profession ; the comb, keys, and shears for
women ; and for men the sword, the horn, the moneyer's
scales, the priest's chalice and paten.   The still earlier emblems were numerous.   Heaven was represented by a seg-
ment of a circle edged with a rainbow, and to symbolize God
with the Creator's hand issuing from it or a cloud (Ezek.
ii. 9 ; viii. 9).   A deep blue globe stood for the universe ; a

ring for eternity; a river, formed by the confluence of four rivers, for eternal life (Ezek. xlvii.; Rev. xxii. 1, 2); an olive-branch for peace; a lily for purity; a heart for charity; sheep, doves, fish, cedars by the watercourses for the beatified; stags at the brook, according to St. Jerome's interpretation of the old legend of the hart that has seen a serpent hastening to drink of a running stream, for souls thirsting for cleansing; the rose of Sharon for incorruption; candelabra for illumination through the Gospel; a palm-branch for victory; a cock for vigilance; the double-necked eagle for the Holy Spirit; an eagle for renovation of grace (Ps. ciii. 5); the resurrection, the neophyte; or as alternated with the dove on the cieling of St. Alban's, the Saviour; a horse for the Christian race; a dolphin for zeal in doing good; an anchor for constancy; the phœnix, said to rise from its ashes with renewed life, for the resurrection; the peacock, said to have incorruptible flesh, for immortality; its beautiful plumage, for Christian virtues, as its scream terrified serpents and their prayers routed demons; a mountain (Dan. xi. 34) for the Church; a vine, a woman in prayer; a house, a vineyard; a ship sailing by a lighthouse, Noah's ark; Susanna, for her militant state; a city for her condition of triumph; water poured by a dove on the cross for holy baptism, the sacrifice of Abel and Melchisedech; the manna, Daniel fed by Habakkuk, the miracles at Cana and of the loaves, a feast (Prov. ix. 2); milk or a milk-pail (Isa. lv. 1; St. Peter ii. 2), fish and bread (St. John xxi. 13), a chalice with three small loaves marked with a cross, or the wafer; and in the ninth century grains of corn and clusters of grapes for the Holy Eucharist; twelve sheep, or a net (St. Matt. iv. 19), for Apostles; four mystic animals, four open books, four scrolls, their symbols set between the arms of a Greek cross; four rivers of Paradise watering the earth, for evangelists; a mountain for Paradise; birds feeding on pleasant fruits for its joys; sun and moon for human life; Orpheus, with his lyre, charming wild beasts, making the wolf lie down with the lamb,—a pillar, a fountain, a lion, a king, a giant, a jewel, a hand for the Saviour; instruments of martyrdom or other accessories for saints and confessors; the pelican, which has a crimson stain on its beak, supposed to be caused by feeding its young with its blood, for the love

of Christ in the Lord's Supper; a lion, for the resurrection;
the olive, for the fruit of good works, and its oil for the lustre
of virtue, mercy, purity, and peace; the gourd, for the Old
Testament; the deathless cypress, for the New; the pine, for
death; the vine, for the ineffable union betwixt Christ and
His Church; the house, for our mortal tabernacle; the lamp
in a tomb, for the rest of the righteous in a place of light;
the wine-barrel, composed of many staves, Christian union;
a harp, for the subjugation of evil passions (1 Sam. xvi. 23);
winter, for the storms of life; spring, for resuscitation; summer, the glow of love to God; autumn, martyrdom, life's
glorious close; an egg, for the resurrection; a nut, with its
triple substance, shell, rind, and kernel, for the bitter passion,
the benign divinity, and the wood of the cross of Christ.
The Holy Trinity was symbolized by a three-coloured rainbow, by three beams of light issuing from our Lord's
head, or by His thumb and fore and middle fingers raised in
benediction, and also by an equilateral or trefoil-shaped
triangle; in the ninth century by three circles interwined,
two above and one below, with the word TRI-NI-TAS in the
outer, and U-NI-TAS in the inner spaces; by three intersecting
triangles, called the Pentacle, though geometrically forming
six points; by three aureoles inscribed with letters P(ater,
Father) at the top, F(ilius, Son) on the right, and S(piritus,
Holy Ghost) on the left-hand. Or a more composite symbol,
an equilateral triangle having curved sides, with the words
Father, Son, and Holy Ghost at the three ends, which are
aureoled; and a central aureole with the one word God,
connected with these by bands inscribed severally "is;" on
the sides the words "is not" were written. The AGONY, by
a chalice, surmounted by a cross of Calvary; the BETRAYAL,
by a sword, club, staff, lantern, torch, the ear of Malchus, a
rope, thirty pieces of silver, and Judas's head; the CONDEM-
NATION, by the basin and ewer, a rope, a pillar, a scourge, a
scarlet robe, a crown of thorns, and reed; the PASSION, by
three nails, hammer, pincers, ladder, sponge, reed, spear,
the scroll, and title J(esus) N(azarenus) R(ex) J(udæorum),
the seamless garment, and three dice; the ASCENSION, by the
imprints of two feet on a hill, and two feet rising in the air;
the RESURRECTION, by a lion. The sacred monogram I H C,
the two first and last letters of the name of Jesus as freely

used, and the sign of contraction above the H, is ingeniously made part of a cross. Birds represented the enfranchised souls of martyrs (Ps. cxxiv. 6), founded on a passage in Tertullian; and in a cage, their sufferings. At a canonization they are still presented to the Pope with this meaning. Sometimes they represent the Passion and Incarnation of our Lord, with the legends (Rom. iv. 25; Isa. vii. 4) in the catacombs. A church in the hand betokens a founder. The dedication of a church is distinguished by an altar with priest, deacon, and subdeacon; the feast of Corpus Christi by a pyx; and that of Cathedra Petri by a figure of the Pope throned and wearing the tiara. The SCALLOP is the sign of a pilgrim; a SCOURGE of penance; a SQUARE a type of the world; the POMEGRANATE, showing its fulness of seed and now bursting, of hope in immortality; the PALM, a SWORD, or ARROWS of martyrdom; a LAMP of wisdom; a SWAN of solitude, its sweet death-song typifying the Christian Nunc Dimittis; a RING of honour; a CROWN of reward; a BOOK of knowledge; the FRUIT-BEARING PALM of celestial rewards; an APPLE of original sin; an ANCHOR of patience; a BANNER of triumph; a SPRINKLER of purity; an OPEN DRAGON'S JAWS of hell. The heart is simply a mark of punctuation. Emblems and armorial charges constantly were used as devices and ornaments for vestments; but in many instances simply became made out of mantles and cloths presented by princes and noblemen. The Saviour has the lion of Judah; the blessed Virgin a fleur-de-lys, or the rose of Sharon depicted on her robe. Faith holds a book, a sieve, a cross, instruments of the Passion, a burning lamp, a chalice, and host. Hope has a ship, a beehive, a rake, and spade. Charity holds a pelican, the sacred monogram, or a flaming heart. Temperance, standing on a windmill, with a gag in her mouth and two eyeglasses in one hand, with the other regulates a clock. Justice with scales, holds one sword poised and another in readiness. Prudence carries a bier on her head, a sieve, a mirror turned to reflect what is approaching, or instruments of the Passion. Fortitude, standing on a press, has an iron anvil on her head, and strangles a dragon which she has drawn out of a tower.

Emblematical Gems. (Exod. xxxix. 8, 14: Rev. xxi. 19, 20.) The Urim and Thummim consisted of four rows of gems—

the cardinal virtues, each containing three jewels—the theological virtues. (1.) Sapphire (blue), truth and heaven, heavenly-mindedness, hope, the single heart. The tables of the law were made of this stone ; St. Paul, St. Andrew. (2.) Chalcedony (grey), humility ; St. James the Great. (3.) Emerald, of victory and hope, immortality, faith, reciprocal love ; St. Simon. (4.) Sardonyx (purple), married happiness, lively charity, martyrdom, humility, grief for sin ; St. Peter. (5.) Sardine (transparent purple), exalted faith, chastity, martyrdom ; St. John. (6.) Chrysolite (green and gold), antidote against madness, charity and wisdom, watchfulness of repentance, wisdom ; St. Matthew. (7.) Beryl (pale bright green), good example, long-suffering ; St. Thomas. (8.) Topaz (yellow), love to God and man, fruitfulness and fidelity, wisdom, good works, contemplation ; St. James the Less. (9, 10.) Chrysoprase (purple), charity in tribulation, love ; St. Jude. (11.) Jacynth (blue), angelic love, heavenly contemplation, preaching to wise and simple ; St. Bartholomew. (12.) Amethyst (violet), sincerity, humility to death, earthly suffering, docility, liberality ; St. Philip. The numbers show their emblematical representation of the Articles of the Creed, according to Marbodus. Agate, health, long life, and purity in the ministry. Bloodstone, carnage. Carbuncle (deep-red), suffering to bloodshed, earnest charity. Chalcedony, secret almsgiving. Cornelian, content. Diamond, innocence, fortitude. Garnet, constancy. Jasper (bluish-green), Christian cheerfulness, faith ; St. Peter. Onyx (bluish-white), truth. Opal, hope. Pearl, purity. Ruby, love, power, and dignity. Turquoise, prosperity.

Emblems of Saints

St. Adrian, with a sword, anvil, and hammer, deprived of legs and arms.

St. Afra, in a caldron.

St. Agapetus, with lions at his feet.

St. Agatha, holding a pair of pincers, and her bosoms.

St. Agnes, holding a sword, a lamb at her feet, a lamb on a book, a dove bringing a ring, a sword and flame at her feet, an angel covering her with a robe

St. Aidan, a stag at his feet.

St. Alban, in a cope, a cross raised on a tall staff in one hand, a sword in the other.

St. Alberic, Patriarch of Jerusalem, founder of Carmelites, in pontificals, with a palm.

St. Alphage, stones in his chasuble; a battle axe.

St. Ambrose, mitred, kneeling, a beehive ; a scourge, in allusion to his repulse of the Emperor Theodosius from his cathedral.

St. Andrew, a cross saltier.

St. Angradesima, as leprous.

St. Anne, teaching the Virgin to read, standing with Joachim before the Temple gate, with a triple crown in the left hand and a book in the right.

St. Anthony, hermit, a demon like a goat.

St. Apollinarius, assailed by a demon with a club.

St. Apollonia, pincers holding a tooth; with a palm.

St. Athanasius, habited as a Greek bishop, holding an open book, standing between two pillars.

St. Augustine, D., holding a flaming heart, or one pierced with an arrow of charity, an eagle.

St. Barbara, a tower in which she was immured, a chalice and host, a tower and palm.

St. Barnabas, holding St. Matthew's Gospel, or three stones, or an open book and staff.

St. Bartholomew, a flaying-knife and book.

St. Basil, a dove perched on his arm; a pen presented by a hand; before a brazier.

St. Beatrice, holding a rope.

St. Benedict, in a black habit, mitred, holding a staff, transfixing a demon with a cross; a sprinkler; a broken sieve; a cup and book; a raven with a book in its beak; a cup with serpents, to represent poison; a loaf; a thorn bush.

St. Benignus, a cross in the background.

St. Bernard de Tolomei, d. 1348, founder of the Olivetans on Monte Oliveto, near Sienna; white, holding an olive-branch.

St. Bernard, founder of the Cistercians; in a white habit, with the tonsure, as an abbot; with the emblems of the Passion; a white dog at his feet; with three mitres, the Sees he refused; writing, an angel holding a cross; kneeling before the apparition of the Virgin, a fettered dragon (heresy) beside him.

St. Bernardine, a tablet or disk like a sun, inscribed with the letters I H S.

St. Blaise, a comb or rake of iron.

St. Boniface, as a bishop, hewing down "the oak of thunder;" a book pierced with a sword.

St. Brannock, a cowl, well, and oak.

St. Bride, conversing with the Virgin, with a book and cross-staff.

St. Britius, carrying burning coals; or a child.

St. Bruno, in a white habit, with the tonsure, and in the attitude of prayer or meditation.

Canute, a king kneeling before an altar.

St. Catharine of Sienna (Dominican), with the stigmata; as a bride at her espousals.

St. Catharine crowned, a sword and wheel with knives.

St. Cecilia, a crown, a garland of red and white roses, and a palm; holding a harp, an organ with pipes, or a lute.

St. Christina, with a millstone round her neck, with which she was thrown into Lake Bolsena, with arrows aimed against her.

St. Clair, carrying a head.

St. Clara (Franciscan), d. 1253, a lily; in dark brown, veiled; the pyx with which she drove the Saracens from Assisi; a cross, staff, and book.

St. Clement, mitred, with a triple cross and anchor.

St. Cornelius, tiared; a horn.

SS. Cosmas and Damian, in togas, carrying an ointment-pot, or instruments of surgery; a bottle and shears; two physicians.

SS. Crispin and Crispinian, a shoemaker's knife and awl.

St. Cuthbert, carrying St. Oswald's head, pillars of light at his side, and swans.

St. Cyprian, a sword.

St. Cyriac, with his hands cut off; a deacon with a dragon.

St. David, a saint preaching from a hill; a dove on his shoulder.

St. Denis, carrying his mitred head; d. 272, in white, with a black mantle.

St. Dominic, holding a rosary; a star on his forehead or breast; a black and white dog setting a globe on fire, allusive to his mother's dream; a crucifix, a book; a fleur-de-lys in one hand, a monastery in the other.

St. Dorothea, with roses and apples of Paradise, sent at her martyrdom to convert a scoffer, Theophilus.

St. Dunstan, a dove lighting on him; a group of angels round him; holding a harp; a furnace and tongs.

St. Eanswitha, carrying fish.

St. Edith, washing the feet of the poor.

St. Edmund the King, pierced with arrows; an arrow in his hand; with a sceptre. (Patron of Bury St. Edmund's.)

St. Edmund, M., a king's head guarded by a wolf.

St. Edward, K and M , holding a cup ; or a dagger or falcon.

St. Edward, Confessor, a sceptre in his right, a ring in his left hand. (Patron of Westminster Abbey.)

St. (Mary) Ægyptiaca, with loose tresses, a monk standing by.

St. Elizabeth, holding St. John the Baptist, saluting the Virgin.

St. Elizabeth of Hungary, crowned with a basket of bread or roses, into which her loaves were changed.

St. Eloi, or Eligius, a hammer and cross-staff, vested as a bishop.

St. Enurchus, a dove.

St. Erasmus, a windlass.

St. Etheldreda, asleep, a tree blossoming over her ; as an abbess.

St. Eustace, a knight ; a dog, a stag with a cross.

St. Fabian, a Pope, tiared, kneeling at the block ; a sword and palm.

St. Faith, a gridiron.

St. Fiacre, as a hermit ; or with a spade and open book.

St. Flora, with her head in her hand, and flowers blossoming from her neck.

St. Francesca Romana, d. 1448, foundress of the Benedictine Oblates, an elderly woman in a nun's dress, with a white veil, and her guardian angel.

St. Francis, receiving the stigmata on Monte Laverna ; with seraphs ; a lamb ; a crucifix, kneeling before a skull ; d. 1226 ; in dark brown, with a girdle.

St. Francis di Paola, d. 1507, founder of the Minims, in a brown habit, with the cowl over his head, and Charitas on a scroll.

St. Frideswide, an ox.

St. Gabriel, holding a lily.

St. Geneviève, holding a candle.

St. German, with dead beasts.

St. Gertrude, a loaf in her hand.

St. Giles, with a wounded hind, the animal which led the French king, in hunting, to discover the recluse in his cave.

St. Giovanni Gualberto, d. 1073, founder of Vallombrosans, dark brown habit, with an embroidered cope, a carved cross and crutch.

St. Gothard, a bishop in a confessional.

St. Gregory the Great, a cross and book ; an eagle ; before him a dove at his ear in inspiration ; Christ appearing over the chalice.

St. Gudule, carrying a lantern.

St. Guthlac, a scourge.

St. Helen, carrying a large cross.

Henry VI., a fawn at a king's feet.

St. Hilary, with three books ; treading on reptiles, that is, heresies.

St. Hippolytus, a gaoler ; a horse.

St. Hubert, a stag, with a cross between the antlers.

St. Hugh of Lincoln, a swan (solitude), with a lantern in his hand.

St. Ignatius, vested for Mass, with a noble type of head ; the monogram I H S on his breast.

St. James the Great, of Compostella, as a pilgrim, with staff, scallop-shell, bottle, and hat.

St. James the Less, a saw ; a fuller's bat in his hand.

St. Januarius, lighting a fire.

St. Joachim, with doves in a basket.

St Joachim, with a staff and basket of doves.

St. Jerome, a lion, his attendant in the desert ; carrying a church ; as a cardinal ; striking his breast with a stone.

St. John the Almoner, with a loaf and rosary.

St. John the Baptist, a lamb on a book.

St. John Chrysostom, a chalice and the Gospels ; a beehive, honey.

St. John the Evangelist, a cup of gold, with a serpent issuing ; as an evangelist ; part of his dress green.

St. John of God, St. Juan Calabita, d. 1550, founder of the Hospitallers ; a pomegranate, surmounted with a cross.

St. John de Matha, founder of the Trinitarians, d. 1213, in a white habit, with a red and blue cross on the breast ; fetters in his hands, or at his feet ; sometimes in a black mantle above white ; or a stag, with a cross, red and blue, between its horns, appearing to him.

St. Joseph, with a flowering rod, and a dove resting on it ; an old man ; part of his dress is always saffron.

Judas Iscariot, the purse ; his hair red, his robe yellow.

St. Jude, a club, with a little ship ; a carpenter's square ; a medallion of the Saviour on his breast.

St. Julian of Mans, a well, banner, palm ; driving a dragon ; a ferryboat.

St. Lambert, a javelin.

St. Lawrence the Deacon, with a gridiron, carrying a cross-staff.

St. Leodegar, a borer or pickaxe.

St. Leonard, an ox; with fetters in his hand.

St. Louis, with a dove and the arms of France ; or washing the feet of the poor.

St. Lucy, carrying a taper (*luce*) or sword; or her eyes. (Called in Scotland St. Tredwald.)

St. Lupus, a bishop giving the Host.

St. Magnan, with an animal eating fruit at his feet.

St. Magnus, restoring a blind man to sight.

St. Margaret, piercing a dragon with a cross-staff.

St. Martha, a vat and sprinkler.

St. Martin of Tours, on horseback, dividing his cloak to give to a beggar.

St. Mary, the Blessed Virgin, with a lily ; an almond-tree ; a star on her shoulder ; in robes of red and blue.

St. Mary Magdalen, robed in red, with the box of ointment.

St. Matthew, as evangelist, an angel ; a purse, as a publican ; a dolphin at his feet ; an axe ; a stone in his hand.

St. Matthias, a halbert.

St. Maurice, in armour.

St. Medard, doves, an eagle; a beggar.

St. Michael the Archangel, as a warrior, in mail, treading on a dragon ; or holding a balance with souls in it ; a cross on his brow.

St. Nicholas of Myra, three children in a tub ; three purses on a book.

St. Nicomede, a club with spikes.

St. Norbert, as holding a chalice, above which is a venomous spider, in allusion to his drinking without harm from it.

St. Olaf, a halbert ; a loaf.

St. Oswald, a dove with a letter, chrism, or a ring in its beak.

St. Oswyn, a sceptre and spear.

St. Osyth, a key; an apse.

St. Pancras, a sword or stone in his hands, a Saracen under his feet.

St. Patern, a serpent.

St. Patrick, treading on reptiles ; with trefoils or shamrocks.

St. Paul, a sword, sometimes two swords, represented with a low, spare body, grave face, weak eyes, bushy brows, and thick beard.

St. Paul, hermit ; ravens bringing food.

St. Peter, two keys of gold (sometimes a third, that of knowledge or this world, is added) ; two keys, one of gold, the other silver ; a key on a book; represented with a pale face, noble head, dark keen eye, and slender, sinewy form, robed in blue and yellow.

St. Peter, M. (Dominican), a knife sticking in his heart.

St. Peter Nolasco, aged, in a white habit, with the arms of Arragon, founder of the Order of Mercy, c. 1230.

St. Petronilla, ministering alms at a table.

St. Philip Benizzi, a triple crown, offered by a cherub.

St. Philip, Ap., a basket with the loaves ; a lance and double cross, with an idol falling at his feet.

St. Philip Neri, a rosary.

St. Polycarp, a flaming pile.

St. Potentiana, almsgiving.

St. Prisca, a sword, a lion, or eagle.

St. Quentin, a spit.

St. Quiriac, pierced with a sword at the altar.

St. Raphael, an archangel leading a youth.

St. Remigius, a dove with a cruse of oil.

St. Rhadegund, two wolves.

St. Richard of Chichester, a chalice falling, with the wine unspilled, at his feet.

St. Roch, as a pilgrim, with a plague-boil on his thigh, a dog beside him.

St. Romuald, aged, with a long beard, in a white habit, leaning on a crutch.

St. Rosalia, embracing a rock.

St. Saturninus, dragged by bulls.

St. Scholastica, with a crucifix, as a Benedictine nun, with a white veil.

St. Sebastian, pierced with an arrow, bound to a tree.

St. Servatus, a sun and a bird.

St. Simon, holding a fish or sword.

St. Stephen, deacon, his dalmatic full of stones ; as the Pope ; a martyr at the altar.

St. Sidwell, a scythe.

St. Sylvester, an ox, or baptizing.

St. Theodora, a demon taking her hand.

St. Theodore, with a halbert and sabre; flogged with rods.

St. Theresa, d. 1582, foundress of Reformed Carmelites ; a dove ; a heart with the sacred monogram ; an angel aiming an arrow at her.

St. Thomas, with a lance or a carpenter's square, allusive to his undertaking to build a palace for Gundafor, king of India, which he explained meant the edification of the Church.

St. Thomas Aquinas (Dominican), a star on his breast, a dove at his ear; a chalice and host in the tabernacle, allusive to his composition of the office for Corpus Christi Day.

St Thomas of Canterbury, a sword in his head.

St. Ursula, an arrow; a white banner with a red cross; a dove at her feet.

St. Valentine, being stoned.

St. Vedast, a wolf and goose.

St. Verena, a flood sweeping past her.

St. Veronica (*vera icon*), the true likeness imprinted on a handkerchief.

St. Vincent, as a deacon, with a gridiron and palm, on a rack.

St. Vitalis, a saint in a river.

St. Waltheof, at the block, the sun rising.

St. Walbruga, oil distilling from her hand.

St. Walstan, a calf; a scythe.

St. Wendolin, a shrine; or with beads and a dog.

St. Wilfrid, destroying idols.

St. William, M., nails in a boy's head and hands.

St. Winifred, with her head in her hand.

St. Wulstan, with his staff fixed in a tomb; a scythe.

Embolismus. The short prayer, against temptation, which follows the Lord's Prayer in every Greek liturgy.

Embrasure. A crenelle, or opening between the merlons, or solid parts of a battlement.

Enamel. Glass rendered opaque by the use of oxide of lead or tin. Limoges was the great school of the art. The Byzantine enamellers, after the fall of Constantinople, went to Russia, and carried with them a distinguished name for skill and beauty in execution. According to the mode in which it is embedded or encrusted, it is termed cloisonné or champlevé.

Encolpia. (*Egkolpizein*, to wear on the breast.) (1.) Reliquaries worn round the neck, and hanging on the breast, which contained relics, or gospels; a fragment of the cross, filings from St. Peter's chains, or oil from the lamps which lighted a martyr's tomb. They are alluded to by St. Chrysostom and Nectarius, patriarch of Constantinople. They were usually square, and bore the sacred monograms of $X\ P$ and $A\ \Omega$. (2.) The bishop's pectoral cross; one lately found bears the motto, "Emanuel, God with us, the Cross is life to me, to thee, Death, an enemy." These reliquaries formerly took the form of a small bottle of gold, contained within a tube; St. Gregory the Great first gave them the shape of a cross; one of his date is still worn by the Provost of Monza at a pontifical Mass; and two smaller phylacteries given to Theodolinda are preserved in the treasury of that church.

Engaged. Having part of a surface attached to a wall, or pillar.

England, Church of. That pure and apostolical branch of the

Church Catholic, derived by lineal succession from the British bishops, and the same before and after the Reformation; a title as old as Magna Charta, and used in a bull of Pope Innocent III. in 1245.

Epact, (Intercalary.) The difference between the last day of of the lunar year and that of the solar year; it is used for calculating the moon's age on any day in the year, and in conjunction with the Dominical letter for finding out Easter Day.

Ependytes *or* **Superaria.** An upper robe worn by the ancient monks, and mentioned by St. Jerome.

Epigonation. An ornament worn by an archimandrite on his left side in the Liturgy.

Epiphany. (Gr. manifestation.) In the Mozarabic and Font-évrault use,—the Apparition; originally the festival commemorative of the Lord's baptism; a tradition as early as the time of St. Clement of Alexandria, but about the fourth century and in the Western Church always observed in memory of His manifestation to the Gentiles, and so in France, Germany, and England it was called the Feast of the Three Kings, and to this day the sovereign sends myrrh, frankincense, and gold, in a crimson bag, which is offered on the altar of the Chapel Royal. The Greek Church calls it Theophany, the manifestation of God—when the voice of the Father proclaimed the Son. St. Jerome mentions it as the Epiphany, the recognized name in connection with the adoration of the magi, but both names occur in his 'Comes' and Pope Gregory's 'Sacramentary'. Bethphany is another title allusive to the miracle in the house of Cana, and Phagiphania, recalling the feeding of the multitude associated with it. In Africa, as St. Augustine says, "the Lights" is a name as old as the time of St. Gregory Nazianzen, connecting it with the rising of the star and the "Light that lighteneth every man that cometh into the world." Balsamon speaks of the lighting of many tapers to represent the glory of the festival, which was kept always on January 6th, as appears from the Fathers and the laws of Valens, Theodosius, and Arcadius. It is alluded to by Ammianus Marcellinus, the heathen. Metropolitans, at Epiphany, sent their paschal letters, announcing the moveable feasts in the coming year, to their suffragans. In England it was known as Twelfth Night, the conclusion of Christmastide, and the morrow as St. Distaff's day, because work was then resumed; in Austria as Bright Day; and in Wales and at Rouen as Star Feast.

Special baptism on this day, a Spanish custom, was abolished by Pope Damasus and Himerius of Tarragona, before the fourth century; but the Greek, Syrian, and African Churches retained the practice, with a solemn benediction of water on the vigil. To this day the custom is preserved in Russia, and attended with innumerable lights and tapers, to symbolize the spiritual illumination to which our Lord, by His baptism, consecrated water. SS. Chrysostom and Epiphanius mention the solemn drawing of water, connecting it with the miracle of Cana,—a tradition alluded to by Chrysologus and Eucherius of Lyons; and St. Paulinus mentions the commemoration of three events—the visit of the Magi, our Lord's baptism, and His conversion of water into wine.

Epistles for Festivals, Fasts, and Sundays, with the Gospels, may have been appointed in St. Jerome's Lectionary day by day, by command of Pope Damasus, who enjoined that order in the Roman Church; but some parties attribute the arrangement and choice to P. Telesphorus or Alexander. Like the Ten Commandments, the epistle and gospel were read in a low pulpit facing the people in the nave, or from the desk attached to the priest's stall in choir, after the Reformation; before that period the rood-loft was used for the purpose. The term 'apostle' was often used to designate the epistle, which is usually part of an apostolical epistle.

Eremites *or* **Hermits.** Dwellers in a Solitary Place. (Gr. *eremos*.) Persons absolutely separated from society. The first was Paul the Solitary, whom St. Anthony visited in the third century, and Hilarion and Pacomius imitated. They usually attended the services of the nearest church, as five at Merkyate did in the twelfth century. The ascetic kept silence and retreat even in inhabited places. Curious rock-cells overlooking rivers were hewn out at the Red and Black Rock, in Worcestershire; at Warkworth, where the neighbouring canons are said to have taken shelter in times of danger; and in Guy's Cliff, Warwick. Hermitages also are found in the Roche Rocks, Cornwall; at Inkerman, Tekerman, Midiah, Gebel-al-Terr, Thelemark, Bretzenheim, St. Aubin, St. Baume, Fontgambaud, St. Antoine de Calumies,

St. Emilien, and Montmajeur, near Arles. The latter is of the sixth century, but was enlarged five hundred years later, retaining, however, its chairs and benches of stone, like a Roman catacomb. The Eremites of St. Paul, founded under the Austin rule by Eusebius of Gran in 1308, came to Colchester in 1310. *See* AUSTIN FRIARS.

Eucharistic Bread. The wafer. (Before consecration, *oblys*, *oblata*; after it, *hostia* and *housl* (Norsk), the sacrifice; used in England in 925); *sancta* in the old Roman Order. In 693 a Council of Toledo required the bread to be made thin so as to be easily broken, and expressly baked for the altar. In the sixth century the Greeks had adopted leavened bread, and in the West the contrary practice of using unleavened bread, said to have been prescribed by Alexander I., was in use between the times of Photius and Cerularius, and during the Papacy of Leo IX. in the middle of the eleventh century, at the period of the rupture between the Greek and Roman Churches. Epiphanius and Severus of Alexandria mention that altar breads were circular. St. Gregory calls them crowns. The *panis deccussatus* of the Roman Christians was divided by incisions into four equal parts. In 1287, Bishop Quivil of Exeter ordered hosts to be whole, white, and round. They at first were usually made before Christmas and Easter, and, until the fifteenth century, by three deacons or priests, with an assistant clerk or lay-brother, fasting with great devotion, and in complete silence, after having said the litany and penitential Psalms. They kneaded the hosts with meal and pure cold water upon a polished table; the assistant baked them, six at a time, with his hands gloved, and from the ninth century used special irons or tongs for stamping them with a cross and monogram (*ferrum oblatarum* v. *ferramentum characteratum*), a pair of of which is still preserved at Braine. The other two cut up the hosts with a knife, and let them fall into a dish covered with a white cloth. Bishop Bleys of Worcester, in 1329, ordered the oblates to be baked in an instrument lined with pure wax, and not with lard. Bona suggests that the wafer was used when the personal offering of the holy loaf fell into desuetude, and the priests provided the element, and that its shape was a memorial of the denar—the betrayal money— and came into vogue when the people offered the Mass

penny as a composition for their oblation. Durandus refers
it to Ps. xxiv. 1 ; xxxix, 8. In 1549 the English Church
ordered the eucharistic bread to be " throughout the realm
after one sort and fashion, unleavened, round, as it was afore,
but without all manner of print, and something more large
and thicker than it was, so that it might be aptly divided
in divers pieces, and every one divided into two pieces, at
least, or more, by the discretion of the minister, and so distributed." Wafer bread was used in the time of Elizabeth,
and at Westminster Abbey in 1643. The altar breads are
called in some Greek liturgies " burning coals," in allusion
to Is. vi. 6, or divine fire of love. The words " holy sacrifice, immaculate host," were inserted in the Mass by Pope
Leo I. The wafer was broken into three portions, as
Casalius says, as an offering to the Holy Trinity : (1) as a
sacrifice of thanksgiving ; (2) a sacrifice propitiatory for the
sins of the living ; and, (3) a sacrifice for the souls in Purgatory, offered immediately to Christ. In the eleventh century
a portion was used for the viaticum, and in the later medieval
Church, according to Bishop Hooper, was carried by the
priests at their breast, their heads being covered with the
surplice. Erasmus says the Host was carried on horseback
round the fields, and from place to place, as a benediction.
Becon relates a painful anecdote, that " if the priest was
weak in his arms the rude people of the country in divers
parts of England would cry out to the priest, ' Hold up, Sir
John, heave it a little higher.' And one would say to another,
' Stoop down, thou fellow afore, that I may see my Maker,
for I cannot be merry (*i.e.* pleasant or happy) except I see
the Lord God once a day.' " And, on the other hand Bishop
Ridley says that blasphemous bills were set round St. Paul's
by the ignorant, at the Reformation, calling the Host " the
sacrament of the halter," " round Robin," and " Jack in the
box." In the Grand Chartreuse the Hosts are passed by
the monks in solemn silence from hand to hand. The phe-
nomenon of the bleeding host was observed in 1004; at
Bolsena in 1264 (the subject of one of Raphael's pictures),
in 1383, 1510; and at Legnano in 1819. In 1848 the
microscope revealed the fact that the stains were made by
myriads of vibrios or monads of a red colour. Houselling
people were communicants. Houselling bread was the

smaller; singing bread (so called from the chanting with which its manufacture was accompanied,) was the larger altar bread. The housel, by Ælfric's canons, was not to be given to men half alive, and was not to be hallowed on Good Friday. The custom of keeping the housel consecrated on Easter Day for a whole year, for communion of the sick, was forbidden, and a weekly or fortnightly consecration prescribed. If it had been by mischance kept so long as to be corruptible, it was burned in a clear fire and the ashes were put under the altar, by Edgar's laws, 960. In 994 the Communion was to be received on every Sunday in Lent, the four last days before Easter, and daily all the next week. In 1009 and 1017, men were required to go to Housel three times a year.

In the Greek Church small, round loaves, or oblations, are used, generally five in number, in allusion to St. Mark, vi. 38, and circular like the money, the price of our redemption. Formerly their number was proportioned to that of the persons offering. From the chief oblation, the Holy Lamb, or Sphragis, which the priest stabs out of the antidoron, are cut a pyramidal-shaped portion for St. Mary, nine portions for prophets, apostles, and martyrs, portions for the dead, and portions for the living. In the time of Maldonati, laymen who did not communicate, at the elevation of the Host, represented in dumb show the earlier custom of touching their eyes, nostrils, temples, and forehead, as the seat of the senses, with it. *See* HOLY COMMUNION.

Eucharistic Vestments. Were first ordered by Pope Stephen in 260, in imitation of the dress of the Jewish priesthood, (Ezek. xliv. 17-19,) out of reverence to God and His Church, to represent the sanctity of the rites administered, as a warning to ministers when wearing them, and to procure reverence in divine worship. In the twelfth century, in Ireland, they were white. By order of Pope Clement old vestments were to be burned, and their ashes buried in the baptistery, under the pavement or in the walls. Gratian says they were washed in special vessels. Their symbolical meaning has been given under their names; the alb, with its two flaps on the shoulders and two beneath over against the feet, behind and before, are the four nails; the flaps of the amice are the crown of thorns, according to Tyndale: the amice is, after the ancient fashion, still worn outside the alb in Holy Week by the Maronites at Lyons and Milan. Rupert says the dalmatic was not worn in Lent or Advent, as a memorial of the disciples' inability to bear the mysteries of the faith until Jesus was glorified. In 1222 and 1322, every church in the Province of Canterbury was ordered to have two sets, the principal for Sundays and feasts, and the rest for week-days.

Eulogiæ, Antidora, Holy Bread, *or* **Holy Loaf.** (1.) In the early Church, at the end of the Mass, the loaves offered by the faithful, which had not been consecrated, were blessed by the celebrant, and distributed as a sign of brotherly communion, as they are now in the Greek Church, to those who had not partaken of the Divine Mysteries, and formerly to cate-chumens, who were not admissible. They were called eulogies or antidora, compensations, by the Council of Antioch, in 341. Sometimes holy bread was sent from the cathedral to its dependent parish churches. The eulogies of unleavened bread were placed on the altar, or on the credence or diakonikon, which stood to the left of it. After certain prayers they were cut up with the holy lance, or eucharistic knife, for distribution. In the fourth century, eulogies in the Western Church were given to catechumens, and St. Austin calls them a sacrament. (2.) Bishops also sent to one another bread set apart with a special blessing and called benediction, as an outward sign of ecclesiastical communion and Christian concord. They might be used by the recipients for consecration afterwards. Paulinus sent such loaves to St. Augustine, and Tertullian mentioned them as pledges of mutual hospitality. (3.) In the sixth century, in France, a meal after grace had been said was called a benediction or eulogy. Certain constitutions of the thirteenth century forbid the giving of eulogies to priests' wives, but at that period women at their churching at Durham received them. Cranmer says, " Holy bread is to put us in remembrance that all Christian men are one mystical body of Christ, as the bread is made of many grains and yet but one loaf, and to put us in remembrance also of receiving the Holy Sacrament and Body of Christ in right charity, which, in the beginning of Christ's Church, men did oftener receive than they do now."

Evangelistic Symbols. The four mystic animals (Rev. iv. 7 ;

Ezek. i. 10; xi. 4) were not drawn earlier than the fifth century. SS. Jerome and Augustine have referred the man to St. Matthew, in allusion to his commencement with the human genealogy; the lion to St. Mark, in reference to his opening with the cry in the wilderness; the ox to St. Luke, from his beginning with the sacrifice of Zecharias; and the eagle to St. John, whose first words are, " In the beginning was the Word." St. Matthew has sometimes an angel, the evangelist of the incarnation, and the other three symbols represent (1) the royalty and resurrection, (2) the priesthood and passion, and (3) the ascension and revelation of the Divine nature. Other interpreters apply them to our Lord, who took our manhood to deliver man; as a lion, trod down His enemies; as a calf, was led to sacrifice; and as an eagle, rose to heaven. The head of the man only has the aureole in most cases, as it was considered wrong to give it to creatures without reason. Stars sometimes are set on the heads of the symbols, which often hold books of the gospels: no precise or invariable order of arrangement was observed, and they frequently appear on the ends of a cross, as witnesses of the godhead and humanity of the Saviour; cherubim have been sometimes pourtrayed as composed of all the four animals.

Evangelists. Missionary or itinerant preachers; assistants of the Apostles in the primitive Church, in distinction to the resident priests and deacons (Eph. iv. 11; Acts xxi. 8; 2 Tim. iv. 5); and the prophets, or inspired expositors of Holy Scripture.

Eve. The day before a festival which is not fasted; so, when a feast falls on Monday, its vigil or fast is kept on the previcus Saturday, but Sunday is its eve.

Evening Celebrations of the Holy Communion are mentioned by the Councils of Agde and III. Orleans. Tertullian speaks of the Eucharist being celebrated " before light;" and the origin, as St. Augustine says, must be traced to the time of the institution at the Paschal Supper. The Greeks followed the custom in Lent, on fast-days, and vigils after noon, that is, possibly, after Vespers. Rabanus Maurus and Micrologus mention that, in Lent, Mass was deferred till Nones in the West. In Africa the same practice prevailed. The Latin Church celebrated on Maundy Thursday at evening; and also on Whitsun Eve, and fast days after Nones. This custom lasted till about 430, when it was forbidden, except on Maundy Thursday, by the Council of Macon; and even that relaxation was removed by the Council of Tarragona. In the East, the Councils of Laodicea and V. Constantinople required Communion to be made fasting, and prohibited evening celebrations with the same view. In 1566 Pope Pius V. deprived metropolitans, cathedrals, ministers, sovereigns, and nobles of the privilege of having such services; to these probably Shakespeare alludes, when he mentions "evening Masses," which no doubt had grown out of the canonical midnight celebrations.

Exarch. The Greek primate, inferior to a patriarch, and superior to a metropolitan. In the third century there were three exarchs—of Ephesus, with the diocese of Asia, twelve provinces, and 300 sees; Heraclea, with the diocese of Thrace, and six provinces; and Cæsarea, with the diocese of Pontus, thirteen provinces, and 104 sees; which were the residences of the imperial prefects. Exarchs had jurisdiction over metropolitans within their diocese, and ordained them; received appeals against their judgments, and decided cases of difference between them and their suffragans. In councils they sat next to patriarchs. In the fifth century the Council of Chalcedon transferred the privileges of the three exarchates to the patriarch of Constantinople, and their titles became honorary. Pope Damasus gave the rank of exarch to the Bishops of Thessalonica; the metropolitan of Cyprus was confirmed as exarch by the Council of Ephesus, in the fifth century, and, like the Archbishop of Bulgaria, who was exempt from the Patriarch of Constantinople, was called autokephalous.

Excommunication. (*Aphorismos*, separation. Exclusion of an offender from the Communion (founded on 1 Cor. v. 11), and his removal from the Church and prayers, being reduced to the condition of a heathen (St. Matt. xviii. 17); he was capable of readmission (1 Cor. xvi. 22; 2 Cor. ii. 5-11). In the medieval Church the general sentence, curse, or execration on all who infringed on the privileges, immunities, rights, and dues of the Church was pronounced with lights burning and the uplifted cross in church, on the Sunday after Michaelmas, Mid-Lent Sunday, Trinity Sunday, and the Sunday

after the Feast of St. Peter Vincula, after the gospel from
the pulpit or rood-loft, by priests, but usually before the
high-altar by a bishop, vested in his alb. The candles were
then thrown upon the ground, whilst the church bells were
rung. and then extinguished; a custom in the eighth century,
as a sign that the souls of the malefactors, unless they made
restitution, would be quenched in torment, and meanwhile
the anathema was laid on them in the field, on the way, or at
home, sitting, sleeping, eating, working, standing, seques-
tered from the light and all the blessings of the Church.
The entire ceremonial probably was not in effect until the
ninth century. The bull In Cœna Domini was read, until
1740, by a cardinal deacon, in the Pope's presence, on
Maundy Thursday, and was a sentence of general excommunication. Tyndale says, that in the Marches of Wales,
when a man had a cow or a calf stolen, he complained to the
curate, who commanded all the parishioners to say, " God's
curse and mine have he." The lesser excommunication removed the person from a participation in the sacraments,
but the greater, called the anathema (Gal. i. 8), which resembled the primitive erasure of a name from the diptychs,
expelled him from the Church, and deprived him of Christian burial. Subjects were absolved from allegiance to an
excommunicated priest. Gregory V., for the first time, inflicted the sentence of excommunication on a king, on Robert
of France, in 998. John, and Henry VIII., and Napoleon,
in 1809, by Pius VII., were excommunicated. The lesser
excommunication was the punishment of sacrilege, lay
usurpation of a church, notorious offenders, or those who
conversed with persons under the greater ban, which was ·
imposed on diviners, heretics, simoniacs, plunderers of
churches, or those who laid violent hands on a clerk. Excommunication is followed by no civil penalty except imprisonment in certain cases.

Exempt, *or* **Peculiars.** (1.) Places and churches privileged by
the Pope from any visitation but his own, as Bury, and many
other abbeys; the Abbot of Westminster had to travel to
Rome for confirmation, and visit Rome once in every two
years or pay a fine. (2.) Churches free from the jurisdiction
of the diocesan and archdeacon, and called peculiars because
not being manors or advowsons of the See, they were reputed

to be subject to the Archbishop of Canterbury and of his diocese, viz., the Arches, thirteen parishes in London, Risborough, Bocking, Shoreham, Pagham, the Pallant (Chichester), Tarring, Poling, and Malling, and parishes in other dioceses, in all 57 in number ; the church of Battle, a donative of the Abbot; and St. Burian's, which was liable to visitation by the Crown only, as Windsor and Westminster are now. From these exempt places an appeal was made after the Reformation to the Queen in Chancery, who constituted a commission of delegates. Some places were exempt solely from archidiaconal jurisdiction. Monastic peculiars or appropriations dependent on great abbeys, until subjected to the diocesan by Act 31 Hen. VIII., c. 13, but he had always the right of institution. In Spain some churches, during part of the year, were under the diocesan, and at other times were said to be *vere nullius*, " truly of none." In England, prebendal churches were visited by the dean of the cathedral (as dean of Christianity), and the representative of the chapter ; these, by 1 & 2 Vict. c. cvi. s. 108, in 1838, are now visited by the diocesan. *See* CATHEDRALS.

Exhortatory Week. The week before Septuagesima.

Exorcism. (*Aphorkismos* in baptism, *exorkismos* in pure exorcism.) In the primitive Church the candidates for baptism coming barefooted, and habited in a single dress, and carrying a taper symbolical of the light of Christ, bowing their heads, and, receiving imposition of hands, were exorcized. The ceremony seems to have been substantially the same as renunciation of the devil, though differing in form. In the fourth century exorcism was recommended as highly expedient. Probably the custom took its origin in allusion to St. Mark xvi. 17; Acts xix. 12–16, and as the persons deprived of the blessings and freedom of the gospel are bond-slaves of Satan, to 1 Cor. v. 3–5 ; 1 Tim. i. 20. The energumens, or exorcized, stood with their faces towards the west, as the symbol of darkness, and stretched out their hands as if pushing away Satan ; the exorcist breathed on them three times. Probably there was a longer form used in the preparation of the candidate, and one shorter previous to his immersion. The Western form was, " I adjure thee, unclean spirit, that thou come out of this servant of Jesus Christ ! in the name of the Father, the Son, and the Holy Ghost." To the last these words were often added, "Make way for the Holy Ghost." In the Prayer Book of 1549 the form was, "I command thee, unclean spirit, in the name of the Father, of the Son, and of the Holy Ghost, that thou come out and depart from these infants." The LXXII. English Canon, of 1603, forbids exorcism without the bishop's licence. "No minister, without licence of the bishop of the diocese, is to attempt, upon any pretence whatsoever, whether of possession or obsession, by fasting and prayer, to cast out any devil or devils, under pain of the imputation of imposture or cozenage, and deposition from the ministry."

Exorcist. One of the minor orders of the ministry, dating from the third century. The exorcist at his ordination, by the Fourth Council of Carthage, was given the forms of exorcizing, and received power from the bishop of laying hands on the energumens, persons possessed, who entered only the forecourt of the church, whether baptized or catechumens; he had charge of the catechumens; he seems to have held a cross when acting ministerially. Peter, who suffered martyrdom in 302, is the earliest exorcist on record.

Exposition. The exhibition of the Host standing manifest in a monstrance or glass viril on an altar. By special privilege it is perpetual at Lugo and Leon, always surrounded with burning lights, and attended by two priests watching. In other large churches the exposition is made during the "Forty Hours," by course or rotation, a privilege restricted to Rome by Pope Clement VIII. in 1562, and introduced at Seville in 1697.

Extreme Unction. Founded on St. Mark vi. 13, and St. James v. 14–15, and universally adopted in the West after the twelfth century; originated in the act of anointing by a bishop or priest, which, in early times, was immediately connected with absolution and the Lord's Supper when administered to dying persons. An anointing of the sick is mentioned by Innocent I. in the beginning of the fifth, and by Felix IV. at the commencement of the next century; but the ceremony did not become universal in the Western Church till after the twelfth century, although it is alluded to by St. Augustine, St. Gregory, Fortunatus of Poitiers, and Gregory of Tours. In the Greek Church it is practised on the authority of oral tradition, and is mentioned by Origen and St. Chrysostom, Victor of Antioch, and St. Cyril of Jerusalem. In the time of Charlemagne several priests officiated, but Innocent III. first defined that one priest sufficed. The pseudo-Dionysius alludes to a practice of anointing the dead before being lowered into the grave. The unction was made in the form of a cross on the brow, the seat of the senses, and that of the disease in the dying. The oil was kept in a tabernacle in the sanctuary wall. The old names for this ceremonial were, the sacrament of the passing, the unction of the holy oil, or holy anointing. The Greeks call it *hagion elaion*, holy oil, and *euchelaion*, the " prayer of the holy oil." In 1322 all persons in England, above the age of fourteen years, were allowed to receive extreme unction.

Fabric, in ancient Statutes. (1.) The material building of a cathedral. (2.) The personal establishment, as when the cope, required to be presented by a dignitary or canon at his installation, was said to be given to the fabric.

Faculty. A dispensation issued by the Archbishop of Canterbury for dispensing with plurality of benefices, or granting ordination, *infra ætatem*, for persons of extraordinary abilities, before the canonical age, or letters dimissory; confirmed by 21 Henry VIII. c. xxi. s. 3; and 44 Geo. III. c. xliii. s. 1. Archbishops Usher and Sharp, Bishops Bull and Jeremy Taylor, and Ven. Bede, were ordained priests before they had attained twenty-four years of age; in the medieval Church similar instances are recorded; and probably St. Athanasius, St. Gregory Thaumaturgus, and Remigius of Rheims, were consecrated at an earlier age than ordinary.

Faithful. The title of a baptized Christian in primitive times, in distinction to a neophyte or catechumen.

Faldstool. (Fr. Pliant.) A folding-stool, or seat, in the form of a cross saltier, like St. Loup's at Sens. At St. Alban's, in the twelfth century, called the faudestole; a bishop's portable and enclosed, or armed chair—from the word ' fold,' a closure : like one preserved at York. Bishop Hacket speaks of the faldestory in the midst of Lichfield choir; and Bishop Andrewes of the faldistory for the Litany. At Rouen, Chartres, Paris, and Vienne, the bishop ordinarily sat on the faldstool. The Litany desk is often improperly called a fald, as if a folding-stool. Queen Mary II.'s faldstool, used at her marriage, is preserved at Winchester; and one of iron, of the fourteenth century, at Bayeux.

Fanon, *or* **Phanon.** (Vannel, mappula, mantile, or maniple; sudarium; from Germ. Fahne, a banner, or vane.) (1.) The orale of old writers; a white silk, gauze-like tippet, with edges and bars of gold lace, and two stripes of blue and scarlet, in imitation of an ephod, worn by the Pope like a hood. It was not used until the time of Innocent III., about 1200, and was a substitute for the amice, which then began to be worn by the Pontiff inside instead of, as before, outside the albe. It is double, and the inner half being put on like a tippet over the albe, the corresponding duplicate is brought over his head until the chasuble is put on, and then it is turned over all the other robes, coming round the back, chest, and shoulders. In lieu of a maniple, he has a succinctory. Tyndale says that it represented the cord with which Christ's hands were bound. (2.) A napkin. (3.) A corporal. (4.) The label of a bishop's mitre. (5.) The maniple, a kerchief formerly carried on the arm, and used by the priest to wipe his face (as Amalarius says), but now a merely ornamental appendage attached to his left hand. In the sixth century it began to be carried on the left arm as an honourable distinction, at Rome. St. Gregory desired John, Archbishop of Ravenna, to permit its use to deacons: in the ninth century priests and deacons indiscriminately, and in the eleventh century subdeacons, adopted it.

Fan Tracery. The peculiar glory of Perpendicular architecture; a vaulting, in which all the ribs at the springing of a vault have the same curve, and diverge equally in every direction, as at Windsor, the Lady Chapel, Westminster; Peterborough New Work; King's College Chapel, Cambridge.

Farced. Kyries and epistles were said to be farced, when they were interlarded with passages, called tropes, which formed, as it were, intercalated anthems between the Kyrie and Eleison, or broke the sentences in the epistle.

Fasts. Abstinence from flesh meat. It was enforced by Queen Elizabeth to promote fisheries, to maintain mariners, and set men a-fishing, and dispensed with by virtue of licences which were sold according to the rank of the applicants by the curates, by an Act of Parliament passed in the fifth year of her reign. By special privilege, the Wednesday fish-day in Lent was dispensed with at Oxford, Cambridge, and Winchester through the influence of Archbishop Parker. Pilkington relates a curious fact, that one side of Cheapside which was in the diocese of London fasted on St. Mark's Day, whilst the opposite side of the street, being a peculiar of Canterbury, were acquitted of abstinence in virtue of the merits of Thomas à Becket. Another singular superstition in England was to observe the fasts of certain vigils of saints' days, such as St. Anthony, St. Brandon, and St. Tronion or Ronan, very strictly as of primary importance. Fastingonge, or Fastens, was the name of Shrove Tuesday.

Fasts were observed differently at Rome and Milan. In the time of St. Augustine and St. Ambrose there was no fast between Easter and Whitsuntide. Epiphanius, in the fourth century, mentions fasting on bread and salt for some days before Easter; and in 1541 the Council of Orleans regarded omission of fasting as an ecclesiastical offence. The ancient fasts were the weekly stations, Wednesdays and Fridays; the monthly fasts, except in July and August, ordered by the Councils of Elvira and II. Tours; fasts on vigils of festivals in the fifth century; the Ember weeks; the rogations; and Lent.

Fathers of the Church. The primitive Fathers are, Clement, Bishop of Rome, d. 100; Ignatius, Bishop of Antioch, martyr at Rome, 107; Polycarp, Bishop of Smyrna, martyr 167, authors of epistles; Justin, martyr at Rome, 163, author of 'Apologies;' Hermias; Hegesippus; Tatian, c. 170; Athenagoras; Theophilus, Bishop of Antioch, c. 169; Irenæus, Bishop of Lyons, 179; Clement of Alexandria, d. 220; St. Cyprian, Bishop of Carthage, martyr, 258; Origen of Alexandria, d. 254; St. Gregory Thaumaturgus, Bishop of Neocæsarea, c. 240; Dionysius the Great, Bishop of Alexandria, d. 265; and Tertullian, of Carthage, died a heretic in 220; Minucius Felix, his contemporary, Arnobius d. 325; Lactanteus, d.c. 325, three apologists against the heathen philosophy; and Eusebius, the historian, Bishop of Cæsarea and Antioch, 319.

The other Fathers are of the Greek Church: St. Gregory of Nyssa, a voluminous writer of treatises, d. c. 400; St. Gregory of Nazianzum, in Cappadocia, Bishop of Sasima, d.

389; St. Cyril, Bishop of Jerusalem, author of catechetical lectures, d. 386; St. Athanasius, Bishop of Alexandria, d. 373; St. Epiphanius, Bishop of Salamis, a writer on heresies, d. 403; St. Basil of Cæsarea, d. 379; St. John, called Chrysostom, Patriarch of Constantinople, d. 407; and Ephraem, the Syrian of the fourth century. Those of the Latin Church are, St. Ambrose, Archbishop of Milan, d. 397; St. Augustine, Bishop of Hippio, d. 430; St. Jerome, d. 420; Pope Damasus, d. 384; and St. Hilary, Bishop of Poictiers, the author of commentaries and treatises, d. 368.

Feast of Fools. On Epiphany Eve the Vicars of Amiens and Senlis chose a pope, at Laon a patriarch, at Noyon a king of fools. Indecent dancing before the porch; infamous songs like those sung on Innocents' Day, and a riding procession followed the election. The Faculty of Theology at Paris had to condemn priests and clerks, entering the church at the the time of the holy office with monstrous masks, wearing the clothes of women or actors, dancing and leaping and singing songs. In the fifteenth century, Menot, a famous French preacher, denounced the custom of priests dancing with women in public after celebrating their first Mass. At Aix, a chorister, until 1543, was chosen yearly on December 21st as king of fools. At the Trinity Church, Caen, a little girl-abbess was elected on that day. At Chalons the king of fools entertained his guests in a theatre erected before the cathedral doors at the expense of the chapter; and afterwards the crowd, singing confused words, and making hideous grimaces, passed through the church and cloisters. When Vespers had been sung in haste, the cantors and choirmaster chanted a ludicrous motet, a parody of sacred language; and then the motley crew, shouting and playing the most noisy instruments, made the procession of the cathedral. In 1346, in England, it was kept on the Circumcision.

Feasts. The Christian festivals are divided into two classes. (1.) Immoveable, those fixed to certain days in the month; (2.) moveable, those which occur at seasons, dependent on Easter or on Sundays.

Fenestral. (1.) A niche containing a drain and credence ledge; (2) a shuttered casement; (3) a low side window; (4) a slanting aperture in the wall, used, probably, as a confessional, found often in England; near Tenby; in Normandy,

and Denmark, and also at Heisterbach, Nuremberg, and
Lecco. The vulgar and modern name is hagioscope or
squint; (5) in some instances, where they are of large size,
or command the view of an altar, they may have been made
to allow persons in the transept, vestry, tower, or other position, to see the altar, as at Minster-Lovell, and Haseley : or,
as at Bridgewater, where there is a series of diagonal
openings, and in the vestry of Merton College, Oxford;
Malvern, and Christchurch, Hants ; and the side chapel of
Chipping Norton, they may have been used as a communication with the ringer of the sanctus bell. At Battle one
of these oblique windows is high up in the nave wall; at
Lynn, in the parvise; at Wittering near the rood-loft; at
Stockbury and Newnham, in the Tower. At Stamford there
are apertures in the west wall of the belfry chamber for the
convenience of the ringers.

Feretory. (1.) The French *fierte*, a reliquary; (2) a shrine
of a saint, from the Latin *feretrum*, a bier or hearse.

Ferials. Week-days ; a term definitely fixed by Pope Sylvester
in 316, thus, Monday is the 2nd, Tuesday the 3rd, etc. The
Orientals, from their love of astronomy, first named the
week-days after the planets. In the fourth, fifth, and sixth
centuries (as appears from imperial laws, Eusebius and
Sozomen), the Christians commonly adopted the heathen
names, but frequently with some qualification, such as "the
day of salvation called by the Greeks," or "commonly, Sunday;" or, the "fast of the fourth or sixth day, which the
heathens call after Mercury and Venus," as St. Cyril of
Jerusalem says. St. John calls Sunday the Lord's Day
(Rev. i. 10), and St Augustine inveighs against the wrong
principle of calling week-days by heathen names. The
Jewish plan of numbers was adopted (St. Matt. xxviii. 1 ; St.
Mark xvi. 9 ; St. Luke xxiv. 1 ; St. John xx. 1 ; Acts xx.
7) ; reckoning Sunday as the first day. These week-days
were called feriæ, as the Council in Trullo, Tertullian, St.
Basil, St. Chrysostom, and St. Augustine understand the
title as days on which we must cease from sin, all days alike
being consecrated to God's service, like the Roman feriæ
(from *ferire*, to strike the victim), days on which all business
was suspended and sacrifices were offered. The greater
ferials are Advent, Lent, Ember and Rogation days.

Fermory. The infirmary.

Feuillans. Reformed Cistercians, founded by Jean-de-la-Barrierre, at Feuillans Abbey, and confirmed by Gregory XIII.

Fillets. (*Peplum.*) (1.) Children, when they went to Confirmation, carried to the bishop, when he was in the neighbourhood, their fillets of sufficient size to dry the chrism and bind their foreheads. On the third day after this they were taken to church, where the fillets or fasciæ were burned, and their foreheads washed in the baptistery by the priest. Tyndale says the bishop or his chaplain knotted the fillets about their necks, and no lay person was permitted to unloose them. (2.) Small bands between mouldings. (3.) The labels of a bishop's mitre.

Finial. (1.) A pinnacle on a buttress. (2.) The knot of foliage surmounting a pinnacle.

Fireplaces occur in sacristies, as at Bristol, for baking the altar bread; and for the same purpose at Lincoln in the transept, and at Rochester in an aisle. Over porches, they were for the comfort of the watchers, as at Winchester; or in towers, as at Rugby.

Fish. I C H T H U S, the word embodying the initials of the five words, Iesous Christos Theon Uios Soter,—Jesus Christ, Son of God, Saviour,—a symbol or acrostic, said to have been invented by the Christians of Alexandria, and used until about the time of Constantine. It is first alluded to by St. Clement of Alexandria and St. Augustine, but only mentioned by Tertullian and Origen in accordance with the discipline of the secret. The fish represented man in the troublous waves of this mortal life: the fish which had the tribute-money typified, according to Optatus of Milevi, the offering of Christ for the world; and the fish broiled on the lake side of Galilee, in St. Augustine's and Bede's explanation, the suffering of Christ. Sometimes the fish bears on its back in the catacombs bread and wine, the ship of the Church, or the elements in two chests; or, when it is connected with baptism, a little child. When it represents a Christian it hangs on a hook, as if caught by the apostolic fishers of men; or is attached to the anchor of the cross, or sacred monogram. Sometimes two fish, symbolical of the Churches of the Jew and Gentile, are pourtrayed. Portable fish were worn as marks of their profession by the newly baptized.

Flabellum. (*Ripidion, esmouchoir, flabrum muscatorium, alara, ventilabrum;* in English, besom.) A fan used in the Greek Church for driving away the flies and other insects at the time of the Holy Communion, and for cooling the celebrant in hot countries. In the East the Syrian monks manufactured the fan. It is still carried by two chamberlains in processions at the side of the Pope on Easter Day, as a memorial of ancient usage; as in the fourth century the deacons, standing at the horns of the altar, used the long brush of peacocks' feathers, which symbolized the many-eyed cherubim, and circumspection (Rev. iv. 6–8); and their waving off the annoyance of insects represented the banishment of distracting thoughts, and the concentration of all looks upon the altar. The waving, St. Germanus, patriarch of Constantinople, informs us did not commence until after the Lord's Prayer had been said. The Greek deacon receives a fan at his ordination; St. Athanasius used it, and the instrument is mentioned in the liturgies of St. Chrysostom and St. Basil; and in the West, where its use was not restricted to deacons in the time of Pope Agapetus, 535; at St. Benignus, Dijon; in the Dominican use; by Hildebert, Bishop of Tours; in the Constitutions of Clugny; and at Salisbury in 1214. It went out of use when, in the fourteenth century, Communion in one kind only was given. The Greeks called it also the hexapterige, the six-winged, because the cherubim (Isaiah vi. 2; Exod. xxv. 18; Numb. vii. 89) were painted or carved on it, or else formed the upper part of the staff. It sometimes bore the words, "Holy, holy, holy," or some other sacred inscription. It was often made of palm fibre, linen tissue, or metal plates, to which bells were suspended; in Armenia it resembled a banner; in France it was wrought with silver, gold, silk, and pearls; and in England its material was silk, vellum, feathers, or silver with figures in enamel, and its shaft was of ivory. One formerly at Tournus, of the ninth century, is preserved at Paris; and St. Theodolinda's is at Monza. In the West it was always round.

Flagellants, or Order of the Penitents of Blood, took their origin, in 1260, at Perugia, and went in procession two and two to the church doors, where they stripped themselves to the waist, the lower part of their bodies being clothed in a long linen habit, and their faces covered; and, having sung hymns, scourged themselves with a knotted rope. Their excesses were suppressed, but again, in 1349, they re-appeared; and in the following century renewed the spectacle of open-air scourging, with metal points to the cords, in Germany, Hungary, Italy, and Spain, in spite of the disfavour of the Popes and Princes, clad in white or sad-coloured dresses and hair cloth, believing that they purchased remission of sins by their voluntary torments; and promulgated heretical opinions.

Flagon. (*Onax, burretta.*) The vessel containing wine used previous to the Lesser Oblation, and sometimes in the consecration.

Flamboyant. A style of architecture so called from the wavy or flame-like lines in the tracery, corresponding in date to English Perpendicular. It prevailed on the Continent; in Scotland from 1371 to 1567; and in Belgium from the latter part of the fifteenth until towards the close of the sixteenth century. There are windows of this character at Oxford, Amport, and other places.

Fleur-de-lys. (*Delices, flos deliciarum,* the delightsome flower— so spelt in the time of Edward I.) A symbol of the Holy Trinity. The derivation from St. Louis is modern and erroneous.

Flowers. (1.) A branching mass of golden needlework used upon vestments; (2.) real flowers in garlands were worn by the choristers of Laon on Corpus Christi Day, and with ivy by the subdeacons of Cologne, at Epiphany; (3.) flowers were laid upon graves (cemeteries were adorned with them, like a pleasant garden), or carved with coronals on vase and corbel, as types of celestial glory; and the mosaics of the apses at Rome and Ravenna, painted the joys of Paradise by a group of saints and a meadow full of flowers and soft, green turf. The ornamentation of the churches built over the martyrs' tomb led to the general use of floral decoration. The floor of the Holy Sepulchre at Jerusalem is always strewn with the fragrant blossom of the mimosa and orange-blossoms. George Herbert had his church, on festivals, "strewed and stuck with boughs," and perfumed with incense; flowers and ivy, on Whitsunday, adorn St. Mary's, Redcliffe, which is strewn with rushes, like the cathedral on Mayor's Day. At Christmas, Easter, and Whitsuntide, churches were always decked with evergreens (Is. lx. 13; St. Matt. xxi. 8); box, holly, ivy, and rushes, no doubt in memory of the Gardener of the resurrection (St. John xx. 15), the second Adam, who keeps the Paradise of the departed, and also in anticipation of the renewal of all things (Solomon's Song ii. 11-13); birch and broom were used on St. John the Baptist's day. St. Jerome says that Nepotian shadowed the basilica and martyrdoms with divers flowers, foliage, and tendrils of the vines. St. Severus decked the church walls with lilies, and Fortunatus speaks of crowns and pendent garlands. St. Paulinus alludes to the same custom; and Prudentius, who also describes the lamps hanging by ropes, and their quivering, glittering light cast on the ceilings, says, picturesquely:—

> "With flowers the pavements strew,
> The doors with garlands wreathe;
> Before its day the year shall bloom anew;
> And purple spring in winter breathe."

Garlands were always used in Cheshire; from time immemorial a garland at Charlton on Otmoor is renewed every May Day; at Grasmere garlands were laid on the altar on July 21, yearly, and the rush-bearing to strew the church on the anniversary of the dedication, on St. Oswald's Day, is still observed, as Glenfield and Heybridge are strewn with grass on their feast-Sundays; (4.) altars were also thus adorned; St. Augustine mentions a person taking flowers from St. Stephen's altar. In the treasury of Aix-la-Chapelle there is a vase of ivory with gold sculptures of the eleventh century, which is supposed to have been used for flowers on the altar; (5.) well-flowering was practised at St. Richard's, Droitwich, till the civil wars; at Tissington; and St. Chad's, Stowe, near Lichfield, flowers and boughs being set about the rim and standing cross.

Flowers were appointed for use on every festival and holy-day, being consecrated to saints and seasons, as parts in the great parables of nature. Our Lord's symbol was a flower in a crown, and flowers symbolical of the gifts of the Holy Spirit were showered down at Pentecost. The two latest

additions to the sacred flora are the Passion flower, introduced by the Jesuits, and the Holy Ghost plant, brought
recently from Brazil. The commoner names are as follows
Herb Trinity, Christ's herb, thorn, palm, our Lord's and
Lady's, Holy Ghost plant, agnus-castus, virgin's-bower, seal,
thistle, lace, finger, slipper, tresses, mantle, mary cost, bella-
donna, maidenhair, fair maid of February, lady of the
night, marygold, pasque and rogation flower, alleluia,
almond of the Annunciation, Lent lily, Christmas rose,
Michaelmas daisy, nun's discipline, nun's flower, monk's-
hood, cardinal's flower, friar's-cowl, angelica, archangel,
arbor-vitæ, rood flower, Passion flower, everlasting, cross
of Jerusalem and Malta, holy tree, thistle of the curse, star of
Bethlehem, balm of Gilead, rose of Jericho, Solomon's seal,
Jacob's ladder, herb of St. Barbara, Benedict, St. Christopher, St. Gerard, St. Andrew's cross, St. Bartholomew's
star, St. Barnabas' and St. Fabian's thistle, St. Catherine's,
St. Louis's, and St. James's flower, St. James's, St. John's,
St. Peter's worth, St. Remy's, St. Jago's, and St. Bruno's
lily, St. Peter's parsley and corn-sweet, St. Basil and St.
William, St. Giles's aspine, St. Eustochium's rod, St. John's
bread, St. Martina's fern, St. Norbert's pink, St. Paul's
betony, St. Patrick's cabbage, St. Timothy's grass and goldy-
locks, St. Veronica, and the Canterbury bells of St.
Augustine. The trefoil, or shamrock, was used as a symbol
of the Trinity by St. Patrick in preaching, and the thorn of
Glastonbury was said to have been imported by Joseph of
Arimathea, and to blow only on Christmas Eve. Boughs of
trees were used at the Feast of Tabernacles.

Font. (Lat. *fons*, a spring or well.) The fountain of the new
life and laver of regeneration; a vessel for baptism—the invention of Pope Pius, according to Archbishop Whitgift—
elevated on a base or shaft, and having a descent to the
water as into a tomb, in allusion to our burial with Christ in
that holy sacrament. It is the counterpart of the Greek
phiale or *pege*, which was raised on arcades and covered with
a cupola, which stood in the close or forecourt of the church.
In order to witness to its sanctity no grave was permitted to
be made near it by a canon of the Council of Autun. Its
material, according to the Council of Lerida and Ivo the
canonist, was to be hard stone, without porousness or any

fracture; the bowl to be of marble, and never of wood, which is absorbent, or of brass, which is subject to tarnish with rust; but if of metal, tin was used. A solitary example of a font of wood, but hewn out of a solid block, is at Evenechtyd, county Denbigh. The font was to be irremovable. A basin was used by the Puritans in the early part of the seventeenth century, but such an indecent appendage or substitute, with dishes or pails, were rigorously forbidden by the bishops. At St. Mary de Castro, Guernsey, there is a small late font of silver, and examples of bronze remain at Frankfort-on-Oder, Münster, Brandenburg, Brunswick, Wurtzburg, Halberstadt, Brussels, Louvain, and Hal. At Chobham it consists of a leaden basin enclosed in oak panelling. A vessel or spoon for pouring water on the child, in case of affusion, was provided. The cover of wood was in allusion to the cross of Christ, which was typified by the ark of Noah, as St. Ambrose says. A railing was to be set round it, and the keys of the font-cover were in the keeping of the curate, to prevent any superstitious abuse of the consecrated water, according to a provincial English synod held in 1236, and to preserve its cleanliness. The water was to be changed every seven days by Edmund's constitutions in 1236, once every month by the rubric of 1549, fortnightly by that of the Scottish Service Book of 1604, but by the present rubric is to be supplied at the time of baptism.

The font of the great baptistery was round or cruciform, with its brim level with the pavement. On the right were three stairs for descending, and as many on the left for coming up; in the centre was a step for the bishop. Sometimes additional fonts, of smaller size, were erected against the walls. The font was sometimes crowned with the figure of a dove, in allusion to Gen. i. 2; viii. 11; St. Matt. iii. 16, as the symbol of the Holy Ghost who, as the Second Council of Nice declared, broods upon the face of the water, bringing peace after the storm and in the death of the world. Napkins were appointed for drying the forehead of the baptized. By the Council of Meaux, 845, every parish priest was allowed to have a font placed in the porch, or, as St. Gregory of Tours mentions was the case in France, on the left-hand side of the entrance-door. At Strasbourg it was placed in the eastern apse, and in many English cathedrals in the second bay of the nave on the south side. Whitgift says the original position was in the midst of the church or in the lowermost post, but never at the church door; but it certainly stood in the last position in 1549, and Cosin says it should be not far from the entrance, and rightly, as baptism admits into the spiritual Church and to a share in the services of the Church militant on earth. The "ancient and accustomed place" is distinctly named in bishops' visitation-articles early in the seventeenth century. At York, however, a medieval dragon-headed beam in the centre of the nave on the north side, and fronting an image of the Christian soldier, held the cover-chain. At St. Peter's, Rome, and in some other cathedrals, the font stands in the north wing of the transept. Constantine the Great built a magnificent font of porphyry, silver-plated, in the Lateran, which had on a pillar a lamp or censer of gold in the centre, in which perfumes were burned at Easter. Water flowed from the mouth of a lamb, near which stood figures of our Lord, St. John the Baptist, and harts thirsting. Pope Damasus, in 384, built another in the Vatican. Detached or separate fonts became common in the eleventh century. Originally they were merely carved basins of circular form, without supports. Some, of lead, remain at Strasburg and Espanburg; other specimens are supported on several pillars, usually five, representing the Saviour and the four Evangelists. In the thirteenth century fonts became octagonal, symbolical of regeneration, the creation of the world having occupied seven days. In the fourteenth and fifteenth centuries they were richly sculptured. Bronze fonts are common in Belgium and Germany, but were always rare in France and England. One formerly at St. Alban's, of copper, was brought by Sir R. Lee from Holyrood Abbey. Another was, in 1651, at Waterford. At Hildesheim a bronze font, of the close of the thirteenth century, rests upon personifications of the rivers of Eden, typifying the cardinal virtues, which appear upon the bowl, and are enforced by the greater prophets, each bearing a scroll (Is. xi. 1 ; Jer. xxiii. 5 ; Dan. vii. 14 ; Ezek. i. 5). Above these are the Evangelistic symbols, with scrolls (St. Matt. i. 21 ; St. Mark i. 18 ; St. Luke i. 32 ; St. John i. 14) ; then occur the Virgin and Holy Child, the Passage of the Red Sea, the Baptism in Jordan, and the Passage of the Ark. The

tiara-shaped cover, which has a knop of foliage, exhibits
Aaron's rod flowering, with Solomon (Eccles. xxiv. 16); the
Martyrdom of the Innocents, with Jeremiah (xxxvii. 15); the
conversion of the Magdalen, with David (Ps. lxxx. 5); the six
works of mercy, with Isaiah (lviii. 7), representing remission
by water, martyrdom, penance, and charity.   At Brussels a
bronze font, 1149, has the baptism, resurrection, and glorifica-
tion of our Lord; that of white marble, 1470, at Florence represents the most remarkable instances of holy baptism; one,
of silver, at Canterbury, used to be carried to Westminster
Abbey for royal christenings.   Leaden fonts, mostly of
the Norman period, occur at Walton-on-the-hill, Clewer,
Wareham, Great Plumsted, Dorchester (Oxon), Parham,
Tidenham, and Frampton-on-Severn, where it has foliage and
sitting figures in low relief.   Some are found in the north of
France.   The stone font of Ashover is covered with leaden
figures.   Sometimes the stone bowls have simple panel-
work on the sides, or an elaborate geometrical pattern, as
at St. Martin's, Canterbury, or intersecting knot-work.
At Winchester the Norman font has the acts of St. Nicholas
of Myra; at Coleshill the crucifix and images; at Horbling
the acts of our Lord; and on those of Lynn, Walsoken, Net-
tlecombe, Norwich, Happisburgh, Worsted, and Dereham
of Perpendicular date, the seven sacraments are represented.
Covers—some of considerable height—are preserved at Fos-
dyke, Selby, Thaxted, Sudbury, Monksilver, Ticehurst,
Walsingham, Castleacre, Trunch, St. John's, Norwich, and
one of Bishop Cosin's time at Durham.

Palindrome inscriptions, capable of being read forwards
or backwards—usually the Greek version of Ps. li. 2,—occur
at Harlow, Warlingworth, Dulwich, Melton-Mowbray, St. Stephen's (Paris), St. Menin Abbey, St. Martin, Ludgate, and formerly at St. Diomede and St. Sophia, Constantinople.   At
Bradley the words "Pater noster," "Ave," and "Credo,"
which the sponsors were bound to repeat; at Dunsby "In prin-
cipio," the beginning of St. John's Gospel; and on a thirteenth century font at St. Anthony, Cornwall, the legend
"Ecce, karissimi, de Deo vero baptizabuntur Spiritu Sancto"
is engraved.   The font was properly erected on three steps.
At Saltzburg it is supported on four lions, and one at Liége,
1112, like the brazen sea of Solomon's Temple, on twelve
oxen.

Foot-pace. (*Haut pas; marche-pied.*) The raised platform or standing-place round an altar. Whilst the altar was raised upon the confession it had no steps; those in the catacombs of Rome and Naples stand on the ground-level. In the fourth century a single step was used, and the num ber was not increased until two hundred years after.

Forcer. A chest or sacred place for vestments, sometimes made of *cuir bouilli*, and of a kettledrum shape.

Foreigns. (*Forinsecus.*) The external court of a monastery. Bathforum is Bath forinsecus.

Forensic Officers. The monastic chamberlain, cellarer, almoner, kitchener, master of the works, and pitancier, their duties lying out of choir.

Form. The wording with which the matter is inseparably accompanied in a sacrament.

Forms of Crosses. The sacred crosses are the following, besides the fylfot, and gammadion; the tau, or anticipatory cross, shaped like a T (*commissa, patibulata*), is typical of life under the Old Testament. Tertullian says that Jacob blessed his children with his arms set in this form, and St. Jerome, St. Augustine, St. Cyprian, Origen, and Isidore refer to it the sign in Ezek. ix. 4–6. Four conjoined make the cross potent, symbolical of the displacement of the Old Testament by the Cross. St. Anthony's cross is a tau cross with a loop or handle (*ansata*). The Saltire (*intromissa*) like an X, when of white, is St. Andrew's; when of red, St. Patrick's. The Greek cross (*decussata*) has four equal arms, the scroll being set on lengthwise; when red, it is called St. George's cross. The Latin cross (*immissa*) has the lower limb or foot longer than the rest, the summit and laterals. The Passion or Calvary cross has pointed limbs. The cross of Resurrection stands on three degrees or steps, faith, hope and charity; the latter is the lowermost, as the cross is rooted in love. The Franciscan cross has its lateral members pommée, ending in balls, and the summit and foot patonce, set between four gammadia. The cross fleury, curved; the cross patonce, straight-sided, each with three pointed leaves; and the cross moline, with two out-curved leaves, represent Christ's Cross flowering, life-giving, and fruit-yielding. The cross crosslet, a combination of four equal crosses, represents the universality of the faith of the

Cross. The Maltese cross consists of four arrow-heads
meeting at the points. The cross ragule represents the
cross budding at the sides. The cross called Irish, or of
Iona, is circumscribed by the circle of eternity. The cross
fleury appears on the shields of the " Thundering Legion"
upon the pillar of Antoninus.

Forth Fare *or* **Passing Bell.** A bell tolled in the thirteenth
century twice in honour of the virgin-born, for a woman,
thrice in honour of the Holy Trinity for a man, and once for
each of his orders in case of a priest, when in extremity,
and mentioned as in use, by Robert Nelson, in the last
century; to summon the priest; to remind the neighbours
of their own mortality; to recommend the state of the dying
to God in their private prayers, and accompany him in his
departure with intercession. In 1605 a benefaction was left
for the tolling of the great bell of St. Sepulchre's, London,
as criminals passed on their way to execution at Tyburn,
whilst the sexton cried aloud, " All good people, pray
heartily unto God for these poor sinners going to their
death." A short peal or knell, by the 67th Canon, was
also rung after death to invite those who heard it to thank
God for the deliverance of the departed out of this vale of
misery. Similar peals were rung before and after the burial.
In the eighth and ninth centuries bells were used at funerals.

Fortified Churches. The churches of Alby, Beziers and Narbonne, Veruela, and the Cordeliers' Church, Toulouse, were
fortified; and on the borders of Scotland many church-
towers, like that of Burgh, Middleham, Ancroft, and Long
Houghton, formed places of refuge in war time to the
parishioners; in the East the monasteries of St. Catherine
and Mount Athos are fortified, as formerly were Black
Abbey, Holy Cross, Bective, Crossraguel, Kilkenny, Aber-
brothock, St. Andrew's, Cashel, Maubisson, St. Germanns,
Auxerre, Marmoutier, St. Martin des Champs, Argenteuil,
Luz, Meissac, Loretto, Medard, Puy, Brionde, Oberwesel,
Münster, Mayfield. In the thirteenth and fourteenth centuries nearly all the French cathedrals and abbeys were fortified, owing to the constant wars. Along the coast of Lucca
all the church towers are capable of defence; in fact, the
church formed the most available fortress in case of an in-
cursion, whether by robbers, the lord of the manor and his

vassals, or by an army. Dol is still strongly fortified, and at Étampes, of the thirteenth century, there are loopholed guardrooms for soldiers built over the side chapels of the nave. The king's licence to crenellate their houses was obtained by bishops and chapters of cathedrals and monasteries, to prevent disorderly meetings, robberies, and the commission of murder in the capitular closes, and the raids of land or sea pirates or armies in the closes. Stately gatehouses and strong walls, in consequence, defended Lichfield, Chester, Battle, St. Alban's, Norwich, Canterbury, Spalding, Thornton, Bridlington, Tynemouth, Clerkenwell, Bury, and Evesham. Michelham Priory still retains its moat and gatehouse, and Hulne, Royat Menal, Sion de Valére, Tournus, Laon exhibit provisions for defence, which were indispensable in unsettled times. In the thirteenth century we read of military assaults and the sack of Boyle Abbey, and the burning of Elphin Cathedral, in Ireland; regular sieges were laid to Binham, Peterborough, Ramsey, and Coventry. W. d'Ypres burned Wherwell Abbey, and a mob of rioters under Jack Straw attacked Bury St. Edmund's; and Norwich cathedral was in imminent danger of destruction during a popular commotion. In Northumberland, churches in the vicinity of a castle were seldom permitted a tower, lest it should be occupied by the troublesome moss-troopers; and peel towers were built along the coast at the cost of Furness Abbey.

Fossores. Clerks who acted as grave-diggers in the catacombs, ranking above the ostiarius; they wore a white tunic girdled, and ornamented with gammadia on the shoulders and skirt. Constantine included them in his 550 guilds of undertakers.

Franciscans. An order of mendicant friars founded by St. Francis of Assisi, between 1198 and 1211, called, from their habit, Grey Friars or Minorites. They were allowed to preach only by licence of the general minister of the order, and with the permission of the bishop of the diocese. They were to work with their own hands and were fordidden to act as missionaries without the sanction of a provincial minister. The general chapter was held at Pentecost yearly. Their first house in England was established at Canterbury in 1224. At Oxford they educated such illustrious students as Archbishop Peckham, John Burley,

Duns Scotus, Oocham, and Roger Bacon. They made choice at first of the suburbs, the poorest and most neglected quarters of a town; their churches were small and unornamented, and cells and poor cottages of mud and wood, fenced by a ditch, formed their convent; but in the fourteenth and fifteenth centuries their houses were luxurious and their churches large, wide, and grand. They held the Immaculate Conception of the Virgin, and were Scotists, because Duns Scotus was of their order. They celebrated only one Mass a day. About the beginning of the fifteenth century they split into two bodies,—the Conventual, who indulged in the laxity permitted by the Pope; and the Observants or Sabbotiers, under St. Bernardino of Sienna, who rigidly adhered to their founder's rule. Of the latter class, were those in England, living without property and begging their daily bread, accepting necessaries, but forbidden to take money. They had an ill repute as spies, frequenting the Court and the houses of noblemen, gentry, and merchants, and were said to toot, that is, look out and pry, for the Pope, hence the nickname of touter. They were the democrats of Christianity. The order came into England in 1259, selling Papal pardons. The Observants wore wooden sandals, a cassock, a narrow hood, a short cloak with a wooden clasp, a brown robe, and a loose girdle of cord with knotted ends, from which they are called Cordeliers. The Conventuals wore a long, grey cassock and cloak, and hood of large dimensions covering the breast and back, a knotted girdle, and large grey hat; but, in preaching, a doctor's cap.

Frankalms. Tenantry by Divine service.

Frater House. (1.) The fratry or refectory. (2.) The calefactory, the common sitting-room of a monastery.

Free Chapels. Usually built on royal manors, exempt from ordinary jurisdiction, but having incumbents instituted by the diocesan.

Freemasons were a corporation in Lombardy in the tenth century, and they appeared as an association in Normandy in 1145.

French Pierre. The Caen stone reredos of Durham.

Fresco. A painting made in oil colours on the fresh mortar of a wall. This beautiful ornamentation has been revived at Mayence.

Fret. A reticulated cieling, like network, forming lozenge patterns.

Friars. A corruption of Fratres, brothers. Mendicant orders in the medieval Church, who adopted more or less of the Austin Canons' rule. Cranmer mentions that persons, in superstitious reverence, used to wear a friar's coat to deliver them from ague or pestilence, or when they were dying; and at their burial caused it to be cast upon them, in hope thereby to be saved. Charles V. was buried in a friar's cowl. Their churches are usually simple parallelograms. The Cordeliers' of Toulouse was an apsidal oblong, with lateral chapel; the Augustines' a parallelogram, with a transept, forming chapels out of all orientation, and opening into two polygonal apses; the Jacobins', like the Dominicans' church at Paris and Abergavenny, consisted of two alleys, divided by pillars, opening on a common apse with chapels; the Dominicans' of Ghent is a long parallelogram, with altar recesses on the side; but, in England, the Friars imitated the Regulars, as in the fine nave of the Dominicans at Norwich, and that of the Austin Friars in London. In Ireland, a tall thin tower parts off the conventual choir from the nave. The regular canon had property in proprietorship, the regular and monk possessed all in common; the friar had none, and was a mendicant.

Frid *or* **Frith-Stool.** The seat of peace; a sanctuary chair of stone, hollowed in the centre, was set near the saints' shrine, or the high-altar, as at Hexham and Beverley, where it is still preserved. Crosses marked the boundaries of the privileged sanctuary at Beaulieu, St. Martin's-le-Grand, Westminster, Ramsay, Croyland, Ripon, St. Burian's, Worcester, Tintern, Jarrow, Leominster, and Whitefriars (London). Sir John Holland, after his murder of Lord Ralph Stafford, sat in the grey chair of Beverley until he had the King's pardon. Leland says the Latin inscription on it was to this effect:—" This seat of stone is called the freedstool, that is, the chair of peace, that the guilty fugitive who cometh to it may have all security."

Frontal. (*Devant d'autel.*) (1.) A piece of metal- or enamel-work; or of mosaics with gilding, jewellery, and glass; or of wood painted or carved, or forming an arcade of images. There is a fine example, of the thirteenth century, at West-

minster, made of wood, painted, gilt, and inlaid with coloured glass or crystal. This was more correctly called a
tabula picture, or table. (2.) The true frontal, like the modern antepane, or antependium, and the ancient pall, was a
hanging of embroidery,—a drapery of the colour of the
festival. There is a specimen of white silk, at the time of
Edward III., at Steeple Aston. The super-frontal, called
the reredos, at Durham (1381), and the super-altar by
Matthew Paris, hung at the back of the altar as a dorsal.
The superb palla d'oro of St. Mark's, Venice, was made at
Constantinople in the eleventh century. At Toledo there is
an exquisite embroidered frontal, with sacred subjects, early
in the fifteenth century: that of Chichester is studded with
jewels. The frontal was the fringed upper covering, or parafront, hanging over the frontal or suffront of an altar.

Fylfot (or *fytfot*, fourfooted). The dissembled cross under
the discipline of the secret ; a cross cramponnée, or rebated,
consisting of four gammas, which as numerals expressed
the Holy Trinity, and by its rectagonal form symbolized the
chief corner-stone of the Church. It occurs on church bells
in the counties of Derby, Lincoln, and York ; and on Edyngdon's effigy at Winchester.

Galilee. In the primitive Church the penitents were plunged
in a "place of tears" near the great doors of the church,
along with the catechumens, from Ash Wednesday until
Maundy Thursday. This custom, however, was discontinued,
and public penance thenceforth forbidden, after a scandal
related by Nectarius, St. Chrysostom, and Pope Leo : a woman, without the priest's permission, loudly confessed her
sins in the hearing of the people. The Galilee sometimes
takes the form of (1) a large western porch, as at Ely and
Chichester cathedrals, or humbler churches as Llantwit, St.
Woolos, Boxley, and Chertsey ; or (2) of a great western
transept, as at Peterborough, Lincoln, Upsala, and Braisne ;
(3) of an ante-church, as in Clugniac Minsters ; or (4) of a
western chapel, as at Durham. The procession took its
origin in our Lord's command, given to His disciples after
His resurrection, to meet Him in Galilee ; and a Durham
MS., quoted by Hutchinson, and Macro in his Lexicon, both
mention that the Sunday procession was held in memory of

the Apostles' journey. But the Durham Rites say that it was called Galilee, owing to the transposition of the eastern chapel to this site. Martene defines it to be "the lower end of the church;" and, in this respect, it may refer to the Galilee of the Gentiles, as being the most remote part from the altar. It served as the place of penitents, and also for the burial of the worthy dead. The true allusion was to the original Hebrew word applied to the outer folding gates of the Temple (1 Kings vi. 34; Ezek. xli. 24), which in Christian symbolism, forming two doorways under one arch, represented the two natures and unity in the person of Christ.

Gallery. Galleries or tribunes were provided in the basilica for women, those of the widows on the left, and those of the unmarried religious on the right; and they are preserved, even in medieval churches, at the west end of the nave at Jumiéges, St. Ursula's, Cologne, Montvilliers, Genoa, Söest, Laach, Le Mans, and Heckington; or in triforia at Paris, Soissons, Rheims, and Noyon; in an arm of the transept at Winchester, Laon, Boscherville, and St. Stephen's, Caen; in the south arm at Hexham, Upsala, and Cerisy; and in the Mannerchör for young men in Rhenish churches, Boppart, Neuss, Zinzig, Heimersheim, Bacharach, St. Goar, Andernach, Ems, Lemberg, and Magdeburg. A gallery in the north wing of the transept of Rheims, which is fenced by a grille, served as a tribune for nuns. In Auvergne the northern with a gallery is common; and in the valley of the Danube as far as Croatia, western galleries of stone, all of the Flamboyant period, are invariably found. A tribune or minstrels' gallery occurs on the north side of the nave at the level of the triforium at St. Juan de los Reyes, Toledo, at Wells and Exeter, where it is still used on Christmas morning for singing the Old Hundredth Psalm; on the south side at Malmesbury; at the east end of the north aisle at Winchester, and in the south aisle of Westminster. At York and at Chichester, till 1508, there was a minstrel's gallery over the reredos. At St. John Lateran, the choir is still seated in a screened gallery. On the exterior of the west front, over a porch, there is frequently a gallery, in which the choir sang, as now at Lisieux, "Laud and Glory" when the procession, on Palm Sunday, returned with the sacrament from the cemetery, or at the reception of a bishop. Sometimes the former ceremonial was held before the altar of the cross in the rood-loft in very bad weather, and this may have led to the construction of the inner gallery. The modern gallery, happily soon to be a thing of the past, was called the scaffold in Bishop Montague's time.

Gammadion. A voided cross, the Greek form of the Fylfot, four gammas in combination.

Gang Days. Rogation days, so called in 1571 from the gangs or processions, recently revived at Colkirk, Norfolk. The gang or cross-flower, so called because it blooms about May 3, the invention of the cross, and was worn by maidens in garlands in rogations, is the milkwort.

Garde-robe, Gong. The latrine, adjoining the calefactory and dormitory in two stages, such as may be traced at Battle, Lewes, and Canterbury, and exists at New College, Oxford.

Garland. (1.) The ornamental band of decorative work round a spire, as at St. Mary's, Redcliffe, Bristol, and Chichester. (2.) A crown or chaplet was carried by two maidens in front of the bier of an unmarried woman, and hung up in a prominent place in a church. It was made of a hoop of wood and two half circles crossing each other at right angles. This frame was covered with long streaming ribbons, artificial flowers, dried horn, and silk ; and in the inside were white paper gloves, inscribed with the name of the departed lady; and, as emblems of mortality, an hour-glass or empty egg shells. · At St. Alban's, the iron which held the wreath remains in the south nave aisle. (3.) At Hathersage Derby, brides still wear a wedding chaplet, which in the seventeenth century was in Westminster called a past or circlet. The nuptial fillet or crown is shown, held by a hand or hovering over the bride's head in the catacombs, and Tertullian alludes to it. It was often pearled and enriched. The Greek Church still uses silver crowns.

Garth. The enclosed green space in a cloister. The centry garth at Canterbury was a corruption of cemetery, as century fields are in Cornwall.

Gates. (1.) Superb entrance gates of bronze, 1400 20, which Michael Angelo said were worthy to be the doors of Paradise, remain at Florence ; others of the eleventh century are at Augsburg, and in a chapel of the Lateran. The monks, although feudal lords, usually gave a pacific character to their gates, as to one at Winchester; but even, when defences were added, they had no drawbridge, barbican, ditch, or outwork, and opened directly on the country, being rather closed than fortified gatehouses, as at St. Leu d'Esserent, of the fourteenth century, and St. Jean au Bois. Michelham possesses a large gatehouse and a moat, but without a permanent bridge or walls. Many fine monastic gatehouses remain at Winchester, Bristol, Chester, Canterbury, Malvern, Tewkesbury, Bury St. Edmund's, St. Alban's, Ely, Carlisle, Wetherall, Castleacre, Reading, Rochester, Hexham. There are three kinds of gatehouses:—(1) the tower-gate at Evesham and Bury, and in colleges; (2) the rectangular, at Lincoln and Colchester, and flanked by turrets at St. Augustine's, Canterbury; Clerkenwell, Battle, and Thornton; (3) the gabled, as Worksop and Norwich. Usually, besides the great archway for carts and horsemen, there is a side entrance, called the postern, for foot-passengers. At Binham the jail gate, at Bridlington the bailey gate, and the gatehouse of Westminster, were used for offending clerks and other prisoners. Occasionally, as at Thornton, Kirkham, and Worksop, the guest-house was in this building. In other places, as at Peterborough, Norwich, Durham, Winchester, Chertsey, and Barlings, there was a chapel in the upper chamber; at Bolton it formed a muniment room. The town monasteries had usually several gatehouses: those in the country but one, except at Furness, and these were usually on the south-west or north-west, but on the south at Worksop. Gatehouses were also attached to bishops' palaces, as at Wells, Chichester, and Hereford; and to the entrance of cathedral closes, as at St. David's, Chichester, Wells, Lincoln, and Salisbury. These were opened before matin Mass, and closed after compline. The pavilion, or pyepowder court, which was held in case of offences by pedlars attending fairs, was held over the Canongate at Chichester.

Gaudied, with large beads. Every decade or tenth large bead in the rosaries representing a Paternoster is a gaud; each smaller bead stands for an Ave Maria.

Gazophylakion *or* **Corbana.** The treasury of the basilica into which the alms and offerings of the faithful were carried, according to the Apostolical Constitutions and Fourth Council of Carthage, and thence transferred to the bishop's house for distribution, as it was forbidden to set them on the altar.

German Architecture. At the termination of the eleventh and the commencement cf the twelfth century a modified basilican arrangement appeared at Worms, Spires, Mayence, Laach, Bamberg, Naumburg, and Ratisbon. The type was a double aspidal cruciform ground-plan, as at Tréves, Besançon, Nuremberg, Liége, andoriginally at Strasbourg. West and main transepts, polygonal domes, and octagonal lanterns at their intersections, octagonal towers flanking the apses, and galleries under the eaves of the aisle roofs, are marked characteristics of the style; the apses also are rarely surrounded with apses or chapels owing to the Teutonic regard for complete orientation. Sometimes, however, the single eastern apse expands into three apses; sometimes there are western and eastern apses; sometimes apses to the choir and east sides of the transept, or apses to the choir and north and south faces of the transept. There are three marked periods of German architecture. (1.) The Romanesque, lasting from 960 to 1000; or 1000·to 1200, according to Lubke, with transitional 1174–1225; it has a circular, domical apse, and apses frequently attached to the ends of the choir, aisles, and the sides of the transept; pairs of towers usually flank the east end, and terminate in pediments, but often are placed at the re-entering angles of the cross, and over its intersection, being generally unbuttressed; spires, or octagonal pyramids, often rise from between the gables; cupolas are also used. The triforia are of enormous size. A western narthex appears in several churches of Cologne, and at Trebitsch and Gurk with a gallery above it. The polygabled spires of the Rhine-land are distinctive features; Sompting is the only English example. (2.) The transitional, or early German style, lasting till the fourteenth century; the apse became polygonal; pairs of towers are placed alongside the eastern and western apses; buttresses, central, octagonal, and western porches came into fashion. (3.) Complete, or decorated German. The nave aisles were frequently doubled, eastern chapels were added, and two western towers became typical of the style. Lubke divides the style, 1225–1525, into severe 1275–1350, declining 1350–1450, in decadence 1450–1525. The earliest churches are St. Gereon, Tréves, Magdeburg, and Marburg. German architects built the Duomo of Milan, and St. John's, Naples.

Gesso. A coating of whiting and size to receive painting and gilding.

Gimmer. A small hinge, or fastening.

Girdle. (*Cingulum, baltheus;* Gr. *zone.*) The cincture of the albe, as old as the days of St. Gregory the Great; formerly ample in size and broad, and often adorned with gold and gems. In the sixth century it was first reduced to its present narrow dimensions. It represented the cord with which our Lord was bound; and alludes to St. Luke xii. 35; Eph. vi. 4; 1 Pet. i. 13.

Glass windows are mentioned by St. Chrysostom and Lactantius, by Fortunatus at Paris, in the fifth century; and by Gregory of Tours, generally in France, as enclosed in wooden frames. Benedict Biscop, and St. Wilfrid imported glass and workmen from France. In 1052 St. Benignus, Dijon, possessed stained glass: but so late as the thirteenth century the windows of Peterborough were closed with reeds and straw; and the unglazed clerestory was long protected only by shutters in most places. Painting on glass was unknown till the eleventh century. At first the design consisted of historical medallions arranged on mosaic glass, which embraced panels with geometrical patterns and borders of scroll-work and leaves. The folds of draperies and details are marked out in bistre colour. The outlines of the designs are formed by the leading. In the fourteenth century the pieces of glass are larger; the slips of lead occur at wider intervals, whilst single figures, placed under canopies, and not on a mosaic ground, but a plain field of red or blue, occupy an entire window. Lights and shadows are introduced in the draperies, and the flesh tints are no longer violet, but of a reddish grey. In the fifteenth, and first part of the sixteenth century, the decorations were increased; hangings are placed behind figures, borders become rare, and when they occur represent a scanty leafage. Grisaille, or silver grey, is freely used. In the second half buildings and landscapes were introduced. The glass windows of Le Mans date from the eleventh century, the earliest now existing, and probably among the first examples of the introduction of glazing in lieu of perforated marble or stone. The art of glass-painting, which took its origin in mosaics, and still more from enamelled work, has been traced back two centuries earlier. At Canterbury, on the glass of the twelfth century (for which Gondomar, the Spanish ambassador, offered its weight in gold), the design consists of panels of Scriptural subjects, on a ground of ruby or deep blue; rich mosaic patterns fill the interspaces, and a broad bunch of foliage and scroll work, in brilliant colours, completes the plan. In the thirteenth century the panels are usually circular, or quatrefoiled, and the colours used are ruby, blue, green, palish yellow, and lilac sparingly. In the Decorated period, the interspaces have flowing foliage; quarries are freely used, and single figures, usually canopied, are frequently represented. Green and lilac are dying out of fashion. In the Perpendicular period yellow became more prominent; the figures increased to a large size, with elaborate canopies, and heraldic cognizances and inscriptions, freely used, mark the style. There is fine glass at Amiens, Chartres, Auch, Bourges, and Fribourg, of various dates; at Burgos and Exeter fourteenth century, Lichfield sixteenth century; Leon of the thirteenth and of the fifteenth, as at Toledo and Avila. There are other beautiful examples at York, Gloucester, Bristol, Lincoln, Canterbury, Fairford, and New, Merton, Lincoln, and Queen's Colleges (Oxford), and King's (Cambridge). In the catacombs ampulles of the blood of martyrs are found; and also glass vessels, like a patera or saucer, the bottoms of which have Scriptural or devout inscriptions, and figures of the Saviour, worthies, and saints, and domestic events etched in upon gold leaf. Some with views of agapæ are said to have served as ministerial chalices, having this inscription:—" Pie, zekais en agathois,"—" Drink, mayest thou find life in these goods," that is, in the Eucharistic elements. Several are of the earliest Christian age, and many were used in times of persecution, as stains of blood still cling to them, rendering their legends illegible.

Glebe. Land enjoyed by an incumbent in right of his church.

Gloria in Excelsis. The great doxology, or angelical hymn. This hymn was ordained to be sung at the time of Holy Communion, on Sundays and martyrs' holy days, by Pope Symmachus, *c*. 510. Some attribute the composition to Pope Telesphorus, *c*. 140, who directed that it should be sung on Christmas Eve. It is certainly older than the popedom of Hilary *c*. 340. The Fourth Council of Toledo attributes it generally to ecclesiastical doctors, but some authors have discovered in it the polyonumos spoken of by Lucian, and the hymn of Christ alluded to by Pliny. It was in use at Matins, and in the Apostolical Constitutions is called the Morning Prayer. St. Chrysostom also alludes to its daily use. However, generally, it was sung only on Sundays, Easter, Christmas, and the great festivals. In the West, Walafrid Strabo says bishops only sung it on such occasions; and Bona mentions that priests never recited it except at Easter. In the East, it was said daily by bishop, priest, and people. St. Athanasius first distinctly mentions the hymn, adding, that it was known by heart by women. When it is sung in Exeter Cathedral on Sundays, Christmas, and Ascension Day, the ten choristers are arranged between the two altar-rails; and, when the bishop is present, the boys precede the procession as it leaves the sanctuary, and place themselves, kneeling, in the aisle, to receive the episcopal benediction, each in his turn. In 1552 the English Church omitted the Hosanna in it.

Glory, Laud, and Honour. A hymn and vocal melody sung on Palm Sunday inside the church, whilst the choir went in magnificent procession from the altar to the closed portals; and composed by Theodulph, an Italian bishop of Orleans, in the prison of Angers, in 835, when confined on a charge of conspiracy against Louis I. the Pious, who is said to have overheard him singing his composition, and at once released him. Some authors attribute the work to Reginald, Bishop of Langres. At Lisieux now, as in English medieval cathedrals, it is sung from a gallery over the great west door.

Gloss. A commentary.

Gloves were worn by bishops in the twelfth century, and are mentioned by Innocent III. They typified the hiding of iniquity by the merits of our Saviour, and the benediction of

Jacob when he wore gloves of skins. William of Wykeham's gloves are preserved at New College, Oxford. Candidates for degrees in medicine formerly gave gloves to the graduates of the faculty in that university, in return for their escort to the doors of the convocation-house. Bishop Ken contributed to the rebuilding of St. Paul's the cost of his consecration-dinner and a hundred pairs of gloves. At St. Andrew's, Holborn, the clergy were given gloves at Easter, and Sir Julius Cæsar used to send a pair to any bishop or dean whom he heard preach. In 1636 the University of Oxford presented gloves to the members of the royal family and King Charles I.

Godfathers *and* **Godmothers** are mentioned by Tertullian and St. Basil; they were called afferentes, sponsores, fidejussores, patres spirituales, paranymphi, and susceptores. Pope Hyginus, *c.* 140, required at least one godfather and one godmother to be present at baptism. Theodore, Archbishop of Canterbury, permitted, in case of necessity, the same person, or one person, to appear as sponsor both at baptism and confirmation. The pseudo-Dionysius mentions the renunciation made by the sponsor, and St. Augustine speaks of the answer on behalf of children brought in the hands of their sureties, who have been compared to the faithful witnesses in Isa. viii. 2. Godfathers are alluded to in Ina's Laws of 693. The name of compater appears in St. Augustine and the First Council of Mayence, the other names were testes, lustrici, sureties, sponsors, offerers, martyres, anadochoi; the later titles were "fathers and mothers at holy illumination," profathers, promothers, patrini, and matrinæ, as those who took the child out of the font as its spiritual parents. Pope Nicholas I. says that there exists a holy fellowship between the child and the godparents, (gossips, *God's sib*, affinity), not to be called kinship, but rather to be regarded as spiritual affinity. It was held to dissolve marriage, but Pope Boniface VIII. restricted the dissolution to marriage not yet contracted.

The custom of having sponsors is traced to St. Philip bringing Nathanael to Christ, but more probably was established by the Church, in order to add security and solemnity to the sacred covenant, as in the civil law sureties were present at contracts. They answered the interrogatories made at baptism, and also as witnesses secured the personal confession of adults in times of persecution. In the fourth and fifth centuries godparents were always appointed, and the the pseudo-Denys mentions that their names were inserted in the baptismal register.

Golden Fridays. The Fridays fasted in the four ember weeks.

Golden Numbers. The lunar cycle, invented by Meton of Athens, and anciently written in gold. It extends over nineteen years. They indicate in the calendar the day of the ecclesiastical paschal full moon; the Sunday letter following marks Easter Day.

Golden Prebendary. The penitentiary of the diocese, who held the prebend of St. Pancras at St. Paul's, the bishop's stall at Hereford, Mathry at St. David's, and Leighton at Lincoln.

Golden Rose. First mentioned by William of Newburgh, about the end of the twelfth century, but dating perhaps one hundred years earlier; an ornament of gold, musk, and balsam, typical of the divinity, body, and soul of Christ; of joy, spring, and Easter, by its sweetness, beauty, and pleasant taste; and of the second advent in the seventh age of the world, as it is consecrated by the Pope on the fourth Sunday in Lent, the seventh after Septuagesima. It was anointed with chrism and sprinkled with perfumed dust; and after benediction, in which allusion is made to the fruit of good works, the flower of the field, the rose, and the lily of the valleys,—the symbols of the Virgin, it was set upon the altar during Mass, and then carried away in the Pope's hands to be sent to some favoured prince, some eminent church, or distinguished personage. Though at first a religious ceremony, it became a Papal acknowledgment of the recipient's sovereignty when sent to a monarch; when the latter was staying at Rome, he carried the rose in procession through the streets, attended by a great retinue of cardinals and prelates, and showing it to the people. The King of the Romans was always crowned immediately after he had received the newly-blessed rose. In 1446 Pope Eugenius sent one to Henry VI; Pope Julius II. in 1510, and Leo X. to Henry VIII.; and Urban V. to Queen Joanna of Sicily, in 1360. In the museum in the Hôtel Clugny there is a a branch of a rose-tree with flowers blooming in gold, of the thirteenth century, which, probably, was a similar gift to some French king.

Golden Star. A kind of monstrance under which, in the Papal Mass of Easter Day, the bread is exhibited on the paten by the cardinal-deacon turning it on every side to the people for adoration ; it is then carried by the subdeacon to the throne. The chalice is exhibited in the same manner. When the Pope celebrates, he gives the benediction to the people with the Host, but does not communicate himself. This is the origin of the ceremony of benediction by priests after Vespers, which is not much earlier than the present century. In 1549 the priest in England was directed at the prayer of consecration to turn to the altar without elevation or showing the sacrament to the people.

Gonfanon. A banner, shaped like Constantine's labarum, sent by the Pope to Baldwin and the Christian army before Jerusalem. It had four pointed ends, and was the sign of a patriarchal church. The Counts of Anjou were hereditary gonfaliers of Tours, the Counts de Vexin, of St. Denis.

Good Friday. The beautiful English name for the day of the Crucifixion; called the Pasch of the Cross by Tertullian ; the parasceve, or preparation (St. Mark xv. 42) ; the day of the Lord's Passion ; Long Friday, owing to its lengthened fast, in Denmark; Ælfric's Canons, 957; and the Saxon Chronicle in 1137; in Germany, Still Friday; and in France, Passion Friday. On this day, it appears from St. Chrysostom, the Greeks commemorated the departed. It is observable that in the catacombs the soldiers crown our Saviour, not with thorns but with flowers, as if the early Christians regarded the triumphant rather than the mournful aspect of his great sacrifice. In the time of Pope Innocent I. Mass was not said on Good Friday or Easter Eve ; but until the tenth century, as by Pope Gregory's 'Sacramentary,' and Ælfric's Canons, 957, communion was permitted to the faithful; in England in 1328 the day was ordered by the Synod of London to be kept as a feast ; and in the reigns of Elizabeth and James I. there was communion. Creeping to the Cross, the altar stripped of its lights, pall, and crucifix, and the use of black veils and vestments marked the solemnity of the day. The Greek Church has a service mainly composed of Scriptural allusions to the Passion. *See* MASS OF THE PRESANCTIFIED.

Crossbuns eaten on this day somewhat resemble the loaf from which the Greek altar-breads are cut, and preserve the memory of the manna, as they are flavoured with coriander seed (Ex. vi. 14-31 ; Numb. xi. 7) and the panis decussatus of the early Christians. Crossbuns are the relic of un-leavened simnel cakes, which were formerly eaten as lamb was on Easter Day in memory of the paschal food of the Jews. In the thirty-sixth year of Henry III. bakers were forbidden to print the cross, the Agnus Dei, or the name of our Lord upon their bread, as a guard against its supersti-tious use.

Gospel. (God's spel, or message; good tidings.) The book of the Gospel, usually splendidly illuminated and bound in jewelled covers, always stood on the altar upon a stand, and the latter is called in 1640 in England a desk; with degrees of advancement, in 1558 it stood in the midst of the altar. Two tapers, according to Amalarius, were carried before the gospeller to represent the light of the Gospel in the world, and other candles, signifying the law and the prophets, were extinguished, to show their accomplishment in the Gospel. In St. Augustine's time the Gospel was read on the north side, in allusion to the prophetical verse, Jer. iii. 12 ; and the old sacramentaries added, because it is preached to those cold in faith; but at Rome, because the men sat on the south side and the women on the north, the deacon turned to the former, as mentioned by Amalarius, probably in allu-sion to 1 Cor. xiv. 35. The Gemma Animæ speaks of reading from the north side as a new custom, but it is pre-scribed by the use of Hereford and Seville. In some parts of England, however, the south side was still observed as late as the fifteenth century. When the epistle was read on the lowest, the Gospel was read on the upper choir steps from a lectern; on principal festivals, Palm Sunday, and the eves of Easter and Pentecost, they were read in the rood-loft. As at St. Paul's ; in cathedrals of the new foundation, also ; and in all cathedrals, by the Canons of 1603, a gospeller and epistolar, or deacon and subdeacon, who are either minor canons or priest-vicars, are appointed ; they are to be vested " agreeably" to the celebrant or principal minister, that is, in copes. In 1159 all these were to be canons at York, by Pope Alexander III.'s order. Anastasius I., c. 405, ordered

all priests to stand and bow reverently at the reading of the
Gospel. In the sixth century the people stood at the reading of both these lections, but standing was retained at the
Gospel only, in deference to Him that speaketh therein.
At the end of the epistle the words are said "Here endeth
the epistle," but no such form follows the Gospel, because it
is continued in the Creed. The custom of saying "Glory be
to thee, O Lord," prescribed before the Gospel in Edward
VI.'s First Book, and saying after it "Thanks be to God for
his holy Gospel," is as old as the time of St. Chrysostom. In
Poland, during a time of idolatry, Prince Mieczlaus ordered
in 968 that at Mass, as a sign of Christian faith, whilst the
Gospel was reading every man should draw his sword half
out of his scabbard, to show that all were ready to fight to
the death for the Gospel. There was a curious English
medieval superstition of crossing the legs when the Gospel
from the first chapter of St. John was read. The Gospel oak
was the tree at which the Gospel was read in the Rogation
processions.

Gown. The ancient academical gown, always wide-sleeved,
was an adoption of the monastic habit from the robe of the
preaching friars, who wore it instead of an albe. From itinerant lay preachers of the time of Elizabeth; the custom of
the universities; the vanity of the richer clergy in the last
century, wearing silk robes out-of-doors and then in the
pulpit; and the introduction of lectures, not provided for by
the rubric,—the use of the gown in English pulpits took its
origin. The narrow-sleeved gown, with a cross-slit for the
arms, was an importation from Geneva, and called the lawyer's
gown, in distinction to the wide velvet-sleeved gown still
worn by other graduates, posers at Winchester, and often
with an ermine hood by proctors at Oxford. Russet white
and black gowns were worn by mourners at funerals.

Graal. The precious dish (*paropsis*) or cup used at the Last
Supper. The vessel in which our Lord turned water into
wine, and Nicodemus or Joseph of Arimathea received the
Saviour's blood at the crucifixion, according to medieval
legends. It often appears in the Arthurian laws, and probably arose from a Druidic origin. The Genoese claim to
have it in the cathedral treasury, where it is known as Sacro
Catino. It is of glass, of hexagonal form, with two handles,

and is 3 feet 9 inches in circumference. It was cracked in its removal from Paris, whither it had passed under Napoleon. Sometimes the graal supports a bleeding spear, as on a crucifix at Sancreed church, Cornwall. The Church is often represented holding a pennon and a graal opposite the synagogue with drooping head, and a banner of three points, the staff broken.

Grace. The benediction of the table, founded on St. Matt. xiv. 19; Acts xxvii. 35; and 1 Tim. iv. 4. The ancient form is in the Apostolical Constitutions, and the collect and medieval versicles are sung at the election dinner in Winchester College, to Reading's setting, c. 1662. The conventual form is Benedictus Benedicat, but a Cistercian abbot, conceiving it to be a slur on his founder, on his return from some Benedictine house to his own convent, gravely said Bernardus Bernardat. The grace-cup was a mazer, and in use at Durham. It is still used with great ceremony at Winchester College in election week. The person nearest to the one drinking, and another opposite to him, stand until he passes the cup.

Gradin. (It. *predella*.) A sort of low retable in Western Europe, of post-Reformation date. Sometimes, in France, it has three steps. In 1486, however, in London, "a shelf above the altar" is mentioned, but this probably was either a rood-candle and relic-beam, or, as at Clapton, Somerset, a stone ledge, supported on columns, running along the east wall, and carrying two brass candlesticks. On the other hand, Bishop Bleys of Worcester, and Bishop Quivil of Exeter, mention two candles on the altar, which, Durandus says—and the custom prevailed in medieval times as late as Queen Anne's reign,—"were set upon the right and left (outer or western) corners (cornua, or horns) of the altar." At William III.'s coronation there were four three-branched candlesticks, such as are preserved at St. James's, Westminster. Two stood at the back of the altar and one on each horn. Possibly the gradin originated in the tabulatus or shelf for the more sacred plate in the Clugniac aumbry, which was lined with precious stuff, whilst the rest of the vessels stood below it.

Graduation. The literary rank given by universities to members of faculties. The system began in the faculty of theology at Paris in the thirteenth century, when bachelors, licentiates, and doctors are mentioned.

Grail. (1.) *Gradale*, gradual, that which follows in degree, or the next step (*gradus*) after the Epistle, a book containing the Order of Benediction of Holy-Water, the Offices, Introit, or beginning of the Mass, the Kyrie, Gloria, Alleluia, Prose, Tract, Sequence, Creed, Offertory, Sanctus, Agnus Dei, and Communion and Post-Communion, which pertain to the choir in singing solemn Mass. In France it denotes the Antiphonar, which was set on the gradus or analogium. (2.) A verse or response, varying with the day. A portion of a psalm sung between the Epistle and Gospel whilst the deacon was on his way to the rood-loft. Their introduction into the Church is attributed variously to Celestine, 430, St. Ambrose, Gelasins, 490, or Gregory the Great, *c.* 600, who arranged the responses in order in his 'Antiphonar.' Rabanus says the name is derived from the custom of singing the grail on the steps of the ambon or pulpit; but others consider it to be taken from the responsory, gradation, or succession, or the altar-step. These verses were formerly chanted, either by a single voice or in chorus. When the chanter sang to the end tractim they were called the Tract; but when he was interrupted by the choir then the name was a Verse, Responsory, or Anthem.

Grandmontines. A Benedictine order under a very composite rule, instituted at Grandmont, near Limousin in 1076, by Stephen, a layman of Auvergne. They came to England in the reign of Henry I., but only had three houses in this country, the chief being Abberbury, founded in 1233. They wore a hard, coarse tunic and a long gown of thick cloth. John XXII. erected Grandmont from a priory into an abbey.

Grange. (1.) The wheat-barn and garners under the charge of the granarer. They remain at Ardennes, Caen, Peterborough, Abbotsbury, Fountains, St. Mary's (York), St. Vigor, Barbery, St. John, Laon, Vauclair, Perrieres, Vincelottes, and Fontenay. (2.) A monastic farm, with a threshing-floor.

Grate. (Lat. *crates*.) A metal screen of ornamental work round a monument; the simple iron railing of Cardinal Langham's tomb; the gate-like screen of Haxey and Archbishop Gray at York; and massive Norman grille of Conques, are in strong contrast with the rich curved closure of Queen

Eleanor's tomb, the metal-work of Henry IV.'s chantry, and the brass gates and screen of Henry VII. at Westminster. *See* CAROL.

Great Entrance. (*Megale eisodos.*) In the Greek liturgies the solemn bringing in of the holy elements in procession to the altar from the prothesis, as the " little entrance " is the bringing in of the Gospels, preceded by tapers and incense. They are the most imposing ceremonies in the Eastern Church.

Grecanic Work. Glass tessellated-work, with all the luxury of gold and tint.

Greces. (Fr. *gré*) Degrees; steps; grissens in Norfolk, and Grecian stairs, a tautology, at Lincoln.

Greek Church. The Church of Russia, Greece, Christian Turkey, Asia, Abyssinia, and the Copts. In the ninth century, owing to the insertion of the Filioque clause in the Nicene Creed; at a later date, from five charges of heresy brought against the Western Church by the patriarch Photius; and finally, in 1059, from a mutual exchange of excommunication by Cerularius of Constantinople and Pope Leo IX.,— ancient feuds resulted in a positive rupture of intercommunion, which subsists to this day.

Gregorian Chant. The music applied by Pope Gregory the Great (591–604) to the service of the Church. St. Ambrose had composed four ecclesiastical tunes, to which the Psalms were sung; those added by the Pope were not rhythmical, like those of Milan, but rather even, grave, and sustained, hence their name of plain or firm chant. The first four modes, invented by St. Ambrose, Gregory called Authentic; those added by himself received the appellation of Plagal, Collateral, or Relative; owing to the insertion of one of these after each of the former, from which it was derived, the order of all was changed; thus the Authentic are now numbered by the uneven, as the Plagal are the even numbers of the eight tones. The ecclesiastical modes, as settled by St. Ambrose, are called, the I. Dorian, III. Phrygian, V. Lydian, and VII. Mixo-Lydian, as modifications of the Greek scales so named; to each of these St. Gregory added a subordinate, or attendant or plagal scale, called II. hypo-Dorian, IV. hypo-Phrygian, VI. hypo-Lydian, and VIII. hypo-Mixo-Lydian, each lying a fourth below the original. Plagal (Gr. *plagios*, oblique), are melodies which have their principal notes between the fifth of the key and its octaves, or twelfth. A ninth tune, to which the Psalm "In exitu Israel" is sung, is called Peregrine, or, from the place of its composition, the Gallican.

Guarded. Garnished, or bordered.

Guardian Angel. (Exod. xxiii. 20; Dan. x. 13; Ps. xxxiv. 7; Heb. i. 14; Acts xii. 15; St. Matt. xviii. 10.) Origen says that a second angel was given to a bishop at his couse-cration. There is a Chapel of the Guardian Angels, with illustrative carvings, in Winchester Cathedral.

Guest House, *or* **Hostry.** The great monasteries had several guest houses, hospices, or hostels, under the charge of the hostillar, or hospitaller; one for monks, another for persons of gentle birth, and a third for poor travellers, who were ordinarily entertained for three days. In some cases a splendid set of apartments was appropriated for the use of the Sovereign, called the King's palace, parlour, or chamber; at St. Alban's; Bristol, and Beaulieu. These visits, and the prolonged stay of nobles, with their retinue, greatly impoverished monasteries which lay near high-roads. Peterborough was cost many thousand pounds by a stay of Edward II. Edward I. spent three months, with his army, at Lanercost; and Glastonbury, on two occasions, entertained 200 knights, arriving with their retainers, and 500 travellers coming on horseback. In fact, the abbey was the only safe hotel when the taverns and hostelry were the haunt of highwaymen and pickpurses, and the lowest of either sex. The Queen was permitted to enter at St. Alban's; but at Durham, Queen Philippa, having entered the precinct claudestinely, was compelled by the monks to rise at midnight, and precipitately betake herself to the rougher accommodation of the Castle. The Benedictine abbot received at his own table the guests of superior degree; the Cistercian abbot modestly dined with them in the hostel, whilst the Clugniac abbot took no notice of their reception. At Abingdon the anthem, "Honor, virtus," or "Time Deum," greeted the guest. The beautiful Guesten Hall of Worcester has been barbarously destroyed; that of Westminster, known as the Jerusalem Chamber, remains; the lesser guest-house, a timbered building, may be seen at Winchester; and portions of the principal hospice at Ely. The great guest-house

usually stood on the west side of the cloister, or else behind
the refectory; it has been preserved in the former position
at Sherborne; sometimes it was removed to a distance from
the cloister, in a base court, as at Durham; or placed in
proximity with the prior's house, as at Worcester; or erected
near the entrance gate, as at Merevale, Furness, and Malling;
or over the gates, as at Chertsey, Finchale, Kirkham, Worksop, and Thornton. The guest-house chapel, in which offerings were made for the poor, and travellers on their arrival
returned thanks to God, adjoined the gate house at Finchale,
Malling, Merevale, and Stoneley; it remains perfect at Peterborough, and in ruins at Furness. The Cistercians admitted
their guests into their minster; humbly bowed and knelt at
their arrival, washed their feet, and sprinkled them with holy
water; they dined with the abbot in the guest house. The
Austin Canons allowed Mass to be specially sung at the
desire of travellers; and the last prior of Christchurch told
Henry VIII. that there was no other house of entertainment
within ten miles for the reception of wayfarers. The Clugniac
abbot dined with guests in hall. The guests were received
by the Benedictines with the "venia" at the abbey gate,
sprinkled themselves with holy water at the minster door,
and, having confessed the sins of their journey in choir and
at the altar of the revestry, were conducted to the parlour;
there the hostillar saluted them, saying the Benedicite, and
having given them the kiss of charity, led them to the guest
house. The guest house usually consisted of a great hall,
divided into alleys or oblong, with a number of sleeping
rooms on the sides, and provided with stables and servants'
apartments. At Gloucester, in 1378, when a Parliament
was held in the abbey, the King was entertained in the
abbot's lodge, the Commons in the guest-house, the Privy
Council in the chief guest-chamber, the Common Council in
the chapter-house, and the Commission on the Law of Arms
in the refectory, whilst the wretched monks were harried for
dinner from the dortor to the school house, and finally took
refuge in the orchard, whilst their cloister-sward was trodden
down by ball players and wrestlers, and the whole precinct
looked like a fair. Monks, friars, and religious lived with
the community. By Ecgbright's 'Excerptions' (740), every
bishop and parish priest had a guest-house near the church.

Guilds. Voluntary associations, combined for the mutual benefit of the members; the bishop's family of clerks was called a
fraternity in 725; and by Bede, in 940–950. Monasteries also
were united in a common bond of fellowship, intercommunion
in prayer, and in prayer for departed members, intelligence
of their demise being communicated by a messenger bearing a brief to the various houses. Brotherhoods, or reli-
gions clubs, maintaining a chantry priest, were also established in nearly every parish church, who formed benefit
societies, kept a yearly feast, met on certain anniversaries at
a common altar, and supported annals for the repose of departed members, whose names were on the guild roll. They
consisted of men and women; in the monasteries kings,
nobles, and benefactors were received in chapter as lay members, and there were also honorary associates of the parish
societies. The members promised fidelity to the guild rules,
and obedience to the superiors, and received a certificate of
admission, signed and sealed by the masters and wardens.
They sometimes maintained a hospital for the relief of decayed members, and always collected alms for their sick
and poor. They met on their anniversary in-livery gowns
and hoods, usually of two different colours, and wearing
the badge or cognizance of their patron saint. On the
morrow of their feast they audited their accounts and transacted the necessary business. At Brecon the guild chapels
had the implements of their various trades carved on the
parcloses, and these remain in a chapel of St. John's (Caen).

Gurgoyle. The legendary name of a monster at Rouen, as
gargouille; reappearing at Metz as granouilli; as kraula
at Rheims, and grand guete at Poictiers. In the old rituals
of Provence the dragon, carried in the rogation processions
as a symbol of heresy, bore this name; it now is applied to
chimeras, dragons, and monsters, wrought into the useful
form of waterspouts. They were also called magots, probably a corruption of magog, in Hebrew meaning "on the
roofs;" and these grinning creatures, perched aloft on roof
and vantage coin, represented the spirits of the powers of
the air endeavouring to assail the faithful, whose sure refuge
is within the Church. One of these figures, at Lincoln, is
called, the "Devil looking over Lincoln." Gurgoyles first
appear in the Early English period.

Gypcer. (Fr. *gibecière*.) A pouch.

Habit of Clergy. In the thirteenth century the rule of the Council of Lateran was adopted, the close cope and cropped hair being enjoined. In the fourteenth century long hanging sleeves not covering the elbow, hair trimmed with fur or cendal, long beards, tippets of monstrous length, broad jewelled belts, chequered hose of red and green, and peaked boots were forbidden; and in 1463 another sumptuary law prohibited neck-tippets of cloth and silk, swords, daggers, purses with gilt embroidery, habits furred, cut off at the hips, or open except at the neck, and bolsters on the shoulders. Archbishop Stratford permitted the use of the sleeved sur-coat or mensal at meal-time, and a short habit in travelling. In the fourteenth century the foreign clergy wore a sleeved tunic closed at the wrists, a supertunic, with long sleeves reaching to the feet, tabard, and black hood; and in travelling a round cloak, black cap, black or brown boots, and socks knotted round the thigh. In 1603 the apparel consisted in England of a square cap, cassock, a gown with standing collar and sleeves straight at the hands, or wide like those worn in the universities; in travelling sleeved cloaks were used. Curates and poor beneficed men had short gowns, and graduates were distinguished by hoods or tippets of silk and sarcenet. George Herbert, when a deacon, wore silk clothes and a sword. *See* CANONICALS.

Halidom. The Gospels, or sacred relics.

Hallow Mass. All Saints' Day. (Fr. *toussaints*, or *touzeins*.) A festival observed at Rome in the seventh century, but not for two hundred years after in Gaul and Germany. Sixtus IV., in the fifth century, gave it an octave. It seems that this commemoration was kept in the East on Good Friday

Hampulling Towels. (From *ampulla*.) Clothes to wipe away the holy oil, chrism oil, and sick-men's oil.

Hanap. A drinking-cup.

Harnessed. Girt, or bound.

Head, *or* **Front of a Church.** The east end. Very rarely the western façade.

Healing. Touching, *i. e.* stroking the patient's face with both hands, to remove the scrofula, significantly called the king's evil, practised by the kings of France as early as Clovis or

Philip I., kings of Hungary, and English sovereigns, from
Edward the Confessor to Queen Anne, who touched Dr.
Johnson. Bradwardine says that crowds resorted to the
kings of England, France, and Germany. Solemn prayer
and the sign of the cross, first laid aside by James I., were
used. Henry II. and Edward I. practised the touch. The
ceremonial took place on a progress, on Good Friday,
monthly, quarterly, or at Michaelmas, Easter, and Whitsuntide, and in 1683 from All Saints till a week before Christmas, and from Christmas till March 1. The first form of
service was drawn up in the reign of Henry VII. The Gospel (St. Mark xvi. 14) was read whilst the king laid on his
hands, and during another (St. John i. 1) at the words "the
light" an angel, noble, or medal with St. Michael stamped
on it, was attached by a white ribbon round the neck of the
patient, who had to produce a certificate of his malady, signed
by the parish priest and churchwardens, and was examined
by the king's surgeon-in-waiting. The faculty of healing was
popularly attributed to the ninth son of a ninth son.

Healing Box. Used for holding the chrism in Extreme Unction.

Heart Burial. The heart was often buried apart from the
body in the place it loved well in life, as Devorgilla founded
Sweet Heart Abbey in memory of the heart-burial of her husband. Richard I.'s heart was buried at Rouen. Robert
Bruce desired his heart to be taken to the Holy Land in lieu
of his pilgrimage, and Lord James Douglas carried it round
his neck in a silver case, hung by a silken cord. He threw
it forward in advance of his men at the great battle of Salano,
and covered it with his body. It was taken to Melrose by
J. Lockhart, and the Douglas still carries a heart.

Hebdomadary. (*Septanier.*) The priest in charge of the services for a week.

Helyng. (1.) A canopy. (2.) A coverlet.

Hermaphrodite Orders. A community of both sexes, living in
different monasteries, separated by a single wall. (1.) Fontévrault, founded by Robert d'Arbissel, Archdeacon of Rennes,
in 1100, under the Benedictine rule. According to the sym-
bolists the abbess presided over the monks, in allusion to the
text St. John xix. 27, but in point of fact because the abbess
held the seignorial lands, as in the early Northumbrian mon-

asteries.   (2.) Bridgetines, founded by Queen Bridget of
Sweden in 1360, and confirmed by Urban V.   The sixty
nuns sat in the choir of the common church of each house.
(3.) Gilbertines of Sempringham, founded by Gilbert, priest
of that village, in 1148, and confirmed by Eugenius III.,
under the Austin rule.

Hermeneutes. An interpreter in the primitive Church, who
translated the liturgy or sermons where people did not
understand Latin, as in Africa, or spoke various dialects, as
in Palestine, or Greek, as in the missions of St. Chrysostom
to the Arian Goths. St. Augustine sent a bishop, who under-
stood Phœnician as well as Latin, to a city, where the inhabitants spoke only the Punic language.

Herse. (Fr. *herce*, a harrow; the Latin *herecius*, a hedgehog;
leichen wagen in German.)   (1.) A triangular candlestick
made of bars, like a harrow, with many branches or candlesticks without feet, varying from seven to thirty-two, and
containing sometimes twenty-four white lights, or else fourteen yellow tapers at the side, representing the eleven
Apostles and three Marys, and a single white light, symbolical of our Saviour, at the top. (2.) A wooden or metal frame,
like a waggon-head, to support the pall laid over a bier in a
church.   It had sometimes seven candles, two on each side,
and three on the ridge.   There are good examples at Tan-
field, Hurstpierpoint, and the Beauchamp Chapel, Warwick.
It was used in offices of the dead at Tenebræ, and in festivals when much light was required.   In the obsequies of an
abbot of Canterbury, at the close of the fourteenth century,
the payment is entered for the image (corpus fictum) and
herse.   Sometimes it was called onzaine when it held eleven
lights, or ratelier (rastrum), a harrow-like rake.   (3.) (A
chapelle ardente, in France; *catafalco,* in Italy; *castrum
doloris*—grief-castle—in medieval Latin.)   A temporary
lofty funeral canopy of timber, covered with waxen figures of
angels and saints, a profusion of tapers in sconces, and
draped with black hangings, flags, and penoncels, under
which a bier was placed, usually before the high altar, with
a balustrade and watchers around it, whilst the departed
were being carried to their burial.   (4.) A horse-litter for
the dead.   A funeral car, covered with black, mentioned in
1556, mounted on four wheels.   Jeremy Taylor speaks of

strewing the herse with flowers. (5.) A dead person: (6.) The frame for the tenebræ candles. A herse-cloth of good needle-work is preserved at St. Gregory's, Norwich, and another at Goldsmiths' Hall, London.

Hibernian Work. (1.) Enamel. (2.) Stud-building.

High Church. (1.) A term professed by the adherents of the Stuarts, in distinction to Low Churchmen, their opponents, about the year 1700. (2.) A cathedral in local usage; as " high prayers," called at Winchester College " Amen Chapel," are those sung to instrumental accompaniment.

Hip Knob. A pinnacle at the top of a gable.

Hip Roof. A gable sloping back.

Hirmos. A strophe in a Greek hymn. The model of succeed-ing stanzas, so called as drawing others after it.

Histories. Anthems composed out of Scripture or lives of the saints.

Hock Tide (*hocken,* to seize), *or* **Hoke Days.** Usually Monday and Tuesday one fortnight after Easter, kept in memory of the slaughter of the Danes by Ethelred, on November 13, 1002, according to Henry of Huntingdon, and mentioned in the Confessor's Laws. Money used to be collected by the parishioners in 1667; and at town gates, as at Chichester, in the last century.

Holosericum. Watered silk.

Holy Bread Skep, *or* **Maund.** A basket for the eulogiæ.

Holy Candle, Blessing with the. Latimer and Tyndale men-tion that dying persons committed their souls to the holy candle, and that the sign of the cross was made over the dead with it, " thereby to be discharged of the burden of sin, or to drive away devils, or to put away dreams and phan-tasies."

Holy Cross. An order of canons reformed by Egerard, Prior of Bologna, under the Austin rule, and confirmed, 1160, by Alexander III., and suppressed in 1656. They wore a cas-sock, patience, gown, and hood of sky-blue colour.

Holy Father. The first person of the Trinity was represented as in Daniel's vision, vii. 9, and vested in a cope, and wear-ing a tiara. It was contrary to our Lord's declaration (St. John vi. 46), and indefensible.

Holy Fridays. Fridays in Ember weeks.

Holy Ghost. The dove constantly represents the third person of the Blessed Trinity (St. Matt. iii. 16); possibly this was the sign or image of the Holy Spirit, which, in the fifteenth century, was carried round the cathedral of Chichester by the dean, or person next in dignity, at the Feast of the Epiphany. He afterwards gave an ornament to the church, as an acknowledgment of the privilege. The dove was first accepted as the type of the Holy Spirit after the Council of Chalcedon (536). Tertullian attributes the adoption to the innocence, and St. Chrysostom to the loving kindness and gentleness of the dove.

Holy Ghost. This is a rare dedication in England, but examples occur at Basingstoke, Walsham; Middleton, Westmoreland, and Newtown, Isle of Wight; and chapels, Exeter and Peterborough cathedrals.

Holy Innocents. This festival is alluded to by St. Irenæus and St. Cyprian, by Origen and Augustine as of immemorial observance. Prudentius, in the fourth century, celebrates it in the hymn, " All hail, ye Infant Martyr-Flowers," and in connection with the Epiphany, as did Fulgentius in his homilies for the day. " Stephen was a martyr before men," said St. Bernard, " John before angels, but these before God, confessing Christ by dying, not by speech, and their merit is known only to God." Violet was used on this day in memory of the sorrow of their mothers, and the Te Deum, Alleluia, and doxologies were forbidden. At Norton, Worcestershire, a muffled peal is rung to commemorate the slaughter, and then a peal of joy for the escape of the infant Christ; and a half-muffled peal is rung at Minety, Maisemore, Leigh-on-Mendip, Wick, Rissington, and Pattington. The Greek menology and Ethiopic liturgy give the number of the involuntary infant martyrs at 40,000.

Holy Night. The night before Holy Day. The first Sunday in Lent. By Theodulf's Chapters, the previous week was employed in shriving penitents.

Holy Oil. In the fourth century oil was brought to Europe from Jerusalem, which had been blessed for use in the holy places. It was carried in cotton within little phials, and distributed to the faithful at a time when relics were sparingly distributed. Oil blessed at saints' tombs was also in vogue in the time of Gregory of Tours; and in the time of St. Gregory oil taken from lamps which burned before the

martyrs' graves in the catacombs. Several of these ampullas,
or vials of metal, are preserved at Monza, which Gregory the
Great gave to Queen Theodolinda. *See* AMPULLA.

Holy Rood. A rare dedication for churches in England, but
it occurs at Southampton, and is the same as St. Cross, near
Winchester. The famous abbey of Holyrood adjoins Edinburgh. Holy Cross Abbey is a ruin in Ireland.

Holy Spear. (*Hagia lonche.*) A liturgical instrument used
by the Greeks, in the form of a spear, with a long handle
ending in a cross, with which the altar-bread called the
sphragis, or holy lamb, is cut out from the loaf for consecra-
cration by the priest with a solemn form in the Liturgy of
St. Chrysostom, founded on Is. liii. 7, 8; St. John xix. 34.

Holy Thursday. The Ascension Day.

Holy-Water. According to the Tripartite History, aqua bene-
dicta and the benediction of salt are attributed to Pope
Alexander I., who had them sprinkled in houses and churches
to exorcise devils. Bishop Marcellus ordered Equitius, his
deacon, to sprinkle holy-water, hallowed by him, for the
same purpose, and, as Theodoret says, by its use caused the
destruction of Jupiter's temple at Apamea. Joseph, the
converted Jew, as Epiphanius relates, used consecrated water
in exorcism. Holy-water was used in all benedictions of
palm and olive branches, vestments, corporals, candles,
houses, herds, fields, and in private houses. By the canon
law it is mingled with salt. The Council of Nantes ordered
the priest before Mass to sprinkle the church-court and
close, offering prayers for the departed, and give water to
all who asked it for their houses, food, cattle, fodder, fields,
and vineyards. By the Capitulars of Charlemagne, Louis,
and Lothaire, on Easter and Whitsun eves all the faithful
might take, for purposes of aspersion in their houses, consecrated water before its admixture with chrism. A novice
carried the holy-water in monasteries before the cross in
procession.

Holy-Water Sprinkler. The Aspergill; a brush for scattering
holy-water. A horrible Tudor mace, with radiating spikes,
was called the Morning Star or Sprinkle.

Holy-Water Stock (*i.e.* pillar) *or* **Stoup** (*i. e.* bucket). A stationary stone basin for holy-water, placed at the entrance of
churches, called by the French bénitier. It succeeded to the

brazen laver used by the Temple priests (Is. i. 16; hi. 2; Exod. xxx. 20; 2 Cor. vii. 1; Ps. li. 2, 7), and cantharus of the basilica [*see* ATRIUM]. Pope Leo III. erected one at Ostia. The vat in a minster next the cloister was used by the mónks, that on the other side by the people. At Durham the church was swept and the holy-water vat filled afresh every Sunday morning. The stoup is found in all periods of architecture, formed in the wall, set on a pillar or in the porch, or standing on a pedestal. At Pylle the leaden basin still remains.

Holy-Water Vat. (*Bénitier, situla, vas.*) A portable vessel to contain holy-water, which was, according to Micrologus, first consecrated by Pope Alexander V., as Cranmer says, to " put us in remembrance of our baptism, and the blood of Christ, for our redemption, sprinkled on the cross." The fixed holy-water stoup was used by those who came too late into church to receive the aspersion by the sprinkler and water carried in the portable vat, which, in the churches of the West, re-presented the bodily ablution made by the Oriental Christians. The bénitier of the Emperor, of gold and ivory, of the eleventh century, remains at Aix-la-Chapelle ; the ivory bénitier of the Virgin, at the close of the twelfth century, at Milan ; and one of bronze, of the same date, at Spires.

Holy Week. The week before Easter, called formerly the Great Week, and in medieval times the Authentic, with the same meaning; in Germany and Denmark the popular title is Still Week, in allusion to the holy quiet and abstraction from labour during its continuance.

Homily. A popular sermon of a colloquial character, used after the time of Origen.

Hood Mould. A label or dripstone over an arch.

Hours, Canonical. Mentioned generally by St. Clement of Alexandria, and as Synaxes in Ecgbright's Excerptions 740. There were four day-hours and three night-hours, in allusion to St. Mark xiii. 35 ; and St. Matt. xxvi. 44. From the fourth century the nocturns embraced three Psalms, one for each watch. The Seven Canonical Hours, so called because fixed by the canon or Church rule, for prayers at each third recurring hour, are founded on David's practice (Ps. lv. 17 ; cxix. 62). Daniel prayed thrice a day (Dan. vi. 10), which St. Cyprian considered was in honour of the Holy Trinity,

and the Jews four times (2 Esdr. ix. 3). Their names are
Matins (*matuta*, dawn), at midnight, called vigils by the
Council of Carthage, 398, but afterwards the first hour after
dawn, and mentioned by St. Cyprian as midnight and
matins, and by St. Athanasius as nocturns and midnight
(Ps. cxix. 62–147; Acts xvi. 25); an office which Cassian
and Isidore say was first observed in the fifth century in the
monastery of Bethlehem, in memory of the Nativity; Lauds,
after Matins, before day, mentioned by St. Basil, and in the
Apostolical Constitutions; in the fifth century nocturns
merged in matin lauds (Ps. lxiii. 6; cxix. 55); Prime, the
early morning, six a.m., mentioned by St. Athanasius (Ps.
xcii. 2; v. 3; lix. 16); Tierce (the third), nine a.m., mentioned by Tertullian with Sexts and Nones, when the disciples were assembled at Pentecost (Acts ii. 15); Sext (the
sixth), noonday, when St. Peter prayed (Acts x. 9); Nones
(the ninth), three p.m., when SS. Peter and John went up
to the Temple (Acts iii. 1); Vespers, mentioned by SS.
Cyprian, Basil, Ambrose, and Jerome, and the Apostolical
Constitutions, (evensong) six p.m., (Ps. lv. 18; xli. 2) when
our Lord instituted the Eucharist, showing it was the even-
tide of the world. This hour is called from evening, according to St. Augustine, or the evening star, says St. Isidore.
It was also known as the office and the hour of lights, as
until the eighth or ninth century it was said in the East, and
at Milan, also when the lamps were lighted (Zach. xiv. 7).
The Roman custom of saying Vespers after Nones then came
into use in the West. Compline, the complement of divine
service, as the office before bed-time (Ps. cxxxii. 3), was first
separated from Vespers by St. Benedict. The Apostolical
Constitutions mention Matins as the thanksgiving for the
dayspring from on high, and the return of light; Tierce,
when our Lord was sentenced by Pilate; Sext, when He
was crucified; Nones, when the great earthquake and
shaking heavens could not endure the Lord's shame; Evening, thanksgiving for the gift of sleep after the day's toil;
and cock-crow, when the coming of the day invites to do the
works of light. Cassian likewise mentions the observation
of Tierce, Sext, and Nones in monasteries. Tertullian
and Pliny speak of Christian services before daylight. St.
Jerome names Tierce, Sext, Nones, Vespers, and Dawn;

and St. Augustine,—for the two latter hours, however, substituting Early Vigil. Various reasons have been assigned for a deeper meaning in the hours; one is that they are the thanksgiving for the completion of the creation on the seventh day. Another theory beautifully connects them with the acts of our Lord in His Passion : Evensong with His institution of the Eucharist, and washing the disciples' feet, and the going out to Gethsemane ; Compline with His Agony and Bloody Sweat ; Matins with His appearance before Caiaphas ; Prime and Tierce with that in the presence of Pilate ; Tierce with his scourging, Crown of Thorns, and presentation to the people ; Sext with his bearing the Cross, the Seven Words, and Crucifixion; Nones with His dismission of His spirit, descent into hell, and rout of the devil ; Vespers with His deposition from the Cross and entombment; Compline with the setting of the Watch ; Matins with His Resurrection. Ado of Tréves says that, even during the Diocletian persecution, the Christians kept Matins, Vespers, Tierce, Sext, and Nones round the graves of the saints. The old English names are, Uht Sang, midnight; Lof Sang, praise or after song, two to three a.m. ; Prime Sang, six to seven, a.m.; and Undern Sang, eight to nine, a.m.; Midday Sang ; Noon Sang, two to three p.m.; Even Sang, six to seven p.m.; Night Sang, eight to nine p.m. The Church of England retains Matins and Evensong, the former containing the canticle for Lauds and the collect for Prime, and the latter the collect and canticle of Compline. In the collegiate churches of Durham, Matins were always sung in the morning. The Canonical hours for marriage by the CII. Canon, are between eight and twelve, except by special licence of the Archbishop of Canterbury. The Canonical hour for the Holy Communion is mentioned by St. Gregory of Tours as Tierce ; at Durham it was nine ; and by the Council of Norwich, 1257, was not to precede Prime. The design was that communicants should be fasting by the Third Council of Carthage, 397, and the advice of St. Augustine. St. Cyprian mentions that the Eucharist was celebrated in the daytime ; Tertullian says before daybreak.

Hour-glass Stand. A post-Reformation invention, existing in the time of Parker, in 1569 ; it is mentioned at Abingdon in 1591 ; a bracket or frame of iron for supporting the hour-glass (found at Wiggenhall, Ashby-Folville, Belton, Stamford, Leigh, Bradeston, South Burleigh, Edingthorpe, (1632), Wolvercot, Stoke-D'Abernon, St. John B., Bristol, Beckley, and some London churches, as St. Alban's, Wood Street), which was necessary when sermons were interminably long,—usually an hour in delivery by Sanderson, Stillingfleet, Tillotson, and Barrow. The hour-glass remains at Wiggenhall, and one has been recently set up in the Savoy Chapel.

Hours of Our Lady. A devotion instituted by Pope Urban II. at the Council of Clermont in 1096.

Hovel or **Housing.** A canopy or niche.

Hospital. (1.) The Greek *xenodochion;* the guest-house used for sick pilgrims. Palladins, Bishop of Heliopolis, mentions one on the Nitrian mountain. St. Chrysostom built several at Constantinople; in the sixth century one was erected at Lyons. One existed at Rome in the fifth century, and bore the ordinary ancient dedication to the Holy Ghost. In the East, priests discharged the office of nosocomi, or prefects of valetudinarians, in such hospitals. (2.) *Hospitium,* or hostry; a monastic guest-house. (3.) A foundation for infirm people, consisting of a series of small dwellings, arranged round a court, with a hall and church, as at St. Cross, (Winchester); or else of apartments opening off a central hall, which terminates in a chapel, so that the sick could hear Divine service even in their beds, as at St. Mary's Chichester, of the thirteenth and fourteenth century; Angers and Ponthlieue of the twelfth, Chartres and Tonnerre of the thirteenth, and Beaune of the fifteenth century. Similar arrangements may be traced at Wells and Sherborne. (4.) *Maison-Dieu;* a guest-house, usually in a seaside town, for poor priests travelling and pilgrims; as St. Mary's (Dover), St. Julian's (Southampton), Holy Trinity (Portsmouth). There were others at Arundel, Beverley, and Elgin; they were governed by a master and brethren, or confraters. (5.) *Maladrerie;* a leper hospital, dedicated to St. Lazarus; so called at Caen and Lincoln. In 1200, lepers were allowed to build a church and maintain a priest. (6.) *Callisses;* almshouses for decayed members of the staple of Calais, at Stamford, Oakham, and in Kent.

Humble Access. Prayer of; that said by the priest kneeling down at the altar before the consecration.

Humiliati. A mixed Italian order, founded in the reign of the Emperor Henry III. in 1017, or in the time of Barbarossa, 1164, by a body of Milanese exiles, on their return to their country. They wore a tunic, scapular, and white cloak; their chief was called a provost, and they adopted the Benedictine rule in part. In 1571 the order was abolished, owing to its dissoluteness. Their name was adopted from the circumstances of their prostration at the feet of the Emperor.

Hutch. An aumbry, or locker.

Hymn. A sacred chant to the praise of God, according to St. Augustine and Isidore of Seville; either a song or metrical composition in prose; mentioned by St. Paul (Eph. v. 19; Col. iii. 16); the verses Eph. v. 14 and Rev. iv. 8 are supposed to represent portions of hymns. A hymn is addressed to God immediately; a canticle celebrates His actions. The Te Deum, Benedicite, Magnificat, Nunc Dimittis, Benedictus, Gloria in Excelsis, and Ter Sanctus, are hymns, as distinguished from spiritual songs and metrical odes; though the latter are now called by the name of hymn, and the first five known as canticles. Philo, as recorded by Eusebius, mentions Christians singing psalms and hymns night and day. St. Ephraem speaks of their use on festivals, c. 379. Socrates, about the same date, mentions that it was the universal practice throughout the East; and the Council of Antioch, in the third century, speaks of such hymns as addressed to Christ as God. Hilary, Bishop of Poictiers, author of "Lucis largitor optime," and Hierotheus, according to Dionysius, Synesius, Bishop of Ptolemais in the fourth century, St. Gregory Nazianzen, Paulinus of Nola, and Prudentius, author of "Salvete flores martyrum," sung at Lauds, were early hymn writers. The most eminent was St. Ambrose, who wrote "Jam lucis orto sidere," "Consors Paterni luminis," and "Deus Creator omnium," and introduced the use of hymns in the West, after the manner of the Greek Church, and not by the choir only. His compositions were formally recommended for use in France and Spain by the Fourth Council of Toledo, in 633. Venantius Fortunatus, Bishop of Poictiers, wrote "Pange lingua gloriosi," and "Vexilla Regis prodeunt." Pope Gelasius, at the close of the fifth century, Rabanus Maurus, Archbishop of Mayence,

Pater Damiani, Cardinal Bishop of Ostia, Odo of Clugni, St. Thomas Aquinas, Adam of St. Victor, St. Bernard of Morlaix, in the West; and in the East, St. Anatolius, St. Andrew of Crete, St. Germanus, St. John Damascene, and St. Cosmas, added to the store of hymns. The " Veni Creator," first found in the works of Rabanus Maurus, in the ninth century, has been attributed to Charlemagne. Paul Warnefrid, the deacon, in his time, composed the hymn for St. John's Day, beginning " Ut queant laxis," from the initial syllables of which Guido of Arezzo composed the Solfeggio musical system. The employment of hymns was sanctioned by the Councils of Agde (506) and Tours (567). St. Augustine says they were used in nearly all the churches of the world; but the Councils of Laodicea (372) and Braga (563) forbade human compositions. St. Hilary of Poictiers alludes to the disinclination of the Gallican Church to adopt them; and years after they were sung at Vienne and Lyons, at Compline only, and sparingly at Rheims and Langres; and Durandus, in the thirteenth century, mentions that in certain churches no hymns were sung. In the sixth century they were used at Matins and Vespers only, but after that date at all the Hours. The Greeks use three hymns in the Liturgy: (1) the Angelic, like the Gloria in Excelsis; (2) Trisagion [which see] ; the Triumphant, or Epinikion, like the Ter Sanctus; and (3) the Cherubic, of the time of Justinian [which see]. The American Church sings hymns during the administration. *See* TE DEUM.

Hymnar, *or* **Hymnal.** A Church book containing hymns; one, according to Gennadius, was compiled by Paulinus of Nola.

Images. (Called in the Greek Church *icons*, whence the name of iconostasis for the altar-screen.) God enjoined the making of cherubim in the Temple (Exod. xxv.). Eusebius mentions a statue of our Lord, erected by the woman who was healed (St. Matt. ix. 20). Tertullian speaks of etchings of the Good Shepherd on glasses, such as are preserved still in the Vatican; and St. Gregory of Nazianzum, Pope Damasus, and St. Augustine frequently allude to paintings and sculptures as common in their time. St. Basil says that by " the beauty of the image the eyes are raised to the fairer

vision of the archetype;" and St. Gregory of Nyssa declared that he never passed the inscriptions of images without tears, and regarded them as efficacious in stirring the
heart and elevating it to virtue; whilst Bede calls them
"the living history of Divine history;" and Beleth "the
literature of the laity." St. Gregory sent pictures of
our Saviour, St. Mary, SS. Peter and Paul, to a French
bishop. Paulinus mentions a picture of St. Martin, in the
baptistery, or place of refreshment; he at Nola, in 460,
adorned the cathedral of St. Felix with wall paintings of the
stories taken out of the Old Testament; and Prudentius,
about the same time, mentions that he saw painted in a
church the history of the Passion of Cassian the Martyr. In
the time of St. Jerome church walls were incrusted with
tablets of marble; the capitals of the pillars and cielings
were gilded, the doors decked with ivory and silver, and the
altars adorned with gold and precious gems. In 305 the
Council of Elvira forbade pictures in churches, or the portraiture on walls of any object of adoration or worship, in
order during periods of persecution to secure them from
profanation; but, from the time of Calixtus, the catacombs
were covered with pictures, because there was no fear of any
desecration. Valens and Theodosius prohibited the use of
the cross; but Constantine restored the paintings of the
Fathers who sat in the first six councils, in St. Peter's
porch of Santa Sophia. In 752 a Roman Council required
images to be erected in churches; and at the end of the
sixth, and again in the eighth century, worship of images
was inculcated, a violent change from primitive simplicity,
wherein they were used only as decent ornaments,—" a remembrance whereby men may be admonished of the holy
lives and conversation of them that they did represent."

In the fourth century the use of images increased until
the eleventh century, so that churches were covered with
mosaic and paintings; St. Mark's, at Venice, will convey
an idea of this method of decoration; and traces of frescoes
remain in the Parthenon at Athens. In the catacombs they
were at once attractive and useful in solemnizing the hearts
of those who kept agape. The subjects are always the same
in different branches of art; a strict uniformity is the evidence of a hieratic tradition in the mural painting, the cut-

ting on glass, the sculpture of the Sarcophagus, and the
mosaic. Wooden figures of saints were probably first introduced into churches in the ninth century, when crowns of
gold were nailed on them, and on sacred pictures. In 1274
the Council of Lyons forbade the practice of veiling altars
in sackcloth, extinguishing lights, and laying relics and
images in places overgrown with thorns, when a church had
been profaned. The II. Council of Nicæa, in 787, ordered
images and crucifixes, whether painted or in relief, should
be placed in churches, in public streets, in private houses,
and on vessels and vestments. The Council of Trent requires the previous approbation of the bishop for the erection of images. The fact is, that the opinions of the early
Christians varied with regard to the use of images, according to their national character; cultivated Rome, re-creating
pagan temples, feasts, and symbols to a worthy use and a
good signification, as if the treasures of the Gentiles were
the inheritance of the Church, approved what ruder countries like Africa and provinces far distant from the centre of
civilization (like men of a more stern nature), regarded with
no favour, as appears from the writings of Tertullian, St.
Clement of Alexandria, and St. Augustine.

Serenus, Bishop of Marseilles, was blamed by Pope Gregory for breaking images in a church, although his zeal in
repressing the adoration of them was deservedly commended.
"In paintings on walls," says Gregory, "they who cannot
read books, can read that which in books they are unable,"
as John Damascene also remarks: Epiphanius, attracted by
a light burning in a church at Anabathla, when about to
enter it, found a curtain-veil before the doors painted with
the image of Christ, or some saint, and desired the churchwardens to remove it because it represented the human
form; and he gave another veil. But his conduct was also
blamed, as contrary to common practice, the custom of
antiquity, and the edification of the unlearned. The
Trullan Council, in 692, allowed pictures of our Saviour in
His human form to supersede merely symbolical representations under the figure of a lamb. The supporters of icons
numbered in their ranks all that was pious and venerable in
the Eastern Church; the iconoclasts were the legitimate development of Manichæism, which, under various names, de-

vastated Christ's fold. Leo the Isaurian began, in 726, and the despicable Constantine Copronymus carried on the persecution; and the Council of Constantinople, in 752, rejected the use of images. The Second Council of Nicæa, in 787, seemed to end the opposition; yet it broke out again when Leo III., the Armenian (813), forbade the images of saint, martyr, or angel in churches; but the feud died out in 842, with Theophilus. Sabinus, king of Bulgaria, provoked a rebellion by an attempt to abolish images. In consequence of the iconoclast movement, great numbers of artists emigrated from Greece to Rome; Gregory II. opened asylums to them; convents were erected for the fugitives from the East; and in the ninth century, under Paschal I., this foreign school produced the pictures of the Madonna, now dark with age, and the famous Volto Santo.

In 1547, " such images as had been abused with pilgrimage or offering made," and " been censed unto," were to be taken down and destroyed; and no torches, candles, tapers, or images of wax," were " to be set before any image or pictures;" and " kissing, licking, and decking" of images were forbidden. Grindal distinguishes "fat images" from pictures, as being solid. The image of St. Mary, of Penrice, near Swansea, had been greatly frequented. In 1539 the image of St. Mary, called " the Block," of Walsingham, was burned at Chelsea. Other famous images were those of our Lady of Ipswich, Doncaster, and Willesden, where the people " made rolls of half an hour long, to pray after that manner" of invocation. Bishop Latimer, in " the Western part," threw out an image which the inhabitants of the country believed eight oxen could not move. The image of Our Lady, of Worcester, was found to be a bishop's effigy. The rood of grace, of Boxley, was shown to be an automaton, by Bishop Hilsey, at Paul's Cross; by means of cords it rolled its eyes, opened its mouth, and nodded its head approvingly, or in dissent. Another vile imposture was practised by R. Leigh, who, by means of a sponge, made the head of a marble rood bleed, at Christchurch, Dublin, when the English Litany was sung for the first time. Archbishop Hugh destroyed it in 1559.

There is an enormous altar-piece, of the fifteenth century, painted in tempera upon panel, and brought from Valencia, in the South Kensington Museum. At Winchester the hooks remain above the base arcade on which the superb suits of tapestry, embroidered with stories of Holy Writ, were hung on solemn occasions. There are at Chichester remarkable wall-paintings by Bernardi for Bishop Sherborne; and at Exeter, in the panels of the screen, thirteen oil paintings of the time of Charles I.; and some figures in distemper, by Damian (1728), at Lincoln. Altar-pieces are far from uncommon in English churches.

Immersion, not affusion, was used by the Apostles and disciples of our Lord (St. John iii. 23; Acts viii. 38); and various passages of Scriptures are applicable only to this form (Rom. vi. 3, 4; Col. ii. 4). Affusion, or sprinkling, was introduced (Grotius says) for the sake of those who were baptized as clinics, bedridden, or at the point of death, but more probably out of consideration to infants, about 875, when adult baptism became rare. St. Chrysostom, commenting on our Lord's command, says, "The Lord, setting as it were a seal on all mysteries in three immersions in water, gave one Baptism to His disciples;" and Tertullian says, "We receive the water, not once but thrice at each name;" and Pope Gregory I. observes, that "by thrice dipping, the mystery of Christ's lying three days in the grave is signified." His 'Sacramentary' prescribes trine immersion, but in consequence of a misinterpretation and abuse of the ceremony by the Arians, the matter was referred to him by the Spanish bishops, and he decided that single immersion was valid, as representing the unity, whilst trine immersion symbolized the Trinity of the Godhead; and this view was embodied in the fifth canon of the Fourth Council of Toledo, in 633. St. Basil, St. Jerome, St. Augustine, and St. Ambrose consider trine immersion to be an Apostolical tradition; and St. Cyril of Jerusalem, St. Gregory of Nyssa, St. Athanasius, and Leo the Great, interpret it as symbolical of the death, resurrection, and ascension of our Lord. Trine immersion was observed by the Greeks in the eighth century.

Beleth says the child was immersed with its face to the water and the head to the east, and then with its face upwards and the head towards the north and the south, at each dipping one person of the Holy Trinity being named;

and at the anointing a chrismal, a round mitre symbolizing the crown of life, or a white robe was set about the child.

The practice of immersion of the whole body, though dying out in the time of Pope Gregory, was retained until the thirteenth and fourteenth centuries; indeed, it has never been abandoned. By the present rubric, adults are to be dipped in the water, or to have water poured over them; and in the case of infants, " if the godfathers and godmothers shall certify the priest that the child may well endure it, he shall dip it in the water discreetly and warily; if they shall certify the child is weak, it shall suffice to pour water upon it."

Possibly immersion was gradually discontinued owing to the ancient custom of baptizing persons wholly undressed, to add significancy to the rite, as we find from the writings of St. Athanasius, St. Chrysostom, St. Ambrose, and Denys the Areopagite. It represented the state of Adam before the Fall, and of Christ on the cross, and the laying aside of the garment spotted by the flesh, and that naked we must enter the Kingdom of Heaven. The old Ordo Romanus alludes to the practice which was followed by Constantine, as Metaphrastes relates; by St. Basil, by Apronianus when baptized in the prison, by Sisinius the deacon, by Tranquillinus when infirm, by St. Polycarp, and other persons mentioned by Surius. About the year 1140 the custom was laid aside in the Western Church. Men were placed on the right, and women on the left-hand of the font.

By the Rubric of 1549, the priest naming the child dipped it in the water thrice, first dipping the right side, secondly the left side, and the third time dipping the face towards the font. In 1552 a single immersion was prescribed.

Impost. The moulding on the top of a pillar from which an arch springs.

Impropriations. Benefices appropriated by monks or regular canons, and served by some of their own body, but at length, through the influence of the bishops, by secular priests. Henry VIII. distributed these livings to bishops, cathedral chapters, colleges, and laymen.

Incense (Mal. i. 2.) was used in processions in the time of Justin the younger, and St. Gregory of Tours; in censing the altar, to represent prayers offered to God; in censing the persons of the clergy and people, to remind them that they should be a sweet savour of Christ (Eph. v. 2; 2 Cor. ii. 15); and even with the dead, in memory of the spices with which the bodies of the faithful were interred, as in the case of our Lord (St. John xix. 39). Bona questions the opinion that Leo I., c. 440, enjoined its use at the altar on solemn feasts; it has been also referred to the year 745 or 876. In the magnificent mosaic of the Church of the Nativity, Bethlehem, on one side of the altar is a candlestick with a lighted taper, and on the other a censer, both on the ground. Incense was no doubt employed, like the lights, in the catacombs, to dispel damp and noisome smell; but it is mentioned during Divine Service by the Council of Chalcedon, the liturgies of St. Peter, St. James, St. Chrysostom, and St. Basil; the Apostolical Canons, Hippolytus Martyr, St. Ephraem, St. Ambrose, Evagrius, Damasus, in the lives of Soter and Constantine the Great, and Germanns, patriarch of Constantinople. It mystically represented, (1) contrition (Eccles. xlv.); (2) the preaching of the Gospel (2 Cor. ii. 14); (3) the prayers of the faithful (Ps. cxli. 2; Rev. v. 8-24); (4) and the virtue of saints (Song of Songs iii. 6). St. Augustine explains the golden censer of the Revelations to mean the humanity of Christ; and the patriarch Germanus adds, the fire, His Divinity; and the fragrance, the sweet savour of the Spirit. It was the deacon's office to incense. The Cistercians used incense only on festivals, whilst the Benedictines and Clugniacs employed it on most occasions. In England and Wales incense-cups of earthenware, with incised ornaments, and apparently adapted for suspension over the sepulchral flame, are not unfrequently found within the cinerary urns of a remote antiquity. Bishop Andrewes, Archbishop Laud, and George Herbert used incense, which was a common article of purchase in the churchwardens' accounts of the period. It was burned at the coronation of George III.; and in a standing censer, at Ely Cathedral, before the altar, about one hundred years ago.

Inclination (Prayer of). (1.) In the Greek Liturgy, that said immediately before the Communion of the people, and corresponding to the English prayer of humble access. (2.) Bowing at the Gloria Patri and the name of Jesus, which was ordered by the Archbishop of Dublin in the fourteenth century.

Incluse. (*See* ANCHORET.) By English Canons of 1236 no one could become an Incluse without the bishop's permission. Those in holy orders celebrated low Masses, and the lay folk assisted in cleaning the church plate and furniture.

Indelible Character. The spiritual sign stamped on the soul which distinguishes clerks in the greater orders from laymen, so defined in the Council of Florence, 1439. St. Irenæus calls it " the certain gift of truth," and St. Augustine " the sacrament of his ordination."

Indiction. A chronological system, including a circle of fifteen years: (1) the Cæsarean, used long in France and Germany, beginning on September 24; (2) Constantinopolitan, used in the East from the time of Anastasius, and beginning September 1; and (3) Papal, reckoned from January 1, 313. The Council of Antioch, 341, first gives a documentary date, the fourteenth indiction. The computation prevailed in Syria in the fifth century, and is mentioned by St. Ambrose as existing at Rome. It is, however, asserted that in the West, the East, and Egypt, with the exception of Africa, the indictions, until the sixteenth century, were reckoned from September 1, 312, and that they commenced in Egypt in the time of Constantine.

Induction after Institution. The admission of a clerk to a benefice by the bishop or his delegate, is performed by the person named in the episcopal mandate or archdeacon's warrant. He takes the presentee to the church and laying his hand on the church key, which is then in the door, and saying, " By virtue of this instrument (the mandate or warrant), I induct you into the real, actual, and corporal possession of the rectory or vicarage of ——, with all its fruits, profits, members, and appurtenances." The clerk is then passed through the open door and tolls a bell. If the key cannot be had, the ring of the door will suffice, and if the church be in ruins, the wall or fence may be touched. At St. Alban's the new abbot touched the bell-ropes to signify his power, and then all the bells were rung.

Indulgences. Remissions of temporal punishment due to actual sins, made without sacramental means, and dispensed from the treasury of the Roman Church to persons not in mortal sin. They are given for so many days or years as it would have taken penance to last in order to exhaust the penalty, some days occasionally being supposed to be observed strictly.

In the early ages penitents used to obtain reconciliation by obtaining the " peace," on intercession of a martyr in prison being made to the bishop on the offender's behalf. Tertullian and Cyprian both allude to the practice. The Councils of Nicæa, Ancyra, and Laodicea, and the Caroline Constitutions permitted relaxations of penance by the bishop. The paschal indulgence regulated the stations of penitents; and from these practices rose up the later system of indulgences. The first mention of the word is in the sixth century by Gregory the Great, when granting indulgence to those who should visit the stations of Rome. In the eighth century Pope Leo granted indulgences to churches in Germany and France. In 884 Pope Sergius granted an indulgence of three years and three-quarters to all who visited St. Martin-at-Mount, in Rome, on Martinmas. In 1116 Pope Urban gave plenary indulgence, in the Council of Clermont, to all who took the cross. In 1213 Innocent III. renewed the grant. Martin V. gave another in the Council of Constance. The wholesale auction of indulgences by Tetzel, in 1517, was the active cause of the Reformation in Germany. According to the Stacyons of Rome of the fourteenth century, at the anniversary of the dedication of St. Peter's, an indulgence of three thousand years was given to citizens, of nine thousand to neighbours, and of twelve thousand to pilgrims from beyond sea. Indulgences, written on parchment and sealed with lead, were found in St. Paul's Churchyard during the demolition of buildings made by the Duke of Somerset to provide materials for his palace in the Strand. One of lead is preserved at Chichester, of the twelfth century, and another, of later date, at St. Omer. *See* BURIALS.

Infant Baptism (St. Matt. xix. 13, 14; Rom. ii. 29) in the sixth century was general; and from the third to the fifth century, and until after the time of Charlemagne, infant communion was permitted. "Mother Church," says St. Augustine, "lendeth to infants the feet of others to come, the heart of others to believe, and the tongue of others to confess."

Infirmarer. He had the care of the sick-house, in which Lent and fasts were not observed, had charge of the burial of the dead, provided physicians and attendance, and flesh meat.

Infirmary. The Benedictine sick-house usually consisted of a small cloister, as at Westminster, Gloucester, and Canterbury, a kitchen, a bath-house, and a hall with aisles to contain beds, and opening at its eastern end into a chapel. At Canterbury, Ely, and Peterborough considerable portions, and at Buildwas and Norwich fragments exist. The infirmarer's house adjoined it, and remains at Westminster and Ely. At Carlisle and Bristol it lay in a second court southward of the refectory. At times, as at Durham and Worcester, it fronted a river. In the infirmary chapel the body of the dead monk was laid, on a stone slab, before the cross, and watched by two of his nearest friends. It was then taken into the chapter-house, and so to the cemetery. The infirm among the Cistercians were required to attend church.

Inquisition, *or* **Holy Office.** A criminal spiritual court for the repression of false doctrine, first appointed in the south of France in the thirteenth century, and about the middle of that period in Spain. In 1484 the Supreme General Inquisitiou was established at Seville, under the control of the Dominicans. The Spanish Inquisition was abolished by the Cortes in 1820, and at the same date that of Portugal, established in 1557. At Rome an inquisition, appointed in 1542, takes cognizance of ecclesiastical delinquents in matters of disobedience, heresy, sorcery, and sacrilege. The standard of the Inquisition was red, with a cross, having a sword on one side, and on the other a palm branch, and the legend (Ps. lxxiv. 23).

Installation. The induction of a canon into his stall in choir and chapter. In the old foundations the order was for the nominee of the bishop to present himself in the chapter-house, where the mandate of the bishop was read out by the chapter-clerk, and the oaths of fealty administered. Then the dean gave permission for his installation, which is performed by the dean or residentiary at CHICHESTER, two canons at EXETER, dean or subdean at WELLS, by the dean, subdean, or subdean's deputy at LINCOLN, by two vicars-

choral at SALISBURY, and by the precentor or succentor at
LICHFIELD,—leading him by the hand to his stall in choir.
At the end of the service the new dignitary or prebendary
is led again to the chapter-house, where he is assigned his
place, with the right of a voice according to his dignity or
the seniority of his prebend. The old form was to say to
the installed, "God preserve thy going out and thy coming
in, now and for ever." The actual admission is made by the
delivery of the text or book of the Gospel, or the statutes,
"the form of regular observance," for spiritual food ; and a
loaf of common or canonical bread, for bodily refreshment.
At LINCOLN and St. PAUL's he was directed to note the Psalm
which he was to recite daily for benefactors, the title or antiphon being written above his stall (Ps. cxxxiii.), except at
Hereford, where the Miserere was always sung after the investiture; and a bond to pay stall-wages to his vicar was
signed, and certain suffrages and prayers used. These customs, in the main, are still observed. At St. PAUL's, when
a prebend was changed, a new installation took place ; and on
promotion to a dignity, the dean led up the canon to the
upper stall, saying, " Friend, go up higher." See COPE.

The installation in cathedrals of the new foundation is very
meagre. The institution takes place in the bishop's palace.
The dean or canon robes in the vestry and, attended by the
verger, mandate in hand, is installed—if a canon, by the
dean; if the dean, by the vice-dean or residentiary—after the
second lessons, the mandate being first read and the statutable oath administered.

Intercessor, or **Interventor.** A bishop in Africa who occupied a see in its vacancy as administrator of the diocese,
and the delegate of the primate; owing to grave abuses
which ensued, such as candidature for the bishopric if of
superior value, unworthy concessions, or protracting the
election of a new prelate, in 401 a Council of Carthage forbade the tenure to exceed one year, and also succession to
the temporary occupant.

Interdict. An ecclesiastical censure by which sacraments,
services, and religious rites at funerals were forbidden. In
the ninth century a bishop of Laon laid an interdict on one
of his parishes. In 1170 Pope Alexander III., and Pope Innocent in 1207, put all England under an interdict. Divine

service was not held in church, the viaticum and ecclesiastical burial were forbidden; eulogia only were administered; old chrism alone was used; infants were baptized in the presence of their sponsors alone; but confessions were received, and dying penitents absolved; sermons were preached and women churched in the yard. On the principal festivals of the Church the faithful were allowed to pray without. In a quarrel with the king, Bishop Ralph of Chichester barred the cathedral doors with thorns.

Internal Dignitaries. The dean, precentor, chancellor and treasurer in cathedrals of the old foundation.

Introits. Pope Celestine, c. 430, ordered the psalter to be sung before the communion antiphonally, which was a new order, as the epistles of St. Paul and the holy Gospel hitherto only had been recited. For about 500 years the Psalm xliii. has been used, the antiphon being verse 4, " I will go unto the altar of God, my exceeding joy." It is an antiphon sung by the choir as the priest goes up to the altar to celebrate. St. Ambrose calls it the ingressa, and it is the commencement of the office which terminates at the prayer after the lesson. The Introit, or entry, is so named in distinction to the verse, by which the return is made to the Introit. The Introit is of two kinds, (1) regular, that sung daily; (2) the irregular, which is chanted on festivals. It should be of grand and solemn character. In a great church there was a procession round the nave to the sound of bells and with incense, passing out by the small gate of the sanctuary and re-entering by the great doors. The deacon then went up with the Gospel elevated in both his hands and set it on the midst of the altar, so as to be seen by the people. Then followed the Introit, composed of several anthems, succeeded by prayers and the Trisagion. The priest and deacon intoned it, the choir and people took it up, and a candlestick with three lights, as a symbol of the Holy Trinity, was lighted. The hymn itself, according to Symeon of Thessalonica, typifies the union of men and angels. The priest at the same time made three signs of the cross over the Gospels with the taper which he held.

Invention of the Holy Cross. A festival on May 3rd, first mentioned in the ' Sacramentary ' and ' Antiphonar ' of Pope Gregory. Some refer its introduction in the Latin Church to

a date later than 720, and still more recent by the Greeks.
In the year 326, according to St. Ambrose, Sozomen, Theodoret, and St. Cyril of Jerusalem, Queen Helena discovered
the Cross of Calvary at Jerusalem. She placed a large
portion in the Church of Holy Cross at Rome, on September
14th, hence called the Exaltation of Holy Cross mentioned by
St. Chrysostom. The Friars Cross-bearers, who always carried a cross in their hands, settled at Colchester in 1244.
Their founder is not known. They wore blue, and kept the
Austin rule.

Invitatories. Short texts interpolated between the verses of
the Psalm, Venite Exultemus Domino, which indicate the
subject of the office to which they invite thought. In the
sixth century the Invitatory at Matins was called the Anthem,
in St. Benedict's rule and the Roman Order. At Lyons, at
Christmas, Easter, and Pentecost, the choir sang Venite
Populi as an invitatory to the clergy and people to communicate after the Agnus Dei, as on those festivals the faithful were required to communicate by the Councils of Agde,
Elvira, and III. Tours under Charlemagne. At Milan this
Anthem inviting to the Eucharist was called the Transitorium. At Lyons, the three contiguous churches assembled
the people with the same bells, and at the same hours ; St.
Stephen's commenced Matins when they were singing in the
cathedral of St. John ' To-day we will hear His Voice,' and
when at St. Stephen's that verse was being sung, morning
service began in St. Cross; so that a canon, if he arrived late at
the cathedral, could go to one of the other churches and not lose
his quotidian. At Vienna on Holy Thursday, after Nones, the
archbishop in albe, amice, stole, and silk cope, and with his
cross, went to the west door of the cathedral and preached to
the penitents, and at the end of his sermon he said three times,
" Venite filii," the archdeacon added " Accedite," whereupon
they all entered the church. The Psalm Venite in the Sarum use is called the Quadruple Invitatory when sung on
principal doubles by four cantors and choir in alternate
verses ; the Triple Invitatory when alternated by three
cantors on the other doubles ; and the Simple Invitatory
when sung between the precentor and the choir. The
Double was sung on simple feasts by two cantors, or by the
precentor and two cantors. In the Roman use, on double

feasts, the antiphon to the Psalms is doubled at Matins, Lauds, and both Vespers.

Jacob's Ladder. The vision of Jacob in the wilderness, pourtrayed in stone on the west front of Bath Abbey.

Jamb. The side of a window or door.

Jesse, Tree of. The emblematical representation of the genealogy of Christ, with a tree growing out of Jesse who lies asleep, on the leaves and branches of which are his descendants, in allusion to Is. xi. 1–10. There is a Jesse in the windows at Winchester College, Rouen, Chartres, St. Cuthbert's at Wells, and in St. George's, Hanover Square, London; in the mullions of the east window of Dorchester, Oxon, and on the reredos of Christchurch, Hants. In the eleventh century the Abbot of St. Augustine, Canterbury, presented to the church a Jesse candlestick of brass which was bought beyond seas.

Jesuits. An order founded by Ignatius Loyola in 1540, confirmed by Paul III. Their superior is called a general, and his subalterns are called provincials. One of their most distinguished members was Francis Xavier. The order has been suppressed in most countries.

John's, St., Day. The nativity of St. John the Baptist, June 24th (in the Greek Church, January 7th), was commemorated as early as the fourth century, and St. Augustine comments upon the peculiarity of observing his birthday rather than his martyrdom. This, under the name of the Decollation, was subsequently kept on August 20th. At Magdalen College, Oxford, an open-air pulpit was used on this day, and at Winchester College, in 1407, the pulpit was surrounded with boughs and green candles, as a memorial of the preacher in the wilderness. In Ireland, as formerly in the North of England, at night enormous bonfires are lighted on the eve. The Greeks represent the Baptist winged, in allusion to St. Mark i. 2. In France wheels were rolled in allusion to the sun's declination, bones of animals burned to purify the air, and torches carried in allusion to St. John v. 35. St. John the Evangelist's Day, December 27th, is first mentioned by Venerable Bede. In 1240 the Council of Lyons directed its perpetual observance. On this evening the boy-bishop was elected, and in France it was called the Feast of Sousdiacres (subdeacons), a pun on *soûls diacres*, drunken deacons.

Journal *or* **Diurnal.** (1.) An ancient name of the Day Hours contained in the Breviary. (2.) A diary of daily expenses in a monastery.

Jubilee. A time of indulgence in which all confessors, with the approval of the ordinary, may absolve in all reserved cases from all censures, greater excommunications, suspensions from offices and benefices, and interdicts, and can commute vows, except those of religion, perpetual chastity, or pilgrimages to Rome, Jerusalem, or Compostella. Boniface VIII. instituted a centenary jubilee in 1300, but some authors insist that it was a revival of the old custom for persons to visit Rome every hundred years. Clement VI. when at Avignon reduced the period to every fiftieth year, owing to the brevity of human life, and for mystical reasons, in allusion to the Mosaic jubilee (Lev. xxv. 9), and to Pentecost. Urban VI., in 1389, enjoined the jubilee to be held every thirty-third year. Nicholas V., in 1449, renewed the former tenure of every fiftieth year. Paul II. reduced the term to every quarter of a century, which was observed by his successors as late as 1625. Jubilees have been held in 1300, 1350, 1390, 1450, 1473, 1500, 1525, 1550, 1575, 1600, 1625, 1650, 1675, 1700, 1725, 1750, 1776, 1826. The jubilee was announced beforehand, on Ascension Day, by the auditor of the Rota. On the recurrence of the jubilee at Christmas Eve the Holy Door of the Station was opened by the Pontiff, after three blows of a mallet, announcing jubilee to the three known quarters of the world, and joy in heaven and earth and purgatory. The anthem, Aperite Portas, and the Te Deum were sung, whilst four deputies opened the doors of the other churches. Boniface VIII. required the four great basilicas of Rome to be visited, and in consequence each had its own holy door. Boniface appointed the following stations :—St. Peter and St. Paul's without. Clement VI. added St. John Lateran ; and Urban VI., Sixtus IV., or Gregory XL, St. Mary Major. In 1300 Charles de Valois, and Charles Martel, King of Hungary; in 1475 Ferdinand, King of Naples, Christian I. of Denmark, and the Queens of Cyprus and Bosnia; and in 1573 Tasso and St. Charles Borromeo, attended the jubilee. In 1550 the numbers of pilgrims were estimated at 1,200,000, but at the close of the century the Popes dispensed with personal attendance on condition that the pilgrims visited stations in their own countries appointed by the ordinary. Magnificent processions, with a representation of the triumph of the Church, in 1575, and in 1600 of the mysteries of the Old Testament, attracted vast crowds, fifty thousand persons of both sexes on the latter occasion following the procession alone. *See* STATIONS.

Judas Light *or* **Judas of the Paschal.** A wooden imitation of the candle which held the real paschal in the seventh branch which stood upright, the rest diverging on either side. The Judas cup was a mazer used at Durham on the night of Maundy Thursday.

Jugulum *or* **Transenna.** A small grated window of marble in the Confession, through which palls or brandea were passed, being first carefully weighed, then, after an interval spent in prayer and fasting by the suppliant, withdrawn from the tomb, in the belief that the divine favour was infallibly signified by the increased heaviness of the garment left in contact with the tomb of a saint. (Judges vi. 38.)

Keys of gold or some rich metal, of small size, and containing the dust of iron filings from the chains of St. Peter and St. Paul, preserved in the remains of the Mamertine prison, now called the Confession, under the Church of St. Joseph at Rome, were formerly sent from Rome to favoured princes since the time of St. Gregory the Great. Pope Vitalian sent a gold relic-key of this kind to the Consort of King Oswy of Northumbria in 667. St. Peter's keys represent his power in heaven, earth, and hell. The crossed keys (the Papal arms) are more usual, one of gold for the power of absolution, and the other of silver as the sign of excommunication.

King Post. The middle part of a roof between the beam and the ridge

Kiss of Peace. A salutation of charity in the primitive Church frequently alluded to by St. Paul (Rom. xvi. 16 ; 1 Cor. xvi. 20 ; 2 Cor. xiii. 12 ; 1 Thes. v. 6) as a token of love, perfect peace, brotherhood, and unity in faith and religion, offered at holy communion, baptism, and marriage, with the words " Pax tecum," peace to thee. In the East, after the recitation of the collect and Creed, the deacon, at the time of the oblation, (St. Matt. v. 24) proclaimed, " Kiss ye one another with a holy kiss," and then the clerks gave the holy kiss to the bishop, and among the lay people men to men, and women to women. In the West it was given after the consecration, and the Lord's Prayer, and is mentioned by Tertullian as the seal of prayer, and by St. Augustine, and Cesarius of Arles. The kiss of baptism is alluded to by St. Cyprian and St. Chrysostom. The Greek Church has retained the marriage kiss, which is spoken of by Tertullian, but the West has long abandoned it. The kiss called Philema by St. Paul, and Eirene by the Council of Laodicea, was omitted at private Masses, on Good Friday, and by persons fasting; because Judas betrayed our Lord with a kiss, and in order to discountenance ostentation of fasting. Charlemagne, King Pepin, and the Emperor Frederic kissed the feet of Popes; and, according to the Papal ceremonial, the emperor elect kissed the Pope's feet in reverence for our Saviour, and so did the empress. The Papal sandal being embroidered with a cross, on Palm Sunday patriarchs, archbishops, and bishops assisting at the throne kissed the Pope's right knee, and mitred abbots his foot, at the reception of the palm. *See* OSCULATORY.

Kitchen. Invariably adjoined the Refectory, behind it in Benedictine houses, and on the side usually in Cistercian arrangements. The ordinary shape was square, but there were exceptions: thus a bottle-form was adopted at Marmoutier, a round at Chartres, Villers, Saumur, and Vendôme, an octagon at Pontlevoy, Caen, Durham, Glastonbury, and with little apses at Fontévrault. At Westminster there was a vaulted way to the hall; at Canterbury a covered alley; but in the smaller orders a hatch or window formed the means of communication. There was also a kitchen for the infirmary, and the abbot had his own kitchen.

Kitchener. The marketer and purveyor who bought the provisions for kitchen use, and was overseer of the cooks, butchery, and fishponds. He visited the sick every morning, and saw that the broken meat was reserved for the poor.

Kneelers. (*Gonuklinontes, genuflectentes.*) The third class of penitents, who knelt in the nave near the ambon or lectern, attended the prayers, and received the benediction and imposition of hands from the bishop.

nife. One with a box-wood handle, which belonged to Thomas à Becket, and was used for cutting the Eulogiæ, is preserved at St. Andrew's, Vercelli. The holy loaf, out of which they were cut, was ordered to be provided by the parish by the Salisbury Constitution of 1254. King Athelstan left his knife on the altar of Beverley, as a pledge for his redemption of a vow of benefaction.

nights of St. John of Jerusalem, *or* Hospitallers. Constituted by King Baldwyn and Pope Honorius II. under the Austin rule, who occupied St. John's Hospital for Pilgrims at Jerusalem, to the capture of which, in 1099, they had materially contributed. They wore a red belt with a white cross, and a black cloak with a white cross of eight points on the left side; but the colour was sometimes black in peace-time and red in war. Their chiefs were called provosts, masters, and at length priors. The knights were required to be of eighteen years of age, of noble or lawful birth, to say the Lord's Prayer a certain number of times daily, to communicate three times a year, to abstain from commerce and trade, to make no heirs, to be gentle to the poor, and repress heathendom. There were three classes in the order: (1) priests and chaplains; (2) knights; and (3) servants. Adrian IV. made them exempt from the Patriarch of Jerusalem, and Alexander III. freed the Cistercians and Templars from payment of tithes to the diocesan, and they were allowed to celebrate in a general interdict. About 1300, being driven out of Palestine, they became Knights of Rhodes, where they established eight Languages under great officers. The grand commander, the treasurer, storekeeper, comptroller, and master of the ordnance were of Provence; the grand marshal, the commander-in-chief, came from Auvergne; the grand hospitaller was of France; the admiral, of Italy; the draper or grand conservator, who attended to the commissariat and clothing department, of Arragon; the turcopolier, the chief of the light cavalry, outposts, and adjutant-general, of England; the grand bailiff, of Germany, including Bohemia, Croatia, Hungary, and Dalmatia; and the grand chancellor, of Castile. The priors presided over the commanderies. In 1523 the Turks drove them from Rhodes, and in 1529 they became masters and Knights of Malta under a grand master, who, like the electors of the empire,

z

were styled His Eminence. Savoy, in acknowledgment of
services rendered by the order, adopted its arms,—gules, a
cross argent. The last prior of England who called himself
first baron of the kingdom and was mitred, ranking after the
abbots of Tewkesbury and Tavistock, died in 1539, followed
by the last turcopolier in 1551. Their gate-house and the
crypt of their church remain at Clerkenwell.

Knights Templars. An order of knights instituted in the year
1118, when Hugo Paynel, Geoffrey de St. Omer, and seven
other Franks undertook to reside at Jerusalem and defend
the pilgrims from interruption on their way. King Baldwin
gave them a home near his own palace, and adjoining the
Temple and its southern gate, whence their name of Templars. The canons and patriarch contributed to their maintenance and endowment. Calixtus II. in the Council of
Rheims, 1119, or Gelasius II. made them exempt from the
patriarch. Their dress was a white cloak, given to them by
Honorius III. in 1128. To it Eugenius, in 1146, added a
red cross, in token that they should be ready to die for
Christ. They ransomed those who were taken by the enemy by a sword and belt only. They were suppressed by
Pope John XXII. after the Council of Vienne, in 1312, on
the most horrible charges. Their nine thousand houses and
their lands, except in Portugal, Spain, and Castile, where
they would do service against the Moors, were given to the
hospitallers and Teutonic knights. In England the king
allowed every member 4*d.* a day; many were quartered on
the monasteries, and others were supported on the proceeds
of their confiscated lands. In France their pay varied from
5*d.* to 12*d.* of the Paris mint. Their chief was called the
Grand Master. Their preceptories were often called temple-
houses. Their churches had a round nave, in honour of the
Church of the Holy Sepulchre at Jerusalem, and four remain,
—Little Maplestead, St. Mary's (London), and the Holy
Sepulchre at Northampton and Cambridge.

The knights of Mountjoye, under the rule of St. Basil,
founded in 1130, and the knights Teutonic or Marianis,
under the Austin rule, founded in 1195, defended pilgrims
to Jerusalem. The knights of Compostella, founded in the
twelfth century, under the Austin rule, protected those visiting the shrine of St. James. The Knights of Christ in the

fourteenth century, under the Benedictine rule, in Portugal; those of St. George, founded in 1470, under the Austin rule, in Bohemia and Hungary; and the knights of Mountjoye and Calatrava in Spain,—defended the frontiers against the Saracens.

Knots. (1.) Trinity knots and St. Katharine's knots and other knots were distinctive badges of guilds. (2.) A boss in a vault.

Kyrie Eleison. Lord have mercy upon us (Is. xxxiii. 2; St. Matt. xx. 30; xv. 22; St. Luke xvii. 13). Called by St. Benedict a minor or lesser litany, and probably meant by SS. Cyprian, Chrysostom, and Augustine when they mention litanies. The supplication, now lifted heavenward by divine music in such strains of adoring rapture, was at first used for catechumens and penitents, the spiritually blind and lepers, as appears by the Apostolical Constitutions, when the deacons and people alternately recited them. The name is used in the Liturgies of SS. Basil, James, and Chrysostom. The introduction of this Greek form into the Latin service has been attributed to Pope Sylvester, c. 320, or Gregory the Great, in the seventh century; but it is earlier than his time, as it is mentioned by the Second Council of Vaison, in 529, as in use throughout eastern Italy, and directed to be used at Matins, Vespers, and Masses. The influence of the Eastern Church on the Western terminology may be traced in this form and in the words pasch, pentecost, parasceve, bishop, priest, deacon, acolyth, epiphany, litany, anthem, hymn, and trisagion, and also in the adoption of the Jewish words, hosanna and alleluia,—the latter so sacred, as St. Augustine says, that the Church scrupled to translate it, and so reverend that St. John heard it sung in heaven. At first the celebrant repeated the Kyrie as often as devotion suggested. From the time of Pope Gregory, the Pope, when he cele-brated, gave the signal for it to cease. The Council of Vaison, 529, sanctioned its repetition in divine service. In the eleventh century it was sung nine times. In the En-glish Litany it is repeated alternately by the priest and choir; at other times the central petition is only recited by the latter. The triple invocation is dedicated to one Person of the Godhead, to show the unity of the Divine Trinity. The Ambrosian rite recites it three times after the Gloria in

Excelsis, and the Gospel, and at the end of the Mass. The kyrie usually designates the passage as chanted at the commencement of the Mass, and in the English Church the responses sung, after each of the Ten Commandments. It was the watchword given by King Henry, in 934, at a battle in Hungary, and soldiers in the Rhine country are recorded to have marched to battle shouting the Kyrie Eleison.

Labarum. Constantine having seen at midday a cross of light in the heavens ordered the first artists of the time to make an imitation of it, which resulted in a gilt pole with a transverse beam, surmounted with a leafy crown of gold and gems, engraved with the sacred monogram of Christ. From the arms drooped a banner of purple tissue, studded with jewels and superbly embroidered with gold, and the heads of the emperor and his sons. Fifty draconarii, or dragoons, so called from the guard of the military standard of Rome, guarded it when it led the army to battle. It was represented on the imperial coinage, and was preserved at Constantinople until the ninth century. Eusebius describes the inspiring effect it produced on the Christian soldiers at the battle of Adrianople, "where the cross went before, victory followed."

Label. A square-headed or straight hood-mould.

Labyrinth. At St. Bertin's in St. Omer there was one of those curious floors, representing the Temple of Jerusalem, with stations for pilgrims, and actually visited and traversed by them as a compromise for not going to the Holy Land in fulfilment of a vow. The labyrinth at Sens was destroyed in 1768; those of Arras and Amiens shared the same fate in 1825. There is a round labyrinth in the centre of the nave of Chartres, inlaid with lead; another, of encaustic tiles, in the chapter-house of Bayeux; and a third, of octagonal shape, in the nave of St. Quentin.

Lady Chapel. The earliest lady chapel in England was that in the western apse of Canterbury, but removed to the north nave aisle by Lanfranc; that of St. Alban's, in the Norman period, was on the east side of the south arm, and also later at Worksop. About the close of the twelfth, or rather the beginning of the thirteenth century, its ordinary position was at the extreme east end, as at Lichfield, Hereford, Wells, Exeter, Chichester, Gloucester, Salisbury. It was included under the same roof as the presbytery at York, Lincoln, Worcester, St. Paul's, Selby, Howden, Hull, Hexham, and Carlisle. At Rochester and Waltham it is on the south side of the nave; at Drontheim, Bristol, Canterbury, and Oxford, parallel with the north choir aisle; at Geneva and Paisley, with the south; at Ely, as formerly at Peterborough, detached on the north side; at Ripon, over the chapter-house; and at Wimborne, in the south arm of the transept. At Bristol there was a second later lady chapel at the east end. In the case of an apse the lady chapel was the central of three radiating chapels.

Lady Day. The annunciation is mentioned in the Greek Church, in the fourth century, by the Council of Laodicea, and also in that called "in Trullo." They observed it like the Sundays in Lent, providing that if it fell on Maundy Thursday or Good Friday, fish and wine might be partaken of by the faithful. In the fifth century Proclus of Constantinople distinctly speaks of the festival. The 'Sacramentary' of Gregory calls it "the annunciation of the angel to Mary."

Lady Fast. A species of penance, voluntary or enjoined, in which the penitent had the choice of fasting once a week for seven years on that day of the week on which Lady Day happened to fall, beginning his course from that day,—or of finishing his penance sooner by taking as many fasting-days together as would amount to an entire year.

Lady Psalter. The Rosary.

Lamb. The symbol of Christ (Gen. iv. 4; Exod. xii. 3; xxix. 38; Is. xvi. 1; Jer. liii. 7; St. John i. 36; 1 St. Peter i. 19; Rev. xiii. 8), who was typified by the paschal lamb, the blood of which was set on the door-posts and lintel of the doors like a Tau cross, to redeem the Hebrews from destruction. In very old sepulchres the lamb stands on a hill amid the four rivers of Paradise, or in the Baptist's hand. It sometimes carries a milk-pail and crook, to represent the Good Shepherd. In the fifth century it is nimbed. In the fourth century its head is crowned with the cross and monogram. In the sixth century it bears a spear, the emblem of wisdom, ending in a cross; or appears, bleeding from five wounds, in a chalice. At last it is girdled with a gold zone of power and justice (Is. xi. 5), bears the banner-cross of the resurrection, or treads upon a serpent (Rev. xviii. 14). At length, in the eighth and ninth centuries, it lies on a throne amid angels and saints, as in the Apocalyptic vision. When fixed to a cross it formed the crucifix of the primitive Church, and therefore was afterwards added as the reverse of an actual crucifix, as on the stational cross of Velletri. In 692 the Council in Trullo ordered the image of the Saviour to be substituted for the lamb. Jesus is now the Shepherd to watch over His flock, as He was the Lamb, the victim for the sheep. (*See* EMBLEMS.) (2.) Walafrid Strabo condemns the practice of placing near or under the altar on Good Friday lamb's flesh, which received benediction and was eaten on Easter Day. Probably to this custom the Greeks alluded when they accused the Latins of offering a lamb on the altar at Mass in the ninth century. In ancient times the Pope and cardinals ate lamb on Easter Day. *See* ALTAR, EUCHARISTIC BREAD, and DISK.

Lammas Day. 1st or gule (feast) of August. St. Peter ad Vincula. From lamb tithing, lamb-mass : or loaf-mass, from the benediction of new bread-corn. A festival instituted by Pope Sixtus III., at the request of the Empress Eudoxia. Lammas lands are commons on which the parishioners have the right of pasturage, commencing on Lammas Day.

Lamps were often placed in graves of the catacombs as a symbol of the eternal light which the departed, it is hoped, enjoy,—a memorial of their shining lights before men and their future glory (St. Matt. xiii. 43). Some of them have the form of a little boat, and a few are inscribed with sacred emblems. These lamps are found in Italy, southern France, Egypt, and North Africa, but always of earthenware. Bronze specimens are much later, and bear only the cross or monogram. At York, near St. Helen's, in the wall, Camden records the discovery of a burning lamp in a tomb, and another was found, in 1833, at Baena, near Cordova. Some Norman stone lamps have been found at Romsey. At Lichfield, in 1194; at Salisbury, by Osmund's Custumal; at Hereford, in the time of Edward III., by bequest; and in all wealthy churches, by episcopal injunctions, in the thirteenth century, a perpetual lamp burned day and night before the high-altar. In the Constitutions of Oxford,

1222, a lamp is first mentioned. Usually, however, lights were placed in the standing candelabra upon the altar-step.

Lantern. *Phare* or *faneau*. (1.) A lamp on a shaft in French cemeteries, probably used during the time of Mass at the interment of persons of importance and rank. Niches for the dead-light remain in the east wall of Ashford and the north wall of the transept of Christ Church, Hants. These were lighted to direct the traveller, to dispossess the fearful passenger of alarm in traversing a churchyard, and to invite the prayers of those who went by for the departed. The Council of Elvira proscribed the use of lights in churchyards during the day-time. (2.) An open central tower of a church, as at Ely, Coutances, Lisieux, Evreux, Lincoln, and York, for showering down light on the choir or rood,—rare in France, rarer in Germany, and unknown in Spain, Scandinavia, and Sicily, where it is replaced by a dome. On great festivals an immense lamp was suspended from the vault of the tower of Beauvais 288 feet above the floor, and being hung about midway down, was visible at great distances from the city at night, symbolizing the true Light of the world—a beacon set upon God's high hill that could not be hid. At Edinburgh and Newcastle the crowns of the towers were illuminated, on festival eves, with coloured lamps, shedding every colour of the prism over tracery and arch. (3.) A turret of open work (Fr. *couronne*), usually octagonal, erected as a beacon on towers, as in the west front of Ely, at Boston, Nantwich, St. Ouen's, Rouen, Tours, Orleans, Valencia, Freiburg, Ghent, and the belfry of Chichester and other places. It is polygonal at St. Gereon's, Cologne. Octagonal lanterns also occur at St. Helen's, and All Saints', York. In the latter a beacon-lamp burned at night to guide the traveller through the Galtres forest; as at Lamborne, for the purpose of directing persons across the bleak downs in winter-time during storms, a bell was tolled. At Cartmel the central tower is low and square, and supports one of the same shape, set upon it diamond-wise. (4.) A lantern [bocca or botta] preceded the priest in carrying the Eucharist to the dying. A beautiful example of a lantern for oil and wax lights, of the fourteenth century, is preserved at Sienna. Portable lamps were carried in the procession of relics and in funerals. (5.) A small gallery, corbelled out and glazed, to

allow persons to be present at services unobserved, as at
Westminster, Worcester, St. Bartholomew's, Smithfield, and
St. Symphorian's, Tours. (6.) A stationary receptacle for a
light near the nuns' cloister-door at Romsey, which retains
its smoke-holes; and another on the stairs of the prior's
lodge at Gloucester, now the deanery, also with smoke-holes
and orifices once closed with horn. (7.) A low central tower,
as at Winchester, Romsey, Peterborough, Boxgrove, Ripon,
Coimbria, Burgos, Piacenza, Monza, Parma, and Asti. It is
octagonal at Caen, Bayeux, Evreux, Antwerp, Cologne,
Haarlem, Batalha, Burgos, Vercelli, and Pavia. In England
the fall of the lofty Norman towers of Worcester, Ely, Winchester, Lincoln, and Evesham no doubt deterred the erection
of similar towers. (8.) A prison, as at Lewes (from *latere*, to
lie hid). Archbishop Arundel tells William Thorpe he shall
be made as sure as any thief that is in the prison of Lantern.
Bocardo, Little Ease, the Gatehouse, and Lollard's Tower, at
St. Paul's, were also terms in common use.

Lapsi. (Fallen.) Apostates. During the Decian persecution
in the third century, when the discipline with regard to
these unhappy men was established, although there are not
wanting examples of earlier defection from the faith. Blas-
phemers openly abjured the creed, incense-burners offered
incense to idols, some sacrificers attended the heathen sacrifices, whilst others, called libellatici, bought attestations of
their relapse to paganism to save their lives, and traditores
surrendered the sacred books and plate, or betrayed the
names of the faithful. There were found persons who re-
lapsed without compulsion. Soldiers, says St. Cyprian, con-
quered without a fight. When the Church had peace, two
extreme opinions were held with regard to the treatment of
these men when they desired reconciliation on the cessation
of the persecution; the one urged total abandonment of
them, the other pleaded for their reception without penitence
or proof of their sincerity. A middle course was adopted;
their readmission after a course of penance proportionate to
the degree in which they had fallen. Members of the clergy
by the Council of Arles, however, were degraded from their
orders, and only in rare instances were they ever reinstated.
In many cases, however, the lapsed obtained libels or testi-
monials from martyrs before their suffering recommending

that they should be received back by the Church. These, however, became available only by the concurrence in their prayer on the part of the diocesan and other suffragans of a province.

Larder. The place where the lard for greasing boots and other purposes was kept in a monastery. Latterly the meat store.

Lardose. The reredos, a corruption of *arrière dos*.

Latten. (Fr. *laiton*.) A mixed metal, resembling copper or brass, gilt, known as Cologne plate, probably imported at first from the Low Countries and afterwards imitated by our own manufacturers. It was extensively used in medieval metal-work.

Lavatory. (1.) A place for washing the dead in the churches of Clugny, Lyons, Rouen, the Chartreux, and Citeaux, in the dioceses of Avranches and Bayonne. (2.) The conduit used by monks for washing their hands before dinner in the cloisters. It remains at Norwich and Westminster. Also a trough for the sacristans to wash the corporals and their hands, as at Chichester, Elgin, and Lincoln. In Spain the lavatory usually stands at the north-west or south-west angle of the cloister, as at Veruela.

Lay Brothers. The servants in a monastery; the Clugniacs wore albs which had not been blessed. Laymen (*laos*, a people) mean the people of God (St. Luke i. 17; Acts xv. 14, xviii. 10; Tit. ii. 14; Heb. ii. 17). The word is used in distinction to clergy by Origen, and generally about the third century. It then corresponds to the use of idiotes (1 Cor. xiv. 16); according to Zonaras and Theodoret, a private, in opposition to a leader or captain (1 Thess. v. 12; Heb. xiii. 17; 1 Tim. v. 17).

Lean-to. A sloping roof, one side of which, as in an aisle, is attached to a taller wall.

Lectern. (*Lectricium*, pulpitre.) A book-desk, which was placed either in the middle of the choir, or at the choir step, and used by the rectors of the choir; by the subdeacon for reading the Epistle at Hereford, for the Gospel according to Beleth, and generally for the Gradual Alleluia, and nine Lections on great festivals. It was of stone at Crowle, Wenlock, of the twelfth and thirteenth centuries, and Evesham *c.* 1218. At Gloucester, one in the north aisle was used to read out the story of Edward I. to the pilgrims visiting his tomb. At St. David's, that used by the bishop rests on the stand of a lectern of the sixteenth century. The stone lectern of Tattershall on the rood-loft faces east, and was probably used for the Gospel, as the Clugniacs, contrary to Cistercian use, also read it in this direction. Beleth says, when a priest was gospeller, he folded his chasuble on the shoulder, to show that he was acting as a deacon. Sometimes the lecterns for the gospeller and epistolar were port· able, and placed in the ambo, or rood-loft. Sometimes the lectern had only one desk for the legendary, and sometimes two for the choir books. In France they were usually of simple form, one at Narbonne, of the thirteenth century, of iron, combining firmness and lightness, has a stand of copper; another, of the fifteenth century, with double legs, is in the Museum, Clugny; and a third, of the same material, is in St. Esteban, Burgos. There is an enormous ancient lectern, with four sides and cresting, at Zamora. At Sens there is an apparel of tissue for the lectern, of the tenth or eleventh century. There are fine specimens of lecterns at Wells (c. 1660), Ditling, Bury, Hunts (decorated), Ramsey, St. Thomas (Exeter), Trinity Church (Coventry), Yeovil, Eton, Campden, King's College (Cambridge), Merton College (Oxford), St. Chad's, Birmingham (formerly at Louvain), Tirlemont (of copper), Hal (with an eagle, of the fifteenth century), Aix-la-Chapelle (of the fourteenth century, an eagle), and Leon. They sometimes rest on lions. (*See* EAGLE and PELICAN.) At St. Ouen's (Rouen), formerly in the cloister, were to be seen two ranges of lecterns, one of wood the other of stone, erected between the vaulting shafts, used by the religious when reading in cloister time. The abbot's desk was distinguished by a carved frontal, or capital.

Lectionary. The book containing the Epistles and lessons read at Mass; called also the Apostolus, because most of the lessons were taken from St. Paul's Epistles; and Comes the collection compiled by St. Jerome, and so called the priest's companion. The Greeks had lectionaries of epistles and gospels, called Apostolevangelia, or Synaxaria, books of the Holy Communion. St. Matthew is read from Whit Monday to the Friday after the sixteenth Sunday after

Trinity; then St. Mark is used; St. Luke is begun on the eighteenth Sunday after Trinity, and St. John at Easter.

Legate. The Pope's deputy. (1.) Legate a latere, a cardinal armed with almost pontifical power, such as Othobon and Otho had, who called national Synods in England, in the thirteenth century; and Cardinals Wolsey and Pole. (2.) *Legatus natus,* a legate without creation, and *ex officio,* as the Archbishop of Canterbury was, from the year 1195 till the Reformation. The one relic of this office is, his power of giving Lambeth degrees. (3.) *Legatus datus,* a special legate, who could hold councils, confirm canons, depose bishops, and issue interdicts. The Councils of London (712), and Cealcythe were legatine. In the time of Henry I. it was agreed that no legate could be received without the Royal sanction. Cardinal Beaufort exercised legatine power. In 1371 no primate or archbishop was allowed to carry his crozier in the presence of a legate. (4.) A mortuary.

Legends. (*Legenda,* lesson.) The lections at Matins; as they contained some unauthenticated traditions and acts of saints and martyrs, the word came to mean vain stories. Usually the word designates a portion of Holy Scripture read and not chanted (hence its name) in Divine service. The reading of lections alternated with psalmody, during nocturns in the East, at least in the fourth century, as appears by the Council of Laodicea. Generally, however, after every nocturn a history, or chapter of the Old or New Testament was read. St. Augustine shows that they were definitely fixed for every season in the year. St. Chrysostom mentions the reading of the Acts of the Apostles, from the fourth century, after the Psalms. In the seventh century, it appears, by the Third Council of Constantinople, that the Greeks substituted the acts of martyrs; a course followed by the Latins in the ninth century, along with homilies of the Fathers. Then, also, the form used by the reader, "Jube domne benedicere" (Sir, give me a blessing), was introduced. In the twelfth century the response after the lesson, "Lord have mercy upon us," was added. In early times, as we learn from St. Ambrose and St. Augustine, the deacon prefaced the lection with a loud cry of "Silence!" or "Attend!" Amalarius adds, that he used the sign of the Cross. (2.) *Capitula,* or little chapters, were shorter lessons used in the day hours;

they date from the fifth century, and the Council of Agde (506); but then longer lessons were also read in the daytime. On feasts of nine lections at Lichfield, the chapter and collect were read out of the last stall on the east. At Canterbury and Wells, the lessons are now read from the stalls.

Lent. Spring; so called in German, Russian, and Dansk, with the same meaning, but in the East called the Fast; it is the Greek *tessarakoste*, and Latin *quadragesima*, both meaning forty (days); and in French, by a corruption, *carême*. Tertullian, SS. Epiphanius, Augustine, Jerome, and Pope Leo contend for an Apostolical origin for Lent, in conformity with the fasts of Moses, Elias, and our Lord (Exod. xxiv. 18; 1 Kings xix. 18). SS. Basil and Gregory of Nyssa mention it as of universal observance; and in the time of Hippolytus Sundays were the only exception to the total fast. Sozomen says that six weeks were fasted by the Illyrians, Egyptians, Libyans, and Syrians; seven at Constantinople, and the countries as far as Phœnicia; others kept three weeks at intervals, or only the three preceding Easter. Charlemagne mentions, that to make up the forty days, those who observed it from Septuagesima omitted Sundays, Thursdays, and Saturdays; if from Sexagesima, Sundays and Thursdays; if from Quadragesima, Sundays, and Maundy Thursday and Easter Eve. Water even was not drunk until after nones, according to Prudentius; except in the case of the sick, as St. Jerome says. At noon in the East, in the fourth century, dry fruits were eaten in addition to bread and pulse, called by the Council of Laodicea xerophagy, dry food; a practice which had prevailed in the West from the second century, and in the Greek Church lasted till the twelfth century in certain places; but in the seventh century the Western Church began to eat cooked vegetables, fish, and water birds, and was imitated in the East. Lent was observed only by the clergy at first, by the decree of Telesphorus. In the second and third century Lent began on the Monday after Quinquagesima, and ended on Maundy Thursday, Saturdays and Sundays being excepted by the Easterns. In the fourth century, at Rome and in other places, Thursdays were not fasted, according to a decree of Pope Melchiades, who, in order to complete a fast of forty days, added Sexagesima; in like manner, Septuagesima was added by the Greeks, when they adopted the exceptional days of the Latins. The Council of Laodicea decreed the keeping of Lent from Monday after Quadragesima Sunday until Easter Eve. Beleth says, the Clergy added two days, and commenced the fast on Quinquagesima: that Popes Melchiades and Sylvester antedated it to Sexagesima, because two meals were eaten on Saturdays; and that Septuagesima was finally observed in lieu of the weekly celebration of Thursdays. Gregory the Great first introduced, it is said, the modern usage of beginning Lent on Ash-Wednesday; but, in point of fact, he says that it began on the Sunday after, and so, subtracting six days, only thirty-six days were fasted. This discipline lasted until the ninth century, as Amalarius says; and the Eighth Council of Toledo conceives existed in all churches of the West, which adopted the Pope's mystical view of Lent as a tithe of the year. In the eleventh century, Ash-Wednesday was taken as the first day in Lent, thus adding four days to make up the forty; but, even now, the rite of Milan commences Lent on the Sunday following. The Greeks and Westerns never celebrated festivals on fasting days in Lent, but commemorated them on Saturday or Sunday, according to the Council of Laodicea. The Latins, by the Tenth Council of Toledo, transferred the feasts; and the Greeks, who did not acquiesce in this rule, nevertheless omitted the fast on such days. Until the sixth century Saturdays were not fasted in the West; but then the Councils of Agde and Fourth Orleans excepted only Sundays. The East still preserves its old tradition. In Russia, monks who keep Lent rigorously, eat only the ANTIDORON. At Lyons and Milan festivals were only commemorated during Holy Week.

Letters Ecclesiastical. (Memorial, dismissory, decretal, pastoral, confessional, commonitory, circular.) Before taking a journey, the primitive Christians presented themselves to their bishop, and received from him letters testimonial, contessaratio hospitalitatis (as Tertullian says), by which they were recommended for communion and entertainment to Christian communities. The Apostolical Constitutions sentenced excommunication on those who received any strangers without this passport and certificate. St. Paul alludes to it in 2 Cor. iii. 1. The practice was indispensable in times of danger, as a precaution; it also cemented the unity of the Episcopate, and the whole Church; from this circumstance they were called pacific, or irenic. In order to preclude fraud by heretics, the Council of Nicæa directed that they should be countersigned with the letters P(ater), U(ios), A(gion) P(neuma), the initials of the three Persons of the Holy Trinity. In the West, by the I. Council of Orleans, the bishops sealed them with their episcopal ring. COMMUNICATORY letters, or letters of SALUTATION, were read publicly in church from the ambon; and the Epistles of St. Paul, except that addressed to the Hebrews, were of this character, being sent from one to the other by the churches (Gal. iv. 16). St. Chrysostom alludes to LETTERS OF PEACE; and Eusebius gives several examples of such correspondence. The letters given to ecclesiastics were called FORMAL in the Council of Carthage (397), CANONICAL in the Council of Laodicea, ECCLESIASTICAL by St. Jerome, because written in a conventional form, which did not admit of counterfeits, and were signed and sealed in a peculiar manner, like the bulls of later date. COMMENDATORY LETTERS, mentioned by the Council of Chalcedon, were given to persons of high distinction. In ancient days readers or subdeacons acted as envoys to carry ecclesiastical letters from one bishop to another, and in delicate cases a priest was employed; and to this day, in Apulia, bishops send their correspondence to the clergy by the hands of clerks.

Library. There were noble libraries at Lichfield, and the Grey Friars, London. Adjoining the monastic library the copyists had cells from the twelfth century. An aumbry with shelves, a chamber having a door opening on the cloister, contained the ordinary books in use for readers during cloister time; and another almery near the altar held the gospels, epistles, and choir song-books. The monastic *librarii*, writers of books, called amanuenses (from *manus*, the hand), or antiquaries (transcribers of old books), which they repaired, used a stylus, or pointed bodkin, and pens contained in a case, to which an inkstand was attached. They formed a numerous class, as the sale of MSS. was no less productive than the multiplication of service books for the use of the community was indispensable. Those who added miniatures, rich borders, and initials in colour, and burnished gilding, were called illuminators.

Licence of Marriage. An episcopal dispensation permitting a marriage to be solemnized without publication of banns, dating certainly from the fourteenth century and confirmed by 25 Hen. VIII. c. 21. A special licence, not subject to these restrictions, is granted by the Archbishop of Canterbury, originally his privilege as Legatus Natus of the Pope, but now confirmed by the marriage act of 1836.

Lichgate, The. (*Lich*, the dead.) Called *Trim train* or *trams, i.e.* "adjust the procession;" in Devon, Cornwall, Wales, and in Hereford, the scallage (from *scallus*, Low Latin, a bench). An old lychgate remains at Stanley St. Leonard's. It was used as a covering for the funeral procession when awaiting the arrival of the priest, or arranging the pall and order of the followers. Examples consisting of three arches and an upper gallery occur at Lampaul, and other places in Finisterre, and possibly served also as preaching tribunes, or places of proclamation of notices when there was no open-air pulpit. The litten, or lichtun, at Marwell and Chichester, as in Lichfield, means a cemetery.

Liernes. Ribs crossing each other and meeting in the keystone, which appear in vaults of the later part of the fifteenth century.

Light. (1.) Space between mullions or tracery, a pane in a cloister. (2.) Joys of Paradise, as in the prayer for the departed, and the inscription on tombs of early Christians, "Grant them perpetual light." (3.) The Holy Communion was always celebrated with lights (Acts xx. 8) in memory of the Light of the World (St. John i. 9, viii. 12; Rev. xxi. 23), without whom we stumble at midday as in the night. There were usually two (Rev. xi. 4) on the altar, but others of indeterminate numbers in different churches were lighted round and above the altar (Rev. iv. 5; Exod. xxv. 37), and on the step; but at Chichester there were ordinarily three, and on greater festivals seven altar-lights. (*See* CANDLES.) In 1276 one, at least, and that of wax, was required by Bishop Bleys with the lamp, and by English canons of 1322. Albertis says the candles, ranged in line, and each of four fingers in length, should be graduated in height from the sides of the altar; a seventh taper behind the cross being added at a pontifical Mass, and the foot of the cross, which was raised on a stem, on a level with the bowls of the nearest candlesticks. (4.) In the fourteenth century private persons often founded a perpetual light to burn before the high-altar, in token that the Church was ever watching (Exod. xxiv. 2; St. Matt. xxv. 7). Cardinal Pole in 1555 required it in every church. In foreign countries there was, Frances says, a similar light before the reliquaries, in allusion to St. Matt. v. 15, 16; Phil. ii. 15. (5.) One light was carried before the Gospel on common days, in memory of St. John the Baptist (St. John v. 35), and on festivals in allusion to the two witnesses, Enoch and Elias. (6.) Mourners at funerals carried a light in one hand, and in the other the offering made after the Gospel had been read.

Limina Vistanda. The obligation laid on all prelates and abbots to visit the apostolical threshold, that is, St. Peter's, Rome, by Pope Anacletus, and renewed by Pope Sixtus in 1585, who enacted times proportionate to the distance of the pilgrim from Rome; that is, from once in three years to once in ten. Pope Benedict XIV. restricted the former term to Italians, and directed that Ultramontanes should visit once in every fifth, and Americans and others once in every tenth year. The Limina were the steps at the entrance of the Confession.

Limitour. A friar who had a certain limit or district assigned him by his convent within which to beg.

Limoges Work. Enamel. The city was a Roman colony, and long eminent for the skill of its inhabitants as goldsmiths and enamellers; the latter trade is traceable back to the tenth century. The effigy of Walter de Merton, at Rochester, and William de Valence, at Westminster, were, in their perfect state, remarkable specimens of this ornamentation.

Lions in marble or bronze are carved at the entrances of cathedrals as emblems of Christian strength, vigilance, force, and courage, as at Rome, Mans, Placentia, Reggio, Bologna, and Foligno. They appear in the twelfth century. One guards the entrance of the pulpit of Wolverhampton, and they often appear at the feet of lecterns and paschal candlesticks. When the lion holds a figure, it typifies the gentleness of the Church to neophytes; when the figure is apparently torn by its claws, her severity is symbolized.

Litanies. (Gr.; Rogations, Lat.) In the fourth century public and private devotions, but eventually public supplications for God's favour and deprecations of His wrath. In the commentary of the pseudo-Ambrose, the procession day is spoken of. Sozomen mentions the procession at Constantinople, instituted by St. Chrysostom with antiphonal chanting and silver standards of the Cross and burning wax tapers. In the East, before the time of St. Basil, litanies were in use. The word litany is first mentioned by Eusebius, St. Chrysostom, and the Emperors Justinian and Arcadius. There were two kinds: (1) general, ordered by the Church, prescribed and ordinarily called Stated Litanies; (2) special or particular, extraordinary, commanded by a bishop according to occasion, and known as Imperatæ. There was a further division into major and minor, the former made through the city streets as a public solemnity, the latter made through the close, cloisters, and interior of a church. Some were sorrowful, deprecations of God's wrath in time of plague or distress, the others joyous, as commemorations of deliverance and thanksgiving. Some say the major litanies were made on St. Mark's Day, and the minors on the Rogation days. Gregory the Great instituted, on April 25th, the greater litany as an annual device, as he had enjoined the septiform procession of seven orders—the clergy, abbots and monks; abbesses and nuns; boys; lay persons; widows; married women, who issued simultaneously to traverse Rome during a flood and pestilence. It bore the name of the Black Crosses, because the crosses and altars were veiled in black, and the members of the procession wore sable mourning. Walafrid Strabo calls this the Great Litany. At the head the cross was carried, and in France bare feet, ashes, and haircloth were prescribed. This order was maintained to invoke God's blessing on the blossoms and fruits of the early summer, according to Amalarius and Albinus, and as major litanies in Charlemagne's "Capitulars", and the Councils of Mayence, 813, and Orleans, 515, expressly mention rogations. The lesser litany has been referred to Mamertus, c. 465, or Claudian, bishop of Vienna, but Apollinarius Sidonius, his contemporary, states that Mamertus only established in a definite form, with fasting, psalm, and prayer, and on the stated three days before the Ascension, a practice hitherto irregular and rare.

2 A

St. Augustine certainly speaks of the Rogations of the
Three Days. The reform of Mamertus was adopted by the
Church of Spain, but observed in autumn and in Whitsun-
week, conformably to the law of the Church which forbade
fast between Easter and Pentecost. In the English Church
rogations before the Ascension were used from the coming
of St. Augustine, who entered Canterbury chanting a verse
from those of Lyons. Beleth says on each of the first two
days a dragon, swollen in body and with a long tail, was
carried before the cross and banners, and on the last behind
them, to typify the broken power of the devil. In 1747 the
English observed the greater litany after the use of Rome on
the seventh of the kalends of May, and also the three rogation
days before the Ascension, according to their ancestral custom. Charlemagne, it is said by the Council of Mayence,
had the Roman litany observed in France on St. Mark's
Day, May 25th ; and Pope Leo III., 795–816, introduced the
Gallican litany of the rogations at Rome ; and it must be
observed that the latter was called the minor at Rome and
the major in France. The litany with candles on the Purification was instituted by Pope Sergius. The plain Litany
was that on which the invocations were often repeated. At
Orleans, on Maundy Thursday, the Grand Penitentiary
headed a procession of penitents who made the circuit of the
choir on their knees, two and two, their faces veiled, and
their bodies covered with sheets, and singing litanies. The
litany was sung on Easter Eve, before the altar, St. Mark's
Day, the Rogation Days, and Wednesdays and Fridays in
Lent, and at Salisbury, on every weekday in the latter
season ; the septiform litany being chanted by six choristers
in surplices on Holy Saturday—the litany in this case, as
at Rome by the Gelasian Sacramentary of the fifth century,
not being confined to a season of humiliation. The septiform litany was also used at Paris, Lyons, and Soissons.
Sometimes seven subdeacons chanted the septiform, and
there were also quinal and ternal litanies for three or five
singers. At Laon and Mans the septenal litany derived its
title from the repetition of each saint's name seven times.

Litre. A band of black paint charged with arms, and placed
in a chantry chapel, round the walls, as a sign of mourning.
It was not to exceed two feet in breadth.

Little Hours. Prime, Tierce, Sext, and Nones.

Liturgy. (Gr. *leitourgia*.) Public offices of religion, and specially the Eucharistic rite foreshadowed (Prov. ix. 5 ; Mal. i. 11). The variations in liturgies are due to several causes ; the privilege used by the early patriarchs and bishops of drawing up the diocesan use, as St. Hilary of Poictiers even in the fourth century drew up a local sacramentary ; the custom, before the second century, of learning and saying by heart great portions which were never committed to writing ; and also the numerous alterations, modifications, and reviews to which they have been submitted before reaching ourselves. The Apostles, also, probably did not restrict themselves to the essential rite. Justin Martyr, *c.* 140, describes the liturgy of his day as embracing the reading of the Acts or Writings of the Apostles, a sermon by the bishop, prayer made standing, the offering of the elements with prayer and thanksgiving, the communion, and transmission of the elements to the absent by the hands of the deacons. The liturgy was always celebrated in the language of the country, in Syriac or Chaldee in Jerusalem ; in Greek at Antioch and Alexandria ; in Latin, in the West ; " Every man praying and praising God in his own tongue," says Origen, " for God is the Lord of all languages, hearing each people as if they used but one and the same language." The Coptic or Egyptian, the Armenian, the Ethiopian languages were used in their respective countries. In Illyria, England, Gaul, Africa, Spain, and Pannonia,—Latin, then the universal language, at an early date was adopted. But nations recently converted used their own tongue, as the Sclaves in the ninth century by permission of John VIII., and the Chinese in the seventeenth century, by grant of Paul V. Liturgies, however, did not follow the modifications in their primitive language, which has been retained unchanged, so that the old national wording still forms an almost hieratic form, as is the case with a not inconsiderable portion of the English PrayerBook.

There are five primitive liturgies : I. St. James', of Antioch or Jerusalem, branching into the (1) Clementine or apostolic, (2) Cæsarean or St. Basil's ; the latter subdivided into that of St. Chrysostom's and the Armenian ; and (3) of Jerusalem or St. James'. II. Alexandrine or St. Mark's, from which are derived (1) St. Cyril's, (2) St. Gregory's, (3) Coptic. III. The

Oriental or St. Thaddeus'. IV. St. Peter's or Roman. V. Ephe-
sine, St. Paul's or St. John's; the latter again divided into the
Gothic, Mozarabic, and Gallican. From the mixture of these
with the Roman sprang, with addition of new rites, (1) the
Ambrosian, still in use at Milan; and (2) the Patriarchine or
Aquileian. The liturgy of St. James is at least fourteen centuries old, and is not only mentioned by the Council of Constantinople, 691, but traceable in the writings of St. Jerome,
St. Chrysostom, St. Cyril of Jerusalem, and Theodoret.
The Clementine is represented in the Apostolical Constitutions of the third or fourth century. St. Chrysostom's is
used in Russia to this day. The Alexandrine can be traced
back to the second century; it received modifications by St.
Cyril. The Roman is substantially one with the three Papal
Sacramentaries of the fifth and sixth centuries. The Ephesine was replaced by that of St. Chrysostom in the fourth
century, as appears by the Council of Laodicea, but was the
foundation of those of Spain, England, and France; in
France, until the time of Charlemagne, and revised by St.
Hilary of Poictiers, Musæus, priest of Marseilles, or Sidonius
Apollinaris; and in Spain, in the pontificate of Gregory VII.;
and it has been preserved at Toledo from the sixteenth century. In England St. Augustine modified the old use by
changes derived from a ritual of the South of France of the
fifth century; having been revised by St. Osmund of Salisbury in 1085, it became for a few years the use of all
England in the sixteenth century, and the basis of that
which we now possess. The communion in both kinds to
the laity certainly had not ceased in the twelfth century, and
probably was not forbidden till after the Council of Constance in 1415. The Eastern liturgies have a distinct invocation of the Holy Ghost at the consecration of the elements
which the Western have not. The Western and that of St.
John have varying gospels and epistles; the Eastern have
not. Those of St. James, St. Mark, and St. Thaddeus have
only one preface for every day in the year. The Mozarabic,
Gallican, and Ambrosian have a different one; the Roman
has several for every festival. The liturgy consists of two
parts, (1) the Proanaphora, including the Mass of catechumens and Mass of the faithful; (2) the Anaphora, comprising
the great Eucharistic prayer, the consecration, intercession

for quick and dead, and communion. Proanaphora (before the oblation) I. (1.) The Mass of the catechumens includes the prefatory prayer, introit, little entrance, trisagion lections, and prayer after the Gospel; (2) the Mass of the faithful consists of prayers of the faithful, the great entrance offertory, kiss of peace, and the Creed. Anaphora II. (1.) The great Eucharistic prayer includes the preface, triumphal hymn, prayer, commemoration of our Lord's life, and the institution; (2) the consecration contains the words of institution, oblation, prayer of invocation of the Holy Ghost, prayer for change of the elements; (3) the great intercession includes prayer for quick and dead, prayer before the Lord's Prayer, the embolismus; (4) the communion comprises the ectene or prayer of intense adoration, sancta sanctis, elevation of the Host, the fraction, the confession, the communion, the antidoron, the thanksgiving, and dismissal. The Western liturgies consist of two portions: I. Ordinary (which was prefaced in the sacristy by the Veni Creator, the collect "Almighty God to whom all Hearts be Open," the XLIII. Psalm, lesser litany, and Lord's Prayer) comprising the office or introit, sung in going to the altar, confession and absolution, the kiss of peace given by the celebrant to deacon and subdeacon, the Gloria in Excelsis, sung while incense was offered, the mutual salutation, the collect, epistle, and gospel, preceded by the gradual, the Nicene Creed, the offertory, oblation of the elements, and secret prayer. II. The canon, including the apostolical versicles, the proper preface, the ter sanctus, the prayer of consecration, the Lord's Prayer, a prayer for deliverance from evil, the Agnus Dei, the mixture of the chalice, the kiss of peace, the communion, the prayer of thanksgiving, post-communion collect, ablutions and dismissal. In the times of St. Augustine and St. Chrysostom, and in Gaul and Italy, the communion Ps. xxxiv. 8 was sung during the administration (see COMMUNION), and at that time, in 1549, passages from the Holy Scripture were chanted in England. (See ADMINISTRATION.) Pope Adrian, 777, is related to have decided on the respective merits of the Gregorian and Ambrosian liturgies by laying them on the high-altar of St. Peter's, sealed with seven bishops' seals, at night, whilst the doors were shut, and prayer was made for a sign from heaven. In the morning both were found open; but the Gregorian book leaves were blown all over the church, whilst the Ambrosian lay still. The decision was that St. Gregory's book should be used throughout the world, and the Ambrosian only in his own church. The Ambrosian was also observed by the Cistercian order. St. Chrysostom's liturgy is used in the four patriarchates and Russia on all Sundays in Lent except Palm Sunday, or Maundy Thursday, eves of Christmas, Easter, and Epiphany, and St. Basil's Day, January 1st, when St. Basil's liturgy is said. The liturgy of St. James, older than either, is used on St. James's Day in some islands of the Archipelago. The Jacobites, Ethiopians, Melchites, and Armenians have peculiar liturgies, all grounded on that of St. Mark. *See* MASS.

Livery. (1.) That which is given out; the dress of the members of a guild or convent. (2.) Liberations; certain portion of meat, drink, money, and clothing delivered at certain times to almsfolk.

Locker. A smaller aumbry for ornaments of the altar in a church wall.

Lodge, Abbot's. This house usually adjoined the west end as at Westminster and Dunstable; sometimes the north-east part of the cloister, like the prior's lodge at Worcester and Durham; the site of the prior's rooms, when he was a subordinate, was usually on the north-east or south-west part of the great cloister.

Loft. A gallery or upper room; the ordinary refectory at Durham.

Lombardics. Uncial letters used in marginal sepulchral inscriptions, each letter at first being of brass inlaid in the stone, but soon after, in the fourteenth century, engraved on brass plates, when the capitals of the style only were retained; these in their turn disappeared in the sixteenth century when Arabic numerals came into use.

Longobardic. The style of Italian architecture which prevailed from the sixth to the ninth century, at length was superseded by the Lombardic, the old churches being rebuilt as Italy increased in wealth. The valleys of the Po and Rhine, we must remember, belonged to the same empire from the time of Charlemagne downwards, and the same style prevailed in both districts, and the churches were almost identical. The Lombardic was well defined in the eleventh and lasted until the thirteenth century. It affected Rhineland in the tenth, and France and England in the twelfth century.

Louvre. A small turret, with apertures for the escape of smoke from the central fire in a hall. Louvre boards, crossbars like Venetian blinds, set in windows as a kind of open shutter. At York Minster the wind blowing through them is said to produce a soft aerial music. Instead of these we should have sound-holes.

Lord's Prayer, The, was ordered to be used at baptism in the Greek Church in the fourth century; at Matins and Vespers by the Councils of Gerona and IV. Toledo, three times a day by the Apostolical Constitutions; and at the Eucharist, according to St. Augustine, St. Jerome, St. Cyril of Jerusalem, and St. Chrysostom. In the Greek and Gallican Churches the priest and people recited it together. By the Roman use the priest alone said it; the English Church uses it in both these ways. In the Mozarabic liturgy the people answer Amen to every petition said by the priest. The Doxology occurs only in St. Matthew's Gospel, and has been supposed to have been introduced into it from the Liturgy. Similar cases are pointed out in the Epistle to the Hebrews (Eph. v. 14, and Rev. iv. 8). It is an old English custom to rise when the Lord's Prayer is read in the second lesson.

Low-side Windows. Small shuttered windows, slightly above the ground level, and usually on the south-west angle of the chancel, for the most part an appendage of an ankerhold; but also added for purposes of ventilation; for communicating with lazars, or persons afflicted with contagious disease; for ringing the sanctus bell where there was no belloot; and used by the friars for confessing penitents. They are rare before the thirteenth century, and were provided with shutters, which could only be opened from within. The earliest examples exist at Caistor, North Hincksey, and St. Giles (Northampton); at Landewednack, in Cornwall a rude block of stone was placed on the outside for a person to stand on. In some instances windows at the east ends of the nave are placed at a lower level than the rest, in order to permit outsiders to see a particular altar. *See* ANKERHOLD and CONFESSIONAL.

Luminare Cryptæ. The shaft for light in a catacomb.

Lup. A black sapphire.

Lustres of Glass. Used in French churches of the seventeenth century, instead of crowns of light.

Magi. The wise men of the East, usually represented as three before the time of Pope Leo. Sometimes four, or only two appear. St. Chrysostom says there were twelve. The ordinary names attributed to the three "kings of Cologne," as they are called from their shrine in that cathedral, are Apellius, Amerus, and Damascus; or Magalath, Galgalath, and Saracin; or Ator, Sator, and Paratoras; or usually Baltazar, Melchior, and Jaspar. On mosaics generally their offerings are a crown of gold (the confession of Christ's royalty), a dish of myrrh (significant of His anointing to burial), and incense, in the shape of a dove (testimony to His Godhead).

Manchet. A small loaf. The name of the wafer in the Mass in the sixteenth century.

Maniple. An appendage of dress, introduced when the use of the stole as a handkerchief fell into desuetude. It now represents the cord with which our Lord was bound to the pillar at His scourging. At Peterborough some maniples were ornamented with little bells and silver acorns. *See* FANON.

Manuaries. Consecrated gloves given to pilgrims.

Manse. (1.) A parsonage, ordered in 1222 to be built near every Scottish church for the reception of the ordinary by the vicars. (2.) The country house used by monks and canons as a convalescent hospital, or for keeping manor-courts.

Mansionarii. (1.) Resident churchwardens in early times, who acted as sacrists and allotted graves. (2.) Clergy assistant to the Pontiff when officiating in a station-church. (3.) Porters, called coliberti in the East, basilicani in Spain, and æditui at Milan. *See* VICARS.

Mantelet. A long cape, with slits for the arms, worn by prelates. Regular bishops wore it without the rochet; and cardinals, vested in rochet and mozzetta, lay it aside when visiting another of their order. The mantellone is a purple cloak with long hanging sleeves. At York certain vicars wore red mantles in the fourteenth century.

Mark's, St., Day. April 25. The day, in commemoration of his martyrdom and the translation of his relics to Venice from Alexandria, was not observed in the Latin Church until the end of the seventh century, and was for the first time formally required to be kept by the Council of Cognac, in the middle of the thirteenth century.

Maronites. A Christian community in the Libanus. The secular clergy are married; the regulars follow the rule of St. Anthony. The bishops are celibates, and their patriarch —who is always styled Peter, and of Antioch—resides in the Convent of Canobiu. In 1736 they formally acknowledged the Canons of Trent in the Synod of Marhanna; they therefore now receive only in one kind, but have retained the Syriac language at Mass, and the priest reads the Gospel in Arabic. Their chant and instrumental music are of a primitive kind. Gregory XIII. founded a Maronite college at Rome.

Marriage of Priest. Pius II. qualified his assertion that marriage was taken from priests with great reason, by adding that it should be restored for causes still weightier. In the East the clergy were allowed to marry within ten years after ordination until the close of the ninth century. Now priests may be married at the time of ordination, but are forbidden a second wife. Bishops must be monks. Syricius first made constitutions for the celibacy of the clergy, and Innocent I. revived it. Gregory I. ordered subdeacons not to marry. Until the end of the seventh century, and the Council of Quinisext forbade it, the African bishops were married. St. Gregory Nazianzen was the son of a bishop, St. Patrick of a deacon, Pope Agapetus of a priest, SS. Cyprian, Basil, and St. Gregory Nyssen were all married men; so were Felix IV. and Adrian II., and several other bishops. Married clergy are mentioned by Socrates, St. Ambrose, and St. Athanasius, and the rejection of their ministrations was forbidden by canon law and the Council of Gangra in 384. The Third Council of Carthage, in 397, mentions the children of clergy, and as late as the sixth century the clergy were married, as appears by an observation of Gratian, who, like John à Ludegna at the Council of Trent, maintained that celibacy was not enjoined by Evangelical law. In 1076 the Council of Winchester, under Lanfranc (whose son is said to have been Abbot Paul of St. Alban's), imposed it; and Anselm —like Stephen IX., in 1059, and Gregory VII. (Hildebrand) had done in 1073, and St. Dunstan endeavoured to achieve— ordered the clergy to part with their wives or their livings. In Lombardy, France, Germany, and Spain the clergy protested against this cruel tyranny, but in 1097 the Council of Piacenza re-enforced it. In 970 the Northumbrian priests were married. Boniface, Archbishop of Canterbury, was married; and Bishop Fitzjocelyn of Wells, and Bishop Peche of Lichfield were bishops' sons. Anselm, in 1102, forbade the marriage of the clergy. The unacknowledged wives of the clergy continued down to the period of the Reformation. In 1281 the Constitutions of Peckham provided that priests' sons should not succeed to their fathers' livings without Papal dispensation.

Marriage, Rites of, are first described by Isidore of Seville in the seventh century, and by Pope Nicholas in 861. The bride and bridegroom, being come into church, offered gifts by the hand of the priest, and received the benediction and "heavenly veil." They then left the church wearing on their heads crowns, which were preserved in the church. (*See* GARLAND.) The betrothal-ring was given at the espousals. In the ancient Church, gifts (*arrhæ*) were made, together with a solemn kiss and the settlement of a dowry, by the man, at the time of the espousals, in the presence of witnesses. At the marriage, the priest united their hands and gave them the benediction. The woman's hair was unloosed; the bride was covered with a nuptial veil, except in the case of re-marriage, as a symbol of modesty or of obedience to her husband, and the twain were united by a fillet of white and purple thread, in token of their being one flesh. Lights were used at marriages, and doles were made to the poor. Women came bareheaded in the time of the Tudors, with bagpipes and fiddlers before them, to be married, and would enter only by the great church-door. In some places they carried wheat-sheaves on their heads; and casting of corn in their faces, with shouts of "Plenty, plenty," was practised. Marriage was prohibited, out of reverence, on high festivals, during Ember weeks, from Advent to the octave of Epiphany, from Septuagesima to Pentecost, by the Council of Eanham, 1009; from Advent to the octave of Epiphany, from Septua-

gesima to the octave of Easter, as times specially solemn or
to be fasted ; and for fourteen days before St. John the Baptist's day, by the Council of Seligenstadt, in 1022 ; but Durandus says in his time three weeks were prohibited, and Beleth
says they were relics of a summer Lent; in Lent, on Christmas, Easter, and Ascension Days; and during Eastertide,
by the Council of Dublin, 1631. The Clementine decretals
and the Sarum use interdicted the time between Rogation
and Trinity Sunday. There was formerly a fast of forty
days, it must be borne in mind, before St. John the Baptist's
Day, and another from Martinmas (Nov. 11) to Christmas.

Martyrologies. A kind of legend read as lections in churches,
and containg the victories of martyrs ; another class of such
narratives is the ' Lives of the Saints.' They correspond to
the ' Menologion' of the Greeks, which was drawn up by
Symeon Metaphrastes. The principal compilers in the West
were Ado of Trèves, Ven. Bede, and Usuardus, in the time
of Charlemagne. Such records were kept in Italian, Gaul-
ish, and Spanish churches, and at Cordova in the time of
Theodosius. Pope Clement instituted seven ecclesiastical
regionary notaries, called from districts assigned to them by
Pope Damasus ; and Pope Fabian added seven deacons and
seven subdeacons as their overseers in writing these acts,
which were preserved in the Church by order of Pope An-
therus, and read on the birthdays of martyrs, that is, on the
day of their suffering, which was their birthday to the new
life. Churches communicated their acts to each other; the
earliest are those of the martyrdom of St. Polycarp, and of
the martyrs of Lyons and Vienne. St. Gregory, in the sixth
century, says, " We possess the names of nearly all the
martyrs in one book, their passions being arranged under
days," probably alluding to the Latin version of Eusebius by
St. Jerome. The Martyrology of Rome was the model of similar compositions in the churches of Smyrna, Vienne, Lyons,
and Carthage. They gave rise to many spurious histories,
itineraries, and acts of apostles and saints, such as those
mentioned by Tertullian, St. Jerome, and St. Athanasius;
indeed Gelasius I., in the Council of Rome (494), distinctly
says that the Church, with singular caution, would not read
certain martyrologies in public of ancient custom, because
the names of the authors were unknown, and their authen-

ticity questionable; and the Sixth Council in Trullo decreed that such writings should be burned. (*See* LEGENDS.) Churches,·besides their own special calendars, had a book containing the acts of other confessors and martyrs, so that on the anniversary of their death the story might be read out in church; and this was the origin of martyrologies. A calendar contained merely the name of the saint, the date of his death, and the day of his commemoration; but a martyrology embraced a notice of his family, the place and date of his suffering, and the name of his judge. All churches had calendars, but very few had a complete martyrology of their own. Eusebius calls it a collection (synagoge) of ancient martyrs.

Masonry. Pre-Norman, Saxon, or Danish. Long and short work in quoins and jambs; blocks laid alternately flat and upright, the latter being the longer. Early Norman, Ashlar with wide joints of mortar; opus reticulatum, diamond-work, square stones laid angularly; herringbone, stones laid slantingwise instead of flat; often found in coarse rubble or rag work, constructed of rough stones, irregular in size and shape. In the Early English period the stones were laid with close fine joints, the first author being Bishop Roger of Salisbury, in the twelfth century. Flint-work appears in the later styles.

Mass. The first names given to the administration of the Sacrament of the body and blood of Christ were the Breaking of Bread (Acts xx. 6, 7), the Lord's Supper (1 Cor. ii. 20), or Communion (1 Cor. x. 18). It was also called, by way of eminence, the mystery, the sacrament, the oblation or prosphora, the sacrifice, Dominicum (the Lord's), agenda (the action), synaxis and collecta (the assembly), the solemnities, the service, the supplication, the mystical or Divine Eucharist or eulogy (the thanksgiving), the office, the spectacle, the consecration, the unbloody sacrifice, the supper, the table, the latria (worship), the universal canon; and by the Greeks also the hierurgia (sacred action), and the good, by excellence, and metalepsis (the Communion) in the Apostolical Canons. These terms served either to explain to the faithful the meaning of the service, or in times of persecution to conceal its real nature from the profane and persecutors. In Acts xiii. 22, it is spoken of as the Liturgy. The term

Mass is ancient, having been used by Clement I., Alexander, Telesphorus, Soter, and Felix (c. 100–275). It has been derived from the Hebrew missach (Deut. vi. 10), a voluntary or free-will offering, or from mincha, an oblation of meal (Levit. vi. 14, 15; Malachi i. 11). The term undoubtedly is employed by St. Ambrose in the fourth century (c. 385), and really is derived from the word missa, low Latin, for missio, the sending up prayers with sacred ceremony to the Most High, the oblations of the faithful being transmitted to God's throne, or from the dismissal of the catechumens, with the words still used in the Roman Mass "Ite missa est," like the Oriental apolusis, "Go, it is the dismissal." St. Augustine says, after the sermon occurs the missa (the dismissal) of catechumens; the faithful will remain. The Fourth Council of Carthage, Florus, Remy of Auxerre, Avitus of Vienna, and Isidore of Seville, coincide in this view. The name of Mass was extended to the day and night offices and festivals, because the Holy Communion formed the great feature in those services, and on those days; and for this reason even fairtimes held on festivals were called sometimes by this name. Hesychius says that the first celebration took place on the day of Pentecost. In 1549 in the English Church the word Mass had given place to the expression High Communion, the Communion of the Virgin or Apostles, but these were forbidden in St. Paul's by the Council very shortly after. From 1549 to 1552, when there was a daily celebration in cathedrals, the heading of the service in the Prayer Book ran, "The Supper of the Lord, and Holy Communion," commonly called the Mass. Melchizedek's sacrifice of bread and wine was a type of the offering in the Last Supper by Christ, the Priest after the Order of Melchizedek (Ps. cx. 4; Heb. vii, 17–21). The manna was another type (St. John vi. 51). The Mass of the Catechumens comprises the preparation at the foot of the altar, the short sermon and succeeding parts as far as the Offertory; the Mass of the faithful commences at the Offertory, or oblations (Cæsarius of Arles says), and continues to the dismissal. Before 960, apparently, the priest said the canon without book, but in that year he was required to have it open before him, for fear of making a mistake in the words.

In the first ages the bishop always celebrated in company

with other bishops or priests; this custom was known as the Lesser Liturgy, or concelebration, and is mentioned in the Apostolical Constitutions and the Council of Ephesus. At ordinations the practice was preserved. The Council of Clermont enjoined that on principal feasts, especially at Christmas and Easter, the country priests, instead of celebrating separately, should assist the bishop in his cathedral; when bishops visited each other, they had the privilege of concelebrating. At Lyons still, at Pontifical or Solemn Mass, celebrated by a dignitary or canon, he has four or six assistant priests vested as for Mass; when the bishop oconpies his throne at the end of the presbytery, the priests sit beside him; and when he goes up to the altar, they aecompany him, and take their places on either side of it. In England, in 1279, when a bishop died, all the bishops at the next council held a concelebration, saying a united Mass for his repose.

At Rome, in times of persecution, Holy Communion was said in prison, in private houses, as St. Paul did (Acts xx. 11), and in the catacombs; indeed, for some time after, from tender and holy association, after the Church had peace, the crypts were still used for the same purpose. By the English Canons of 994, Mass was to be said in churches only, except in the army, and then under a tent, with a hallowed (portable) altar. In 1076 an English Council again forbade the saying of Mass, except in a consecrated building. In 1342 noblemen, if aged or living far from a church, received the bishop's licence to have Mass in their private chapel, or oratory.

At first, celebration occurred only on Sundays (1 Cor. xvi. 1); and in the time of Justin Martyr, after the second century, the Western Christians communicated on Sundays and Wednesdays and Fridays. In the fourth century the Greek Church added Saturday; now it maintains daily celebration. St. Augustine says that the practice differed in various countries; in some celebration was daily, in others on Saturdays and Sundays, but in some on Sunday only; the daily celebration existed in Africa and Spain, and at Constantinople; in the sixth century, it was general. St. Ambrose mentions three celebrations in the week, St. Francis one daily Mass, at Rome. After the fifth century, priests

were allowed on certain days, called Polyliturgic, to celebrate twice. Pope Deusdedit first enjoined a second Mass
in a day. Alexander I. permitted a priest to celebrate only
once a day. Leo IV. forbade private Masses; but still there
were several festivals besides Christmas when the priest said
Mass three times in a day. Leo III. sometimes celebrated
seven or eight times within twelve hours; and it was not
until the close of the eleventh century that Alexander III.
directed that the same priest should say no more than one
Mass on the same day, Christmas excepted. The Council of
Seligenstadt forbade a priest to exceed saying three Masses
in a day. From the sixth century these repeated Masses
said by the same priest may be dated, when private Masses
were not in common use; and were permitted (as St. Leo
says) in order to satisfy the need of crowds of communicants,
and he calls it a form of tradition from the Fathers. At
length, when the pressure no longer existed, in the eighth
century there were four Masses at Christmas, two on the
Circumcision, and three on SS. Peter and Paul's Day, and
on Maundy Thursday. In France every priest was allowed
to say two Masses every day in Holy Week. Three Masses
were said on St. John Baptist's Day, one on the eve, in commemoration of his being the Lord's messenger; a second on
his Feast, in memorial of the Baptism in Jordan; and the
third because he was a Nazarite from his birth. In 1222, in
England, Mass might be said twice by a priest on the same
day at Christmas, Easter, and in offices of the dead. The
three Christmas Masses were in honour of Christ, as the only
begotten of the Father; His Spiritual birth in Christians,
and His nativity of a woman. A restriction by the Council
of Autun (613), was in force until the tenth century, against
celebration by a priest at the same altar twice on one day, or
where Pontifical Mass had been said. Priests who celebrated
more than once collected all the ablutions of their fingers in
one chalice, and the contents being emptied into a cup, were
drunk at the last Mass by a deacon, clerk, or layman in a
state of grace, or innocent. The day when no Mass was
offered, except that of the Mass of the Presanctified, which
was called aliturgic.

The Holy Communion was celebrated at first at night, out
of pure necessity, or, as Pliny says, before daybreak; and

Tertullian calls the meeting the Night Convocation, or that before light. But in time the Church prescribed the Mass to be said at tierce on festivals, but always after tierce in England in 1322; on common days at sexts, in Lent and on fasts at nones, or 3 P.M. In the middle ages, the nightly celebrations were permitted on Christmas Eve, on Easter Eve, on St. John Baptist's, principally in France, and Saturdays in Ember weeks, when ordinations were held; and Easter and Pentecost, on the hallowing of the candle. In 1483 Archbishop Bourchier, from regard to his infirmity, received permission to celebrate in the afternoon. There are several Masses. Beleth says each day had its Mass, commencing on Sunday; those of Holy Trinity, Charity, Wisdom, the Holy Ghost, Angels, Holy Cross, and St. Mary; and that at Rome, and in the province of Ravenna, the Mass of Easter Eve was not said until after midnight. He adds, that the Greek Church excommunicated all who failed to partake of the Eucharist for three Sundays. *See* INVITATORY.

(1.) High Mass, grand mass, the principal, capitular, canonical or conventual Mass, is sung with music and solemn ceremony, and the assistance of numerous ministers. The priest is assisted by a deacon and subdeacon, two taper-bearers, a thurifer or censer-bearer, a master of the ceremonies and sacristan. Communion is seldom given at high Mass. Pontifical high Mass is sung by a bishop. (2.) Low Mass is said by a priest attended by a single clerk. (3.) Private Mass is said in a private oratory on any day by a priest who alone communicates, and with, perhaps, a single assistant. St. Ambrose celebrated in a private house; the father of St. Gregory Nazianzen celebrated in his room; so did Paulinus of Nola; and Constantine the Great had a private oratory in his palace, and a moving chapel which accompanied him to the wars. The English Church requires two other communicants at the administration to a sick person. Becon says Masses were called private or special, golden, and canonical. (4.) Mass in honour of St. Mary and saints. (5.) Votive Mass said by way of supplication or thanksgiving. (6.) Mass for the dead. These, of course, are all comparatively modern, more or less. The holy communion was said at funerals, it appears from Tertullian, St. Ambrose, St. Epiphanius, St. Augustine, St. Cyril of Jerusalem, and St. Chrysostom. The present "collect" in the English burial service is provided for this purpose; and a form of service was drawn up in the reign of Elizabeth. (7.) The Mass of the Presanctified: celebration with a portion of a Host, sometimes called the Familiar, previously consecrated on Maundy Thursday and placed in a chalice of unconsecrated wine; used in the Latin Church from the time of St. Augustine on Good Friday only, but in the Greek Church from the time of the Council of Trullo, or possibly that of Laodicea, every day in Lent except Sundays, Saturdays, Maundy Thursday, and the Annunciation. The Ambrosian rite prescribes it on all Fridays in Lent. On Sunday five additional loaves are consecrated. In imitation of the Roman use, at evening on the weekdays the faithful meet at Vespers, and during the prayers consume ·the elements, having recited the gradual, psalms, certain hymns, lections, and prayers prescribed by the Euchologion. In the time of Pope Innocent I. *c.* 450, Mass was not said on Good Friday or Easter Eve, through grief at our Lord's death, and in memory of the dispersion of the terrified Apostles. (8.) The Mass at cock-crow was the first Mass on Christmas Day at Sens and Wells. (9.) The Mass of the Holy Ghost, a solemn Mass for the Pope, the Sovereign, and all in union with the Church or a religious order; sung before councils, or the election of a bishop or abbot, and also at consecrations and coronations. In general chapters of the great monastic orders, there were three Masses sung: 1, of the Holy Ghost; 2, for all the faithful dead; and, 3, for departed brethren of the order. (10.) A dry Mass—missa sicca—one in which there was neither consecration nor communion. (11.) St. Mary Mass in harvest (so called in 877): the feast of the Assumption, August 15th. (12.) Matin Mass, the first Mass said in the day, at the matin altar in choir, or the rood altar in the nave. At Lichfield it was also called Our Lady Mass. (13.) Mary Mass were the Annunciation and Purification; in 1017 there was a daily Lady Mass in cathedrals, minsters, and most large churches. (14.) Peter Mass, August 1st, when Peter Pence were collected. (15.) The Mass of the Overthrow of the Idols is the name for the Mass on Circumcision in the south-east part of Europe, in allusion to the destruction of paganism.

2 B

Massa Candida. Quicklime or burning oil by which martyrs were put to a terrible death.

Massarius. A chamberlain; massa communis was the common fund of a cathedral.

Mass Penny. A conventional name for the offering made by a chief mourner at a funeral.

Mass Priests. Mercenaries hired at a certain sum, who undertook an immoderate number of annals or trentals, and were unable to say them, and sold them to be offered by others. This abuse was forbidden in 1236 by Archbishop Edmund's Constitutions. (2.) In 960 the mass priest was the secular and the minster priest the conventual, and this is the earliest meaning of the term.

Master of Ceremony. An officer of the Pope who superintends the order of processions and religious ceremonial. He wears a purple cassock and surplice; on festivals his cassock is red. The master of the ceremonies is a clergyman who acts as director at a High Mass. His place is at the south-west angle of the altar steps, behind the subdeacon.

Masters of the Church. Mentioned in 673; learned clergy who sat as advisers of the bishops in synods. (2.) The residentiaries at Chichester and Lincoln; Master of the Sacred Palace, the Pope's theologian and licenser of the press, a Dominican since the time of Pope Honorius III. There were several masters in a minster, Master of the Lady Chapel, being its keeper; Master of the Choristers; Master of the Common Hall, Calefactory, or Parlour; Master of Converts, the superintendent of lay-brothers; the Master of the Novices, always an elderly monk; Master of the Song-school; Master of the Shrine, at Durham called Feretrar, Tumbarer at Worcester, and Keeper at Norwich; Masters of the Order or Custodes, the great officers of a monastery (at Evesham the vineyard-keeper and gardener were included); Masters of the Anniversary and of the Table are mentioned at Canterbury; Master of the Works or Fabric (Fr. Proviseur de la Fabrique; Lat. supervisor operis, operarius, Magister operis, Sp. obrero). The names of the designers, Flambard, Poore, De Berrington, and Billesleigh at Durham; Godfrey de Noyers, at Lincoln; Gower and De Leia, at St. David's; Parys, at Peterborough; Elias de Dereham, at Salisbury;

and of Alan de Walsingham, and J. de Wisbech at Ely, are still preserved. R. Farleigh, "mason or builder," at Salisbury, as guardian of the fabric under the Master of the Works, received 6*d.* sterling a day, and 10 marks quarterly. The Domus Operaria (the designing house) remains at Gloucester in the Close; and at Lincoln, adjoining the passage to the cloisters; and at Christchurch, Hants, over the transept chapel. Every cathedral and monastery had its own regular, but not numerous, gang of workmen, in its employ, regularly at work every day, year after year, large numbers being taken on upon special occasions only. The monks and canons sometimes worked as masons or carpenters, and the bishop or prior, or one of the body, usually the sacristan or treasurer, was architect, the clerk of the works being the practical architect (apparailleur du maitre des œuvres, or contre-maitre; Lat. constructor).

Mastlin. A kind of brass.

Matricula. The canon of church register, containing a list of the clergy. The term matriculation for admission on the list of undergraduates is still used in our universities. The matricular was (1) the sacristan's servant, who rang the bells and woke the convent; (2) A chaplain priest in Italy who was registrar, and had charge of the baptistry, cemetery, and belfry; (3) The almoner at Corbey.

Matthew's Day. September 21st; in the Greek Church, November 16th. Is mentioned in St. Jerome's Comes, and was generally observed in the eleventh century.

Michaelmas. The commemoration of the dedication of St. Michael's Church on Mount Gasganus, kept on September 29; mentioned in the 'Saxon Chronicle' in 1011, and in Ethelred's Laws, 1014. The apparition of St. Michael, "the prince of seraphim, leader of the angelic hosts, prefect of paradise," and "conductor of souls" to the place of repose, to whom cemetery chapels and churches on hills were in consequence dedicated, was observed on May 8. In the tenth century there was a curious superstition that on every Monday morning St. Michael sang High Mass in heaven. There is a tradition that the feast was instituted by Alexander, Bishop of Alexandria, in the fourth century. It was generally observed about the eighth century, and recognized, in 813, by the Council of Mayence. The emperor Manuel Comnenus, in the twelfth century, formally established it in the Greek Church.

Matutinal. A book containing the Matin office.

Maundy. A dole of alms and food given weekly or daily to the poor at a convent gate.

Maundy Thursday (Cœna Domini, the Lord's Supper; or Feria Quinta in Cœna Domini), so called from the mandatum, our Lord's new Commandment of Love (St. John xiii.), through the first antiphon, Mandatum novum do vobis, or Manducando, from eating the supper (1 Cor. xi. 24), was the Thursday in the week before Easter. In medieval times it was called the Birthday of the Chalice or the Eucharist, in memory of the institution of the Eucharist; in England Sheer (or affliction) Thursday; and in Austria Remission Day, from the reconciliation of penitents previous to restoration to communion at Easter. The altar stones were washed with wine and water, in allusion to St. John xix. 34, and dried with bloodwort, hard box, or yew brushes, in memory of the crown of thorns. At Chartres and Autun they were rubbed with fragrant herbs on Good Friday after this cleansing. The day was observed as early as the fifth century by the celebration of holy communion and washing of the feet of others (lavanda); catechumens also publicly recited the Creed in the presence of the bishop and clergy; and the sermon of the day is still called mandato in Portugal. A large illuminated cross, as it still is at Venice, was let down inside the cupola of St. Peter's until the Papacy of Leo XII. In the East and West the monks used to sup together after the Maundy. (*See* CLOISTERS.) The Archbishop of Moscow still performs the ceremonial. Cranmer says, " Our Lord did wash the feet of His disciples, teaching humbleness and very love and charity by His example. It is a laudable custom to wash the altars and to prepare with all cleanness the places where the most blessed Sacrament shall be ministered; and also to be for us a remembrance that as those things inanimate are washed and cleansed for that purpose, so we ought much more to prepare and wash our minds and consciences at all times, and especially at this time for the more worthy receiving of the same most high Sacrament. We, in like manner, as Christ washed His disciples' feet at His maundy, should be ready at all times to do good unto our Christian brothers, yea, even to wash their feet, which seemeth to be the most humble and lowly act that we can do unto them." At Lichfield, and probably in other cathedrals destitute of clois- ters the ceremony of the maundy took place in the choir. At York there are some stalls and aumbries in the north side of the choir, which were probably connected with the ceremo- nial. The Clugniacs merely touched with wetted fingers the feet of three poor men. The Benedictines and Cistercians scrupulously washed the feet of the brethren, the abbot him- self not being excused. King James II. was the last English king who performed the maundy at Whitehall. In lieu, maundy money, consisting of silver pence, is still given on this day by the Lord Almoner to a certain number of poor persons cor- responding to the years of the sovereign's age. (*See* p. 17.)

May Bishops. Nullatenses, having only bare titles of bishop- rics. A term derived from the May lords in the rustic summer games.

Mazer. A broad standing cup or drinking-bowl of maple or walnutwood. There are several examples still existing—one at Oriel College, Oxford; and another belonging to the Iron- mongers' Company, the St. Mary bowl of the fifteenth century, with silver bands; a third of the time of Edward I., at Harbledown Hospital, Canterbury, with rims and bases of silver gilt, which was used on St. Nicholas's Day for the common feast. (*See* BOWLS.)

Mediety *or* **Portion.** A division of a rectory church into several parsonages or vicarages, reprobated in England in 1237 by the Legate Otto, who ordered that where it was of old order the bishop must see that the income was properly divided, and regions or districts carefully assigned. The decrees of Pope Dionysius, the Councils of Toulouse, Rheims, and Lateran, under Alexander III. and Innocent III., forbade pluralities of benefices with cure of souls to one man.

Mediocres *or* **Second Grade.** Monks from 24 to 40 years of age who were exempted from being taper-bearers, the read- ing of the epistle, gospel, martyrology, and collation in chapter, and parva cantaria, chanting the offices.

Member. (1.) A moulding. (2.) A subordinate portion of a building.

Memorial. (1.) A prayer of oblation; the prayer in the order of the Communion beginning "O Lord and heavenly Father," which follows the communion of the faithful. (2.) The tomb of a martyr, or a church dedicated to his memory. (3.) The commemoration of a concurrent lesser festival by the use of its collect. (4.) Exequies, an office for the dead said by the priest in the fourteenth century in England.

Mensa. The upper immoveable slab of stone of one piece laid on a cube of stonework in an altar. The lower part of the altar of St. Dunstan in the Pyx Chapel, Westminster, is of the eleventh century, square and unadorned.

Merenda. (From *meridies*.) The midday meal; dinner.

Meridian. The siesta or noonday sleep in a convent, allowed to be taken during one hour after hall time.

Mesorion. An intermediate office in the Greek Church after Proton, Triton, Ekton, Ennaton; but omitted after Luchnikon and Hesperinon; Apodeipnon; Mesonuktion (matins); and Orthron (lauds).

Metropolitans were called primates, first bishops, heads in the Apostolical Constitutions, bishops of the first see by the Third Council of Carthage, bishops of the first chair by the Council of Seville, and in Africa seniors. The name of arch bishop does not occur before the fourth century, when it is mentioned by St. Athanasius. Beveridge, Ussher, Wolf, Schelestrate, and De Marca recognize Titus and Timothy as the earliest metropolitans, and Eusebius and St. Chrysostom speak of the one as president of the Churches of Crete, and the other as chief governor of those of Asia. St. Cyprian speaks also of the bishops of his province. St. Paul sent epistles only to the chief cities in each province, and St. John in the Revelation addressed the principal cities. Corinth and Thessalonica were evidently regarded by the former as the metropolitical cities of Macedonia and Achaia. St. John fixed his see at Ephesus; St. Peter at Antioch and Rome; and St. Mark, his disciple, at Alexandria. The metropolitans exercised a veto on the election of a bishop. The dignity is purely of spiritual creation, and cannot be made by grant of the civil magistrate or royal patent. The Council of Chalcedon enacted that any bishop who attempted by court favour to have his see erected into an archbishopric should be deposed, and any one made by the imperial authority should hold only the bare title, without power or jurisdiction. Metropolitans were also archbishops, which is, in fact, the generic title for them, as for patriarchs and primates, ranking after a patriarch; a primate being their chief, and the metropolitan presiding over a certain number of cities in the mother city or chief town of a province, as Rome, Ravenna, Aquileia, and Milan, and, in Charlemagne's time, nineteen other towns, whereas an archbishop might have no suffragans. The Archbishops of Saltzburg, Hamburg, Oviedo, and Bourges, and other cities in France, were metropolitans. The right of erecting a cathedral into a metropolitical church was reserved to the Pope, as Adrian I. erected Lichfield into a metropolitical see with six suffragans, Worcester, Leicester, Stow, Hereford, Elmham,. and Dunwich, leaving Canterbury only London, Rochester, Winchester, Sherborne, and Selsea, in 785, till Leo III., in 803, restored the jurisdiction to Canterbury. But St. David's, like Caerleon before it, was an archbishopric without the pall, until Henry I. reduced Wales to dependence on Canterbury. During the quarrel between the king and à Becket, Gilbert Foliot endeavoured to secure the title of metropolitan for the see of London; in 1093 Thomas of York, claiming the same title, successfully contested the claim of Canterbury to be the metropolis of all Britain. Pope Sixtus IV. made St. Andrew's metropolitan and independent of York; and Pius IV. created Utrecht, Malines, and Cambrai. The term is first used by the Council of Nicæa in 325, and corresponds to that of the Greek exarch. The Bishop of Alexandria was metropolitan in Egypt, the Bishop of Cæsarea in Palestine, and Chalcedon was made metropolitan in the time of the Emperor Marcian. Until the time of Alcuin Apostolical was used as a synonym. The rights of a metropolitan were to consecrate suffragans, to convene provincial councils, to settle disputes among bishops, and to superintend the faith and discipline in his province.

Maturines *or* **Trinitarians.** An order for the redemption of captives, founded by John de Matha, of Provence (born 1154, died 1214,) under the Austin rule, and confirmed by Innocent III. It was called in England the Order of Ingham, and established itself here in 1357. It had twelve houses. The Order of Mercy was also founded for the redemption of captives.

Miniature. Pictures illustrating the text of a MS., so called because filling up the outline sketched in vermilion (mi-nium.

Minims. An order of Franciscans (least of all), founded by Francis di Paula (born 1416), and confirmed in 1473 by Sixtus IV. They were often called Bonhommes. The habit was tawny, with a hood, a scapular, and leathern girdle. Their superior was called a corrector.

Minister. (1.) An inferior clerk in a cathedral. (2.) An officiating clerk in holy orders, ministering God's Word and Sacraments. (3.) A priest until the last review of the Prayer Book, and in the Canons of 1603.

Minister of the Altar. The server at Mass, in 1195, provided pure bread, wine, and water for the Mass.

Minor Canon. Petty canon, petty prebendary, or sub-canon. (1.) A vicar in priest's orders in the old foundations; a representative and auxiliary who celebrated at the high altar in the absence of a canon. Generally there were four, as at Hereford and Lichfield; eight at Rouen. In most cases they were the vicars of the four dignitaries, but at Hereford represented the abbots of Lyra and Cormeilles. At St. Patrick's they were founded in 1431, and there were petty canons also at Toledo. At Salisbury the word designated the prebendaries who were in minor orders, and at York a major canon was one who had kept the greater residence. At St. Paul's they form a college, instituted in 1395, over and above the thirty vicars. The latter sung the Matin and Lady Mass, but the minor canons chanted the Mass of requiem for their founder, as well as the Apostles' and high, or chapter Masses, being required in addition to attend all the hours. All were priests under a superior, called the warden. Their almoner looked after the choristers. The two cardinals, who had a double stipend, were parish priests of the close. They furnished the librarian, subdean, succentor, and divinity lecturer, and the perpetual gospeller and epistoler. In 1378 they wore surplices, dark almuces of calabre, lined with minever, with a black cope and hood, trimmed with silk or linen. (2.) A subordinate and stipendiary priest, appointed by the dean and chapter, in the new foundations; and by the original constitution the number equalled that of the canons, and the stipend half that of the latter. They had a share in the quotidian. In the time of Charles I. their numbers were reduced, and still further by the recent Act of Spoliation. They lived in a common hall, until the time of the civil wars, along with the schoolmasters, lay singers, and choristers. The minor canons of Chester alone possess an estate. Minor canons are removeable by the dean and chapter, and are now choral substitutes of the canons residentiary, officiating in turn, under their authority, jointly with the dean.

Minster—münster, moustier—meant originally, as in the writings of Cassian, St. Athanasius, and Jerome, the cell of a solitary; but the word was extended by Eusebius to embrace the church or abode of a religious community. (1.) A church of regular canons. (2.) A church formerly served by monks, as at Durham; in Germany the term Münster is still employed, and Marmoutier in France—majus monasterium—(great minster). (3.) A cathedral, as York, Salisbury, Lincoln, Ripon, etc. (4.) Many large churches, as Beverley, Wimborne, Southwell, though held by secular canons, were dignified by the title of Minster. (5.) Parish churches, in 960, were called minsters, and several churches retain the name in Dorsetshire. These were the original outposts of the Church, isolated stations of priests living under rule and in community, which in time became parishes.

Minster Ham. A sanctuary-house, in which persons might have refuge for three days. If it was burdened with the king's purveyance, they might remain for a longer period.

Minstrel. A name, in the thirteenth century, given to musicians and poets. The minstrels formed a corporation, under the patronage of St. Jullien; and their chiefs, appointed by the prince of the country, were called kings of the minstrels, and wore a crown. At St. Mary's, Beverley, one of the nave pillars bears the inscription, in Latin, "Pray for the souls of the players;" on the capital there are five figures, habited as minstrels, and bearing musical instruments painted, the harp, lute, treble and bass flute, and tabor. (*See* GALLERY.) The minstrels were incorporated by King Athelstan to control all minstrels between Trent and Tweed. They held a congress annually at Beverley to choose an alderman and other officers of the fraternity. These waits or histriones gradually degenerated, and in the time of Elizabeth were ranked with rogues, and within recent times wore a municipal dress, a chain, and badge, confining their duties to a serenade at Christmas-time, and playing before the mayor and civic authorities at processions and local festivities. The angel-choir of Lincoln represents, in the spandrils of the triforia, the angelic minstrelsy.

Miracle Play, The. French and German Mystery. The representation of the acts of a saint. The earliest on record, that of St. Katharine, was played at Dunstable in the twelfth century, by a graduate of Paris and his scholars. But in the tenth century such representations had been not unfrequent in that university. Archbishop Langton, Bishop Grostête, and Baston, a Carmelite, in the thirteenth century, wrote plays in Norman-French; and John Lydgate, a monk of Bury, in the fifteenth century, produced similar dramas. At the close of the twelfth century London was famous for its scenic representations of the miracles wrought by confessors, and the sufferings of martyrs. In the fourteenth century Chaucer and the author of 'Piers Ploughman's Crede' show that these plays were the popular amusements of the day. At the Clerken-well the parish clerks then acted before the king, and the choristers of St. Paul's besought the royal protection for their Christmas play of the history of the Old Testament, which was to be produced at a considerable outlay. No doubt the idea of the mystery was derived from the liturgical drama,—the symbolical representations prevalent within the Church of sacred events. The sculptures of St. Etheldreda round the octagon of Ely are a mystery in stone. Plays are said to have been represented on Sundays at St. Paul's and in the Chapel Royal until the time of Charles I. In the Middle Ages, when the Church was unable to repress the popular taste for the stage, we find, side by side, two classes of dramas, one laic and secular, the other ecclesiastical, religious, and moral. The two motives meet in the 'Morgante Maggiore' of Pulci. A German abbess, Hoswritha of Gandersheim, in the tenth century, introduced plays, written in Terentian Latin, and representing nuns reclaimed to the cloister from a life of vice. During the eleventh and twelfth centuries the religious drama spread rapidly through England, France, and Spain; and the scene sometimes extended from the sanctuary to the porch. At length the adoption of the vernacular and the introduction of action instead of expressive dumb-show, led to vulgar diction and buffoonery. In 1548 the French Parliament prohibited all except honest plays, owing to the scandals which arose during the play of the 'Acts of the Apostles,' in which five hundred actors took part. It occupied forty days in representation at Bourges. In 1417 the English bishops had plays acted before the Council of Constance, and the clergy took part in such representations, just as the monks (and notably Benedictines) and canons did at Thetford, St. John's, Beverley; Lincoln, in the time of Edward III., Woodkirk, St. Florian, St. Benignus, Dijon; Corbey, and Eisenach. In 1492 the Franciscans of Coventry acted miracles on Corpus Christi Day, as their brethren in London played the Passion in 1556. In 1519 Cardinal Wolsey forbade the Austin canons to act, but at a later date the chaplains and choristers of the Duke of Northumberland acted at Easter and Christmas. In 1526 the canons of Lille acted a comedy (that is, a play in acts) in the open air. At Veletri and other Italian towns mysteries long lingered. In the church of Ara Cœli, at Rome, the representation of the Præsepe and Bambino still takes place at Christmas. At Ober Ammergau the Passion-play is a decennial representation, and at Barcelona very recently the mystery was still in vogue. The 'Autos Sacramentales' of Calderon hold the highest rank in this remarkable class of literature. They were acted on Corpus Christi at Seville, Toledo, and Madrid.

Mysteries were commonly played on saints' days, and degenerated into monstrous abuses and licence. At Nivelles, on Whitsun-Monday a young girl sitting by a horseman, represented St. Germanns, whilst a youth, playing a thousand fantastic tricks, did all in his power to make her laugh. At Courtrai, on Good Friday, a poor man received £25 to personate the Saviour bearing His cross and endure the blows inflicted by six Capuchins on one side and six Recollects on the other. Similar exhibitions took place at Brussels in the church of the Augustines; in honour of the rosary, by the Dominicans at Venice; and on Corpus Christi Day, with burlesque pantomimes, in Spain, carried on by the Discipliners. These plays soon overpassed the traditional language of the Church, and adopted the homely vernacular, becoming so popular that they were acted no longer in the close, which became too strait for the audience, but on hillsides, in cemetories, and public places where scaffolds could be erected.

In fact, one part of the population was often engaged in amusing the rest. The transition from the church to the exterior was gradual. On Whitsunday 1313 the guilds of the skinners and curriers of Paris, within the aisles of Notre Dame, performed in dumb-show, with musical accompaniment, the mystery of 'Reynard the Fox' and 'Paradise and Hell,' in which the performers wore the disguise of various. beasts. The Church tried to check the people, but the temporal soon leavened the spiritual element.

The acting of plays was not confined to the clergy. Secular actors, as in the Præmonstratensian refectory at Paris, or guilds, represented the mysteries. Menestrier thinks that the first impulse was given by the pilgrims returning from the shrines of Compostella, St. Michael, or Le Puy, and chanting recitative songs of a sacred character, a spectacle which so excited the interest of the citizens of Paris that they built a permanent theatre for plays on festivals. In England the trading companies shared the expense, and each guild took its part in what was called the pageant,—a lay show or spectacle of detached scenes, acted by relays of independent brotherhoods, almost invariably on Corpus Christi Day, but at Chester at Whitsuntide. In 1313 the guilds had a dumbshow, with musical accompaniments, at Paris. At St. Quentin, in 1452, a mystery was played. But England was the home of such shows. They are mentioned at Cambridge in 1355, in London in 1348; at Chester they were commenced before the abbey-gate so early as 1268. They lasted till 1577, at Coventry till 1591, at Newcastle till 1598, and at York from the close of the thirteenth until late in the sixteenth century. At the dissolution of the guilds they passed into the universities. In 1564 Queen Elizabeth witnessed one at Cambridge, and at Ely House the 'Passion of Christ' was acted on Good Friday in the reign of James I., and about the same period Corpus Christi plays were acted at Preston and Lancaster. That which had been the delight of kings, however, had descended to the amusement of the common people only. At Tewkesbury plays were acted in 1583, and the Guary (play) Miracles in Cornwall about the same period.

Misericord. (1.) Subsellia, Sp. subsilia, the folding seat of a stall. (*See* STALLS.) There is an Early English specimen in the Lady Chapel at Westminster. (2.) A compassionate mitigation of full penance. (3.) According to Lyndwood, a custom in certain monasteries of relieving a number of monks, in alternate weeks, from attendance in choir and claustral duties. (4.) A hall for eating flesh-meat in a monastery at Tewkesbury, Westminster, Worcester, and Peterborough. Some convents, as Canterbury and Westminster, had country hospitals for convalescents. In the latter case it was at Chelsea.

Missal. Called in early times the Sacramentary, and in Scotland the Cursus. The book of prayers and chants used in the Mass, compiled by Gelasius and Gregory the Great, and revised by Celestine, c. 422, and Leo the Great. Salvian, Musæus, a priest of Marseilles, and Voconius, Bishop of Castellana, drew up sacramentaries. Some copies, as required in every parish by the bishops, contained the gospels, the sacramentary, prayers, prefaces, benedictions, and the canon, the lectionary, a book of epistles, and the antiphonar —in a word, all that was to be sung by the priest at the altar and by the minsters in the ambon. These books were called Plenars (complete, or full), but usually their contents were distributed into separate volumes, the gradual, collectar, benedictional, hymnar, etc. The complete missal was requisite when priests, from the ninth century, began to say low Masses, and especially for country clergy; as laymen, by the Capitulars of 789, were forbidden to sing the lessons and Alleluia, and the priests were required to sing the Sanctus with the people before the canon was commenced. The earliest Frank, Gothic, or Gallican missals, of the sixth century, contained only the portion of the liturgy recited by a bishop or priest, that is, the canon, prayers, and prefaces. At a later date those of small churches comprised the Introit, Gradual, Alleluia, Tract, Offertory, Sanctus, and Communion, where, although there were a deacon and subdeacon, yet the smallness of the choir required the celebrant and his two assistants to chant together. The missal, mainly compiled by Pope Leo, was amplified by Gelasius, corrected by Pope Gregory, and reformed by Pius IV. Celestine required the psalter, besides the epistles and gospels, to be said, but his successors, to avoid wearying priest and people, substituted collects and versicles, e. g. the Introit, Gradual, Offertory,

and Post-Communion. St. Augustine insisted on uniformity
of ritual in Africa.

Mistral. A corruption of ministerial. A provost at Vienne
who acted as prefect of the city, delegated by the archbishop.
A canon who looked after the prebendal estates.

Mitre. The mitra or mitella was worn by virgins like a
kind of veil, and is mentioned by Optatus of Milevi;
and the mitre was used by some Eastern sovereigns;
probably it was the same as Aaron's tiara (Exod. xxix. 6 ;
Lev. viii. 9), "the mitre upon his head; upon his forehead the golden plate, the holy crown ;" "the holy crown
upon the mitre ;" and in early times it was simply a
small band or narrow plate of precious metal (petalum)
tied about the head, such as St. John the Evangelist,
St. James the Less, and St. Mark are said to have worn by
St. Jerome and Eusebius ; the latter terms the mitre " ste-
phanos," or crown, and St. Gregory Nazianzen calls it the
kidaris, or diadem ; corona was its name in the fourth
century, and a synonym for the episcopate. The Pope's
mitre is called the tiara. Until the sixth century it lost
nothing of its early simplicity, but at that date John of Cappadocia added to it ornamental embroidery, and images of
saints painted or in needlework. For some time, until the
twelfth century, it was merely a crown hollowed out in front
like a crescent, a modification of the horned or pointed cap,
which was its shape before the tenth century. The earliest,
of a cloven shape, were very low ; about the twelfth century
they were blunted, and usually white. In the fourteenth
century they were heightened and sumptuously enriched ;
the points ended in jewelled crosses, and the edges ornamented with crockets or leaves. In the fifteenth century
they became broader and higher. From 1300 until the
latter half of the century the outlines were very graceful.
The present shape is exceedingly ugly, and, as a witty
French cardinal observed, strongly resembles the undesirable
san benito. The two points symbolized the two Testaments, which are diverse in rites and ceremonies ; or the
hypostatical union of Christ ; or the helmet of salvation.
The two fanons or labels hanging down over the shoulders
represent the literal and spiritual sense of Scripture. They
originally were brought round like strings or ribbon-bands,

and tied under the chin to secure the mitre firmly on the head; their ends or pendants became in time mere ornaments. The open top and jewellery have been considered emblematical of the intellectual decoration of the prelate's head, and the richness of the knowledge of Scripture, in which precious examples of varied virtue blend their lustre with the tissue of the sacred history. The mitre was formerly of linen, as St. Bruno, Honorius of Autun, and Hugh de St. Victor describe it; but Durand, in the thirteenth century, observes that this was "the former custom." The privilege of wearing the mitre was a concession of the Popes, as to the bishops of Hamburg by Pope Leo IV., and to those of Utrecht by Pope Alexander III. Pope Leo IX. gave it to canons of Bamberg in 1053. Pope Alexander II. is said to have given it to a duke of Bohemia; he undoubtedly gave it to Egelsin, abbot of St. Augustine's, Canterbury, in 1059, renewed 1173. The grant of the mitre was made to Westminster, 1167; Waltham, 1191; Thorney, 1200; Winchester, 1249–53; Evesham, 1163 and 1230; Battel, 1370; Malmesbury, 1380; Chester, 1324–49; Durham, 1374–91; Peterborough, 1397; Gloucester, 1400; Tavistock, 1458; Worcester, 1351; and Canterbury in 1378. In 1154 Adrian IV. transferred the precedency from Glastonbury to St. Alban's. The first summons of ecclesiastics to Parliament was made in the forty-ninth year of Henry III., the king calling up such as he thought fit. The Abbot of Jorevalle and the Prior of Durham (in 1374) received the mitre, but had no seat in Parliament. The religious summoned were reduced by Edward III. in number to twenty-five abbots and two priors, there having been in the reign of Henry III. sixty-four abbots and thirty-six priors in Parliament. The privilege was far from desirable to the greater abbots, who looked upon it as a burden, and endeavoured by every means to be excused from it. The omission of names in the rolls of Parliament may be attributed to a vacancy in their houses, and the fault of the clerks. The priors of St. James, Northampton, and St. Mary de Pré, Leicester, the abbots of Middleton and Burton, were occasionally summoned. The abbots of Monte Cassino and St. Denis were mitred. The first French mitred abbot was Hugh of Clugny, in 1088, by permission of Urban II. Innocent III. granted the distinction to Vendôme, but the honour had become so common in time, and the bishops so seriously complained of the abuse, that Pope Clement IV. confined the precious mitre (orphreyed, and plated with gold or silver, but unjewelled)· to exempt abbots; and to others, not so privileged, simple white mitres, undecorated, and without the indent. In synods and councils jewels marked the episcopal mitre. There is a good example of a mitre of the fourteenth century preserved at Beauvais. In 1217 the dean, matrescuela (chancellor), treasurer, and archdeacon of Toledo; the provost, dean, and chanter of Mayence; since 1244 the provost, celebrant, deacon, and subdeacon at Vienne and Macon; the provosts of Ghent, St. Die, and Lavantz; and the celebrant of Cambrai were mitred. There were several kinds of the mitre: (1.) The precious, made of gems and gold and silver plates; (2) the orphreyed, of white damask, covered with pearls and gold thread; and (3) the simple, made of damasked silk, bokeram (boquerammus, fine material of goats' hair), or pure white linen (byssus), with red fringes (laciniæ), and hanging fillets (vittæ). In 1386 the Prior of Winchester wore a ring and plain mitre in the presence of the bishop, and in his absence a silver mitre, pearled and jewelled. Mitres and staffs of silver-gilt were carried at the funerals of Juxon, Duppa, Frewen, Cosin, and Wren, Trelawny (1721), and Lindsay (1724); the mitres only at the burials of Monk and Ferne, of bishops of Bristol in the present century, and Bishop Torry at Perth. The effigies of Hacket, Magrath, Harsnett, and Lamplugh had mitre and staff in the seventeenth century; those of Sterne, Dolben, and Sharpe (1721) are mitred. The bishops appeared mitred at the coronation of George III. In 1645, at York, the vestry contained two double-gilt coronets, the tops with globes and crosses, to set on either side of his grace, which are called his dignities, upon his instalment when he takes his oath. Two, of the earliest bishops of America, are preserved in the United States. (*See* CANON, CARDINAL, CORONET.)

Mixed Chalice of water and wine, in memory of water and blood flowing from the Saviour's side, was instituted by Pope Alexander I., of which the Jewish atonement was typical (Heb. ix. 19, 20); it is also said by Cranmer to signify the union of Christ's strength with the weakness of His people, or 'the union of His two natures in one person. Our Lord drank of a cup with wine and water mingled. The 3rd Council of Braga, 675, forbade the use of milk or a sop. Lanfranc in 1071 prescribed mingled wine and water, and prohibited the use of beer or water only. In 1549 a little pure and clean water was added to the wine in the chalice before the prayer for the Church after the offertory. Bishop Andrewes used a ton set upon a cradle on the altar, and a tricanale, a round ball with a screw-cover, whereout issued three pipes for the water of mixture. In 740, in England, the practice of mixing wine with water in baptism was forbidden.

Mixtum. A light meal of bread and wine taken in a Benedietine monastery before hall by the servers who had communicated. Houselling sippings of unconsecrated wine were given to communicants at the end of Mass. Becon calls them bottom blessings.

Modus. A payment in money which is by custom or prescription made in lieu of the whole tithe in kind.

Mola. (From the sacramental immolation of Christ, Beleth says.) The middle of an altar, signed with the dedication cross, and covering the sepulchre of relics.

Monastery. The monastery took its origin in the cell of the hermit or solitary; gradually others were grouped round it, and at length a community was formed. The little chapel grew into a church; the relics or grave of a sainted superior or king attracted pilgrims and visitors, for whose accommodation guest-houses were erected; traders and pedlars came to sell their wares; their booths were converted into stationary shops; fairs and markets granted to the abbot by the king or feudal lord led to fresh accessions to the population; the village grew up, and at length developed into the town, or even city. Such is the origin of most great towns in England and on the continent. In the monastery of Tabenna, founded by St. Pachomius, which was presided over by an abbot for spirituals, and an economist or provost for temporals, it was divided into houses, each having a prior. These contained separate cells for three or four monks, and as many cells made a clan or tribe. A large house contained forty monks, and great monasteries had thirty or forty houses. At Nitria, where there were 5000 solitaries, there was but one church, served by eight priests. When there was a small community there was but one president; where it was numerous they were divided into centuries under a centurion, or deaneries under a dean, and obeyed the canon or chief abbot (father), hegoumenos (president), or archimandrite (chief shepherd). From the fourth century, in the West, at the request of the people or their abbot, the monks frequently took orders, and in the East at the instance of the bishops, the archimandrites being sometimes elevated to the episcopate, or acting as bishops' deputies at councils, and their monks ranking after priests and deacons, who frequently came to study in their cloister. It was not until the fifth century that the cœnobites left the desert for the suburbs of cities and towns; after the next century they established their houses in them. Gregory in the sixth century, and Boniface IV. in the seventh century promoted monks to holy orders without transition through the lower grades, and in consequence they bore the name of clerks. It was then that St. Benedict restored the ancient discipline of the cloister. The earliest written rule was that of St. Basil, who was followed by Cæsarius of Arles, Cassian, and St. Martin of Tours, in France, and by Isidore of Seville in Spain, the latter being retained until the eighth century. The ancient dress was the colobium or lebitus, a linen sleeveless dress; a melotes or pera, a goatskin habit; a cowl covering the head and shoulders; the maforte, a smaller cowl, cross-shaped over the shoulders; and a black pall. St. Benedict introduced during manual labour the lighter scapular reaching from the shoulders down the back, and the cowl became a habit of ceremony and worn in choir. Borrowing the language of the regular and secular canons, the monks at length, when in their common habit they attended choir, called it on ordinary service days "dies in cappis," in distinction to "dies in albis," days in surplices or festivals, the cope being black like the frock. The origin of monasticism is attributed to Christian solitaries called Therapeutæ, who settled on the shores of the lake Mareotis; but the founders of hermits were St. Paul and St. Antony of Egypt in the Thebaid, about the middle of the fourth century, as described by St. Jerome, when the Nitrian desert was crowded with monks and nuns; Erigenes or Hones in Mesopotamia; Pachomius and Hilarion in Palestine ; Æmatha and Masarius in Egypt and Syria. In Rome monastic observance without restriction to the cloister is referred to Athanasius and some priests of Alexandria, when they fled from their Arian persecutors, c. 341 ; and St. Jerome says that women adopted a similar life. St. Augustine mentions houses of prayer and labour at Milan. St. Martin of Tours founded the first monastery in the West, at Ligugé, near Poictiers, c. 360, and Marmoutier. The chiefs only of these monasteries at this time were in orders. Until the sixth century women were allowed to relinquish their state and marry. The regular life of community was introduced by Eusebius of Vercelli, c. 350. Theodoret mentions a large number of monasteries both in the East and West, some founded by St. Basil, c. 358; others by St. Augustine in Africa, c. 390; and some by St. Ambrose at Milan in 377. In 550 the rule of St. Basil, followed by all Greek monasteries, was introduced at Rome, but St. Benedict gradually absorbed all other monks into his great rule. In 585 St. Columban's rule of prayer, reading, and manual labour was founded in Gaul. In 649 the Monothelite persecution in the East furnished many monks to the Western Church, and in the eighth century the Iconoclasts were the cause of a still larger migration. In the thirteenth century St. Dominic prevailed on women to observe a still stricter rule. The first written rule—that of St. Basil, Bishop of Cæsarea in the fourth century, who embodied the traditional usages—was derived from that of Pachomius, aimed at the combination of prayer and manual toil, and was modified by St. Benedict, the patriarch of Western monks, but in the eleventh century was still vigorous in Naples. Polydore Vergil says that in 373 St. Basil first enacted the triple vows of chastity, poverty, and obedience. In 410 Lerins was founded. The Benedietine rule spread rapidly in Italy before his death, in 543. Maurus and Placidus spread it in France and Sicily ; others introduced it into Spain, where monasteries are said to have existed in 380 ; and in less than two centuries all the monastic orders in the West were affiliated to it. St. Columban built the first abbey in England in 563, as he had done in Ireland ; in the latter instance it was preceded only by the St. Bridget's Cell at Kildare, which was famous in 521, and

established probably by St. Patrick. In 802 the Council
of Aix-la-Chapelle decreed that the Benedictine rule should
be universally adopted. From the tenth century it put forth
branches; Clugny, in 910, under its abbot, embraced the
rule; so did the Camaldolesi in 1020, from St. Romuald; the
Cistercians in 1098, from St. Robert; the Carthusians in
1080, from St. Bruno; the Valombrosans in 1060, from John
Gualberte; the Celestines in 1294, from Peter di Merona;
and the Olivetans in 1319. At Bangor in 603 there was a
monastery with seven portions, each consisting of three hundred monks, with their provosts or rectors. Benedict Biscop
in 677 built the monasteries at Wearmouth and Yarrow of
stone; and in 1035 Lanfranc united all the English abbeys
into one congregation. St. Maur in 1621 was the last instance of its reform. In the seventh century the rule was
observed in the East. Monasteries were called ingenua if
exempt from their foundation, or libera if the grant or privi-
ledge had been made subsequently. Those which were not
exempt were compelled to render to the bishop obedience;
annual fees called jus synodale, or circadas; procurations, or
the provision of entertainment; solemn processions, and
the right of celebrating Mass in their minsters. All abbots,
however, despite their repugnance, certainly after the ninth
century, were compelled to make the profession of canonical
obedience to the diocesan when receiving his benediction,
and this implied his right to give holy orders, consecrate
churches, altars, and cemeteries, and grant chrism, and
dimissory letters when the abbots travelled out of the diocese.
The foundation of the monastery was the dictate of religious
motives in the youth of the Church, but the reward of piety
was temporal also; the estates of the founder were improved,
the vassals educated, order introduced, the sick and aged
tended, and handicrafts and useful arts taught. The in-
trigues of the friars, the accumulation of wealth, and the
decay of discipline wrought the fall of the monasteries,
which was commenced by Wykeham, Fisher, Alcock, Chichele, Beckington, the Countess of Salisbury, and Wolsey
for university foundations. " What, my lord," said Oldham
to Fox in 1513, " shall we build houses and provide liveli-
hoods for a company of bussing monks, whose end and fall
we may live to see ?" It was a great and fatal error of the

Reformation, Leighton thought, that the great abbeys had not been preserved for places of education, and retreats for men of mortified temper without vows. Henry VI. dissolved the alien priories; Henry VIII., in 1535, the lesser, and in 1538 the greater monasteries. The extravagant waste of the commissioners, the expense of bringing down special juries from London to assess the value of each monastery, the destruction of superb churches, ancient monuments, and works of beauty, and the cost of pensions assigned to the late occupants rendered the proceeds of little value to the Crown, and the loss to the country and the poor irreparable. In France, Spain, Austria, and Italy the same suppression has taken place in less than a century.

Money Stone. The upper slab of a tomb, as at Carlisle, York, and Dundry, on which payments were made.

Monk. (*Monachos,* solitary.) (1.) The title of a metropolitan. (2.) The ascetic, or continent, who, living on bread and dried fruits in the week, and cooked pulse on Sundays, withdrew into the Egyptian and Syrian deserts for purposes of religious meditation, manual labour, and study, was the prototype of the medieval monk, whose name he bore, and also of the anchorite, or solitary, and hermit, the dweller in a solitude; the remobothi, mentioned by St. Jerome, lived in towns, in parties of three or four. Cassian says the monastic life was the child of mystic theology, which was the fruit of a burning sun and a sky without rain. Since the third and fourth centuries the name of monk designated a member of a religious community, more correctly described as a cœnobite (one living in common), or conventual. The Gyrovagi, or wandering monks, are reprehended by St. Benedict as worse than the Sarabaitæ, monks of the time of St. Jerome, who lived in small societies of two and three in castles and towns. In islands, because of "the hardness of monastic life," St. Gregory the Great fixed the age of admission at eighteen, and it was the English rule in 1222; in other countries it was fourteen. King Sebbi was the first unprofessed layman buried in the monastic habit. At a later period still more frequently persons adopted the monastic habit when life was in danger, and those who recovered were bound to enter the cloister, and known as monachi ad succurrendum. An incorrigible monk was sent for punishment to a neighbouring convent, which had to spend two-pence a day on his maintenance.

Monogram of the Saviour. A combination of X and P, the first two letters of the name of Christ, also forming a cross; sometimes it takes the appearance of a P set upon a Tau cross in the East. It is often set within a crown or palm-branch, or has the letters A and Ω on either side (c. 355). Ancient writers recognize in it the mystic seal (Ezek. ix. 4–6; Rev. vii. 2, xiv. 1). It is clearly of Eastern origin, and was adopted by Constantine as one long consecrated to Christian use. The letter P began to be disused, and the X was retained only in the form of a Latin or Greek cross; and even now Xmas and Xians are common abbreviations. The letters A Ω represent the initials of Alpha and Omega, the designation of our Lord as the Beginning and the End (Rev. i. 8, xxii. 13). St. Clement of Alexandria, and Tertullian both allude to this monogram; St. Ephiphanus and Origen explain it as symbolical of the two natures of Christ.

Monstrance. (*Ostensorium;* Sp. *viril.*) A species of vessel used for showing the Eucharist to the people; it is composed of a stem, which supports a crystal case surrounded by rays of glory, a transparent pyx, or tabernacle. At Conques there is a silver-gilt monstrance, with a large disc and a double patriarchal cross above it; the lower portion is of the fourteenth century, the upper part is a later remodelling. In the fifteenth century the custom of carrying about and exposing the Host began to be universally observed. The festival of Corpus Christi, which occurs in June, was instituted in 1264 by Pope Urban IV.; and in certain churches a procession was enjoined on that day between 1320 and 1330, and even in the eleventh century the Eucharist had been carried in procession; but the Council of Cologne first, in 1452, mentions that the Host was set up and carried visibly in monstrances, showing that formerly the wafer was not exposed, but borne in a closed ciborium. The necessary alterations were made in the earlier examples at a later date. At first it took the shape of an ordinary reliquary, but at length was made like a tower of crystal, of cylindrical form, and mounted on a foot like that of a chalice, and covered by a spire-like canopy, with flying buttresses. Inside the cylinder was a crescent held by an angel, in which the Host was set; in some cases the cylinder was replaced by a quatrefoil, or was surrounded by foliage like a Jesse-tree, and at a later date by the sun, a luminous disc, with rays alternately straight and wavy, set upon a stand. Upon the vessel itself the Doom was often represented, and relics were placed in it. The monstrance did not become common till the fifteenth, and is probably not earlier than the fourteenth century; it bore different forms: (1) a little tower, jewelled, and having four apertures of glass or crystal; (2) the figure of a saint, or the Holy Lamb, with St. John Baptist pointing to it; (3) a cross; (4) a crystal lantern, or tube, mounted on a pedestal of precious metal, and covered with a canopy in the fifteenth century; (5) a sun with rays, containing in the centre a kind of pyx (this is found as early as the sixteenth century).

Months' Minds. Monthly commemorations of the dead. Trentals.

Montjoy. Mounds serving to direct travellers on a highway, probably often originally tumuli, or funeral mounds of an elder people; heaps of stones overgrown with grass, which had been piled over a dead chieftain. They often were crowned with a cross. Montjoie St. Denis was the French war-cry; Montjoie St. Andrew, of Burgundy; Montjoie Notre Dame, of the Dukes of Bourbon; and Montjoie St. George, of England.

Morality. A paganized miracle play. In 1680 the London pageant revived the "Morality," when Sir Patience Ward, Lord Mayor, exhibited in his procession the Virtues, some of whom made poetical addresses. In 1687 the Goldsmiths presented a hieroglyphic of the company, representing St. Dunstan, in full pontificals, working at his forge; and in 1689 the Skinners in Guildhall gave a pageant, a wilderness with beasts and birds, with some horse-play. The modern Gog and Magog, or Corineus, were made in 1708, and are substitutes for wicker giants of old processions.

Morrow Mass Priest. The priest who said early Mass, morrow being equivalent to morning.

Morrow of a Feast. The day following.

Morse. (*Firmaculum*, formal, owche.) A clasp for a cope or pectoral.

Mortmain. An exemption from rendering feudal military service. Lands held by a religious corporation were under this tenure, which deprived the crown of such service as if the land were held by a dead hand. The Act 7 Edward I., 2, was directed against such holdings, except with the king's sanction.

Mortuary. A composition for oblations wrongly detained, or forgotten tithes; a principal legacy or bequest for the soul of the dead made to the Church. Henry VIII. abolished the practice, which was a constant source of contention between the clergy and executors. These payments were called St. Hubert's rents, St. Alban's lands, St. Edmund's right, and St. Peter's patrimony. Mortuaries were paid in pursuance of a council held in 1009. It was fixed to be the second best animal of the deceased, to be paid to the parish priest or church; the best went to the lord, by constitutions made in the thirteenth and fourteenth centuries. In Venice a tithe of the personal property went to the Church, but in England only one-third; probably the mortuary was a composition for it. Innocent IV. mentions that in England the third part of the goods of intestate persons passed to the fabric of the church and the poor. As early as 840 a white horse and the arms of a dead knight were given to the church in which he was buried.

Mosaic, Musivum. The production of a design or painting by the combination of small pieces of glass, paste, stone, or marble, naturally or artificially coloured. A composition, by means of coloured and solid materials, representing objects of nature. (1.) Opus tesselatum, of various shapes, used in pavements. (2.) Opus sectile, of one or two colours, in thin marble slabs, used in pavements or on walls. (3.) Opus vermiculatum, so called from the minuteness of its fragments, and employed in grand groups and figures. Vitreous mosaic (*crustæ vermiculatæ*) was substituted for that in coloured marbles or terra-cotta. Mosaic work is mentioned in the book of Esther, and was known as opus Græcum, from the workshops of Greece and Byzantium. Mosaic enamel is attributed to the Persians. St. Mark's, Venice, is a treasure-house of mosaics. At Byzantium mosaics, formed of cubes of enamelled glass, were made to adorn the interiors of churches, with a magnificent effect. There is good glass mosaic upon St. Edward's shrine, *circa* 1269; and stone mosaic before the altar, *c.* 1268, at Westminster. There is also a similar pavement at Canterbury.

Motet. A little word; play on words. A medieval composition, formed upon an anthem, to which different parts were sung, as if improvised; a movement or counterpoint upon the plain song. It was also called pulpitre in the fifteenth century. When counterpoint was first introduced there were only two parts, the tenor and discant; then a third, called triplum, was added; then a fourth, the quadruplum or motet. The latter word, in the thirteenth and fourteenth centuries, was a synonym for contralto.

Moulding. The face or outline of the angles of cornices, capitals, jambs, and bases.

Mozarabic. Most-Arabe, "Arabic by adoption;" a term applied to the Spanish or Gothic liturgy, of Ephesine origin, which was coeval with the introduction of Christianity into Spain, and possibly received some additions from the Goths. At Braga, in 538, the Roman office was adopted; but at Toledo, in 589, St. Leander of Seville reformed and digested the national use, and introduced some orientalisms. St. Isidore of Seville improved and developed it. In 633 the Fourth Council of Toledo extended its use to all Spain, and so it continued until the eleventh century. At the time of the Mahometan invasion it received its present title, possibly from the right being a concession within the Moorish pale. Cardinal Ximenes, in the sixteenth century, restored it from almost total decay, and it was revived in six special chapels at Toledo, Salamanca, and Valladolid; but it is now extinct in the latter place. In the time of Queen Costanza the Papal legate endeavoured to introduce the Gallican Breviary. Two parties were formed on the question, and the Toledan and French books were put to the ordeal, first of a duel, in which the Toledan champion won the day; and then of fire, out of which the Spanish book came unharmed, whilst the French book suffered some injury. The decision was that Toledo might preserve its ritual, which, in after years, Cardinal Ximenes had carefully transcribed.

Mullion. The upright divisions between the lights of a window or screen, rarely found of earlier date than the Early English period.

Mozetta. A short cape worn by Italian bishops. There is no actual distinction between the mozetta and camail; the former is used in all dioceses of France by bishops and canons, and the latter only in a few. It is edged with crimson; the episcopal camail is violet.

Mumpsimus. The nickname for persons obstinate in religious matters; used by Henry VIII. in Parliament, and founded on a story, related by Pace, of a priest who refused to abandon the practice of saying "quod ore mumpsimus" on the plea that he would not give up the usage of thirty years for any correction.

Muniment Chamber. Register-house or treasury. A room for the preservation of charters, fabric and matriculation rolls, terriers, and registers. At Salisbury it is detached, on the south side of the cathedral. At Chichester it was over a chapel of the transept, dedicated to the Four Virgins, and at a later date, next the chapter-house, and furnished with a sliding panel. At Durham it adjoined the stairs of the prior's lodge. At Winchester and New College, Oxford, it is in a tower, as at St. Martin des Champs, Clugny, and Vaux des Sernay. At Fontenelle it was over the church-porch, as now at Peterborough. Where there was a provost that officer kept the key. Muniments are, as it were, the defences of church property, hence the name.

Murmuring, as a sign of disapproval or pleasure, was once common in churches. Bishop Burnet and Bishop Spratt were both hummed when preaching at St. Margaret's, Westminster. Burnet sat down and enjoyed it, rubbing his face with his handkerchief, but Spratt, stretching out his hand, cried, "Peace, peace; I pray you, peace." At Cambridge a witty preacher, in the time of Queen Anne, addressed his congregatien at St. Mary's as "Hum et hissimi auditores." At Hereford this unseemly practice, which greeted every person arriving late in choir, was prohibited. *See* AMEN.

Mynicens. (Fem. of *munuc;* Lat. *moniales.*) Classed with monks in England in 1009 and 1017, and probably Benedictines, differing from nuns in being of younger age and under a rule more strict.

N. *or* **M.,** in the office of baptism, probably designate N(omen), a single name, or NN, nomina, (fused in M, a printer's blunder), a double name. In the marriage service N only is given.

Nable. A stringed instrument with a triangular sonorous-box. It only differed from the psaltery in form and having shorter strings.

Nails in the Crucifix. In the thirteenth century three are pourtrayed, one foot of the Crucified overlying the other, without the hypopodion. James de Voragine first mentions the change, which Ayala, Bishop of Galicia, attributes to the Albigensian heretics. Benedict XIV. pronounced the nail preserved in St. Cross, Rome, to be authentic. (*See* CRUCI-FIX.) On Irish crosses the Saviour's feet are represented tied with a cord, and His arms drooping.

Naos. The inclusive name for the trapeza, or nave, and the choir in a Greek church.

Napery. Linen.

Narthex. The porch or portico in front of a basilica. So called from its narrow oblong shape, resembling a rod or ferule. It contained three doors, the central for the clergy, the north for women, and the south for men. These were imitated at a later period in the three western porches of St. Mark's, Venice, and elsewhere. The narthex itself reappears at St. Front, Périgueux, Romain Mortier, of the tenth century, Jumiéges, and Neuchatel; and a similar narrow porch has been traced at Fountains and Beaulieu. At Moissac and Petersburg, Halle, 1124, it supports a parvise in the west tower. It is a portico of insulated columns in several Roman churches of ancient date, reappearing in the Palladian porticos, and growing, still earlier, into the portal cloister which was added round the courts of several Roman churches, at Ravenna, Novara, Milan, Parenzo, Laach, Lorsch, and Tournus, churches at Cologne, Trebitsch, and Gurk, and in the latter instances with a gallery above it. In the large basilicas there were two kinds of narthex, one at each end of the atrium or forecourt. The exterior, called the vestibule, horopulaion, propylos, or first entrance, was a large porch or colonnade of three, five, or seven pillars, sometimes double, with an upper and lower range, as at Tournus; in it the dead were buried, after the Council of Nantes permitted intramural interment, in 658. In smaller churches an outer narthex was added for the use of the penitents, called weepers.

The interior narthex was the ferula proper, divided from the nave by a wall. It was the place of the second class of penitents, the hearers.

Natalitia. Birthdays (*i. e.* into immortality). Days on which the martyrs had suffered.

National Council. An assembly of all the prelates of a country. The earliest in England was that of Hertford, in 673, and the last was held by Cardinal Pole in 1555.

Nave (Lat. *navis, gremium, cumulus;* Germ. *hoch schiff;* It. *nave;* Fr. *nef;* Sp. *coro,* the choir being called *capilla mayor*) derives its name from Gr. *naos,* or Lat. *navis,* symbolically of the ship of Christ, the Church—an idea as old as the Apostolical Constitutions, and preserved in the English baptismal service. The church of SS. Vincent and Anastasius at Rome has its walls curved like the ribs of a ship; and the nave of Payerne is of uneven width, to represent a vessel beaten with the waves. In France naves were first subdivided by ranges of pillars about the fifth century. At St. Paul's, in 1385, persons bought, sold, and played ball in the nave, which, two centuries later, was put to abominable desecration. At Durham and Worcester there was a common thoroughfare, and in York and the northern minster the country gentry and townsfolk made the nave a fashionable walk.

Navette. An incense ship or boat. A vessel for containing incense, as we use the word vessel and (butter or sauce) boat now.

Necrology. When the diptychs fell into desuetude, necrologies, obituaries, books of the dead, books of annals or anniversaries, and books of life took their place, in which, in cathedral and collegiate churches and minsters, the names of the departed were entered. The Benedictines adopted them at the beginning of the sixth century. When an abbot or distinguished monk died, a messenger, carrying a brief or roll, a kind of encyclical letter, rode to the various associated abbeys or churches to apprise them of his decease, and left a schedule, containing his own name and that of the dead and the date of his arrival. The new name was then inserted in the several obituaries. These were read after the martyrology at prime, but in a monastery after the rule. The names were recited on their several anniversaries, and in case of a benefactor the De Profundis and a special prayer were sung. The abbot was commemorated by the words, "The deposition of Lord Abbot N." All others had the simple affix "obiit," he died. First were read out the names of abbots, then monks, provosts, præcentors, and in succession those of sacristans, bishops, priests, sovereigns, and soldiers. Saints were also included; and for convenience a single volume generally comprised the monastic rule, the martyrology, and obituary. The gifts of benefactors were often recited; but sometimes only a general commemoration of all brethren and familiars of the order was made, followed by the words, "Requiescat in pace," may he rest in peace, uttered by the president, and closed by an "Amen" chanted by the whole chapter. Cowel says that at the Prayer of the Prothesis the Greeks had their names inserted in the catalogue and deposited a present in money, which formed a considerable portion of a country priest's income.

Neophyte. (Newly planted.) (1.) The name of the newly baptized, grafted into the true vine (Ps. xcii. 13; St. Matt. xv. 13; Rom. vi. 5; 1 Pet. ii. 2). (2.) A catechumen, in distinction to the faithful or baptized. (3.) A clinic, as St. Cyprian's phrase is; a grabbatarian, in that of the Sixth Council of Paris,—one who put off baptism until on a sick-bed, an abuse reprobated by the Council of Neo-Cæsarea, St. Gregory Nazianzen, and St. Chrysostom. (4.) A clerk or novice promoted to a bishopric without proceeding through the inferior orders (1 Tim. iii. 6).

Neuma. The sequence. A musical prolongation of the last syllable of the word Alleluia, sung after the gradual, and so called from its following the rhythm of the Alleluia, or from the words of the deacon which succeed, "Sequentia Sancti Evangelii," etc. (here followeth the Gospel). To these notes Notkar, who died in 912, wrote words, which were called "sequences." The latter were substituted, Beleth says, for the neuma, by Papal authority.

Newel. The central column round which a circular staircase winds.

New Fire. On Easter Eve the new fire was kindled for relighting the lamps in church, which were extinguished on Good Friday, though in some places the upper candle of the Tenebræ was reserved for the purpose; and in others, as at

Rome, in 750, in the pontificate of Zosimus, three lamps were concealed, emblematical of the three days in which our Lord lay in the tomb; but usually the new flame was kindled by a burning-glass from the sun, as a type of the Orient on high; or as mentioned by Leo IV., in the ninth century, from a flint, symbolical of the Rock (1 Cor. x. 4), as at Florence from one brought from Jerusalem in the time of the Crusades. The rekindling represented both the resurrection and the fire which our Lord came to cast upon the earth (St. Matt. xii. 49). The fire was used to light three tapers branching from a common stock in the top of a lance. *See* HALLOWING.

Nicene Creed was first recited in the time of the Eucharist by Peter the Fuller, Bishop of Antioch, in 471; and adopted by Timothy, Bishop of Constantinople, in 511; in Spain by the Third Council of Toledo, in 589; in France in the time of Charlemagne; and all the Western Church by Pope Benedict VIII. in 1014. It is based on the Creed of Cæsarea, which was adopted by the Council of Niexa in 325, and afterwards received the addition of the words from " the Lord and giver of life " in the Second Council of Constantinople in 381. It was enjoined to be sung in the Mass by Pope Marcus, *c.* 340, but Pope Innocent III. and others say that it was introduced by Pope Damasus, after the custom of the Greeks. Its characteristics are the insertion of the term " of one substance," directed against the Arian heresy, the insertion of the words " and the Son," and the omission of the clause " He descended into hell," which occurs in the Athanasian Creed. The question was raised in the Council of Aix, 809, whether the Spanish and French churches were right in adding the Filioque clause in this Creed, and it was referred by Charlemagne to Pope Leo, who allowed the Creed to be sung, but without the addition; and Walafrid Strabo says that the Creed was chanted in France and Germany after the condemnation of the Felician heresy in Gaul. Leo the Great, however, in consequence of the opposition of the Patriarch of Aquileia and Photius, at length authorized the use of the clause, and uses it in letters to the Bishop of Astorga and the monks of Mount Olivet. Charlemagne decreed that the interpolation was to be used; the Council of Toledo, 447 and 580, adopted it; and it was inserted by the

Catholic Visigoths and Franks. In 680 Archbishop Theodore and an English council accepted the clause. Pope Benedict, in 1024, at the request of the emperor, required the Creed to be chanted in Italy. It is the custom for the priest alone to intone the words, " I believe in one God."

Niello. (Black; from Lat. *nigellum*.) An imitation of pencil-drawing in black on metal, by the use of lead, silver, and copper, an art brought to high perfection at Florence, and practised by Benvenuto Cellini. The monk Theophilus speaks of the art. The patriarch Nicephorus of Constantinople sent, in 811, to Pope Leo two jewels adorned with niello. Marseilles was eminent in this art during the reigns of Clovis II. and Dagobert.

Night-Watch. (Lych-wake, death-watch, or vigil). It was the custom for the faithful to observe night-watches for the departed until the funeral, and make intercession for their souls; but in 1343 this practice was forbidden in England, as it had degenerated into an occasion for assignations, thefts, revels, and buffooneries in private houses, under pain of excommunication, the relations of the dead, and those who said psalters, only excepted. In 1363 these wakes were kept in churches, under the close supervision of the parish clergy. The wake still lingers in Scotland, Ireland, and Wales.

Nihil Prebends. At Bangor, unendowed canonries, held by the præcentor, chancellor, and three canons, who were maintained by corrodies, pensions, and oblations.

Nimbus. A cloud, called a diadem in an inventory of Bourges in the fifteenth century; the attribute of sanctity, or of power; a circle or disc of light surrounding the head, as a reflex of celestial glory. It was at first a heathen symbol for deities and emperors, and then became a mere conventional ornament of the heads of personifications; in the third century it was Christianized, and attributed to the Saviour; then to angels, evangelists, to their symbols, apostles; lastly, St. Mary and all saints. In the fifth century the nimbus of our Lord is distinguished by a cross pattée, and sometimes by the insertion of His monogram. In the sixth century, Isidore of Seville first mentions that angels were nimbed; at the close of the seventh century the other classes received the nimbus, which was given to the mystic dove, and the phœnix. Herod and sovereigns have the nimbus of power designated by red or green colour, gold being reserved for Christian saints. The nimbus of our Lord represents His dominion, the splendour of the Divinity, and glory of the Sun of Righteousness. Honorius of Autun says, " In saints it pourtrays their heavenly joys and imparted glory; and its round buckler shape typifies the Divine protection which guarded over them. *See* AU-REOLE.

Nine Lections. Three lections are said on each of the three nocturns, the first three taken from Holy Scripture, the second from the acts of a saint, the third from homilies of the Fathers. Justin Martyr alludes to the commentaries of apostles and writings of prophets, the Council of Laodicea to lections, the Third Council of Carthage to the passions of martyrs on their anniversaries, and St. Jerome to the works of St. Ephrem, as being read in the sacred assemblies. The nine had reference to the orders of angels, with whom the Church joined in adoration, and, as a tripled three, bore allusion to the Holy Trinity. But from the time of Cassian there were twelve lessons, until Gregory VII. reduced them to nine, with eighteen psalms, on Sundays, except Easter and Pentecost; on festivals, nine psalms and nine lessons; on ferials, twelve psalms and three lessons; in Easter-week and Whitsun-week, three psalms and three lessons, according to ancient use. Among these days were included the Epiphany, the Circumcision, Conversion of St. Paul, Purification, St. Matthias, the Annunciation, SS. Philip and James, St. Barnabas, St. Peter, All Saints', St. Andrew, and sixty-eight other commemorations of saints and holy days, such as the Exaltation of the Cross and the Name of Jesus.

Nine Worthies of the World. (1) Hector of Troy; (2) Alexander the Great; (3) Julius Cæsar: heathens. (1) Joshua; (2) David; (3) Judas Maccabeus: Jews. (1) King Arthur; (2) Charlemagne; (3) Godfrey of Boulogne: their arms are on Duke Robert's tomb at Gloucester.

Norman Architecture. (William I. to Richard I., 1066–90.) The cieling, of timber, with beams reaching from side to side, is flat; the ribs are broad massive flat bands, crossing the vault at right angles, but occasionally are enriched with zigzags; the choir ends in a semicircle or apse; the doors are generally deeply recessed, with grotesque and various mouldings above the arch, which is invariably round; the windows have no divisions; the pillars are round or octagonal, sometimes channelled; the buttresses have but a slight projection, and are flat and broad; arcades are common; the roofs are steep; turrets are tall, and terminate in conical spirelets; mouldings consist of alternate rounds and hollows, with splays and few fillets, are broken into zigzag lines, or form billets and beak-heads. The last ten years of the century belongs in architectural character to that which succeeded. Arches at first squared were then chamfered, and later ornamented in various ways. Pillars, at first with a diameter equal to their height, were gradually increased to six or eight diameters high, as in the crypt under A'Beckett's crown, and in the Galilee of Durham. The ornamentation of pillars and shafts was introduced in the reign of Henry I. Capitals were plain and circular, and in this century have a plain piece of stone projecting from the centre of each face, to be painted or carved subsequently, but later in the style were imitations of the Corinthian capital. Doors follow the same order; deep rich doorways are always late. The windows at first were small and plain. The earlier masonry is distinguished from later stonework by coarseness, and wide joints of mortar between the stones. Surface ornament is found only in late work. Sedilia are peculiar to England. Aisles only were vaulted until the middle of the twelfth century, and were made barrel-shaped, often of herring-bone work, without mouldings, or groined simultaneously. Ribs were introduced after 1100. The naves are of great length; the choirs apsidal, without radiating chapels, and often without a surrounding aisle. The ground plan included a central lantern and western towers. Oxford had a square end. The development of the Norman style in the twelfth century was a natural expansion—not the invention of a single mind, but the gradual work of many—an indigenous work, aided by hints drawn from different countries and various sources. Pointed arches occur previous to 1150, but with Norman details and mouldings; the progress of the Early English style was rapid after 1184, and established before 1200. The reign of Henry II. was the chief period of the transition (1154–89). The masonry is coarse, as if hewn with a hatchet, until 1110, when Roger of Sarum, according to William of Malmesbury, used a form of construction that gave the building the appearance of being built with one stone. The style became light, as in Durham Galilee, about 1180; and rich doorways occur at Rochester about that time; and the Corona of Canterbury, of that period, is the first real Gothic building.

North Side of the Church. The east was regarded as the gate of the prince (Exod. xliv. 1–3); the south as the land of light, and the soft warm wind (Acts xxvii. 13); the west as the domain of the people; but the north, as the source of the cold wind, was the abode of Satan. In some Cornish churches there is an entrance called the Devil's door, adjoining the font, which was only opened at the time of the renunciation made in baptism. In consequence of these superstitions, and its sunless aspect, the northern parts of churchyards are usually devoid of graves. The north side of the altar corresponds to the Greek *boreion meros*, and Latin *sinistrum cornu*.

Notaries acted as recorders of the acts of councils, and shorthand writers of sermons; as Socrates tells us the homilies of St. Chrysostom were thus preserved. (2.) The acolyth who registered the names of persons to be baptized. Pope Julius I. required the notaries, or the primicier of notaries, to digest the history of the Church. In 1237 there were no public notaries (tabelliones) in England. *See* MARTYRO-LOGIES.

Novena. A religious service continued during nine days consecutively.

Novices. The novices were lodged in a dormitory at the far end of the monks' dortor, generally in Benedictine houses. The Cistercians and Austin Canons usually placed them apart, under their master, at the west side of the cloister; and this was the case at Winchester exceptionally. In the old cathedral of Canterbury their school was in the north tower of the nave; but in Benedictine monasteries, at a later date, they studied in the western alley of the great cloister. The age of a postulant in a Benedictine house was eighteen, and the term of a novice's probation one year, as in Cistercian abbeys. The Clugniacs remitted part of the time; but in all cases they were subjected to a sharp discipline and menial duties, such as carrying a lantern before a procession; they occupied an inferior place in church and hall.

Numbers, Sacred. One is the Unity; two represent Unity repeated; three, the Creator, Trinity; four, the world, and, by the Second Adam, Paradise; five, the Synagogue; six, perfection and creation, the hour when Jesus was crucified; seven, rest, as in the Sabbath, love, grace, pardon, composed of three and four; eight, beatitude and resurrection (eight persons were saved at the Deluge); nine, angels; ten, the law of fear, or salvation, in allusion to the denar given to the labourers in the vineyard; twelve, Apostles; fourteen, perfection; three hundred, redemption; fifty, beatitude; and one hundred, virgins; sixty, widows; and thirty, wives, according to St. Jerome, on Matt. xiii. 8; 888, IESOUS the Saviour. The uneven number of the collects in the Mass, three five, or seven, was symbolical of the Church's desire of unity.

Numerale. The same book as the compotus, the kalendar.

Nuncio. Like the apocrisiarius, a Papal envoy in a civil capacity, accredited to a royal court.

Nun. (*Nonna*, a grandmother; or *nonis*, a maiden; Egypto-Greek.) A holy woman, unmarried and elderly, or widow, dedicated to God's service under the veil. In 1009 and 1017, in England, they are mentioned with canons, so that their rule was less strict than that observed in myncheries. St. Jerome uses the word nonna in the sense of a religious widow. There were two kinds of nuns: one made on a promise of virginity spontaneously, on the part of a young woman about twelve or sixteen years of age, called henceforward "Deo devota," devoted to God, who lived in their own homes, and wore simply a dark dress. The other was by formal profession, at the age of twenty-five years by the Council of Carthage, or at forty as other councils required; these nuns were called "Deo sacratæ," consecrated to God. They received the veil from the bishop on festivals, and specially on Epiphany, Low Sunday, and saints' days. In 745 they were called the Lord's handmaidens in England; spouse of Christ was a later title. Nuns are said to have been established by St. Syncletica, c. 363, near Alexandria, and to have existed in England in 630. In the fourth century St. Macrina, sister of St. Basil, c. 340, St. Anthony, and St. Pachomius built nunneries;

but Marcella was the first (St. Jerome says) who occupied a convent for women ; and St. Augustine speaks of communities at Rome and Milan devoted to a life of labour, prayer, and self-denial, but not bound by vows. There were others in Africa, and at Vercelli. In the fifth century there were nuns in France. Even in the sixth century nuns were unfettered in the cloister. In 721 a Roman council anathematized married nuns, and the regular conventual life for women does not date earlier than the institution of St. Dominic, in the thirteenth century. Until the fifteenth century, nuns, under proper restrictions, in England were allowed to visit their friends, and to receive callers of their own sex in their convent. In 1127, in England, they were allowed to use lambs' wool, fox or catskin, but in 1138 were forbidden grey, sable, marten, beaver, or ermine fur, or a gold ring, or curiously plaited hair ; their dress was in 1200 determined to be a black-hooded cope, without a cap. In 1222 their confessors were appointed by the bishop ; they were allowed to wear a ring, but neither a silk veil nor gold or silver needles in their hair. St. Aldhelm condemned the extravagant costume of nuns, the soft violet skirt, beaded tunic, crimson hood, sleeves with fur, and red silk bands and hanging ornaments, curled hair, and coloured mafortes flowing down to the feet, whilst the nails were worn as long and sharp as the talons of a bird of prey. The Benedictine nuns, founded by St. Scholastica in 530, had a house at Wilton in 773. The Franciscans, or Minoresses, founded 1212, came to England in 1293; they were first established in the Minories, London. The Poor Clares, founded 1225 by St. Clara of Assisi, were another branch. The Bridgetines were established at Sion, Middlesex, in 1415; Clugniacs, c. 940 ; Cistercians by Humbertina, sister of St. Bernard, c. 1118; the Præmonstratensians, c. 1121; the Dominicans, c. 1206; the Carmelites, c. 1122; the Carthusians, by Beatrice, a Frenchwoman, in 1309; and the Béguines, by St. Begga, c. 698, under the Austin rule. Fine nunnery churches of the Benedictines remain at Jesus College, Cambridge, Romsey, and St. Helen's, Bishopsgate, and one of smaller dimensions is at Minster, island of Sheppey. The parishioners occupied one aisle, divided from the rest of the church. The conventual buildings of Easebourne, Sussex, are tolerably perfect. St.

Rhadegund's, Poictiers, founded in 567, was the first French nunnery.

Nunneries. The local name for the triforium at Durham, Westminster, and Christchurch (Hants). At Paris recently nuns occupied this story on great occasions.

Nut. A cup made out of a cocoa-nut; examples remain at Corpus Christi and Exeter Colleges, Oxford.

Obedience. A place or office with the estate and profits belonging to them in a monastery, subordinate to the abbot, whence the name, and corresponding to a dignity in a cathedral or collegiate church. In 1222 the incumbents were required to render half-yearly or quarterly accounts, as well as the greater prelates, abbots, and priors. The obedientiares were usually the subprior, præcentor, cellarer, sacristan, chamberlain, kitchener, infirmarer, keeper of annals, hostillar, almoner, pitanciar, tumbarer, and master of the Lady chapel. But the obediencies varied according to the size of the monastery; sometimes the gardener, fruiterer, or keeper of the orchard was included.

Obit. The commemoration of a saint's death, called also his celebration, departure, falling asleep, birthday, or, if a martyr, his passion. The Assumption is ascribed to the Blessed Virgin, and Deposition to St. John, from the tradition that he laid himself down in his grave.

Oblates. (1.) Children dedicated from infancy to the cloister; the parents wrapped their boys' hand in altar cloth, with a petition. (2.) The dying who assumed the cowl. In 1191 Celestine III. freed children from such vows. (3.) Lay persons who offered themselves with a rope or bell round the neck, or four coins in their hands, or else laid their heads on the altar, and there engaged themselves, resigning all their property. (5.) Benedictine Oblates, an order founded by St. Frances Romana, d. 1443, neither cloistered nor bound by vows.

Oblationar. The shrine-keeper who received the offerings.

Oblations. (1.) Offerings for the maintenance of the ministers of the Church in kind, such as oil, vegetables, fruit, milk, honey, and farm produce, which, with offerings in money, were delivered to the bishop, and he made the redistribution of the residue in three parts—one for himself, the second for the fabric, and the third for the poor and pilgrims, according to the rule

of Pope Simplicius, in 476. (2.) Offerings of bread and wine
for the Holy Communion; and also of wheat, grapes, incense,
and oil for the lights. All the faithful who intended to communicate brought their offerings every Sunday, according to
the Second Council of Macon, in 582, under pain of anathema, the custom being founded on Exodus xxiii. 15. They
carried them to the oblationarium or gazophylakion, a kind
of portable aumbry placed near the diakonikon, where the
deacon received the offerings made by men, and a deaconess
those of women, strictly scrutinizing those who came, and
rejecting usurers, heretics, notorious sinners, those under
Church censure, persons not in a state to communicate, public penitents, and such as had invaded the Church rites.
During the scrutiny the offertory was chanted by the choir.
In the Ordo Romanus, the Pope, with considerable ceremony,
received the offerings; and by the Ambrosian rite, at High
Mass, six aged men offered three hosts, and six women presented white wine, each on their proper side. Strictly
speaking, the oblation was an offering to God; the oblata
an offering for the service of the altar. In 1549 the parishioners in England were required every Sunday to " offer the
just valour and price of the holy loaf, with all such money
and other things as were wont to be offered with the same."
In 1552 the bread and wine were to be provided at the
charges of the parish, and the parishioners were discharged
of such sums of money or other duties which hitherto they
had paid for the same, by order of their houses, every Sunday. In some French churches the *l'offrande* is made still.
Large round cakes are carried up with lights to the altar by
the assistants, and after benediction are cut up, as *pain béni*,
into pieces, which are distributed from a basket to the congregation. At Milan ten bedesmen and two aged women
carry up the oblations to the altar, where they are received
by the deacon. In the primitive Church the people offered,
probably in consecutive order, bread taken from the offering
made at the love-feast. In the medieval Church the wine
was brought in an amula or cruet, wrapped in the fago, a
white linen cloth.

The word oblation also designated sops or portions of
bread formerly offered at the altar before the Holy Communion and blessed by the priest. Some were given to the

poor, and others reserved for the clergy and poor, or distributed in the church as a sign of corporate unity. The lesser oblation comprises the typical offering up of the elements of bread and wine, and of the alms and other devotions of the people for special purposes, in the Holy Eucharist. The greater oblation is the act of spiritually offering the body and blood of Christ in the Eucharist. Small round loaves are used in the Greek Church for the Eucharist. In the West houselling bread was used for communion, and singing bread for the oblation. Offerenda is the layman's offering. The oblation was restricted to the priest's part at the altar.

Obligation, Feasts of. Holydays on which work was suspended. In 1362 forty-one are named, including Christmas, Circumcision, Epiphany, Ascension, Pentecost, and Easter (each with the three following days), Good Friday, St. Stephen, John the Evangelist, Holy Innocents', Purification, Annunciation, St. Mark, SS. Philip and James, John the Baptist, SS. Peter and Paul, St. James, St. Bartholomew, St. Matthew, St. Michael, St. Luke, SS. Simon and Jude, All Saints', St. Andrew, St. Thomas the Apostle, Invention of Holy Cross, St. Thomas the Martyr, Corpus Christi, Translation of St. Thomas the Martyr, St. Mary Magdalen, Assumption, St. Lawrence, Nativity of the Blessed Virgin Mary, Exaltation of Holy Cross, St. Nicholas, Conception of the Blessed Virgin Mary, the dedication of the church, the patron saint of the church, and feasts ordained by the ordinary. In Worcester diocese the labour of the plough only was allowed on seven days; and women's work was forbidden on the feasts of SS. Agnes, Lucy, Margaret, and Agatha.

Occurrence. When two festivals fall on the same day the lesser is either omitted or anticipated, or translated, that is, deferred to the nearest vacant day. Festivals concur when at Vespers the office of one commences before the other is terminated. The lesser day is then only commemorated.

Octagonal Chapels or churches occur at Stony Middleton, Wisby, Milan, Perugia, Ravenna, Hierapolis, and the modern St. Dunstan's-in-the-West of London. There was formerly one at Ayot St. Peter's. The form is mentioned by Eusebius at Antioch in the case of a church built by Constantine, and was a modification of the principle of the round church. There is an octagonal porch at St. Mary's, Redcliffe, and a chamber, in modern times called the baptistery, but really connected with the water-system, at Canterbury Cathedral.

Octave. The eighth day after a great festival, as Easter, Christmas, Pentecost, etc.

Œcumenical (*General*). In·1179 the English bishops stated that four only were required to attend a general council.

Offering Days. ˙Christmas, Easter, Whitsuntide, and the feast of the dedication of the church, or, as Beleth says, All Saints', when the alms were allotted for the priest's stipend and the purchase of the paschal. By Henry VIII.'s Injunctions, 1538, the four general offering days were changed to Christmas, Easter, Nativity of John the Baptist, and Michaelmas, when money offerings at the altar were given for the support of the clergy. In the last century, attended by the Knights of the Garter, and heralds in their tabards, the king offered, at Christmas, Easter, Whitsuntide, and All Saints', a bezant in his private chapel; on six other days gold; and on Circumcision and Epiphany gold, frankincense, and myrrh, in three purses.

Offertory, The, in the Mass (1) commences with the Dominus vobiscum, after the Creed, ending with the Preface. It contains the oblation of the bread and wine by the celebrant, the censing of the oblation, altar, and attendants, the washing of the fingers, the subsequent prayers, the invitation to pray, and the secret prayer. Originally it was usual for the faithful to bring to church the provisions which they contributed to the support of the clergy, and the necessaries for the Holy Communion and the church use. The offering was made at this time. The deacon selected what was required for the altar, and the residue was taken to the bishop's house for distribution to the clergy at his discretion. The candles given at ordinations and the bread and wine at the consecration of a bishop are remnants of the ancient practice. Walafrid Strabo says that it was lawful to offer new wheat-ears, grapes, oil for lamps, and incense at the time of celebration. (2.) The anthem sung after the Gospel or Creed, during which the people formerly offered their alms and oblations. Such was the custom in Africa, c. 400, in St. Augustine's time. Hugh de St. Victor and Honorius of Autun attribute the introduction and arrangement of the offertories to Pope Gregory the Great, but it has also been referred to Eutychian, *c.* 280; Celestine I., *c.* 430; or Adrian I. Singing is used in allusion to Eccles. 1. 12–18. Pope Gregory II. ordered oblations to be made as God had directed by Moses (Exod. xxiii. 15). In the first four centuries the offering was made in silence. When a bishop celebrates he goes to the altar after the offertory, and, taking off his gloves, makes the ablution of his fingers. (3.) A silk napkin in which the deacon wrapped the chalice when offered to him by the priest. The sub-deacon now has a large scarf placed upon his shoulders and takes the chalice, over which an attendant spreads the end of the scarf. He then carries the offerings to the deacon, presents the water-cruet, and receives the paten from the celebrant, which he holds enveloped in his scarf, standing behind him since the custom of consecrating upon the corporal was introduced.

Office. (1.) An administration without precedence in choir or chapter; the financial provost and procurator; the præcentor, chancellor, and treasurer of Beverley; monks elected by the prior and seniors, and confirmed in authority by the bishop, in a conventual cathedral were called officers, the term designating now the vice-dean, treasurer, and receiver-general of the new foundations. (2.) The Introit. (3.) Vespers. (4.) The canonical Hours, called by St. Basil and the Greek Church the Canon; by SS. Jerome and Benedict God's Work; the Cursus or Course in the Roman rite; the Collecta by St. Pachomius; Synaxis by Cassian; and Missa, in 506, by the Council of Agde. (5.) A service. When two "concurred" on one day the latter was called "dies duplex," a double day.

Official. A judge ecclesiastical, for the most part in priest's orders, acting as the deputy of a bishop or archdeacon, to hear causes in their courts. Archbishop Becket mentions his vicar; and, in 1195, Archbishop Hubert's officials held pleas of Christianity at York. In 1222 the archdeacon's "officials in consistory" are mentioned. The principal official heard causes only, and in 1343 is distinguished from the vicar-general, who exercised all voluntary episcopal jurisdiction, except what the bishop reserves to himself as collations.

Ogee. (*Ressaunt.*) A moulding, partly convex and partly concave.

Oils. There were three—(1) holy oils; (2) chrism oil; and (3) sick men's oil—kept in different bottles in every church, and fitted into an oblong "ointing-box" with a crested lid like a church roof.

Omophorion. A kind of scarf or stole, worn by the Eastern bishops. It resembles the Latin pall, but is broader, and tied round the neck in a knot.

Option. The choice by the archbishop of any dignity or benefice in the gift of any bishop consecrated or confirmed by him. The right is now extinct.

Opus Alexandrinum. An invention of the Egyptians, or, as others say, made in the time of Alexander Severus. A kind of mosaic pavement, made of squares and circles of porphyry, coloured stones, and marbles, of brass, silver, and gold. Opus Græcum, mosaics. Opus Teutonicum, metal work. Opus intextum, irregular masses of stonework. Opus reticulatum, stones arranged diagonally. Opus vermiculatum, chequer-work, latticed embroidery. Opus Anglicum, embroidery.

Orale (from *ora*, a stripe) or fanon. An ornament of the Pope, introduced by Pope Innocent III., *c.* 1200, as a substitute for the amict, which then began to be worn inside the albe. It is of thin silk, striped in four colours, and edged with gold lace and worn double, the inner part serving as a tippet over the albe, and the duplicate being laid on the Pope's head until after the chasuble is put on, and then turned over the back, chest, and shoulders.

Orarium. The stole of a deacon, as epitrachelion marked that of a priest originally. The name designated originally a handkerchief, but was applied to a new form of the white robe (Rev. iv. 4) used by the Christians in prayer, which was fastened on the chest, flowed over the shoulders, and concealed the hands. It derives its name from *orare*, because used in prayers; but the Fourth Council of Toledo, Ven. Bede, Alcuin, and Raban derive it from the preacher or Christian orator; others from *ora*, care, or *orao*, to observe. More probably it comes from *ora*, the ornamental band, of purple and gold, from the neck to the feet. The Council of Laodicea, *c.* 366, forbade the use of the orarium by subdeacons or readers. Gregory the Great interdicted it, as well as the chasuble, to subdeacons, who, like acolyths, had previously worn it. The Council of Braga, 563, ordered deacons to wear it on the shoulder over the dalmatic, to distinguish it from the tunicle of the sub-deacon; the Fourth Council of Toledo defines the left shoulder, and forbids it to be coloured or adorned with gold. The priest wore the stole at all times, the deacon only at the time of Holy Communion. The Greeks wear it hanging behind and before; the Latins scarf- or sash-wise, from the shoulder to the right side.

Oratorio. A spiritual opera, holding an intermediate place between religious and secular compositions, and invented by St. Philip Neri in the house of the Oratorians, c. 1540, at Rome, in order, by the use of good music and singers, to attract people to church, especially during the time of the Carnival. Handel, in 1720, Haydn, Mendelssohn, Bach, Beethoven, Cimarosa, and Jomelli have composed oratorios. The first religious drama of this kind, having recitatives, was the ' Body and Soul ' of Emileo del Cavaliere, which was represented at Rome in 1600. Of the unmusical religious play Racine's ' Athalie ' and ' Esther,' Milton's ' Sampson Agonistes,' Alfieri's ' Saule,' and Chocquet's ' Les Actes ' are well-known examples.

Oratory. (1.) The private chapel, usually an upper chamber (Acts xiii.), in which the early Christians worshipped for safety, to preserve their secret discipline from the knowledge of the heathen, and in distinction to the pagan exhibition of graven images on the ground-floor of buildings, and also in memory of the place of the Last Supper. The use of private places of worship, called euteria, outlasted the times of persecution, and were permitted, under certain restrictions, by the Councils of Saragossa, 381, and Gangra. (2.) A chapel in which no Mass may be said without permission of the ordinary. There are several kinds—(1) a monk's cell; (2) a private chapel, recognized by the Council of Agde, 506; (3) a chapel in the country without a district; (4) the private portion of a minster reserved to the use of the convent; the choir; a chapel attached to the chapter-house; in 1027 Alexis, patriarch of Constantinople, condemned the abuse of oratories, in which persons of power had assumed to have baptism administered and to assemble congregations under a licence; (5) in the sixth or seventh century a burial chapel, or a chapel in a cemetery, in which Mass was said at times, when the bishop sent a priest to celebrate; (6) a chantry chapel in a church. The private chapel of the dukes of Burgundy was rebuilt as the cathedral of Autun; the château of the Bourbons became that of Moulins. The ancient Cornish oratories are simple parallelograms, and contain a stone altar and well; they are sometimes raised on artificial mounds.

Ordeal. (*Urtheil, urdell,* judgment, the judgment of Heaven.) There were two kinds in 925, one of red-hot iron for freedmen, the other of boiling water for slaves. In the latter he dived his hand to bring up a stone, with his arm bared to the elbow or wrist, according to the accusation; in the former he took the iron from a stake of iron or stone and made three strides of three feet each, and at the last threw down the iron. His hand was then sealed up for three days, and then was examined, to see if there was any mark upon it. The ceremony was accompanied by prayer, the use of holy-water, and the kiss of the cross. It was forbidden on holy days in 878; embers; from Advent to the octave of Epiphany; and from Septuagesima until a fortnight after Easter, in 1009; and in 1064 was required to be performed in presence of the bishop's representative and the civil magistrate. In the Council of Mayence, 847, a slave had to traverse twelve red hot ploughshares; but Stephen V. and Alexander II. forbade ordeals altogether. Montanus and St. Britius are said to have carried live coals in their dress to prove their innocency. Remigius, as was customary with persons of rank, passed the ordeal by deputy. At length, owing to the condemnation by the Church, by the Council of Lateran, 1215, this superstition fell into desuetude during the reign of Henry III. An ordeal, prohibited in Italy in 816, consisted in two persons standing before a cross until one fell down from weariness. The ordeal of hot water was in use amongst the Salian Franks as early as the fifth century; that of the ploughshares is mentioned in 803. There were also ordeals by lot, when two dice—one a blank, the other inscribed with a cross—were used; and by the bier, when the person of the dead was supposed to bleed at the touch of his murderer. Henry II.'s assizes established the ordeal in lieu of compurgation, in which the accused produced witnesses in his defence, whose worth was estimated at one pound of old English money. The wager of battle was claimed in 1817, and abolished by 59 Geo. III., cap. 46. *See* CORSNED.

Order. (1.) Ecclesiastical office. The hierarchy includes (1) priests; Pope, superior, bishops, inferior, priests; (2) ministers in sacred orders ; deacons, and subdeacons ; (3) minor orders. Those in the greater or sacred orders are bishops, priests (reckoned as one sacerdotal order), deacons, and subdeacons ; and in minor or unsacred orders acolyth, exorcist, reader, and porter or ostiarius, as detailed in Ælfric's Canons, 957. The singer was regarded as a clerk only in a large sense. In 1281 it was not permitted to give the four minor orders and one of the superior orders to the same person on one day, and it was declared desirable that the minor orders should be conferred at intervals, or at least only two at one time. The English Church regards the orders of bishop, priest, and deacon as three and distinct. With this determination the canonists generally coincide, though some have ranked the episcopate only as a degree or grade of the priesthood. (2.) In the tenth century a certain form or rule of monastic discipline. Afterwards the word denoted an association of several monasteries with the same rule and under the jurisdiction and superintendence of one common chief.

Ordinal *or* **Custumal.** The use of Salisbury. The ecclesiastical offices comprised in a single volume by Osmund, Bishop of Salisbury, which John de Brompton, in 1198, says was in general use in England, Wales, and Ireland.

Ordinary. One who has authority to take cognizance of causes in his own right, and not by delegation, as the bishop in his diocese, and the archbishop for hearing appeals in a province, and the crown in royal peculiars.

Ordination. The laying on of a bishop's hands, with prayer, to put a candidate in the order, grade, or rank of the ministry (Gr. *telesiourgia, kathierosis, cheirotonia :* Acts xiii. 3; xiv. 23; 1 Tim. iv. 14; 2 Tim. i. 6; Numb. viii. 10; xxvii. 18, 19; Deut. xxxiv. 9; Exod. viii. 6, 7). The hand represented divine aid (Ps. lxxxix. 21, 22; Ezek. iii. 14). The right hand only is used in the Greek Church; but in the Western, after the sixth century, both hands were employed. The priests lay on their hands at the ordination of a priest merely as a sign of approval and reception. The earliest form of prayer was called the consecration. In the Greek Church the words are, "The Divine grace, which helpeth them that are weak and supplieth that which lacketh, choesed this godly subdeacon (or deacon) to be deacon (or priest)."

For nine hundred years after Christ there was no express statement of the Church respecting the power of consecrating Christ's body and blood in the ordering of priests. The form conveying the power of absolution is later by three hundred years, but took the shape of a prayer. It appears first in a pontifical of Mayence in the thirteenth century, and the consecration of the Holy Eucharist in a pontifical of Caetan before the year 1000. Unction of the priests, however, and the investiture with robes occur in St. Gregory's Sacramentary. The delivery of the Gospel or the Bible was probably introduced from the East into the Gallican Church. Beleth says that minor orders were given on Sundays and festivals, but holy orders on Saturdays only. Ordination of a church is its settlement under a parish priest—a term used as early as 1237, but in 1126 signifying his institution to a benefice.

Organ.   The original of this instrument has been traced back to the syrinx or pipes of Pan and the hydraulos or water-flute, which was the invention of Ctesibius, a mathematician of Alexandria, B. C. 520. It derives its name from the fact of its being the instrument of all instruments. It was often called organs, in the plural, and at a later date in the singular, organ. St. Augustine and Isidore mention the organ, which is said to have been introduced by Pope Vitalian into churches in 666, but Spain is recorded to have possessed it two centuries before that date. St. Aldhelm, who died in 709, describes one with golden pipes in England; and in the time of Dunstan, Canterbury and Ramsey, and at the close of the tenth century Winchester, Magdeburg, Ghent, and Halberstadt, in the thirteenth century Bury St. Edmund's, and somewhat later St. Alban's and Crowland possessed organs. King Pepin received an organ in 757 from the Greek emperor Constantine Copronymus, which was set up at Compeigne. In 826 Louis le Débonnaire ordered an organ from George, a Venetian priest, for the church of Aix-la-Chapelle. Pope John VIII., elected in 872, begged Anno, Bishop of Friesing, in Bavaria, to send to him an organ and organist. The introduction of organs in Italy, Germany, and England, and a great part of Europe, dates from the close of the tenth or beginning of the eleventh century. In 951 Elphege, Bishop of Winchester, built one for the minster, which required several men to set the keys in motion, probably with hammers, and fill the four hundred tubes with air. Wolstan celebrated its magnificent tones in Latin verse. Organs, though not mentioned in the inventory prescribed for English churches in 1305, were objected to by the Lollards. Aquinas says that the Church had not established musical instruments for the praises of God, and they are not mentioned in the canon law. Marinus Sanudo, called Torsellus, who flourished in 1312, introduced in Germany a kind of wind organ, called after him a torsel. The regals was a small portable organ to accompany the singers. It had a single row of treble pipes and a small bellows, worked by the left hand. The larger organs are often called "a pair." The Benedictines employed a choir of boys to sing the Lady Mass in the morning to the organ, with most harmonious modulation, and the bishops also maintained choirs in their domestic chapels. At Milan, Padua, Bergamo, Venice, Florence, Verona, Ferrara, Bologna, Santiago, Seville, and Burgos there is an organ on either side of the choir, to carry out more emphatically the antiphonal chanting of the psalms. At St. Alban's and Crowland there were large organs at the west end. This position is still common in Germany and France, as a small instrument is used to accompany the choir at Autun, Caen, Bayeux, Amiens, St. Omer, Sens, Fécamp, Paris, Lausanne, Haarlem, Trèves, Courtrai, Vienna, and Prague. At Durham and Gloucester the choir-organ was on the south side, as now at Hereford, Canterbury, and Faenza. A pair, called the cryers, were on the north side at Durham, as is now the case at Chichester, Ely, Durham, Lichfield, Bristol, St. Paul's, Winchester, Sherborne, Armagh, and Burgos. Since the Reformation, at York, Westminster, Lincoln, Chester, and Worcester, the organ was placed on the north side, and in the medieval period at Winchester, as now at St. Paul's and Genoa, in the south wing of the transept. At the Restoration organs were placed upon the rood-screens, to the utter destruction of internal effect. At Braga, Batalha, and Chartres the organ is on the south side, at Strasburg on the north side of the nave, at the west end of the choir at Antwerp, and the east end at Ratisbon and Perugia. At Lyons, Liége, and St. Peter's, Rome, no organ was used in choir, and the Cistercians proscribed its use. Two bands

of musicians on either side of the choir at Liége accompanied
the singers.   In the thirteenth century four priests who sang
the Alleluia were called its organizers, as those who sang it
in parts.   Organs in the middle ages were constantly borrowed by smaller churches.

Organ Cases are not earlier in date than the fifteenth century.   At St. James's, Liége, is an early example of the beginning of the sixteenth century ; that of Amiens was made
1422–9 ; one at Old Radnor is carved and of the early part of
the seventeenth century.   In Spain the organ-pipes are arranged in stepped compartments, with those of one stop projecting from the principal range.   They have often painted
wings or shutters.   At Rotterdam the organ (1840) has
90 stops, and 6500 pipes ; that of Haarlem (1738) 60 stops,
5000 pipes ; that of Friburg 64 stops, 7800 pipes ; that of
York 4500 pipes.

Organist. At Durham a monk played at Nocturns and Matins,
and the master of the song-school at High Mass and Vespers.   The more ancient names of this official are Master of
the Song-school, Clerk of the Chapel, and in the thirteenth
century at Hereford, Clerk of the Organs.   He ranked as a
vicar, and usually was also master of the choristers.

Orientation.   The position of a church facing the east, a rule
of the northern nations ; is an ancient custom and approved
tradition, according to the Council of Milan.   Rievalle alone,
in England, is built nearly north and south.   Pope Virgilius
ordered the priest to celebrate towards the east.   God is everywhere present, but the east is, as it were, His proper dwelling-
place, and that quarter where heaven seems to rise.   The
window in the ark is believed to have faced the east.   Prayer
was made to the east in the primitive Church (according to
Justin Martyr, Tertullian, and Origen, SS. Augustine and
Basil) : (1) in allusion to Ps. cxxxii. 7 ; Zech. xiv. 4, " His
feet shall stand in the Mount of Olives, which is before
Jerusalem on the east ;" (2) toward sit as the dayspring (St.
Luke ii. 78) ; (3) as the place of light ; and (4) of Paradise
(Gen. ii. 8) ; and (5) of the Crucifixion and Ascension, Pentecost and the second Advent.   Churches, therefore, faced
the east, and the dead were laid with their faces to the east.
The altar represents the Holy of Holies of the Temple ; at it
the death of Christ is commemorated, and from it the sacred

food is administered to the faithful. Leo I., 443, condemned the custom of the people at Rome who used to stand on the upper steps in the court of St. Peter's and bow to the rising sun, partly out of ignorance, and pàrtly from a lingering paganism. In later times the custom continued of turning eastward before entering St. Peter's, but with the intent of praying to God. To avoid, however, any suspicion of super-stition, in the time of Boniface VIII. a mosaic of the ship of Christ was erected, towards which devotions were to be made. Urban VIII. placed it over the outer great door. In some early churches (as those of the Holy Cross at Jerusalem, erected by Constantine, and Tyre, built by Paulinus at the beginning of the fourth century) three great gates faced the east, the central being the loftiest, like a queen between her attendants. The arrangement adopted was that of the Jewish Temple. In several early Roman churches, and in the western apses of Germany, the altars face westward, but the celebrant fronts the congregation. *See* EAST.

Oriflamme. (*Auri flamma*, or *fanon*.) A red flag of sendal, carried on a lance shafted with gilt copper. It was preserved in the abbey of St. Denis, and said to have been lost at Agincourt, in the Flemish wars by Philip de Valois. It passed with the County of Vexin, the counts having been the protectors of the Church, and became the standard of France in the time of Philip I. Other accounts state that it was last seen in the battle-field in the time of Charles I.; and Felibien says that in 1535 it was still kept in an abbey, but was almost devoured by moths.

Orphrey. (*Auriphrigiata*, gold of Phrygia.) An ornamental border of a cope or albe, so called as an imitation of the famous Phrygian embroiderers. England was famous for this work, and M. Paris relates that the Pope, struck with its beauty, directed the Cistercian abbots to buy up all the specimens they could, saying, "England is our garden of pleasure and delight; its treasure is inexhaustible; where much is, thence much may be taken." His order was obeyed, and his choir vested in cepes thus ornamented. In some English inventories the rich apparels (apparatus) of the albe for the neck and hands are called spatularia and manicularia.

O Sapientia. The first of the seven antiphons of the Magni-

2 E

ficat sung in Advent, on December 16th. The others were,
December 17th, O Adonai; December 18th, O Radix Jesse;
December 19th, O Clavis David; December 20th, O Oriens;
December 22, O Rex Gentium; December 23rd, O Emmanuel,
St. Thomas's Day being omitted.

Ostiarii. Doorkeepers; porters; the lowest of the minor
orders in the Western Church, spoken of in the third or
fourth century. The Fourth Council of Carthage prescribed
as the form for their admission to office the delivery of the
church-key to them by the bishop, with these words, " Behave
thyself as one who must render account to God of the things
locked under these keys." They arranged catechumens
in their places, announced the hours of service, and had
charge of the church. From this word ostiarius are derived
the words huissier and usher. The second master of Winchester is still called hostiarius. The Greek Church only
partially adopted the institution of porters, and soon let it die
out. In the West they always lived near the church.

Owch. A precious brooch.

Ox, The, and the ass are often represented round the cradle of
the Nativity, in allusion to Is. i. 3. Beleth says the lion and
ox in front of doors and a cock or eagle upon the church
were common representations.

Pace Haut. A broad step before an altar.

Palace. A bishop's house, called before the Norman invasion
the minster-house, in which he resided with his family of
clerks. It was provided with a gatehouse at Chichester and
Hereford; at Wells it is moated and defended by walls; at
Durham an actual castle; at Lincoln and St. David's it exists
only as a magnificent ruin; the chapels remain at York,
Winchester, Chichester, Durham, Wells, and Salisbury; and
the hall is preserved at Chichester; a few portions remain at
Worcester. There is a very perfect example at Ely. Bishops had town houses mostly along the Strand, as well as
numerous country houses, like Farnham, Rose, Hartlebury,
and Bishop's Auckland. The chapels of Lambeth, and Ely
Place (Holborn), the abbots' houses at Peterborough and
Chester, converted at the Reformation into palaces, retain
many ancient portions, like those of Bayeux, Sens, Noyon,
Beauvais, Auxerre, Meaux, and Laon.

Paled *or* **Paned.** (Lat. *pannus,* cloth.) Striped or rowed.

Pall. (1.) A band of honour, "the plenitude of the pontifical office," was first worn by Linus, or Sylvester, in the reign of Constantine. In 336 St. Mark gave it to the Bishop of Ostia, when officiating at the consecration of a Pope, when the pontiff was not a bishop at the time of his election. It is made of wool shorn from lambs which are blessed on St. Agnes' Day; it receives the Papal benediction on the feast of SS. Peter and Paul. All the previous night it is laid on the altar of St. Peter, after certain antiphons have been sung and certain candles lighted. If there was a morrow Mass at the high-altar it was laid upon it, and afterwards returned to the Pope; and the canons of the Basilica received three shillings of Provence, for claret, as the fee for their service. The tapers were the chamberlain's perquisite.

It is the peculiar mark of primates, metropolitans, and archbishops, and a few privileged bishops, to be worn by them at councils, ordinations, and on certain occasions in church. The Council of Macon, 581, forbade archbishops saying Mass without the pall. About 600 Autun received it, but Arles had the privilege from time immemorial. Isidore of Seville says that it was once common to all bishops, but at length it was only an exceptional honour in their case, as when St. Boniface received it from Pope Gregory II., the Bishop of Bamberg in 1046, and the Bishop of Lucca from Alexander II. in 1057. Pelagius or Damasus required all metropolitans to fetch their pall within three months after consecration; Pope Gregory I. forbade the reception of money by any official at its delivery, but the journey and fees in time became a sore tax, which cost the Archbishop of Mayence 30,000 gold pieces. Pope Gregory sent a pall to St. Augustine of Canterbury, and in 734 Ecgbright of York, after great difficulty, procured the same distinction, which had been withheld since 644. In 1472 the archbishops of St. Andrew's became independent of York and metropolitans of Scotland in right of the pall. Four palls were given for the first time at the Council of Kells, 1152, to the Irish archbishops by the Papal legate, this being their earliest acknowledgment of the Pope's supremacy. The pall represents the lamb borne on the Good Shepherd's shoulders, and also humility, zeal, a chain of

honour, and pastoral vigilance. Its other names were ano-
phorion, superhumerale, and, in the writings of Theodoret
and St. Gregory Nazianzen, hiera stole. It is a circular
scarf of plain lambs' wool worn like a collar about the neck,
and having two falling ends fastened over the chasuble by
three gold pins fixed on the left shoulder, the breast, and
back, the number signifying charity or the nails of the Cross.
Before the eighth century it was ornamented with two or
four red or purple, but now with six black crosses, fastened
with gold pins, which superseded an earlier ornament, the
Good Shepherd, or one cross, in the fourth century. It has
been supposed to be the last relic of an abbreviated toga, reduced to its laticlave by degrees. In the time of Gregory
the Great it was made of white linen cloth without seam or
needlework, hanging down from the shoulders. It has pendants hanging down behind and before to represent the
double burden of the Pope. (2.) (Gr. *endute, trapezophoron,
aploma.*) The frontal hanging in front of an altar; the
modern antependium, like the blue cloth of the golden altar
(Numb. iv. 11). In 1630, at Worcester cathedral the upper
and lower fronts, and the pall or middle covering, are mentioned. There is one with the acts of saints of the fifteenth
century at Steeple Aston, Oxon. (3.) The corporal. (4.)
Wall hangings, according to Rupert, betokening the future
glory of the Church triumphant. (5.) The linen cloth covering
the table or slab of the altar, ordered by the Councils of Lateran and Rheims, and by Pope Boniface III. In the Greek
Church, on the four corners of the holy table are fixed four
pieces of cloth called the Evangelists, because stamped with
their effigies, symbolizing the Church, which calls the faithful
to Christ from every quarter of the world. Over these are
laid the linen cloth, called the body cloth, representing the
winding-sheet of the Lord in the tomb (St. John xx. 7); a
second of finer material, symbolizing the glory of the Son of
God seated on the altar as His throne; and a third the corporal proper. The use of three cloths in the Latin Church
is said to have existed in the time of Pius I. St. Optatus of
Milevi mentions an altar cloth. In the sixth century silk and
precious stuffs were used, as St. Gregory of Tours informs us.
Constantine gave a pall of cloth of gold to St. Peter's; and
Zachary presented one wrought with the Nativity and studded

with jewels. A fair white linen cloth, and a carpet of silk or decent stuff, are required in the English Church. The form is the ancient pall, and should be fair, that is, damasked or ornamented, and so beautiful (Is. liv. 2; Ezek. xvi. 17); it is white (Rev. xv. 6; xix. 14), like the Saviour's raiment, exceeding white as snow (St. Mark ix. 3). It ought to hang slightly over the front of the altar, but at the ends nearly to the ground. Decent, the canon explains, means "such as becometh that Table," therefore rich and of price. (6.) A herse-cloth laid over a coffin and bier, ensigned with a cross of yellow or white material, often of bright blue colour. In 1386 Lord Neville's coffin had a russet pall ensigned with a red cross. Another pall is described as made of black fur with gold embroidery. The Clothiers' Company at Worcester preserve one made of two copes of the early part of the reign of Henry VII.

Pallant. An independent jurisdiction, like the Archbishop of Canterbury's peculiar at Chichester.

Palmer. A pilgrim who carried a palm-branch in token that he had visited the holy places. He differed from a pilgrim in having no home, with no definite shrine to visit once for all, and in being never free until death released him from his vow. Palm was the symbol of triumph after confession of Christ (Rev. vii. 9).

Palm Sunday (Palm Easter; *Pascha floridum,* the Easter of flowers), a name as old as the time of Amalarius, for the Sunday before Easter, as the commemoration of the palm-strewn entrance of our Lord into Jerusalem. It was observed in the Greek Church as early as the fourth century; the first allusion to it in the West occurs in an epistle of St. Ambrose. Bede records its observance, which was general in the time of Charlemagne. In the middle age a priest seated on an ass was often led in procession through the streets. The blessing of the palms is mentioned in Italy in the fifth century, but was of earlier date in the East. In England it is not noticed until the eighth century. In some places this ceremony took place outside the city, and the procession was stopped at the entrance by finding the gates closed, as at Paris, until they were opened after having been struck with the cross. In other churches, as Salisbury, St. Alban's, Canterbury, and Bec, the Holy Eucharist was car-

ried before the procession, which, at Angers, in the eleventh
century, was made with especial ceremonial, owing to hostility
to Berangar; but in Germany and the East the Holy Scripture led the van; and Alcuin, in the eight century, says the
Gospels, encircled by palms and laid on a richly-ornamented
litter, were carried in procession by two priests vested in
albs. The ashes of the palms were used on Ash Wednesday
for sprinkling penitents. Indulgence Sunday in St. Jerome's Lectionary, from the reconciliation of penitents, but
more probably connected with the word indulgentia, remission of sins, which occurs in the Preface in St. Gregory's
Sacramentary. Great Sunday. Hosanna (save us, we pray)
Sunday, in the East and Southern Europe, in allusion to
St. Matt. xxi. 9–15; St. Mark xi. 9, 10; St. John xii. 13.
Pardon Sunday. Dominica broncherii. In Italy it is called
Olive Sunday; in Wales, Flower Sunday; in Spain, Portugal,
and France, Branch Sunday; in Russia, Sallow Sunday; in
land, Willow or Yew Sunday, because of the respective
substitutes for the Oriental palm in the procession on this
day, commemorating our Lord's triumphal entry into Jerusalem. At Malmesbury they still go in procession, carrying
catkins of the willow, to St. Martin's Hill on this day.
Flowers, box, or laurel were used in France. It was also
known as Pasch of Competents and Tradition Sunday, because the catechumens were taught the Creed on it; in Hert-
fordshire, as Fig Sunday, in allusion to our Lord cursing the
fig-tree; and at different times it has been characterized as
Capitilavium (head-washing), by Isidore and Alcuin, from the
washing of the heads of infants who were to be anointed
on Easter Eve. "In the beginning of the procession,"
Becon says, "the people goeth out, having every one a palm
in their hand, following the cross, which is covered with a
cloth," to signify "Christ adumbrated, shadowed, prefigured
by types, etc.," and "the fathers of the Old Testament."
"They go forth until they reach unto a certain stead of the
churchyard, where they stand still, and in the meanseason
the priest read the Gospel;" this signified the prophets
which prophesied of Christ's coming. "Then goeth forth
the people with the cross that is covered, and even straitways not far from them come other people (δ), and the priest
with the Sacrament, which have with them a cross, bare (a)

and uncovered, pricked full of green olives and palms (γ), and certain children before singing En Rex Venit (β)," to signify (a) Christ born; the prophets (β) that prophesied a little before He was born ; the innumerable abundance of virtues which are in Christ (γ), and His victory; and (δ) the people of the New Testament. " They are not so soon met but the bumbled cross vanisheth away and is conveyed from the people straitways. Then all the whole people inclose together with great joy, singing and making melody, triumphantly following the naked cross, bearing in their hands every one a palm ;" in some places they also bore green herbs instead of olives, to signify that types have vanished away, that there is now but one fold, and that the victory is won, and Christians may bring forth fruits of righteousness. " Then the people goeth somewhat further unto the churchyard, and there standeth still ; immediately after certain children (1), standing upon an high place right against the people, sing with a loud voice a certain hymn in the praise of our Lord, Gloria laus (2) ; at the end of every verse they cast down cakes or bread (4) with flowers (3)," to signify that Christians (1) should be simple and humble in heart as children. (2) glory in Christ, (3) showing an honest conversation towards God, and (4) mercy to His people. Then goeth the procession forth until they come to the church door, which when they come unto it is opened and certain children in the church singing. The song being once done, the priest taketh the cross in his hand and putteth the door from him with it, and so openeth it, and entereth it with all the other people after him," to show that Christ is the entrance to heaven, where the ransomed are with their everlasting songs. "When they are once entered into the church, then doth all this people kneel down, and the priest, plucking up the cloth wherewith the crucifix was covered, singeth a certain song," to signify the beatific vision revealed to the faithful departed. Cranmer says the ceremonial was designed to teach us to receive Christ into our hearts, as He was received into Jerusalem. The "stead" in the churchyard was sometimes called the pavilion, a tent being erected in bad weather, but occasionally there was a permanent structure like that called St. Germoe's chair in Cornwall, which is Early English in date and oblong in plan 6.3 × 3.6 feet, having two arches in front, and at the back a blind arcaded wall and a bench of stone. At Eyam the churchyard cross formed the station. At Caistor on this day a man holds over the priest's head a whip with a leathern purse at the end containing thirty pieces of silver, signifying the price of blood paid to the traitor, and with four pieces of witchelm tied upon the cross to typify the Gospel. Whilst the first lesson is being read he cracks it three times in the porch to commemorate St. Peter's denial, and during the second lesson waves it thrice over the reader in honour of the Holy Trinity. Upon the performance of this curious ceremony the tenure of Hunden Manor depends. There was also a custom of casting cakes from the church tower amongst boys assembled below, and of blessing palm crosses to be set on doors or carried in the purse. The veil was also drawn from before the rood during the processions. At the Reformation in England the making of crosses of wood on Palm Sunday during the reading of the Passion was forbidden.

Panagia. Bread cut crosswise, and distributed to Greek monks in refectory after every meal.

Pancarea. A representation of the six general councils painted on the walls of St. Peter's, Rome, in the eighth century.

Pane. A light in a window; a bay in a cloister; the side of a tower; a panel or compartment of wainscoting, or cielings.

Panteon. A Spanish term for a crypt behind the altar, serving as the burial-place of bishops.

Parabolani. District visitors, especially at Alexandria, in times of dangerous disease.

Paradise. A garden; "a place of Divine pleasantness, destined for the reception of the spirits of saints," Tertullian says. *See* CLOISTER.

Paramonàrius. In the East, a bailiff of Church lands; in the West, a resident verger and porter.

Parapet. A low breastwork to protect the gutters and roofs of churches, in England commonly battlemented or panelled, but in France usually pierced.

Paratrapezon. A side-table for the additional chalices in the Greek Church.

Parcel Gilt. Partly gilt.

Pardon Bell. The same as the Ave, which was tolled three times before and thrice after service; it was suppressed by

Bishop Shaxton. It derived its name from the indulgences attached to the recitation of the Angelus.

Pardoner. (*Quæstor.*) A missioner, usually a friar, who carried a seal, and sold Papal pardons and indulgences, and pretended to absolve from all punishment and guilt. Their wickedness was condemned by the Council of Lateran (1215), Pope Clement V. in the Council of Vienne, and Archbishop Neville in 1466. They buried suicides, remitted penances, and dispensed with vows, for money. The Council of Trent abolished their very name. At Segovia, St. Paul's Cathedral, and St. Helen's, Bishopsgate, there was a pardon-door, where indulgences were sold. At St. Paul's Cross a general absolution was pronounced after sermons, usually at Pentecost.

Pargetting. Ornamental plastering on walls.

Parish (*Paroikia*), as the word is used by St. Athanasius, St. Basil, St. Gregory Nazianzen, Eusebius, Irenæus, and even in Corboyl's Canons in 1127, in England; in the first three centuries the circuit of a bishop's jurisdiction, extending over a city and a district round it, whereas a diocese was the see of an exarch, or patriarch, embracing several provinces. In the fourth or fifth century parish sometimes designated both the city and rural divisions, and diocese marked a single church, as if it was the priest's diocese. Title was also a name given to distinguish the parish priest's church from the cathedral or see, because the clergy, being permanently attached, derived their title from it. As the population became Christianized, these parish churches were multiplied; but those in the city, for many centuries, were served by the cathedral clergy. Innocent I. used to send the Eucharist by acolyths to priests in Rome upon Sundays, and in the time of Justinian the capitular clergy served in the three basilicas of Constantinople in courses. The country parish clergy at first remitted the offertory to the bishop, who assigned to them a portion annually or monthly, until the middle of the fifth century; for a hundred years later in Spain, and for a yet longer period in Gaul and Germany. Pope Dionysius (*c.* 267) is said to have divided to priests churches and churchyards, and appointed parishes and dioceses. The African Canons, in 418, and the Council of Sardica, required the sanction of a primate, the provincial

synod, and the bishop of the district for the erection of a
new parish in the sense of a diocese; in 747, parishes, that
is districts, first assigned to priests by Theodore in the
South, and Wilfrid in the North, existed in England, and
are alluded to in 970 and 994.

Parish Chaplain. An assistant stipendiary, temporary or permanent; the medieval curate, whose pay was six marks a
year in 1347. In 1362 they had become scarce, preference
being given by unbeneficed clergy to the office of Mass
priests, who celebrated annals only, without cure of souls;
very stringent regulations were then made, in order to secure curates, whilst the pay of the others was not to exceed
five marks a year.

Parish Church. In a monastic or cathedral church, as at
Norwich, Kilkenny, Carlisle, Chester, Salisbury, and Hereford. Spanish cathedrals have usually an attached sagra-
rio or parroquia, or parish church, which communicates
with the main building; at Strengnäs, in the south aisle,
there is a peasants' church. Nice, like Manchester and
Ripon, are also parish churches. The Austin Canons of
Thornton, Carlisle, and Christchurch, and the secular canons at Hereford and Chichester, left the naves open for the
parish altar; the Benedictines, who, at Rochester, Westminster, St. Alban's, and other places, built a separate parish
church, yet tolerated it within the nave at Bodmin and Tynemouth. At Romsey, Marrick, St. Helen's (Bishopsgate),
Croyland, and Dunstable, the north aisle, and at Leominster
the south aisle, formed a parish church. At Lincoln, Bishop
Sutton removed the parishioners of St. Mary Magdalene out
of the nave. In order to give still further relief at Chichester, Scarborough, and Manchester, side chapels were
erected externally to the nave aisles; a large chapel at York,
and a church of St. Cross at Ely, were appended on the
north, as at Rochester and Waltham on the south, of the
nave; and at Sherborne, a western ante-church.

Parishioners, in 1250, 1281, and 1305, were required to find
in every church a chalice, principal vestment, a silk cope
for principal festivals, two others for rectors of the choir on
those days; a processional cross, a cross carried before the
dead, a bier, a holy-water vessel, with salt and bread; osculatory, paschal candlestick, censer, lantern, and little hand-

bell (for preceding the viaticum) ; two candlesticks for acolyths before the gospel; a legendary, antiphonar, grail,
psalter, tropar, ordinal, missal, and manual; high-altar
frontal, three surplices, a pyx, rogation banners, bells and
ropes, a font with lock and key, chrismatory, images, the
image of the patron saint, the church light (before the altar) ;
the repairs of the nave and tower, glass windows, aisles, and
churchyard fence. In 1014, parishioners were called the
priest's hyrmen, or hyremen. In 994 the only church furniture expressly required comprised holy books, housel, vessels, and mass vestments. The Sovereign is the parishioner
of the Archbishop of Canterbury.

Parish Priest. (1.) A medieval reader in a parish church,
in 1127; a temporary assistant in choir to a resident incumbent, without cure of souls; in 1287 he received forty shillings a year, whilst the chaplain had five marks, and the
mass priest was paid fifty shillings ; he is called a temporary
vicar in 1408. (2.) In 1362, a curate in a parish church.
(3.) A rector or vicar, in 1268; called by John de Athon
perpetual curate or perpetual vicar. The temporary parish
priests only preached if they had a licence; either of the
three meanings of the word can only be ascertained by the
context of the passages in which it occurs. Annual chaplains, in 1236, were required not to be removed by the
rectors without reasonable cause. In 1305, these stipendiaries, or chaplains, often were maintained by their friends ;
they attended choir in surplices, and could only celebrate
Mass, bury, and hear confessions by the permission of the
incumbent. *See* CURATE.

Parlour. (*Locutorium, spekehouse.*) At Durham, where it ocen-
pied the usual site of the slype, and St. Alban's, the monks
communicated in this room with visitors and tradespeople ;
there were two chambers bearing the same name : the private,
forensic, or outer parlour, was used for this purpose, and was
almost invariably near the western side of the cloister, or the
abbot's lodge ; whereas the regular parlour, or calefactory,
used as a withdrawing-room by monks or regular canons,
adjoined the refectory and chapter-house, and usually formed
a portion of the cellarage under the dormitory. In it also
monks communicated with the obedientiaries during reading
or cloister time. At Lincoln the canons had a common

chamber, in which part of the ceremonial of installation took place. In the outer parlour, a fugitive monk was revested in his habit after his reception.

Parson. (*Persona*, a word designating at first the King's chaplains and capitular clergy.) The parson was represented by the vicar (Tyndale says), and the latter, when he obtained a dispensation for non-residence, put in a parish priest, "who had most labour and least profit," taking " the mass-penny, trental, dirge money, bead roll, and confession penny." In 1164, parsons are said to hold of the King in capite, and the election of a bishop was made by the chief parsons in the King's chapel; in 1236 the title included rectors and vicars. In 1363, Thoresby mentions archdeacons, deans, plebans, provosts, chanters, and other parsons; the plebania was a rectory, with dependent chapelries.

Partibus, in, Infidelium. Bishops of some see in which there are few if any Christians, residence being dispensed with.

Particular Feasts. Festivals only locally observed, as St. Hilary's was in Aquitaine, in distinction to general feasts, which were kept universally.

Parvis. (1.) An enclosed space, paradise, or atrium; occasionally elevated above the ground; in front of a cathedral, as at Rouen, before the north front of the transept. It is a relic of the primitive arrangement; the ancient basilicas had a forecourt, surrounded with porticoes, and containing in the centre tombs, wells, fountains, and statues. At the close of the twelfth century the parvis became open, and only slightly marked out, to show the episcopal jurisdiction. On it scaffolds were erected, on which delinquent clerks were exposed, and criminals did open penance; the relics were exhibited, and the inferior clergy were ranged, whilst their superiors occupied the open galleries above to sing the Gloria. At Rheims, and Notre Dame, Paris, the parvis was enclosed with a low wall; at Amiens and Lisieux the raised platform exists; and at Rhadegund's, Poictiers, the coped wall, with kneeling angels, dogs, and lions, and its five entrances remain perfect. A trace of the same plan may be seen in front of Lichfield. At Laach, and St. Ambrose's, Milan, the parvis and cloister remain; and the forecourt at Parenzo, Salerno, Aschaffenburg, St. Clement's, and other churches at Rome. Staveley derived the word *a pueris parvis*, from little boys educated in the parvise, and the song-school at Chester was held over the south porch; but the true derivation is paradise, the term applied to the cloister garth at Oxford. Bishop Cooper says the sophisters kept logic disputations in the parvise school. (2.) A chamber over a porch, as at Drontheim, Paisley, Christchurch (Hants), and Hereford.

Passionists. An order founded, 1779, by Paul of the Cross.

Passoire. A cullender, or strainer, for the wine and water when poured into the chalice. It dates from the seventh century.

Pastophoria. (1.) That which is borne on a shrine. (2.) Paston, a small chapel, the sacristy of the Greek Church; from *passo*, in the sense of an embroidery, which was wrought upon the curtain which hung before it. It comprehended the diakonikon and skeuophylakion. (3.) The watchers' chamber.

Pastoral Staff. (*Baculus pastoralis, cambuca, pedum, crocia, virga, ferula, cambutta* in Gregory's Sacramentary.) A symbol of episcopal authority, resembling a shepherd's crook, and pointed at the end as an emblem both of encouragement and correction. In the fourth century it resembled a simple cane with a knob, or else a crutch-like staff, like a Tau. The Russian bishops use one with two curved heads. After the twelfth century the staffs increased in height and ornamentation, but the abbots, especially those of the order of St. Anthony, long retained the Tau-shaped one. The Pope gave up the use of the staff in the middle of the twelfth century, and cardinal-bishops no longer carry it. The early staffs were made of cypress-wood generally, and afterwards of ivory, copper-gilt, crystal, and precious metals richly carved, jewelled, or enamelled. The silver cambuca of St. Remi is mentioned in the sixth century. The staff has either a simple crook or volute, or one enriched with foliage, or with a sculptured subject. Between 1150 and 1280 the crook was often formed of a serpent (the old dragon), or contained St. Michael or the lion of Judah, and at a later period the prelate praying before his patron saint. Beautiful crocketed work also was added on the exterior of the crook. The banner (*sudarium, vexillum*) on the staff originally was a handkerchief. The bishops of Oxford, Chichester, Rochester, Salisbury, Honolulu, Capetown, and some other colonial

prelates have resumed the use of the staff. Fine specimens
are preserved, those of Wykeham, of silver-gilt, enamelled,
at New College; of Fox, at Corpus Christi College; of Laud,
at St. John's College, Oxford; of Smith, of the seventeenth
century, at York; of Mews and Trelawney, at Winchester;
and are represented on the effigies of an archbishop at Cashel,
four archbishops of York, and Bishop Hacket of Lichfield, all
of the seventeenth century. The British Museum contains
the head of a staff with Limoges enamel, of the thirteenth
century, and the coronation of the Virgin in the head; another, of the same date and character, with an inscription
only, from Peterborough; Lyndwood's wooden staff with
delicate foliage, of the fifteenth century; and a bronze staff,
with a silver head and crestwork of birds, which was used
by Archbishop Finnen of Leinster, who died in 1108. At
Chichester the head and pommel of a staff of obsidian and
jet, and an ivory crook with a bird and foliage, A'Beckett's
at Sens, two at Maryland and Connecticut, two in the
Museum Clugny, and three, of the twelfth century, at
Hildesheim, are of great interest.

The staff of a præcentor had a double curve by way of distinction. The oriental staff is straight and surmounted by a
globe and Tau cross, or has two interlaced serpents. The
French abbot's staff has its crook turned inwards, to show
that his authority extended only over his house, whilst the
bishop's crook turned outwards, to denote his external
jurisdiction over his diocese. At Worcester the mitred prior
was allowed to carry only a blue-and-white staff in the presence of the bishop. The wooden staff of Abbot Sebroke of
Gloucester, who died 1450, is now preserved at Newcastle,
and is nearly five feet in length. The crook has projecting
bosses and two tabernacled figures in the centre. The Tau-
shaped staff of Morand, Abbot of St. Germain des Prés in
the tenth century, was of hazel, with a cross-piece of ivory.
In the Penitential of Theodore and the Ordo Romanus the
bishop gives the abbot his staff and sandals. The former
was then curved back like a bishop's. The veil on the
abbot's staff was covered in the presence of the diocesan.

Paten, so called from its open shape. A small flat plate for
holding the sacred element of bread, formed of the same
material as the chalice, and invented by Pope Zephyrinus.

Walafrid Strabo mentions some of glass, which was forbidden by the Council of Tribur. But long before this date patens were of gold and silver, and such are spoken of in the times of Pope Urban, Damasus, and Sylvester, but were formerly of larger size than at present. They were consecrated, as Moses, by God's command, sanctified the vessels of the Tabernacle. In some places the deacon, after the Lord's Prayer, having received the paten from the subdeacon, lifts it up so as to be seen of the people, in order to notify the congregation that the communion is about to commence. In the Greek Church it stands on the left of the chalice. Besides the altar patens there were (1) ministerial, of larger size, for containing the breads given to the people; (2) chrismal, hollow in shape, and used for containing chrism for baptismal confirmation; (3) ornamental, with carvings and symbolical images, set on altars as decorations. Church plate of medieval date is necessarily rare. In 1070 William I. robbed all the English minsters of their shrines and chalices, and in 1193–4 another raid was made upon them for the ransom of Richard I. There are three ancient specimens at York, one engraved with a hand upraised in benediction. Another, at Chichester, of the twelfth century, has the same design between a crescent and star; another has the Agnus Dei; a third, of pewter, was taken from a bishop's grave, with a chalice of the same material. A paten and chalice, once at St. Alban's, remain at Trinity College, 1527; others at Nettlecomb, of the middle of the fifteenth century; a communion chalice, of the same date, at Monk's Kirby, Warwickshire; a paten and chalice, of Elizabethan date, at Wymondham, St. Mary's, Bedford, Hillmorton, Withybrook, Caxton, Long Itchington, Churchover. In 1685 Archbishop Sancroft consecrated church plate at Coleshill.

Patriarch. A local title, of Eastern origin, almost synonymous with primate, and derived from Acts vii. 8. The successors of the Apostles were so called, as if the fathers of all other Churches. These were Rome, Alexandria, Antioch, and Jerusalem in the third century, but the name and duties were hardly established before 440. At first each quarter of the world had its patriarch—Europe, Rome, Asia, Antioch, Africa, Alexandria. At a later period there were two more —those of Jerusalem, as the mother of all churches, "the

Apostolical See" of St. James the First, founded by the
Council of Chalcedon; and Constantinople, by the Council
of Constantinople, 451, as Byzantium was another Rome
and imperial city. The patriarch of Constantinople took
the title of œcumenical, or universal (587), and in 934 received
the honour of the pall from Pope John XI. St. Gregory enumerates only four patriarchs. The bishops of Aquileia became
patriarchs in the sixth century, and were confirmed in their
rank in the eleventh century. The bishops of Lyons and
Bourges whilst their cities were capitals of kingdoms, the
Archbishop of Toledo at a later date, enjoyed the title.
Antioch, the metropolis of the East, the first see of St.
Peter, embraced five provinces. Alexandria, the evangelical
see founded by St. Mark, contained Libya, Pentapolis, and
the Thebaid, but in the seventh century lost the distinction.
Jerusalem embraced Syria and Palestine; the rule of Constantinople extended over Pontus, Thrace, and Asia, the
metropolitans of Cæsarea and Heraclea being deprived of
their power over their suffragan sees. To the patriarchs
lay appeals; they consecrated metropolitans and convened
national councils. The five Roman patriarchal churches are
St. John Lateran, "the chiefest of all," St. Peter, St. Paul,
St. Mary Major, and St. Laurence. There are also patriarchs of Venice, Lisbon, and the Indies. The dress of the
four patriarchs at Rome, Constantinople, Antioch, Alexandria, and Jerusalem, ranking next to cardinals, resembles
that of cardinals except that the colour is purple. In the
Papal chapel they wear over their soutane and rochets amicts
and a purple serge cappa, gathered up with a fold under the
left arm, with a white ermine tippet, and when the Pope
officiates, plain linen mitres and copes of the colour of the
day. The Greek patriarchs have a lampadouchon, or lighted
candlestick, carried before them. In the twelfth century
the right, hitherto exclusively attached to the pontificate, of
having a cross borne before them was conceded to all patriarchs and metropolitans, and granted to all archbishops from
the time of Gregory IX.

Patrons (helpers in diseases, etc.) :—

St. Agatha presided over fire and valleys; St. Barbara, over hills; St. Florian, over fire; St. Anne over riches; St. Osyth, over house-keys; St. Sylvester, over woods; St. Vincent and St. Anne, over lost goods; St. Urban, over vineyards; St. Anthony, over pigs; St. Gall, St. Leodegar, or St. Ferrioll, over geese; St. Leonard, over ducks; St. German, over hen-roosts; St. Gertrude, over eggs; St. Huldeth, over mice; St. Hubert, over dogs; St. Magnus, over locusts; St. Pelagius, over oxen; St. Wendoline, over sheep. St. Barbara took care that none died without the viaticum.

St. Judocus preserved from mildew; St. Magnus, from grasshoppers; St. Mark, from sudden death.

St. Leonard broke prison chains.
St. Otilia watched over the head; St. Blaise, over the neck; St. Erasmus, the chest; St. Catherine, the tongue; St. Laurence, the back; St. Burghart, the lower members.

St. Romain drove away spirits.

St. Roche cured pestilence; St. Apollonia, toothache; St. Otilia, bleared eyes; St. Eutropius, dropsy; St. Chiacre, emerods, St. Wolfgang, the gout; St. Valentine, the falling sickness; St. Erasmus, the colic; St. Blaise, the quinsy; St. John, Shorne; St. Pernel, the ague; St. Vitus, madness; St. Laurence, rheumatism; SS. Wilgford and Uncumber, bad husbands.

St. Susanna helped in infancy; St. Florian, in fire.

Patron Saints (*Defensores*) of professions, trades, conditions, and callings. Several are clearly connected by a sort of pun (as St. Clair, of lamplighters; St. Cloud, of the nailmakers; and St. Blanc, or Blanchard, of laundresses), or are derived from some incident in their life (as St. Peter, of fishmongers), or in their legends, as St. Dunstan, of goldsmiths; St. Sebastian, of archers; St. Blaise, of combmakers; St. Laurence, of girdlers and cooks; SS. Hubert and Eustace, of huntsmen; St. Cecilia, of musicians; St. Catherine, of philosophers. Some preside over different trades, as St. Eloi, patron of hangmen, coachmen, tinmen, nail and shoeing smiths, and metalworkers; St. George, of soldiers, clothiers, and horsemen; St. Anne, of grooms, toymen, turners, and combmakers; St. Michael, of fencing-masters and pastrycooks; St. John at the Latin Gate, of printers, attorneys, and papermakers; IV. Coronati, of masons and builders; SS. Cosmas and Damian, of physicians and surgeons; SS. Crispin and Crispinian, of cordwainers and embroiderers; St. Nicholas, of butchers, scholars, seamen, and thieves; St. Vincent, of vinedressers and vinegar-makers.

Artillery, and engineers, and mechanics, and married women, St. Barbara.
Bakers, SS. Wilfred and Honorius.
Basketmakers, St Anthony.
Blind men, St. Thomas à Becket.
Bookbinders, the Ascension.
Booksellers, St. John the Evangelist.
Boys, St. Gregory.
Brewers, SS. Honorius and Clement.
Brokers, St. Maurice.
Builders, SS. Coronati, Severus, Severianus, Carpophorus, and Victorius.

Butchers, SS. Anthony the Abbot and Francis.
Carpenters, SS. Joseph and Andrew.
Carters, St. Catherine.
Chandlers, the Purification (Candlemas).
Charcoal-cutters, St. Anthony.
Children, The Holy Innocents, St. Felicitas.
Chinamen, St. Anthony of Padua.
Common women, SS. Bride and Afra.
Confectioners, the Purification.
Coopers, SS. Mary Magdalen and Hilary.

Captives, SS. Leonard and Barbara.
Curriers, SS. Simon and Jude.
Divines, St. Thomas Aquinas.
Drapers, SS. Blaise and Leodegar.
Drunkards, SS. Martin and Urban.
Falconers, St. Tibba.
Ferrymen, St Christopher.
Fools, St. Mathurin.
Fullers, St. Severus.
Gardeners, SS. Urban of Langres and Fiacre.
Girls, St. Catherine.
Glaziers, St. James of Germany.
Granarers, millers, St. Anthony.
Grocers, the Purification, St. Anthony.
Hairdressers, St. Louis.
Hatters, SS. James and William.
Horsedealers, St. Louis.
Hotelkeepers, St. Theodotus.
Jockeys, St. Euloge.
Labourers, SS. Walstan and Isidore.
Lawyers, St. Ives.
Locksmiths, St. Peter-ès-Liens.
Lovers, St. Valentine.
Master-shoemakers, St. Martin.
Matmakers, the Nativity.
Mercers, St. Florian.
Millers, SS. Martin and Arnold.
Mowers and reapers, St. Walstan.
Nurses, St. Agatha.
Painters, SS. Luke and Lazarus.
Pavlours, St. Roch.

Peasants, St. Lucia.
Physicians, St. Pantaleon.
Pilgrims, St. Julian.
Pinmakers, St. Sebastian.
Plasterers, IV. Coronati.
Ploughmen, St. Urban.
Potters, St. Gore.
Saddlers, St. Gualfard.
Seamen and fishermen, SS. Nicholas, Dismas, Christopher, and Elmo.
Shepherds, SS. Neomaye, Drugo, and Wendolin.
Spinners, St. Catherine.
Spurriers, St. Giles.
Students, scholars, SS. Jerome, Laurence, Mathurin, Mary Magdalene, Catherine, Gregory the Great, Ursula.
Tailors, SS. John Baptist, Goodman, and Anne.
Tanners, SS. Simon, Jude, and Clement.
Taverners, St. Laurence.
Theologians, SS. Augustine and Thomas Aquinas.
Thieves, St. Dismas.
Travellers, St Julian.
Virgins, St. Winifred.
Washerwomen, SS. Hunna and Lidoise.
Weavers, St. Stephen.
Woolcombers, SS. Blaise and Mary Magdalene.

The dedication of a church often commemorates the patron of the staple trade of the vicinity.

Patrons of Countries, Cities, and Towns:—

Asturia, St. Ephrem.
Austria, SS. Colman and Leopold.
Bavaria, SS. George, Mary, and Wolfgang.
Bohemia, SS. Norbert, Wenceslaus, John Nepomuc, Adalbert, Cosmas, Damian, Cyril, and Methodius.
Brabant, SS. Peter, Philip, and Andrew.
Brandenburg, St. John Baptist.
Brunswick, St. Andrew.
Burgundy, SS. Andrew and Mary.
Denmark, SS. Anscharius and Canute.
England, SS. George and Mary.
Flanders, St. Peter.
France, SS. Mary, Michael, and Denis.
Germany, SS. Martin, Boniface, and George.
Hanover, St. Mary.
Holland, St. Mary.
Holstein, St. Andrew.

Hungary, SS. Mary and Louis.
Ireland, St. Patrick.
Italy, St. Anthony.
Leon, SS. Isidore, Pelagius, Ramiro, and Claude.
Luxembourg, SS. Peter, Philip, and Andrew.
Mecklenburg, St. John the Evangelist.
Naples, St. Januarius.
Navarre, SS. Fermin and Xavier.
Norway, SS. Anscharius and Olaus.
Oldenburg, St. Mary.
Parma, SS. Hilary, John Baptist, Thomas, and Vitalis.
Poland, SS. Stanislaus and Hedariga.
Pomerania, SS. Mary and Otho.
Portugal, SS. Sebastian, James, and George.
Prussia, SS. Mary, Adalbert, and Andrew.
Russia, SS. Nicholas, Andrew, Wladimir, and Mary.

Sardinia, St. Mary.
Savoy, St. Maurice.
Scotland, St. Andrew.
Sicily, SS. Mary, Vitus, Rosalie, and George.
Spain, SS. James the Great, Michael, Thomas à Becket, and Edward.
Suabia, St. George.

Sweden, SS. Bridget, Eric, Anscharius, and John.
Switzerland, SS. Martin, Gall, and Mary.
Venice, SS. Mark, Justina, and Theodore.
Wales, St. David.

Many cities and towns bear the name of their patron saint, to whom the principal church is dedicated, as St. Remo, St. Sebastian, St. Malo, St. Omer, St. Quentin, St. Die, Peterborough, Bury St. Edmund's, St. David's, St. Asaph, St. Alban's, Boston (St. Botolph's town), Kircudbright (St. Cuthbert's church), Malmesbury (Maidulph's town), St. Neot's, St. Ive's, St. Burcan's, St. German's, St. Marychurch, St. Andrew's. Others have special saints: St. Fredeswide, of Oxford; St. Sebald, of Nuremberg; St. Giles, of Edinburgh; SS. Peter and Paul, of Rome; St. Mark, of Venice; St. Stephen, of Vienna; St. Geneviève, of Paris; St. Januarius, of Naples; St. Nicholas, of Aberdeen; St. Gudule, of Brussels; St. Norbert, of Antwerp; St. George, of Genoa; St. Ursula, of Cologne; St. Bavon, of Ghent; St. Ambrose, of Milan; St. Vincent, of Lisbon; St. Boniface, of Mentz; St. Domatian, of Bre; St. Romuold, of Mechlin.

Pavement. From the fourth century churches were carefully paved, as the Jewish temple had a wooden floor. The narthex was laid with plaster, the nave with wood, and the sanctuary with mosaic. The custom of burying within churches between the seventh and tenth centuries led to the practice of covering the pavement with memorials of the departed; and at length the floors were laid with stone, marble, or tesselated or plain tiles. Rich pavements, like marqueterie in stone or Roman mosaic, occur in most parts of Italy, at St. Omer, St. Denis, in the Rhine country, at Canterbury, Westminster, and in the churches of St. Mary Major, St. Laurence Without the Walls, of the time of Adrian I., and St. Martin of the period of Constantine at Rome. The patterns are usually geometrical, but figures, flowers, animals, and the zodiac are frequently introduced with an effect equal to the richest tapestry. This decoration lasted till the twelfth century, but at that time, and in the subsequent period, marble became rare, and hard blocks of freestone were used, and lastly tiles. There is a magnificent

pavement at Rheims, commenced in 1090. Pliny called
these beautiful additions to buildings aserota (Gr., not to be
swept); and in the time of Cicero they were known as
emblemata vermiculata and opus musivarum, and the invention is attributed to Sosias of Pergamus. In England
rushes, hay, straw, and on great feasts ivy-leaves, were
strewn on the floors of the noblest minsters. Tessellated
pavements occur at St. David's, Malvern, Salisbury, Worcester, Prior Crauden's Chapel (Ely), Stone Church, and
Chinnor. The sacred monogram, the fish, the lamb, the
interlaced triangle, the fleur-de-lys, and the pelican are
found at Gloucester, Hereford, and Evesham. Letters werē
found at Beaulieu, portions of inscriptions and mottoes,
which are complete at Malvern and Gloucester; figures, as
at Tintern, and Romsey, and Margam; armorial bearings,
c. 1450, at Gloucester; quatrefoils at Shrewsbury; birds,
grotesques, and animals at Christchurch, Hants, St. Alban's,
Beaulieu, Evesham, Romsey, Salisbury, Kirkstall, and
Shrewsbury; and sometimes large designs, made up of a
large number of separate tiles, as at Haughmond, St.
Alban's, Haccombe, and Shrewsbury. The use of marble
pavements in choirs commenced in the seventeenth century,
and at Canterbury in 1704. At Lichfield (formerly paved
with cannel coal and alabaster) and Chichester there are
superb pavements of marble and tile recently laid down.

Pax. (*Deosculatorium, osculatory.*) In lieu of the ceremonial
kiss of mutual salutation and affection at Mass. Owing to
its abuses, about the twelfth or thirteenth century, when
Low Masses came into vogue, and the division of the sexes
in church began to be neglected, a tablet of metal, usually of
latten, and sometimes of precious stone, was introduced.
It was kissed by the celebrant after the Agnus Dei, and
offered by the acolyth, serving-boy, or parish clerk, to all
the clerks in choir, to be kissed after the prayer and Pacem,
and then by the congregation, in order. Beleth says that
the priest first kissed the Eucharist, or the seal of the altar,
and transmitted it by the deacon to the congregation, but
men were not to kiss women. At Milan a prayer followed,
said aloud, and not as in the Roman use, in secret. The
new fashion pervaded Italy, Spain, Germany, and France,
but it has now altogether fallen into disuse among the laity,

and in several places among the clergy, except those engaged immediately about the altar or in choir, as at Caen, in St. Stephen's Abbey. In England the pax was sometimes called the pax bread (*brede*, *brœde*, a board), because made of wood. The pax, mentioned at York, c. 1250, and in the Constitutions of Peckham, c. 1280, is called the osculatory in 1250; the asser ad pacem in a Council of Oxford, 1287; the paxillum at St. Paul's, 1298; in the Council of Merton, 1300, tabula pacis; and in France the porte paix. There is one of silver-gilt, of the date of Henry IV., at New College, with an engraving of the crucifix; another, enamelled with jewels, of the fifteenth century, at Arezzo; and a third at Cologne. Other subjects were also employed, such as the Annunciation, the Trinity, the Adoration of the Magi, the Baptism in Jordan, or the patron saint of the church. One of glass was given by Chichele to his College of All Souls, Oxford. At Doncaster, in 1548, "the clerk took the pax without the church door, and said to the people, This is a token of joyful peace betwixt God and man's conscience. Christ alone is the Peacemaker." At Durham the embossed cover of the Book of the Gospels and Epistles served as the pax.

Pax Vobis. (St. John xix. 19–21.) The salutation made by the bishop at Pontifical High Mass, in place of the customary Dominus vobiscum, used at other times after the Gloria in Excelsis. A Council of Rome in 561 restricted the salutation to these times, but St. Chrysostom and St. Cyril of Jerusalem show that the Greek clergy invariably used this form.

Pedalia. (1.) Foot-cloths in front of the altar. In 1092 we find bearskins used for this purpose. (2.) Collections of the creeds and canons of general councils in the Greek Church.

Fedaries. Consecrated sandals for pilgrims.

Pedilavium. (1.) Feet-washing, a ceremonial at Milan, and in other places, observed at holy baptism. (2.) The lavanda, in the fifth century, which followed the Holy Communion on Maundy Thursday.

Pedules. Shoes or slippers.

Pelican. One supporting the lectern is at Wimborne. At Waterford there was a great pelican for the Bible, with two great standing candlesticks above a man's height, and a brass eagle, until 1651. At Sefford and North Walsham a pelican crowns the font cover. *See* EMBLEMS and LECTERN.

Pelvicula Amularum. Metal stands for the cruets.

Penance. (*Pœnitentia.*) Punishment for sin: (1) private, enjoined by a confessor; (2) special, enjoined by the priest for notorious crime; (3) solemn, enjoined by a bishop alone, and ordinarily restricted to Lent, the offender being put out of the church, and reconciliation, or absolution, given on Maundy Thursday; in 1281 it was made with imposition of hands. Years—seven, ten, or twelve—were formerly appointed for penance for sin; the Council of Elvira determined five as the number for accidental homicide, and seven for murder or malice prepense; ten years for adulterers, or unchastity in a priest. Sewal, Archbishop of York, used to sit in the minster porch upon Maundy Thursday, when the penitents were tied up to two large pillars and publicly scourged. In the early Church there were three kinds of penance: (1) segregation, *aphorismos*, prohibition of offering at the altar, for lighter offences; (2) deprivation of communion for graver faults; (3) effacement of the name from the list of the faithful, and exclusion from church, for great sins. At first the deacons interposed, and besought the bishop to reconcile the penitent; if the bishop assented, after examination of the offender, he imposed a fast of a fortnight, three, five, or seven weeks, and at length gave absolution; after three episcopal monitions a sinner was regarded as a heathen man and a publican. In the third century penance became a subject of canonical legislation. Canonical penance was inflicted for idolatry, adultery, and homicide, but required great prudence in its administration, and was only imposed after a solemn judicial act. Reconciliation at first was restricted to bishops; but at the time of death St. Cyprian, and the Councils of Seville, Agde, and Elvira gave power of private reconciliation to priests and deacons. In the ninth century, priests obtained the right of public absolution. In the East, public absolution was given on Good Friday or Easter Eve; in the West, the day was Maundy Thursday, and in both Churches at the time of Mass, before the Lord's Prayer. The penitents, in haircloth and ashes, stood before the ambon, and from it the bishop laid hands upon them, after being entreated by his clergy in set forms of address. Public penance for secret sins was remitted in the seventh century; in the eighth century it was commuted for alms and prayers; and in the twelfth century, for pilgrimages; 'and then at length indulgences were given. The two latest instances of public penance in England occurred at Bristol in 1812, and Ditton, Cambridgeshire, in 1849. In 1554 the penitents stood wrapped in a white sheet, with a taper in one hand and a rod in the other, during a sermon, after which they were struck on the head at Paul's Cross, and so reconciled. In 1389, men in shirt and breeches, and women in their shifts, holding sacred images, stood during Mass barefooted and bareheaded, and finally made an offering to the priest. Weepers, audientes, kneelers, consistentes, were the names of the classes of penitents in the early Church. There are several Italian orders of penitents, or of mercy, who attend criminals; one at Florence dates from 1488. The Canons of Rouen and the Abbot of Battle could reprieve a criminal going to execution, if they met him. The Friars of the Penitence, or Sack, came to Cambridge in 1259. In a monastery a monk was separated from the common table for a small fault, but for a greater fault was thrice scourged in chapter, put on short commons, had his head cowled, put in solitary confinement, and lay prostrate at the hours before the choir door (1092, 1298, 1343). In 960, in severe penance, a pilgrimage was made by a man never passing two nights in one place, never eating meat, clipping his hair or nails; if rich, he was to found a church, build a bridge, make roads, or emancipate his serfs.

Pendant. (1.) A hanging ornament in Perpendicular vaults or cielings. (2.) A spandril in a Gothic canopy.

Pendentive. (1.) The spandril or triangular space of a vault left between the intersections and crossings of the ribs. (2.) A corbelling out in angles which are formed by arches carrying a square building into an octagonal or circular form. (3.) The part of a vault between the arches of a dome.

Penitentiary. The office of general confessor or penitentiary priests in a diocese, mentioned by Sozomen and Socrates, was abolished by Nectarius at Constantinople in the reign of Theodosius, and generally in the East, but was retained in the West for regulating penance and hearing confessions. Deans and priests of penitents are mentioned by the Council of Agde, in the ceremonial of Ash Wednesday, as imposing penance on offenders. In England, in 1237, as at Salisbury, general confessors were appointed in all cathedral churches, and others in every rural deanery were nominated by the bishop to receive confessions from parsons and minor clerks who were reluctant to make them to the rural deans. In 1281 the common penitentiaries heard cases reserved to the bishop in the case of both clergy and laity, and Lyndwood says secular canons confessed to the bishop, the dean, or persons appointed by the bishop or the dean and chapter. The external penitentiary was a diocesan confessor acting within a certain district; the internal penitentiary regulated penances and absolved in graver cases reserved to the bishop. At Canterbury and Peterborough there were two, at Dunkeld four grand penitentiaries. At Exeter the dean, in 1225 and in 1284, as at York the subdean, yearly visited the sick who could not attend at the cathedral. At Salisbury the penitentiary on Maundy Thursday, standing at the church door, besought the bishop to reconcile penitents; at Worcester he distributed the ashes on the first day of Lent. In foreign cathedrals he was to be forty years of age. The office existed at Siguença, Bayeux, Sens, Lisieux, Orleans, Amiens (1219), and Rouen, where he preached on Holy Thursday, and was præcentor, as at Hereford. In the latter instance he could not leave the city, even with chapter licence. *See* GOLDEN PREBENDARY.

Pentacle of Solomon. A five-angled figure, composed of two triangles interlaced. The legendary seal or sigil of Solomon, carved on an emerald, by which he ruled the gins or demons, representing the five fingers of the hand of omnipotence. David's shield has six angles.

Pentecostal. A contribution or duty paid by every house or family to the cathedral church at Pentecost, in consideration of a general absolution then pronounced.

Perambulation of the circuit of parishes made on the Rogation Days; mentioned in 926, and ordered in 1616; now known as beating the parish bounds, as the marks are struck with a stick.

Per Annulum et Baculum, bishoprics were given by the tradition of the staff and ring.

Per viam Compromissi. Election of a superior by the sworn delegates of a convent, who retired into a secret chamber, and, after invocation of the Holy Ghost, named the person on whom their choice had fallen.

Per viam Spiritus Sancti was an unanimous election by the whole convent, as if by Divine inspiration.

Per viam Scrutinii was when each monk voted singly in the chapter-house, in the presence of the bishop.

Perch. (1.) A bracket. (2.) A tall candle. (3.) *See* pp. 64, 229.

Perpendicular Style. Early, 1375–1425. Late, 1425–1524. Professor Willis believes that this style may be traced first at Gloucester, but it is usually attributed to William of Wykeham when clerk of the works at Edyngdon. The fine open timber cielings and fan-traceried vaults of stone are peculiar to England. The tracery from the window usurps walls and roofs; piers and arches are no longer in justly-balanced proportion; some members disappear, as the triforium—others are exaggerated, as the clerestory. Panelling is profusely employed; fan-tracery is much used; the pillars are clustered and of lozenge shape; pinnacles are usually square, the arches obtusely pointed, ogee, and four-centred; window-tracery is vertical; transoms cross the mullions at right angles; the vaulted and depressed roof becomes very complicated; doors have a square moulding, forming a spandril, which is generally feathered or has tracery; large hollows are in the jambs on either side; the upper parts of capitals are often battlemented, or have the Tudor flower, a sort of angular fleur-de-lys; parapets are battlemented, gurgoyles universal; capitals are frequently octagonal and composed merely of mouldings; pillars grow taller and are of lozenge form, standing west and south; arches are narrower; buttresses are bold and projecting; and windows of great size form a majestic range, nearly occupying the space of every bay between them; there is an absence of fillets, and rounds and hollows are fused. Its marked characters are angularity and squareness; arches are ordinarily four-centred; doors are generally panelled; mouldings become flatter, rarely splayed, and have large shallow hollows, form ogees or undulate, or are concave in the centre and convex at the ends; splays are unfrequent; members are separated by quirks. Enrichments are very various, formed of foliage,

grotesques, and heraldic devices; cielings are flat, and usually divided into square compartments by ribs; and bosses
and pendants are profusely employed. Large richly-cano-
pied recesses are employed for tombs, and chantries and
screen-work introduced about them. The decadence of
medieval art was contemporaneous with the discoveries of
natural science and the commencement of a new order of
studies. It shared the transitory lot of ideas to which it
had subjected immortal thought. Its revival in a century
rich in ample mechanical resources will possibly rival, perhaps exceed, all its triumphs in the past.

Perpent. A through or border stone of ashlar, appearing on
either side of a wall, which it pierces. A perpeyn wall is a
buttress or pier projecting to support a roof, or a corbel.

Personati. A term not earlier than the eleventh century,
which came into use after the time of Alexander III. (1.)
Persons, canons holding office with precedence in chapter
and choir after dignitaries, either by institution or custom.
A dignitary was also a person because his person was ho-
noured and he was a person constituted in dignity. The
quatuor personæ were the four internal dignitaries. Until
recently the dignitaries were called the parsons at Hereford.
(2.) Stipendiary clerks or chaplains perpetually resident in a
cathedral or collegiate church, like the chantry priests of
St. William at York and the rectors of choir at Beverley,
holding offices for life. At Grenoble, Sens, Arles, and
Nevers they had the responsibility of the ordinary choral
services.

Peter's, St., Day (June 29) has been traced back to the third
century. In 348 Prudentius mentions that the Pope celebrated the Holy Communion in both St. Peter's and St.
Paul's churches at Rome on this festival, which in the
sixth century was observed at Constantinople, and was kept,
until the Reformation, associated with the name of St. Paul;
whose Conversion was not generally commemorated on January 25 until the twelfth century. Cathedra Sancti Petri is a
commemoration virtually of SS. Peter and Paul, but its title
is the Chair of St. Peter, wherein he first sat at Rome, January 18. On February 22 his chair at Antioch is commemorated.

Peter Pence, paid on Peter Mass, August 1, were granted by

King Ina of the West Saxons at the close of the seventh
century for the maintenance of the English College at Rome.
King Offa, about sixty years later, gave one penny of every
hearth to the same purpose in the kingdom of Mercia as a
penance for his murder of King Ethelbert. In Northumbria,
in 950, a priest and two thanes collected this tax and paid it
in at the bishop's see. In 958 the defaulter had to go on a
pilgrimage to Rome, for which the payment was a composition, and moreover pay a heavy fine. They were discon-
tinned by Edward III. whilst the Popes were at Avignon,
but afterwards revived, and finally abolished by Henry VIII.

Pew. A bench, or stool (like Dutch *puy*, a desk-front to
kneel at). Open benches are mentioned at Exeter in 1287,
but at Durham, somewhat later, the enclosed cloister carols;
and, in the fifteenth century, "parrocked" seats in churches,
with garnets, or hinges, to the doors, were called pews.
In 1215, in Durham diocese, patrons of churches, and in 1225
in Scotland, nobles were allowed seats in the chancel. In a
London will, dated 1453, we read, "*sedile vocatum pew,*"
which probably was allotted to women. The old French
word *puie* meant a balcony, a gallery built on balks or posts
of timber; and it has been unnecessarily suggested that pew
may only be a form of podium, a book-desk, or the crutch used
by monks before sitting was permitted. Pepys speaks of
the bishop's raised throne in St. Paul's as the pue. Weever,
in 1631, first mentions "high and easy" pews as a fashion
of no long continuance, and worthy of reformation. Pews
probably did not come into fashion until the fifteenth century, when stationary pulpits were erected. Previously to
that date people sat on the bench tables in the aisles, or
knelt along the floors, as in a miniature of Archbishop Arundel represented as preaching; and the engraving of the Litany prefixed to Bishop Sparrow's ' Rationale.' There are
ancient carved pews, or benches, at Caxton, Finedon, Net-
tlecombe, Talland, Lavenham, Shellesley, Walsh, Long Melford, and Langley Marsh. At Bottesford there were circular
stone benches round the nave pillars. Latimer and Bradford,
in 1553, speak of timeserving and unwilling conformists at
the Reformation, neither worshipping nor kneeling, but
" sitting still in their pews" at the time of Mass. And it is
quite clear that the seats were open and unscreened at that

time; but in the next reign, Bishop Corbet of Norwich speaks of pews, instead of stools, which had "become tabernacles, with rings and curtains, casements, locks and keys, and cushions," and suggests the addition of pillows and bolsters. "They are," he says, "either to hide some vice or to proclaim one, to hide disorder or proclaim pride." In the fifteenth century three-legged stools were in use; and wooden seats are mentioned in a constitution of Bishop Grostete. In 1509 six and eightpence was paid for part of a pew at St. Margaret's, Westminster. The reading pue, first mentioned in the rubric of 1662, was the reader's stall in the chancel. It had two desks—one on the west for the Holy Bible, and the other for the Prayer Book facing eastwards, as in Hooker's Church at Drayton Beauchamp. In 1571 Grindal called it "the pulpit, where prayers are said." Calamy applies the word to designate an open-air pulpit. George Herbert made his pulpit and reading pue of equal height, so as to be of equal honour and estimation, and agree like brethren.

Philip and James the Less (or Jacob), SS. (May 1). This festival dates possibly from the sixth or seventh century, and may be traced back to the burial of St. Philip's relics, brought from Hierapolis, in St. James's grave. At Rome, in the fourth century, two hundred years later, Pelagius built a church under their common dedication. The Greek Church observes their days separately; in the Lectionary of St. Jerome, and the Sacramentary of St. Gregory, their names are associated. At Angers on this day the cathedral vicars sacked the citizens' houses, and compelled them to redeem their property.

Phylacteries. (Gr., preservatives.) (1.) Amulets. Cæsarius of Arles couples the word with "devilish characters" and "fortune-telling." (2.) Reliquaries.

Piscina. The Latin rendering of the pools of Siloam and the Five Porches; from the curative nature of their water, baptism was symbolically called the piscina of regeneration, and the vessel into which the water of the font was poured took the same name; perfusorium was the name of the drain for ablutions. The priest at the lavabo still washes the tips of his fingers in a piscina, a small vessel placed near the tabernacle; but the Carthusians and bishops wash their whole hands during the recitation of verses from Ps. xxvi. The remarkable triple piscina of Rothwell had drains for all these purposes.

Pie. (*Pinax*, Gr., a board.) (1.) A wooden table, on which the directions for service were written in early days. (2.) The Pica, Ordinale, or Directorium Sacerdotum. Becon talks of a priest being "well seen in the pie," and Ridley calls it the "rubric primer;" it was both a table of daily services, and a summary of the rubrics of the Mass. (*See* BOOKS.) The Dominican Friars, from their black-and-white dress, were called friars pied, or of the pie.

Pier. Solid masonry between doors and windows.

Pilgrim. (*Pelegrin, peregrinus,* a stranger.) In Bishop Mayo's tomb at Hereford, and St. Richard's at Canterbury, pieces of hazel-wood wands, memorials of pilgrimages, were found. The pilgrim's weeds consisted of a hood with a cape, a low-crowned hat with two strings, a staff or bourdon four or five feet long, made originally of two sticks swathed together, a bottle strung at their waist-belt, and scrip. Those whose pilgrimage was self-imposed walked barefooted, and begged their daily bread, let their beards grow, and wore no linen. The palmer was distinguished by two leaflets of palm; the pilgrim to Mount Sinai wore the St. Catherine's wheel; he who went to Rome came back with a medal, graven with the cross-keys, or vernicle; the pilgrim to Compostella brought home the scallop shell of Gallicia; those who went to Walsingham were distinguished by a badge; and from Canterbury the pilgrim carried, as a memorial, an ampulla full of Canterbury water, which was mingled with one tiny drop of A'Becket's blood. Latimer mentions "the piping, playing, and curious singing, to solace the travail and weariness of pilgrims." At Gloucester the pilgrims' door, with its colossal warders, remains in the south arm of the transept. In the holy wars the French Crusaders were distinguished by a red, English by a white, and Flemings by a green cross. Penitents paid Peter's pence as a composition for a pilgrimage to Rome, or commuted it by a visit to Peterborough, St. Alban's, or St. David's. In 1064, persons going to visit a saint had the protection of the Church. At Hereford, a canon might be absent on pilgrimage in England for three weeks; and once in his life for seven weeks to visit St.

Denis; ten weeks, Rome and Compostella; eight, Pontegnes; and one year, Jerusalem. In some Continental countries pilgrims and priests sometimes inscribed their names on the altars which they visited. These were called inscripta, or literata, but must not be confounded with those bearing the donor's name; the first instance of the latter custom occurred in the case of Pulcherius at Constantinople, as Sozomen relates. The pilgrim's tomb sometimes bore the print of two bare feet, as emblematical of his safe return. The pilgrims, having been first shriven, prostrated themselves before the altar whilst prayers were said over them, and stood up to receive the priest's benediction on their scrips and staves, which he sprinkled with holy-water and delivered into their hands. If going to Jerusalem, a cross was marked upon their garment; the ceremonial terminated with a solemn Mass. In 1322, a priest who betrayed a confession had to go on pilgrimage as a penance. Monks were not allowed to become pilgrims in 1200. " Divers men and women," said W. Thorpe in the fifteenth century, " have with them both men and women that can well sing wanton songs, some other have bagpipes, so that in every town, what with the noise of their singing and with the sound of their piping, and with the jingling of their Canterbury bells, and with the barking out of dogs after them, they make more noise than if the King came there away with all his clarions and many other minstrels." The staff had sometimes a bronze socket, inscribed with these words in Latin, " May this cross direct thy journey in safety."

Pilgrimage. SS. Chrysostom and Augustine mention pilgrimages to Rome to the " Memorial of the Fisherman," and St. Jerome and Socrates pilgrimages made to Jerusalem, and Theodorus those made to the martyrs' tombs and churches. In the fourth century serious evils were found to attend these journeys. In 744 St. Boniface advised Cuthbert, Archbishop of Canterbury, that a provincial council should be held forbidding Englishwomen, especially nuns, for good reasons of morality, to go on pilgrimage to Rome; and a law of Charlemagne forbade wandering through the land by pedlars and feigned penitents, wearing iron rings or chains, as if they were the marks of penance. Beleth says pilgrimages began on Saturday in the Ember week of Advent.

Pilgrimages were made to the roods of Bermondsey, Boston, Dovercourt, and Chester; that of Beccles was made to sweat, bleed, and smell sweet. The " gaping rood," or " bearded crucifix," called also the "rood of grace," of Boxley, was exposed at St. Paul's Cross. The shrine of St. Mary of Walsingham was of wood, in the shape of the Holy House of Nazareth. Henry VIII. walked barefoot to visit her image, and offer it a necklace from Barsham, in the second year of his reign. The shrine of St. Thomas A'Becket, at Canterbury, in one year, when there was no offering at the Saviour's altar, received £964 in gifts. The Pilgrims' Road from London to Canterbury is still pointed out along nearly its entire extent. The Milky Way in the sky, from its brilliancy and position, was called by the pilgrims from the southward Walsingham Way. In the monastic guest-houses the travel-worn pilgrim and serge-clad palmer, footsore and bronzed with Eastern suns, were ever welcome, and repaid their hosts for bed and fare by telling wondrous legends, miracles, perils from the Moslem, and tidings of other lands, which found their way into many a medieval chronicle.

Pillory. One, like stocks, for brawlers' fingers, is preserved at Ashby-de-la-Zouch, and a brank or gag for scolds at Walton-on-Thames.

Pillow-beres. A pillow-case, usually of rich material.

Pinnacle. A small turret or tapering spirelet, used as a covering of buttresses, parapets, and towers. The earliest occur at Caen and Rochester Cathedral. In the Early English period they are sometimes shafted, crocketed, and tabernacled for statues. In the Decorated style they have finials, and are usually square. In the Perpendicular period they often end in figures or have ogee-shaped tops.

Pitanciar. The furnisher of the gaudies; the distributor of the pittance (*pietancia* or *pite*, a coin of Poitou) or extra commons, as caritas was an additional beverage to the generale, the usual fare.

Pity, Our Lady of. A pietâ, a representation of St. Mary holding the dead Christ.

Placebo. The antiphon at Vespers in the office of the dead, as the dirge is at Matins.

Plain-Song (*canto fermo, cantus planus*) is a monotonic recitative, being the Cantus Collectarum. The Cantus Prophetarum Epistolarum et Evangelii admitted certain inflections. The Cantus Psalmorum adopted inflections in the middle and end of the verse. An unrestricted melody was used in prefaces, anthems, and hymns.

Platform. A ground plan.

Plays of a religious character were written at an early period. One, of the close of the second century, by Ezekiel, a Jew, represented the Exodus. St. Chrysostom composed the 'Dying Christ;' St. Gregory Nazianzen wrote plays, substituting hymns for the ancient choruses; Apollinarius, Bishop of Laodicea, with his son, who was a priest of the diocese, turned portions of Holy Scripture into tragedies and comedies upon the Greek model. In later times the word "play" designated a drama founded on Holy Writ and containing an aggregate of pageants. At length it degenerated into the ridiculous form, with amusing or grotesque accessories, and at last fell deservedly under episcopal censures. The statutes of Exeter condemn grave irregularities in choir, banquetings and drinkings and irreverence. In 1360 Bishop Grandison peremptorily forbade the acting of plays at Christmas. At Lichfield on Christmas Eve the representation of the Shepherds, the Resurrection (as at Rouen) at dawn on Easter, and the Pilgrims to Emmaus on the following day; at York the Three Kings at Epiphany, and the Shepherds at Christmas, stars being employed in the scene,—were popular Church mysteries. In the intermediate stages of the miracle play the actors used a scaffold, built over the steps of the porch, with the inside of the church representing the heaven out of which the Deity comes. At Gloucester and Durham the Ascension was represented by a figure drawn up through an aperture in the choir vault. These lively representations led to other "spectacles." At Wells, during Whitsuntide, laymen in choir wore absurd masks, and at Christmas the vicars made ridiculous gesticulations, convulsing the congregation with laughter. At Pentecost there was an "interlude" representing the descent of the Holy Spirit. In 1310 Pope Gregory desired the bishops to extirpate the custom of priests mumming and acting in churches, and the Council of Basle, in 1436, forbade scenic plays in consecrated places. In 1384 William of Wykeham prohibited spectacles in the cemetery of Winchester. In 1446 the Council of Rouen condemned the disguisings and

fools'-play which had grown into an intolerable abuse.
Spectacles with low songs prevailed at Sens and Trèves.
At Toledo, and in other Spanish cathedrals, at Christmas,
during High Mass, masks and monstrous shapes, cries and
humorous verses, were freely bandied in choir in the beginning of the sixteenth century. The feasts of the Ass and
Fools were grossly indecent. In 1542 Bishop Bonner prohibited common plays, interludes, and games in the London
churches, but interludes were certainly acted in English
churches in the reign of Elizabeth, and probably for the last
time at Witney, by means of puppets, as in the show of the
Creation of the World, which was fashionable at Bath in
the time of Queen Anne. Jack Snacker, the watchman, who
clapped two sticks, was the popular character at Witney.
In 1316 the Bishop of Worms condemned the masks and
plays used on the festivals of St. John, and required the mystery of the Resurrection to be acted before the entrance of
the people, and in 1834 the Bishop of Cambrai prohibited
the plays of the Shepherds at Christmas or the Passion at
Easter on religious grounds.

THE EPIPHANY. The Three Kings were represented at
Rouen by three canons, habited in royal ornaments, mitre on
head and sceptre in hand, descending westward from the
altar and followed by attendants carrying gold, incense, and
myrrh. Opposite the altar of the cross, in the nave, was a
tent containing a figure of Christ in His cradle, and overhead was a star in the vault. Before this figure, which was
discovered to them by two other canons, they kneeled
down, whilst a boy in the rood-loft, habited like an angel,
sang verses to music. They then returned along the south
aisle and re-entered the choir by the north entrance.

THE SEPULCHRE AT ROUEN. Three deacons in dalmatics,
with amices on their heads and perfumes in their hands,
represented the Three Maries, and traversed the choir,
where at the sepulchre a boy, vested as an angel, was sitting.
As they turned away a priest-canon, one of the great dignitaries, in his albe and holding a cross, met them and represented the Saviour. The ceremony concluded with the Te
Deum. From these ceremonies and those exhibited on
Palm Sunday, Christmas, Good Friday, and other days the
sacred drama took its origin. These mysteries were sung to

2 G

the plain chant. It was not until the thirteenth century that the stage-play, composed by troubadours and acted by laymen, was introduced.

Plicata. The "folded" chasuble worn on Good Friday by the deacon and subdeacon, or by a priest, folded on the shoulder, when acting as a deacon. It is a relic of ancient usage, anterior to the use of the dalmatic and tunic, when they wore the trabea rolled up in front to leave their hands free and unencumbered, and is also a peculiarity belonging to times of penance.

Plinth. A square stone forming the lower part of a base of a pillar.

Plough Monday. Called in Belgium Lost Monday, from its revellings. Old ploughs are preserved in the belfries of Bassingbourne and Barrington. Plough alms were one penny paid for every plough harnessed between Easter and Pentecost in 878, and in 960 payable on the fifteenth night after Easter.

Pluralities. The tenure of many benefices by one person, abolished by 1 and 2 Vic., c. 106. Throughout the thirteenth century the Archbishops of Canterbury inveighed against the gross disorder and evils produced by the prevalence of pluralities; but it was not until the present century that the blot was removed from the system. In the middle ages, notably at Lincoln and York, and in other cathedrals, many of the stalls were possessed by non-resident foreigners; and even such a man as William of Wykeham held as many as fourteen benefices. Bogo de Clare, Præcentor of Chichester, held 16 churches in the reign of Edward I., besides other benefices. Offenders who had not Papal dispensation were excommunicated in 1279.

Pocularies. Consecrated drinking-cups.

Poderis or **Talaris.** (Reaching to the heels.) The albe.

Pointed Style. The Pointed arch, mentioned as an architectural term in the fourteenth century, occurs in Egypt, Italy, Greece, and Mexico in ancient buildings, merely as a freak of the architect, an accident, or irregularity. Some authors have traced its origin to the avenues of a forest; others have seen it in the palm, in the wooden churches of an earlier period, or the intersecting arcade. Some refer it to the Goths, like Warburton; to the Saracens, like Christopher Wren; to

Asiatics, like Lord Aberdeen and Hallam; to the period of Rome, like Payne Knight; to England, like Carter; to Germany, like Palladio; to Italy, like Smirke; in fine, to Egypt, the Hebrews, the Normans, the Lombards, or the Freemasons. There are strong objections to every one of these views, either on historical grounds or from the reasoning of common sense. The true origin, no doubt, lay in the aspiration of the Christian builders to attain height in construction, when vaulting had become common. It was simply the application of a well-known form to a new and loftier purpose.

Pointing. The choral pause in the midst of a verse of a canticle or psalm denoted by a colon or two points.

Pole-Axes. The ensigns of legates à latere, carried with silver pillars (Gal. ii. 9) before Cardinals Wolsey and Pole.

Polychrome. The application of colour to ornament a building.

Polygonal Towers. Octagonal towers occur in all countries, as at Oppenheim, Liége, Barcelona, Wymondham, St. German's, Lausanne, Dijon, and Pisa; hexagonal towers at Lynn; a triangle at Maldon; and two bisecting polygons of 16 sides above an octagon, at Swaffham Priors.

Pome. (*Pomum*, Lat., an apple.) (1.) A cup or ball filled with perfumes. (2.) (Calefactorium, calepungnus, scutum; Fr. *rechaud*, a chafing-dish.) A ball of metal filled with hot water and used by the priest to warm his hands at the altar, sometimes made fourfooted, with rings of silver.

Pomel. A knop or boss of round shape.

Pontiffs, Confraternities of. In the twelfth century guilds of associated masons for building churches and bridges, which appeared first at Chartres, and spread through France, England, Switzerland, and Germany. When their Christian character died out they became lodges of Freemasons.

Poor Men's Box, The, for alms (*uniculus, pyxis ad oblationes faciendas*) in lieu of pilgrimage, was affixed near the high-altar, by Cranmer's orders. It was enjoined in every church in 1559. There is a curious almsbox in St. Helen's, Bishopsgate, supported by the figure of a mendicant, and another at Outwell with a grinning mouth. The idea of these boxes was probably derived from such objects as the bracket of the fifteenth century, adjoining the tomb of Edward II. at Gloucester, and the oaken box with a slit for alms, used at St. Richard's shrine at Chichester, which is of the sixteenth century, although the ironwork dates back three hundred years earlier. There is a wooden almsbox of the fourteenth century at Fribourg. There is a stone box at Bridlington. A flasket or box of wood for collecting alms is mentioned in England in the seventeenth century. At Selby there is a chest made out of the bowl of a single tree. In 1292 such hutches were forbidden at Chichester, as the oblations hitherto made at the altar were placed in them. At St. David's, two centuries ago, old people could remember having seen basinfuls of oblations made by seamen and passengers.

Pope. (*Papa*, father.) The name in early ages, until the sixth century, used by all bishops. It was first given to the Bishop of Alexandria in St. Mark's Liturgy, where Patriarch designates the Metropolitan of Antioch, and Archbishop, him of Constantinople. St. Jerome addresses St. Augustine as "very holy lord, and most blessed pope." The Bishop of Constantinople was called pope of the city, as the Bishop of Rome bore the title of Pope of the City of Rome. In the time of Leo the Great, Pope was the official title of the latter, and was, in 1076, decreed by Pope Gregory VII. in a council of Rome to be the peculiar appellation of the Supreme Pontiff. Benedict III. assumed the title of Vicar of St. Peter; and his successors assumed that of Vicars of Christ, in the thirteenth century. In the fifth century Pope Hilary called himself "bishop and servant of Christ;" Gregory III. appears as "most holy and blessed Apostolic Pope," or "by the grace of God, bishop of the Catholic and Apostolic city Rome." Agatho, in 679, called himself Universal Pope; and Boniface accepted the title of Primate of all Churches. Gregory I. condemned the name of Œcumenical Bishop. Up to the ninth century, and during it, Pope of Rome was adopted, to distinguish the Pontiff from other prelates bearing the title of papa. Eugenius III. and Leo IV. first were thus designated. The Greek bishop is called pápas; a priest, papás, with a different accentuation. Père (father) and abbé are also used for priests. John VIII., 872–882, called the Primate of Sens "Second Pope;" and Anselm of Canterbury was invited by the Pope to sit next him in the apse of Bari, as "Pope of the other orb." In 1163, at the Council of Tours, Alexander III. seated A'Becket at his right-hand. The Bishop of Rome was formerly chosen by the clergy of the city. The Gothic kings and the Eastern empe-rors at length interfered in his nomination or confirmation. Until the eleventh century the Roman people took part in the election of the Pope; and the latter had to pay a tribute into the Byzantine treasury. The Conclave was first esta-blished by Gregory X. at the Council of Lyons, 1274, when it was ordered that, during the first three days of seclusion, the cardinals should dine on only one dish, and after five days, on bread and water. The cardinals, in 1299, refused to sub-mit to seclusion; and in 1351 Clement VI. forbade them, on pain of excommunication, to promise their votes beforehand. In the eleventh century the parish priests and regionary deacons, with the suffragan bishops of the province of Rome, acquired privileges subsequently developed into the Ecclesi-astical Senate of the College of Cardinals; but it was not until 1179 that their special prerogative as electors was con-firmed and assured to them by Alexander III., at the Lateran Council. The limitation to the agency of the Sacred College dates from 1174, but the strict organization of the Conclave in secrecy and seclusion came into practice early in 1276, in the popedom of Innocent V. In 682 the tribute claimed by Justinian at the election of a Pope was relinquished by Constantine, but a veto is still exercised by France, Spain, and Austria, through the mouth of a cardinal. Stephen IV. decreed that only a cardinal, priest, or deacon could be raised to the pontificate. Nicholas II., in the Lateran Coun-cil, 1059, and Gregory X., in the Council of Lyons, in 1271, gave the form for assembling the Conclave of Cardinals. Pope Innocent III., in 1200, regulated the mode of election, which was to be by scrutiny, compromission, and inspiration; and Gregory XV., in 1621, and Urban VIII., in 1625, intro-duced several modifications. The Pope was set upon the altar of St. Peter's by the cardinals, and his feet, hands, and lips kissed by them. After being enthroned, in the twelfth century, he was led to a stone chair outside the porch of the Lateran, called the seat of the dunghill, in allusion to 1 Sam. ii. 8. He then stood up and scattered three handfuls of pence, using these words: Acts. iii. 6. At St. Stephen's Church the Prior of St. Laurence gave him the keys of the Lateran; a rod, the ensign of authority; and a girdle, with a purse containing twelve jewelled signets, and musk, symbolical of chastity, mercy, power, and fragrancy in Christ. A belt with seven keys and seven seals of the seven basilicas, in the eleventh century, was presented. He then scattered silver, saying the verse Ps. cxii. 9. On the morrow he was consecrated by the Cardinal Bishop of Ostia, from the ninth century; or by the Archpriest of Ostia or Velletri, having the pall, the fulness of the pontifical office, with three little gold nails with turquoise heads, fixed by the Prior of St. Laurence before, behind, and on his left side. At St. Stephen's tower the Jews presented the Book of the Law, and received £20 of Provence. At his coronation the master of the ceremonies lighted a piece of tow, saying, " Blessed Father, thus passeth away the glory of the world." So the Greek emperor at his coronation carried akakia, a purple bag filled with dust. The first Pope who changed his name was Octavianus Conti, who took the title of John XI., in allusion to St. John i. 6. The Pope has been carried on men's shoulders since the time of Leo or Sylvester II. At Peterborough in medieval times, and in France at an early date, prelates were carried through the church after their consecration or benediction. In going a journey the Pope carried the Viaticum, and was preceded by a bell. When he celebrates he receives a purse of white velvet for having sung the Mass well from the Chapter of St. Peter's.

Poppy Heads. (*Popis, poppœa;* Fr. *poupées.*) Ornaments of the elbows of seats, first appearing in the Decorated period, and deriving their name from their resemblance to a bundle tied in the middle, and latterly the fleur-de-lys.

Porch. (*Porticus.*) When infant baptism became prevalent in the West, and the discipline of catechumens had fallen into desuetude, the narthex was still retained in the form of a vestibule, frequently closed, and sufficiently capacious to contain a large number of persons and permit the celebration of different ceremonials. Few churches, cathedral, conventual, or parochial, were, until the middle of the twelfth century, unprovided with a central porch in front of the principal entrance, but after the thirteenth century they were not so common. The earliest porches in the West, dating from the eighth to the eleventh century, are shallow, and extend across the church front, as at Clermont. One of the earliest is at St. Front, Périgueux. In some cases they were recessed under the tower, as at St. Germain-des-Prés (Paris), Limoges, Poissy, of the ninth or tenth century, St. Benet-sur-Loire, Moissac, and St. Savin. During the eleventh century this became the rule; in the thirteenth century it was rare, but at a later date it reappeared at Caen, Fribourg, and Cranbrook. At St. Savin the porch is defensible and protected by a ditch, just as the castellated palace stands in front of the western entrance of Cashel Cathedral. The giant porch of Vienna, imposing as it is, is far exceeded by the three magnificent Early English porches of Peterborough, which accord with the entire work, whilst those of many of the great French cathedrals are mere afterthoughts, noble but accidental additions. At Fribourg, Rheims, and Chartres (1250–80) the porches are covered with statuary. Towards the close of the twelfth century the ceremonies performed within them fell into desuetude, and they in consequence dwindled into a mere appendage of the nave. Then, from the exclusive use of western doors, large lateral porches, usually in cathedrals, as at Chartres, Mans, Bayeux, Puy-en-Velay, Chalons-sur-Marne, Wells, Salisbury, Lincoln, and Hereford, were built for the convenience of worshippers when entering or leaving the church, for benedictions, and the preliminaries of marriages and baptism, and the passage of funerals. The monastic churches in towns imitated the arrangement. These porches were usually closed at the sides, as in the Norman examples of Kelso, Selby, South-well, Sherborne, and Malmesbury, although that of Alençon is open. At Hereford the outer porch, c. 1513, is open, but the inner Decorated porch is closed. Until the close of the fourteenth century porches, generally of open form, were commonly built. The lateral porch fronted the side which faced the more populous portion of the city—at Gloucester, Canterbury, Malmesbury, Chester, and St. David's, on the south; at Durham, Hereford, Exeter, Christchurch (Hants), and Selby, on the north. At Chichester it is on the south side, opening on the cloister to admit processions to the shrine; at Westminster (called from its beauty Solomon's Porch) it stood in advance of the north front of the transept; at Lincoln the bishop's porch is in the presbytery. There

are Early English porches at St. Alban's and Barnack, the
latter, like All Saints', Stamford, Albury, and St. Mary's,
Nottingham, having external and internal stone roofs.   At
Tewkesbury the vast western arch may have formed a
gigantic porch.   At Lincoln three recessed porches exist, as
once at St. Alban's.   Wooden porches occur at all dates,
fine examples remaining at Chelvington and Warblington.
There are large porches at Tours, Pol, St. Leon, and Ul-
richsk, and smaller specimens in several churches at Cologne.
English cathedrals and minsters are remarkable for the
homeliness of their doorways, resembling those of parish
churches on an enlarged scale.   The cathedral, in distinction
to a minster, in the twelfth century, was built with many
porches and western doors opening directly on the close, as
if inviting the entrance of crowds.   Noyon, at the end of the
thirteenth or beginning of the fourteenth century, is a solitary exception to this rule in possessing large porches in
advance of its principal front.   Up to the sixth century
children were exposed in the porch, and the Council of Arles
required those who adopted them to place in the priest's
hand a letter of contestation with regard to the sex and age
of the child; and the Council of Vaison, complaining that
the children were exposed to dogs, for fear of scandal required the priest at the altar to announce on Sundays the
name of the adopter.   Kings and princes were permitted to
be buried in porches by the Council of Nantes (658), and
interments were forbidden within church walls till the twelfth
century.   At Ely, as in many ascertained examples in France,
probably the recesses above the arcading were used as char-
nels, fenced in with an iron screen; and at Chichester there
are still lateral tombs.   Gradually incense was used and
litanies were chanted in porches.   Fonts and basins for the
ablutions of the faithful before entering the church were
erected, and exhibitions of relics and sacred images were
made.   Markets were permitted, just as objects of piety are
still sold in foreign porches on festival days.   Feudal and
other courts were held.   At Sandwich a school was taught
and books sold, and even in 1519 pedlars hawked their wares
at Riccald.   Chapters and religious bodies appealed to the
civil power to put an end to such irregularities, and the
great abbeys of Clugny, Maulbronn, and Citeaux, about the

beginning of the twelfth century, began to erect large inclosed porches in front of their churches. The Clugniacs
built large ante-churches of two stories, as at Lewes; at
Tournus, of the close of the eleventh century, the latter consisting of a nave and aisles of thirteen bays, with an upper
chapel of St. Michael, in which the altar was used for a Mass
attended by penitents; and at Clugny in the thirteenth century, where an altar and pulpit adjoined the church door.
Their influence is perceptible in the large upper chapel over
the porch at Puy-en-Velay and Autun and the tribune for
an altar at Châtel Montagne, Monreale, and Dijon, which
are said to have been used by women and minstrels. In
many instances the view into the nave was unimpeded.

The Cistercians built western porches deep and longitudinal, in imitation of the narthex, according to the desire of
St. Bernard, at Toury, Moutier, Charité-sur-Loire, Fountains,
and Beaulieu. At Vezelay, in the thirteenth century, the
porch, of two bays in length, forms a nave with aisles, lateral
galleries, and a tribune for an altar over the minster door.
In many French parish churches this plan was followed in
order to accommodate mourners at funerals. In England
an upper chamber sometimes occurs over porches, as at
Southwell, Christchurch (Hants), and in parish churches used
as a schoolroom or a chaplains' or watchers' dormitory.
Placentia, Parma, and Modena have porches of two
storeys.

In the foreign examples pilgrims or penitents were marshalled on the ground floor in order to hear an address from
the pulpit, or Mass said at the upper altar, whilst those who
came from a distance found shelter in these vaulted porches,
just as the country people on the eves of great festivals pass
the night under the porticos of St. Peter at Rome. At
Paulinzelle, c. 1150, there is, and at Sherborne there was a
large parochial ante-church. At Glastonbury and Durham
the Lady-chapel was placed in a similar position. It is possible that these outer buildings served the same purpose of a
place of previous assembly, just as the great western transept
of Ely or Lincoln may have been also occupied on occasions
when large multitudes flocked to the church. In some
monastic churches it served as the forensic parlour for conversation with persons inadmissible within the inner portions.

The children of the abbey serfs were baptized and the office at which their domestic servants and labourers attended was said. In all large churches the processions were arranged in the porch on Palm Sunday, on Holy Cross Day, and in Rogations. Sometimes it formed a sanctuary, containing a ring in the door to which the fugitive clung, as at Durham, and at Cologne there was an inscription to this effect, " Here stood the great criminal." *See* GALILEE and DOORS.

Portable Altars. (*Viatica, gestatoria, itineraria.*) One is preserved at Santa Maria in portico d'Campiteili, and another, of carved porphyry, at Conques, *c.* 1106. During the Crusades the bishops and ecclesiastics who took part in them carried an " itinerant altar." The portable altar-stone or table was used on unconsecrated altars in private chapels. Bede mentions a consecrated table in lieu of an altar. The monks of St. Denis carried a table of wood, covered with a linen cloth, in Charlemagne's campaign against the Saxons. There were examples also of stone, metal, and terra cotta. The reposoir is used in the street to rest the Sacrament on in the procession of the Fête Dieu in France.

Portable Bells. Handbells were of Celtic origin and used in Brittany, in St. Patrick's time in Ireland, and in that of St. Teilo in Wales. Unlike the small altar-bells, which were square, these were hexagonal or oval, without clappers, like the original cloc, usually of bronze and sometimes jewelled, being regarded as specially sacred and possessed of miraculous powers, as St. Iltyd's, the bell of Armagh of the close of the eleventh century, the golden bell of St. Senanus, St. Ewin's or Bernan at Monastevin, which was tied with a cord to prevent its automatic flight, and used as an ordeal for swearing criminals by the justices of Munster. The cloc was cylindrical, and in the eighth, ninth, and tenth centuries often gemmed. In Wales the bangu was used at Caerleon at a funeral recently. Hand-bells are preserved at Perros, Guirec, and St. Symphorion's, Côte du Nord.

Portal. (*Avant-portail.*) An external arched canopy, usually gabled, raised in front of the principal doors of a church by way of shelter, whereas a porch is a projecting outwork independent of the door. There are fine examples at Rheims, Paris, St. Ouen's, and the cathedrals of Rouen, Amiens, Sens, Senlis, and Bourges, Westminster, and of smaller dimensions at Salisbury, Lichfield, Verona, and other Italian churches. Penniless porch, the resort of beggars, was the local name of the cemetery gate of Wells.

Portatives. Candlesticks carried by hand.

Portesse. A breviary. From the Latin portiforium (à portando foras), through the French porté hors, hence portusse, portas. The foreign breviaries were divided according to the four seasons, but in England into winter and summer parts.

Porticus. A porch; an apse; an inclosed end of an aisle; an anker's cell.

Portion. The mediety of a parish, which was divided into several vicarages or parsonages.

Portionist. A beneficed person in a cathedral, who received only half or a moiety of his prebend, called in France a demi-prebendary and in Spain a rationero. Bursaries in Scottish universities and the German bursch were portions of money given to poor students, while the Cambridge pensioner lives at his own cost.

Poser. A bishop's examining chaplain. The annual examiners at Winchester and Eton still bear the name.

Præcentor. (1.) (Gr. *Protopsaltes, canonarcha,* and *domesticus cantorum;* Fr. *grand chantre;* Sp. *chantre, caput scholæ,* or *capiscol,* leader of the school of singers; Germ. *primicier;* at Cologne, *chorepiscopus.*) The præcentor led one part of the chant and the sub-chanter responded in the other, in some French cathedrals being sub-chanter of canons. The dignitary collated by the diocesan and charged with the conduct of the musical portion of Divine service, and required, on great festivals and Sundays, to commence the responses, hymns, etc., to regulate processions, to distribute the copes, to correct offences in choir, and to direct the singers. In France, England, Germany, and Spain he ranked next to the dean. He gave the note at Mass to the bishop and dean as the succentor did to the canons and clerks. He superintended the admission of members of the choir and tabled their names for the weekly course on waxen tablets. He corrected and had charge of the choir books. In England when he ruled the choir he wore a rochet, cantelor cantor's cope, ring, and gloves, and carried a staff; and the rectors followed him in soutanes (often of red colour), surplices, and copes. He installed canons at Exeter, at

York the dean and dignitaries, and at Lichfield the bishop and dignitaries. He attended the bishop on the left-hand, as the dean walked on the prelate's right-hand. At Paris he exercised jurisdiction over all the schools and teachers in the city and respondents in the universities. In the French cathedrals, upon high festivals he presides over the choir at the lectern, and carries a baton of silver as the ensign of his dignity. At Rodez, Puy-en-Velay, and Brionde he, like the other canons, wears a mitre at High Mass, and at Cologne was known as chorepiscopus. At Chartres during Easter week all the capitular clergy go to the font, with the sub-chanter preceding the junior canons, carrying white wands, in allusion to the white robes of the baptized. At Rouen the chanter carries a white wand in certain processions, and no one without his leave could open a song-school in the city. In England his stall faces the dean, being on the north-west. In foreign cathedrals he occupied either the same position or sat next to the dean. The Greek præcentor at Christmas wore white, and the singers violet. The exarch was the imperial protospaltes. The dignity of præcentor was founded at Amiens 1219; at Rouen in 1110; at Exeter, Salisbury, York, Lincoln, in the eleventh century; at Chichester, Wells, Lichfield, Hereford, in the twelfth; and at St. Paul's in the thirteenth century. The præcentor was required to be always resident, and usually held a prebend with his dignity. The Clugniac præcentor was called armarius because he was also librarian, the treasurer being aprocrisiarius. The singers of the primitive Church were regarded as a minor order by Pope Innocent III., by the Council of Laodicea, 360, and in Trullo. When the service of song was intrusted to lay persons in course of time, the title of chanter was preserved in cathedral chapters and collegiate churches as that of a capitular dignitary, having precedency, rights, and duties. (2.) The monastic præcentor had similar duties and privileges in choir. He also was chief librarian, registrar, secretary of the seal, registered obits, regulated processions and the order of the monks, ordered the monthly shaving, had charge of the charters, sent out briefs announcing the demise of a brother, gave out the books, noted the chants and ministers, presided over the carols and studies, and rode with young monks going to be ordained. (3.) In the new foundations a minor canon appointed and removable by the dean (as rector chori) and chapter. Whilst there was a common hall he presided at table as censor morum. He, like the German and Italian punctator, was to note absences. His duties now are to select music for the choir, subject to capitular revision, to recommend men and boys for the choir, and to instruct them in music, assisted by the organist. At Vienne and Beverley the precentor was only a person.

Prælector. (Fr. *Théologal.*) A divinity reader in the cathedrals of Vich, Bayeux, Sens, and Lisieux; at Chichester, attached to the prebend of Wittering, 1259. The lectures were read in cloister, but now, in Lent, in the cathedral; and at Valencia in the chapter-house. At St. Paul's, in 1394, he was a B.D. At Hereford, the prælector lectures in Lent, on saints' days, and other times. He was paid by the bishop's prebendary, and succeeded to the first vacant residentiary stall, except the last-named. At Westminster there is a term lecturer, and at Canterbury six preachers are appointed by the Archbishop to deliver annual sermons.

Præmonstratensians. An order of regular canons, founded by Norbert of Cleves, afterwards Archbishop of Magdeburg, at Premontré, in the diocese of Laon, in 1120, under the rule of St. Austin, and confirmed by Honorius II. and Innocent III. The title was taken from a legendary tradition, that an angel showed aforehand the site for the new monastery in a meadow. The white canons wore a white cassock and rochet and a long white cloak. The abbots never wore pontificals; and any member promoted to the Cardinalate or Popedom retained his habit. Until 1273 their monasteries were double, a house of women always adjoining the convent of men. Their churches and conventual buildings, as at Eastby, Leiston, Bayham, Wendling, and Eggleston, were very irregular in plan, the greater portion of the minster being aisleless, and the transept unimportant, as they eschewed all processions. There is a fine ruin at Ardaines, near Caen, which gives a vivid illustration of the farming arrangements of the order, which was to the Austin Canons what the Cistercians were to the Benedictines, homely and retired lovers of the country, and enterprising farmers. Their principal houses were Torre, East Dereham, and Hales Owen. They carried the almuce over the right arm ; the Canons of St. Victor wore it like a tippet round the neck.

Præmunire. An Act (28 Henry VIII.) directed against those who refuse to elect the Crown nominee as a bishop, involving outlawry, imprisonment, and confiscation of goods.

Preachers. Non-resident rectors were required in 1281 to maintain a steward to relieve the poor, and entertain preaching friars. Every priest was bound four times in the year to expound in the vulgar tongue to his people the fourteen articles of faith (*i.e.* with regard to the Holy Trinity, seven ; and to Christ's humanity, seven), the Ten Commandments, the two evangelical precepts (love to God and man), the seven works of mercy, the seven capital sins, the seven principal virtues, and the seven sacraments. In 1408 no secular or regular was allowed to preach, except with the licence of his diocesan, after due examination ; the Dominicans and Franciscans were authorized by written canon law to preach in the churchyard and public street, and of common right anywhere ; and Carmelites and Augustines enjoyed special privileges. The perpetual curate (that is, the rector or incumbent) preached by right and virtue of his office ; temporary vicars and chaplains were restricted to the topics prescribed in 1281. Until the Restoration, the preacher and academical congregation wore their caps in sermon time at the Universities.

Prebend. (*Præbenda*, provender, an allowance of food.) (1.) The right of receiving a stated income in a church, attached to a member of a college or chapter, in reward for the discharge of ecclesiastical duties. (2.) A certain portion of dues and fruits of lands accruing of right to such an incumbent and beneficiary. (3.) A church, all the tithes and profits of which were impropriate to his maintenance. In the time of Henry III. the bursaries, prebends paid out of the bishop's purse, were reconstituted at Lichfield, and endowed with lands. It is a separate endowment impropriated, as distinguished from the communa, manors or revenues appropriated to maintain all the capitular members. When regular canons only existed, all were maintained from a common stock, from which they were prehended or fed. When the common life was given up by canons on their becoming secular, each canonry became a benefice, with its fixed revenues and stated allowance; before the arrival of William I. there is a trace of the tenure of distinct lands, afterwards made prebendal at St. Paul's; but the definite names of prebends is not much earlier, in England, than the time of Edward I. These names were derived from their corps in land; the church or altar from which the income was derived; their founder; their portion, or the amount of their value; thus we find such titles as Littlemead, Consumed-by-the-Sea, Arthur Bulkeley, Holy Cross, Combe the first, Lesser-part-of-the-Altar, Llanfair Portion, One Hundred Shillings, etc. The earliest prebend on record was that of Neauflé, founded in 1095, at Rouen. As the parish priests had secured their glebes and separate incomes, the capitular clergy claimed a similar independence; and the custom at length took such a hold that no person was admitted to a canonry unless there was a vacant prebend, as the wages of church service, for his support. Prebends are in the gift of the bishop ordinarily, but in some cases, when attached to offices or certain stalls, were in the patronage of the dean and chapter, as at Chichester. In 822 the Bishop of Lichfield assigned prebends to his secular canons; at Lindisfarne, at the close of the tenth century, the clerks received prebends after the manner of secular canons. At Lincoln, in the eleventh century, forty-two prebends were founded; in the twelfth century, at Wells, the prebends were formally distinguished, and the dignities founded; in the thirteenth century fourteen prebends were founded at Llandaff. At York, Archbishop Thomas divided the lands of the common fund into separate prebends; these were augmented by Archbishop Grey and Romaine, who added the last stall in the thirteenth century. In the sixteenth century Bishop Sherborne founded four stalls at Chichester, the latest endowed in England.

The prebends were divided into stalls of priests, deacons, and subdeacons, a certain number coming up to reside in stated courses; but in 1343 all the stalls of York were declared to be sacerdotal. Dignitaries almost invariably held a prebend attached to their stall. The great chapter included twenty-seven prebendaries at Lichfield, at Hereford and Exeter twenty-four, at Chichester twenty-eight, at Salisbury thirty-two in 1092, and latterly fifty-three, at Lincoln forty-six, at Wells forty-nine, at St. Paul's thirty-nine, and at York thirty-six; but at different times stalls were merged or lost, and Exeter retained but twelve, Salisbury thirty-six, and York twenty-eight. Every prebendary is a canon.

Precedence. A recognition of superiority in certain acts due to one person over another. Thus priests precede deacons; and rectors, vicars; and vicars, perpetual curates; and incumbents assistant-stipendiary curates. Rectors rank with each other according to the size and importance of their livings, or the date of their induction; bishops according to the precedence of their sees, in the case of London, Durham, and Winchester, and of Meath in Ireland, where the incumbent bears the title of Most Reverend; or, otherwise, of the date of consecration, by the Councils of Milevi (416), Braga (573), Toledo (633), and London (1075), unless their sees were privileged by ancient custom. Priests and deacons rank according to the date of their ordination. For a cathedral of the old foundation in England the order runs— dean, præcentor, chancellor, treasurer, archdeacons, canons residentiary (subdean, subchanter of canons), and canons non-resident. In chapter the bishop sits with the dean, chancellor, archdeacon, and residentiaries on the right, and the præcentor, treasurer, archdeacon, and residentiaries on the left; the rest of the canons in order of installation. At Salisbury two extra archdeacons sat on either side of the entrance. In all processions the members walked two and two, at regular distances—dignitaries in copes, canons priests in chasubles, canons deacons and subdeacons in dalmatics, with one pace between collaterals, and three paces between each rank; juniors first and seniors last in going, but in reverse order on their return; the right-hand side is the place of honour. At St. Paul's the dean walked last, between two dignitaries. The parish clergy go first, then follow vicars, canons, dignitaries, the dean, the bishop, and last the lay persons. Each parish had its cross or banner. Abbots took precedence according to the date of their benediction; Glastonbury, St. Alban's, and Westminster at various times challenged the first place among those who were mitred. Rural deans and honorary canons have only local precedence in a ruridecanal meeting or cathedral respectively.

In 1383 it was ruled that the Archbishop of Canterbury should sit at the King's right-hand, and rest his cross against the right side of the throne, the Archbishop of York being on the left side; where the place admitted they should walk side by side, but if the passage was too narrow then Canterbury should have precedence. In 1075 the Council of Canterbury ordered that York, in synod, should sit at the right, and London on the left of Canterbury; but if York was absent, then London occupied the right, and Winchester the left-hand side.

Preces. The verses and responses at the beginning of matins and evensong.

Prefaces in the Mass. (*Immolatio;* the Gallican *contestatio missæ,* the priest's witness to the *vere dignum* of the people; the Mozarabic and Gallican *illatio* or *inlatio.*) The Prefaces were composed by Gelasius, in memory of our Lord singing a hymn with His disciples after the Last Supper, the Jews at their Paschal Supper singing seven psalms (Ps. cxiii.-cxix.). Pope Sixtus added to them the Ter Sanctus. Pope Victor calls them capitula. The Preface is a thanksgiving before the act of consecration, to which it is the preparation, as an invitation to praise God before the Canon, or principal part of the Liturgy; it begins, "It is very meet." The Greeks use only one Preface. From the sixth to the end of the eleventh century the Western Church had Prefaces for every festival, but after that date they were reduced to nine, and are enumerated by Pope Pelagius and Alexander on Easter, the Ascension, Pentecost, Christmas, the Apparition of our Lord (Epiphany), the Apostles, Holy Trinity, Holy Cross, and Quadragesima. In 1175, by Archbishop Richard's Canons, the Tenth for the Blessed Virgin, added by Pope Urban at the Council of Placentia, 1095, was sanctioned in England. The Eucharist of St. Paul (1 Cor. xiv. 16) and St. Justin is probably the germ of the Western Preface, and the long thanksgiving prayer corresponding to it in the Greek Church.

Prelates. Bishops, abbots, deans, priors, archdeacons, or their representatives, exercising ecclesiastical jurisdiction.

Prenorman Architecture. In a large class of buildings anterior to the Norman Invasion of England, besides the Cornwall oratories, the walls are of rag or rubble, of herringbone-

2 H

work frequently, and unbuttressed; the quoins present long and short work; strips of stone or pilasters bisect or relieve the towers; the imposts of the shafts are rude, massive, and ornamented either with classical mouldings or rude carvings; the arches are round or angled, and sometimes constructed of bricks; and baluster-like pillars are introduced in the windows, which are often deeply splayed within and without. Two pillars from Reculver Basilica are standing in the Green Court of Canterbury. The churches of Lyminge, Barnack, Bosham, Bradford (Wilts), Brixworth (the oldest remaining church in England, and possessing a Basilican type), Stanton Lacy, Dover Castle, Brytford, Corhampton, Dunham Magna, Caversfield, and part of the crypt of York, those of Ripon and Hexham, the towers of Deerhurst, Barton, St. Benet's (Cambridge and Lincoln), Cholsey, St. Mary (York), Bolam, Brigstock, Earl's Barton, and the steeples of Bosham and Sompting, and portions of many other churches, exhibit some or other of these peculiarities. The base storey of the tower of Barnack formed a judicial and council chamber, with an angle-headed sedile on the west, with stone benches for the assessors on either side. They were erected either by the English, or possibly by the Danes under Canute, as that king ordered churches of stone and lime to be built in all places where the minsters had been burned by his countrymen, and out of the hundred, which is the number of these buildings, two-thirds are in the Eastern Counties and Lincolnshire, where the compatriots of the French Normans settled before the latter arrived. In the first half of the eleventh century churches so rapidly multiplied in France and Italy that a chronicler says the world seemed to be putting on a new white robe. Westminster Abbey was built by the Confessor in the Norman style; whilst in Lincolnshire the Prenorman mode was preserved late in the eleventh century, just as Perpendicular lingered in Somerset in the time of Elizabeth, and produced Wadham College Chapel by the aid of west country masons.

Prerogative Court. The Archbishop's Court for proving wills and giving administration, when the person within the province has goods in another diocese than that within which he died.

Presbyter. (Gr., an elder; Lat. *senior*; a title of honour, like ealdorman or seigneur.) One in the second order of the ministry; with bishops, priests make up the one sacerdotal order; sacerdotes is used in the Latin version of the English Articles, in allusion to the sacra, holy things, which they have to handle. Prester John was a fabulous King of Abyssinia or Tartary, first mentioned in the earlier part of the twelfth century; Alexander III. sent an embassy to him. Some have identified him with Unk Khan, a real Nestorian shepherd ruler. In modern times even the Majesty—the Saviour sitting in Doom—has been absurdly called a Prester John. Bishop Pilkington gravely talks of him as a heathen prince, living in his time; so does Harding. Jewel speaks of Peter Gran in Ethiopia, and Becon improves it into Precious John, in whose dominions there was daily Communion.

Presbyteress. (A priestess.) Presbutis (Titus ii. 3), a woman appointed to superintend women-members of the Church, and before the Council of Laodicea ordained with imposition of hands; their office consisted in teaching and catechizing, and was superior to that of the deaconess, or ministra. (2.) An abbess, according to the Council of Rome, 721, and the Excerptions of Ecgbriht, 740.

Presbytery. (Sanctuary; *capitium, secretarium,* and *sancta sanctorum;* the space between the choir and altar.) An ascent (*gradus presbyterii*) from the choir led to the presbytery, and a second flight of stairs (*gradus altaris*) led from the *planum presbyterii* to the altar. The presbytery usually stands on a higher level than the choir, being raised upon the crypt, the choir in turn being raised above the level of the nave. Clement I. says, " It is not lawful for any layperson to sit in the place where priests and the other clerks sit (which is called the presbytery) at the celebration of Mass, in order that they may decently and conveniently do the holy office." At Norwich, the orifice for the chain of the altar-light, and at Ely, Salisbury, and Gloucester, a rich boss on the vault, marks the site of the high-altar.

President in Choir. The dean's deputy, usually the senior residentiary or vice-dean, in his absence for the correction of offences, who acts also as president in chapter, and choragus or director of the services where there is no dignitary-præcentor.

Pricked-Song. Written in musical notes; musical composi-

2 H 2

tion was divided into descant, pricksong, counterpoint, and faburden, the latter being a highly pitched key.

Pricket. A spike on which candles were fixed; there are specimens from Kirkstall Abbey in the collection of the Society of Arts, London; and another of Limoges enamel of the thirteenth century is in the British Museum.

Prie-Dieu. A small lectern or book-desk, introduced in the fifteenth century.

Priests' Rooms. The chaplains frequently had chambers over porches or sacristies, as at St. Peter's-in-the-East, Oxford; in Ireland, over the vault of the church, as at Cashel, Mellifont, Holy Cross, and Kilkenny; in Scotland, at Iona, over the aisles.

Primate *or* **Exarch.** Beleth says, the president of three archbishops; one of any inferior grade of patriarchs; presidents of provinces, appointed by the Council of Nice, and recognized by Charlemagne; several bishops in Greece, and Illyria, Thessalonica, Carthage, and Milan, in the third century; those of Arles and Mayence, Tarragona and Carthagena, by Pope Zachary's order; Pisa, by that of Alexander III.; Armagh and Dublin, and Papal legates in the South of Europe, were primates. In Scotland there is an elective primus. In the African province, except Carthage, the primate was simply the bishop who had been consecrated earlier than the rest; and the registers were kept in his See, and in the city of the metropolitan. In the fifth century the greater metropolitans sought the title of primate, which implied no more than legatine authority. In the Eastern Church a change of precedency was made by secular power : the vicegerent of a patriarch became autocephalous, and every prelate exarch of some province. In France the Archbishop of Rouen was called Primate of Normandy; the Archbishop of Auch, Primate of Gascony; the Archbishop of Lyons, Primate of all Gaul; the Archbishop of Vienne, Primate of the Primates of Gaul; the Archbishop of Cæsarea, the Most Excellent of Most Excellent; the Metropolitan of Heraclea, First of the Most Excellent. The Archbishop of Saltzburg became Primate of Germany in 792, and metropolitan. In the seventh century Seville was compelled to resign the primacy, held for two hundred years, to Toledo. In the time of Charlemagne, Bourges received the primacy of.

Aquitaine, and Narbonne of Aix. At Bourges the archbishop appointed two vicars, one a metropolitan, and the other a primate. By John VIII. Sens was endowed with the primacy of Gaul. In the same century Hamburg and Oviedo became metropolitan, and Hincmar of Rheims contended for the primacy of France. At the close of the eleventh century the Archbishop of Lyons became Patriarch of Tours, Sens, and Rouen. Calixtus II. advanced Vienne to the primacy of Bourges, Bourdeaux, Auch, Narbonne, Aix, Embrun, and Tarentaise. In 1085 Toledo received the primacy of all the Spains, but Braga still claims the precedency, and uses the double-barred cross. By Innocent VI., in 1354, York and Canterbury were respectively declared to be Primate of England and Primate of all England and Metropolitan, but in the eleventh century York carried his cross through the southern province ; but in 1280 the official of Canterbury broke the cross of York in pieces. The northern primate, however, replaced it and again carried it before him. In 1300 Archbishop Winchelsey ordered that bells and divine service should cease when the Archbishop of York was passing through the province of Canterbury, that no layman should ask his blessing, and that every diocesan should prevent him from carrying his cross. In 1325 Archbishop Walter excommunicated the Archbishop of York for an infraction of this rule. (*See* CROSS.) The Archbishop of Canterbury had the right of carrying his crozier unconditionally in the province of York. Clement III., in 1188, dissociated all Scotland from the province of York. Canterbury absorbed the archiepiscopal sees of St. David's and Lichfield. From 1072 to 1125 York was also subject to it. Before the irruption of the Moors Spain was divided into five provinces, now increased to eight in number. Portugal has three. The primate always occupied a principal city, and had archbishops under him, but need not himself be an archbishop. In France they ranked thus : Bourges, Sens, and Bourdeaux.

Prime, Canons of. Twenty-nine short lections taken from synodical injunctions, and read in France instead of capitula, at Prime.

Primer. The reformed version of the Little Office of the Virgin, or Enchiridion, which was revised by Peter Damians in the eleventh century. The latter name also denotes the breviary of the Greek Church.

Primicier. The first singer enrolled on the tablets of wax, primus in ceris; a title dating from the ninth century. In the Greek Church there are two primiciers, who stand with the domestics. The Præcentor of York, in 1226, was addressed as primicier by Honorius III. At Constantinople the chartophylax and archdeacon bore the same title; and the primiclerus in Spain, who was both provost and principal of the college of inferior clerks and ministers, as in the primitive Church the præcentor, was called Prior of the School of Singers. The archdeacon was at first called Primicier of Deacons : the latter at length discharged many of the functions of the subdeacon, as the bishop's vicar, presiding over the minor clergy at the hours, directing the lections by the clerks, and controlling the music. In Italy, therefore, the archdeacon, archpriest, and primicier were regarded as the three chief dignitaries; but on the other side of the Alps, at least for some time, the archdeacon retained these duties, and, with the archpriest and custos, was regarded as the principal in a cathedral. At Metz the primicier superintended all the city and diocesan schools. At Braga he is both præcentor and chancellor; at Aberdeen he was præcentor, taking that name eventually; at Forli his office was founded in 1562 ; there is also a primicier at Venice, Milan, Naples, Cremona, Bergamo, Toul, Verdun, Arles, and Metz, who is the grand chanter, and at Barcelona, master of the choir, having his deputies the precentor and succentor, who thus correspond to the subchanter of canons and succentor.

Principal Vestment. The suit of robes used on principal or chief feasts, including, in 1250, a chasuble, fair albe, amict, stole, maniple, cincture, with three towels, corporals, and vestments for deacon and subdeacon.

Prior. (1.) A vice-abbot, so called where a bishop, as at Coventry and other conventual cathedrals, sat as abbot. At Ghent, in 1536, he became a dean. (2.) Prior-major, elected by the convent; the second in authority to the abbot in a monastery. (3.) A conventual prior, chosen by the monks of a small convent; and holding the power of an abbot. (4.) A claustral abbot presided over a cell of a greater house, and was nominated by the abbot of the latter, his own being

subject to it; all these, in 1126, were required to be priests.
(5.) The prior-major had under him the prior of cloisters,
who held chapter in his absence, visited the infirmary, inspected the brethren after Compline, and made the circa
(grand rounds or patrol) of the monastery after nightfall; there
were usually two other subpriors, who held the rank of custodes, or masters of the order. (6.) Subprior, the vicegerent
of a conventual or claustral prior. (7.) The mitred head of
the order of Hospitallers. (8.) The chief provost at Cefalu,
Osma, Cremona, Urgel, Burgos, Astorga, Tarragona, and
Siguença; and at Cologne, Seville, Brechin, Dunblane, St.
Andrew's, and Merewell College, a vice-dean; called senior,
or ancien in some German and Italian churches. Probably
the title was a relic of a conventual establishment formerly
existing at Brandenburg, Littomissel, and Pampeluna. The
Council of Aix, in the ninth century, required that those who
had formerly been priors, subordinate to other prelates,
should be called provosts, whereas at Canterbury, after Lanfranc's arrival, the provost was named prior; and in the
middle of the twelfth century priors in secular chapels began
to be known as deans.

Prison. A bishop was required to have one or more prisons
for criminous clerks in 1261. That of the Bishop of Chichester remains over his palace gate; and the Bishop of
London's gatehouse stood at the west side of Westminster
Abbey. The south-western tower of Clugny was used as a
prison. There were various names for prisons : (1) Little Ease,
in which the prisoner could neither sit, lie, nor stand;
(2) Bocardo, as over the gate near St. Michael's, at Oxford ;
(3) Hell, as at Ely ; and (4) the Lying House at Durham. At
Durham, Berne, and Norwich, the conventual cells adjoined
the chapter-house; at Durham the term of imprisonment
lasted sometimes during a year, and was often attended with
chains, food being let down by a rope through a trap-door.
In all cases solitary confinement was practised, and in some
cases the guilty were immured, after the pronunciation of the
sentence Vade in pace, " Go in peace." At Thornton the
skeleton of Abbot de Multou, c. 1445, with a candlestick,
chair, and table, was found built up within a recess in the
wall ; and a cell, with a loop looking towards the high-altar,
remains at the Temple, in which William le Bachelor, Grand

Preceptor of Ireland, died. At Clugny the prison had no stair, no door, and no window. At Hirschau the prisoner could barely lie down; at St. Martin-des-Champs the cell was subterranean; at St. Gabriel, Calvados, under a tower. The prisons remain at St. Gabriel, Calvados, Rebais, St. Peter-sur-Dives, and St. Benet-sur-Loire; at Caen, near the great gate; and over it at Tewkesbury, Binham, Hexham, Bridlington, and Malling. The prison was under the charge of the master of the infirmary. "Criminous priests" were imprisoned in 740 in England, and in 1351 their meagre fare was prescribed. *See* LANTERN.

Private Baptism. In case of danger or sickness, baptism might be administered at any time or in any place. In Thessaly, when baptism was restricted to Easter, many died without it, and, in consequence, the old prohibitions were mitigated, the font being hallowed at Easter and Pentecost for occasional use. Children, if in danger, might be baptized on the day of their birth, by the Councils of Gerona, 517; and Winchester, 1071; and the Constitutions of Othobon, 1268.

The vessels in which any have been baptized are to be carried to church and there applied to some necessary use, and not to any common purpose, out of reverence to the sacrament (Langton's Constitutions, 1223); and the water with which baptism was ministered was to be thrown into the fire, or carried to the church to be put into the font. The vessel, Lyndwood says, was to be large enough to permit immersion, and was to be " burned or deputed to the use of the church" by Edmund's Constitutions, 1236; that is, as Lyndwood explains, "for washing the church linen." Wooden vessels were burned. Children, if sick, were brought to the priest, by Ælfric's Canon's, 957, who was to baptize them, from whose district soever they were brought, without delay, by Theodulph's Capitulars, 994.

Privileged (1) Sundays. Those on which "histories" (lessons from Holy Writ) were read. (2.) **Days** signalized by peculiar ceremonies or commemorating particular events; the first, fourth, and fifth Saturdays in Lent, and Easter Eve, Ash Wednesday, first and fourth Sundays in Lent, Palm Sunday, Good Friday, and Holy Week.

Procession. A choir in movement, marshalled by the sacristan, comandatore, preceptor processionum, or terminator. The origin of processions may have been an imitation of the motion of the heavenly spheres, the courses of the stars, and the revolutions of seasons, and more immediately of ancient religious dances. They were always accompanied by singers, and generally by musicians. Procession is progression, says Durand, when a multitude, headed by the clergy, goes forth in regular order and ranks to implore the Divine grace. They represent the pilgrimage of man upon earth on his way to the better land, from the cradle to the grave, as St. Paul says that we are pilgrims and sojourners in this world. Processions round cloisters and cemeteries still more vividly brought before the mind the thought of the last home to which man must come at length, as waters, after the most devious course, are lost in the great sea. In a procession to the altar, in reverse order to that of the recession, first went the verger, the cross-bearer, attended on either side, by acolyths carrying candlesticks and lighted tapers; then came the censers, or thurifers, the chanters in copes and carrying batons, the subdeacon, deacon, and celebrant; then choir boys, clerks of the second grade, and the more honourable following. In a cathedral the præcentor, the sub-chanter of canons (*prechantre*), and the succentor of vicars (*sous-chantre*), each with his chanter's baton, preceded the bishop, carrying his cross, or staff. In the middle of the fifteenth century the capitular tenants went in procession on St. Peter's eve at Exeter, preceded by the choristers carrying painted shields of arms. Processions were introduced for public prayers when the faithful people went in order to implore Divine help (Joshua vi. 15; 2 Sam. vi. 15; Ezra ii. 12–30; 1 Kings viii. 4, 5; Numbers x. 33–36), with a form at setting out and when halting; or when rendering thanks to God (2 Chron. xx. 27, 28, 21; St. Matt. xxi. 9). Christian processions commenced in the reign of Constantine. Justinian required the formality of a public procession at the consecration of a church, to add dignity to the ceremonial and suppress conventicles. Processions are mentioned by Tertullian, SS. Augustine and Jerome, and the Third Council of Braga, and were protected by Justinian's edict in 541. The word processio is used by Tertullian and St. Jerome in the sense of church-going. Ruffinus mentions processions

to the various shrines made by Theodosius.   Sozomen speaks
of the alternate chants used, and Nicephorus, Socrates, and
Theodoret, of hymns.

Processions were made with litanies and prayers, (1) for
the prosperity of the King; (2) the wealth of the realm;
(3) for pureness of the air; (4) for the increase of the fruits
of the earth.   Two processions for the good success of a king
were made on Sundays about the church and churchyard,
by English canons, in 1359 and 1298.   On Ash Wednesday,
after confession in church, there was a solemn procession
for ejecting the penitents, who were not readmitted until
Maundy Thursday.   On Easter Day was a grand procession
in memory of the disciples going to meet our Lord in Galilee, and in imitation of it there was a humbler procession
on every Sunday.   The other great procession was annual, on
Palm Sunday.   Bishops were also met with processions of
the chapter and vicars; or a convent; at the west door of the
church and the cemetery gate, by decree of Honorius III.,
1221.   In 1471 all curates of the diocese were required to
visit the high-altar of Lincoln Cathedral in procession, and
make their offerings.   In the nave the great processions were
arranged; at Canterbury two parallel lines, and at Fountains, Lincoln, Chichester, and York were two rows of circular processional stones, arranged at proper intervals, and
specifically allotted.   At Exeter the antiphon was sung daily
at the screen, and the procession passed through the north
gate of the choir to the vestibule of the Lady-chapel, and
then by the south gate of the choir near the throne to the
high-altar; it afterwards traversed the nave and cloisters,
concluding before the rood-loft; and if there was no sermon
the procession returned to the altar.   Carpets were strewed
along the way on great festivals.   Bishop Edyngdon desired
to be buried at Winchester where the monks stood in procession on Sundays and holy days. These monks, being aggrieved
by a bishop, on one occasion went round their cloisters from
west to east, out of their usual manner, in order to show that
all things were out of order.   At Chichester at Epiphany an image " of the Spirit " was carried round the
church by the dean or senior canon and two vicars.   On
Whitsun Monday the parishioners in the diocese often came
to blows about right of precedence, so that Bishop Storey

made injunctions (1478) for order on this occasion, when the shrine of St. Richard was visited annually. Crosses and banners were permitted, but the long painted rods with which the contending parties had hitherto belaboured each other were proscribed, as well as laughing, crowding, and noise. The pilgrims entered by the great south porch and assembled in the choir at 10 A. M. and left the building by it, having duly visited " the chancel and church." In 1364 the primate forbade such dangerous contentions throughout England. On Easter Monday at Kinnersley and Wellington the parishioners, adult and children, joined hand-in-hand, surrounded the church and touched it with a general simultaneous embrace, called " clipping the church." They afterwards attended Divine service. The procession at Wolverhampton on Monday and Tuesday in Rogation week, in which the children bore poles dressed with flowers and the clergy chanted the Benedicite, only ceased in 1765. Some of the Gospel trees or holy oaks where the stations were formed still remain. The office for Corpus Christi Day was drawn up by Alcuin with a hymn, and prose by Alcuin for Urban VI. One hundred years after, at Pavia, the Host was carried in procession upon that day, and the custom passed into Anjou and other countries. As late as 1551 the city companies of London went in procession, the Fishmongers' to St. Michael's, Cornhill, with three crosses, a hundred priests, and the parishioners and members of the guild carrying white rods; and the parish of St. Clement Danes displayed eighty banners and streamers, and was preceded by the city waits. A processional cross was carried in front certainly in the fourth century, and in the fifth century, both in the East and West, banners and lights were also used. Usually this staff ended in a tall pinnacle on which was a small cross, to distinguish it from a crozier. The gilt and tapering end of a modern churchwarden's wand is the last relic of the older staff. The deacon for the Gospels followed the cross; the priests and bishops walked last; the rest moved in the following order, clerks, monks, laymen, women, religious, and children, all barefooted. The Rogation procession of each parish in Franconia was called a cross, from its banner. The reliquary cross is usually detached from the foot or stand, which is either round or square, supported by the Evangelists, and was placed upon the altar beforehand. It was presumed to contain a portion of the True Cross. In the treasures of St. Omer there is a cross with two bars (a double traverse), of the thirteenth century, resembling in form one formerly at Bourges. On the lower bar was a crucifix, and on the upper Christ in glory. Another double cross, once in the abbey of Aignies, of the twelfth century, is at Namur, and a stand of the same date at Lunebourg, in Hanover. The celebrant in some churches, as at Rheims, carried a small relic-cross in coming out of the sacristy to proceed to the altar or walk in procession. When the reliquary cross was set upon a staff it became a processional cross; when set upon a stand it was an altar-cross. Three beautiful examples remain, that of Maestricht, of the twelfth century, made of rock crystal, which in the sunlight blazes up and shines like fire; another at Vernassal, of silver, embossed and carved, of the close of the thirteenth century; and another at Ahetze, of the sixteenth century, silver-gilt, with niello-work and bells, which are a favourite adjunct in the south of France, in order to call attention to the passing procession. At Orleans on Easter Day two processional crosses were carried at Mass and Vespers. "In processions," said Cranmer, "we follow the cross of our Saviour, professing ourselves, as true Christian people, ready to bear our cross with Christ, willingly to suffer all troubles and afflictions laid upon us for the love and cause of our Saviour, like as He suffered for us."

Processional Cross, The, or **Cross of the Station** (*Crux gestatoria* or *stationaria*), is mentioned by Socrates, Nicephorus, Cassiodorus, in the Life of St. Porphyry by Durand, and by Baronius under the year 401, and in the Canons of Cleveshoe in 747, when regulating the Rogations. A cross made of ash, silver-plated, engraved or enamelled, without a crucifix, was at an early date, after the introduction of the Labarum of Constantine, carried in processions by the staurophoros. The evangelistic symbols were usually set at the ends of the arms, which terminated in fleurs-de-lys. In the fourth century they had short handles, and candles were attached to the arms. Charlemagne gave such a cross, of pure gold, to the churches of Constantine at Rome. In the twelfth century at Rome a subdeacon, regionarius, carried down the cross, inclined so that the faithful might kiss it, from the altar to the porch, where he held it upright in his hands during the procession. At Durham the chief cross was of gold, with a silver staff, and the cross used on ordinary days of crystal. A novice followed it, carrying a benitier. A cross of the fifteenth century is still preserved at St. John's, Lateran; another, of the time of St. Louis, is at St. Denis; and a third, of silver and beautiful design, with statues and evangelistic symbols, at Conques; and another at Burgos. In England, no doubt, many were destroyed during the Wars of the Roses and at the Reformation. At Chichester the aumbry for them remains. In England, from Easter to Ascension, the cross was of crystal or beryl, but in Lent of wood, painted blood-red. No parish could carry its cross into a monastic church; and in funerals in a collegiate church the cross of the latter only is set before the bier. *See* STATION.

Processional Path. (*Spacium vel via processionum a retro altaris; latus pone chorum;* Fr. *partour de chœur,* behind a choir.) The transverse aisle in square-ended churches is commonly doubled, as at Lichfield, or even tripled, as at Winchester and St. Mary Overye, in order to provide room for chapels as well as a passage for processions. At Hereford this aisle resembles a low transept. The eastern screens at Fountains, the Lady-chapel of Hexham, and the Nine Altars of Durham seem to have been further developments of the same idea, which appears also in the longitudinal new work of Peterborough. At Canterbury, pilgrims to the martyrdom passed up the south aisle of the nave, and through the passage under the platform of the crossing.

Proctor. (*Procurator,* a proxy.) (1.) The master of the works and general bursar in a monastery. (2.) The procurator fabricæ at Lunden and Roeskilde, at Lincoln, Salisbury, and St. David's, had charge of the houses of the inferior ministers. (3.) An economist, like the cellarer of St. Asaph (1372), who presided over the granary from which the canonical bread or wheat was furnished. At Nola there are two procurators or quæstors, one for the canons, the other for the numerals. There was a similar officer at Otranto, Rieti, and Littomissel. (4.) The president of the vicars' college at Salisbury. At St. Bertin's he defended the privileges of the vicars. (5.) Two representatives or proctors from each diocese were summoned to a provincial council in 1279. Members of Convocation, not being deans or archdeacons, are called proctors.

Procuration. (1.) An entertainment given to the archdeacon with provision for seven horses and six men. (2.) An equivalent in money; according to Lyndwood, 7s. 6d. to the archdeacon and 1s. to each of the other six at his visitation. (3.) An entertainment made at a visitation for a bishop. In 1336 a money composition was permitted to be offered by Pope Benedict XII., but only one procuration could be demanded if several churches were visited in one day. The amount varied in different countries. In England an archbishop received 220 turons, a bishop 150, an archdeacon 50, and an archpriest or rural dean 10.

Profession of Faith made in baptism. (Lat. *promissum, pactum, votum*; Gr. *suntassesthai Christo.*) The form following a renunciation.

Profesti Dies. Days without any special service, in distinction to solemn or officiated days, which include stations, litanies, fasts, and feast-days or festivals.

Prokimenon. The short anthem before the Epistle, consisting of verse and response, usually taken from the Psalms. Used in the Greek Church.

Prone. (*Præconium.*) Publication in the pulpit of banns of marriage, pastoral letters, coming fasts and feasts, and a sermon (the dominicale or homily for Sunday) after the Gospel in France.

Proper Psalms. Psalms adapted by their contents to the subjects of particular Sundays or festivals and holy days. St. Chrysostom refers to ancient prescription in this matter, and St. Augustine mentions as an old custom the use of Ps. xxii. on Good Friday. Cassian informs us that Ps. lxiii. was sung at Matins, and the 141st at Evensong. St. Athanasius and St. Augustine appointed special Psalms on certain occasions.

Prophecies, *or* **Exercises.** (1.) Conventicles of the Puritan clergy, borrowed from Scotland about 1560, for sermons and Scriptural study, in market towns or other places. Forbidden under pain of suspension for the first fault, of excommunication for the second, and of deposition from the

ministry for the third by the 72nd Canon of 1603, and previously by Grindal in 1577, owing to its abuses. (2.) The
lections from the prophetical writings read and sung by the
deacon and choir on Easter Eve before the lighting of the
Paschal, a relic of the primitive custom of Scriptural instruo-
tion given to catechumens on this day in the early Church.
(3.) A church dedicated to a prophet, as apostoleia were to
Apostles.

Prosar. The service-book containing the proses.

Prose. The French name for the Sequence. (1.) The prayer
sung in the Mass after the Gradual and before the Gospel
on great festivals. It required the licence of the diocesan
or the superior of a monastery before it could be used. (2.)
A canticle in which no metre is defined. An expression, in
loose measure, of the principal circumstances of a festival
to be added to the pneuma or adapted to its notes. St.
Cæsarius of Arles required the laity in the diocese to sing
proses and antiphons in church—some in Greek and some in
Latin—aloud like the clergy, in order to introduce among
the people a love of psalmody and hymns. Notker, Abbot
of St. Gall, c. 880, composed and favoured the use of proses,
but certainly did not invent them. He says that he found
one in an antiphonar brought from a Benedictine abbey near
Rome, which had been burned by the Normans in 841.
Pope Nicholas first authorized their use. Proses in the middle ages were written in the vulgar tongue for the edification
of the people. These proses, having become exceedingly
numerous, and in some places even ridiculous, were retrenched
by the Councils of Cologne in 1536, and of Rheims in 1564.
The four proses used since the time of Pius V. are Victimæ
Paschali Laudes, for Easter ; Veni Creator Spiritus, appointed
by Pope Innocent III., at Whitsuntide ; Lauda Sion Salva-
torem, for Corpus Christi Day, written either by Bonaventura or St. Thomas Aquinas ; and the Dies Iræ, Dies Illa,
used in the commemorations of the dead, and attributed to
Thomas de Cellano, or Salerno, a Franciscan, c. 1230, Cardinal Ursin (who died 1204), Cardinal d'Aquasporta (who
died 1302), Humbert, general of the Dominicans (who died in
1277), Augustus Buzellensis, or Bonaventura. The Stabat
Mater Dolorosa, written by Pope Innocent III., or Giacomo
da Toda, a Minorite in the fourteenth century, is a prose.

Possibly the chants used by St. Aldhelm, Bishop of Sherborne, sitting on the bridge of Malmesbury, to win the attention of the passers-by, were of the nature of proses. In the twelfth, thirteenth, and fourteenth centuries rhythmical chants were sung at the end of a banquet which the Pope gave to his clergy. At Sens, Lyon, Paris, and Rouen proses were in frequent use (unlike the Roman custom), but they were mere rhapsodies, as we have in one instance preserved to us "Alle—necnon et perenne celeste—luia." After the prose, the Mass-book is removed from the Epistle to the Gospel side, to represent the translation of authority from the Aaronitish to the Apostolical priesthood.

Protection of the Church prevailed in 1064 in England from Advent to the octave of Epiphany, from Septuagesima to the octave of Easter, from Ascension to the octave of Pentecost, in Ember weeks, throughout Sunday, on the vigils and feasts of Apostles and saints which were bidden on the previous Sunday, All Saints', the dedication day of a church, in going to synods, chapters, on pilgrimage, to a consecration, or to church.

Prothesis. (1.) A small side-altar in a Clugniac church on the Epistle side, at which the ministers of the altar on Sundays and festivals partook of both kinds, using a silver calamus to drink of the chalice. (2.) The chapel of the credence in the Greek Church.

Province. The diocese of an archbishop, including a certain number of suffragan episcopal sees. Russia forms one province with three eparchies, (1) Kieff-Novgorod; (2) Moscow; and (3) St. Petersburg. Archbishops form the second, and bishops the third episcopal class.

Provincial Synod. An assembly of the metropolitan and his suffragans, which, by the Council of Nicæa, was to meet twice a year. By 25 Hen. VIII., c. 12, the royal licence is now requisite.

Provision. The destination of an ecclesiastic by the Pope for promotion to a see, living, or stall not yet vacant.

Provisor. (1.) A chamberlain. (2.) The Clugniac bailiff of the vill or manor and receiver of rents.

Provost. (*Præpositus.*) A prelate or president. (1.) The bishop in the time of Tertullian and St. Cyprian bore the name of provost, and in the early monasteries the title was transferred to the subordinate of the superior (præpositus per episcopum), nominated at first by the bishop, and at a later date by the abbot. He was a priest in the earlier cathedrals; the bishop's representative, who held charge of the estates, had cure of souls, and took care that the constitution and revenues were maintained unimpaired, the statutes obeyed, and divine service religiously observed. (2.) The major or grand provost had the first seat in choir, installed the canons, and gave them leave of absence for a week; he punished their excesses; saw that the daily distribution, the oblations, and fees for anniversaries were given only to canons and vicars present at the daily services; celebrated on great festivals; acted as president of chapter, but usually without the right of a vote; and held precedence in choir and processions. At Lichfield and Worcester, and in the seventh century at Ely, there was a provost besides an archpriest. In fact, the same office was called by Chrodogang, and the Councils of Aix and Valence in the ninth century, archdeacon, provost, and primicier; and at Utrecht and Deventer, centuries later, and in twenty-five Italian and German cathedrals, the archdeacon was still called also provost, and dom-prost in Sweden; but at Utrecht the major provost presided over four archdeacon-provosts. The inconvenience of the tenure of many offices by one person was at length sensibly felt. The provosts became too powerful, owing to their administration of the financial affairs. They were seen to represent too strongly the bishop's influence in the chapter, and their temporal duties conflicted with their spiritual headship and continuous residence. The office of dean as president in choir was therefore established. In 1020 the president at Canterbury, and in 1080 at Wells, was still called the provost; even in the sixteenth century dean was regarded as a synonym for provost, and the latter Cranmer proposed to revive in his own cathedral. At Vienne, and in the provinces of Aix, Arles, Toulouse, and Rheims, and in twenty churches of Germany, Holland, and Scandinavia, and in many English collegiate foundations, he was still president, as he is still in many colleges, at Pesth, and since 1536 at Ghent. (3.) Provost of canons. From an early date there was an inferior provost. The Council of Mayence calls the office a mastership or ministry, and at length it subsided into a

2 I

benefice and obedience, with rank, but without compulsory residence, and the Council of Rheims classed provosts and vidams as secular officers. The German cellarer, the French economist (a name occurring also in Ireland), and Spanish primiclerus corresponded to the English provost, a steward of estates and bursar. The dean superseded the provost at Auxerre 1117, in England and Norway between the close of the eleventh and middle of the twelfth century, at Upsala 1285, Urgel 1299, Solsona 1409, and gradually in France, the Peninsula, and Italy. At Forli the provostship was created in 1466. There were frequently several provosts, as at Hildesheim and Padua four, at Spires three, and in the tenth century twelve at Vich, Urgel, Barcelona, and Gerona, each acting for a month. At Wells in 1135, owing to the fraudulent conduct of the presiding provost, two were appointed, and then one, by Jocelyn's statutes, to pay the prebendaries of Combe, ranking next to the subchanter of canons. At Vienna, Milan, Seez, Amiens, Chartres, Tours, Lincoln (where he found the choir books), at Tuam, Elphin, Killala, Kilmacduagh, Achonry, and all cathedrals in Connaught a provost, at Brechin a pensionary, and at York and St. Paul's a chamberlain discharged the same temporal office of bursar. At Toulouse the provosts acted as gospeller and epistoler. At Beverley the provost was a dignitary, having charge of the bedern and granary and paid the canons who had quarrelled over their dividends by the chamberlain. In 1536 the monastic provost became the præcentor of Ghent. (4.) In England in 696 and 740, and by the Council of Orléans, and later, the church reeve and warden. (5.) In 1305, a rector or perpetual vicar in an English church. (6.) In 1308, an ordinary. (7.) In some French monasteries, the claviger.

Psalmody. (1.) The singing of the Psalms. Pliny, mentioning the Communion before dawn, speaks of the antiphonal strain (*carmen invicem*). (2.) It is used on the Continent in the sense of the English saying.

Psalms, Burial, in the time of St. Augustine and St. Chrysostom were xxiii., xlii., xliii., lix., ci.; in the Roman Church are xxiii., xxv., xxvii., and the seven penitentials; in the English Church, xxxiii., xc.; in the Greek Church, xci., cxix., and for clerks, xxiv., lxxxiv. Beleth mentions Ps. cxiv. and Confitemini; he says charcoal was placed in the grave to show the ground could never again be occupied. PSALMS GRADUAL, Pilgrims' Songs, or Psalms of Degrees : the Psalms cxx. to cxxxiv., which were sung in ascending the fifteen steps of Solomon's Temple. HALLELUJAH : cxlvi. to cl., each beginning with the words "Praise ye the Lord." PSALMS LUCERNAL : those sung in the primitive Church at the lighting of the lamps, the first hour of the night. The Clementine Constitutions, Cassian, and St. Chrysostom mention the office said at this time under the same appellation. PSALMS OF PRAISE (Hallel.) : Ps. cxiii. to cxviii., the hymn sung by our Lord before His agony. PSALMS PENITENTIAL,—St. Augustine when dying and lying speechless on his bed had the Seven Psalms painted on the walls of his chamber, that, looking towards them, he might resist any temptations of the devil,—Ps. vi., xxxii., xxxviii., li. (Miserere), cii., cxxx. (De Profundis), cxliii. PSALMS PROSTRATE, during the saying of which the seniors knelt in their stalls and the junior monks lay prostrate on the floor or forms. Those after Vespers and in Lent before the Collects of the Hours and Verba mea auribus percipe. Twelve psalms, called the Dicta, were sung (with three lections and responsories and six anthems) on the nocturns of ordinary days, one for each hour of the night. Six, says Beleth, are sung at Matins, Lauds, and other hours, in memory of the six works of mercy; five at Vespers, one for each of the senses; and four at Compline, the number of perfection.

Psalter. The Psalms of David, divided by the Jews into five books, ending respectively with Ps. xli., lxxii., lxxxix., cvi., cl. Seventy-three are attributed to David, one (xc.) to Moses, two (lxxii. cxxvii.) to Solomon, twelve to Korah's sons, and fourteen to the chief singers Asaph, Heman, and Ethan (1 Chron. xv. 19). The Psalms in the East, from the first to the fourth century, were recited in the version of the Septuagint, and by the Latins, until the time of St. Jerome, in the Italic. St. Jerome, c. 382, rearranged and corrected the Psalter, which was adopted by the Greeks and called Horologiai, under Theodosius; Horologion is their Book of the Hours. In the fifth century Pope Gelasius made a new revision. The 91st Psalm at Compline was formerly (we learn from St. Basil) sung at Vespers till the fourth century. In the ninth century the 31st was added to the 41st, 91st, and 134th. The Prayer Book version was made by Tyndale and Coverdale, and published in Cranmer's Bible in 1539.

Psaltery *or* **Canticum.** A stringed instrument played with the fingers or plectrum, the sonorous body of brass or wood being placed at the top. It was either square or triangular, with ten strings. From the ninth to the eleventh century David is represented playing on this instrument, but after the latter date carries a harp.

Pugillaris. The reed of gold, silver, or ivory used for drinking from the chalice.

Pui. The name of a fraternity, partly religious, in honour of St. Mary, and partly literary, established in Picardy and Normandy, and translated to England about the beginning of the fourteenth century, deriving its name from the Virgin of the Cathedral of La Puy, to which pilgrims greatly resorted. They yearly elected a prince, who was crowned with garlands or circlets, like those still used on certain occasions by the City Companies; the loving cup was gaily passed at the election, and the author of the best ballad-royal was also crowned. They had a chaplain-priest to sing Masses, maintained a grand feast annually, and kept a common hutch for the contributions of the brotherhood. There was a chapel of St. Mary de Pui at Westminster. No woman was admitted at their meetings. Perhaps Puits, another form, may allude to Song of Solomon iv. 15.

Pulpit. (Fr. *chaire, pulpitre,* meaning a lectern, lection being a book-desk, an elevated place for preaching.) Ezra, when reading the Law, stood on a pulpit of wood high above the people (Nehem. viii. 4); and Solomon prayed on a brazen scaffold (2 Chron. vi. 13). In medieval times the word designates the rood-loft. Becon uses it in its modern sense. It is said to remind the hearer of our Lord going up on the mountain to preach His Sermon of Beatitudes. The earliest pulpit was the ambo, tribune, or tribunal, as it is called by Prudentius. Epiphanius says that St. Chrysostom preached usually from the ambo; so did St. Ambrose and St. Augustine; and Nicephorus records that Macedonius, Patriarch of Constantinople in 489, mounted the ambo when he desired to clear himself of a charge of heresy. The ambo was placed in the centre of the church by the Greeks. It is in the middle of the nave at St. Pancras', Rome, on the left side, but on the right at Milan and Ravenna; at St. Clement's, Rome, the epistle desk is on the left, and that of the prophecies on the right. At Chartres, Bayeux, and Roiament the Matin lections were sung on the left side of the choir-entrance, and the desk was called the legend at Chartres. At Bourges an eagle stood in front of the Matin-altar. A pulpit at Orléans and Châlons-sur-Marne was used for reading the Epistle, Gradual, Tract, and Alleluia; the Gospel was sung on the west side of the jube at Chartres, Châlons, and Lyons, that for the lections facing the east. At Bayeux and Noyon there were several desks. At Lyons and Vienne the Gospel was read in the lower part of the choir, and the Epistle from the ambo; but the latter was used at both times at Rheims, Cambrai, Tours, Rouen, Sens, Châlons, Laon, Soissons, Noyon, Amiens, Beauvais, Senlis, Orléans, Meaux, Tournay, Bayeux, and St. Denis. The desk for reading the Gospel was called the pulpit; the lectern held the choir-books. The former was moveable, so as to be transferred from the one side to the other of the choir, and used by the subdeacon for reading the Epistle, whereas the lectern stood in the centre of the choir as a fixture, and was common to all the cantors in time of singing. Both, from their common ornament, the symbol of St. John Evangelist, were called the Eagle, and it appears on the ambones of Pistoia, of the thirteenth century, and in three ancient churches at Rome. The deacon, taking the text, the Book of the Gospels, richly bound in ivory, metal, and jewellery, carried it processionally, preceded by thurifers and taper-bearers, to the north side, where the pulpit stood. Fulk, Abbot of Lobbes, in the ninth century, made a wonderful eagle, on which burned four tapers in the form of a cross; a censer was contrived in its neck, which poured fragrant smoke from the beak and flaming eyes of the bird; and the head and wings were moveable, for the convenience of turning the book. Often the other three Evangelists were represented as writing the words sung by the deacon; at Messina there is one with the pelican, as the symbol of the Saviour, above all. At Narbonne, in the cathedral, is a moveable pulpit of the fourteenth century, consisting of two iron supports set saltierwise and supporting a bookstand of supple leather. Those of St. Augustine's, Canterbury, and Bury St. Ed-

mund's, mentioned in the twelfth century, were moveable
until the fourteenth century. In Belgium the ambo or
a faldstool set before the altar served as a pulpit. According
to John de Garlande, who wrote at the close of the eleventh
century, a pulpit is the ascent of steps to the lectern, upon
which the chant- or reading-book was laid. The double pulpits of Milan, Narni, and Perugia connect the tradition with
the ambones; those of Toledo are of bronze, and at Seville
(1518) are still used for singing the Gospel and Epistle. In
three of the ancient churches at Rome the Epistle ambon is
square, and stands on the north, whilst that for the Gospel
is round, and stands on the south side, with flights of stairs
leading up to it. The ordinary pulpit also stood on the
south side, as at Toledo, because the Gospel was preached
from it. The jube for the gospeller and epistoler in large
churches took the place of the ambo, and within two centuries was used by the preacher at Rouen, but in smaller
churches a pulpit was used, but there is no existing example
or record of such furniture until the thirteenth century.
The church-pulpit is usually hexagonal or octagonal, and of
wood, possibly in allusion to our Lord preaching from the
boat (St. Luke v. 1). Early pulpits were, no doubt, moveable,
and kept in corners until required for use, like that still
preserved at Hereford; and at Bury the analogium, or pulpit,
we know was removed from the chapter-house into the
church when it was necessary. This, no doubt, is the cause
of their present rarity. There are fine examples of pulpits
at King's Sutton, Kingsbury Episcopi, Wolvercot, North
Kilworth, Dartmouth, and Frampton, which has images of
saints. Those of Sudbury, Southwold, Hereford, and Winchester are of wood, and of the sixteenth century. The
earliest Jacobean example is at Sopley, 1606. There are
stationary pulpits of stone at Wells of the sixteenth century,
Worcester (1504), Ripon, Combe, Nantwich, and Wolverhampton. The oldest wooden pulpit is at Fulbourne, c.
1350. In Italy there are examples of the thirteenth and
fourteenth century at Sienna and St. Miniato, Florence; in
Germany there are stone pulpits at Fribourg, Ulm, of the
latter part of the fifteenth century; at Avignon, in France;
and Nieuport, in Belgium. There is a Byzantine pulpit,
said to have been brought from St. Sophia's, Constantinople,

at St. Mark's, Venice. Romanesque pulpits may be seen
in St. Ambrose's, Milan; St. Mary, Toscanella; and St.
Sabino, Canova. There is an octagonal pulpit, dated 1482,
at Ratisbon; that of Kidrich is *c.* 1491. An hexagonal
pulpit is at St. Andrew's, Pistoia. The octagonal pulpit of
Perugia is used for giving the benediction. There is a
superb thirteenth-century pulpit on seven pillars in the baptistery at Pisa, with lecterns for the Gospel and Epistle on
the stairs. Abbot Wygmore's pulpit (Gloucester) was on
the north, and placed against the third pillar westward of the
crossing. The south or men's side is the most common position, as at Wells, Chartres, Haarlem, Aix, and formerly at
Winchester, Peterborough, Gloucester, and Worcester. In
England the pulpits were copied from those of the refectory,
and such as stood in the open air, like those of Paul's Cross,
Worcester, and Norwich. In cathedral churches the pulpit
was often large enough to contain several persons, as the
bishop when preaching was accompanied by his two archdeacons. Gilding and colour were not employed on pulpits
until the fifteenth century. Many of these pulpits were
highly enriched with carving; that of Worcester has the
New Jerusalem, and one of stone at Newton Nottage has
the Scourging sculptured upon it. One at Burnham Norton,
of wood, is painted with the Doctors of the Church. In the
sixteenth century stone pulpits were introduced. There are
magnificent wooden pulpits at Strasbourg, 1481; Mayence,
Antwerp, Faye la Vineuse, Nuremberg, Brussels, 1699; and
Vienna, from which John Capistran preached a Turkish crusade in 1451. At Durham there was an iron pulpit or ambo
in the Galilee, from which the Sunday sermon was preached
to women. There is another on the north-west at San Gill,
Burgos; and two like ambons, fitted with desks, of the
fifteenth century, flank the screen of Zamora; the two
pulpits of Milan are of metal, and circular. At Aix the
choir-pulpit is silver-gilt and jewelled. At Lugo one of the
two metal ambons has an eagle on the south. (2.) Refectory
pulpits remain at Beaulieu, of the fourteenth century, Chester, Shrewsbury, Walsingham, Chichester, Carlisle, Easby,
and in part at Oxford. (3.) Open-air pulpits in France, overlooking a cemetery, are not uncommon, and were probably
used when the friends of the departed came to visit their

graves. One at St. Die remains in the cloister; another, in the outer court of Magdalen College, Oxford; and there are other examples at St. Lô, Des Carmes, Paris, De Vitre, Laon, Prato, Pistoia, Viterbo, Spoleto, and Wraxall. That of the Dominicans at Hereford is canopied, as a protection against bad weather, as that of St. Paul's was. (4.) Cranmer desired the lessons to be read from the pulpit, and Cosin ordered the Commination to be read from the lower pulpit, clearly a synonym for the reading-pue.

Pupilla Oculi. A clerical manual written by John de Burgh, and very popular during the fifteenth and sixteenth centuries.

Purfles. (*Pour filles.*) Embroidered borders.

Purgation. A clearing of an accused person from impeachment by oath of himself and others; this, in 696, was done at the altar. The number of witnesses or consacramentals varied; the common man had four. In Wales three hundred were required; and in 1194, the Bishop of Ely purged himself with one hundred priests' hands. The practice was general among the Teutonic nations; in England it was called the atha. If the offence was alleged to have been committed in Lent, or on a festival, a triple purgation in 1018 was enjoined.

Purification. February 2nd; called also Light Mass, and, in the Greek Church, Hypapante, as commemorating the meeting of our Lord by Simeon and Anna. It probably dates from the close of the fifth century in the Latin Church. In England a jocular name was St. Blaise, derived from the blaze of candles. (*See* CANDLEMAS DAY.) In Germany St. Blaise's Day, from its bonfires, was popularly called Little Candlemas. Candles were offered at his altar, as Beleth relates.

Purifier. (*Purificatorium.*) A napkin of linen to cleanse and dry the chalice, the lips and fingers of the celebrant.

Purlin. Horizontal timbers resting on the principal or main rafters of a cieling, and supporting the common rafters.

Putlog Holes. Apertures for scaffolding left in walls.

Pyramid. A sepulchral monument in imitation of a spire of flame. Beleth mentions one built at Tours, and another, called St. Peter's Needle, at Rome. *See* EFFIGIES.

Pyx. (A box of boxwood, *puxos*.) The custody, or vessel for the reserved Host, so called as early as the Councils of

Tours and York, 1179, and enjoined by Pope Innocent III. in 1215, and by Odo of Rouen in 1266, to be over or near an altar. The Clugniacs had a pyx of cork or bark and a pendent gold dove. In 1322 the Archbishop of Canterbury required the pyx to be made of silver or ivory. Bishop Bleys of Worcester, a century before, required two pyxes, one of those materials or of Limoges work for the reserved Host, and the other, decent and honest, for the oblates. At Durham the pendent pyx was lifted or lowered by cords of white silk. Gervase, Hoveden, and W. Malmesbury mention the pendant pyx. Only two English notices of a dove-like shape occur—one in an inventory of Salisbury, the other in Matthew Paris. The ciborium, custodia, or corporax cup is, as it were, the chalice of the Host, a vessel to contain the consecrated altar-breads for Holy Communion, or the communion of the sick. The monstrance contains a single Host for exhibition to the people, and when the ceremony of adoration is over the Host is returned to the ciborium. The tabernacle contains the pyx, sacred plate, the chalice, and ciboria, and is, in fact, an aumbry.

The great ciborium, or cup, contained all the altar-breads for Communion; the small ciborium, or pyx, held only those for the Viaticum. The larger kind, like one at St. Omer of the twelfth century, had covers, and often were receptacles or tabernacles for the pyxes. The pyx was usually a cylinder with a cone-shaped cover. Up to the thirteenth century the material was ivory, but subsequently, when it became rare, gold, silver, or enamelled copper. A few rare cup-shaped pyxes are preserved at Sens of the thirteenth century; Munster and the Louvre, of the twelfth century. The latter came from Montmajeur, and the second serves now as a reliquary. They were usually crowned with a cross, or a jewelled diadem of precious stones. There are fine examples at New and Corpus Christi Colleges, and in the Bodleian, Oxford. The pyx was the casket for jewels used by the Greeks and Latins, and made of boxwood: hence the name. In the fourteenth century an apothecary of York uses the word for an unguent-box. (*See* TABERNACLE.) At that date, in Germany, the true pyx often resembled a small turret and spire. A wooden pyx held the Hosts at St. Paul's, and another served as an alms-box.

Quadripartite. The divisions of a vault into four triangular spaces. Sexpartite includes six of such divisions.

Quarrel *or* **Quarry.** (1.) A diamond-shaped pane of glass. (2.) A wax taper of ¼lb in weight.

Quarter, Stud, *or* **Punchion.** An upright support in a screen.

Quatrefoil. An ornament of four leaves or featherings, as cinquefoils have five, and trefoils three foils.

Quirk. A sharply-formed recess or channel between mouldings.

Quisshion. (*Pulvinar, cussinus, culcitrum.*) A cushion, usually of velvet, and stuffed with wool or horsehair, for the service-book, on the south side of the altar, appears in Henry VI.'s Book of the Hours, and was used by Bishop Andrewes. In the former it is on the south side, in the latter on the north. Albertis mentions the wooden desk, plated (legile), as a modern substitute. The book was first set on the right side, and afterwards moved to the left side of the altar at Mass.

Quoin. The outer angle of a wall.

Quotidian. (*Secta chori.*) Payment for duties performed in choir, and personal attendance at divine service. The præsentiarius paid it in foreign cathedrals.

Rabat. A linen neck-collar.

Rafters. Inclined timbers, forming the sides of a roof.

Rails, Altar, date from the time of Bishop Andrewes, who calls them "wainscot banisters," and Laud, who intended to preserve the altar from profanation by their use. They are, in fact, the cancelli moved eastward, resembling the medieval reclinatorium, and answer to the primitive altar-veils and Greek Iconostasis. At Leamington Priors, St. German's, and Wimborne they are covered with a white linen cloth at the time of Holy Communion, a relic of the custom for communicants to hold the houselling cloth (*dominicale,* for the Lord's body) below their chin for the purpose of retaining upon it any portion of the Sacrament which might fall during the administration. The custom was disused at the coronation of William IV. St. Augustine and Cæsarius of Arles mention a linen cloth (*linteamen*) used by women for the same purpose. *See* CHURCH BOOKS and HOLY COMMUNION.

Rationale. (*Pectorale, logion.*) An ornament worn by a bishop on his breast. It was in the form of a trefoil, quatrefoil, or oblong square, like the piece of stuff worn by the Aaronic high-priest. It appears on Bishop Gifford's monument at Worcester, 1301. It was worn perhaps for the last time on record at Rheims. The Pope has a formal, and cardinals and Italian bishops wear superb brooches to clasp their copes. The Greek peristethion worn by patriarchs and metropolitans over the chasuble is an oblong plate of gold or silver, jewelled.

Rattle. (*Crécelle, tarturelle, rattelle; semantron; crotalus.*) The Celtic cloc, which preceded the use of bells, was a board with knockers. The Greeks used the hagiosideron (sacred iron), a mallet and plate of iron, and the hagia xula (sacred wood), two clappers, as summons to prayer; the latter are mentioned by John Climacus as used for rapping at the cell doors in the monasteries of Palestine, in the sixth century, as a night signal and waking-hammer; at University and New Colleges, Oxford, fellows are summoned to a meeting in common room by the blow of a hammer at the stair-foot. By the rule of Pachomius a trumpet was used. At Burgos the clappers are called matraca, in Italy serandola, and in some parts of France symandres, which sound for service between the Mass on Maundy Thursday and the Gloria in Excelsis, sung on Easter eve in the Mass after Nones, when the bells are disused, in memory of our Lord's silence in the tomb and the speechless timidity of Apostles, a custom dating from the eighth century. At Caen the ceremoniar gives the signal for censing with tablets. Neogorgus says that boys carried rattles in the procession of Good Friday. *See* BELL.

Ravle. A cloak worn by women mourners.

Rayonnée. Rayed; a line in zigzags, vandyked, like sunrays.

Read. To recite, whether in monotone or with a musical inflection of voice, which are respectively expressed by the terms saying and singing; read is the generic and inclusive term, embracing the more ornate and simpler forms of recitation, whether cum notâ or sine notâ.

Reader. (*Anagnostes.*) (1.) The teacher of the hearers. The office ranking next to subdeacons; is mentioned by Tertullian, and in Spain by the Council of Toledo. St. Cyprian speaks of their ordination. In the West the subdeacons assumed the office, which became at length almost extinct. Their duties were to read Scripture from the ambon, and in the East to act as acolyths. They were often very young, and in primitive times were selected from confessors. (2.) The chaplain of an Inn of Court.

Receptorium, or **Salutatorium.** A parlour attached to the basilica, where the bishop and priests received persons who came to ask their benediction or advice.

Reconsecration of a church was required by Ecgbriht's Excerptions, c. 740, in case of the removal of an altar, or its violation by murder or adultery. If the walls only were altered, reconsecration was made with holy-water and salt.

Rector. (1.) The recipient of the great tithes. John de Athon says that in his time, and certainly in England before 1126, any clerk might be appointed to a rectory; but Pope Boniface VIII., in 1299, permitted a subdeacon by dispensation to hold one for seven years. In 1273 the Council of Lyons prohibited any one from accepting a benefice whilst under twenty-five years, instead of the previous requirement of only fourteen years of age. A rector, or vicar, in 1250, was required to maintain the chancel, with its desks, benches, windows, walls, and glass windows. (2.) In 747, in England, a conventual president or parochial incumbent. (3.) The superior of a Jesuits' seminary, and some foreign universities. (4.) The head of Exeter and Lincoln Colleges, Oxford.

Rectors of Choir. The vicars provided on great festivals four subordinate rectors, the principal rector and collateral on one side, and the secondary rector and collateral on the other side of the choir, the præcentor (the chief rector of choir) being in the midst, before the altar-step. They stood at the bench and lectern until the chant began, and then walked in copes to and fro, with staffs of ivory and boxwood in their hands, to mark the time. Their folding faldstools of iron were covered with leather. At Lincoln the slab inscribed "Cantate hic," ("sing here,") remains; and Pugin discovered the marks of their seats. They also acted as markers of absence for a week at a time. At Chichester the two high-rectors were chosen from the vicars, who wore the calabre almuce, and the two second rectors were selected from the priests' stall on great festivals; on lesser days the latter acted as high rectors, and two from the second form as second rectors. The præcentor taught them the antiphon, intonation, and difference of the Psalms. At Lichfield, on doubles, the two principals were chaplains, and the others secondaries, deacons, or subdeacons; on greater doubles the former were vicars of the dignitaries, chosen by the præcentor; on ordinary days only two secondaries acted. On alternate weeks the dean's and præcentor's choirs led; but the dean's if he were present, except at Christmas, Easter, and Whitsuntide, when both choirs were united.

Redemptorists. An order founded by Alfonso Liguori, 1787.

Refectory. The dining-hall of a monastery, which remains at Chester and Worcester as a schoolhouse, at Carlisle and Durham as a library, and at Beaulieu as a church. Portions of its beautiful arcaded walls remain at Peterborough. It was at Lanercost, Rievalle, and usually, raised upon cellarage, which at Clugny contained the bath-rooms; and in Benedictine friars' and regular canons' houses it lay parallel to the minster, in order that the noise and fumes of dinner might not reach the sanctuary; but in most Cistercian houses, as Beaulieu, Byland, Ford, Netley, Tintern, Rievalle, Furness, and Kirkham, Maulbronn, Clairvaux, Braisne, Savigny, and Bonport, it stood at right angles to the cloister, as it did in the Dominican convents of Toulouse and Paris. A few foreign monastic refectories were of two alleys, as Tours, Alcobaça, the Benedictines', and St. Martin des Champs at Paris. At St. Alban's an abbot, on his resignation, went to reside in a chamber which he had fitted up under the refectory. The usual dinner-hour was 3 P. M. The small bell rang and the monks came out from the parlour and washed at the lavatory, and then entered the hall, two and two, taking their appointed places at the side-tables. At the high-table on the dais the superior sat, in the centre of the east wall, under a cross, a picture of the Doom, or the Last Supper, having the squilla-bell on his right-hand, which he rang at the beginning and end of dinner. Usually the number of each mess varied between three and ten persons. Each monk drew down his cowl and ate in silence. Whilst the hebdomadaries or servers of the week laid the dishes, the reader of the week began the lection from Holy Writ or the lives of saints in the wall pulpit. During dinner all the gates were closed, and no visitors were admitted. After dinner the broken fragments were sent down to the almonry for the poor and sick, and the brethren either took the meridian sleep, talked in the calefactory, read, or walked, but in some houses went in procession to the cemetery and prayed awhile bareheaded among the graves of the brotherhood. At Durham the frater-house was used only on great occasions. It was fitted with benches and mats. The ordinary fare was pulse, fruit, vegetables, bread, fish, eggs, cheese, wine, or ale; and the evening meal, the biberes, collation, mistum, or caritas, consisted of bread and wine, and was followed by prayer in church before bedtime. The dinner-hour at length became put back to noon, and the supper was continued at the old time, about 5 P.M. At the entrance of the hall there was a large aumbry for the mazers, cups, and plate. The Clugniacs distributed the unconsecrated hosts in hall. The Last Supper of Leonardo da Vinci, painted for the Dominicans of Milan, represents the high-table of a refectory of the order. French or Latin only were allowed to be spoken in hall or cloister, and in 1337 meat was not eaten on Wednesdays and Saturdays, during Advent, or from Septuagesima to Easter Day. The hall of a guest-house was lined with beds at Clugny and Farfa, for men on one side, and for women on the other, whilst moveable tables down the centre were laid out at meal-time. *See* LOFT.

Registers of Ordination were first ordered to be preserved in 1237 in the bishop's house or in the cathedral.

Registers, Parish, were required to be kept as a record of baptisms, marriages, and burials in 1538 by Cromwell, by the Royal Injunctions of 1547, and the 70th Canon of 1603.

Regnum. The tiara or diadem of the Popes, encircled with three crowns. It is, says Innocent III., c. 1200, the imperial crown, representing the Pope's power as plenary and absolute over all the faithful. According to some authors, Hormisdas first wore a crown which had been sent to him as a mark of fealty by the Emperor Anastasius, to whom Clovis had presented it in 550, whilst some refer it to a gift of Constantine to Pope Sylvester. At the entrance of a church the Pope, when borne on his litter, laid aside the regnum and put on a precious mitre, but resumed the former when he left the building. Paul II. made a new regnum, and enriched it with precious stones, when its use had long lain dormant. At first it was a tall round or conical cap, ending in a round ball and wreathed with a single gold crown, representing regal and temporal power. It is mentioned in the eleventh century. In the ninth century, on mosaics, Nicholas I. is represented wearing two circles, the lower labelled, "The crown of the kingdom, from God's hand," and the upper inscribed, "The crown of empire, from St. Peter's hand." Boniface VIII., 1294-1303, added a second or spiritual crown, whilst Benedict XII. (1334), others say John XXII. or Urban V., contributed the third coronet of sacerdotal sovereignty, and about that time the ornament assumed an oval form and was no longer straight-sided. The patriarch of Constantinople wears two crowns on the tiara. On putting on the tiara the cardinal deacon says to the Pope, "Receive the tiara, adorned with three crowns, and know that thou art father of kings and princes, the ruler of the world." The crowns represent the three realms of heaven, earth, and purgatory, according to Becon; but as Jewel explains it, the three divisions of the earth, Europe, Asia, and Africa. Pope Adrian V.'s effigy at Viterbo has no crowns on the tiara.

Regular Canons. Prosper of Aquitaine and Pope Gelasius introduced the order of canons into France. Baudin at Tours, and Wolfgang at Ratisbon adopted the common life. The real fact, no doubt, was that at first monks lived outside the city and the canons resided in towns, at first with the bishops and then independently, receiving the monks in time of war or persecution, and adopting from them portions of their rule, so that from the growing similarity their houses were familiarly called monasteries and their churches minsters. They wore black almuces, and canons secular had white until the latter adopted grey fur. *See* CANON.

Regular Clerks. Modern orders founded for preaching, meditation, or education. The principal are the Theatines, founded by Paul IV., and the Oratorians, instituted 1550 by Pope Neri of Florence.

Relics. Remains of a saint's body. Objects which had touched such remains or tombs. Called also benedictions, insignia, lipsana, xenia, patrocinia, pignora sanctorum, or sanctuaria; and objects which had been used or handled by a saint. In the seventh century Gregory sent the bones of a saint to Britain for the consecration of a church by St. Augustine, but he reprobated the dismemberment of the remains of the holy dead. At first a handkerchief, a flower, or veil laid on the sacred tomb, filings from a chain or instrument of torture, oil from lamps that had burned round the grave, stains of the saints' blood on stone, or dust from the spot, had hitherto been regarded as gifts worthy to be sent to prelates or carried home as heirlooms by devout pilgrims. Relics of saints were regarded as the palladia of cities, as St. Martin's body was carried out to the gates of Tours in 845 to repel a siege by the Danes. St. Werburgh's relics were borne in procession to quell a fire at Chester, and the canons bore them through the diocese to invite alms for the erection of Salisbury Cathedral. At Lichfield the bells were rung at their departure and return. In the ninth century, it is said, the sale of relics and holy images, with occasioual traffic in MS. codes, formed the chief trade of Rome. Theodosius, in 386, forbade the sale of relics by itinerant monks. In 855 Leo IV. ordered that on altars should be placed only the book of the Gospels, the pyx, and relics. In the sixth century the custom of swearing upon relics, as later upon the Gospels, began.

Relic Sunday. The Sunday after the Translation of St. Thomas (July 7), for worship and reverence of all saints' relics left here on earth, and the third Sunday after midsummer day.

Religious. Monks, friars, canons living under the bond of a rule (*religio*).

Reliquaries. Vessels for holding relics, and enclosing always in the thirteenth century three grains of incense, in honour of the Holy Trinity. Reliquaries, called by a French author the souls of churches set in the midst of the great body of the Church, usually took the form of the material building, reproducing that in which it was kept, as at the Sainte Chapelle, Paris, and Nivelles, of the end of the thirteenth century. At Tournay and Cologne they assume a conventional form. In the fourteenth century cathedrals adopted the form of a church, whilst in chapels and parish churches preference was given to images of gold and silver. Sometimes they take the shape of a coffer; or a transparent bier, carried by ecclesiastics; a case-like cruet; a rose; a quatre-foil; a canister in an angel's hand; horns, at Canterbury; a triptych, like the triple entrance of a church; a lantern tower and spire; a campanile; cylinders of crystal, as at Rheims, and one in the museum, Clugny; or a strong castle, with towers. A beautiful specimen is preserved at Ovieto. In some cases the church bearing the name of a saint, as St. Denis, St. Omer, St. Hilary, St. David, St. Asaph, has his monument; sometimes great shrines, as St. Remi's at Rheims, St. Front at Périgueux, the Three Kings at Cologne, St. Edward at Westminster, St. Cuthbert at Durham, St. Edmund at Bury, rose over their tombs; but in other cases the relics only were preserved in portable shrines. Very small relics were inclosed in the figure of some popular saint. Sometimes a large wide chest, like a gabled coffer, contained all a saint's bones. In other instances the reliquary was of stone, or of plated wood set with gems. There was a superb reliquary, shaped like an altar, which had been used by kings for military Mass in the field, given by William I. to Battle Abbey. At Limbourg there is a beautiful Byzantine reliquary, referred variously by German and French antiquaries to the tenth or thirteenth century. At Chichester the relic-chest of St. Richard is of oak, contains a door which was opened when the relics were exposed, and a slit for the reception of offerings in the cross-bar below it. It is of the sixteenth century, of oak, with ironwork of the thirteenth century. At Kewstoke there is a mural relic-aumbry in the nave, and at Gloucester, in the south arm of the transept, a beautiful screened relic-chamber or treasury. At first the reliquaries were portable, to form accessories of a procession. The Third Council of Braga in 560 notices the procession of " the ark of the Lord " and the relics carried on the shoulders of a deacon, but Anjou was the principal if not earliest imitator of the custom of carrying the Host in procession, a ceremonial which began at Pavia. In 745 relics and the cross were carried in the Rogation processions in England. At Rome the "three relics" are exhibited on Good Friday, the portion of the True Cross, the blade of the lance which pierced His side, and the veronica. About the beginning of the thirteenth century reliquaries were placed upon the altar instead of

2 K

under or in the centre of it, the tabernacle being also placed
upon the mensa, and retables, palls, banners, books, veils,
curtains, burses, and phylacteries introduced. The reliquaries took the form of the limb or bust, called a corset or
corselet, which they contained, incased in crystal or mounted
with precious metals. (*See* CHEF.) Statues on a portal or
west front, as at Wells, are ranged in order, those of the
Old Testament on the left, and those of the New Testament
on the right hand of the Saviour, who occupies the centre.
Reliquaries were arranged on great festivals in a similar
manner in their case or aumbry on the rood-beam, or upon a
kind of retable, with a number of apertures, set above the
high-altar, being brought from a low altar of relics placed behind it, at the east end of the sanctuary, or from the sacristy
or the treasury, their most appropriate place, innumerable
lights being kindled in their honour. *See* PROCESSIONAL
CROSS.

Renunciation in Baptism. (Gr. *apotaxis.*) An abjuration
of the deceits of the world, the works of the devil, mentioned
by Tertullian, SS. Cyprian, Ambrose, Jerome, Cyril of Jerusalem, the Apostolical Constitutions, and Salvian, and made
three times (according to Dionysius, St. Ambrose, and the
Gregorian Sacramentary), with turning to the west as the
place of darkness.

Repentinæ. (*Feriæ.*) State holidays.

Reposoir. (1.) A receptacle for the tabernacle in the procession of Corpus Christi. (2.) A chapel and shelter for travellers on the wayside, common in Italy ; one of the thirteenth
century is near Fismes ; a pilgrims' chapel remains on Lans-
downe, near Bath.

Repousse. Hammered work.

Requiem. A musical Mass for the dead, so called from the
words of the Introit, Requiem æternam dona eis, Domine,
" Give them eternal rest, O Lord," etc. (2 Esdras ii. 34, 35) ;
and the antiphon for the Psalms in place of the Gloria
Patri.

Reredos. (*Retroaltare, retrotabularium, postabulum, postaltare,
posticum, reyretaule, retaule, retable, reredos, lardose, l'arrière
dos ;* Sp. *retablo ;* Ger. *postergule.*) Called by Bishop
Andrewes the backpiece. An ornament behind an altar,
of hanging, carved metalwork, or drapering ; on it were

often ranged innumerable lights "ultra magnum altare." It is not earlier than the fourteenth century in its later form, nor under any description previous to the end of the eleventh or beginning of the twelfth century. As long as the old ritual lasted the altar stood free from the east end, in the chord of the apse. Until the fourteenth century it was still of the ordinary form of a table, and had only the Gospels and ciborium set on it at the time of Holy Communion, both in the Western and Eastern Churches. The tabernacle was an addition in the seventeenth century to the retable; the latter about the end of the eleventh century was introduced, being moveable and made of wood or precious metal, and set on the altar to contain relics at certain times. Even the fixed retable, a mere upright slab of stone masking a little shrine behind it, does not date further back than the beginning of the twelfth century, and was never attached then to the high-altar of a cathedral, but only used in minsters to which pilgrims were to be attracted by the exhibitiou of relics. Before this, curtains, dossals, or ridels (Fr. *rideaux*), which had fenced in the back and sides of the altar, gave place to the stone reredos at Exeter, Lincoln, Brecon, Beverley, Bristol, York, Canterbury, Durham (1380), Westminster, and those now lost at Peterborough, Tewkesbury, and Gloucester, and still .grander structures, the germ of which may be seen in the panelled walls of Ludlow and Wells, or at Christchurch (Hants), Winchester, St. Alban's, and St. Mary Overye, of the fifteenth century, covered with tabernacle-work, images, and sculpture round a central crucifix, once lighted by pendent lamps. Whilst they obstruct the view of the eastern limits of the church, which hitherto augmented the sublimity of the sanctuary, they resemble a gorgeous veil before some further holy of holies which our earthly services faintly shadow. There are superb reredoses of the sixteenth century, with wonderful carvings in wood, at Schleswig, Nuremberg, and Bamberg, where colour is employed. Other beautiful examples in stone remain at Seville (1482–1550), Keyserburg, Bodilis, Lampaul, and Crozon. In parish churches there was a panelling often over the altar, or an arcade, as at Hanwell, Enstone, Solihull, and St. Michael's, Oxford. At Arundel there is a passage behind the wall or reredos of the altar, as

2 K 2

originally at King's College, Cambridge, and still at Brilley and Michaelchurch, where there are carved oak posts against the east wall, which, with corresponding posts in the sanctuary screen, supported a beautiful panelled canopy as wide as the chancel and resembling the baldachino of the Basilica. There is a beautiful carved reredos and painted triptych of the sixteenth century over St. Agilophus's altar at Cologne. The contre-retable faced the celebrant. *See* ALTAR.

Reservation. (1.) Amphilochius mentions that St. Basil divided the Eucharist into three portions, one to be buried with him in his grave, and another suspended in a gold dove above the altar. The Council of Nicæa mentions the place for the reservation of the Holy Sacrament, and the Clementine Constitutions speak of the tabernacle. An instance of burial of the Eucharist with the dead is related by St. Gregory, but the practice was forbidden by the Councils of Carthage, Hippo, and the Third of Constantinople. Satyrus, brother of St. Ambrose, carried the Eucharist in a cloth (orarium) on shipboard, as did St. Birinus of Winchester in his pall. Innocent IV. prohibited the reservation for the sick of the Eucharist consecrated on Maundy Thursday, but allowed the practice during fifteen consecutive days, in order to provide against the Host becoming mouldy. In the time of St. Basil, in the absence of a priest or deacon, persons in Egypt kept it in their own houses, and took the Communion for themselves; but this practice of carrying the Eucharist out of church was forbidden by the Council of Toledo in 400. Irenæus says that the Eucharist was sent by various Churches to each other as a sign of Communion, but this again was forbidden by the Laodicean Council in the fourth century. In the primitive Church reservation was unavoidable, owing to the scattered and persecuted state of her members; hence Justin Martyr says that the eucharistic elements (probably from one central altar) were sent to the absent by the hands of the deacons; and Tertullian relates that the priest gave them to pious persons, who partook of them at home daily in secret, for fear of their enemies, when it was impossible to hold religious assemblies. St. Cyprian thus speaks of a woman keeping the Eucharist in her chest; Origen and Augustine, of it borne to private houses in a linen cloth; and Eusebius, of a lad carrying it to a dying Christian. St. Jerome says that Bishop Exuperius of Toulouse carried it abroad in a basket. In St. Chrysostom's time, however, both elements were reserved, and communicated either on the morrow or very shortly after. In Greece during Lent consecration was made only on Saturdays and Sundays, so that reservation, in order to meet the case of reconciled penitents being at the point of death, was a necessity; but by the Apostolical Constitutions, written when the Church had peace, the residue of the elements was given to the clergy. St. Jerome says they were consumed by the communicants. Hesychius mentions that their remains were burned, as in 960, by Edgar's Canons; but in Constantinople, according to Evagrius, and by the Council of Macon in France (585), and Tours in 813, the young, and (by the testimony of Nicephorus) children, partook of them. Reservation was usually made in the chapel of the Holy Sacrament. A chapel under that dedication remains at Chichester. Pope Innocent III., in the Lateran Council, 1215, c. xx., first ordered that chrism and the Eucharist in all churches should be reserved (*conserventur*) under faithful guard and keep. Honorius III. renewed the order. The Council of Tours, under Pelagius in 566, required the Lord's body to be reserved on the altar, not in the aumbry or among the images, but only under the cross. The practice of reservation was intended to serve three purposes—to quicken the love of the faithful, to have the elements ready for the Communion, and to furnish without delay the Communion of the sick. Leo, in a letter to the Emperor Michael, says that reservation at Jerusalem was for the convenience of pilgrims. At Christchurch, Hants, masses were allowed to be said specially at the arrival of strangers. In 1195 the Legatine Constitutions, at York, require the Host to be kept in a clean and comely pyx, and renewed every Sunday; and Archbishop Reynolds, in 1322, renewed this injunction. In 1229 reservation was made for seven days. On Good Friday, after the adoration of the cross, Beleth says the reserved Host was set on the altar, and after Communion Vespers were sung. In 1549, in England, reservation for the sick was made when there was "open Communion" on the same day in church, and also if more private Communions than one were to be administered, at the first celebration. In 1558 reservation was made in an aumbry, on the right side of the altar, either in the wall or framed in it, with the chrism and oil for the sick. (2.) The appointment of a bishop to a see reserved, or claimed beforehand by the Pope for his donation. (*See* PROVISION.) Devolution was a claim to appoint made when a chapter omitted to elect, or the person elect was declared unworthy.

Residence. In former times the following words, explanatory of their duties, were required to be read over frequently by canons :—" All canons are bound to perpetual residence in their church, in obedience, chastity, charity, prayer, reading psalmody, contemplation, and sobriety. Some of them are priests, some deacons, and some deacons always abiding : at God's altar the priests by course serve for a week, with deacons and subdeacons likewise ministering in turn" (but latterly in quarterly courses). "They, with a common counsel, treat of all matters touching the Church ; and in their food there should be a fair distribution ; they should not be absent from their church or live elsewhere, neither ought they to leave the world nor follow the fashion of its generation, since the whole Church is set in their hands, that by God's grace they may rule and govern it."

The love of canons died out in the twelfth century, when prebends had become common, non-residence the rule, and vicars were appointed as their deputies, the burden and heat of the day, as they were pleased to call it, falling upon the residentiaries, who in turn absented themselves often for half or even one-third of the year. The practice became still further deteriorated by the permission for only two-thirds of the residentiaries to be present at the cathedral ; and so common were absences and pluralities of stalls that the commune system was introduced, with a share in the diary, sequence, petty commons, or livery of bread and wine furnished by the church manors, and the money payment on Saturdays, called the great commons, quotidian, or manual, varying in different cathedrals, and apportioned to the number of times of attendance and the occurrence of festivals ; and in the quarterly distribution, annual dividend of fines for absence, and in the residue arising from offerings, rents, legacies, obits, fees, and the prebend of a canon for one year after his demise. The constant presence of some of the capitular members was thus secured; but in the fourteenth century unstatutable expenses were laid upon residents which amounted to a prohibition, in order to secure a larger dividend, so that non-residence was almost openly encouraged, except that the non-resident member paid a proportion of his prebend to the common fund by way of fine. At first a precious cope, or composition in money, like the emphanisma at Constantinople, was made to the fabric; but at length the new resident, on his protestation or offering to reside, received no income for his first year beyond his prebend, but had nevertheless to bear the burdens of the church in the shape of fees and entertainments to the dean and his brethren, vicars, choristers, and in some cases the citizens. These impositions sometimes amounted to several thousand marks in a year; and in consequence Richard II. was compelled to threaten a fine of £4000 on St. Paul's chapter, and prebendaries were prayed, for love of God, to come into residence. If a prebendary missed Matins or Mass on a single day in his year of probation, he was compelled to commence it anew. In some cathedrals there were two annual residences, of unequal duration, called in consequence the greater and less. The dean, præcentor, chancellor, and treasurer were resident during eight months of the year in most cases, and each had his own house, called the deanery, præcentory or chantry, chancery, and treasury. The numbers of residents varied, but the quarterly courses of priests, deacons, and subdeacons, one-fourth of the whole number at a time coming up to their duty, was long preserved. The grounds of excuse were teaching school, service in the King's chapel, attendance on an archbishop or bishop, absence on church affairs, or for prebendal residence; and then three parts of the year were allowed as the term of non-residence. The requirements for attendance in choir were met by presence at Mass and one canonical hour daily, or, sometimes, at Matins and Prime Mass, and Vespers, great stress being laid on the attendance at Matins.

In the new foundations the dean celebrated on the principal feasts, the subdean on greater doubles, and the canons on other feasts, in their order; the bishop officiated when he pleased in some of these cathedrals, as Peterborough. The

residence was either statutable or ordinary; the former permitted absence varying between eighty and ninety days in the
year, with a quarterly attendance of twenty-one days continu-
ously; the other was regulated by bye-laws; now the legal residence is three months. The quotidian varied: at Carlisle it was
10d.; at Chester, Worcester, Rochester, and Gloucester, 8d.;
at Durham, 1s. 4¼d.; and at Ely, 3s. 4d. daily. Commutation of residence was sometimes allowed for fifty days' continuous attendance in choir, but the usual rule was that one-
fourth or one-third of the canons should be always resident.
At Ely and Durham the canons had prebends; and in the
latter cathedral the investiture was made by the delivery of
the loaf and statute-book.

Responds. (1.) Short anthems giving the key-note of the fes
tival. (2.) Half-pillars set against a side-wall for the support of an arch.

Response. A chant earlier than the antiphon, in use by the
Benedictines in the sixth century, and brought from Italy.
It was sung in any part of the choir, unlike the gradual,
which was restricted to the ambon. In the antiphon a single
voice sang the verse; in the response the whole choir sang
alternate verses.

Responsory. (1.) The verse sung after the Epistle, which is
followed by the Gradual. (2.) The answer after the lections
at Matins.

Return. (1.) The end of a hood-mould, often in the shape of
a mask or leaves. (2.) A stall set against the east side of a
roodscreen.

Reveal. The side of a window or door-frame.

Reverend. A titular designation of the clergy below the rank
of bishop and dean, in the seventeenth century almost invariably associated with the adjunct "learned." In the last
century judges were sometimes spoken of as reverend, as
now they are called honourable. In 1727 the dignitaries,
archdeacons, and canons of Chichester with superior degrees were called venerable, and the rest masters; in 1733
the former only; but in 1742 all were indiscriminately styled
reverend. South, in 1693, speaks of Dean Sherlock as very
reverend, but the ordinary almanacks do not give deans the
distinction till 1807. Dean Nowell in Elizabeth's reign
mentions only the titles reverend and most reverend; at

the same time the Dean of York was called " right worship-full." Pope Gregory called St. Augustine "your holiness." In 673 the Archbishop of Canterbury mentions a Bishop of Worcester as most reverend. Six years later the Council of Rome speaks of the " glorious and most holy bishops." In 747 Cuthbert of Canterbury is called honourable; priests are termed venerable, and bishops most reverend, approved, honourable, and venerable. The Bishop of Meath, like archbishops, is called most reverend. The primitive bishops were often called makarioi, blessed. In 1709 an Archdeacon of Lincoln was called very reverend, whilst his brother of Leicester was simply reverend. A Bishop of Peterborough in 1630 was most reverend, whilst his predecessor in 1594 was reverend. In 1696 a Canon of Peterborough is described as very reverend; and a Prebendary of Hereford in 1497, and the Chancellor of St. David's in 1622, are dubbed venerable.

Rib. A projecting band in a vault or cieling which covers the groin or junction of the stones or timbers.

Ridge Piece. The upper rib running along the centre of the inside of a cieling.

Ridge Tiles. Cresting upon a roof.

Ring. (1.) Pope Adrian sent a gold ring to Henry II. as the sign of investiture with the realm of Ireland. (2.) An ornament adopted by bishops in the West in the fourth century, but unknown in the East. It is the sign of fealty to the Spouse of Christ and alliance with the Church, contracted by election, ratified by confirmation, and consummated by consecration, when it is blessed and placed on the fourth finger of the right hand, which is used in benedictions. The ring was formerly worn on the middle finger of the right hand, as that indicative of silence and discretion in communicating the mysteries, in giving the benediction, but was shifted to the annular finger in celebrating Mass. In 827 Gregory IV. required it to be worn on the right hand, and no longer, as before, on the left hand. The ring is mentioned by the Councils of Orleans, 511; Rome, 610; the Fourth of Toledo, 633; Hincmar of Rheims, Isidore of Seville, and the Sacramentaries of Gelasius and Gregory the Great in 590. St. Augustine speaks of his signet. These rings usually had monograms (siglæ), or engraved subjects, and were used as signets till the eleventh century in official correspondence, and for signing a neophyte's profession of faith, and, by Pope Sergius's order (687–701), for sealing the font from the beginning of Lent to Easter Eve in France and Spain, a custom alluded to by Optatus, and in France for sealing the receptacle of relics in an altar. They were called sometimes, in consequence, church-rings. Every bishop had also a jewelled pontifical ring, which Innocent III. in 1194 required to be of gold, solid, and set with a plain precious stone, usually a sapphire, baleys, or ruby, which was uncut. Durand says they were not to be engraved; but the ring of Pope Eusebius, c. 310, had his monogram and that of our Lord upon it; possibly the rule was directed against the use of pagan antiques. This ring represented fidelity to Christ, the bridegroom of the Church; the duty of sealing and revealing; and, lastly, the gifts of the Holy Spirit. The best rings of suffragans at their decease were the perquisite of the primate, and, in the vacancy of the archiepiscopal chair, of the Crown, at least as early as the time of Edward I. In 1163 the Pope, Alexander III., granted all the episcopal insignia to the Abbot of Evesham, except the ring. The rings of Pope Caius (c. 296), St. Birinus (d. 640), and St. John of Beverley (d. 721), were found in their graves. The following episcopal rings are preserved :— Athelstan's, c. 867, in the British Museum. At Winchester, Bishop Gardiner's ring, with an intaglio, 1531–55; two gold rings, set with a sapphire; one is of the thirteenth century, the other belonged to William of Wykeham, 1367–1404. Chichester, three rings, two having sapphires, the third set with a Gnostic gem of the twelfth century. At York, two rings with rubies, one of the thirteenth, the other of the fourteenth century; and a gold ring with the chançon " Hennor et joye" of the fifteenth century. At Hereford there is a ring set with a sapphire, and with the chançon " En bon an " of the fifteenth century; another with a ruby of the sixteenth century. St. Cuthbert's ring at Ushaw. A ring at Metz, with a cornelian engraved with the fish, earlier than the fourth century. Priests, as friends only of the Bridegroom, did not wear rings. Italian canons wore a ring without a stone, except at Mass. FISHERMAN'S RING. That worn by the Pope as the descendant of St. Peter, with an engraving of St. Peter casting his net. THE DECADE RING. A modern substitute for the rosary during the existence of the penal laws, being more easily concealed. It has on it ten knobs, on each of which as it passed under the fingers an Ave was said, and on the eleventh, which is distinguished by a cross, a Paternoster. THE GIMMEL, OR BETROTHAL RING, or a coin, was broken by the two contracting parties; and rings were interchanged at espousals in England, to which Shakespeare alludes in 'Twelfth Night.' They are usually made of two circlets; on the front there is usually a heart clasped by two hands. Herrick, in the 'Hesperides,' speaks of returning a ring of jimmals for a true-love-knot; the latter was the well-known Stafford knot. Wedding-rings, certainly from the time of the Tudors, and betrothal rings at an earlier date, bore posies or loving inscriptions upon them. THE MARRIAGE RING was formerly given at the espousals (as Pope Nicholas says), being placed on the finger of fidelity, or, as Isidore of Seville explains, on the fourth finger, whence a vein runs to the heart, as a token of love and union of hearts. In the tenth century the ring was given at marriage, probably as an amulet, and in imitation of the bishop's ring. In George the First's time it was worn on the thumb. In the sixteenth century " other gifts of spousage, gold and silver," were presented by the man at marriage, and at Cosin's time in the north of England. SANCTUARY RING. One remains at Pampeluna; it is of the Flamboyant period, and in the form of writhing serpents, set upon a richly-perforated plate. *See* KNOCKER.

Rite. (*Riht*, an ordinance ; *jus;* Gr. *reton,* prescript.) (1.) The right rule and settled custom observed in ceremonies ; the essential part in their ministration. Ceremonies are for decency and order. (2.) A special order of office peculiar to a single church.

Rites of Baptism. Tertullian mentions (1) renunciation; (2) trine immersion ; (3) tasting of milk and honey ; (4) abstinence from bathing for the space of a week ; and (5) unction with oil. The milk and honey were given to signify that, Christ being our Captain, and having passed over Jordan, the baptized have the sure hope of inheritance of the better land of promise (Exod. iii. 8-17 ; xxxiii. 3). St. Jerome says in his time, in the Churches of the West, wine was mingled with the milk, as a type of infantine innocency, in allusion to Isaiah lv. 1, or in reference to 1 St. Peter ii. 2, the spiritual nourishment of God's Word, which is pleasant to the renewed (Ps. xix. 11; cxix. 105; Rev. x. 9, 10). The custom died out in the West in 725, but prevails in the Ethiopic Church still. St. Augustine mentions the interrogatories, exorcism, and blowing away of all adverse power, i.e. the devil, by the clergy. Rabanus Maurus mentions the placing of consecrated salt in the mouth as the seasoning of wisdom (St. Matt. v. 13; St. Luke xiv. 3; Coloss. iv. 6). Beleth says that at the church door males were placed on the right side, and women and children on the left, and when they were brought into church one of either sex was led up into the chancel, to show the salvation of the baptized. He adds that, after the unction, a chrismal or round mitre like a head-dress, symbolical of the crown of life, and a white robe like a cowl, of pure white cloth with a thread of crimson, were put on the baptized. After the renunciation a black pall instead of the toga was given to the candidates as a sign of humility. Shoes were given, symbolical of the life of the dead and of entrance on a new path of life. The tapers carried by the candidates for a week after baptism were deposited in the baptistery and used in the church-service. On the day of baptism the churches in early times were carpeted, perfumed with balsam, scents, and incense, and lights were kept burning. Offerings in kind or money were made to the priest; litanies were said in going to the font. At first the candidates fasted till evening, but, in consideration to the feebleness of infancy, the morning was appointed for the administration. The names of the candidates were recited by the bishop or notary in the order in which they had been given in. Friends offered their congratulations, hymns were sung, and the Lord's Prayer was said. Ten siliquæ, coins of small value, were given by the Pope to the baptized, to show divine grace was not to be bought. The pax was given for about 700 years. The baptized, then called the elect, because placed on the Church register, were placed in an elevated position in front of the sanctuary, within the chancels, or at the altar: the custom is preserved in the East. A crown, as a symbol of joy and victory, was set on their heads. A banquet was given to the sponsors and priest, but was restricted by the Second Council of Mayence. Signs of joy were exhibited by friends. The Alleluia sung in the Roman office on the octave of Easter is a relic of this exultation. The baptismal day was observed as an anniversary. Cranmer describes the old ceremonial, which was extremely ancient :—(1.) The minister, after signing a cross upon the forehead of the child, "makes another cross upon his breast, for that it is not enough to confess Christ with mouth openly unless he does steadfastly believe in heart inwardly." (2.) "The minister makes the sign of the cross in the child's forehead, adjuring the devil to depart and no more to approach him." (3.) The minister wets with spittle the noise-thurles (nostrils) and ears of him that shall be baptized, putting us in remembrance of the miracle of the deaf and dumb wrought by Christ, and signifying the grace and godly influence descending from heaven by the operation of the Holy Ghost. (4.) After the exhortation to the sponsors "the minister makes the sign of the cross in the right-hand of the infant, which cross shall in all our lifetime admonish us valiantly to withstand the devil and all our corrupt and perverse affections and desires; and, so blessing the child in the name of the Holy Trinity, takes it by the right-hand and bids it enter into the Church, there to be admitted as one of Christ's flock and congregation, and so proceeds to the font." (5.) After the interrogations "the minister anoints the child with holy oil upon the breast and betwixt the shoulders, behind, with the cross, which (1) signifies that our heart and affections should be wholly dedicated to Christ; and (2) that we should bear the cross of our Lord, and patiently sustain such cross of persecution, trouble, and affliction as our most merciful Lord shall lay upon us." (6.) After the baptism he is anointed with holy chrism on the head, signifying thereby that he is made a Christian man by the head of his congregation, and that he is anointed with the spiritual unction of the Holy Ghost (or as anointed as a Christian wrestler, and graffed into the true vine). In some church-towers fireplaces occur which were used for heating the towels used in wiping off the chrism, or tempering the water of the font. (7.) "Then he is clothed in a white vesture, in token of his manumission and freedom from the former captivity of the devil, and of Christian purity and innocency." (8.) "The minister puts a candle-light in his right-hand, in token that he should through all his lifetime show before all men a light of good example and godly works, and be in readiness with the saints to meet his Lord, and receive the fruition of everlasting joy."

Ritual Choir. The part of a church actually used for the choir, and distinct from the architectural or constructional choir.

Robertines. An English order of eremites founded by Robert of Knaresborough, c. 1169.

Rochet, The. (Gr. *rouchion*; Ger. *rock*, a little frock.) The word appears first about the thirteenth century. At Cambrai it was called sarcos, and John of Liége speaks of it as a saroht. The Council of Buda, 1279, mentions it as the white camisia or rosetta which was to be worn over the breast and round the neck, under the cappa or mantle, by prelates when walking or riding. This, says Catalani, was the rochet which the bishop promoted was to wear in the city and in the church according to the Council of Lateran IV., under Pope Innocent III., A.D. 1215. It might be red, but was then to be quite concealed by the mantle. Between 1305-77 the Popes introduced it at Avignon, but it is of far earlier date, having been identified with the linea prescribed by the Ordo Romanus, and worn by St. Cyprian. It was in common use in the seventh century. Bede, comparing it with Aaron's ephod, says that the closeness of it at the hands denotes that he that wears it ought to do always something that is profitable. In the following ages the bishops were obliged by the canon law to wear their rochet whenever they appeared in public. This practice seems to have been kept up in England more than in other places, as Hody says it was only laid aside in hunting, and Erasmus mentions as a singularity of Bishop Fisher that he left off his rochet (linea vestis) when he travelled. Since the Reformation the bishops have not worn their rochets in any public place out of the church, except in Parliament, and, in Convocation, over their scarlet habit. Secular prelates, prothonotaries, and canons who had the right to use it put it on over the vestis talaris before robing for Mass. The rochet, according to Lyndwood, was sleeveless, and worn by the server to the priest, and by the latter in baptizing; and Ducange mentions it as worn by bishops and abbots with straight sleeves.

The modern full sleeve is not earlier than the time of Bishop Overall. Bale describes the clergy wearing fine white rochets of raines (linen of Rennes or Rheims) or fine linen cloth, costly grey amices of calaber and cats' tails, fresh purple gowns when they walk for their pleasures, and red scarlet frocks when they preach in the pulpit. In the thirteenth century in England a priest was buried in the ferial rochet of the church with a chalice of tin that had not been blessed.

Rogation Days. The three days before Ascension Day, in 747, in England, were observed by the people on bended knees after a procession with the cross and relics, and with fasting till three p.m., and celebration. Games, horse-races, and banquetings, which had desecrated the observance, were then forbidden. In 1014 processions were made barefooted on the three days before Michaelmas, which were rigorously fasted. Crosses and banners were carried in memory of the power of the ascended Saviour, and the prayers were offered with stronger hope of being heard, in faith of His promise, "Ask and ye shall have." In 1559 processions about the church and churchyard were forbidden, "to avoid all contention and strife, by reason of fond courtesy and challenging of places." In 1572 and 1576 Grindal forbade "wearing any surplice, carrying of banners or handbells, or staying at crosses," but the common perambulation of the circuits of parishes was retained at the time accustomed in the days of Rogation, and in the procession were to be sung Psalms ciii., civ., with the Litany and suffrages. At certain places the curate was to admonish the people to give thanks to God for the increase and abundance of His fruits upon the face of the earth, and inculcate these sentences : "Cursed be he which translateth the bounds and doles of his neighbours." A sermon or homily of thanksgiving was to follow, and divine service said in the church. At Paris, Rouen, Laon, and in Provence they carried two serpents in rogations, but the accidents which resulted from placing fusees in the eyes and between the jaws of the monsters led to their disuse. The procession with the dragon was observed at Dublin. *See* LITANIES.

Roman Manner. The custom of building churches of stone, spoken of in 675 when Benedict Biscop, Abbot of Wearmouth, went to France to engage masons. It was about the same time called the Gallican mode.

Rome Land. A large open roomy space in front of the minster of Waltham, St. Edmund's Bury, and St. Alban's, called the forbury at Reading, and probably the original of the tombland of Norwich, so called since 1302.

Rome Scot, *or* **Rome Fee.** An annual tribute of a thousand marks paid by King John to the See of Rome.

Rood. In the fifteenth century a cross surmounting the jube or screen of St. Sophia's at Constantinople is described as being of gold and jewelled, and carrying taper-stands. The rood itself was usually of wood. On the arms of the cross were the evangelistic symbols facing the nave, but busts of the four doctors towards the choir. About the fifteenth century the figures of SS. Mary and John were added on either side of the rood. Three chains, let down from the vaulting, supported its head and arms. A light always burned before it during Matins. The black rood of Scotland was of silver, and derived its name from having been smoked black with the tapers before it after its removal to Durham. Many superstitions were connected with roods, "with rolling eyes and sweating brows, with speaking mouth and walking feet." The more celebrated crosses were, according to Calfhill, "the rood of grace of Boxley, the rood of Winchester, the very cross of Ludlow, and Jack Knacker of Witney" (which Lambard says was the name of the watchman in the puppet play of the Resurrection). There were also St. Saviour's of Bermondsey, the rood of Chester (which gave name to the rood eye), and the speaking crucifix of Calne in St. Dunstan's time. *See* IMAGES.

Many churches were dedicated to the holy rood, as the abbey near Edinburgh, and at Daglingworth, Caermarthen, Bettws-y-Grôg, Capel Crist, Llechyd, Cuxham, Southampton, Combe Keynes, Thruxton, Wood Eaton, Swindon, Shillingstone, Malling. The Church of SS. Vincent and Anastasius, after it received the addition of a transept, was called Holy Cross, from its new shape. The rood was set before the feet of the dying, stretched on straw or ashes, emblems of mortality, and also, Beleth says, erected at the head of graves.

Rood-Beam. (*Trabes crucifixi.*) A screen of lighter construction than that which fenced the entrance of the choir parted off the sanctuary at the extremity of the stalls, like a chancel-rail. A solitary instance remains at St. David's, and at St. Alban's the beam was of the thirteenth century, and an altar of the holy cross, inclosed within an iron screen, once stood beneath it. At Malmesbury a similar screen existed. At Northleach it stands over the chancel-arch. At Worcester, on the western piers of the lantern, are stone brackets for the rood-beam, at a height of twenty-eight feet from the floor. It was, in point of fact, a rafter eastward of the altar to support a crowd of tapers, (according to the dignity of the day,) the cross, and reliquaries. When the space below it was filled down to the floor it was developed into a reredos. At Lubeck the screen is on the east side of the crossing, whilst the beam spans the western arch.

Roodloft. A screen with a gallery supporting the rood. (*Ambo, pulpitum, alleluia, gradus, tribune, jube, lectrier, doxale.*) The roodscreen had no upper loft or solar. For the first three centuries there is no direct evidence of the separation of the choir from the nave, but after the time of Constantine, tapestry, a veil, or a balustrade, like an altar-rail, was employed, like the modern Greek iconostasis. These screens, which are mentioned by St. Augustine, St. Gregory Nazianzen, Theodoret, Sozomen, Synesius, St. Germanus, St. Paulinus, St. Gregory of Tours, and the Council of Chalcedon, had three doors, one facing the altar, a second fronting the Gospel side, and a third the Epistle side. Before them veils were dropped at the consecration. That of the Apostles, at Constantinople, was a lattice of gilt brass; that of Tyre, erected by Paulinus, of carved wood; one of stone, *c.* 340, remains at Tepekerman. In Spain, Italy, Greece, and the East they were in use in the fifth century. There is one, of the date of Justinian, at St. Catherine's, Mount Sinai; and that of St. Sophia was imitated, in the eleventh century, at Novogorod, Kieff, Chernigoff, and Cutais. The Benedictines and Cistercians preserved the use of the Lenten veil, drawn between the choir and the altar, and the Gilbertines divided the brothers and sisters by a veil at sermon-time. During the greater part of the first seven centuries probably the iconostasis was used in Italy, but when the apsidal arrangement was definitely adopted this screen was pushed westward, until the altar was placed in the middle of the church, as in the large Italian churches, in southern France, and even in Burgundy, the screen now being placed under the chancel-arch, (as in other parts the rood-altar was erected,) and no longer within that of the sanctuary, like the rood-beam. When the choir was thus extended into the 'nave, the roodscreen was erected westward of the crossing—in the first bay at Ely, Durham, Gloucester, Chester, Fountains, Tintern, and Chichester; in the second, at Norwich, Worcester, and Peterborough ; in the third, at Melrose, Binham, St. Alban's, and Westminster; in the fourth, at Jorevalle and Merevale ; and in the sixth, at Tynemouth. At York, Lincoln, Lichfield, Wells, Salisbury, Hereford, Exeter, Canterbury, Rochester, Winchester, Oxford, Carlisle, and Christchurch (Hants), the crossing was left free, and the screen erected under the eastern arch, but at St. David's under the western arch, of the crossing, which was regarded as the natural division between the nave and choir. The screen was built in the twelfth century at St. Alban's, and in the thirteenth at Bury St. Edmund's, the addition being made when choir-screens were multiplied for the purpose of giving warmth and seclusion to the canons or monks. With the introduction of permanent stalls, walls were erected between the intercolumniations for their support at Ghent, Poitiers, Auch, Bourges, Christchurch (Hants), Canterbury, Rochester; and at Carlisle wooden parcloses, with paintings. In Belgium at the close of the thirteenth century, and in France, at Troyes and Paris, in the fourteenth, and generally in the fifteenth as at Rheims and Rouen, and in the sixteenth century at Auch and Rodez, the roodscreen was adopted to furnish the accommodation for the gospeller and epistoler hitherto given by the ambons. The latter fell into desuetude in Italy and France about the time of the removal of the Popes to Avignon in 1309. There are other examples at Limoges (1593), Alby, Lierre, Rodez, St. Pierre-sur-Dives, Laon, Beaune, St. Etienne du Mont, Arles, Tournay, Bonn, Tournus, Dixmunde, Bamburg ; Louvain, of the fifteenth century ; and double, of stone, of the fourteenth century, at Oberwesel. At Clugny, Paris, Sens, and Milan, the name of jubé (from the words, Jube domne benedicere) was adopted, and the episcopal benediction was for the last time given at Bayeux. The Clugniacs communi-

cated the laity at a grille in the screen. The loft was used
for reading the Gospel, Epistle, certain lections, letters of
communion, pastorals of bishops, proclamation of treaties,
and acts of councils; from it penitents were absolved, the
episcopal benediction pronounced, and elect abbots presented to the people. At a later date the organ and singers
were placed in it. In France the paschal taper was blessed
in this place. Bishops sometimes preached from the loft.
At Peterborough the abbots after benediction, and some of
the Kings of France before their coronation at Rheims, were
presented to the people from the loft. A screen existed at
St. Alban's in the twelfth century. The desk for the reader
of the fifteenth century remains at Merevale, and at Esslingen facing the choir, and by the Salisbury use the eagle
lectern for the Gospel stood in the loft; at Gloucester the
stone pulpit, of the fourteenth century, was over the west
choir-door. The usual arrangement was to have either a rood-
altar with side processional doors, as at St. Alban's, or else
a central door with lateral altars, as at Chester, Exeter, St.
David's, Chichester, and Norwich; sometimes, as at Carlisle, Lincoln, Clynog Vawr, Canterbury, Ripon, Southwell,
Christchurch (Hants), and York, there is only a central door;
at Hexham the panels above it represented the Dance of
Death; and at York the side-niches are filled with statues of
kings. There is a beautiful screen, elaborately painted, at
Ranworth. Screens were erected at Bristol (1541), Rodney,
Stoke (1625), and Durham after the Restoration. At Canterbury and Winchester magnificent stairs, and a lesser flight
at Rochester, led up to the screen, as the choir is elevated,
as in a basilica, over the crypt. The single rood-altar occurred at Clugny, Lyons, Zamora, Munster, Milan, and
Florence, and for the laity at Dunster and Ewenny. (See
PARISH CHURCH.) The central tower, from the cross below
it, was often called the rood-tower, as at Lincoln and Hereford: a blaze of sunlight was thus showered down upon the
altar of the rood. Many lofts and screens were destroyed in
England after the Reformation, but up to the year 1571 the
beam was allowed to remain with a cresting on it. The rude
hand of innovation, however, has removed as many or more
screens bodily from German and French churches. Some
beautiful examples of screens exist at Southwold, Worstead,

Shellingham, Old Radnor, Bradninch, Collumpton, Plan-
borough, Beverley, Hexham, St. Burian's, Gresford, Chinner,
Thame, Northfleet, Gilston, and Swinbrook. A loft of
the thirteenth century remains at Stanton Harcourt, but the
finest specimens date back to the early part of the fourteenth
century, and the most common now to the fifteenth century.
Many retain beautiful colouring and rich decoration. Drains
have been found in roodlofts at Maxey, Frome, and Eastbourne, but probably they are mere insertions from some
other place, or, if in their original position, were used for the
ablutions of pavements and linen, or the ashes of tow, palms,
etc.

Rood-Stair. The staircase to the roodloft. It winds at Bur-
lingham round a pier at the entrance of the chancel. At
Christchurch, Gloucester, and Carlisle it is constructed
within the loft on the north side, which is the general arrangement in a large church. At Sopley and other places
an aperture is pierced through the pier towards the transept
on the north side, and was reached by a wooden staircase.
At Battle there is an external stair-turret, having a bridge
within the north nave aisle which communicated with a
similar opening. In Norfolk there are frequently two stair-
turrets. The stairs at Lupworth, St. John's (Chester), and
the external flights at Christchurch (Hants), adjoining the
Lady-chapel, led to an upper chapel, like that of Henry V. at
Westminster. There are good stair-turrets at Stamford and
Eastbourne. There are stairs in the chancel-pier at Girton
on the south; and on the north at Belleau. Fribourg and
Manchester have noble rood-turrets. Sometimes there were
four, but ordinarily two flights of stairs, one used by the
deacon-gospeller, and the other by the subdeacon-epistoler,
as at Sens, Ravenna, St. Sophia (Constantinople), and St.
Pancras (Rome). In England one flight was probably used
for ascending, and the other for descending.

Roofs. Several churches in Norfolk and Suffolk, and Somersby
in Lincolnshire, are modestly thatched; and Rampston is
covered with reeds, formerly abundant in the fen country, and
resembling the sea mat-weed. Wooden cielings consist of
common rafters next the tiles. Parallel with these are the
principal rafters; the tiebeams extend longitudinally from
wall to wall; the wall-plate runs along the top of the wall,

under the tiebeam, as the pole-plate under the common rafter; the ridge in the centre of the meeting of the common rafters; the struts are diagonal timbers joining the tiebeam to the principal rafter; the posts are upright timbers rising from the tiebeam; where there are two posts a collar unites them at the top; the hammer-beam was a tiebeam not extending across from wall to wall, and was of Perpendicular introduction when panelling came into fashion. There are Early English cielings at Hales Owen and Rochester Cathedral; of Decorated date at Chartham, Sparsholt, Addington, Stourbridge, and Temple Balsall; and of the Perpendicular period at Cirencester, Devizes, Faringdon, Godshill, and Wear Gifford; and groined wooden cielings at Selby, St. Alban's Lady-chapel, and Winchester College chapel. In the twelfth century the height of the chancel-roofs was elevated, to the utter destruction of the old symbolism of the low ridge, indicative of the drooping head of the Saviour. The deflection at St. Etienne du Mont was to the traditional position of the penitent thief, the north. *See* DEVIATION.

Rosary, The, *or* **Lady Psalter,** consists of fifteen decades (or 150 Ave Marias and fifteen Paternosters), in honour of the fifteen mysteries, or events in our Lord's life, in which St. Mary is said to have borne a part—five glorious, five joyous, and five sorrowful. The "usual prayers," mentioned in Arundel's Constitutions of 1408, were probably beads; a Crown had six decades and sixty-three Ave Marias, the Psalter fifteen decades and 150 Ave Marias, the Little Psalter three gauds and fifteen Ave Marias, and the Chaplet three gauds and fifteen Ave Marias.

Rosette. An ornament in front of the hat, worn by prelates, dignitaries in a cathedral, and archdeacons. Savage, in the 'Progress of a Divine,' 1735, says "he gains a cassock, beaver, and a rose;" and Archdeacon Sharp specifies as the clerical badge "the band, hatband, and short cassock."

Rose Window, *or* **the Marygold,** was derived from the round window, called the eye in the basilica, pierced through the gable over the entrance, and imitated in the Norman period, at Canterbury in the transept, at Southwell in the clerestory, at Patricksbourne, Iffley, Barfreston, and the Temple Church, London, but is unknown in Rhenish architecture. About the thirteenth century, at first in Picardy, Champagne, and the Isle of France, and at a later period in Burgundy and Normandy, the rose became of large dimensions. There are fine examples at Paris (1220–1257), Mantes (1220), Laon, Rheims (1239), Amiens (1325), St. Denis, Sées, Clermont, Montreal, Soissons, and Rouen. They bore the names of the elements—the northern being called the rose of the winds; the west, of the sea; the south, of heaven; and the east, of the earth. In England the rose usually occurs in the transept, as at York, Lincoln, Winchester, and Beverley; of the Decorated period, at Chichester; and of the Perpendicular, at Lynn and Westminster. When there were two of these transeptal windows in a cathedral, that on the north was called the bishop's, and the southern one the dean's eye, as representing their respective jurisdiction, one watching against the invasion of the diocese by evil spirits on the north, and the latter as presiding as censor morum over the capitulars and close. At St. Paul's exceptionally the Lady-chapel had a superb eastern rose, and one still adorns the nine chapels of Durham.

Rota, Auditors of the, formerly called auditors of the sacred palace, and by Pope John XXII., in 1450, apostolic chaplains, reduced by Sixtus IV. A judicial tribunal at Rome, having cognizance of civil and ecclesiastical causes; its decisions always state the grounds on which they are made.

Rouel *or* **Rowel Light.** The device for moving the star in the Epiphany play of the Three Kings with a pulley-wheel (*roue*), as the spiked wheel in a spur is called rowel.

Round Churches were imitations of the Holy Sepulchre at Jerusalem, the nave being round and forming the vestibule of an oblong chancel, as in the Templars' churches at Laon, Metz, and Segovia, 1208. Other examples are found in Ludlow Castle, Cambridge, Northampton, of the end of the twelfth century; Little Maplestead (built by the Hospitallers), St. Gereon's, Cologne, of the thirteenth century; Trèves, Bonn, Aix-la-Chapelle (a copy of St. Vitalis, Ravenna, and more remotely of St. Sophia, Constantinople), Salamanca, St. Benignus Dijon, London, built in 1185; Neuvy St. Sepulchre, *c.* 1170; Lanleff, Rieu Minervois, of the close of the eleventh century; Brescia, Pisa, Rome, Bergamo, Bologna, Thorsager, and several other churches in Scandinavia. In many cases the shape may have been merely a mechanical contrivance to carry a dome. (*See* KNIGHTS TEMPLARS.) Circular churches occur of all dates, and distributed over most parts of Europe, either insulated as baptisteries, in a mystical allusion to the Holy Sepulchre, attached as chapels to churches, or existing as independent buildings. They are sometimes of a simple round or polygonal form, either without recesses, except an apse or porch, such as the church of Orphir, Orkney, and the baptistery of Canterbury, or with radiating recesses, rectangular or apsidal, as the baptisteries of Novara and Frejus. Sometimes a circular or polygonal centre is supported by pillars, and surrounded by an aisle of corresponding form; this aisle is repeated at St. Stephen's, Rome, and Charroux. The Crusaders, or pilgrims, imitated the plan of the Sepulchre of Jerusalem, surrounded by a circular church, and the Martyrdom, or place of the Crucifixion, by a chancel eastward of a round nave. At Bury St. Edmund's, at the close of the eleventh century, the abbot removed the body of St. Edmund from the "round chapel" to the new church; and this circular termination is still seen in Becket's Crown at Canterbury, at Sens, Burgos, Batalha, Murcia, and Drontheim. After the middle of the thirteenth century round churches were no longer built. Almost all the German churches of the time of Charlemagne were circular, like Aix, Nimeguen, Petersburg, and Magdeburg.

Round Towers occur of the time of Justinian, attached to the Church of St. Apollinaris-ad-Classem, in Verona; two in the same city, *c.* 1047; others of minaret-like shape, and divided by string courses, at St. Mary and St. Vitalis, Ravenna; also at Pisa, Bury, near Beauvais, and at St. Desert, near Châlons-sur-Saône. The French round towers appear to have come from the north of Italy. In the ninth century they were erected at Centula, Charroux, Bury, and Notre Dame (Poictiers), Gernrode, and Worms. Those of Ireland are mainly of the eleventh or twelfth centuries, though some are of an unknown date, and were at once treasuries, belfries, refuges, and places of burial. Round towers are found in East Anglia, at Rickingale Inferior, at Welford and Shefford, Bucks; Welford, Gloucestershire (thirteenth century); in the Isle of Man, at Bremless, Breconshire, Brechin, built by Irish ecclesiastics (c. 1020); Abernethey, and Tcherni-god, near Kieff (c. 1024). The East Anglian form, and those of Piddinghoe and Lewes, have been attributed to the peculiar character of the material employed, and a desire to evade the use of coigns. At Brixworth a round is attached in front of a square tower.

Rubble. Coarse walling of rough stones.

Rule, the Choir. (Fr. *régir le chant;* Sp. *regir los clerigos.*) The duty of the præcentor, as director of the musical ser-vices on greater doubles, and of the hemdomadary on simple feasts. The choir was ruled for the invitatory on Sundays, doubles, feasts of nine lections, and other principal feasts. Canons present at the service were said to keep choir.

Rural Deans. Innocent III. first mentions that the officers hitherto known as archpriests were sometimes called by this name, and were subject to archidiaconal jurisdiction; they are appointed by the bishops as his removable overseers of certain small districts; their office terminates with the life of the bishop who nominates them. In 1279 they held quar-terly chapters; in 1337 they were required to have seals graven with the title of their office or deanery, but without their personal name, their office being temporary only. In 1222 they are described as "deans constituted under bishops," and "archdeacons' deans." Probably the deanery rural took its rise out of the local guilds of priests, con-sisting of geferan or mates, mentioned in 950 and 960, both in Northumberland and King Edgar's dominions. Rural deans are unknown in Italy.

Russian Architecture. A debased style of Byzantine. The plan of the churches is an oblong, the Greek cross being marked by cupolas; three long alleys terminate in apses, which are screened by iconostases; in front of the latter the choir is arranged. Under the great central dome are thrones, one on the right for the emperor, and the other on the left for the bishop. The principle of one altar only is preserved, but small bye-churches are often erected in groups, as in the Kremlin, and convents usually have a double church.

Sabanus. A white chrism-cloth in which infants were wrapped at baptism in the Greek Church.

Sacrament. (*Sacrum,* a sacred thing.) (1.) "The word is added to the element and it becometh a Sacrament, as if a visible word," says St. Augustine. (2.) The reserved Host. The seven sacraments—the Eucharist, Holy Baptism, Confirmation, Penance, Orders, Matrimony, and Extreme Unction—are pourtrayed on many fonts, and in a reredos in the Lady-chapel of Paisley. Sacramentals are oil, salt, and other matters used in the administration. Beleth says priests are called sacerdotes, as though sacra dantes, ministers of sacred things.

Sacring-Bell (*campanella, timbele*) was rung at the elevation inside the church, in England, by the Constitutions of Cantelupe in 1240, as a warning of devotion. Becon says while the elements were blessed the serving-boy or parish clerk rang the little sacring-bell, at which the people knelt down whilst the Host was elevated. The second sacring was the crossing of the chalice with the Host. The custom has been attributed to Cardinal Grey when legate in Germany, *c.* 1203; it was confirmed by Gregory IX. in 1259. At the beginning of the thirteenth century, at Paris, the bells were rung at this time. The Armenians use a cymbal, with little bells, called the quechouez. A sacring-bell was found in the wall of Deddington church, and that of Hawstead still hangs above the roodscreen. The use of this bell has been traced back to the eleventh century, and before 1114 Ivo, Bishop of Chartres, thanked Queen Maud of England for the bells which she had given to Chartres, and says they were rung at the elevation. The custom is confined to Western Christendom, and is unknown at Rome. In Spain they use a melodious peal of bells, which chime a silvery music, instead of the ordinary tinkling of a single bell, at the moment of consecration, when the Divine words of institution are recited by the celebrant; and at the elevation of the Host Aubrey mentions that at Brokenborough, Wilts, there were eighteen little bells rung by pulling one wheel. Such wheels, it is believed, are still preserved at Yaxley and Long Stratton. In the Roman Church it is rung thrice at the Sanctus, once before and three times at the elevation of the Host, three times at the elevation of the Chalice, and at the Domine non sum dignus, and once before the "Pater" (the latter dating from the sixteenth century), and also at Benediction with the Sacrament.

Sacristan. (1.) The monastic treasurer and churchwarden.
He provided all the necessaries for Divine service, was
keeper of the church keys, relics, fabric, plate, furniture,
and ornaments, secretary, and chancellor.   He arranged the
way of processions for the præcentor, superintended the
bell-ringers, and received the rents, oblations, and burial-
fees.   At Canterbury he delivered the crozier to the new
archbishop.   At Ely he received the candle-corn (one sheaf
of corn in every acre), to supply the lights, and, as the
bishop's vicar, exercised archidiaconal jurisdiction over the
city chaplains.   At Peterborough his fee was the horses of a
knight buried in the minster, if under four marks in value;
otherwise they accrued to the abbot; and at Worcester, the
abbots of Gloucester, Tewkesbury, Pershore, and Evesham
gave him a cope of profession at their benediction.   (2.)
Vice-custos, the vicar of the treasurer, or sub-treasurer at
York in 1230.   He opened the doors of the sacristy in the
morning, admitted the rectors of choir and sick members
who desired to say the Hours privately.   He warned canons
of chapter, kept the doors shut during its session, rang the
bells, and led the procession.   Bishop Storey mentions the
use of the word sacrist in an inferior sense as recent in the
fifteenth century.   Where there was no permanent sacristan
in a cathedral a canon was appointed, called præfect of
sacristy.   In the Decretals of Gregory IX. and at Lyons
(1269) the sacrist was the inferior of the sacristan.   In the
new foundations he furnished the sacred elements, administered sacraments, officiated at marriages and burials, was the
curate of the chapter, like the foreign parochus, and had
charge of the bells, church goods, furniture, and lights.   At
Girgenti there are four sacrists; at Mayence he was a vicar,
and at Angers a cubicular or chamberlain, who administered
the sacraments to sick canons and the choir clergy.   (3.)
The sacristan at Mass has charge of the vessels, and attends
in a surplice at the credence-table, which is placed on the
south side of the altar, and arranges on it the chalice, covered
with the linen cloth called the purifier; and by the paten,
which is covered with a stiff cloth and a rich veil of silk; the
cruets for wine and water; the Gospel and Epistle books; the
ewer, bason, and water for washing the celebrant's fingers; the
corporal, or cloth on which the chalice and Host are placed,

and contained in a burse, or embroidered case ; a crucifix, and two tapers. (4.) A church servant, now called sexton.

Sacristy. (*Vestry, revestry, sacristia, sacrarium, secretarium, mutatorium, metatorium.*) A chamber near the choir, or transept, as at Chester, Westminster, and Gloucester, used for robing by the clergy and clerks. A receptacle for the hangings, aumbries, cope-stands, presses for vestments, and altar furniture, usually having very narrow windows and strong iron screens or bars externally, and an altar, at which minor clerks or suffragans were ordained and young priests learned to celebrate Mass. At Lichfield the Early English hooks for the store of lamps remain in the vault, and a chamber for the priest-vicar in course above it. At Christchurch a loop in the wall commanded a view of the processional aisle, to allow the watcher to ring the small bell in time to announce that the celebrant was coming out. At Chichester an Early English laver, for washing his hands, is set in the wall. At York there are a well and drain, c. 1350; and at Bristol, c. 1334, the fireplace for baking the altar-breads still exists. Occasionally there was a second sacristy, or a muniment-room, communicating with the treasury. There are fine examples at Rouen (twelfth century) ; Worcester, under an upper chapel, of Early English date ; Laon and Tours, of the thirteenth century ; at Chartres, of the fourteenth century ; at Paris, with an upper storey, forming a treasury, choir-library, and gaol ; at Amiens, communicating with a cloister ; at Carcassone, retaining aumbries of the fourteenth century ; at Hereford, and, with narrow strongly-barred doors at Châlons-sur-Marne, of the twelfth century ; at Selby, of grand dimensions, with a double doorway ; and at Salisbury, octagonal in form, with a muniment chamber above. At Ludlow, Eastbourne, Hawkhurst, Malvern, and Warwick behind the altar there is a small sacristy. At Crewkerne and Arundel it intervenes between the east wall and the altar. Formerly at York and Chichester there was a sacristy behind the high-altar, used by the bishop at his enthronization and on solemn occasions. There were always two sacristies, one for the canons, and the other for vicars, chaplains, masters of choir, and assistants. The latter was often called the vestibule. The Greek sacristy is on the south side of the choir, fronting the credence chapel.

Before the twelfth century the canons came from their houses chorally habited, attended by their vicars, so that vestries or sacristies were not so indispensable as at present. In some churches, as at Clugny and St. Denis, the aumbry adjoining the altar was called the sacrarium, forming a small inclosure of wood or stone.

Saddle-back Roof. A covering to a tower accommodated to the pitch of the gables on the north and south, which appears at St. Nicholas, Caen, New, Sweetheart, and Pluscardine abbeys. It is very rare in England.

Saint. (*Hagios*, holy.) The appellation of Christians (Eph. iii. 5; Rev. xviii. 20). From the fourteenth century the Pope has exclusively been called His Holiness, but the title was given by a Pope to an archbishop in 465, and to a patriarch in 590, and by Constantine to the senate in 326, in a calendar of the Church of Carthage and Pamelius, c. 449. The appellation is given to Christian worthies. It seems to have superseded the earlier form of dominus. Beleth mentions that at Venice and in Greece many of the Old Testament worthies give titles to churches. The Breviary contains a proper of time and proper of saints, that is, offices appropriate to a day, whilst the common of Apostles, a martyr, etc., is an office used in common for saints, arranged in classes, who had no special festival. In 1494 it was ordered that at a canonization offerings should be made of four loaves, four barrels of wine, wax tapers, and two cages of doves and singing-birds. The two former offerings were made by bishops at their consecration, except in England. In 1298 Pope Urban made saints' days doubles. Beatification is a permissory but unjudicial act of the Pope, allowing religious veneration to be paid by an order or community to a reputed saint until the tedious details of canonization can be concluded and the authoritative judgment of the Pope pronounced.

Saint Barnabas's Day. (June 11.) Mentioned in the Calendar of Ven. Bede. The Greek Church observes the festival, in conjunction with that of St. Bartholomew's, on August 24.

Saint Bartholomew's Day (August 24) appears first in the Sacramentary of St. Gregory. It is observed on this day in the Greek Church, St. Barnabas's name being associated with that of St. Bartholomew, who has been identified with

Nathaniel since the twelfth century, against the opinion of many of the Fathers. Owing to a horrible massacre of the Huguenots at Paris in 1572, the day was known as Black Monday. In 1662 the revised Book of Common Prayer came into use on it.

Saint Stephen's Day (December 26) is first mentioned in the sixth century by St. Gregory Nyssen. Beleth says the deacons sang the Magnificat and night office and gave the benediction in honour of the first deacon.

Sakkos. A tight sleeveless habit worn by Greek patriarchs and metropolitans.

Salt was mingled with holy-water, in allusion to 2 Kings ii. 21, and was used at baptism and in exorcisms. In 1223 children who were exposed by their parents had salt laid upon them in token that they had been baptized.

Salut. An evening office, which took its origin in Southern Europe, Spain, and Italy, consisting of an exposition of the Sacrament, accompanied with chanting and a brilliant display of tapers. It varies in different churches; at Lyons it is not followed by benediction, and in France generally is only used in a solemn form on the eves of great festivals. Grancolas, writing in the seventeenth century, says that benediction with the Holy Sacrament was not earlier than a century before his time. The Roman rite requires the sign of the cross to be made with the monstrance in silence; but in some parts of France the priest used a form of benediction. At Cadiz and other Spanish churches the monstrance doors open by mechanism for the salut, as the chant commences. The most sumptuous monstrance extant is at Aichstadt, being profusely jewelled.

Salve Regina. An antiphon written by Bishop Peter of Compostella, in the twelfth century, or by Adhemar, Bishop of Puy, who died 1098. It is said that the last words were added by St. Bernard when he heard it chanted in the cathedral of Spiers. It was sung from Trinity Sunday to Advent, but at Châlons between the Purification and Maundy Thursday. The Dominicans spread the custom.

Samit. Satin; rich silk, with gold or silver thread interwoven.

San Benito. A tall painted cap, worn by persons condemned by the Inquisition to an *auto da fe*, or death by burning at the stake. Their sleeveless dress was yellow, with a cross saltier, flames of red serge if they were to be pardoned, or figures of demons if they were to be executed.

Sancered. The bead-roll, or list of Church benefactors and founders.

Sanctuary. (1.) The presbytery, or easternmost part of the choir, containing the high-altar. (2.) A graveyard, in which fairs and markets were prohibited by Parliament in 1258. (3.) The right of asylum in a church, mentioned as ancient by the First Council of Orange; the "Church's peace," so called in 605, and extended in 945 as the King's protection for three miles three furlongs and three broad acres from the gate of the city in which the palace stood. The protection afforded by a church and its precincts to accused persons was first granted by the Emperors Honorius and Theodosius in 392. It received the Papal sanction from Pope Boniface in 620. King Ina, in 693, recognizes the immunity of sanctuary; King Alfred, in 887, allowed it for seven nights, in order to allow composition by the offender; King Canute, in 1017, confirmed the right of sanctuary. The felon was suffered by later enactments (as the Constitutions of Clarendon, in the reign of Henry III.) to confess before the local coroner, and abjure the realm for perpetual banishment into some Christian country by Canute's laws; and he went forth bearing a crucifix, or white cross, for his protection. At Durham, Westminster, Carrow, Ramsey, Crowland, Ripon, Tintern, Leominster, and Worcester the privilege of asylum was restricted to the precinct, at Paris to a quadrangle, but at Beverley extended to a leuga on every side. At Hexham, and St. Gregory's, Norwich, where the sanctuary ring-knocker, or hagoday, remains on the north door, the church only was a sanctuary. St. Burian's and Beverley were privileged by Athelstan, Westminster by Edward the Confessor, St. Martin's-le-Grand in 1529. By the Act 22 Henry VIII., c. 14, the person abjured was not allowed to leave the realm, but was transferred to some other sanctuary. All persons accused of high treason were declared incapable of sanctuary by Act 26 & 28 Henry VIII., and in the twenty-first year of the reign of James I. the privilege was wholly abolished. Alsatia, the precinct of Whitefriars, London, was the last sanctuary in use. In 1540 sanctuary was removed from Manchester to Chester. Margaret of Anjou and Perkin Warbeck took refuge at Beaulieu; the queen of Edward IV. and Skelton the poet, at Westminster. At Durham the fugitive fled to the north door of the cathedral, and laid hold on the knocker, or hagoday. At Cologne the place was marked, "Here stood the great accused." The watchers, who occupied two chambers over the porch, gave the fugitive admission, and tolled the Galilee bell. He was then provided with a black cloth gown, with a yellow cross on the shoulder, and lay in a screened or grated chamber near the Galilee, being provided with food for thirty-seven days. At Beverley he would have been fed in the refectory and lodged in the dormitory for thirty days. He was bound to wear no weapon, to hear Mass, and assist as a bell-ringer. He might go thirty paces from a church and forty from a cathedral with immunity. At the end of the time he was forwarded by the under-sheriff, under the constable, to the nearest port or seacoast, and put on board ship. If the same person claimed sanctuary a third time, he became a servant of the Church. There are sanctuary knockers on the doors of Durham, Pampeluna, All Saints' Pavement at York, and St. Gregory's, Norwich; the Norman sanctuary chair is preserved at Hexham. At Westminster there was a double-storeyed building, detached on the north-west side, containing a chapel in the upper stage. In 1261 all persons who prevented victuals from being brought to the fugitive, or killed him after he had forsworn the kingdom, were excommunicate.

Sanctus- *or* **Saunce-bell,** was rung in the sancte bellcot, outside the church, at the singing of the Ter Sanctus in the High Mass, whence its name, as a warning that the Canon of the Mass is about to commence. It has been attributed to William of Paris, in 1097, confirmed by Gregory XIII., or to Cardinal Guido, 1200, confirmed by Gregory IX. in 1230. In 1281, in England, all the bells were to be tolled at the elevation, in order that the absent from daily Mass in house or field might bow their knees at the sound; and it is said that his people would let their plough rest when George Herbert's saints'-bell rang to prayers, that they might also offer their devotions unto God, and would then return back to their plough. A bell rung now after Matins in country

churches is a relic of the sanctus bell; the bells remain at
Long Compton, Whichford, and Brailes, and the frame of
one is over Nykke's chantry at Norwich.

Sandals became an episcopal ornament in the ninth century,
bishops having previously worn black shoes. If bishops
made an uncanonical sequestration they were deprived of
tunic, dalmatic, and sandals. A pair worn by Bishop Lynd-
wode (d. 1446) are in the British Museum. In 970 the
Bishop of Metz procured the use of sandals and dalmatic for
the Abbot of St. Vincent in that city. Richer, Abbot of
Cassino, obtained the Papal permission to use, as his predecessors had done, sandals, dalmatic, and gloves on great
feasts in time of Mass; and Fulco of Corbey, and Warin of
St. Arnulph, at Metz, received the same indulgence, with the
exception of gloves, from Leo. IX. The monks wore latchet
sandals (*sotulares corrigiatos*) as well as boots (*calceamenta,
botæ*). In former times they had a tie or latchet; those of
priests had none. They were supposed to indicate firmness
in God's law, and the duty of lifting up the weak. In later
times the priest celebrant was forbidden to be sandalled. In
1379 the Abbot of Malmesbury, and all other exempt abbots,
wore sandals and the rest of the pontifical habit.

Sarantari. (Greek.) Masses for the dead during forty days.

Saturday. The seventh or Sabbath day. Regarded by the
Greek Church as a festival and working day, but in the West
as a fast day, except by the Ambrosian rite. The Jews
made it a holiday, with cessation from business and long
journeys; one of cheerfulness and hospitality. The Saturdays in Ember weeks are called " in XII. Lections," from the
six Gospels read both in Latin and Greek.

Savagarad. An Armenian priest's cap, of cloth of gold, with
an orb and cross on the top.

Saye. (1.) Silk and wool mixed. (2.) Serge, woollen cloth
made at Sudbury in large quantities.

Savigny, Order of. Grey brothers, founded by Vitalis of
Tierceville, near Bayeux, 1105. They came to England
1120, and were united to the Cistercians in 1148.

Saying. A distinct or sustained monotone, analogous to the
old "saying without note," neither singing nor reading.

Saviour. The so-called portrait, engraved on an emerald, which
was said to have been made by Pilate's order for presenta-

tion to Tiberius, and, further, to have been given by the Sultan, from the Byzantine treasury, to Pope Innocent VIII., is a forgery, of the time of the Italian Revival, and the head is copied from one in Râphael's cartoon of the Miraculous Draught of Fishes. St. Augustine says there was no record of His likeness. *See* VERONICA.

Scala Cœli. A staircase at Rome, ascended by pilgrims on their hands and knees, in the belief that our Lord went up it in His Passion. Certain churches in England had similar staircases, which enjoyed the privilege of affording composition for a visit to Rome,—at Westminster Abbey, in 1504; St. Mary's Chapel at Boston; St. Mary's Chapel in the Austin Canons' Church, Norwich; and at Windsor, with a college of ten priests, until 1504.

Scandinavian Architecture. Many of the earlier Norwegian and Swedish cathedrals were built by English or French workmen. There are six basilicas in Norway, with towers at the ends of the choir-aisles. In Denmark there are eight round churches and one octagonal. Roeskilde, Ribe, and Thorsager are apsidal, but the general characteristics of the Danish churches are a square east end and an immense south porch and parvise. The wooden churches of Norway are probably of Byzantine origin, the plans having been brought back by the Varangians.

Scapular, *or* **Patience.** (Gr. *analabos.*) Two bands of woollen stuff—one going down the breast, and the other on the back, over the shoulders—worn by the religious. The original scapular was first introduced by St. Benedict, in lieu of a heavy cowl for the shoulders, designed to carry loads. It was cruciform in the eighth century. The tongue-scapular, on which twelve tongues of red cloth were sewn, was put upon a Cistercian who had offended with his tongue.

Scarf. A broad stole-like ornament of silk, folded three times, properly belonging to the D.D. and dignitaries, but assumed by chaplains of noblemen in the time of Queen Anne, as appears by an amusing paper in the 'Spectator.' In Italy and Malta it is called talaga, and worn by the doctors of theology. *See* ALMUCE and TIPPET.

School. (1.) The clergy-house adjoining the church in the early ages, when, as in the capitulars of Charlemagne, clerks were called scholastici, students of the various sciences, which they pursued under the rule of the bishop. (2.) The choir.

Scotch Architecture. The churches of wicker-work in the fifth century gave place to stone churches, built by monks from Jarrow, Frenchmen, and other strangers. Whitherne derived its name from its bright white stone church. From the middle of the sixth to the middle of the eleventh century was the age of a Scoto-Irish style, with round towers, small churches grouped, beehived houses, and dome-roofed cells. The successive styles then are (1) English-Romanesque (1124–56), as at Dunfermline, Kelso, and Leuchars; (2) Lancet (1165–1286); (3) Decorated (1286–1370) and Flamboyant (1371–1567). The marks of foreign art and influence are everywhere manifest after the War of Independence, in the saddle-back roof to towers, the double aisles of Elgin, the polygonal apse and the shallow transepts. At Holyrood, Aberdeen, and Dunfermline were the only instances of western towers. The spires are few and poor; that of Glasgow is the best. The imperial crown of Edinburgh is almost unique. The naves of Kelso and Paisley were shorter than the choirs. Aisleless choirs occur at the latter, Dunkeld, Sweetheart, Dunblane, and Whitherne; and the two latter cathedrals, like Brechin, are not cruciform. Roslyn was built by architects from the north of Spain. There are fine porches at Aberdeen, Paisley, and Dunfermline.

Scottish Manner. Bede calls by this name church-building with planks of oak and roofing of rushes.

Screen. (Fr. *grille*; Sp. *reja*; Germ. *schrage*; It. *tramezzo*; *parclose, intermedia, murus*.) According to 'Eulogium Historiarum,' Pope Boniface II., c. 533, first made a distinction between the clergy and laity at Mass. By the Councils of Tours (566) and Nantes (658) lay persons were forbidden the choir. Martene complains that the laity, interdicted from approach, except for communion, pressed into the choir, and women sat on the altar steps; and this probably occasioned the introduction of the side-screens of the presbytery, as at Winchester (1528), at Carlisle (1484), and another, of cinquecento work, c. 1540. They also gave access to the aisles by means of doors, and permitted the passage of processions without interruption to the choir service. There is a transitional Norman screen, of wood, c. 1180, at Compton,

Surrey, and others, of Decorated date, at Chester, Stanton, Harcourt, Dorchester, Oxon, Morden-Guilden, Northfleet, Bignor, and Sparsholt, and of the Perpendicular period at Fyfield, and St. Mary's, Leicester, and Worcester. The Early English screens were of stone, as at Canterbury. Conrad built one of marble slabs. Metal screens occur in France, at St. Germer, St. Quentin, Braisne, Rheims, Noyon, St. Denis, Auxerre, Conques, Beziers, and Puy. At Westwell, Kent, there are three tall arches of stone in front of the chancel. The superb screens of metalwork in Spanish cathedrals date between 1530 and 1600.

Scriptionale, Scriptorium. (1.) Desks used by the monks who were copyists. Those which were round and moved on a pivot were called the roue. Some had a central pricket for a taper. Some with two sloping sides, of the sixteenth century, are preserved at Oxford. (2.) The monastic copyists' room.

Scrutiny. The inquiry into the faith and manners of candidates for baptism; it was made in the presence of the congregation on seven days, the last being the Wednesday before Passion Sunday. The name of each candidate was called; then the deacon bade him prostrate himself five times and rise, in memory of the five wounds of Christ; and the sign of the cross was made on his forehead by the sponsor and acolyth; lastly, he was sprinkled with ashes. The custom died out in the year 860.

Seals (intaglios, in distinction to cameos, which are bas-reliefs cut in the substance of the stone) were in the middle ages made with beeswax, not as now with lac. (1.) Archbishop Reynold's private seal was round, with the mitred heads of eighteen bishops engraved upon it. There is a seal of an early bishop preserved in the chapter clerk's office at Chichester. A chapter used two seals, one for capitular business, the other for letters and daily missives. In 1237, owing to the prevalence of forgeries and the absence of public notaries in England, abbots, priors, deans, archdeacons, their officials and rural deans, capitular bodies, colleges, and convents, were required to have seals. If the office was perpetual, then the name of the man who bore it was engraved on the seal; but rural deans and officials whose office was temporary had only the name of their office engraved upon it, and were to resign their seal at the expiration of

2 M 2

their tenure to him by whom they had been commissioned. (2.) The little stone which covers the sepulchre of relics in an altar. (3.) Seal of confession; the obligation on a priest never to reveal the secrets of the confessional.

Seasons. According to Lyndwood, winter commenced on November 23; spring, Feb. 22; summer, May 25; autumn, August 24; and, as custom in various places prevailed, winter lasted from Michaelmas to Lady Day, or from All Saints' to SS. Philip and James.

Secondary. At Exeter a class of twenty-four clerks of the second form, who were, if learned and expert in music, eligible for promotion by the dean to the place of vicar; he was the canon's personal attendant. At Chichester the secondary sang the daily Mass of Requiem in the Lady-chapel.

Secret, Discipline of the. A systematic and organized reserve used by the primitive Church, seen in the mysterious language, the allegory and symbolism, the reticence of writers, and the hieroglyphical character of the productions of art (St. Matt. vii. 6; 1 Cor. iii. 1), which only the initiated could understand.

Secret of the Mass. A prayer in the Canon of the Mass before the Preface, since the tenth century said secretly in a low voice by the celebrant after the Orate, fratres, and having much the same tenor as the collect. In France it was marked with the mystic letters V. D. St. Gregory calls it the Canon of the Secret. According to some writers it represents that the working of God in the Holy Communion passes man's understanding, but, as Cranmer explains it, Christ's secret conversation which He kept with His disciples before His Passion. The bells in England were forbidden to be rung at this time in 1071. The secrets were formerly called super oblata, and may have taken their name from the secretion of the gifts and oblations. *See* CANON OF THE MASS.

Sedilia. (*Prismatories*, presbyteries.) A single stall near an altar is sometimes found in the catacombs; Ducange mentions a sedes majestatis, and Trivet says that Edward I. gave the royal chair of Scotland as the celebrant's chair at Westminster; several authors mention it as thus occupied. The sedilia are canopied and graduated stalls for the celebrant, with the subdeacon on his right and the deacon on his left; or, in England, more usually for the priest on the east, and then the deacon and subdeacon; when on the same level, they mark the date when priests acted as assistants. They are always on the south side, and generally have a water-drain beyond on the east side. They occur in the twelfth, and were common in the next century. Sometimes they are divided by pillars, and sometimes by a wall with apertures; at Dorchester, Oxon, there is a small triangular window at the back of each seat. The eastern stall is generally raised above the level of the others. The earliest form in the catacombs, and repeated at St. David's, was a bishop's throne flanked by collateral seats. At Beckley and Lenham there is only a single elbowed seat, in other cases two are found. The earliest stall in England, used however for judicial purposes, is in the Prenorman west tower of Barnack. At Westminster the stalls of the thirteenth century are enriched with paintings. Sedilia are comparatively rare on the Continent, but there are examples at Leon, Stuttgardt, Boppart, Augsburg, Marienburg, Oberwesel, the Certosa (Pavia), and Corbeil, four at Esslingen and Sens, and five at Padua and Ratisbon. Three stalls remain at Exeter (1320), Rochester (Late Decorated), Selby, Ripon, St. David's, St. Mary's (Leicester), Binham, Worcester (c. 1500), and Tewkesbury, the latter still retaining their colour; four at Westminster, Durham, Furness, Paisley, Gloucester, Bolton, Rothwell, and Ottery in the Lady-chapel, and five at Southwell. The chaplain, deacon, and subdeacon or crossbearer, and, on great days, a canon with the mitre, were thus accommodated at an Episcopal Mass; and on great festivals, when the dean was celebrant, the assistants were doubled; but at Durham there are four sedilia on either side of the altar (these were probably used by the four acolyths in the Pontifical Mass, one with the mitre, the thuribler, and taper-bearers, and two deacons and subdeacons). At York the dean on greater festivals was assisted by three deacons and three subdeacons; and the archbishop by seven deacons at Toul, Vienne, and Lyons.

Seeded (*i.e.* dotted over) with pearls; a vestment is said to be semée or sown, when they are more thickly placed together.

Selour. (*Cyling, ciel, cileo.*) Cellar; a canopy; inner roof of a room, which is sealed or closed with planking.

Semifrater. A benefactor, who was regarded as in confraternity, having a share in conventual prayers during life, and in Mortuary Masses after death.

Sempecta. A monk who had passed fifty years in a monastery. At Westminster and Crowland he lived in the infirmary, and had a young attendant.

Sendal. A kind of taffeta, used for quilts and banners. The clergy in 1343 were forbidden to wear their hair rolled with fur or sendal.

Seneschal, and Receiver Monastic. (1.) He seated the guests in the guest-hall, sent presents to strangers of degree, and in some cases had charge of the bishop's palace. (2.) The Steward of the Liberties at Canterbury held an annual court, to which he cited tenants holding of the See by knight service. (3.) The High Steward of Chester was the Earl of Derby, and at Canterbury the Earl of Gloucester. (4.) Stewards of the year or months, minor canons or vicars, who catered for the common table.

Senior. (1.) Monk from the age of forty to fifty years, who was excused from the external offices of provisor, procurator, cellarer, almoner, kitchener, master of the works, and pitanciar, but took his turn in singing Masses. (2.) The head of a college of secular canons, as at Christchurch, Hants, 1099. (3.) At Osnaburg, Trent, Lubeck, and in some Italian cathedrals, the antianus, or senior, corresponds to the archpriest of certain French cathedrals, in which he acted in the bishop's absence as his representative in administration of sacraments and benediction of ashes, palms, and the font. Such an archpriest was required in every cathedral by the Council of Merida.

Sequestration. Execution for debt on a benefice, issued by the bishop, by which the profits are paid to the creditor.

Sequence. (1.) The later name of the pneuma, a melodious and varied prolongation of the Alleluia. (2.) The announcement of the Gospel of the day when taken from the middle of the Gospels, but called Initium when the opening words were to follow. On the four days of Holy Week the words, " The Passion of our Lord Jesus Christ," replaced the ordinary sequence, or initial. *See* PROSE.

Serge. (Fr. *cierge ;* Lat. *cereus,* a wax taper.) Those in a low basin were called mortars, and burned during Matins at the choir-door. Lyndwood says in very many churches "the two" (*i.e.* on the altar) were found by the curate. .~

Serjeants. (*Servitores.*) Servants in monastic offices; those of the church, the guest-house, refectory, and infirmary were subordinate officers. The first was the bell-ringer, except for High Mass, Vespers, Matins, and obits; the candle-lighter, except round the high-altar (he also laid out the vestments for the celebrant at the high-altar), was the chandler, making all the wax candles, and assisted the subsacrist in baking the hosts. The serjeant of the infirmary was the barber, and, with the clerk and cook of the infirmary, waited on the monks who were sick or aged.

Sermons were called tractatus (expository), disputations (argumentative and controversial), allocutions, and by the Greeks didaskaliæ (doctrinal), or homilies (familiar addresses). The preacher used the sign of the cross and a short prefatory prayer, as St. Chrysostom says; and St. Augustine used to say, " God give me some worthy word to say. May the Lord make known His mysteries. The Lord aid our prayers, that I may say what I ought to speak and you to hear." The sermon ended with a doxology to the Holy Trinity, in the time of St. Gregory Nazianzen. In some places the prosresis, " Peace be unto you," with the response, " And with thy spirit," was in use; and in Africa, before and after sermons, St. Chrysostom mentions that sometimes the form was "Blessed be God," and the blessing of the bishop was asked. An hour was the appointed limit to the preacher, who sat or stood at his pleasure. Laymen occasionally were allowed to preach, like the catechists of Alexandria. Sermons formed a part of the Sunday and festival services, and were delivered on special occasions and in times of penitence and rejoicing alike. The pulpit was the front of the bishop's chair, the steps of the altar, as St. Gregory of Nyssa and Sidonius Apollinaris inform us, or the ambon. In the East the people frequently sat, and not uncommonly gave audible signs of approval or the reverse. When St. Chrysostom preached the people waved their handkerchiefs, threw up their robes in the air, laid hands upon their swords, and shook their plumes, exclaiming "He is worthy, worthy." (*See* MUR-MURING.) At Durham the galilee-bell was rung on Sundays from twelve to one, to announce that a sermon was to be

preached, the duration of which was from one to three p.m.
Thorndike says that a quarter of an hour is long enough for a
sermon, and Herbert would restrain it within an hour, a limit
which Barrow and South must have often exceeded. Funeral
sermons were not very uncommon in England, immediately
before and after the Reformation. Sir Julius Cæsar always
sent a broadpiece to the preacher, or a pair of gloves to a
dean or bishop, because he would "not hear God's word
gratis." Beleth says that in some churches the sermon immediately followed the Gospel.

Server. (*Adjutor.*) The priest's assistant at a low Mass. The
Clugniacs allowed one, but the Cistercians, in obedience to
Pope Soter's injunction and the plural wording of the Domi-
nus vobiscum, required always two.

Service-Books of the Greek Church. (1.) The Euchologion,
corresponding to the Missal. (2.) The Menœa, answering to
the Breviary, without the ferial offices, and full of ecclesiastical poetry in measured prose. (3.) Paracletice or great
octoechus, the ferial office for eight weeks, mainly the work
of Joseph of the Studium. (4.) Triodion, the Lent volume,
from the Sunday before Septuagesima to Easter; and the
Pentecostarion, the office for Eastertide.

Services. (*Canto variato* or *modulato*, harmonized, as opposed
to *canto fermo*, unisonal or Gregorian singing; a kind of
anthem.) (1.) Arrangements of the Canticles, Te Deum,
Benedictus, Benedicite, Magnificat, and Nunc Dimittis,
and the Psalms sung by substitution for them, consisting of
a succession of varied airs, partly verse and partly chorus,
sung in regular choirs, of which, probably, the germ is to be
found in the Ambrosian Te Deum, a succession of chants
which is mentioned first by Boethius, who lived a century
after St. Augustine. The simplified notation of this music,
as used in the Salisbury and Roman breviaries, was composed
by Marbecke. Tallis's Service is an imitation rather than an
adaptation of the original arrangement. Probably the first
was the setting of the Venite by Caustun in the time of
Henry VIII. In 1641 complaint was made of "singing the
Te Deum in prose after a cathedral-church way." There
are two classes: (1) full services, which have no repetitions, and are sung with an almost regular alternation
by the two choirs; (2) verse services, which have frequent

repetitions, no regular alternations, and are full of verses, either solos or passages sung in slower times by a selected number of voices. (2.) The domestic officers (servitia) of a monastery were the cook, baker, brewer, laundrymen, and tailor. At Rochester the bishop appointed them.

Servites. Servants of St. Mary. A mendicant order under the Austin rule, founded 1285 or 1304, by Philip Tuderti, a physician of Florence. Their dress is a close black tunic, a plaited black cloak, a scapular, and alms-pouch.

Set-Off. The projecting portion of a buttress, the nosing marking the successive stages, made of skew-stones.

Seven Capital or Deadly Sins. Pride, envy, anger, slothfulness, covetousness, gluttony, luxury.

Seven Principal Virtues. Faith, hope, charity (theological), prudence, temperance, justice, fortitude (cardinal).

Seven Sacraments. Baptism, Confirmation, Penance, Eucharist, Extreme Unction, Orders, and Matrimony.

Severy. A bay or compartment of a vault or cieling.

Shaft *or* **Virge.** The portion of a pillar between the base and capital.

Shalloon. (From Châlons.) A medieval stuff.

Shaving of the monks was performed at certain fixed times, the razors being kept in an aumbry close to the entrance to the dormitory. At Christmas and Easter, after shaving, baths were allowed.

Shawm. A pipe or hautboy.

Shier Thursday. Char or Sheer Thursday, Maundy Thursday, commonly said to mean Shrift Thursday, deriving its name from the custom of men polling their beards on this day as a token of grief for our Lord's betrayal. In Saxony it was called Good Thursday, and in the North of England Kiss Thursday, in allusion to the Judas kiss. "Oil and chrism are consecrated on this day," Cranmer says, "which signifies principally the imperial and priestly dignity of Christ, and His being anointed with the spiritual unction of the Holy Ghost above all creatures, admonishing us of our state and condition; for as of chrism Christ is named, so of Christ we are called Christians; and it signifies defacing and abolishing of the rights and consecrations of the old Law, which were done in oil, and therefore at this time the old oil is burned and destroyed, and new consecrated, signifying thereby our new regeneration in Christ and holy inunction which we have by His Holy Spirit."

Shingles. Thin tiled-shaped pieces of wood used as coverings for roofs or towers.

Ship. (*Navis, navicula, acerra.*) For incense; so called from its pointed oval form, often carved and enamelled. After the twelfth century it was furnished with a foot, and a cover jointed in the middle, and often ornamented with angels. A spoon or ladle was used with it.

Shire. In the tenth century a bishop's diocese, a parish being known as a priest's shrift or shriftshire.

Shrift. Confession of sins to a priest. Greek, exomologesis.

Shrine. (*Feretrum, feretory.*) (1.) The continuous prolongation of churches eastward led to the formation of feretories in place of the bishop's throne behind the high-altar, and furnished with their own altar on their west side, as at St. Alban's; St. John's, at Bridlington and Beverley; St. Guthlac's, at Croyland; St. Paulinus', at Rochester; St. Thomas', at Canterbury; St. Cuthbert's, at Durham; St. Edward's, at Westminster; St. William's, at York; St. Erkenwald's, at St. Paul's; St. Ethelbert's, at Hereford; St. Richard's, at Chichester; St. Edmund's, at Bury; St. Chad's, at Lichfield; St. Osmund's, at Salisbury; St. Olaf's, at Drontheim; St. Hugh's, at Clugny; St. Louis, at St. Denis; and the Three Kings, at Cologne. St. Sebald's shrine, of the sixteenth century, however, is in the centre of the choir of Nuremburg. Sometimes bouquets of lights were arranged on staples in the vault, and at Ely, in 1378, the triforium was cut through for larger windows to shower down light on a shrine. At Canterbury bandogs were employed to guard its treasures. At Westminster and Chester (of the fourteenth century) the shrines still remain perfect; and at St. Alban's and Oxford the watching-chambers remain perfect. At Durham the effect must have been very imposing; flags and standards drooped over the shrine, and nine cressets burning in front of the great eastern marygold threw a soft radiance over its gold, and gems, and colours. The shrine usually consisted of two storeys, the lower forming a marble or stone basement often enriched with porphyry, crystal, serpentine, alabaster, and mosaics, and provided with lateral niches for the sick folk who came to be healed to lie in; the pilgrims simply knelt. The upper stage had a marble coffin or chest enclosing the saint's body, and concoaled by a painted cover of wood, plated with precious metal, ridged like a church-roof, gabled, and provided with tapers at each end, which was visible above the reredos to all entering the church, and in some cases the west end of the shrine was the reredos of the high-altar, as at York, St. Paul's, and Lincoln. On great festivals and the anniversary of the patron the veil was drawn up at Matins, High Mass, and Vespers, by means of a rope to which sweet-sounding bells were attached. Around the basement, on precious cloths, hooks, and gilded or silver rods, were laid jewels, ivories, corals, rings, girdles, slippers, rich tapestries, trindles, tapers, models of limbs supposed to have been healed by the saint, besides offerings of brooches, lances, swords, ships, chains, necklaces, women's hair, and images. At Santiago 1000 lamps burning incense were kindled round the subterranean shrine of St. James. At Malmesbury a troop of cavalry kept order among the crowds who came to pray at St. Aldhelm's tomb. Musicians often sat harping and singing at a shrine, as Edward I. found Lovel, the minstrel, at Chichester, in order to awaken emotions of gratitude in the pilgrim, or celebrate the praises of the saint. The largest shrine now existing is the Camera Santa of Oviedo. At the entrance of the aisle at Gloucester there is a stone lectern, at which a monk recited the story of King Edward's death to the pilgrims. (2.) Subordinate positions were also selected :—a side-chapel for St. Frideswide's, at Oxford : the transept, as for St. Amphibalus', at St. Alban's ; St. Francis', at Assisi ; St. William's, at Rochester ; Little St. Hugh's, at Lincoln ; St. Caradoc's, at St. David's : and the fine tomb of Cantelupe, at Hereford, with its effigies of knights in the basement, and an upper canopy resting on open arches. Venerable Bede's shrine was in the galilee of Durham ; and at Ripon, St. Wilfrid's was in the choir-aisle. There are two interesting stone-coped shrines left, of Norman date, at Canterbury and Peterborough, in the latter case enriched with figures. (3.) A portable shrine (*bahut, theca, chasse, locellus, scrinium*), shaped like the mortuary chests on the choir-screens of Winchester. These shrines were carried in procession about the church, or on the town-walls to scare an enemy, or quench a fire, or round the diocese to collect alms, and upon their return were greeted by the chiming of the bells. Many were arranged upon the roed-beam or about the retable. Several are still in existence, as St. Heribert's, at Deutz; St. Taurin's, at Évreux; St. Emilbert's, c. 1635, at Cologne; Charlemagne's, in the Louvre; St. Romain's, at Rouen, c. 1305; St. Yvet's, of the eleventh century, formerly at Braisne, and now in the Museum Clugny; three of the thirteenth and one of the twelfth century, enamelled, in the British Museum; another of the thirteenth century in the Museum of the Society of Antiquaries of London; some at Goodrich Court; one of the close of the twelfth century, with plates of enamelled copper, and engraved with the rood, at Shipley, Sussex; St. Ethelbert's, at Hereford, ornamented with the acts of A'Becket; two of the eleventh century, at Hildesheim; one of the ninth century, and the Notre Dame of the twelfth, the gift of Barbarossa, at Aix-la-Chapelle; St. Elizabeth's, at Marburg, of the thirteenth; and one at Orvieto, of the fourteenth century; St. Ursula's, of the fifteenth, at Bruges; the Three Kings, of the twelfth century, at Cologne; and a fine example at Orsa Michele, Florence. From the richness of the enamel, these were often called Limoges coffers. The shrinekeeper or his clerk sat at the shrine to watch the jewels and palls on an enclosed seat, or in a pentice, or chamber, with his book, or in prayer.

Shrove Tuesday. In Italy called San Martedi dì Carnovale; in France, Mardi Gras, and Carême (Quadragesima) entrant. The pancake-bell was rung at noon on this day.

Sibyls. (*Siou boule* or *bulle*, the counsel or fate of God.) Twelve ancient sibyls, in various parts of the world, were believed to have foretold the history of our Lord; and in medieval decorations their figures are often introduced, as at Sens, Aix, Autun, St. Ouen at Rouen, Beauvais, Auch, and Auxerre. They are thus distinguished:—(1) the Persian, treading on the serpent, and holding a lantern; (2) the Lybian, with a lighted taper, allusive to Christ, the Light of the world; (3) Erythrean (*i.e.* of the Red Sea), with an expanded white rose, with a bud of the same flower, allusive to the Annunciation; (4) Cumæan, with a crutch or manger; (5) Samian, with a cradle; (6) Cimmerian (*i.e.* the Black

Sea), with the suckling-bottle; (7) European, with a sword, allusive to the Slaughter of the Innocents ; (8) Tiburtine (*i.e.* Tivoli), with a gloved hand raised to buffet ; (9) Agrippa, with a scourge; (10) Delphic, with a crown of thorns ; (11) Hellespontine, with a cross ; (12) Phrygian, with a precessioual cross and scarlet flag, bearing a cross of gold. In the Prose for the Dead allusion is made to these traditions in the words, " Teste David cum Sibylla." They are represented as of commanding stature, and in the prime of life, habited in tunic, mantle, and robes, jewelled and richly embroidered. The Sibylline verses date from two hundred years before the Christian era to the third century after it, and are a strange medley of heathen oracles and Jewish traditions. They were quoted against paganism by Tatian and SS. Clement of Alexandria, Clement of Rome, and Justin; and SS. Jerome, Augustine, and Gregory Nazianzen, and Tertullian, Arnobius, and Lactantius allude to them. St. Ambrose attributed them to demoniacal inspiration.

Sicilian Architecture. The prevalent styles are Byzantine, Saracenic, and Pointed Norman. There are no central towers, the cupola being their substitute, and the windows are very small.

Sidemen *or* **Questmen.** (O. Eng. *sithesmen,* or *sithcundmen,* country officers of the king.) Like foreign testes synodales, mentioned in the ninth century, assistants of the churchwarden in making presentments to the bishop at a visitation, and chosen annually. They are mentioned first in 1595 as synods men. The churchwarden's office became necessary in the fourteenth century, when the parishioners had to repair the nave.

Signs. (1.) The great bells at Canterbury in the twelfth century ; one took twenty-four and another thirty-two men to sound it. (2.) A most intricate system of talking with the fingers, used by the Clugniacs to indicate their wants in hall. (3.) Gerbert furnishes a minute account of a similar manual telegraph made use of by the præcentor in choir.

Simony. Selling the grace of the Holy Ghost (Acts viii. 20), which Simon Magus desired St. Peter to do. The buying or selling of holy orders, or any ecclesiastical office with cure of souls, forbidden in England in 740 and 1075, or with promotion to any dignity in 1127.

Simple Feasts. According to Salisbury use, those on which only the initial words of the antiphon to the Benedictus and Magnificat were sung, comprised under three classes: (1) "of nine lessons," with triple or double invitatory; (2) of three lessons, with double invitatory; (3) of three lessons, with simple invitatory; the latter, in distinction to the former two, were marked "sine regimine chori." Simple feasts, like ferials and vespers, had no first vespers.

In the Roman use simple feasts, without ruling the choir, are classed as simples; the simple, with ruling the choir, as semi-doubles. Accordingly, the highest class of Salisbury simples became the Roman doubles, to which succeed greater doubles, doubles of the second and doubles of the first class.

Sinecure. (1.) A benefice held by a rector in a parish where there is also a vicar. (2.) A benefice where there is no church or no population

Singers (*hypoboleis*, psalmists, monitors) were appointed with these words by the Fourth Council of Carthage, 398, " See what thou singest with thy mouth that thou believest in thy heart, and what thou believest in thine heart thou confirmest also in thy life." They formed a distinct order, and are mentioned in the fourth century, by St. Ephraem, and in the Liturgy of St. Mark. They were at length called canonical or registered singers. In the sixth century song-schools were erected at Tours. That of St. Gregory at Rome, frequented by students from Britain, Gaul, Spain, and Italy, became the model for Europe. Some Spanish singers only ate pulse before singing, and were called in consequence fabarii, whilst the Clugniacs used liquorice juice and electuaries to improve the voice.

Si Quis. (If any one.) A notice of requirement put forth for any objector to dispute the fitness of a candidate for holy orders, formerly set on church doors, but now read from the altar. It corresponds to the prædicatio of the primitive Church, and epikeruxis of Chalcedon, 451.

Sir. This, as the English of dominus, was the style adopted by priests, as dom by monks, and in consequence they were commonly called Sir Johns. There were three Sirs, Sir King, Sir Priest, and Sir Knight. At the Reformation, Sir appears generally to have marked literates, in distinction to Magister.

Solar. (1.) A terrace on the roofs of Greek churches. (2.) An upper chamber or loft.

Solaria. (*Gynecœa, hyperoa, katechoumena.*) The upper galleries for women in a Greek church, which, St. Chrysostom mentions, had screens of wood. They remain at St. Laurence, St. Agnes, and the Four Coronati, at Rome.

Solea. (A corruption of *solium*, the ground.) The space in a Greek church between the ambon and sanctuary, where the laity communicated, afterwards appropriated to monks, and at length to the lesser orders. In a Latin church, between the choir and presbytery. In the basilica it was raised several steps above the ambon and the choir of minor clerks. Here the communion was given to all but the clergy, and subdeacons and readers sat, and the candidate for the priesthood was led up from this part to the altar.

Sommer. (*Summarius*, a beast of burden.) (1.) A main beam or girder. (2.) Sommier is the French term for an abacus, the support of an arch. (3.) Summissarius, the chanter of High Mass.

Soul Cake. A sweet seed- or oat-cake, of triangular form, formerly eaten on the eve of All Saints' Day and All Souls' Day, and given by the rich to their poorer neighbours, probably in return for prayers for the departed, for whom also the bells were rung at this time.

Soulscot. A mortuary payment made to the church which the dead had attended, at the open grave, in 1009.

Sound Holes. Ornamental perforations in belfries for the emission of the sound of the bells.

Span. The breadth of an arch at its base.

Spandril. The triangular space between an arch and the outer rectilinear mouldings.

Spanish Architecture. In the South few early Gothic buildings remain, and those which exist were mainly erected in the fifteenth century; but in the North the obra de Godos (Gothic), the Romanesque, and Geometrical Pointed (Tudesco) are represented. The German Middle Pointed, as well as French art, clearly influenced the designers in Spain. The old system of parallel eastern apses gave way to the affection for a chevet, with its processional path and circlet of chapels. The constructional choirs are usually very short. Moresco designates the leaven of the Moorish style, and Plateresque, so called from its plate-like tracery in flat relief, is the Spanish style of the Renaissance, of the sixteenth century. The choir in a Spanish church occupies the eastern half of the nave. The westward portion of the latter is called the trascoro; the part eastward of the choir is called entre los dos coros. Under the cimborio or lantern is the crucero or crossing. A passage, fenced with screens of metalwork, afford the clergy a means of access to the screen in front of the altar in the sanctuary or capilla mayor. In the centre of the coro are several lecterns for the choir-books, and on the west, north, and south are stalls, the bishop occupying a central stall facing east. Pulpits are erected against the western faces of the eastern pillars of the crossing. This curious arrangement, which has been followed at Westminster Abbey, is probably not earlier than the sixteenth century. About the same time, in parish churches, large western galleries, of stone, were erected for the choir, as at Coimbria, Braga, and Braganza, and provided with ambons at the angles. The choir was in the centre of the nave at the Lateran, St. Mary the Great, St. Laurence's, and St. Clement's, at Rome, by a basilican arrangement.

Sparver. (A.S. *sparran*, to enclose.) A richly-embroidered cloth. A bed-canopy.

Spear, Holy. A lance with a serpent twined about it, carrying a lantern for the new fire. *See* EASTER EVE.

Spire. (1.) *Flèche*, a spirelet; a small central spire, as at Haarlem, Cologne, Brussels, Amiens (130m. 54 centimetres in height), St. Benignus (Dijon), Rheims, Orleans, Évreux, the Sainte-Chapelle, and Notre Dame (Paris), and formerly Rouen. This is quite a Continental feature. (2.) *Aiguille*, a spire of stone, as at Peterborough, Lichfield, Salisbury, Chichester, Norwich, Oxford, Strasburg, Chartres, Semur, Vienna, Freiburg in Brisgau; or of wood, as one at St. Benet, Holm. Bramante said, when building St. Peter's, "I will put your marvel, the Pantheon, in the sky." The Gothic architect had already pierced heaven with the spire. The tower showed at first merely a top covered by a roof; and then by a low spire, which in time grew higher, lighter, sharper, requiring buttresses, increasing in breadth from the summit to the ground-line, until, as at Vienna, Ratisbon, Ulm, Freiburg,

Strasburg, Autun, Chartres, Mechlin, Antwerp, and Brussels, by a succession of retreating arches, buttresses, and pinnacles, gradually receding behind each other to the top, it pyramidized, like a magic growth of stone shooting up—the natural development of the higher out of the lower structure. In France a very frequent form of spire is a high coved roof of wood, bounded on two sides by triangular and on the other by quadrilateral faces. In Germany a low many-gabled covering, with facets such as jewellers cut on precious stones, is common. In France there are superb examples at St. Denis, Chartres, Coutances, Autun, Cambrai, Harfleur, Caudebec, Caen, Langrune, and St. George, Boscherville. The central spire of Lausanne is covered with metal or brightly-glazed tile. An ingenious lover of symbolism has discovered that the north-west spire of Lichfield is hollowed inwards like a trumpet, as though the church bells sounded from it like the silver trumpets of the Temple on Zion. Chesterfield spire, 228 feet high, has been warped into a twisted shape by the sun-heat; but the most extraordinary appearance is presented by the south-western spire of Gelnhausen, clearly a whim of an eccentric architect.

The spire is the noblest ornament of a tower, without which a tower can hardly claim to be complete. The conical capping of the turret, or the sharp pediment of a dormer window, may have suggested the original idea, but it already existed in the top of the obelisk and the bulk of the pyramid. Before the Norman period rude spires appear in England, and in the west of France in the eleventh and twelfth centuries, some being supported on an octagon rising from a square tower. The earliest and latest English steeples are destitute of spires. Towers first received a low capping, then a low timber spire, as in Kent, Sussex, and Herefordshire. This was again changed into stone, which became perfect in the Decorated period, often overhanging the tower; and in Perpendicular broach spires lingered on in Northamptonshire. In the Decorated period the spire grew reduced in breadth and more lofty; the spire-lights project less, and mount from the base along the sides; the squinches are smaller and are pinnacled, or are no longer visible; while the junction with the tower is not marked by a corbel table. At length the broach merges into the true spire as an essen-

tial portion of the tower from within a parapet which is sometimes pierced. The spire is sometimes ribbed, sometimes
crocketed, united to angle turrets by flying buttresses; or
bold and massive pinnacles are grouped round it inside the
parapet with consummate skill, as at Chichester, Peterborough,
and St. Mary's, Oxford. The conjunction of a tower and
spire forms a steeple. Height of steeples above the ground :—
Old St. Paul's, 527 feet; Salisbury, 404 feet; St. Michael's,
Coventry, 320 feet; Norwich, 309 feet; Louth, 294 feet;
Chichester, 271 feet; Strasburg, 500 feet; Vienna, 441 feet;
Antwerp, 406 feet; Freiburg, 385 feet; Chartres, 353 feet;
St. Patrick's, Dublin, 223 feet; Glasgow, 225 feet. The spire
of Amiens, called the golden steeple, from its gilded crockets,
is 422 feet; of Cologne, 510 feet; the highest pinnacle of
Milan, 355 feet; the dome of St. Peter's, 434 feet; Florence,
387 feet; and Segovia, 330 feet.

Splay. The slanting side of a doorway or window-frame.

Sponge, Holy. The *mousa* of the Greek Church, corresponding to the Latin *purificatory ;* it is used to gather the various "portions" in the disk under the holy bread, and to
cleanse the chalice in memory of the sponge of the Crucifixion. It is carefully wrapped in a linen cloth.

Spoon. (*Cochlear.*) (1.) One is sometimes used in pouring in
wine and water into the chalice. (2.) *Colum, colatorium ;*
a spoon-shaped implement, with holes in the bowl, used for
straining the eucharistic wine (St. Matt. xxiii. 24) as early
as the fifth century. It is mentioned as late as the ninth
century. (3.) *Labis ;* a spoon used in the Greek Church
for giving the sop in the Eucharist. Apostles' spoons had
their stems ending in figures of Apostles, and were usually
made for christening gifts.

Sprinkler. A little brush made of hyssop, with which the altar
and congregation are sprinkled with holy-water at Mass;
but in some places the water is blessed in the sacristy, and
placed at the entrance of the church in a stoup; it is used to
invoke the protection of God on the church and people, and
to typify the internal disposition required in the worshipper.

Spur Money. A fine levied formerly by choristers of St. Paul's,
Westminster, Lichfield, and Windsor on persons entering
the church.

Square Cap. This was first used by clerks in the fifteenth century.

Squinch *or* **Sconce.** Small arches formed across the angles of walls in towers to support the alternate sides of an octagonal superstructure.

Staff. There are three kinds used by a præcentor : (1) ornamented with a pommel of gold, like one preserved at Limburg-on-the-Lahn, and within memory at Rheims ; (2) having a carving like those of St. Gereon's, and the Dom at Cologne ; the latter has a staff of the twelfth century, with the Adoration of the Magi added in the fourteenth century ; (3) terminating in a Tau-shaped head, usually of boxwood, like St. Servais', of the twelfth century, at Maestricht ; sometimes they were made of ivory, adorned with bands of silver, gilt-edged, with gems, and ending in a crystal ball. It was sometimes called serpentella, from a figure of the Virgin treading on a serpent, as at Paris. The slightly-curved top of the " cross of St. Julliene" at Montreuil-sur-Mer, of the eleventh century, marks the transition from the staff to that borne by a bishop. The chanter's baton of St. Denis, now in the Louvre, was carried by Napoleon I. and the French kings before him at their coronation as " the golden sceptre of Charlemagne," from a seated figure of the monarch on the top ; it is dated 1384. There was another of the time of that king at Metz ; the grand chantre used it in certain ceremonies, when wearing an ancient cope covered with golden eagles in general processions. At Amiens the choristers carried little silver crosses, and the priest-chanter and chanter had staffs with figures in a dome-like niche, but formerly used batons of silver of the Tau-shape, which at length descended to the hands of cantors and choristers on certain days. The dean of Messina and the senior canon of Palermo carry a silver staff. The præcentor on great festivals used the staff at Paris, Rouen, Angers, Lyons, Catania, Neti, Messina, and Syracuse. *See* BATON *and* PASTORAL STAFF.

Stairs. Large flights of stairs, called in Spanish *gradas* (the English grees), lead up to the west fronts of Amiens, Lisieux, Barcelona, Salamanca, and Seville, and the transepts of Chartres and Beauvais. There are fine internal staircases at Burgos, Rouen, Hexham, and Beverley. The terrace at Seville was desecrated by money-changers even in the sixteenth century. At Tamworth, where the church was collegiate and parochial, there are double stairs to the tower,

for the use of the several ringers before the respective services; and at Lynn there are two stairs in the double chapel,
one for the priest and the other for the people. Two sets of
stairs also lead to the upper chapel at Christchurch, Hants,
probably for the accommodation of persons visiting the relics,
one being for access and the other for egress. At Barnack
there is an octagonal Early English staircase within the
Prenorman tower, and at Whitchurch a similar wooden staircase of the fourteenth century. At Wolverhampton the
pulpit stair winds round a pillar. There were usually three
stairs to an altar; at Salisbury on Palm Sunday the benediction of palms was made on the third step, flowers and
palms were presented on the altar for the clergy, and for
others on the stair only.

Stalls. (Fr. *stalle,* Sp. *sillar,* Germ. *stuhl,* It. *stallo;* at Chichester locally called books.)   Ranges of seats placed in
the choirs of churches, or chapter-houses, for the use of the
clergy, for the religious in a monastery, or for canons.   In
the most ancient churches of the West, in the cathedrals
and great minsters, the abbot or bishop sat at the head of
the choir, behind the altar.   Around them, on semicircular
benches of stone, marble, or wood, were ranged the capitulars. The arrangement survives in some of the oldest Italian churches. Since the thirteenth century the seats of the
clergy were placed in front of the sanctuary, on either side of
what is now called the choir; and is comprehended between
the crossing and the steps of the sanctuary leading up to the
altar. In Italy and Sicily the stalls were generally of marble
or stone, but in Germany, France, and England were always
of wood. The ancient rule was that the clergy should stand
during the greater part of divine service, when the Gospel
was read and the Psalms sung. SS. Chrysostom and Athanasius mention this custom in the East, and St. Benedict in
monasteries; Chrodogang at Metz in capitular churches, and
the Council of Aix (816) in all churches, required canons and
monks to observe it in the West; but a relaxation occurred in
course of time, for at Besançon, in the eleventh century, we
find that Peter Damian condemned the practice of the canons
sitting. To this day at Tours a vestige of the old practice
prevails, where the canons stand at the Compline of Holy
Thursday, and during the Lesser Hours of the two following

days. In Greece the aged monks are allowed the concession of a T-shaped staff, on which they lean during service. In the West a similar indulgence in the use of a staff by the infirm was the first modification of the ancient severity of practice. St. Benedict and Chrodogang, however, furiously inveighed against such effeminacy, whilst on the other hand Amalarius, who took a foremost part on the reorganization of cathedrals as well as the old Ordo Romanus, merely required the resting-crutch to be laid aside during the reading of the Gospel. At length some of the monks or canons at a time were allowed to sit at Clugny, Citeaux, and St. Benignus, Dijon. At Lichfield, in the fifteenth century, and in Austin canons' minsters, half the choir stood and half sat during the Psalms, or one between two sat at the Psalms, Alleluia, Gradual, and Epistle, and those who could not endure the fatigue sat in a place set apart for them. At Ratisbon and Braunschw, and elsewhere, sitting, standing, and genuflection only are recognized; but we find also prostration on forms, or bending over the misericord, occasionally mentioned. The words for the seat preserve at once the traditionary rule and the indulgence—stall from the Latin *stare*, to stand; and *misericord*, mercy; the latter forming a compromise to rest the canons without their deviating from a standing position. St. Gregory of Tours first used the word " form" in a sense analogous to that of a staff; from the ninth to the eleventh century it became morè and more familiar, as the designation of a bench with a back and desk, and divided by arms of wood into separate seats. The stall is mentioned at Maestricht in 1088, at Antwerp in 1201, at Meaux 1240, by Matthew Paris in 1250, and at Paris 1388. In 1121 Peter of Clugny appears to allude to the misericord when he speaks of the scabella sediliis inhærentia which were raised at a particular part of the service; about the same time, at the Convent of Hirsaugh, in Germany, the word misericord is distinctly mentioned, and the stalls are called sedilia. The dignitaries and senior monks only occupied such stalls, the simpler canons and junior monks sat on benches, the choristers and vicars knelt on the floor. At Amiens stalls (116) date 1508–22; Poictiers (70), *c.* 1237; Auch, 1529; Civita Vecchia, *c.* 1330–40; Roeskilde *c.* 1420; Sanlieu, of the thirteenth century; Rodez, of the fifteenth century; Rouen (86), 1457-1467;

Solesme, 1553; Ulm (92), c. 1459–1462. At Ratisbon there
are some specimens, of the middle of the twelfth century, of
very coarse workmanship, and in a dilapidated condition; at
St. Gereon, Cologne, and at Bamberg, of the fourteenth century; Flavigny and St. Claude Jura, of the fifteenth century;
Alby and Montreal, of the sixteenth century; Auch, 1520–
46; Lisieux (50), of the fourteenth century; St. Mary De-la-
Roche, near Paris, of the thirteenth century; Bruges, 1477;
Gerona, Palencia, Tarragona, and Zamora, with a series of
Scriptural subjects, of the fifteenth century; and Toledo,
carved with the Conquest of Granada, 1495–1543; Civita,
of the fifteenth century; Burgos (103), 1497–1512; Cadiz
(63), 1527; Leon 1468–81; Saragossa, 1452; Seville (125),
1475–1548. Early English benches may be seen at Rochester; three unique shafts, with capitals of gilded wood, are
preserved at Peterborough. At Chichester (40), Exeter(51),
are stalls of the thirteenth century; at Lincoln (62), c. 1380;
Winchester (60), Early Decorated; Worcester (52), 1379,
misericords and elbows; Hereford (60), temp. Edw. III.;
Gloucester (60) and Ely of the fourteenth; at Carlisle (46),
St. David's, Ripon (32), Norwich (62), Chester (48), of the
fifteenth; at Manchester (30), Beverley, and Bristol, of the
sixteenth centuries. Perpendicular stalls still remain at
Cartmel, Sherborne, St. Helen's Bishopsgate, Westminster,
Selby, and Dorchester; of the Cinque-Cento period, at
Christchurch; Jacobean at Wimborne; and of the seventeenth century at Salisbury and Durham. There are also
some stalls preserved at Hexham, Hull, Ottery, and Tewkesbury. Stalls with panelled backs remain at Etchingham,
but more commonly the side-screens divide them from the
aisles; at Capel-le-Ferne, St. Margaret's Westminster, and
St. Mary's Oxford, there are simply long benches with desks.

The introduction of tabernacles and canopied backs was
of later use than the stalls or forms. Bishop Lacy, at Exeter,
in the fifteenth century, gave hangings, to be placed behind
the canons and vicars, of damask for summer use, and of green,
powdered with flowers, in winter time, to preserve them from
wind and cold, and sixty years later cloths were hung in the
choir for a similar purpose. In the thirteenth century the
stalls of Peterborough had paintings of Scriptural subjects. The wall at Rochester, Bamberg, and Llandaff, and

the stone screen at Canterbury, c. 1304, enabled the occupants to dispense with canopies.

The stall consists of (1) a misericord, patience, subsellium; Gr. sumpsellion, sediculum, or sellette, a folding seat turning on hinges or pivots; (2) the book-desk, prie Dieu, podium; (3) the parclose, sponda, the lateral pillar or partition, the upper carved part forming the museau; (4) croche, accoudoir, or accotoir, the elbow-rest; (5) the dorsal, dossier, the wainscot back; (6) dais, baldaquin, the canopy or tabernacle work. In the east of France and Germany there is usually only one range of stalls. Gangways with stairs, entrées, are openings permitting access to the upper stalls, which are raised on a platform. The lower stalls stand on the ground, or upon an elevation of one step. The upper or hindmost range of stalls (hautes stalles, or formes) were restricted to the capitulars or senior monks, from the time of Urban II., sitting in order of installation or profession. In cathedrals the four dignitaries occupy the four corners to overlook the choir, the dean on the south-west, the præcentor on the north-west (hence the term decani and cantoris to designate the two choirs), the chancellor on the south-east, and the treasurer on the north-east; next to them sat archdeacons, and in some places the subdean and subchanter of canons occupied the nearest stalls to them westward, as the priest-vicars did on the eastern side, but the latter had no kneeling •mats or cloth-covered hassocks, but sometimes they sat in the central stalls. In the middle range, basses stalles, were canons, deacons or subdeacons, and their vicars, annuellars, and chaplains; and in the lowermost range were clerks and choristers (bas-chœur or clergeons at Vienne), occupying forms or benches without arms or backs. At Pisa the canons' stalls were distinguished by coverings of green cloth, and in Italy generally by cushions. The hebdomadary, principal cantor, and master of the choir sat at the head of the second row. The ranges were reckoned as first, second, and third, sometimes from the wall and sometimes from the floor. The cantors had their folding chairs in England and France, and the celebrant was provided in many places with an elbow or armed chair. In some cathedrals the archdeacon fronted the bishop as his " eye." At Exeter books for devotional use were chained before the altar; antiphonars chained before the dean, chancellor, and treasurer; ordinals in front of the præcentor and succentor; and books chained, like those still remaining at Selby, between the choir-step and altar-step. At Durham there was a bell behind the stalls for signalling to the sacrists the time for ringing or stopping the church-bells. The name of his prebend and the antiphon of the psalm which each canon was bound to recite daily for benefactors and departed canons were written up over his stall, as at St. Paul's, Lincoln, Chichester, Wells, etc., to which was added afterwards a notice of his preaching turn at Hereford. Citations to residence were affixed by the pre-bendary's vicar upon his stall. At Lichfield every canon was provided with his own light and book in choir.

Staurophylax. The keeper of the sacred cross on the Church of the Resurrection at Jerusalem.

Stanchion. An iron bar between mullions.

Standard. A massive standing candlestick in front of an altar. A large chest. An iron bar in a window.

Standing at the Gospel. Pope Anastasius ordered that at the reading of the Gospel the people should not sit, but stand with heads bowed. Formerly those who had staves laid them down, as a sign of submission to the Gospel, and the military orders, after the example of the Polish king Mieeze-laus in 968, drew their swords. When the Gospel was commenced all in church crossed themselves on the brow, lips, and breast, and the reader kissed the book. [At Car-lisle, in 1686, at the name of Jesus all bowed or knelt, and in 1641 " bowing towards the east, with three congées in every motion, access or recess, and advancing candlesticks upon the altar, and crucifixes and images upon the parafront or altar-cloth," and " standing at the Gloria Patri " are men-tioned.] All said, " Gloria Tibi, Domine," and at the conclu-sion, " Deo Gratias " or "Amen." Men bared their heads and the clergy had their hair short, that they might hear the better. Unmarried women covered their heads, and if they had no veil their mothers placed a cloth upon them. The sign of the cross was also made at the end of the Creed, the Lord's Prayer, Gloria in Excelsis, and evangelical canticles, which were all said standing.

Standing Cup. One that stands upon its foot, in distinc-tion to a tumbler, which must be emptied at a draught.

There is a fine specimen, of the time of Edward III., at Lynn.

Star, Golden. A vessel for the exhibition of the Host at the Communion of the Pope on Easter Day. One, with twelve rays, is used to cover the paten when carried by the cardinal deacon to communicate the Pope. From their roofs, powdered with golden stars, the chancels of St. Mary's, Stamford, and Tonge are called the golden choirs. Seven stars—the Great Bear, which never sets—is the emblem of the everlasting state of the Catholic Church (Rev. i. 20).

Stations. (1.) According to Rabanus, the observation of stated days or times; but, as Beleth says, so called because the participants stood and rendered praise, unlike the penitential posture and supplication of a litany. General stations were the visits of the members of a diocese to the cathedral church in Whitsun weeks; particular, those made in thanksgiving to a saint, whose prayers had been invoked in time of national distress or peril. The choral habit was used by the clergy. Tertullian thus calls the Wednesdays and Fridays of the Lent fast; the fast accompanying visits to the martyrs' tombs. In the Greek Church on these days, and also on Saturday, the stational Mass in Lent is celebrated, and they were called semijejunia, half-fasts, because the fast was broken after communion. St. Athanasius mentions the Saturday as a station. (2.) Station (in distinction to collecta, the rendezvous or place of assembly) denoted the halting-place of a pilgrimage, or processions, carrying relics of saints, usually marked by a cross, stone, or one of those buildings which served both as a place of shelter and prayer for travellers, called in France reposoir. Gang days meant stations or visits to shrines or relics. (3.) Bishops, before their enthronization, paused to pray at a station (like knights before their creation), either at the cathedral gate, as at Chichester, or in some adjoining church, as at Winchester, Bourdeaux, Tours, Rouen, Autun, Noyon, Laon, Quimper, Rennes, Clermont, and Paris. In some parts of France the vassals carried the new bishop to the church-door. (4.) Solemnities, stated masses and litanies, were sung in stated churches at Rome on stated days, by enactment and statute, or, as Tertullian suggests, from the watch of a Roman sentinel, as the Christians " keep to their station in church until noon," that is, on the fast days or anniversaries of martyrs. So station meant also the actual procession to the station or church. The Lenten and "uptide" (bumbled or veiled) crosses were used in the stations of Palm Sunday. On certain occasions when a procession was made through the city it set out from the principal church and halted at certain churches, where the great doors stood open, and the clergy appeared to receive it as it stopped to make a station, with the measured chant, sung by multitudes, rising and falling with slow sonorous rhythm, filling the streets with mournful music or the solemn cadence of the Latin litanies. The Roman churches in which the Pontiff officiates on stated days are called churches of the stations or mansionary, and the assistant clergy are spoken of as stationars, a name derived from the body-guard of the emperors. Gregory I. ordered masses and litanies to be sung on certain days in the principal Roman churches. These, being continued on stated occasions, were called stations. At Rome Malmesbury mentions a sanctuary church of Jerusalem, at which on three Sundays, called the Jerusalem stations, the Pope sang Mass, and at Westminster a Jerusalem chamber adjoined the sacristy. In Clugniac processions on Sundays there were four stations —(1) in the Lady-church; (2) before the dormitory; (3) in front of the refectory; (4) in the porch or vestibule. The stations of the way of the cross, since the end of the fifteenth century, greatly promoted by Benedict XIV., are—(1*) the condemnation of our Lord; (2*) Christ bearing His cross; (3) Christ falling under the cross; (4*) the meeting of Jesus and the Virgin; (5) the Cyrenian bearing the cross; (6) the veronica; (7) Jesus falling to the earth; (8) He consoles the daughters of Jerusalem; (9) He falls again; (10) He is stripped of His dress; (11*) He is crucified; (12) He dies; (13*) the taking down from the cross; (14*) the entombment. Those marked with a star may be traced back nearly three centuries earlier. The Franciscans and Capuchins were especially privileged with making stations, the former having had charge of the holy places in 1342. If in a church, they commence on the Gospel side and terminate on the side of the Epistle. In 1730 Pope Benedict XIII. required a cross to be set up over each picture. The pilgrims who returned to Nuremberg constructed stations on a hill-side. Pavements were constructed with labyrinths, representing the pilgrimage to Jerusalem. Alvaro, a Dominican, established stations in his convent at Cordova. He died in 1420, and, years after, the Franciscans once more revived the idea and disseminated it far and wide. *See* JUBILEE.

Statutes. The particular and domestic rule binding members of a cathedral with regard to Divine worship, or capitular property, made as occasion required, confirmed by the bishop, and committed to writing, after receiving the assent of the dean and greater part of the chapter. Those of the new foundations are codified into chapters, and were mainly drawn up by Bishops Heath, Day, and Cox, Tonstal, Thirlby, and Bonner, and Mawson, and Laud.

Stayned. Painted. Stained cloths are paintings on linen.

Step of Satisfaction. The choir-step on which a delinquent knelt in acknowledgment of a fault.

Sticharion. The Greek albe or tunic, used by bishops and priests flowing and ample, and narrow and close by deacons. It is purple in Lent, except on Sundays, Saturdays, and the Annunciation.

Stichos. A short varying versicle and response in the Greek liturgy, answering virtually to the Latin Gradual. The koinonikon is a sacramental hymn and stichos, sung a little before the Communion.

Stilted *or* **Surmounted Arch.** One which has the capital below its curve, the moulding in the interval being straight.

Stocking. (*Caligæ.*) A footed legging, reserved to bishops after having been forbidden to the clergy when of a green colour.

Stole. [*Sudarium, stola, orarium,* so called by the Councils of (Fourth) Toledo and Braga.] The name of Orarium is derived either from *ora,* denoting its strip-like appearance, or, as Bede suggests, from its use at the hours of prayer, but according to Rabanus and Alcuin, because it was worn by preachers (*oratores*). Probably it was, like the maniple, at first a kerchief or towel. It denotes the yoke of Jesus, or, as Tyndale states, the rope with which our Lord was bound to the pillar of scourging. The Fourth Council of Toledo says that it was worn by deacons on the left shoulder " because he preaches," and by a priest on the right shoulder that he may be ready for his ministrations. The Council of

Braga requires it to be worn over both shoulders. Stoles have been worn by priests, crossed in front under the cingulum (the part thus covered being the subcingulum), since the end of the fourteenth century. A bishop, as he wore a pectoral cross, wore his stole straight. In Flanders the stole was narrow, and worn uncrossed. Two of the time of Henry VI. are in the possession of Lord Willoughby de Broke. The stole of the Eastern priests, called orarion or epitrachelion, is merely a long strip of silk or stuff more than double the width of the Western stole, and with a hole in the middle of the upper part, through which the celebrant puts his head. It has an embroidered seam down the middle.

Stone of Dedication. The original stone, inscribed with the date of the dedication, 1192, remains at Clee Church, Lincolnshire.

String. A thin projecting horizontal line of masonry on walls.

Stuffs used in the middle ages. The names Damask ; Sarcenet (*Saracenorum opus*) ; Sypers, cloth of Cyprus ; and Levantine brocades of silver and gold, made in the Lebanon ; Orphreys, "the gold of Phrygia;" Attalic robes, splendid cloths of Asia Minor; and the embroidery, veils, silks, and cloths of Alexandria, bespeak the place of manufacture. Byzantium was also a considerable producer. The earlier patterns are Byzantine, with flowing and geometrical designs, animals, birds. In the thirteenth century arms of donors were introduced, and in the fourteenth century splendid borders, representing saints, angels, and evangelists, were added to vestments. In England embroidery of Alexandria, Indian samit, color de Painaz, Turkey work, cloth of Antioch, Tripolis, Tartaryn, Tiretaine, cloth of Tyre (so called from its bright red tint), Tarsus, India, Tarse de Nak, Tuly, Inde di Gangi, Moire de Tarse, are mentioned as used in vestments, all being of Eastern importation.

Stylites. (Pillarists.) Monks who lived on the top of a pillar (*stulos*). Symeon, "the ambassador between earth and heaven," spent thirty-seven years on the summit of a column in Asia Minor, and crowds of admirers came to see him. A bishop of Adrianople spent sixty years in a similar position, assisted in his devotions by choirs singing below ; and so did a Longobardic deacon, near Trèves, until his bishop wisely called him down. Evagrius mentions one who lived sixty-eight years on his eminence, but there were not a dozen persons who became imitators of this strange humour.

Subchancellor *or* **Scribe.** The notary of Italian cathedrals is the chancellor's vicar, called also registrar or matricular, and at St. Paul's in 1280 as scriptor librorum. He acted as assistant-secretary, librarian, lecturer in theology and law, and teacher of reading.

Subchanter, Succentor. (Gr. *hypoboleus;* Fr. *chantre;* Sp. *sochantre;* Ger. *unter-cantor.*) (1.) One who sings after the præcentor. (2.) The deputy of the præcentor; the principal among the vicars in choir. The præcentor sat on the right-hand side of the choir, and the succentor on the left. His office was usually in the gift of the chapter; occasionally, however, he was nominated by the præcentor. There were two kinds of subchanters: (1) The succentor of canons, or succentor-major (first mentioned in the eleventh century), at York, Bayeux, Paris, Amiens, Glasgow, Châlons, Girghenti, Wells, and Salisbury, acted as præcentor's deputy with regard to the canons; he ranks after the subdean; the office was given by the diocesan. At Amiens he installed canons in the lower stalls; at Rouen he holds a prébend and regulates processions; he often is called pre-chantre, in distinction to the grand chantre; (2) a vicar, the deputy and assistant of the præcentor. At Seville and Placentia, and in England, he tables the ministers for service. At Chichester and Hereford he chastised the boys, and ordinarily his duties were confined to ordering processions, delating offenders, and general supervision of the lower choir; he could not correct a canon. His office appears at Chichester and St. David's in the thirteenth century; he corresponds to the precentor of the new foundations. At Lichfield and St. David's the subchanter is head of the Vicars' College.

Subdeacons. The term is first used by St. Athanasius to designate a clerical order hitherto known as that of hyperetai. In the end of the third century the order existed. In the fourth century, both in the East and West, subdeacons were appointed to assist deacons. Eusebius mentions seven at Rome, but at length their number was tripled about the eleventh century, and divided into three classes: palatines, the immediate assistants of the bishop; stationaries, those connected with the arrangement of stations and processions; and regionaries, occupied in particular districts of the city. At Constantinople there were ninety in the time of Justinian, who were reduced to seventy by Heraclius. In the Greek and African Church the subdeacons did not receive imposition of hands at ordination, and are still regarded as in minor orders. In the West they were at first, as in the East, the bishop's messengers, doorkeepers, servers at the altar, but in the twelfth and thirteenth centuries began to be classed with the superior orders. At their ordination a book of the Epistles and an empty chalice and paten were given to them. They were not allowed to distribute the sacred elements. The subdeacon is not allowed to wear a stole. His vestment at Mass is a narrow tunic, called by Sicard the subtile; this author also mentions his maniple, of larger size than that of a priest. In the twelfth century in England he was forbidden to marry. The Apostolic subdeacons were established by Pope Fabian in 240. In the year 1057 their number amounted to twenty-one. Owing to their irregularities, they were suppressed by Pope Alexander VII. in 1656; the auditors of the rota have succeeded to their ecclesiastical functions. The voters of the signature, since 1656, have replaced the apostolic acolyths; they furnish the bearers of the incense-cruets, lights, the Papal gloves and ring, when the Pope officiates. In 957 his duties in England were to bring the vessels to the deacon, and minister with him at the altar. The newly-crowned emperor acted as subdeacon at Milan, and offered the chalice and paten to the archbishop. The Circumcision was called in France the Feast of Subdeacons, held also on Epiphany or its octave. There were four solemn dances after Christmas in church: those of priests, deacons, subdeacons, and boys or minor orders. *See* St. John's Day.

Subdean. (*Sous-doyen,* the *deutereuon* of the Greek.) (1.) There were three kinds of subdeans: (1) the vice-dean; (2) the dean's vicar, his sub-officer, assistant when present, and deputy when absent; vice gerens in choir, as at Lichfield; both had a similar office, that of supplying the duties of the dean in his absence, but the one was personal delegation made to an individual named, the other was real, being appointment to an office; in some cathedrals the dean, with the consent of the chapter, nominated a locum tenens to a perpetual office; in the other case the dean simply deputed a person temporarily, and as capable of removal; (3) the capitular subdean; the perpetual subdean, who is said to hold a place which is a quasi dignity in the gift of the bishop. He has a stall, and corresponds to the foreign archpriest having parochial charge of the close. The office was founded at Salisbury in 1021; at Wells and Lincoln in the twelfth century; at St. David's, York, and as penitentiary at York and Exeter, in the thirteenth century. In all these instances he ranked after the dignitaries, and sat in the third stall on the dean's side at Exeter. At Chichester he is mentioned in 1383 apart from the dean's vicar; he was vicar of St. Peter's the Great in the cathedral, and had a seal of office. At Cologne there is a subdean. In the absence of the dean, the senior canon at St. Paul's, the præcentor at Lichfield, and the archdeacon of Llandaff was president of chapter. At Salisbury and Wells the subdean exercised archidiaconal authority in the city and suburb, but not in the close, and over schools, except those of the cathedral. At Llandaff, till recently, the archdeacon was subdean, the bishop being dean. At Exeter and York he was the penitentiary. At Lincoln he took his turn in celebrating on greater doubles. At Wells he could give leave of absence and promote the vicars. The Council of Autun mentions an arch-subdeacon, and subdeacon is the term applied to the subdeans of St. Paul's, Chichester, Lincoln, and York, and used by Innocent III. Probably, as there were archpriests who became deans, and archdeacons who held external authority in the diocese, these subdeans were, in point of fact, arch-subdeacons with a limited jurisdiction within the cathedral city, outside the close, and apart from the archdeaconry, acting as confessors, and representing the dean, in his absence, within the cathedral. At Dunkeld he was commissary and rural dean of the diocese; and at Utrecht there were four arch-subdeacons or chorepiscopi. At Cologne, Brechin, Ross, Glasgow, Elgin, and at Chartres, where they ranked after the præcentor, there were subdeans. (2.) The dean's vicar, that is, his substitute in choir only, is mentioned at Lichfield in the twelfth century; this subdean was necessarily in priest's orders, and is a minor canon at St. Paul's. The subdean of Hereford acted as a kind of provost or bailiff of manors. At St. David's he is a vicar.

Subucula, Poderis. A cassock like a rochet worn under the albe.

Subsacrists. Servants of the treasurer, usually acolyths or ostiarii; a later name than that of hebdomadary servers, and not earlier than the fifteenth century. They were keepers of the vestry and sacristy, church-cleaners, bell-ringers, door-openers, lamplighters, and searchers at nightfall to see that all was safe; they kept order during divine service, and attended to the good condition of the cemetery. At Lincoln they were called stallkeepers, and at York, clerks of the vestibule and sacrists; and at Canterbury, vesturers.

Substrati. The prostrate or genuflectentes, kneelers; the second class of candidates for baptism, who after the sermon had part in the prayers, or, rather, because they sought baptism prostrated.

Subtreasurer. The deputy receiver of certain rents in a cathedral of the new foundation, and deputy treasurer; the sacrist; a minor canon who had charge of the church goods, acted as parish priest in the precinct, provided necessaries for divine service, and was librarian. The office is still partially preserved as an assistant in divine service and parochial cure of souls. At Hereford he ranked after the succentor, and sang the Founder's Mass. He is mentioned in 1290 at York, and at Chichester in the fourteenth century, being the treasurer's vicar, where he made the chrism of oil and balsam.

Succinctory. (1.) The part of the priest's stole (subcingulum) passed under the belt. (2.) A peculiar ornament of the Pope, resembling a maniple, and embroidered with the Holy Lamb, and worn on the left side, either as a substitute for an alms-purse or the ancient belt of chastity, which was the cincture of the albe. In the East bishops wear one pendent, of a lozenge form, tasselled, and with a cross on it called epigonation.

Sudary. (1.) The purificatory for wiping the chalice. (2.) The mappula; the maniple. (3.) The veronica. Blessing the priest's eyes with the sudary was forbidden 1549. (4.) The banner of a bishop's staff.

Suffragan Bishop. (1.) A diocesan prelate who has the right of suffrage or voting in a provincial synod or at the election of a metropolitan. (2.) A coadjutor. By 26 Henry VIII. c. 14, suffragan sees were proposed to be erected at Cambridge, Hull, Gloucester, Taunton, Shaftesbury, Bedford, Bristol, Berwick, St. German's, Thetford, Ipswich, Grantham, Huntingdon, Southampton, Guildford, Leicester, Nottingham, Marlborough, Dover, Shrewsbury, Penrith, Molton, Bridgenorth, Isle of Wight, and Colchester. The following were actually for awhile suffragan sees :— Taunton, 1538 (Bath and Wells); Shaftesbury, 1537 (Sarum); Marlborough, 1537 (Sarum); Bristol, 1538 (Worcester); Dover, 1537, again till 1558, again 1569–97 (Canterbury); Bedford, 1537–60 (Lincoln); Shrewsbury, 1537 (Lichfield); Ipswich, 1536 (Norwich); Thetford, 1536–70 (Norwich); Colchester, 1536 (London), again 1592–1607; Hull, before 1552 (York), again 1553–79; Berwick, 1536–70 (Durham); Penrith, 1537–9 (Carlisle); Nottingham, 1567–70 (York). An archbishop or bishop presented two names for the selection of one of them to the crown. A permissive Act for bishops suffragan in Ireland was passed in the early part of the present century, and others have recently been consecrated in the colonies. In 1210 the Council of Newtown enjoined the appointment of archpriests (rural deans) in place of chorepiscopi and bishops of small sees.

Suffrages. The versicles after the Creed.

Sunday. First of the week, St. John xx. 26; Acts xx. 7; 1 Cor. xvi. 1, 2. Dies Dominions, the Lord's day (Rev. i. 10), in 1064, began at Nones (eight p.m.) on Saturday and lasted until Monday. In 994 parishioners were required to attend Evensong and Nocturns on Saturday. In 696 the Lord's day was reckoned from evening to evening, but in 958 from Saturday Nones till light on Monday morning. Islip's Constitutions and the Councils of Aix (789), Frejus (791), and Frankfort (794) assign as the cause that Vespers are the first office of the morrow. The medieval tradition was that our Lord was born on Sunday, baptized on Tuesday, and began His fast on Wednesday. In the English Church, before the Norman invasion, markets and work were forbidden on it. No malefactor could be executed, but friendly entertainment of strangers and neighbours was

permitted.   Public business, in 321, and labour, by the
Council of Laodicea (360), confirmed by Theodosius in 420,
were prohibited on this day.   The Christians reinterpreted
the heathen name as implying the Sun of Righteousness.
St. Chrysostom called it the day of Bread, as the Eucharist
was always celebrated.   No one fasted or knelt on Sunday
from the fourth to the seventh century, as a sign of joy, in
the West.

The Sundays in Advent and Epiphany are called in the
Greek Church by a certain number, in connection with St.
Luke's Gospel; thus Advent Sunday is the " Tenth of Luke,"
and the Second Sunday after Epiphany the " Fifteenth of
Luke." (*See* Lessons.)   The Third Sunday in Advent is
called Gaudete, from the Introit.   In the Greek Church
most Sundays are called after the Gospel, but in the Western Church they are designated from the Introits.

Sunday after Epiphany.   Gr. Sunday after the Lights.
At Brough on Epiphany Eve the hollins, or holy tree, an
ash illuminated with rush torches, was drawn, to the sound
of music, through the streets.   In the north of Italy, Marriage Sunday, from the Gospel.

Sunday before Septuagesima.   In the Greek Church the
Sunday of the Publican and Pharisee.

Septuagesima.   (Seventieth.)   So called either in allusion
to the captivity of seventy years, as the counterpart to the
forty years of wandering in the desert, to which Lent corresponded, or as reckoning, in round numbers, from Quadragesima to the First Sunday in Lent, including Sexagesima
and Quinquagesima by analogy.   It is the third Sunday before
Ash Wednesday (sometimes in England written Pulver Wednesday), and called by Greeks the Sunday of the Prodigal,
from the Gospel, and in the West (in the sense of the Greek
apodosis) the Close of Alleluia, which Beleth says was accompanied by a solemn dance ; and at Toul a sod of turf
was carried in procession and buried in the cemetery.   The
week following was called Apocreos or Carnis privium, because meat was forbidden.

Sexagesima (Sixtieth.)   The Sunday of Apocreos of the
Greek Church, because meat is not eaten beyond it.

Quinquagesima.   (Fiftieth.)   Dominica in Capite (Quadra-
gesimæ) ; De Carne Levanda ; Esto Mihi (Ps. xxxi. 2), from

the Introit; in Germany, the Priests' Fortnight, ecclesiastics commencing their fast on this day; and in the Greek Church, Tyrophagus, because cheese is no longer eaten. In France the morrow was called Collop Monday, as the last day in which meat (and then only in small quantities) was permitted.

The name of Shrove-Tuesday, instead of Fastens, occurs in 1512. It was derived from the shrift or confession practised on this day, which was popularly devoted to the coarse and wild merry-making from which the carnival took its origin.

SUNDAYS IN LENT:—(I.) *Invocavit*, from the Introit (Ps. xci. 15); in France, from an ancient ceremonial, Sunday in Brandons (torches) or of Heârths; Germ. Spark Sunday; Quadragesima; in the East, Orthodoxy Sunday, from the overthrow of the Iconoclasts; in 994, in England, Holy Day, because all parishioners were shrived on the evening before, and in 877 "the day on which Christ prevailed against the devil;" in Germany, Freed Sunday, from the freedom permitted to servants. This week was called Chaste Week, or Clene Lenton. (II.) *Reminiscere*, from the Introit (Ps. xxv. 16); in France, Transfiguration, from the Gospel in the Paris use. (III.) *Oculi*, from the Introit (Ps. xxv. 15); in the East, the Adoration of the Cross, which was then kissed with great reverence. (IV.) *Lœtare*, from the Introit (Is. liv. 1); Refreshment Sunday, from the Gospel and lection at Matins (Gen. xliii.); Mi-Carême; Midlent Sunday; Mediana; Sp. Mediante, Pasques Charnicula; in the Greek Church, from a special hymn, Sunday of the Great Canon; and at Rome, Sunday of the Golden Rose. (*See* that word. Henry VI. received one in 1446 and 1452.) In England, Care Sunday, as it were Penance Sunday, from *kar*, a penalty; Mothering Sunday, in allusion to the Epistle (Gal. vi. 21), when all persons made their offerings in the cathedral or mother-church, until the thirteenth century, when other churches or stations were appointed. From eating fine wheat-cakes or beans on this day Simnel, or Carling Sunday. The popular name was Mid. Tid. Mis. ra, a corruption of Mid-Tide-Miserere, the Psalm used in Lent continually. (V.) *Judica*, from the Introit (Ps. xliii. 1); Passion Sunday; Dimanche Reprus, from veiling the images; the Sunday of

the Quintain, from the sports of the day, in France; in
Germany, Black Sunday, from the veiling of the crosses when
the words of the Gospel are read, " Jesus hid Himself."
The Saturday before is called in southern Europe Alms
Saturday, because our Lord said on this day, " The poor ye
have always." In the East it is known as St. Lazarus's Saturday. The Greeks call it Acathisti, from a hymn to the
Virgin sung standing. (VI.) (*See* PALM SUNDAY.) The week
was called " Greater " from the length of the services. Beleth
says that on the previous evening the Pope and bishops made
the Maundy. On Easter Day, Beleth says, in some places
in the yard or porch a large vessel was placed to contain all
that was to be eat and drunk by the parishioners, and these
were blessed with the cross and holy-water, the priest taking
what he would. After communion also a morsel of bread
and sip of wine were given to each of the faithful on leaving
church. At Rheims and other places the bishops and clergy
played at ball, a game known as the Liberty of December,
in imitation of the heathen Saturnalia. Women beat their
husbands on Easter Monday, and the men retorted on the
next day. On the following Saturday, called, like Easter
Eve, the Sabbath in Albes, white dresses were worn. Easter
Eve was called the Sabbath of Lights.

GREATER SUNDAYS. The First Sunday in Advent, the First,
Fifth, and Sixth in Lent.

SUNDAYS AFTER EASTER:—(I.) *Low Sunday;* Quasimodo,
in allusion to man's renovation by the Resurrection (1 Pet.
ii. 2), from the Epistle; Anti-Pasch; Missæ Domini; Quinquagesima of Joy; Neophytes' Day; Sunday in Albes; and
Octave of Infants, in allusion to the newly-baptized. On
this day, or the Fourth Sunday after Easter, was kept the
commemoration of the last Easter baptism, called the Annotine Easter. Fordun says Easter Monday was popularly
called Black Monday, and the ' Chronicle of Dunstable'
derives the name from a great blackness of the sky at Paris
on April 14, 1361. (II.) *Three Ointment Bearers*, from the
Gospel; St. Thomas, or Renewal Sunday (St. John xx. 27); in
the Latin Church, Misericordias Domini, from the Introit
(Ps. xxxiii. 5); Sunday of White Cloths, or after the exhibition of relics. (III.) *Of the Paralytic*, from the Gospel, in the
Greek Church; in the Latin, Jubilate, from the Introit (Ps.

lxvi. 2). (IV.) *Mid-Pentecost ;* Of the Samaritan, in the Greek
Church, from the Gospel; in the West, from the Introits,
Cantate (Ps. xcviii. 1), Rogate (Sol. Song ii. 14), Exaudi
(Ps. xxvii. 7). (V.) Rogation; in the Greek Church, from the
Gospel, "Of the Blind Man."

SUNDAY AFTER ASCENSION. In the East, Sunday of the 318,
in allusion to the Nicene Fathers; at Rome, the Sunday of
Roses, so called by Innocent III. in 1130, as roses were
thrown down from the roof of Santa Maria Rotunda, symbolically of the gifts of the Spirit. This week was called
that of expectation (Acts i. 4).

TRINITY SUNDAY. In the East, All Saints' Sunday; in
France, the King of Sundays, or Blessed Sunday.

Super-Altar. (*Altare, viaticum, gestatorium, portatile, para-
tum, itinerarium,* and propitiatory until the ninth century.)
(1.) The supertable of Cranmer. Becon says both the altar and
super-altar were covered with "cloth of hair." Mass might
not be celebrated but upon an altar, or, "at the least, upon
a super-altar, to supply the fault of the altar." "Superal-
teries," or trentals of communions, were forbidden by Ridley,
1550. The ornamental slab of an altar, often jewelled and of
jasper. It was a removable, precious, and often a very costly
covering of marble or metal upon a frame of wood, which
was placed on an altar for purposes of magnificence and devotion. St. Cuthbert's grave was found to contain a portable table of oak. Another was discovered in St. Acca's
grave at Hexham, also of wood. One of ivory was given to
Exeter in 1050. The slab was usually quadrangular or circular, with a sepulchrum or hollow for relics, and was made
of jasper, marble, or ebony. Hincmar, in 867, allowed the
use of a consecrated slate, marble, or a black stone slab,
probably owing to the needs of the Crusaders and the defi-
ciency of churches. It was large enough to contain the
chalice and host. Guilds, the merchants of the staple, and
private persons had the privilege under certain restrictions
by special favour. (*See* ANTIMINSION, anti-mensa.) (2.)
The reredos or retable in the twelfth century at St. Alban's,
carved, with a cross over it, and colouring, and wrought
sides, over the Mary-altar: this is either a local term or an
application of the word by Matthew Paris.

Superfrontal. The tabula superfrontalis, retro-tabula, or post-tabula, was the decoration attached to the wall behind and above the altar, as the tabula frontalis was the permanent ornament of its forepart. (2.) Modern name for the decorative hanging which overlaps a frontal. Lyndwood defines the frontal to be the pall or apparel hanging in front of an altar. In 1641 the Puritans objected to " crucifixes and images on the parafront or altar-cloth," and bringing up " children from the baptism to the altar to offer them up to God," and " making three congées " to it eastward " at every access and recess and motion."

Superstitions. In 960 the Church forbade the worship of fountains, groves, trees (especially elders), and stones, or the drawing of children through the earth on the " night of the year." St. Agatha's letters were used against burning houses and fire ; a holy candle on the hawthorn was a charm against lightning ; and the hallowed bell rung in thunder ; St. Blaise preserved horses, and saved men from the ague and choking. According to Becon, " If we fast the blessed saints' evens . . . St. George will defend us in battle ; St. Barbara will keep us from thundering and lightning ; St. Agape will save our house from burning ; St. Antony will keep our swine ; St. Luke will save our ox ; St. Job will defend us from the pox ; St. Gertrude will keep our house from mice and rats ; St. Nicholas will preserve us from drowning ; St. Loye (Eloi, Bishop of Noyon) will cure our horse ; St. Dorothy will save our herbs and flowers ; St. Sith (Osyth, a princess of East Anglia, martyred by the Danes) will bring again whatever we lose ; St. Apolline will heal the pain of our teeth ; SS. Sweetlad and Agnes will send our maids good husbands." Prayers are also mentioned :— " Unto Rock (St. Roche), for the pestilence ; to St. Christopher, for continued health ; to Clement, for good beer ; St. Germain's, evil ; St. Sithe's, key ; St. Uncomber's (Rhadegund's or St. Wylgeforth), oats ; Master John Shorne's boot (into which he conjured the foul fiend ; preserved at Merston, near Gravesend) as a cure for the ague ; St. Fiacre, for the ague ; St. Galltian, for lost thrift ; St. Walstone, for good harvest ; St. Cornelis (Cornelius, Bishop of Rome), for the foul evil ; St. Hubert, for dogs ; beans were offered to St. Blyth and St. Blaise, and children to St. Clement." " Invocations were made to Anne for a husband ; unto Margaret, for women with child ; to Blaise, for the ague ; to Catherine, for learning; to Crispin and Crispinian, for shoes making; to Cosmas and Damian, for physic," and St Barbara, for gunshot. The following were " extolled " :—St. George's colt, St. Anthony's pig, St. Francis' cowl, St. Leonard's bowl, St. Cornelys' horn, and St. Parson's breech. St. John's Gospel was hung as a charm about the neck. The (Redeemer's) Blood of Hales (Abbey), like that of St. Januarius at Naples, was exhibited as liquefied to persons not in a state of mortal sin ; to those that were it appeared opaque.

Surplice. (Over the pelisse; Lat. *super-pelliceum*; the Greek *samisia* or *epiraptoria*; Fr. *surplis*; Sp. *sobrepelliz*; Ger. *chorhemd*, a choirocke, is a vestment; sirpcloth in the north of England in the seventeenth century). Paulinus sent a lambs'-wool coat to Severus, and St. Ambrose complains of the use of beaver skins and silk dresses. The monks probably adopted the pelisse in allusion to Heb. xi. 37, and wore it in the eleventh century. The white garment of the clergy is mentioned by St. Gregory Nazianzen, Jerome, and Clement of Alexandria, Honorius, and Ivo of Chartres. It was used only in ministering at the altar, or in proceeding to church, or carrying the Eucharist. Angels and other blessed persons are recorded in Scripture to have appeared in white linen (St. Matt. xvii. 2 ; xxviii. 3 ; St. Mark xvi. 5 ; Acts i. 10 ; Rev. iv. 7, 9, 10). The name and colour signify holiness of life joined to penitence, denoted by the skins of dead beasts, the evil affections of the heart. The name is first mentioned by Odo of Paris and Stephen of Tournay, in the twelfth century, and by Durand. The Council of Basle required the surplice to reach below the middle of the thigh. The Gilbertines wore a hooded surplice. At Burgos, in summer, the canons wear, instead of a cope and mozzetta (their winter habit), a sleeved surplice raised on the shoulders. In 1322 Reynold's Constitutions order the server at the altar to wear a surplice. Lyndwood says it was worn by a priest who went to the altar to do anything with regard to the Eucharist. In 1305 chaplains or conducts wore it in choir.

Surrogate. The deputy of a bishop for granting licences of marriage and probate of wills.

Surcingle. (1.) The part of the stole crossed under the girdle. (2.) A belt with two purse-like appendages, used in the old English Church.

Sursum Corda. The words "Lift up your hearts," with the response "We lift them up unto the Lord." They occur in St. Cyprian, St. Cyril of Jerusalem, St. Augustine, St. Chrysostom, and Cæsarius of Arles.

Susceptores. (St. Matt. xviii. 16; Is. viii. 2.) One man and two women for each child. Beleth says, godparents who held the child at the font and took it from out the priest's hands after its baptism, a custom alluded to by Walter's Constitutions, 1195, and those of Langton, 1223. They in early times, according to Albinus, held the child on their left arm whilst the priest wiped the child's face with a linen cloth. Sureties who undertake, as the Canons of Cealcythe in 785 explain, renunciation of Satan and acceptance of the Creed. The religious, heathens, persons unconfirmed, and a husband and wife together were not permitted to be sureties.

Swords and a ducal cap (It. *stocco e beretto*) are blessed on Christmas Eve at the midnight Mass by the Pope, in order to be sent to favoured kings, as Edward IV., 1478; Henry VII., 1505; Henry VIII., 1517. The last gift of this kind was made by Leo XII. to the Duc d'Angoulême in 1825.

Symbol. The Creed, as the bond of intercommunion and test of fellowship and brotherhood among Christians; that distinctive sign by which they recognized each other when it was not as yet committed to writing, and was restricted to the initiated.

Symphony. Simple melody, in opposition to diaphony.

Synagogue. The Jewish Church is in the Catacombs represented as a woman of majestic presence in flowing robes; but in medieval examples, as on a doorway at Rochester Cathedral, with her eyes bandaged, the Tables of the Law falling from one hand, and holding a broken staff in the other (Jer. v. 16, 17). The Church is crowned and sceptred, and holds a church and a cross. *See* GRAAL.

Synapte. The Greek collect in the Liturgy of St. Mark, resembling the ectene in those of St. James and St. Chrysostom.

Synaxarion. An abridged form of the Greek menology; an account of the festival being celebrated.

Syncelli. Household clergy living with a bishop as witnesses to his pious conversation.

Synod. (Gr. *sunodos*, an assembly.) A diocesan assembly, as a provincial synod was called a council: in 1070, the bishop was to summon them twice a year. By the Apostolic Canons and the Council of Antioch there were to be provincial councils convened by the metropolitan in the third week after Pentecost, and on October 15th. Theodore's Canons in 673 enjoined a yearly synod at Cloveshoe on August 1st, in place of the usual half-yearly meetings; but in 785 the latter were restored by the legate at Cealcythe.

Synodals. (1.) Provincial constitutions or canons read after the synods in parish churches. (2.) Procurations, so called because formerly the bishop held his synod and visitation together.

Tabernacle. (*Repositorium, theca;* Gr. *skene;* Germ. *sacramenthaus.*) (1.) A niche or hovel for an image. (2.) An aumbry on the right side of the altar or behind it, for the reservation of the Host, chrism, and oil of the sick. It was always locked. (3.) A throne carried like a litter on the shoulders of Spanish priests in the procession of Corpus Christi, and supporting the Host. (4.) A small temple over the central part of an altar, for reservation of the Eucharist, contained in the pyx, and often decorated with a crown of three circlets.

The name is allusive to the ark of the testament contained in the Mosaic tabernacle, and holding the pot of manna. The Third Council of Braga calls the tabernacle the ark of the Lord, and so the Apostolical Constitutions name it the pastophorion, which in Ezek. xl. means the priests' dwelling, in allusion to our great High Priest. Possibly the word may refer to Ps. lxxxiv. 1. Its earliest form was a coffer of wood or a little arched receptacle, then it became a tower of gold, or of circular shape, being a casket for the chalice and paten, in fact a ciborium. At Amiens and in the north of France a dove suspended by chains over the high-altar, or a vessel like an elongated aumbry, was employed. The Greek skene, a box surmounted with precious stuff, is sometimes suspended in a bag, but more commonly is set upon the high-altar. In Italy the tabernacle is set upon the altar-shelf, flanked by the accessory lights, the two candles used at Mass being set, as usual, upon the altar. In the thirteenth century the tabernacle almost universally was placed near the altar. Two tabernacles, before the twelfth century, were often placed in churches, one to hold the reserved Eucharist, and the other to contain the Gospels, according to the Church proverb, " Verbum Dei sicut Corpus Christi." At St. Alban's, about that date, there was a gold vessel, richly jewelled, for the Host, hung above the high-altar, and Henry II. gave a cup of price to contain this " theca." There was a similar cup at Chichester in the twelfth century. On Palm Sunday the Eucharist was carried in a shrine-shaped vessel to a tent in the cemetery, then to the chapter-house, and back into the church, by an old monk in a white chasuble, supported by two others in copes. Lyndwood says that in Holland and Portugal the aumbry near the altar formed the taber- nacle, [and Moleon mentions similar instances in France], whilst the English custom of having a pendent pyx was better for adoration, but worse in respect to danger of theft or falling down. Bonner, however, ordered the pyx to be " hanged upon the altar," and Cardinal Pole desired that the tabernacle, under lock and key, should be elevated in the midst of the high-altar, or near it, with a light before the Sacrament,—a lamp or taper ever burning in honour of the Host; but even then common usage did not sanction such a position upon the altar. In the fifteenth century the tabernacle became a magnificent piece of furniture over or on the left side of the high-altar, with statues, towers, foliage, buttresses, and superb work full of grace and delicacy, as at Grenoble, St. John Maurienne, Leau, Tour- nay, Louvaine, Augsburg, and St. Laurence, Nuremberg, the latter sixty-four feet high and of white stone, "like a foaming sheaf of fountains," made by Adam Kraft. At Moltot there is a tabernacle, of the time of Louis XII., serv- ing both for reservation and for exposition. Another of the same kind at Senauques, of the thirteenth century, resembles a tower of wood. At Kintore, Foulis, and Kinkell are taber- nacles like aumbries, with angels kneeling before a mon- strance, of the sixteenth century ; and others remain on the north side of the choir at St. Clement's, Rome, Cologne, Ulm, Esslingen, Louvaine, Frankfort, and Bonn. *See* CIBO- RIUM, CUP, DOVE, PYX, CORPORAX CUPS.

In Italy the Host is carried in a box enveloped in a precious veil. (*See* CANOPY.) By Edmund's Constitutions, 1236, the Eucharist was carried to the sick in a clean decent box, containing a clean linen cloth, and Peckham, in 1279, directed the employment of a tabernacle or a covering of purple silk or clean linen, with a decent enclosure, within which the Lord's body was to be laid, not in a purse or bag, but in a fair pyx, lined with the whitest linen. In many Cistercian churches, and at Marseilles, in the procession of the Fête Dieu, an image of the Virgin held the tabernacle. The Greeks use a pendent silk bag over the altar.

Table, Holy. (1.) The altar, "the table at which the holy bread which came down from heaven is eaten," as Othobon defined it in 1268. That in the Vatican is of firwood, which was considered incorruptible. The words table and altar are indifferently applied (Ezek. xxiii. 41 ; xli. 22 ; xliv. 16), as priest and minister were (Joel i. 9). In regard to the oblation it is an altar, and in respect to the Communion, God's board, or the table of the Lord (1 Cor. x. 21). The earliest altars were of wood. The martyrs' tombs in the catacombs served as altars. After the edict of Felix I., who died in 274, they were covered by a slab of tufa and called by Prudentius the mensa. The church built over St. Cyprian's tomb was called Cyprian's table. Gregory of Tours speaks of an ancient stone table, set on two upright slabs, as "the ark." The Greek Church has always called it hagia trapeza. It is simply a wooden table, with a rich cloth ; on it are laid the tabernacle for the Eucharist reserved for the sick, the enkolpion in which it is carried round the neck by the priest, the antiminsion, folded, and the Book of the Gospel. (2.) A flat piece of board ; a level surface ; any construction for superficial decoration. (3.) A frontal to an altar at St. Alban's in the twelfth century. Such tables were partly of metal and partly of wood. Some had rich carvings, and some were coloured. One given to Glastonbury in 1071 was of gold, silver, and ivory. Another, of the same date, at Ely was bordered with jewels, and represented the throne of God, and figures. (4.) Mensa, the upper stone altar-slab. (5.) Pensilis contained the names of benefactors, registers of miracles, a list of indulgences, and the course of officiants, officiating clergy at the Hours, and celebrants of Masses. *See* ALTAR.

Table Tomb. A raised solid structure erected over a grave, and shaped like a table, closed at the sides.

Taper-Stand *or* **Sconce.** (*Pro torticiis.*) A socket to hold a pricket, on which a taper was set. They occur on the sides of windows and in brackets, being used for night-lights in church, or the offerings, by the devout, of candles, which were kept burning before a shrine. The Greeks call the hand-candlestick manoualion, and a group of lamps poleielaion.

Tapestry. (Sp. *colgaduras.*) Hangings are still used in the coros of Spanish churches. The hooks for them remain along the nave walls of Winchester, and examples are preserved at Beauvais; St. Peter's, Mancroft (1573); Denbigh, a dorsal (1530); at Chester, of French manufacture, till lately used as a dossal; at Merton College, Oxford; and Westminster, of the time of James II. Polydore Vergil, in the sixteenth century, gave hangings, embroidered with his arms, for the stalls at Wells. Those given by Prior Goldstone to Canterbury are now at Aix. The screen-hangings used for shelter and ornament at Exeter represented the story of the Duke of Burgundy, and were blazoned with the arms of the Courtenays. At Peterborough, in the transept, tapestry, with the deliverance of St. Peter out of prison, of the time of Henry VIII., is the solitary relic of sixteen pieces used on festivals, and suspended, till 1643, from the choir triforium. At Manchester there is tapestry, *c.* 1661. From Christmas to Purification, from Easter Eve to the octave of Trinity Sunday, from the Assumption to Michaelmas, and on St. Chad's Day, Lichfield was adorned with silken hangings and cloths. At York Archbishop Lamplugh gave tapestries for hanging the reredos. At Westminster tapestries were hung round the easternmost bays at the coronation of Charles I., and remained till the last century. Until 1765 the bays between the pillars were hung with tapestry at Carlisle. The tapestry hangings remained at Norwich till 1740.

Tassels. (*Tasse,* a hay-mow.) In the twelfth century chasubles and copes were ornamented with gold tassels. The word also denotes a thin plate of gold or silver worn as an orphrey on the back of a cope or glove, like the Greek antipanon.

Tawdry. A necklace of thin silk worn in memory of St. Audrey or Etheldreda, who mourned for her vanity in wearing gold necklaces, when she was smitten with swellings in the neck.

Te Deum. This hymn (commonly called that of SS. Ambrose and Augustine, and said by Dacius, Bishop of Milan in the time of Justin the Elder, to have been first sung at the baptism of the latter's father in the basilica of Milan) occurs in the Matin service, but has also been frequently used as a separate thanksgiving with a procession or litany, as at St. Paul's, for the victory of Musselburgh, 1547, and at the close of the Coronation Service. This glorious hymn certainly dates a century later than the time of St. Ambrose, and the chronicle of Dacius is regarded as not genuine. It probably was written in Gaul, and has been variously attributed to the monk Sisebutus, and Nicetus, Bishop of Treves in 527. The first mention of it occurs in the Rules of St. Benedict and Cæsarius of Arles.

Te Igitur. The beginning of the Canon of the Mass after the Ter Sanctus and Secrets was written by one Scholasticus in the time of Gregory I. It was also called Obsecratio.

Tenebræ. (*Tenables.*) The usual office of Nocturns and Matin Lauds for Thursday, Friday, and Saturday in Holy Week, said at the Vespers of the preceding day. At the end of the Benedicite the top candle of the Tenebræ candles was removed and placed behind the altar; at the prayer Respice it was brought out again by the cærimonar, to kindle all the church lights at a signal from the officiating priest and those in choir, by making a sudden noise with books, or beating on their desks, symbolically of the confusion of disciples at the Lord's betrayal, and the convulsion of nature at His death. In Florence and other places the laity joined in with discordant noises and irreverent levity. At Seville a volley of musketry customarily is fired. The name of the office has been traced to the fact that it was formerly celebrated at midnight, as an allusion to Christ walking no more openly with the Jews, as Cranmer says; others suggest that it is derived from the gradual extinction of lights which originally were put out one by one as the morning began to grow clear; or in symbol of grief and mourning; or, as Beleth suggests, of the eclipse of three hours at the Passion.

About the year 840, Theodore, the archdeacon of Rome, told Amalarius that the lights were not extinguished on Maundy Thursday in St. John's, Lateran. These lights are arranged on a large candlestick supporting a triangular frame or herse; along its sides are fourteen yellow candles, and one of white colour on the point itself. These are variously interpreted, the lower lights as the Apostles and disciples who fled from the Saviour at His betrayal, or the patriarchs and prophets whose light was dark to the infidel Jews, whilst the upper light is said to represent the Virgin, who remained constant, or the True Light Himself. The upper light is not extinguished, but concealed until Easter, under the altar, which is left in darkness on the Epistle side The number of lights varied. In some churches there was a candle corresponding to each psalm and lesson of the office. Thus we find seven, nine, twelve, fifteen, twenty-four, twenty-five at York, thirty, seventy-two, or even as many as each person thought fit to bring. These were extinguished sometimes at once or at two or three intervals. At Canterbury there were twenty-five, but since the twelfth century the usual practice is to light fifteen on the triangle, besides those on the altar. In some places they were quenched with a moist sponge, and in others with a hand of wax to represent Judas. St. Gregory of Tours says that on the night of Good Friday the watchings were kept in darkness until the third hour, when a small light appeared above the altar. Cranmer explains that the Lamentations of Jeremiah were read in memory of the Jews seeking our Lord's life at this time. The Reproaches and Trisagion were not sung until the fourteenth century on Good Friday.

Tenths of ecclesiastical benefices and lands were first paid in 1188 towards Henry II.'s. Crusade.

Terrer. The local name of the hostillar at Durham. The Greek guest-houses adjoining churches are called anakampteria.

Terrier. A register or survey of Church property ordered by the 87th Canon to be made and preserved in the bishop's registry.

Ter Sanctus. (Thrice holy; Is. vi. 3; Rev. iv. 8.) The invocation of God sung before the Canon of the Mass, at the end of the Preface, alluded to by St. Cyril of Jerusalem. Pope

Sixtus in the sixth century ordered the people to sing the Sanctus with the priest. Charlemagne forbade the priest to commence the Canon before the people had sung the Sanctus. The Sanctus Deus, Sanctus Fortis, sung daily by the Greeks, is chanted by the Latins on Good Friday only. *See* HYMNS.

Tester. (1.) The upper hanging over a bed. (2.) Housings for a horse. (3.) Covering of a trunk. (4.) A flat canopy, co-opertorium. The co-operculum was the wooden case enclosing a precious shrine. The latest instance of a tester, perhaps, is that over Bishop Montague's tomb at Bath, *c.* 1615.

Tetragammaton. The name of God in four letters, יהוה.

Texts. The Book of the Gospels, which Rupert says were enriched with precious metals and jewels.

Thanksgiving, The, is the prayer after the Memorial in the Communion office.

Theca *or* **Burse.** (Lat. *bursa,* a purse.) A case-cover containing the corporals, and presented to the priest at Mass; it was of square form, made usually of rich stuff, and lined like a bag with fine linen or silk; on the upper side was a sacred image or cross. One of the fifteenth century, of canvas, remains at Hessett, painted with the Veronica and Holy Lamb.

Thomas's, St., Day. (Dec. 21.) Observed by the Greek Church on Oct. 6, is mentioned by Theodoret, and in St. Gregory's Sacramentary.

Throne. (1.) The bishop's chair was often decorated with bronze and gold ornaments up to the thirteenth century; in Germany, England, and France, stone or marble was employed, and, from a tradition of curule chairs, ivory in Italy alone. At Vienne, Lyons, Autun, Metz, Arras, and Rheims, where a cross was laid in it during the vacancy of the See, the throne, provided with lights, was at the east end of the church, as in Istria and Dalmatia since 1510, and at Milan, Augsburg, and Monreale; at Canterbury it was in the same place, and occupied by the archbishop until the Offertory or Consecration; he returned to it to give the benediction. When a bishop celebrated pontifically in his own church he read the Mass of the Catechumens from his throne, but when in the church of another bishop had a seat on the Epistle side of the altar. St. Martin of Tours sat in the sacristy, where, at Ravenna, a seat of stone remains. At Autun, York, Monreale, Parenzo, St. Mark's (Venice), Malta, and Gerona the throne was of stone or marble, like those at St. Stephen's (Verona), at Avignon, of the fourteenth century; at Ravenna, at Torcello, of alabaster, with a cross between stars and flowers, of the eleventh century; and at Toul of the thirteenth century. The throne given by Charlemagne is preserved at Aix-la-Chapelle; Bernini's bronze throne adorns St. Peter's, Rome; St. Maximian's throne, of ivory, of the sixth century, is at Ravenna; and the Royal Museum of France contains the gilt and bronze chair of St. Dagobert, formerly at St. Denis, the folding part being of the seventh century. St. Sylvester's throne is in St. Martin's-at-Hill, and another enriched with mosaics, of the thirteenth century, at St. Laurence's, Rome. The thrones of Milan and Augsburg rest upon lions, one at Sabino on two elephants, and a third at Bari on three kneeling figures. At Ely and Carlisle the bishop, being abbot, sat in the south-west stall, but his ordinary place was at the end of the stalls on the south side of the choir during the daily office, as the central position of dignity; but at a Pontifical Mass his faldstool was placed on the north side of the altar. The throne of Durham is erected, with a solemn meaning, over a tomb. Those of Hereford, of the fourteenth century; Exeter and Wells, of the fifteenth century; and a chair of the thirteenth century in the former cathedral, are of wood; that of Exeter has a superb-canopy. At St. David's the throne (c. 1500) has side stalls for the collateral canons, and a low inclosure (c. 1342) round it. In England three or two candles were set on the side of the throne. The throne of Susa is of the thirteenth century. The Greek thrones are domed. Wilfrid, at his consecration, was carried, after the French custom, by bishops through the church in a gilded sella. Casalins mentions, in the seventeenth century, that the four principal magistrates carried the Archbishops of Tours, Bourges, Poictiers, and Auch at their first entrance into the metropolitical city. On certain days the Pope is carried on a sedes gestatoria, which is canopied by eight prelates referendaries, and escorted by two attendants waving feather-fans. The larger Greek churches have a throne for the sovereign prince, and at

Monreale and Palermo the kings, having legatine power, occupied enormous thrones near the altar. In Spain, since the fifteenth century, except at Barcelona, the throne is at the west end of the choir. Rodez retains a flamboyant throne, and Tarragona one of Renaissance date.

Thumbstall, *or* **Pouncer.** A ring with pearls, rubies, or rich ornament, worn by a bishop on his thumb, when it had been dipped in chrism, out of respect to the holy oil, and to preserve his vestment from stains.

Thurible. A censer (Phiale, Rev. v. 8; the thumiaterion, Heb. ix. 4). In the eighth century pans of incense were carried about, and the censer was whirled round with short chains, as by the Greeks. Charlemagne gave gold censers to Charroux, and Chosroës made a similar gift to Jerusalem. Pope Sixtus III. presented silver censers to the Liberian basilica. There is an ancient silver thurible at Louvaine, and another of silver-gilt and German workmanship at St. Anthony's, Padua. Cowel supposes that the word "treble" came from the shrill voice of the thuribler, and that the boy carrying a little bell might give the name of treble to a smaller bell. High up in the crossing of Westminster Abbey there are gigantic angels censing.

Tiles, Encaustic. Used in pavements about the thirteenth century for the first time apparently; there are some fine examples at Winchester, Gloucester, Christchurch (Hants), Westminster, Worcester, Ely, Romsey, Tewkesbury, Tintern, Malvern, Warblington, and Bredon; and in France, in the Hall of the Guards, Caen. Some early specimens are preserved in the British Museum, which came from Castle Acre. At Great Malvern tiles have been employed to form a reredos; in the Gaunt's Chapel, Bristol, Spanish ajuleios are found like those of Granada. Heraldic ornaments, sacred emblems and figures, are the usual decorations. In the sixteenth century Flemish tile was introduced, and in the sevententh century there was a local manufactury in Devonshire; in medieval times Droitwich and Malvern were the chief producers. At Hamburg there was an ancient tomb, with an effigy of a pope executed in tilework.

Tinsel. (Fr. *estincelles*, Lat. *scintilla*.) Sparkling stuff; spangled.

Tippet. The tip of a hood, or timp. (*Liripipium* or *colli-*

2 P

pendium; Germ. *zipfel.*) A tail-like appendage, lengthened out so as to lie on the shoulder, and become a neck-wrapper. In 745 cocculæ round the head and wraps (*fasciolæ*) round the legs were forbidden to monks in England, because worn by laymen. The liripip (which the statutes of Ratisbon explain as capitium vel cleri peplum, vulgo poff) lingers in the ordinary hatband and that used at funerals. The tippets of the almuce had rounded ends, to distinguish it from the squared terminations of the stole; they were worn hanging down in front by canons, but by monks behind by way of distinction. Latimer calls a halter the Tyburn tippet. The tippets, or liripips, disappeared from the hood in the time of Henry VII. At an early period the cape had only a bell-shaped ornament, and at a later date an edging of tails. The liripip is not earlier than the time of Edward III., and was worn by canons and rural deans; it is mentioned in connection with a hood in the Constitutions of Bourchier (1463), and Stratford (1343). Grindal uses it in the sense of a stole; Ducange explains it as an epomis. The short liripip, or cornet of silk or cloth, was worn by preachers in Queen Elizabeth's time, and according to Act 24 Henry VIII. enforced by Parker, of sarcenet by certain ranks. Latimer talks of his cloak and tippet, Grindal and Whitgift mention caps and tippets as distinctive of the clergy, and Cranmer complains of a petty canon "jetting" or strutting about London in side (long) gown and sarcenet tippet, the ensigns of dignitaries and graduates. Grindal, in 1571, says the clergy were required to wear commonly a square cap, and a kind of tippet over the neck hanging from either shoulder, and falling down almost to the heels. In Convocation the clergy wore long gowns and tippets, 1553. Pilkington and Cranmer call the time-serving clergy turn-tippets. A small triangular piece of folded cloth, called the tippet or epomis, at Oxford is worn behind the left shoulder by proctors, and should be by noblemen and baronets. Harding, in Queen Elizabeth's time, says some wear square caps, some round caps, some button caps, some only hats; some wear side gowns, having large sleeves with tippets; some Turkey gowns, gaberdines, frocks, or nightgowns of the most lay fashion. The stuff tippet, liripipium, of the canons of 1603, worn by literates, is the stole.

Tiron, Monks of the Order of. Founded by St. Bernard at Tiron in 1109; their habit was light-grey, but afterwards black. They had one house in this country, St. Dogmaël's, in Wales.

Tithes. St. Augustine calls them the tribute of the Church and of needy souls. Before the Norman invasion they are mentioned by Boniface, in 693; and besides them were paid plough alms at Easter, within a fortnight of the festival; of young, at Pentecost; of fruits of the earth, at All Saints'; Rome fee, or Peter's pence, on August 1; Church scot, at Martinmas; light-soot, first mentioned in 878, a halfpenny worth of wax for every ploughland, paid on Easter Eve, All Hallows', and the Purification; and soul-soot, given at the grave of each parishioner. In 957 the bishops had surrendered their fourth, and the tithe-payer attended at church, and of his offerings one part went to the church repairs, a second to the poor, and a third to the clergy. Tithes were formally enforced within the Pale after the Synod of Cashel, in 1172.

Title of the Cross, St. Augustine says, was written in Hebrew for Jews who gloried in God's law; in Greek for the wise of the nations; in Latin for Romans, the conquerors of the world. Hence churches were called titles, not only because the clergy took titles from them which fixed them to particular cures, but as dedicated to the Crucified. The appellation is first used by the Council of Braga in 572. The dedications (as distinct from consecrations to God) were chosen with care : churches standing on a hill bore the name St. Michael or St. Catherine, in allusion to the apparition of the Archangel on Mount Garganus, and the angels carrying of the virgin saint's body to Mount Horeb; those by the ferry were called after St. Christopher, who carried the infant Christ across the ford; those near the sea were named after St. Nicholas; and such as were connected with the factory of Hamburg merchants, St. Bodolph. The dedications of Holy Trinity and Christchurch were synonymous. A title was also a right to serve some church from which an ordained clerk took his title, a name derived from the titles of the martyrs' tombs, at which service originally was said, and so called for the reason given above, or the fiscal titulus which marked buildings belonging to the sovereign; and thus, also, churches dedicated to the King of kings. Pope Cletus, c. 81, appointed twenty-five priests for Rome; these Evaristus, in 112, divided as cardinal priests among the churches of the regions or quarters in which they resided; he also instituted cardinal deacons; and Stephen IV., in the ninth century, appointed cardinal bishops for distinct sees. The earliest title was St. Pudentiana, now called St. Praxedes. The Roman Cathedral had in 142 a title or parish church (as in many modern instances) attached to it by Pope Pius I. The Council of Lateran, 1179, enforced ordination on a distinct title.

Titular Bishops. Bishops bearing the name of a See, but whose diocese was extinct, or held by the heathen. They were employed as suffragáns or assistants to diocesan bishops in consecration of churches, reconciliation of penitents, ordination, and confirmation. Irish and Scotch bishops in the middle ages, driven out of their sees by violence, or compelled by poverty, often thus assisted in England. The Roman Church has 229 titulars and 865 effective prelates; the College of Cardinals should contain 6 bishops, 50 priests, and 16 deacons.

Tone. (Gr. *echos.*) The ecclesiastical modes in the Greek Church correspond to those of the Latins, and are numbered the even, as II., Plagios A; IV., Plagios B; VI., Plagios G; and VIII., barus (grave); and the uneven, as I., A; III., B; V., G; VII., D.

Tonsure. Dionysius Areopagita first mentions the tonsure (cutting of the hair of the priests), and St. Athanasius speaks of the hairs cut in a round; St. Jerome and St. Ambrose allude to the cutting of the nuns' hair in Italy, Egypt, and Syria. The custom has been referred to the practice of persons in sorrow among the Jews making themselves bald, as related by Isaiah and Micah, which prevailed also in Argos, Egypt, Syria, and other places. Penitents were shorn, as appears from Paulinus and the Third Council of Toledo, and, in consequence, in the fourth and fifth centuries, it was censured as unbecoming spiritual persons by St. Jerome and Optatus. In the time of Julian it would appear by the Tripartite History that the Christian clergy polled their heads short. In 740 the Excerptions of Ecbright derived the tonsure from the practice of the Nazarites, and an imitation of Christ's crown of thorns. The Irish used the Pauline or Greek tonsure, shaving the head from the front to the ears, in distinction to the Western or Petrine, which is on the crown, and large in proportion to the rank of the wearer. By the Law, priests and Levites were forbidden to shave their heads in a round (Ezek. xliv. 20). St. Jerome uses this fact as an argument against the fashion. Optatus brands the Donatists for shaving the crown, whilst the Council of Elvira permitted priests who had been shorn like the heathen sacrificers' "crown" to be admitted to communion only after a penance of two years. Casalius explains that the tonsure betokens the sorrow of the priest for his own sins and those of his people. At first the lowest Church servants wore their hair short as a mark of servitude, and the monks, out of humility, imitated them, and in the sixth century the clergy adopted the fashion. The clipping of the priests' hair, which was derived from the practice of the Nazarites, is alluded to by Isidore, the Fourth Council of Carthage, that of Agde, Evagrius, Ammian, Marcellus, St. Gregory Nazianzen, Cyril, Eusebius, St. Augustine, St. Ambrose. St. Paul had his head shaven. Pope Anicetus, c. 200, required the French priests to shave their heads like a ball; and Bede says the custom for the Greeks to be shorn square was derived from St. Peter. Germanns, Patriarch of Constantinople, and Boniface of Canterbury, in 1261, compared the tonsure to the crown of thorns set on the Saviour's head, and the second tonsure to that of the Apostle. Isidore of Seville and Gregory of Tours allude to the crown, and the Fourth Council of Toledo, 633, enforced it. In 1195, in England, beneficed priests who did not keep their tonsure and crown were deprived, and the archdeacon or rural dean clipped the heads of all others perforce. Hubert Walter, in 1200, enforced its observation. The little round on the top of the head is a modern abbreviation of the ancient tonsure, which embraced the whole upper part of the head. Bishop Hacket would not admit candidates to holy orders who wore extremely long hair; and the Statutes of Oxford, as edited by Archbishop Laud, forbid long locks to undergraduates. The old English councils repeatedly proscribe long hair and beards, in accordance with the Council in Trullo and the Fourth of Carthage. In 1102 and 1168 the hair was to be clipped so as to show the ears and not overlap the eyes. The tonsure of a monk is mentioned in England by King Withred's Dooms, 696, and the Excerptions of Ecbright. The crown was to be of an approved breadth, that is, worn larger by regulars than seculars, and by priests than by deacons, being, according to the legate Othobon, in 1268, tokens of their laying aside worldly things and of the dignity of their royal priesthood; coifs, with which the crown was concealed, were forbidden, except on a journey. Peckham, in 1281, calls it the distinguishing mark of a soldier of the Church, and of a heart enlarged and open to the celestial rays, but complains that the clergy covered it out of sight with hair laces. Concealment had been already forbidden in Edgar's Canon, and by Anselm in 1102.

Toothing Stones. Projecting stones left in a wall for an additional building to be made to it.

Torch. (*Torticius.*) A large altar-taper; two, provided from the alms of the faithful, were required, according to common practice, to burn in the Canon of the Mass, by the Synod of Exeter in 1287; and two in France, at the same period, were lighted at the time of the elevation. It has been authoritatively ruled that the expression " before the Sacrament," beyond the sense of " in front " or " in presence of " the consecrated elements, in distinction to the reserved Sacrament (as suggested in page 96), means also that before the time of actual consecration two candles set upon the altar are to be lighted. In the Greek Church, Goar says, the perpetual light is kept burning between the altar and the place of the Sacrament, in reverence both to it and to the Book of the Gospels. In England, where there was not a single pendent lamp, the number of sacrament-lights before the reserved Host was unequal. *See* LAMP, GRADIN, LIGHTS.

Totquots. An abuse of annates, whereby the Pope required firstfruits, not only of a new preferment, but also of all other livings held with it, so that the annates were paid over and over again for the same living.

Touch-Stone. A name given to dark marbles, hard black granite, or limestone, used for tombs and effigies.

Towel. (*Tuella.*) (1.) A rich covering of silk and gold, laid on the top of an altar, except at Mass. (2.) A linen cloth. Two were frequently placed on the altar, under the corporal, and a third (the lavabo) was used at the lavatory for wiping the hands. As the canon law required four towels (Cecco-pelius says three), the corporal was usually doubled back. (3.) Tela stragula was a coverlet of the altar after Mass. (4.) A cloth in which the font was wrapped at its hallowing on Easter and Whitsun Eves.

Towers obviously preceded the spires, but they were rare until the eleventh century. The Roman mortuary pillar may have suggested them as a monument of the martyr to whom the church was dedicated. Belfries were not mentioned till the eighth century by the monk of St. Gall, and by Amalarius. The earliest on record is one built either by Pope Stephen III. in 770, or Adrian I. in 772, as a belfry, which was imitated in that of St. Frances Romana, at Rome, in 836. Becon, in his 'Potation for Lent,' fancifully suggests that "bishops in early times lived near unto the church, that the poor people, beholding the steeple, which is the poor man's sign, might know where to be relieved;" but M. Viollet le Duc and M. Lenoir regard them as having been designed as land-marks and ensigns of power; and it is known that the Cis-tercian order considered them pompous, and, in consequence, forbade their construction. The earliest towers consist merely of a succession of stages, pierced with windows, a monotonous elevation relieved by discontinuous arcades. The western tower was the immediate imitation of the Lom-bardic campanile. Owing to a faulty foundation or a subsi-dence of the soil, several towers lean considerably out of the perpendicular, as that of St. Marian at Este, Pisa, and the Garisenda at Bologna, of which Dante says that when a cloud passes over its summit it seems to stoop to one standing beneath the leaning side, and the towers of Vienna, Delft, Saragossa, Weston (Lincolnshire), the Temple (Bristol), Wynunbury (Cheshire), and Surfleet. Taking advantage of the slope of the building at Pisa, Galileo, in the presence of the learned, made from the summit his famous experiments to calculate the direct fall of falling bodies; and the oscilla-tions of the great lamp under the cathedral dome suggested to him the idea of measuring time by means of the regular movement of the pendulum. Like the towers of New and Magdalen Colleges, Oxford, or in the South of France until the middle of the thirteenth century, and in Italy and Spain,

they generally remained isolated.   But in time, for the purpose of enabling the bellringers to avoid the inclemencies of
the weather in countries north of the Alps, they were connected with the church, at first on one side of the western
front or in advance of it.   Then, out of regard to symmetry,
two western towers were built, and at last a tower rose out
of the very centre of the church, the most effective position
it can occupy.   At a later period it would seem that the
central tower was the mark of a religious community, or its
dependency.   The tower at the side of the nave was erected
by a lord of the manor, and the western tower by the
parishioners.   At Lisieux, Chartres, St. Denis, St. Germain's, and Llandaff the towers are unlike in size and
outline.   At Clonmel, and St. Patrick's (Dublin), Auxerre,
and Sens, one tower only was completed.   Lyons has four
towers.   Lincoln, Durham, and Ripon formerly possessed
two western spires, and they exist at Igregia Matriz, Vienna,
Chartres, Burgos, and St. Jean des Vignes.   At Rouen, Wells,
Salisbury (though small), Chichester, Lincoln, and Drontheim the towers extend beyond the aisles, thus giving
great breadth to the western front.   The Angel Tower of
Canterbury derived its name from a gilded figure of an
archangel crowning it, like the statue of the Faith does
the Giralda of Seville.   Three towers mark cathedrals,
and, with rare exceptions, Benedictine minsters. So pleasing
was the additional charm afforded by the multiplication of
towers that towers were built at the re-entering angles of
the nave and choir round the transept.   Rouen has seven
towers (as Clugny had) in memory of the seven Churches of
the Apocalypse; Rheims has six and a flêche; Chartres,
Peterborough, Tournay, and Canterbury have five.   M.
Viollet le Duc has traced two schools of towers, one of the
West, and the other of the East.   One at Perigord probably
was derived from Venice, and the other from the banks of
the Rhine, which, in the middle of the twelfth century, gave
place to a national school.   The monastic towers in Ireland
—Jerpoint, Kilconnel, Clare, Galway, and Knocking—have
a remarkable feature, a series of oblong holes pierced through
the parapet for carrying off water.   A similar arrangement
prevails in the north of Italy.   The parapets are crenellated
and stepped, like those of Maestricht.   In the fourteenth

and fifteenth centuries narrow central towers were added to churches. They are usually square, and inside the battlemented parapet the roof rises with a high pitch, and is provided with a flight of stone steps, as at St. Étienne, Caen, up one side and down the other, at the ends, thus affording easy communication and the opportunity of using the embrasures with effect and safety. The enormous height of many foreign towers may be due to the incentive for constructing such ambitious structures afforded by rival towns, or the flatness of the surrounding country, which rendered them visible at vast distances; but in many instances, as at Amiens, the height of the roofs dwarfs the towers. On the leads of the Magdalen Tower, Oxford, on May morning, at sunrise, the choir still sings the eucharistic hymn, Te Deum Patrem colimus," in lieu of a mass for the soul of Henry VII., formerly celebrated on it. Anthems used to be sung round the spire of Old St. Paul's, and are still chanted yearly on May 29th, after evensong, on the great rood-tower of Durham, in memory of the monks singing Te Deum upon it after the victory of Neville's Cross, 1346.

Towers as Places of Refuge. At Adare, c. 1230, the central massive tower has a large turret at each angle as places of safety for life and property. The only access is by a wall staircase, which can only be reached by a ladder from the interior. St. Doulough's, near Dublin, contains several rooms. Many border towers, as at Newton Arlosh, are fortified like that of Olite, in Spain.

Heights of Towers. Mechlin, 348; Bruges, 442; Tournay, 320; Utrecht, 321; Grantham, 274; Ludlow, 294; Boston, 268; Newark, 220; Canterbury, 229; Lincoln, 262; York, 198; Durham, 216; Gloucester and Westminster, 225. A steeple is a tower covered with a spire.

In the province of Toulouse the earlier churches had a single western tower, as at Limoges in the eleventh, and Alby in the fourteenth century; and the same arrangement occurred at Ulm, Studtgart, Fribourg, Mechlin, Rotterdam, Liége, Dort, Ghent, Frankfort, Aarhuus, Strengnas, Avila, Zamora, Limerick, Stirling, Poictiers, Puy, Périgueux, and Limoges. Those of Bangor and Manchester marked a parochial nave. (See Austin Canons.) Where there is a low central lantern, or the inconvenience of tolling the bells from the crossing is to be avoided, a western tower was attached to the front as a belfry, as at Soignies, Leominster, Ely, Hereford, Wymond-ham, and Furness. In France the cathedral towers served as municipal belfries.

Tracery. (1.) The ornamental stonework in a window, formed by the intersection of the mullions. This is called bar tracery, in distinction to plate tracery, a ruder and earlier kind, which looks as if cut out of a plate of metal. Flamboy-ant tracery is so called from its combination of wavy, flame-like lines. In Germany stump tracery is formed of flowing lines ending abruptly. The noblest windows in England are of Decorated date—at York, $78+33$; Lincoln, $53+30$; and Carlisle, $58+32$; and of Perpendicular date at Gloucester, $72+38$, and Winchester, $55+32$. (2.) Decorative patterns on wood and metal work. Tracery was a gradual develop-ment. First a circle was set above two arches, without com-bination by any external mark; then lancets were grouped together, followed by their union by a hood; and then a reduction of the intervening wall into an incipient mullion; next a combination under one comprising arch succeeded; and then the space between the comprising arch and the lights below were occupied by apertures; and finally the complete development took place by piercing the spandrils or eyes.

Tract. (1.) Plain-chant, introduced by SS. Ambrose, Gregory, and Gelasius, and sung sadly and slowly (whence its name), instead of the Alleluia, on fasts, or after the Alleluia at other times. (2.) A psalm, or portion of a psalm, sung between Septuagesima and Easter, and at the office of the dead. (3.) The pointing in the Psalter. It is said that the psalm or hymn chanted by one voice was the Tract, and when the singer was interrupted by the choir his part was known as the versicle, and the portions allotted to them were called responsories.

Transept. Across the bar (the lantern); or cross-alley. A word derived from the balustrade in the old basilica, which divided the place of the lawyers from the people standing in the nave and aisles; usually ill-defined in France, Spain, and Scotland; it is in England a feature of great importance in the ground plan. The early type was that of an aisleless oblong, with a single or double apsidal chapel to the east, and denoting the arms of the cross in a church, called aisles at Rochester, Gloucester, and Hereford. The Latin ala or brachium were used, the former in a constructional, the latter in a symbolic acceptation. Transept towers at Barcelona, Exeter, Ottery, Angoulême, St. Germain des Prés, Clugny, Alet, Châlons-sur-Marne, and Geneva were designed to consult the convenience of the canons or monks in tolling the bells for the Hours and choir services. The western towers contained the great bells used on festivals and for summoning the laity.

Transfiguration *or* **Jesus Day.** Kept on August 6, and in stituted in 1456 by Pope Calixtus III. in memory of the victory of Uniades and the Hungarian army over Mahomet and the Turks. In France, after consecration, the chalice was filled with new wine, or, as at Tours, received some of the juice of the ripe grapes, and the clusters are blessed in Germany and the East on this day.

Transitorium. The antiphon in the Ambrosian rite sung after the Communion.

Translation. (1.) The transference of a saint's day which concurs with a greater festival to an unoccupied day. Gregory III. removed the feasts of All Apostles from May 1 to November 1, because at the former time food was often scarce. (2.) The removal of a saint's body to another grave. Deposition was the death of a saint not a martyr. (3.) Or of a bishop to another See. The first canonical instance was that of Bishop Foliot, transferred from Hereford to London in 1163.

Transom. A horizontal cross-bar in a window for the sake of strength, which was sparingly used at first in the Early English period, in glazed windows of the Decorated period rarely, but generally in the Perpendicular style.

Trappists. Reformed Cistercians, founded in 1140 at La Trappe, Orne, by Rotrow, Comte du Perche. About the middle of the sixteenth century they were known, for their disorderly lives, as the brigands of La Trappe, but in 1662 were displaced for Brethren of the Strict Observance, who still maintain the most rigorous discipline.

Traverses. Costers. Side curtains for the altar, used by Bishop Andrewes.

Trayled. Trellised latticework. At Durham one of the inner doors was thus grated, and provided with a row of spikes for protection against thieves.

Treasurer. (1.) The keeper of the muniments and relics. The fourth dignitary, by custom, not by canon law, in a cathedral, called cheficier or chevet-keeper; sacrist, from charge of the sacristy; cellarer, as providing the eucharistic elements and canonical bread and wine; matricular, as keeper of the inventory; coustre in France and Germany; custos and cimiliarch in Italy; the Greek skeuophylax. The custos had charge of all the contents of a church, but at length became superintendent of deputies, discharging his personal duties, and at length took the title of treasurer, as having charge of the relics and valuables of the church. He is the Old English cyrcward, and medieval perpetual sacristan, and now represented by the humbler sexton. Every necessary for the church and divine service was furnished by him. The old title of custos descended, before the thirteenth century, to his church-servants. His dignity was founded at York in the eleventh century; at Chichester, Lichfield, Wells, Hereford, St. Paul's, in the twelfth; and at St. David's and Llandaff, in the thirteenth century. At the Reformation the dignity fell into disuse at York (where he had installed canons), Lincoln, and Lichfield, and at Exeter, Llandaff, and Amiens is held by the bishop. (2.) The monastic treasurer or bursar received all the rents, was auditor of all the officers' accounts, paymaster of wages, and of the works done in the abbey. (3.) An annual officer, like the vice-dean and receiver-general of the rents, elected from the residentiary canons in the new foundations—as paymaster, master of the fabric, sacristan, keeper of the muniments, statutes, and chapter-seal.

Trecanum. An anthem sung after the Communion before the sixth century, in honour of the Holy Trinity; called by this name in Gaul. Some think it was the Apostles' Creed. In the Greek Church there is a Confession of the Holy Trinity sung after the Hagia Hagiois. The latter form is mentioned by St. Cyril of Jerusalem, St. Basil, and the Mozarabic and Gallican liturgies.

Trefoil. A three-lobed figure.

Trendles. Long rolls of wax candles or tapers.

Trental. (*Tricennalia, trigintalia.*) A service of thirty Masses said for thirty days successively after the death of the departed, or a Mass on the thirtieth day only.

Tribunal. (1.) The ambo, pulpit, or step on which the deacon read the Gospel, mentioned by St. Cyprian. (2.) The choir tribunal was the bema. (3.) The monastic court-house.

Trichorum. The triapsidal ending of a chant.

Triforium. (*Forus*, Low Latin for a gangway.) A word used first by Gervase to describe the thoroughfare or wall-passage and middle storey of Canterbury Cathedral. It is probably connected with the Italian traforare, to pierce, as if transforium, and represents the foreign tribune. The Cistercians seldom had a triforium, and where it existed it had no wall-passage. The triforia of Christchurch, Durham, and Westminster were called the nunneries. In the latter church they are said to have been occupied on certain occasions by the nuns of Barking and Kilburn. At Notre Dame, Paris, within the present century they have been used for a similar purpose; triphoriatus or trifariè means a border. The triple arrangement of the base arcade, triforium, and clerestory is analogous to the three storeys of the ark (Compare Ezek. xli. 16; xlii. 3, 6). The nave, aisles, and clerestory are often locally called the upper and lower walks, in distinction to the triforium. At Paisley and in one bay at Ely the clerestory-walk is carried on brackets. The galleried triforium, for the accommodation of spectators, occurs at St. Ambrose (Milan), Amiens, St. Michael's (Pavia), St. Gereon's (Cologne), Coblentz, Tournay, Bonn, Paris, Châlons-sur-Marne, and Laon, and noble galleries exist at Norwich, Ely, and Peterborough. The simply arcaded triforium is found in Cistercian churches, St. Mary Overye, Lausanne, and in the Perpendicular period, except in Spain. At this time the triforium was treated only as a portion of the clerestory window, whereas before it had been designed to combine additional height with constructional security. At Westminster and Lichfield the windows are triagonal, and round at Southwell. At Brioude there is a fireplace in the tribune or triforium of the transept, of the thirteenth century.

Trikerion. (Gr. *tria kerata*.) A three-headed taper used by the bishop when he signs the Gospel crosswise, to show that the doctrine of the Trinity is contained therein at the Trisagion. He previously crosses the Gospel with the dikerion or double taper, to represent the illumination to pass both in heaven and earth by the incarnation of the Lord Jesus in His two natures.

Trinitarians *or* **Robertines.** An order for the redemption of captives, founded by Robert Rokesby at Mottingden in 1160.

Trinity Sunday. The office of the Holy Trinity was composed by Alcuin in the reign of Charlemagne; it was not observed at Rome in the Pontificate of Alexander III., and was even in 1268 in England known as the Octave of Pentecost. In some churches the festival was kept on this Sunday, or on the Sunday next before Advent. In 1305 it was established by Pope Benedict XIII. as it is now observed, or, according to others, by John XXIII., in 1334, or by Thomas A'Becket.

Triptych. A picture with two folding-doors set over altars. A Russian example is in the museum of the Society of Antiquaries of London.

Triquetral (*i.e.*, three-cornered). A censer used by Bishop Andrewes, in which the clerk put incense at the reading of the first lesson.

Trisagion. A hymn attributed to the Patriarch Proclus in the fourth century; mentioned in the Apostolical Constitutions. Theodosius the Younger ordered it to be sung in the Liturgy, after his vision of a child chanting it during an earthquake at Constantinople. At the Council of Chalcedon the form was amplified thus—"Holy God, Holy and Mighty, Holy and Everlasting, have mercy upon us," as a proclamation of the Trinity. Then, to oppose the heresy of the Theopaschites, the words "Christ the King, who was crucified for us," were inserted before the "have mercy upon us," but many churches rejected them, and in their place in Europe was sung "Holy Trinity have mercy upon us." After the Preface this hymn was always sung, and, according to St. Cyril of Jerusalem, St. Chrysostom, and the Second Council of Vaison, also at all Masses, Matin Lenten or of the dead; the Epinikion, the same as the Western Tersanctus, the triumphal hymn, and the longer and more modern, the Trisagion; the former to be used at the Masses of the faithful, and the latter at those of catechumens.

Trisantia. One side of a cloister, mentioned at St. Alban's at an early date; a recess in it screened off in Clugniac houses.

Triumphal Arch. The division between the nave and transept in old St. Peter's at Rome, containing a rood beam.

Tropar. A Greek service-book containing anthems, hymns, and responses, the trope being a short hymn not taken from Scripture; several made an ode, and many of the latter made a canon. The Cathisma was one during which the congregation sat; at the Catavasia both choirs came down together and stood singing it in the midst of the church; the Theotokion celebrated St. Mary, the Stauro-Theotokion, her standing at the cross.

Trope. (*Tropos*, a change.) A verse sung on great festivals immediately after the Introit, as if a continuation of it; or interposed in the Kyrie and Gloria. It was at first a mere modulation, to which words were set afterwards, so that it may have derived its name from the change into a kind of antiphon. The trope is not more ancient than the eleventh century, and probably commenced in the monastery of St. Gall. The Council of Limoges in 1031 mentions its use in secular churches. At Rouen, on certain days, acclamations or praises were added to the trope, and such feasts were said to be held with trope and laud. At Lyons, Sens, and Soissons the trope was such words as " Orbis factor, fons bonitatis," put between Kyrie and Eleison.

Truce of God. A suspension of hostilities for hours or days, in the eleventh century, and recommended by the Council of Lateran in 1179.

Trullus. The dome under which is the choir in a Greek church.

Trunk. (*Truncus;* Fr. *tronc*.) (1.) An alms-box made out of the trunk of a tree. (2.) A low seat, at which the novices did penance at Bury St. Edmund's, in the choir.

Tudor Flower. An acute-angled fleur-de-lys, used as cresting in Perpendicular work.

Tufa. A porous stone (called travertine when compact) found in calcareous streams, and used, from its lightness, in vaultings, as at Bredon and Canterbury.

Tunic *or* **Tunicle.** (*Roccus*, subtile; the mass-cope.) (1.) A dress worn by the subdeacon, made originally of linen, reaching to the feet, and then of an inferior silk, and narrower than the dalmatic of the deacon, with shorter and tighter sleeves, and devoid of the stripes or embroidery of that vestment,

but for some centuries the assimilation has grown so complete as to render the slight difference subsisting almost im-
perceptible. Bishops wore both the tunicle and dalmatic
at Pontifical Mass. (2.) Tunicle, the parva tunica, or cotta,
a linen habit reaching to the knees, used at all kinds of services by simple clerks and others; it differed from the rochet,
it being fuller. Amalarius speaks of a blue tunicle of jacinth
colour, or subucula, worn by the bishop, Rupert says, under
the chasuble, as emblematical of the seamless robe of Christ.
(3.) A dress worn by monks.

Truckle- *or* **Trundle-bed.** That used by an attendant, and run
under the standing bed when not required.

Typica. Ps. ciii., cxlvi., and the Blessings on the Mount, recited on Sundays from Low Sunday to Trinity Sunday in the
Greek Church, instead of the ordinary two anthems.

Typicum. (1). A book of rubrics and ecclesiastical order, directing what shall be said or omitted. (2.) Anthem from
the Psalms, sung on twelve vigils in the Greek Church.

Ultramontanes. The Italian theologians who uphold the para-
mount authority of the Pope, in distinction to the Cismon-
tines (on the north side of the Alps); the French and German doctors who regard the general council as superior to
the Papal decisions.

Umbrella. A privilege of bishops in Italy, in processions and
ecclesiastical sittings and acts: a kind of baldacchino of red
velvet, with golden summits, erected in 1550 over the altar
of Winchester College; in 1641 it was called " a canopy over
the altar, with traverses and curtains on each side and before
it." In the eighteenth century it was used to shelter the
officiant at funerals.

Uniformity, Acts of, are 1 Eliz., c. ii., and 13 & 14 Charles
II., c. iv.

University. (*Generale* or *solemne studium.*) An assembly of
students of all countries, students in every branch of learning
in one great society, under one government, having a common chest, their own seal, and place of business. Camden
says the term was generally used in the reign of Henry III.
During the twelfth century, besides our two English Universities, Paris for theology, Bologna for civil law, and Salerno
for medicine were eminent. Italians, Spaniards, and French

rallied to Bologna, the English and Dutch went to Paris. Spain and Germany had universities of schools, where the students formed part of the corporation. Paris and England had universities of masters only; some in Germany and France were of either kind. Paris had four "nations"; Oxford was divided into two—Northerns and Southerns. The two earliest Colleges in our Universities were organized in the thirteenth century. Canons and beneficed clergy were allowed by the bishop's licence to be absent from their duties to read in the University, sometimes for three years.

Ursulines. An order combining conventual seclusion with education; called after St. Ursula of Naples, and founded in 1537 by Angela de Brescia.

Use. The ritual of a Church. In England there were five—those of York, Lincoln, Hereford, Bangor, and Salisbury: the latter was followed in the south of England; at Durham, out of jealousy to York; and in Portugal from 1300, owing to the influence of Philippa, Duchess of Lancaster. St. Paul's, London, was made the model of Peterborough and Carlisle at the Reformation. Lincoln Use was followed in some parts of Scotland. *See* LITURGIES.

Vacantivi. Clerks who left their diocese.

Vacant Sundays. The four Sundays after Ember weeks, which have no proper office, owing to the protracted service of ordination on the previous night; the Sundays between Christmas and January 1st; and the Fourth Sunday in Advent—the former because preoccupied with another office, and the latter because the Pope devoted himself to almsgiving, as on Vacant Saturday, the day before Palm Sunday.

Vair. Minever, the white fur of the ermine, with spots of the black wool of Lombardy lambs.

Valance. Say, or serge, for bed-curtains or valances. A stuff made at Valence or Valencia.

Vault. (*Volta.*) (1.) A vaulted chamber, like the refectory of St. Martin's, Dover, or a crypt. (2.) (*Testudo, fornix;* Sp. *boveda;* It. *volta* or *cielo;* Fr. *volte;* Germ. *Gewolbe.*) The stone covering of an alley, nave, or choir. The earliest kind was cylindrical, and called barrel or waggon. Groined vaulting is where vaults intersect each other at right angles. At a later date ribs were introduced to cover the groins in the Early English style, and as thus it consists of four or five or more vaults, it is called quadripartite, quinquepartite, etc. In the Perpendicular style pendants and fantracery were introduced. The span at Gerona is 73 feet; Toulouse, 63 feet; Perpignan, 60 feet; York, 52 feet; Chartres, 50 feet; Amiens, 49 feet; Paris, 48 feet; Cologne, 44 feet; Canterbury, 43 feet.

Veil. (1.) A cloth, called by St. Gregory the white birrus, shot with red thread in memory of Christ's Passion, and worn like a crown to preserve the chrism by the baptized; it was laid aside with the albe. In 1090 it fell into disuse, as the chrism then was wiped off with some light material like silk. St. Augustine and Theodore of Canterbury mention them. (2.) A hanging in front of a church door, such as Nepotian was so careful to see in their place, as St. Jerome says. (3.) Bankers at the sides of altars, let down when the priest entered the sanctuary, and raised every Saturday during Lent when the Sunday office began. Dossals and frontal veils (so called in allusion to the Temple veil) were also in use at the high-altars of large churches until the end of the sixteenth century. Three ancient pillars with carved capitals, used for the veils, remain at Monreale. (4.) Curtains of great richness, used only in Lent; one veiled the altar, a second the sanctuary, and a third the choir. They were raised by the subdeacons or porters, according to the Council of Narbonne, to represent the removal of the veil (Ephes. ii. 14). They were succeeded by permanent screens; hence in Spain, as marriages were permitted or forbidden, such seasons were called veilings open or shut. (5.) The bridal veil (*poele*, *palla*), mentioned by St. Ambrose, and worn (as Durandus says) as a symbol of maiden modesty and obedience to the husband. (6.) A nun's veil (*maforte*, *mitra*; *flammeum*, because of the colour of pure flame), an ornament used in the time of St. Gregory, and given only to a woman of twenty-five years of age, and, except in case of extreme sickness, at no time but Epiphany, an Apostle's day, or Low Sunday, in 740. The colour was sometimes purple. (7.) A scarf in which, at a solemn High Mass, the subdeacon muffles his arms and shoulders as a sign of humility and reverence when he elevates the paten, to announce the time of communion; also that used by a priest to envelope his hands at the time of the Benediction. (8.) *Dominicalis*, a woman's veil or coif in church, and at the time of communion, called in Provence a domino, and ordered by the Councils of Autun (578) and Angers. (9.) The churching cloth, used in the latter half of the seventeenth century at the churching of women in England; it was of white damask, fringed. (10.) A black veil for the head, used by the Greek priest in reading the prophecies, in allusion to 2 Cor. iii. 13–16. (11.) In the Greek Church three communion veils are lifted over the eucharistic bread on a paten by the cruciform and folding star —(1) the diskalumma, (2) katapetasma, (3) the nebula or aër, being made of very fine material, and of cloud-like appearance, in allusion to the cloud of Transfiguration. (*See* AIRE, ASTERISK.) (12.) At Christmas and Easter, in France, formerly three veils were laid upon the altar and then removed— (1) black, to represent the time before the law; (2) pale, to signify the time of the law; (3) red, showing the time of grace; one was removed at each nocturn of Christmas. (13.) A covering for the cross and images during Lent. This, Cranmer says, "with the uncovering of the same at the resurrection, signifies not only the darkness of infidelity which covered the face of the Jews in the Old Testament, but also the dark knowledge they had of Christ, who was the perfection and end of the law, and not yet opened until the time of His death and resurrection. The same is partly signified by the veil which hid the secret of the Holy of Holies from the people." Becon says that they were covered to stir the people to repentance, that they might "be found worthy against Easter, *i.e.* against the time of passing and going out of this world, clearly to behold and openly to see in the kingdom of heaven the shining face of God and His saints;" "to declare the mourning and lamentâtion of sinners for their ungodly manners, the clothes that are hanged up in church have painted on them nothing else but the pains, torments, passion, bloodshedding, and death of Christ, that the mind should be fixed only on the passion of Christ." Beleth says the ornaments of the altar were veils, crosses, shrines, gospels, and reliquaries; and in Lent two veils were used, one round the choir and the other before the altar, which were folded back on Sundays, and at Tenebræ on Maundy Thursday all were removed, in memory of the rend-

ing of the Temple veil, except one altar-cloth, which commemorated the seamless vestment of Christ. He also mentions a veil, a pall, or table of metal before the altar, and a
veil which was removed from the front of the crucifix, behind which a pall was set, to show that the mystery of the
passion had been made manifest. In some churches banners of triumph were hung about the cross. (14.) A veil
for the chalice, which in England was elevated without it;
in some French churches the chalice was covered at that
time (Gr. *poterio kalumma*). (15.) (*See* CORPORAX CUPS.)
Sindon, pyx, or Corpus Christi cloth. At Winchester College
a canopy of linsey-wolsey, powdered with stars of gold, was
used to fall over the pyx on Palm Sunday and Corpus Christi;
a Sacrament-cloth of guipure lace, with a fringe of gold and
scarlet, and gilded balls at the four ends, and a small central
aperture for the chain, remains at Hesset, of the sixteenth
century. Another is in the South Kensington Museum.

Verdour. Hangings for a bed, representing trees and grass.

Verger. (*Virgifer, bastinarius.*) A servant of the church who
carries the virge, usually a staff of silver, the fasces of the
dean and chapter, a sign of their authority, and formerly
hollow, and containing the rod with which the offending
choir-boys were whipped. At Wurtzburg the postulant for
a canonry had to run, bare to the waist, between two lines
of canons, who struck him sharply with virges. The verger
precedes the bishop, dean, and canon in residence in processions, there being usually one for each of those persons.
When Bishop Sherborne visited his cathedral pontifically
he was preceded by a verger ringing a small handbell. At
Palermo an apparitor or beadle carries a silver mace before
the canons. When Bishop Cameron, in the fifteenth century, visited Glasgow, he was preceded by twelve fertors
carrying his staff, and eleven large maces were borne before
him. The Suisse in foreign cathedrals is dressed in an old-
fashioned habit and cocked hat, and carries a halberd and
sword.

Veronica. (Lat. *vera*, true; Gr. *icon*, image or likeness; Fr.
suaire.) The sudary of the holy Veronica. A towel or
handkerchief with which a Jewish woman, named Prounice
or Berenice (Latinized Veronica), who had been cured of the
issue of blood, is said to have wiped the face of our Lord

when going to His Passion by the Way of Sorrows. Wet with blood and spitting, on its triple folds His likeness was stamped, and the cloth was brought in a wooden coffer from Palestine to Rome, and eventually removed from the Rotunda to St. Peter's, where it is still preserved under the charge of the canons, having been placed by Urban VIII. in an upper chapel adjoining one of the great piers which support the dome. It is exhibited in a silver case ten times in the year to the Pope, cardinals, and faithful, who are placed in the nave. As early as the fourteenth century painters represented a woman holding a linen cloth, on which is a radiating face, surrounded by a nimbus, with the cross. The attribute has become the subject, and the accessory the principal object; the inanimate substance has taken life, and the woman is only known as the Veronica. There were icons or veils preserved at Laon, Cologne, and Milan. The earliest fresco of our Lord is in the catacomb of Calixtus, of the fourth century. There are several so-called portraits—one said to have been sent by our Lord to Abgarus, king of Edessa (first mentioned by Evagrius, who died 590), in the church of St. Sylvester in Capite; another, by St. Luke or angels, in the Benedictine sacristy at Vallombrosa; and a third, given by St. Peter to Pudens, shown every year by the Abbot of St. Praxedes on Easter Day; and a fourth in St. Bartholomew's, Genoa. They are all indistinct and faded, and the latter was covered with a crystal by Innocent III. All the portraits painted by order of Constantine reproduced the portraiture given in a letter by Lentulus to the Roman senate, and the familiar features since the eighth century follow the description of St. John Damascene.

Versicle. Written as V. (1.) A portion] of a psalm, *e.g.*, " O Lord, open thou our lips." (2.) A short antiphon sung towards (*versus*) the altar. (3.) The prayer or acclamation at the beginning of the Hours. The word is derived from verse, a sentence in a single line. Cassian first mentions " O God, make speed," and St. Benedict added the response, " O Lord, open thou." The verse of Compline, " Converte nos," is first alluded to by Durand in the eighteenth century.

Vesperal. A division in an antiphonar containing the chants for Evensong.

Vessels for Holy Oil were arranged like three towers round a central crown-topped spire, with which they are connected. Each contained a small phial, which could be detached when wanted, and a spoon. One of these phials held the oil for baptism; a second, chrism for confirmation; and the third, oil for the sick. They were made in copper or silver-gilt. At Laon they were kept in an aumbry next the piscina, but very frequently, as in the Sainte-Chapelle at Paris, and usually in England, this recess was in the north wall of the sanctuary. The ampulla for chrism was sometimes made of ivory and crystal, to distinguish it from the vessels containing the oils.

Vessels, Sacred, of the Altar. The priests and Levites only might touch the vessels of the Temple (Is. lii. 11). Subdeacons were forbidden to handle the plate or enter the sacristy by the Council of Laodicea; a reader or ostiarius, by the Second Council of Rome; and all not in orders, by the Council of Agde.

Vexilla Regis Prodeunt. (The kingly banners forward go.) A hymn sung in procession on Good Friday before the Mass of the Presanctified.

Vexillum. (A banner.) (1.) The crucifix carried before the Pope, with the figure towards him, to remind him that he should have Christ crucified (who is always regarding His Church) ever before his eyes. (2.) The banneroll attached to a pastoral staff. (3.) A processional banner.

Viaticum. (Gr. *ephodion*.) A word mentioned by Bede, Egbert, the Council of Auxerre, and Giraldus Cambrensis, and rendered by Bishop Jewell "voyage provision," or "viand for the way." It was originally the Communion sent to excommunicate persons at the point of departing, but is now the last Communion, where the sick man cannot long survive or be able again to receive. The custom is traceable to the Councils of Nicæa and Vaison, 442. By the Capitulars, priests carried the Eucharist about them for emergencies, and St. Laurence, an archbishop of the twelfth century, did so. By the Council of Westminster, 1138, the Eucharist was to be reserved for not more than eight days, and then carried by a deacon, priest, or any person in case of necessity; but in 1195 the Synod of York required a priest in his habit, with a houselling light, and that of Durham enjoined the use of stole and surplice, a bell and lantern, and a pyx and burse, and clean linen cloth; in 1322 a processional cross was required when the Viaticum was carried. Cardinal Pole desired "a little sacring-bell" to be used before it. In 1281 Peckham recommended that it should be given to persons in a frenzy or alienated in mind with good assurance. Archbishop Edmund required the use of a clean, decent box and a pure linen cloth, and desired, like the Synod of Exeter, in 1287, the ablutions of the priests' fingers to be given in a silver or tin cup to the sick. In the Greek Church seven priests in the patient's room consecrate the holy oil with the euchelaion.

Vicar. (1.) Pope Boniface III. called himself the Vicar of St. Peter. The Vicar of Christ was a title assumed in the thirteenth century. (2.) The archpriest who presented candidates for Orders to be examined by the archdeacon, and in the Celtic monasteries of Northumbria offered nuns at their profession. (3.) A substitute in a parish. The word originally signified a temporary vicar or assistant curate, as in 1261 we read of vicars or chaplains of parish churches. (4.) A perpetual vicar. The representative of a rector as regards cure of souls. Usually the permanent incumbent appointed by a monastery or college which held the great tithes after they were impropriated. The word in this sense of a perpetual curate is not earlier than the thirteenth century. In 1237 he was required to be competent to take the diaconate at the following ordination, and to swear residence. His assistant in 1306 is called a deputy. In 1268 the Cistercians were compelled by Othobon to nominate, within six months, vicars who should be instituted by the bishop. In 1439 the voluntary offerings, which formed a chief source of a vicar's income, had become greatly diminished, owing to the spread of Lollardism. Perhaps the earliest intimation of a subordinate cyric-then or church-minister is in 963, when a mention occurs of "young men" or juniors appointed to officiate and minister to God in certain newly-built churches. In 1222 no perpetual vicar was to have a less income than five marks a year, but in the fifteenth century a temporary vicar had eight or ten. (5.) A substitute in a cathedral. When the common table and home was given up by canons, and the common fund, about the middle of the

twelfth century, was divided into prebends or portions, hired
deputies were employed by those absent from the cathedral
to chant in their place in the daily services, and this led to
the permanent establishment of vicars-choral in the following century. At first these substitutes were only temporary,
but about a century later the rule of having a vicar became
permanent. These assistants within another century had procured incorporation as a college under their own president,
and holding their own lands, just as the chapter rendered itself
as independent as possible of the bishop, and each member
of it secured his own separate prebend, patronage, and local
jurisdiction. Each dignitary and prebendary had his vicar;
the former were called subdean, subchanter, vice-chancellor,
and sub-treasurer. These were, in fact, minor canons celebrating at the high-altar in the absence of their masters.
In some cathedrals there were perpetual vicars, who received
a certain portion in the church from a foundation; they
were actual ministers of the church, who attended all the
Hours. Again, there were minor or petty vicars, who were
removable, vicars of the first, second, and third form, according to their place in church : these ordinary vicars-
choral, and conducts stipendiaries without endowment, received from their masters stall wages, which ranged from
£40 to 40d.; two marks at Wells; at Exeter, five shillings
quarterly; forty shillings a year at Lincoln. At Urgel they
were called statores, from standing in their masters' places
or stations. After their maintenance at their masters' table
fell into disuse, along with personal household service, they
received a payment called quotidian, varying from 1d. to 3d.
a day, dependent on their attendance at High Mass and the
Hours, known as petty commons, and an allowance of bread,
and at an early date wine or ale. If they officiated as priests
they had an additional mark. Those in deacon's and subdeacon's orders acted as gospellers and epistolers; those below this rank served as ministers at the altar and instrumental and vocal musicians. At Canterbury two sackbut-
teers (players upon the pipe; Sp. *sackbuche*) and two
corneteers were appointed by Laud's statutes, and about the
same time instrumental music was in use at Exeter, Lincoln,
and Westminster, and at Durham after the Reformation, and
even now drums, trumpets, and trombones are used at St.

Paul's and Westminster on special occasions. (*See* CHO-
RISTERS.) Within memory parish churches retained musicians. Vicars were admitted to probation for a fortnight
without wages if unknown, or if known with pay at once,
by the dean, præcentor, or succentor, and the majority of
the residentiaries or vicars, and for one year were engaged in learning the antiphonar, psalter, and hymnal under
the charge of an auscultator appointed by the præcentor.
If guilty of absence or misbehaviour they were discommonsed;
if they revealed chapter secrets, were excommunicated; and
if absent from choir during six months, were deprived. The
tabler marked their names for weekly duty, and if they sang
or read badly at Hereford the deacon or subdeacon was
flogged on the bare back "like the religious" by the hebdomadary; a priest was compelled to beg pardon on bended
knees; those in inferior orders received a yet sharper chas-
tisement. If any failed in reverence to the dean, they stood
for a day and night before the rood-light. The vicars furnished the weekly hebdomadary, celebrant, and his assistants, and the rectors of choir on festivals, and attended all
processions. The chamberlain, custos, or hebdomadary
noted their absence. If a canon did not appoint a vicar
within a month (or two months in some churches) after his
installation or the demise of a vicar, the patronage lapsed to
the dean. The vicar could be dismissed by his master at a
notice of three months, but the dean and chapter might
retain him at their own charges. In most cathedrals they
formed what was called the lower chapter. At Wells there
were fifty-two, incorporated in 1347 under a principal; at
York there were thirty-five (with nine persons, six deacons
and subdeacons, two vestry clerks, twelve thuriblers and
choristers), incorporated in 1252, and again in 1461 under a
custos; at Exeter there were twenty-four (and twelve secondaries), incorporated under a custos in 1401; at Chichester
there were twenty-nine (and twelve choristers), incorporated in 1277, and 1334 under a principal; at Lincoln
there were twenty-five, incorporated under a principal in
1396; at Lichfield there were thirty-one, incorporated in
1240; at Hereford, twenty-seven, incorporated under a
custos in 1396; at St. Paul's, thirty vicars; and at Salisbury, twenty-one priests, eighteen deacons, and eleven sub-

deacons, incorporated under a procurator in 1410; at Kilkenny there were four vicars and four stipendiaries, founded in a college in the thirteenth century; at St. Patrick's, sixteen, incorporated in 1431; at Waterford there were twelve, and at Aberdeen twenty vicars. Vicars wore a surplice, a black almuce of cloth or Calabrian fur, and by day a doubled cap, but no hood. The title of lay clerk or vicar, as distinct from priest-vicars, dates only from the Reformation, and a trace of his having once been in minor orders lingers in the unseemly practice of a layman singing the litany in some places with a priest.

In the foreign cathedrals the system of vicars also exists there are mansionarii or assisii in Spain and Italy; perpetual vicars, the inferior beneficiaries, called in Spain chaplains of the cope, numerales at Nola, demies; at Beauvais, Sens, Seez, and Auxerre; quartans; millenarii and centenarii at Palermo; portioners, assizars, from their holding a portion or allotment of food of the commune, and mace canochi (canons of the massa or common fund) at Milan and Genoa; and machicots at Paris. Stipendiaries having no freehold were called altarists at Wells, and frequenters of choir at Hereford. At Christchurch and Manchester, both collegiate churches, the vicars are called chaplains, as at Rouen, where there were forty-eight chaplains choral, who lived in four colleges, sixty-nine chanting priests, and seventy chaplains, like English annuellars, who took their titles from the chapels in the cathedral. At Pisa there were two classes, that of the quinterno or register being the higher, and having a share in the daily distribution. In Germany the name was convicars, socii vicarii, as at Salisbury in former times. At Paris the perpetual priests, and at Vienne the chanter-priests sat in the upper stalls. At Lyons, Angers, Bourges, and Rouen they were called chanters, or semi-prebendaries; at Dunkeld and St. Patrick's, choristers or personists. In 1480 the vicars of Chichester wore uniform caps or almuces; and in 1391 vicars of York were forbidden to use clogs or pattens (long-peaked boots) in choir. *See* ALMUCE.

Vicars' College. The residence of the non-capitular members of a cathedral; at Wells the court, entered by a gate-house and lined with the houses of the vicars, remains, with its hall, chapel, and library; at Hereford it forms a beautiful cloistered quadrangle, with the same adjuncts; at Chichester and Exeter the halls of the fourteenth century only have been preserved; and at York the bedern retains considerable portions of the ancient buildings. Until the civil wars the collegiate life was everywhere maintained, and at Hereford so lately as 1828. At Lincoln Bishop Oliver built the college. There were colleges at St. David's, Armagh, Dublin, Kilkenny, Limerick, Cashel, Tuam, Cork, Cloyne, Lismore, Ross, Ardfert, and Glasgow at the close of the fifteenth century.

Vicars Apostolic. Eight were appointed in England and Wales by the Pope in 1840; there were four in 1688, superintendents of districts. The vicars apostolical of Arles, Seville (in the fourth and fifth centuries respectively), Mayence, and Canterbury first received the pall, the first having it *c.* 500; Mans in 685, and all metropolitans of Gaul in 743 were given the privilege. In the time of Henry I. the Archbishop of York paid £10,000 for it. Gregory VII. made the grant of the pall the condition of a metropolitan's right to consecrate churches or ordain clergy.

Vicars Episcopal. The Greek chorepiscopus. In Africa the city priest was one of the cathedral body, who ministered in the adjoining villages. According to Sidonius, he was the bishop's chaplain, vidam, notary, treasurer, theologian, and steward.

Vicar-General. A principal official, now called chancellor of the diocese; an ecclesiastical judge in the bishop's court, as the official belonging to the archdeacon.

Vicars of the Holy See. First appointed in Gaul by Pope Zosimus in 417.

Vice-Dean. An annual officer elected from the residentiaries in cathedrals of the new foundation, ranking next the dean, acting as his representative and locum tenens, and regarded as a paterfamilias. In his absence the senior residentiary acts; he usually sits in the north-west stall, although that is properly appropriated to the hebdomadary or canon in residence. At Pistoia a prefect of choir is annually elected, and the city prior, senior dignitary, or senior canon is the deputy of the dean when absent.

Vidam. (*Vice dominus*, vice-lord.) (1.) The bishop's steward in the administration of the Church revenues, as the viscount represented the count; at Rheims and Chartres the vidams

raised their office into a fief. (2.) The provost or bailiff of
the capitular rents, as at Lincoln, Cambrai, Rouen, Chartres,
Sens, Laon, Beauvais, Amiens, Parma, Piacenza, Halberstadt,
and Münster. (3.) Heirs of founders of religious houses who
had certain rights over their estates and attached churches.

Vigil. (1.) An office sung anciently at night. Honorius of
Autun says that in former times there was on great festivals
an office sung by the bishop before midnight, and another
by the clergy about that time, and the people watched all
night in praise; but the custom ended in dancing, drinking,
singing, and impurity, and was therefore abolished, so that
the day of the previous fast, which was the compensation for
its disuse, alone retained the name of vigil. In Beleth's
time, in Poitou, all the young people, with players and
minstrels, attended on the day before the feast of dedication
of a church. (2.) The office for the dead. (3.) The night
watch. St. Ambrose, in his commentary on the 109th
Psalm, says, " We fast on the Saturday, keep vigils, and remain in prayer through the night." St. Augustine has a
homily on the vigils of St. John Baptist and SS. Peter and
Paul; St. Bernard, on those of St. Andrew and the Nativity.
They were called vigils because the faithful passed the night
before a festival watching, in prayers, hymns, spiritual reading, and fast; they also had the name of lucernariæ preces
or gratiarum actiones, the prayer and thanksgiving of
lamp-light. (4.) The fast-days before a festival. The holydays of the English Church having vigils correspond nearly
to the doubles of the ancient use, and on such days the
first Vespers of the feast commence on the evening next
before, but if a Sunday intervenes, then on the Saturday
also. The festivals of Circumcision, Epiphany, and the
three feasts of St. Stephen, St. John, and Holy Innocents,
which follow in sequence, as occurring within the octave
or season of Christmas; St. Mark, SS. Philip and James,
and St. Barnabas, falling within Easter and Whitsuntide;
St. Michael and All Angels, as those who have not entered
into joy through suffering; the Conversion of St. Paul, as not
connected with martyrdom; and St. Luke, from the preceding day being that of St. Etheldreda, or because he is not
believed to have been a martyr,—have no vigils. Beleth
says neither St. Barnabas, because he was not of the number

of Apostles, nor St. Matthias, because his festival often fell in Lent, had a vigil. (5.) In Beleth's time the first nocturn and the day before a feast. Vigils, otherwise called watchings (says Cranmer), remained in the calendars upon certain saints' evens, because in old times the people watched all those nights. The vigil begins at Vespers, and lasts till the first Mass of the morrow is said. Beleth says that if a Sunday and vigil coincided, the Vespers of both were said in that order; or, as at Mayence and in minsters, the proper collect of the saint's day with the Magnificat; but if there was no vigil the collect and antiphon were used.

Virtues and Vices. A favourite impersonation under human forms, in the middle ages, as in the chapter-house of Salisbury. Prudentius alludes to figures of Love and Hope, Despair and Hate, in churches; and the Roman de Rose describes personifications of Envy and Sorrow.

Virgin, the Blessed, in the Catacombs, is depicted in a pall, tunic, and dalmatic, and at a later date in a blue mantle, a white veil flowing over the shoulders, an inner tunic scarcely showing, a long wide-sleeved robe, and cincture. The traditional features are copied from a description given by Epiphanius. The portraits attributed to the hand of St. Luke are of the Greek school, of the seventh or eighth century, and were brought to Italy during the crusade after the Latin siege of Constantinople. In the catacomb of St. Agnes, in a mosaic of the fifth century, without nimbi, the Virgin is veiled, and, praying with hands outspread, the Holy Child stands before her. Her old English designation of "Our Lady" is retained in the Table of Lessons. In the ninth century sometimes she appears of advanced age, and sometimes as a queen; and in the seventh century as a central figure among Apostles and saints. The first invocation addressed to her is attributed to Justina, in the Diocletian persecution; the first representation of the Assumption, a legend recorded by Gregory of Tours and John Damascene, is at Assisi; in one of Pisano's frescoes, c. 1230, the Mater Dolorosa is represented, as in St. Luke ii. 35. *See* PIETA.

Virgin Chimes. The bells rung in peal on Christmas Eve.

Visitation. The inspection of a province, diocese, archdeaconry, or parish church. In 1179 Pope Alexander III. forbade, in the Council of Lateran, an archbishop to visit with not more than forty or fifty horses or men, bishops with above twenty or thirty, an archdeacon with more than five or seven, and a rural dean with more than two. This rule was enforced in 1200-1268 in England, and again in 1342, when it is said that archdeacons used to arrive on the previous night at a rectory or vicarage with a numerous retinue and horses, indulging by the way in hunting with hawk and hound; the order was made that the expense thus incurred was to be deducted from his procuration, and that if he visited several churches in a day they should all contribute their quota to make up a single procuration. Innocent III. and Gregory X. forbade procurations in money, but they were allowed in 1298 by Pope Boniface VIII. In 1250 his namesake of Canterbury was repulsed before the doors of St. Bartholomew's, when his breastplate was seen gleaming through the folds of his rochet. In some cases the sum was fixed by immemorial custom or privilege. In England they paid eighteenpence for the archdeacon and his horse, and one shilling for each of the other horses and men. The archdeacon might require supper and dinner, but was not allowed to invite guests. The Council of Toledo forbade the payment of procurations if the visitation was not duly made. In the early English Church, as for instance in 747, bishops were required to make an annual visitation, teaching in assemblies of the people convened by him. By the sixtieth Canon they must hold triennial confirmations. In the old foundations a bishop might visit triennially with eight persons and demand two entertainments. By the Laudian Statutes of Canterbury the archbishop may hold a visitation, with a retinue of thirty persons, and demand two refections, once in every three years; and in the new foundations the bishop may visit as often, with eight or ten persons, and, if desired, by the dean or two canons.

Voice Tube. Set at an angle in confessionals. Said to exist at Beauchamp Chapel, Warwick, Yarmouth, Colton, and Hagham, on the north side of chancel.

Volowing. From the response "Volo," baptism was called volowing, and the priest a volower.

Voluntary. A piece of music played on the organ after the Psalms, and so called because the choice of the music is left to the organist. It is a kind of gradual, accompanying the reader to the lectern or eagle. It should cease when he reaches the desk.

Voussoir. (*Claveau.*) A wedge-shaped stone used in the construction of an arch or vault.

Vulgate (*i.e.* for vulgar or common use). The Latin version of the Bible, by St. Jerome, used in the Roman Church. The authorized edition is dated 1592.

Waits. (1.) Watchmen, from *guet*, a sentry, outpost, or night-watch. There is a waits' tower at Newcastle. At York they were minstrels who assisted the choristers in the minster. At Durham they wore a regular livery and a silver badge. (2.) Musical watchmen at York, who played on the cornet, fiddle, curtel, and theorbo to pipe the Hours: hence their conversion into minstrels. (3.) Angelic musicians with horns represented on corbels and cielings.

Wake. (Goth. *weihan*, to consecrate.) The anniversary of the dedication of a church; the vigil and revel on the day, also called revel-day and feast-day. It was usually kept, for convenience of people meeting, between Lady Day and Michaelmas, but at Chichester in October. The Irish call it a " patron " (saint's day). In 1229 in the diocese of Worcester every altar had its patron's name written round it. In 1225 wrestling matches, lawsuits, and dances were forbidden in Scottish churches and cemeteries, and in 1364 the Primate in England prohibited the mummeries of the Feast of Fools on January 1, sports, and raising rams upon wheels, and follies. In 1367 Archbishop Thoresby condemned the indecent merriment at vigils of the dead.

Wall Arcading. A series of niches added as an ornament in the interior walls of aisles. At Leuchars, and All Saints', Stamford, it adorns the exterior of the church. At Battle, Merton, Rochester, and Brecon there is a very lofty series of arcading.

Wall-Paintings were added at an early date to ornament the building and teach the people. It was not till the close of the thirteenth century that the hideous practice of whitewashing churches became common. St. Wilfred, however, employed it in England, whilst Benedict Biscop painted the walls of his churches with figures of our Lord, the Apostles, St. Mary, the incidents of the Gospel and Revelation, and the harmony of the two Testaments. St. Gregory of Tours and St. Paulinus mention pictures near the altar, probably on the ciborium, and also on the walls. The Popes John III. and Pelagius II. adorned the churches of Rome with mosaics, and the catacombs with paintings. The painting in the underground church of St. Nazarus at Verona is said to be of the sixth or seventh century. Charlemagne sent out royal envoys as commissioners to inspect yearly the churches and paintings on vaults and walls. There is a remarkable series of wall-paintings on the clerestory of Battle Church, of the twelfth century, and some fine specimens at Winchester. A common embellishment was the morality of the Trois Morts et Trois Vifs, the living in their pride and only skeletons in their death, as at Bardwell, Charlwood, and Ditchingham; the Dance of Death, as at Croydon, Hexham, Newark, Salisbury, and Wimborne; the Angelic Hierarchy and legends of saints, as at Barton-Turf, and Carlisle; the Months, as at Salisbury, and on the font of Burnham, Deepdale; the Rota Fortunæ (Wheel of Fortune), at Rochester; the Doom or Last Judgment, and the Tree of Deadly Sins. The Vintage appears on the baptistery of Constantine at Rome. At Royston, Yorkshire, the Creed, the Lord's Prayer, and Ten Commandments are painted in black letter on the chancel walls. At Catfield, Norfolk, there is a most interesting series of mural decorations, and at Exeter the panels above the rood-screen have paintings of the time of Charles I.

Wall Passage. (1.) A covered way, sometimes with an open arcade leading to a refectory pulpit, as at Beaulieu, Chester, and the Minims' Church at Toulouse. (2.) A passage through the triforium for admission to its galleries, in front of the clerestory, used by the sacristan to close the shutters of the windows when unglazed or simply filled with trellice-work, in case of storms; or through the walls of the base storey, as at Westminster, for the supervision of the priests at the minor altars in the chantry chapels. At Marburg there is an external passage all round the church in front of the windows, with apertures through the buttresses, and another in the lower storey, no buildings being allowed to stand before it. These were intended for the use of processions carrying the relics of St. Elizabeth in sight of thousands of pilgrims assembled in the open air below. An altar is placed in the whispering gallery of Gloucester, a passage formed above the porch of the Lady-chapel. In the choir and transept aisles of Westminster and in the chapter-house of York there are wall passages. The former are said to have been used for purposes of supervision.

Warden (1) of the Courts, or Curiarius. At Abingdon a monk, who had charge of the court of the abbey, acted as hospitaller, and had charge of the larder and granary. (2.) The title of heads of colleges at Winchester and Oxford. (3.) The principal of the vicars at Exeter, Hereford, and St. Paul's.

Watchers, or the Sleepless. (*Akoimetai.*) (1.) Monks who lived in the monastery of the Stoudion, near Constantinople.ʹ (2.) Also the keepers of the Easter Sepulchre. Usually there were two or three, who sang psalms and maintained the watch. In the early monasteries the cross was laid on Good Friday in a space within the altar, across which a curtain or veil was drawn until Easter morning, but at length the fuller ceremonial already described came into vogue. Moleon says the watchers at Orleans, habited as soldiers, broke their lances before the third stall, in presence of the chanter, and marched round the church with bare swords, and the subdean began the Te Deum. (3.) The keepers of the church, who went the rounds at night. A curious pierced cross in the east wall of the choir of St. David's was used by them for looking eastward or westward.

Watching Lofts, from which the great shrines were observed, remain at Oxford, Nuremberg, Lichfield, St. Alban's, Westminster (over Henry VI.'s chantry), Worcester (in the north aisle), and other places. Those of St. Alban's and Oxford are beautiful structures of wood; that of Worcester is a stone oriel; at Lichfield it is a gallery over the door of the sacristy. A smaller watching loft remains in the transept of St. Alban's. At Bourges there was ˉone on the left side of the altar. (2.) At Exeter, Hereford, and Christchurch (Hants) there is a room over the north porch. The watchers at Lincoln went round the church at nightfall to see that all was safe.

Wayside Chapel. These buildings were commonly attached to bridges at the entrance of towns, as at Rochester, Stamford, Elvet, Durham, Exeter, Newcastle,.and London. Two still exist at Castle Barnard and Wakefield, the latter being of the fourteenth century; it has a remarkable carving of the Resurrection. In France, Switzerland, and Italy they are still common; there is a good example at Pisa, c. 1230. They were frequented sometimes as objects of pilgrimage, but more commonly by pilgrims going and returning from a shrine, and by ordinary travellers when the dangers of the highway and bypaths were considerable. Until recent times the Bishop of Chichester was met at St. Roche's Hill by the civic authorities on his return from Parliament, to congratulate him upon his safe arrival home.

Wayside Cross usually marks the boundary of a monastic or capitular or parochial jurisdiction. One, removed from the site of the abbey, is preserved in Langley Park, Norfolk. The Weeping Cross at Shrewsbury was a station on Corpus Christi Day, when the various guilds, religious and corporate bodies visited it, and there offered prayers for an abundant harvest, returning to hear Mass in St. Chad's. There was a weeping cross at Caen, erected by Queen Matilda in memory of her sorrows at the cruel treatment of her husband, William of Normandy. Sometimes it commemorated a battle, as the Neville's Cross, near Durham, erected in 1346; or a death, like the memorial of Sir Ralph Percy, who was killed on Hedgeley Moor in 1464; or the halting-place of a burial procession, like the fifteen Queen Eleanor Crosses, erected c. 1290, of which only three remain, at Geddington, Northampton, and Waltham. There are remains of wayside crosses near Doncaster, and at Braithwell, with inscriptions inviting the prayers of the passing traveller. In Devonshire alone there are 135 places called by the name of the cross. At Pencran and St. Herbot, Brittany, there are superb specimens; and others, carved richly, at Nevern, Carew, and Newmarket. Valle Crucis Abbey took its name from Eliseg's sepulchral cross of the seventh century. These crosses served as stations at Rogations, preaching places, and at every meeting of roads, to remind the folk who went by of Him who died upon the cross. In Spain, Italy, Lubbeck (near Louvaine), Willebroek, and on Boonhill, Berwickshire, they are memorials of a violent death. By the roadside, and on the rocky summit of the mountain, the wanderer, or the traveller returning home, may greet it from afar, and breathe his prayer. In the life of St. Willebald the English labourers are said to have gathered round a cross in the middle of a field for daily prayer as an ordinary custom.

Weepers. (*Prosklaiontes, flentes.*) The class who lay in the porch weeping, and beseeching the prayers of all who entered.

Wells occur in crypts, some of which were regarded as possessing waters of miraculous powers, as at Pierrefonds; but very possibly they were made in imitation of the baptismal wells of the Catacombs. There was usually a well or fountain in the centre of a cloister garth. There is a highly-enriched well in the south nave-aisle of Strasbourg. Probably these wells, as in cathedrals, served to drain water and supply the baptismal font, as in St. Patrick's, Dublin, and at York, Carlisle, Glasgow, and Winchester. Wells were forbidden to be worshipped without the bishop's authority in 960, 1018, and 1102. In 950 they were made sanctuaries. Round them were frithgeards, for sanctuary, which were reputed holy ground. They were determined as holy by the diocesan, by canons passed in 960 and 1102, and abuses were condemned by the Synod of Winchester in 1308. In many of the small Cornish oratories or baptisteries there is a well. St. Keyne's well was an object of frequent visits, as was St. Winifred's, which was built in 1495, and contains a star-shaped basin, formerly surrounded with stone screens, and contained within a vaulted ambulatory under an upper chapel. In many of the ancient Cornish churches of the fifth and seventh centuries, at Marden, Kirk Newton, and Durham there are wells. Joubert's well at Poictiers is a good medieval specimen. At Ratisbon, in the south wing of the transept, there is a well with figures of the Saviour and the Woman of Samaria. There is an ancient well in the cloister of Arles. St. Aldhelm's well, at Shepton Mallet; St. Chad's, at Lichfield; St. Julian's, at Wellow, Somerset; St. Thomas's, at Canterbury, and numerous others in Wales, are still regarded as possessing medicinal virtues.

Wells of Pity. The five wounds of Christ, distilling His sacred Blood,—for grace, from the right foot; for ghostly comfort, from the left foot; for wisdom, from the right hand; for mercy, from the left hand; and from the heart, for everlasting life: each represented by a drop of blood in rich ruby glass, issuing from a gash which bears a golden crown, as in a pane of Perpendicular glass at Sidmouth.

Whimple. (*Bindæ.*) A linen cloth passing under a nun's chin, and across her brow.

Whipped Work. Needlework.

Whitsun-Day, *or* **Pentecost,** of which the first name is a corruption through different dialectic forms. The commemoration of the descent of the Holy Ghost upon the infant Church, and, according to St. Ambrose and Hilary, instituted by the Apostles (Acts xx. 16.) Hesychius says the first celebration of Holy Communion occurred on it. The Poles called the day Ziclone Swiatke, green holly; the Finns speak of it as Hellun Tai; and the Welsh, as Y Sulgwyn, with the idea of brightness and bliss; but all other European nations preserve the original word Pentecost, either plainly or under a thin disguise. By the law of the Younger Theodosius, the Acts of the Apostles, and by the Council of Toledo, 633, the Revelations were read during the great forty days between Easter and Whitsun-Day; alms were distributed, slaves liberated, and all prayer was made standing. At length, in the fourth century, the word Quinquesima or Pentecost was restricted to the actual day of commemoration, as, in round numbers, the fiftieth after Easter. At Lichfield, 1197, " On Pentecost and the three days ensuing, whilst the Sequence was being sung, clouds were by custom scattered." A circular opening still exists in the centre of the vault of Norwich, and there are similar apertures at Exeter. Through it, on Whitsun-Day, a man habited as an angel was let down to cense the rood. At St. Paul's a white dove was let to fly out of it, and a long censer, reaching almost to the floor, was swung from the west door to the choir steps, " breathing out over the whole church and company a most pleasant perfume." At Dunkirk, in 1662, the ceremonial was always performed during the chanting of the Veni Creator, as in Spain. Balsamon alludes to the loosing of the dove in the East. At Orleans, on Whitsun-Day, during the singing of the Prose, birds, lighted tow and resin, wildfire, and flowers were thrown into the cathedral. At St. Jullien's, Caen, until the end of the sixteenth century, seven kinds of flowers were showered down. In Sweden churches are on this festival still decorated with the wind flower and Pentecost lily—the daffodil. The eves of Easter and Whitsun-Day were occasions of solemn baptism ; and Pentecost was one of the three great feasts appointed for the reception of Holy Communion by several councils, as Gloucester in 1378, and Paris in 1429. At Durham the convent went in procession with two crosses, one of gold and the other of silver, and St. Cuthbert's banner going foremost ; every monk wore a rich cope, and that of the prior, being of cloth of gold, was so heavy that his attendants bore it up on either side, as he walked mitred, and holding his golden cross in his hand ; then followed the shrine of Bede, carried by four monks on their shoulders ; then the picture of St. Oswald, and the cross of St. Margaret, and the relics, through the great north door, down Lydgate, up the South Bailey, and so home through the abbev gates, amid a crowd of spectators. In most cathedrals the country folk came in procession on this day, and Sir Thomas More mourns over the unwomanly songs of the women who followed the cross ; their offerings then made were called Whitsun-farthings or Pentecostals. On Monday, Tuesday, and Wednesday in Whitsun week the famous Whitsun plays of Chester were acted from the fourteenth century until 1574, on Whitsun Wednesday " Whitsonday, the making of the Creed," being performed. Tilts and tourneys amused knights and fair dames ; the morris-dancers delighted the common folks ; and in many a rural parish the church ale, a sort of parochial picnic, was kept in an arbour called Robin Hood's Bower, followed by dancing, bowls, and archery. Eton Montem was kept on Whitsun Tuesday, and until the present century the scholars of Winchester sang their Sweet Song of Home round the college courts on the evening before Whitsuntide, at the time when the swallows come. Whitsun-Day was also called the Easter of Roses. A Whitsun ale was a feast such as that sculptured on the porch of St. John's, Chalke. At Angers, in 1448, the cathedral clerks used to drag out the bed-furniture of the citizens into the streets and deluge it with water.

Widows were consecrated to the estate of perpetual widowhood by the bishop on any day, and in the sacristy only, where they received a peculiar dress if they became ecclesiastical, that is, did not live in the world. From this class deaconesses, priestesses, were selected. They wore at one time the whimple veil and brow-band.

Wig, Episcopal. An innovation of the time of Tillotson, and first laid aside by Dr. Shute Barrington, but Archbishop Sumner was the last Primate and Dr. Monk the latest bishop who used it, although in recent times Bishops Bagot and Blomfield had given it up. In 1668 the use of wigs by priests without episcopal licence was forbidden in France.

Wilkyn. Weak ale, the commons of minor canons of St. Paul's.

Windows. In the Norman period windows are deeply splayed within, often elaborately ornamented with carved mouldings, and sometimes divided by shafts. In Early English they are mostly long, narrow, and lancet-headed, and often grouped together, sometimes under a comprizing arch, or in such proximity that the intervening stonework becomes almost a mullion, and the jambs are shafted. In the Decorated period mullions are used as the window space is enlarged, and filled in the head, which is of different shapes, with tracery. In the Perpendicular style the heads become flattened, the mullions extend from the base to the top, and transoms, often embattled, are constantly employed. A dormer window (*lucarne*) lights rooms under the roof. There is a fine example at Chapel Cleeve.

Wine, Eucharistic. The Greeks use warm water and the Latins cold water in the mixed chalice. Red wine was prescribed in order to avoid accidents by the use of white wine, and also more sensibly to represent the mystery. The Roman Church now uses white wine. In the seventeenth century claret, and in the eighteenth century sack was employed in England.

Women, Churching of (Gr. *to ecclesiasthenai*), is alluded to by Pope Gregory in 601 as the thanksgiving, and by the Emperor Leo's Constitutions, 460. The Salisbury use calls it the purification after childbirth at the church door, evidently in allusion to the purification of St. Mary. In 1549 the "quire door" was substituted for the original place. A veil or churching-cloth, of white material, was used in 1560 by the woman, and a pew or seat was allotted to her from an earlier date.

Wooden Churches. Nether Peevor, built in the time of Henry II.; a chapel at Bury St. Edmund's until 1303; St. Ald-

helm's, Durham, 998 ; St. Stephen's, Mayence, 1011 ; a stud
Lady-chapel at Tykford, and another at Spalding in 1059,
were all built of wood, as many of the Norwegian churches
(like Little Greenstead, 1013 ; Newtown, Montgomeryshire ;
and Newland, Worcestershire) are to this day. The latter
may have been a grange altered to form a church. Ribbes-
ford has wooden nave-arcades. The excellence of English
carpentry is conspicuous in the woodwork preserved to us in
roofs, as at Peterborough, Ely, Old Shoreham, Polebrooke,
Warmington, and St. Mary's Hospital, and the palace kitchen, Chichester ; the Guesten-hall, now in a church, at Worcester ; and St. Mary's, Reading ; doors, as at Beaulieu and
Luton ; cloisters, like the dean's at Windsor, of the fourteenth century ; lychgates, as at Beckenham ; windows, like
those of Englefield ; stalls, as at Lancaster, and some of
Early English date at Salisbury ; screens, as at St. John's
Hospital, Winchester, Roydon, Ewerby, the palace chapel,
Chichester, Lavenham, and St. Margaret's, Lynn ; or early
stall-desks, like one preserved at Rochester of the twelfth
century. The curious "fish-scale" ornament of Norman
spires is an imitation of the oaken shingle so common in
Kent and Sussex, a clear proof that there were earlier spires
of wood. Probably the Gothic stone spire was derived from
Normandy, where the earliest—the pyramid of Than—forms
a succession of steps, of the end of the twelfth century, and
was the prototype of Comornes, Basly, and Rosel. But
England never produced such a grand example of ornamental carpentry and lead as the flèche of Amiens.

Wrest. A screw in a cross or banner-staff.

APPENDIX

ADDITIONS AND CORRECTIONS.

———◆——

P. 7, l. 12. **Archangels** often have a cross on the brow St. Raphael carries a pilgrim's scrip and a fish (Tobit v. 4; vi. 3) Chamael, a staff and cup (St. Luke xxii. 43); St. Haniel, a cross, crown of thorns, and reed (St. Matt. xxvi. 53); St. Jophiel, a flaming sword (Gen. iii. 24).

P. 8, l. 17. Each company contained 6666 legions!

P. 11, l. 33. For 492, read 429.

P. 22, l. 9. For 1458, read 1485.

P. 43. A Frank priest addressed St. Aldhelm as archimandrite. There was an archpriest at Armagh in the thirteenth century.

P. 65. **Bedel.** A verger (from *pedo*, a staff, or *bede*, a prayer). He gave notice for academical devotions at Cambridge in 1276.

P. 74. **Barretta** is the French form of biretta, bis rectum, from its original two-folding sides by which it was handled. It has now four sides and a central tuft, as in the time of Louis XIV. The Council of Basle allowed the use of caps, and they appeared in England *c.* 1224.

P. 80, l. 3, and p. 33, l. 12. The genuflexion at the words "and was made man" was introduced by St. Louis after the First Crusade. Raoul of Tongres mentions that it lasted from "came down from heaven" to "He rose again."

P. 90. **Buttress.** A projection from a wall to give additional support, classed as face- or angle-buttresses, according to their position. Pilaster buttresses are the shallow forms used in the Norman period. For the various characters of buttresses, see under the several styles of architecture. Owing to a defective spacing at Amiens on the north-east angle of the nave, the first side-chapel external to the aisle was erected as a mask. Buttressing arches at Canterbury, Wells, and Salisbury are subsidiary arches set under the grand arches of the lantern.

P. 91, l. 31. The doors are sometimes described as (1) holy, between the bema and choir; (2) angelic, between the choir and nave; (3) royal, between the narthex and nave; and (4) beautiful (or aioi), the outer gate of the narthex.

P. 104, l. 14. *For* Repitz, *read* Hippo.

P. 106, l. 8. *Add*, the Count of Barcelona in that cathedral.

P. 113. **Cardinal.** No doubt the name comes from the assistants at the cardines or horns of the altar.

P. 121, l. 24. *For* canons, *read* catechumens.

P. 122, l. 31. Several abbeys in France became cathedrals, as Aleth, Vabres, Tulle, Luçon, Condom, Castres, and Rochelle. Utrecht was once monastic, and the Benedictines of Ghent in 1536 were made seculars. Farfa, Subiaco, and Urbania were monastic.

P. 142, l. 38. At St. Pierre-sur-Dives, Fontenay, Badeix, and the Jacobines, Toulouse, which is apsidal, of the fourteenth century, pillars divide the building.

P. 145. At Chester there is a chest with ironwork of the thirteenth century.

P. 151. **Chrismal.** A small receptacle for the Host within a pyx.

P. 158, l. 6. Ruffinus mentions the cross over the altar.

P. 177, l. 6. Nuns, in 1279, were confessed near the altar in England.

P. 183. Lyndwood says the priest wore the cope when incensing the altar or saying the collects.

P. 184. Sleeved copes were forbidden in the twelfth century by Pope Innocent III. The Greek bishop's mandyas is waved with red and white bands, like the stream of the word of God which should ever be in his mouth. Festa in Cappis denoted special festivals in secular minsters, when the precious copes were worn by the ministers of choir. On the richness of the sacristy depended the frequency of such days in the local rite. *See* p. 386.

P. 186, l. 26. The other names were the pyx or Corpus Christi cloth. There is one in the South Kensington Museum.

P. 188. **Credence.** In 1641 a "credentia or side-table" was objected to by the Puritan party in England. Prothesis is the term used in St. Matt. xii. 4; Heb. ix. 2.

P. 208. So late as 1611 mention is made of "maidens dancing after evensong in churchyards" in England.

P. 193. Preaching crosses remain at Iron Acton (fourteenth century), and Didmarton. The Sailors' Cross, which mariners saluted when sailing up or down the Severn, remains at King's Weston. The Wayside Cross of Calmsden (fourteenth century) stands near an elm-shaded spring. A cross, formerly at Bristol, is now at Stourhead; and that of Cirencester in Oakeley Park. Yarnton and Bisley retain their crosses.

P. 203, l. 25. At Bamberg there is a large opening to the crypt behind an altar which stands between the two flights of stairs leading up to the choir platform.

P. 223, l. 18. Gabriel Biel. THE SCHOOLMEN (*Scholastici*, doctors of the church schools.) Professors of scholastic, in distinction to positive theology, in which divinity was codified and treated after a philosophic manner. There were three distinct periods, one from Abelard to Albert the Great; the second, from Thomas Aquinas to Durand, the age of Scotists and Thomists; and the last, from Durand (d. 1333) to Gabriel Biel. Most of these teachers were friars—Anselm, Lanfranc, Hildebert of Tours, St. Lombard ("Master of the Sentences"), W. Burly (sometimes called "the Invincible," the title of "Subtle" being given to W. Occham), and G. de Colonna, the "most profound," are among the prominent teachers of the system which St. Bernard and Gregory IX. opposed.

P. 227. Fillets, by the Council of Worcester (1240), were worn for three days, and, if not burned, were retained as cloths on which the priest wiped the chrism from his fingers. The water used in washing away the unction was poured into the font. Staurogatha crosses, of red and white ribbon, are attached for eight days to the dress of the newly-baptized in the Greek Church.

P. 229. The Golden Rose was sent to King Ferdinand of Naples in 1849, and to Queen Isabella of Spain in 1868.

P. 240, l. 19. At Bamberg, a church peculiarly rich in bronze effigies, there is a sarcophagus of the third or fourth century under the tomb of Pope Clement II., who died 1047.

P. 249, l. 14. *Add,* Bishop Beckington's, at Wells.

Ibid. Bona says the Latins elevate the Host and Chalice after consecration, and the Greeks, following ancient precedent, just before the Communion. William of Paris, in the thirteenth century, ordered that a bell should ring at the elevation or just before, to stir the minds of the faithful to prayer.

P. 256. **Emblems.** *Add,* St. Anselm, the apparition of the Madonna; St. Apollinaris, amidst flames; St. Bibiana, a dagger and palm; St. Bridget of Scotland, a flame on her head; St. Corbinian, a bear carrying a wallet; St. Columban, a bear and sun;

St. Emerentiana, stones in her cap ; St. Eulalia, a cross-hook and dove ; St. Eustace, with a bugle ; St. Martina, an iron comb and temple ; St. Maurice, a flag with seven stars ; St. Geneviève, a candle and a demon with bellows ; St. Richard, King, a pilgrim with two sons.

P. 262, l. 4. The antiphon Psalm xlvi. 4, Beleth says, was sung in allusion to this rite.

P. 266, l. 2. *Read*, by the Maronites, and at Lyons.

P. 271, l. 26. The " forty hours," with the salut, special prayers and exposition, were instituted at Rome to counteract the licence of the carnival on the three days previous to Lent.

P. 282, l. 4. There is another at Claydon, Oxon. The Guernsey font is of the time of George II. There are leaden fonts at Walmsford, Wolstane, Pyecombe, Churton, and Brundall.

P. 291. The transept of Boxgrove has screened galleries.

P. 293. There are fine examples of gatehouses at St. Vigor, St. Gabriel, Ardaines, Longues, and Penmarch.

P. 303, l. 8. Strictly speaking, the prayer before meals is the benediction of the table ; the grace (*gratias*), thanksgiving, follows at their conclusion.

P. 309, l. 28. This festival, which is mentioned by Bede and St. Gregory on November 1, was enforced by Gregory II. at Rome, and in 835 on the other side of the Alps. In 998 the feast of All Souls was first observed in Clugniac monasteries. In 603 Pope Boniface established a festival of St. Mary and All Martyrs, which was kept on May 13. All Martyrs' Day is observed in the Greek Church on the octave of Pentecost.

P. 315. **Hood.** (*Caputium.*) The badge of a graduate in a university (*see* Cowl), derived from the fur edgings or colours of the lining of almuces, used in cathedrals which had schools, the chapter being termed a university. The hoods of Aberdeen and Paris, of St. Andrew's and Louvaine, and of Glasgow and Bologna were identical ; just as Dublin adopted that of the Oxford D.D. and M.A., although the lining of the latter has of late years been converted by the tailors into a deep blue. The D.D. hood is of scarlet cloth, lined with silk, black (Oxford, Dublin) ; pink, like that of D.M. and LL.D., and LL.D. Dublin (Cambridge) ; purple (Durham). The D.C.L. hood is of scarlet cloth, lined with silk, of rose-colour at Oxford ; the LL.D hood is scarlet, lined with white (Durham) ; the B.D. (Oxford) is of black silk, but shaped like that of a D.D. ; at Cambridge it is of the same shape as that of an A.M., and common to the B.M., and, as at Dublin, to the LL.M ; the D.M. hood is of scarlet cloth, lined with silk, crimson (Oxford) ; rose-coloured (Dublin). The

B.C.L., B.M., and Mus. Bao. hood is blue silk, edged with white fur (Oxford) ; and for LL.M., purple, furred (Durham) ; the B. Mus. hood is blue, lined with black silk (Cambridge) ; the B.M., black silk, lined with rose-colour (Dublin) ; the M.A. hood, black silk, lined with crimson [coccineum] (Oxford) ; white (Cambridge) ; episcopal purple (Durham) ; dark blue (Dublin) ; the B.A. hood is black silk (Oxford) ; or stuff (Cambridge, Dublin, Durham), edged with fur ; the S.C.L. hood, blue at Oxford ; the same as A.B. at Cambridge. The full-dress M.A. hood at Oxford, since the seventeenth century only worn by the proctors, is of ermine, as that of the Cambridge LL.D. was formerly scarlet, lined with that fur ; the Mus. Doc. hood is white brocaded silk, lined with pink (Oxford) ; buff silk, lined with cerise (Cambridge) ; white figured satin, lined with rose-colour (Dublin) ; and purple cloth, lined with white silk (Durham). At Paris, the præcentor and chancellor of Notre Dame held office in the university.

P. 333. **Irish Architecture.** The churches have little or no richness of ornament, probably owing to the hardness of the material employed. Spires and pinnacles are rare and exceptional ; apses and vaulting are unknown ; parapets consist of battlements tapering in steps ; and tracery usually consists of intersecting mullions, and is unfoliated. Rooms occur frequently above the chancel and other parts. The conventual remains embrace churches of Austin canons, Cistercians, and Friars. The churches of the latter exhibit a nave, with or without an aisle ; a choir, usually aisleless ; a large transept ; and a central tower, generally slender and oblong, frequently a later insertion (about the fifteenth century), and always blocking off the chancel, which was reserved for the convent, from the nave, which was used for preaching to the people, whereas the Cistercians absorbed a large portion of their naves for their choirs. It is difficult to trace any buildings before the thirteenth century ; two chapels, however, at Killaloe and Cashel are, like the former cathedral, of the twelfth century. The English at that date, and the Cistercians from Clairvaux, introduced the styles of their respective countries, which the Irish gradually modified, as it is suggested, by influence derived from Wales and Italy. The only crypt existing is at Christchurch, Dublin. St. Cormac's chapel, Cashel, c. 1135, and the round towers are genuine examples of early national architecture, which comprises (1) oratories, square or of beehive shape ; (2) small aisleless rectangular buildings, often in groups of seven ; the windows are of one light, often triangular-headed, with sides battering inwards, like those of the doorways, which have a monolithic lintel; the smaller churches (*basilicæ*) had stone roofs, but no chancels; (3) Romanesque, ninth to twelfth century, *c.* 1150, with a throne or bench table in the east wall, and a detached altar.

P. 339, l. 28. *Add*, Sabaoth.

P. 342. The mortar was an iron vessel filled with oil and a wick, which was lighted during Matins, before the choir door at Salisbury, as at Durham one of twelve cressets on a stone pillar, set against the south-east pillar of the crossing, was lighted from sunset till the close of Matins.

P. 347, l. 18. A legendary from the patristic writings was drawn up by Paul the Deacon in 883 at the command of Charlemagne for use in church.

P. 352, l. 9. St. Jerome says, " At the reading of the Gospel, even whilst the sun is shining, lights are kindled, as a sign of joy," and cites Scriptural authorities.

P. 352. **Linen Pattern.** An ornament like a plaited linen cloth used on panelling in the Perpendicular period.

P. 360. **Manciple.** A provider of victuals in a college. Mancipia includes generally all subordinate university officials in the Cambridge charter, 1276.

P. 382. **Mitre.** Bishops had not commonly the use of the mitre until the eleventh century; commendatory abbots, who were always secular, used the mitre only on their coats of arms. The prior and chanter of Loches were mitred.

P. 396, l. 9. *Add*, corpus (body).

P. 402, l. 38. *For* laws, *read* lays.

P. 405. **Ogival.** [From *ogive*, a diagonal rib, or the structural aid (*augere*) afforded by the pointed arch.] The French medieval style of architecture, which succeeded to Romano-Byzantine. (*See* pp. 91, 92.) (1.) Primitive, or lancet, thirteenth century. (2.) Secondary, or radiating, fourteenth century. (3.) Tertiary, or Flamboyant, fifteenth century. (*See* also pp. 91, 22.) The ill-developed transept, the chevet with its radiating crown of chapels, the chantries set between the large buttresses which stride out to support the enormous height of the vaults and roofs, and frequently unfinished or discordant western towers, are the chief characteristics of the style. The mutual debt of France and England in architecture, which began with Wilfred, Lanfranc, Ernulph, and William of Sens, and was reciprocated by the English during their occupation of several French provinces, is so intimate that the greatest living French authority pronounces part of Lincoln to be English, whilst his English rival regards it as French. In Hungary, Servia, and Austria many churches have no pointed arches even late in the fourteenth century.

P. 431, l. 25. A paten of the early part of the fifteenth century, enamelled with a crucifix held by the Ancient of Days, remains at Cliffe, Kent. A silver paschal candlestick (1216) five feet high, a monstrance and vestment of the fourteenth or fifteenth century, an ivory crucifix of the eleventh century, and some ancient reliquaries remain at Bamberg.

P. 432. Venice was made patriarchal by Nicholas V., and Paul III. created the patriarch of the Indies.

P. 442. **Per-saltum.** Ordination immediately to the superior order without passing over the intermediate orders, on the principle that the episcopate virtually contains all others.

P. 457, l. 22. There is a superb Perpendicular example at Cirencester.

P. 468. The Bishop of Gran was Primate of Hungary, and the Bishop of Magdeburg, for a time, of Germany.

P. 469. Canterbury was the imperial capital of the Bretwalda at the coming of St. Augustine: hence its archbishopric became the ecclesiastical metropolis of the Primates of All England. So York, the chief city of the Northumbrian princes, became metropolitan, with the primacy of England in the northern province.

P. 511. **Rock Monday.** The Monday following August 16th, St. Roche's Day, the general harvest home.

P. 520. **Rubric Rules** and instructions for the conduct of divine offices inserted in Church books, sometimes in red letter (*rubrica*) or Italics, to distinguish them from the text. The word is derived from the old Roman law, in which the summaries or contents of chapters were written in red. Gavanti says that in the Vatican few missals have rubrics in red letter. Formerly the rubrics were marginal directions, like those in the Alexandrine Codex, and were only by degrees inserted in the text.

P. 566, l. 8. The orarion is properly the deacon's stole, embroidered with the word " agios " (holy) thrice repeated.

Dimensions of the chief churches in the world in internal length, breadth at transept, and height:—Rome, St. Peter's, 613 × 450 × 152; Canterbury, 514 × 130 × 80; [Old St. Paul's, 590 × 300 × 102; New] St. Paul's, 460 × 240 × 88; Winchester, 545 × 209 × 78; St. Alban's, 543 × 175 × 66; Ely, 517 × 185 × 72; York, 486 × 222 × 101; Lincoln, 468 × 220 × 82; Durham, 473 × 170 × 70; Westminster, 505 × 190 × 103; Salisbury, 450 × 206 × 84; Florence, 458 × 334 × 153; Cologne, 445 × 250 × 161; Milan, 443 × 287 × 153; Saltzburg, 466; Seville, 398 × 291 × 132; Granada, 425 × 249; Valladolid, 414 × 204; Amiens, 442 × 194 × 140; Paris, 432 × 186; Rouen, 415 × 176 × 89; Chartres, 418 × 200 × 114; Lubeck, 316 × 206; Drout-

heim, 334 × 166 ; Upsala, 330 × 140 × 105 ; Dublin, St.
Patrick's, 300 × 157 × 58; Glasgow, 282 ; Vienna, 337 × 115
× 92 ; Ratisbon, 384 × 128 × 118; Palermo, 346 × 138 × 74 ;
Constantinople, 360 ; Venice, 205 × 164.   Interior diameter in
feet of CHAPTER HOUSES :—Circular, Worcester, 56 ; Margam, 50 ;
octagonal, Lichfield, Early English, 47 × 28 ; Salisbury, Early
Decorated, 58 ; Wells, c. 1298, 59 ; Westminster, c. 1250, 62 ;
decagonal, Lincoln, Early English, 62 [Hereford was 40] ; York,
c. 1320, 60.   Scotland has some square chapter houses with central pillars.

SUPPLEMENTARY INDEX

OF

SYNONYMS AND MINOR TERMS.

Abat Voix, 111.
Accotoir, 551.
Accoudoir, 551.
Acerra, 126, 538.
Acrostic, 277.
Acu plumario, 11.
Adjutor, 536.
Admiral, 337.
Adoration of the Cross, 563.
Advowson, 73.
Æditua, 360.
Aer, 595.
Afferentes, 298.
Affusion, 324.
Agenda, 364.
Aiguille, 544.
Aithrion, 46.
Ajuleios, 577.
Akakia, 453.
Akathisti, 564.
Akoimetai, 609.
Akroteleuteia, 6.
Ala, 587.
Alara, 278.
Albe, 345; flaps of, 265.
Album, 101.
Alexandrine Liturgy, 355.
Aliturgic, 367.
Alleluia, 339, 509, 513, 586.
All Saints' Sunday, 565.
Alms Saturday, 563.
Altar-Breads, 263, 264.
Altar of Revestry, 307.
Altars Washed, 372.
Amanuenses, 350.
Ambon, 336, 484, 544.
Ambrosian Liturgy, 356, 357.
Amice, flaps of, 265.

Ampulles, 296, 309, 445.
Amula, 202, 406.
Anabologion, 26.
Anadochoi, 298.
Anagnostes, 491.
Anakampteria, 574.
Analobos, 529.
Anaphora, 356.
Anathema, 269.
Andrew's, St., Cross, 285.
Andron, 61.
Angel Choir, 378.
Angelic Door, 91.
Anointing the Dead, 272.
Annotine Easter, 564.
Ansata, 200, 285.
Ante-Church, 457.
Antependium, 33, 290.
Anthem, 304, 332.
Anthony's, St., Cross, 285.
Antidora, 266, 349, 357.
Anti-Panon, 572.
Anti-Pasch, 564.
Antiochene Liturgy, 355.
Antiquarii, 350.
Aphorismos, 268, 438.
Aphorkismos, 270.
Aploma, 420.
Apocreos, 562.
Apocrisiarius, 403, 460.
Apodeipnon (Compline), 374.
Apolusis, 365.
Apostle, the, 262, 346; Spoons, 546.
Apostoleia, 479.
Apostolical, 375; See 432.
Apostolical Liturgy, 355.
Apostolo-Evangelia, 346.
Apotaxis, 498.

2 s

Decollation, 333.
Decree, Gratian's, 106.
Decretals, 106, 349.
Decumans, 102.
Decussata, 285.
Defensores, 433.
Deflection, 517.
Degrees, Psalms of, 483.
Delices, 279.
Deo Devotæ, 404; Deo Sacratæ, 404.
Deosculatory, 436.
Deposition, 397, 405.
De Profundis, 483.
Deputy, 597.
Descant, 468.
Deus Creator, 319.
Deutero-Canonical, 35.
Deuteroon, 558.
Devant L'Autel, 289.
Devil Looking after Lincoln, 250, 308;
    Devil's Door, 402.
Devolution, 502.
Diadem, 382, 399.
Diakonikon, 406, 429.
Diaphonia, 221.
Diary, 502.
Diaspro, 218.
Didaskaliæ, 535.
Dies in albis, 386; Dies in Cappis, 386;
    Dies Iræ, 480; Dies Dominicus, 561.
Dicta, 483.
Dignities of York, 384.
Dimanche Reprus, 563.
Dimensions of Churches and Chapter-
    houses, 623.
Dipsalma, 6.
Diptera, 9.
Directorium Sacerdotum, 445.
Discant, 393.
Discipline of the Secret, 56.
Diskalumma, 595.
Dismes, 235.
Dismissory Letters, 349.
Disputations, 535.
Distaff's Day, 262.
Diurnal, 335.
Doctor Audientium, 121.
Dog-tooth, 237.
Domicellars, 103.
Dominica Broncherii, 422; Dominica
    in Capite, 562.
Dominical, 175, 490, 594.
Dominican Nuns, 404.
Dominicum, 157, 179, 364.
Dominus, 524, 542.
Domus Operaria, 371.
Dorian, 305.
Dorsal, 144, 551.
Dortor (dormitory), 307.
Dossal, 498, 572.
Dossier, 551.

Double benefices, 73; Double Cross,
    Double Monasteries, 461; Double
    Invitatory, 332.
Doxale, 230, 513.
Doxology of Lord's Prayer, 359.
Draconarii, 340.
Dragon, 308, 354.
Draper, 337.
Drop Arch, 237.
Drum (tympanum), 224.
Dry Mass, 369.
Duomo, 224.
Duplex, 409.

Echos, 580.
Eileton, 186.
Eirene, 336.
Ekton (Sext), 374.
Eleanor Cross, 193.
Elect, 508.
Embering Thursday, 46.
Emblems of Apostles, 256.
Embolismus, 357.
Eminence, 115.
Enchiridion, 469.
Endute, 420.
Energumens, 270.
English Mode, 105.
Enkolpion, 571.
Ennaton (Nones), 374.
Entre los dos coros, 544.
Entrées, 551.
Eparchy, 480.
Ephesine Liturgy, 356.
Ephodion, 598.
Epigonation, 560.
Epikeruxis, 542.
Epinikion, 320, 590.
Epiraptaria, 567.
Episcopium, 101.
Epitrachelion, 410, 556.
Epomis, 577.
Eremites of St. Paul, 263.
Esmouchoir, 278.
Estincelles, 577.
Esto Mihi, 562.
Et cum spiritu tuo, 226.
Eucharist, 364, 465.
Euchelaion, 272.
Eulogiæ, 337, 364.
Euteria, 411.
Even Sang, 317.
Exaltation of Holy Cross, 332.
Exarch, 219, 375, 460, 468.
Exaudi, 564.
Executades, 221.
Exedra, 38.
Exequies, 84.
Exercises, 479.
Exomologesis, 538.
Expectation Week, 565.

X81835

Lightning Source UK Ltd.
Milton Keynes UK
UKOW06f1937050116

265873UK00014B/358/P